EVERYMAN, I will go with thee, and be thy guide,
In thy most need to go by thy side

CHRÉTIEN DE TROYES, commonly regarded as the father of Arthurian romance and a key figure in Western literature, composed in French in the latter part of the twelfth century. Virtually nothing is known of his life. Possibly a native of Troyes, he enjoyed patronage there from the Countess Marie of Champagne before dedicating his last romance to Count Philip of Flanders, perhaps about 1182. His poetry is marked by a learning and a taste for dialectic acquired in Latin schools; but at the same time it reveals a warm human sympathy which breathes life into characters and situations. Whilst much of his matter is inherited from the world of Celtic myth and the events notionally unfold in the timeless reign of King Arthur, the society and customs portrayed are those of Chretien's own day. In his last, unfinished work, *Perceval*, the mysterious Grail makes its first appearance in literature.

D.D.R. OWEN, currently Professor of French in the University of St Andrews, has taught there since 1951. He studied at the Universities of Nottingham and Cambridge, where he obtained his Ph.D. in 1955, and in Paris at the Sorbonne and the Collège de France. Among his books are *The Evolution of the Grail Legend, The Vision of Hell, Noble Lovers* and a translation of *The Song of Roland*. Joint editor, with R.C. Johnston, of *Fabliaux* and *Two Old French Gauvain Romances*, he has also edited *Arthurian Romance: Seven Essays* and has published chapters on Arthurian Romance and Chrétien de Troyes in *European Writers: The Middle Ages and the Renaissance*. He is General Editor of the journal *Forum for Modern Language Studies*, which he founded in 1965.

EVERYMAN CLASSICS

CHRÉTIEN DE TROYES

Arthurian Romances

Translated, with an introduction and notes,
by D. D. R. Owen
Professor of French, University of St Andrews

Dent: London and Melbourne
EVERYMAN'S LIBRARY

© J. M. Dent & Sons Ltd, 1987
All rights reserved

Made in Great Britain by
Guernsey Press Co. Ltd, Guernsey. C.I.
for
J. M. Dent & Sons Ltd
Aldine House, 33 Welbeck Street, London W1M 8LX

First published as an Everyman Classic, 1987

British Library Cataloguing in Publication Data

Chretien, *de Troyes*
  Arthurian romances: Erec and Enide, Cligés,
  Lancelot, Yvain and Perceval.
  I. Title   II. Owen, D.D.R.
  841'.1   PQ1483.G3E4

ISBN 0-460-11698-3

No 1698 Paperback ISBN 0 460 11698 3

CONTENTS

ACKNOWLEDGMENTS

In offering a new translation of Chrétien's romances, I am very conscious of the great debt I and many others owe to my predecessor W. W. Comfort, whose elegant versions have for so long graced Everyman's Library. So it was with mixed feelings that I undertook to replace them with my own renderings, where some gain in accuracy may prove insufficient compensation for his engaging if now rather dated idiom. With the work behind me, I can look back with pleasure on long periods spent in the stimulating company of Chrétien himself, and with gratitude for the encouragement, advice and often tolerance afforded me in many quarters. My thanks are due not least to my colleagues and students at the University of St Andrews, to the Library staff for their ready help, and to my wife Berit for many patient hours spent in tidying and improving my typescript. Finally, at journey's end, I must express my appreciation of the work of my two editors, Jocelyn Burton and Judy Tagg, under whose discreet but reassuring guidance it has been accomplished.

INTRODUCTION

In France from about the middle of the twelfth century the new genre of romance came to challenge the heroic epic, or *chanson de geste*, as the favourite form of literary entertainment among the aristocracy of the northern courts. The romances were long tales of chivalric and sentimental adventure presented in verse until the fashion shifted to prose in the following century. With a style less aggressively terse and formulaic than the *chansons de geste*, they were not composed, like them, for dramatic recitation by jongleurs, but to be read, either privately by the educated or more often, no doubt, aloud to a listening group. Some took their themes from Classical Antiquity—stories of Aeneas, or of Thebes or Troy; others exploited Greco-Byzantine material and occasionally more recent history; but from an early date it was the Matter of Britain that gripped the imagination of writers and public alike: legends of Tristan, of King Arthur and his knights, of the marvels of the Celtic world.

Chrétien de Troyes may not have been the progenitor of Arthurian romance, but he is usually thought of as at least its adoptive father. As such he has a rightful place among the greatest and most influential figures of world literature. Yet he is also one of the most enigmatic. To begin with, although he was much revered, probably in his own day and certainly by his successors, we know virtually nothing of his life. It is assumed from his dedication of *Lancelot* to Marie, Countess of Champagne, that in the 1170s he had some connection with her court at Troyes, the town with which he had associated his own name in the prologue of *Erec et Enide*. On the other hand, the last of his acknowledged romances, the unfinished *Conte du Graal* or *Perceval*, he was to offer to Philip of Alsace, Count of Flanders. Does this mean that by about 1182 Chrétien had left Marie's entourage to work for another patron? It is possible, though not certain, for Philip was in close touch with the house of Champagne, and a commission from him does not necessarily imply a change of residence on the poet's part. In any case, this was an undertaking that Chrétien never brought to fruition, since, if we are to believe a continuator, it was death that took the pen prematurely from his hand.

He was fortunate during his lifetime to have worked for two patrons of such quality and distinction. Marie, great-granddaughter of the first known troubadour, had inherited from her mother, the remarkable Eleanor of Aquitaine who was queen successively of France and England, a taste for culture and the sophisticated manners of the southern French courts. In Count Philip, Chrétien served a man who not only wielded great power in the land, but was also much noted for his piety and liberality (a signal virtue in a patron) and for the richness of his court. The poet moved, then, in a world of high aristocracy, although whether he lived solely by his literary activity or whether he held some other office, we cannot say. It is plain from his works that he had received good training in the discipline of the Latin schools, and indeed Wolfram von Eschenbach was later to dub him *meister*; so he need not have relied entirely on his verse for his livelihood.

While for our knowledge of Chrétien our almost only resource is his works, even with them there are perplexing questions to be considered. He prefaces *Cligés* with a list of his earlier compositions, although this is less precise than we would like and has to be deciphered. It looks as though he found his literary touch by exploiting the vogue for Ovid in the third quarter of the twelfth century, producing French versions of at least the *Ars amatoria* and the stories of Pelops and Philomena as found in the *Metamorphoses*. Of these early works the first two are lost; but it is surely his *Philomena* that has survived, in 1,468 octosyllabic lines, embedded in the *Ovide moralisé*, a long allegorical treatment of the *Metamorphoses* compiled late in the thirteenth century. Chrétien further tells us in *Cligés* that he had written something on King Mark and Iseut (there is surprisingly no mention of Tristan) and also the story of Erec and Enide, which may well have been the first of his full-scale romances.

Erec is nowadays thought to have been composed in about 1170, and the approximate dates of his other major works are: *Cligés* 1176, *Lancelot* and *Yvain* 1177, the *Conte du Graal* 1182. Another romance often ascribed to him on grounds of linguistic similarity and more especially the fact that the author names himself as Chrétien is *Guillaume d'Angleterre*, a rather pious and homiletic tale far enough removed from our poet in content, style, length, and indeed in general artistry, to raise grave doubts as to his responsibility. We are on much firmer ground in ascribing to him two lyric *chansons* treating of love in the troubadour style, and in one of which he alludes to Tristan's fateful passion. Whatever the nature of his own treatment of the

Tristan legend, it seems to have been something of an obsession with him, encouraged perhaps by a professional rivalry with his contemporary Thomas of England, who also produced a version.

We have not yet done, however, with problems of authorship and composition. It is generally accepted that Chrétien's last romance was the *Conte du Graal*, left still unfinished after more than 9,000 lines. Yet there are good, though many think insufficient, grounds for supposing that what we have here is not one but two incomplete romances, run together only after Chrétien's death. The first deals with Perceval and the Grail quest, the second with the amours and frustrations of Gawain, related in a tone of gentle burlesque. In much the same vein as the truncated adventures of Gawain there exist two shorter poems also concerned with him and composed in the usual romance metre, although seemingly intended for recitation rather than reading like most representatives of the genre. They are *Le Chevalier à l'épée* and *La Mule sans frein*, and both show detailed knowledge of Chrétien's main works. Here might seem to be a case of flattery through imitation by one or perhaps two short-winded disciples. However, in each poem the author appears to name himself in the prologue: in the *Chevalier* directly as Chrétien de Troyes, in the *Mule* as Paien de Maisières, which can be shown in its context to be a play on the full name of Chrétien. So here is yet another puzzle to do with our elusive author. Did he compose one or both of these minor but interesting works? If not, he most certainly inspired them.

If we are faced with these doubts in the simple enumeration of Chrétien's works, their assessment and interpretation are just as open to controversy, subject as they are to the vagaries of critical fashion. Introducing his own translations over seventy years ago, W. W. Comfort was surprisingly harsh in his judgment: "The modern reader may form his own estimate of the poet's art, and that estimate will probably not be high. Monotony, lack of proportion, vain repetitions, insufficient motivation, wearisome subtleties, and threatened, if not actual, indelicacy are among the most salient defects which will arrest, and mayhap confound, the reader unfamiliar with medieval literary craft." Most critics today would spring eagerly to Chrétien's defence.

Bound as he was to the tradition of octosyllabic verse in rhymed couplets, he managed to achieve a remarkable variety of rhythms and a fluency of expression without lapsing like so many of his contemporaries into formulaic *cliché* or a rigid, predictable style. He was a master of dialogue, which he handled with all the skill of a dramatist. And in an age when descriptions tended to be stereotyped he had the ability to set scenes briefly yet vividly, with usually enough distinctive touches and richness of vocabulary to avoid the monotony of which Comfort complained. In the presentation of crowd scenes, dress, and the effects of light and sound he showed particular talent. His physical portrayal of people seldom overstepped the conventional, it is true, but he did go further than most in the interior portrait. Psychological investigation was still in its infancy in Chrétien's day, but we see him experimenting with various techniques: direct dialogue, monologues and interior debates in the style of Ovid, and even, notably in his first romance, the calculated use of silence. As a result we do meet real characters in his works, people we feel to be further removed from us in time than in humanity.

Comfort complained of "vain repetitions". There is admittedly an element of repetition in the romances, ranging from the use of two or three words expressing the same idea to the recurrence of recognisable motifs from one poem to another or even in the course of the same work. As far as verbal repetition is concerned, we have to remember the rhetorical tradition within which Chrétien worked and which might welcome as an elegance what we would deem superfluous. As for the re-use of motifs, which could be a more serious matter, he may well have shown a certain parsimony, a lack of outright inventiveness; but he did nevertheless go to great pains to disguise this procedure under a mask of new detail. He was a more brilliant re-creator than creator.

Another charge is of "insufficient motivation", which brings us back to the question of psychological plausibility. What, we might ask, is sufficient motivation in a world of marvels? But this would be to defend Chrétien on the wrong grounds, for instances abound where he appears to have gone to much trouble to rationalise a supernatural element he had inherited and to introduce as much plausible motivation as the chain of events would bear. We shall turn to his sources in a moment, but in the case of *Philomena* the position is clear, for we have Ovid's tale to compare with the French redaction. In the latter we find situations and events that Ovid had too brusquely introduced now subtly prepared for far in advance with elements of what may be called preliminary motivation. The same technique can be followed in the romances presented here. It may be, as in the first part of *Yvain*, that Chrétien's concern for plausibility on one level may trap him into an improbable circumstance on another. At least, though, he usually does his best. I say "usually" because the case of *Lancelot* may be different. For the most part, Chrétien shows the care of a playwright in his manipulation of time and place; but in *Lancelot* normal scales seem so strangely distorted that the charge of careless-ness has often been levelled against him. This, however, is a romance so full of incongruities that one suspects them, far from being the result of negligence, to belong to some total and original artistic design.

A counter-suggestion would be that Chrétien left *Lancelot* unfinished and so never gave it its final polishing. To this I would reply that he had one notable failing, and a failing that surprises in an artist who seems to have been very anxious to give his works not only unity, but balance and proportion. It was that he apparently found it difficult to bring his romances to a satisfactory conclusion. *Erec*, though ending with fine pomp, gives the impression of having been stretched artificially over the last couple of thousand lines. *Cligés* finishes on a note approaching bathos. *Yvain*'s ending is better, though contrived and psychologically barren. *Lancelot* was not finished at all by Chrétien but by a colleague, Godefroi de Leigni. The *Conte du Graal* was likewise left incomplete; or, as I believe, neither of its two constituent poems (the one on Perceval, the other on Gawain) runs its distance. It looks as if Chrétien had a target length for each of his major romances of something near 7,000 lines, and that this put a strain on his endurance. If I am right, and right too about his unfinished Perceval poem, then we must look beyond the incompleteness of *Lancelot* for an explanation of its apparent lapses in composition (the most admirably organised of all Chrétien's works I would hold to be the Perceval fragment). Is it too rash to suggest that the incongruities here are being used deliberately to heighten a sense of ambiguity, in the service perhaps of some ironic intention? This is a point to which I shall return.

There is no reason not to take Chrétien at his word when he refers in each of his romances to some source—in the case of *Cligés* and the *Conte du Graal* to books, for the other works to either written or oral material. Unfortunately (since comparison with a source can often reveal much of an author's methods and aims), no text exists which

he could have used as his prime model for any of the romances.
However, the Welsh *Mabinogion*, a collection of prose tales which, in
their present redactions, were written down well over a century after
Chrétien's death, do offer three texts of great interest for students of
his works. They are *Gereint Son of Erbin*, *Owein* (known also as *The
Lady of the Fountain*), and *Peredur*; and they tell much the same
stories as *Erec, Yvain*, and the *Conte du Graal* respectively, but in
much shorter space. What, then, is their relationship to the French
romances?

After many years of debate, the question is still far from being
resolved to everybody's satisfaction. There are those, though their
ranks are now depleted, who hold that the Welsh tales are all corrupt
and abbreviated versions of Chrétien's. It is more usually supposed
that each pair is derived from a common source; but a refinement in
the discussion is to claim that the Welsh author or authors knew
Chrétien as well as the shared models. Yet another possibility, which I
would defend, is that whereas *Gereint* and *Owein* reflect fairly
faithfully the sources from which Chrétien developed *Erec* and *Yvain*,
Peredur lies downstream from him and contains garbled material
from the *Conte du Graal*. The assumption follows that such stories as
were used both by him and by the Welsh author or authors were
composed in a form of French, probably Anglo-Norman, but
whether in verse or prose and whether for oral or written transmis-
sion we can only surmise.

So for *Erec* and *Yvain* Chrétien appears to have reorganised and
elaborated two already fairly well developed tales of ultimately Celtic
origin, the "tales of adventure" of which he speaks in his first
romance. The cases of *Cligés* and *Lancelot* are rather different. When
he composed *Cligés*, Chrétien seems to have been very much preoccupied with the Tristan legend. In *Philomena* he had expressed
strongly moral views on the evil of an unlawful passion; and the
adulterous relationship of Tristan and Iseut, prompted not by the
spontaneous attraction of noble hearts and still less by reason, but by
the accidental consumption of a love potion, was viewed by him with
extreme disfavour. This was not mitigated, it seems, when Thomas
made it the subject of his own Anglo-Norman romance, thought to
have been composed just before *Cligés*. There may, then, be a hint of
rancour about the way in which Chrétien frames his new work partly
to mirror and partly to rival the Tristan story; an element too,

perhaps, of penance for having himself once flirted with the legend.

Yet though its influence on *Cligés* was strong, it was only one of several diverse sources exploited there by Chrétien. Whilst the delicate account of Alexander's wooing of Soredamors seems chiefly of Chrétien's own devising, the young man's martial exploits owe much not only to Wace's account in his *Roman de Brut* of Mordred's betrayal of King Arthur but also to the *Chanson de Roland*. On the other hand, the central inspiration for the Cligés-Fenice affair is to be found in a widespread tale concerning a wife who feigned death to dupe her husband. One version was to be used by Shakespeare in *Romeo and Juliet*; another, alluded to by Chrétien, makes King Solomon the cuckold. But a variant form much closer to his own narrative is found in a rather later text, *Marques de Rome*, and here again scholars favour the theory of a common source. Chrétien's treatment of the apparent death and "resurrection" of Fenice is, however, strongly and startlingly influenced by yet another model: the scriptural account of the Passion and Resurrection of Christ.

In Caradoc of Lancarvan's *Vita Sancti Gildae*, composed certainly before 1160 and probably before 1136, we read how Melwas or Maelwas, king of the summer country, abducted Queen Guenevere and held her in the City of Glass or Glastonbury before restoring her to King Arthur on the intervention of the abbot there. A sculptured archivolt in Modena cathedral, which may be even earlier, depicts a scene in which Guenevere seems to have suffered a similar abduction, while knights including Arthur, Gawain and Kay ride to her rescue. Some such story must have furnished Chrétien with the central plot of *Lancelot*, a story still clearly marked by the ancient Celtic motif of an otherworld captivity. As with *Cligés*, though, the matter of the main source was eked out by the introduction of extraneous elements, including again one of the central Christian events. This time it was the story of Christ's Harrowing of Hell as known in the Middle Ages through the popular *Gospel of Nicodemus*. We may well wonder what Chrétien was about in *Cligés* and *Lancelot*: two stories of adulterous love, and both played out in terms, barely disguised, of the ultimate Christian mystery.

It is generally assumed that his purpose in the romances went beyond merely supplying for public consumption entertaining tales of fantastic adventure, and that in using the word *sen* in his prologue to *Lancelot* he referred to some implicit meaning, even moral, he wished to convey. The assumption is not unreasonable, even though some doubt has been cast on that precise interpretation of *sen*. For Chrétien was plainly a man of intelligence, a keen observer of his fellow-humans, a man moreover of moral principles. Yet there has never been full agreement on what he was trying to say in these works.

Was his main concern with sexual relationships? He, if it is he, is at his most forthright in *Philomena*, inveighing against blind passion and the treacherous undoing of young girls, and pressing the moral issues more firmly than Ovid himself. *Erec* is the story of an idyllically happy marriage in which the husband luxuriated to the detriment of his duties as an active knight. To regain his good name he set out to prove his valour in the presence of his forbearing wife, the innocent source of his temptation. In *Yvain* the situation is to be reversed, with the hero winning a bride who is all too soon abandoned for a round of athletic chivalry, so that this time love itself is endangered, to be finally restored only after the truant has turned from tournaments to gain the reputation of being a bold champion of women and so a worthy husband after all. Meanwhile, *Cligés* had presented two sentimental tales, the first showing the timorous radiance of young love and the second an extra-marital passion that won its way through suffering to an ultimately honest fulfilment. *Lancelot*, on the other hand, dealt with adultery impure and unsimple: the love of a knight for his lord's wife and her haughty and capricious reciprocation. In the first part of the *Conte du Graal* there is seen a young man's progress from flirtation with his mother's chambermaids to a true meeting of hearts, while in the second part we are shown through the person of Gawain how a philandering disposition can deflect even the best of knights from the straight course of duty.

Love, then, would seem to be the golden thread running through each romance. Yet a case might be made for chivalry being the more dramatically interesting element. Has a knight like Erec the right to withdraw into a private world of love, or must he be energetic in the service of the society where he is shortly to become king? Is Yvain's quest for adventure and glory too self-centred to merit public as well as domestic approval? Although love might seem the dominant element in *Cligés*, chivalry is by no means eclipsed, and questions of honour are seriously examined. In *Lancelot* is love even held to ridicule and shown to make a wise man foolish? If the *Conte du Graal* had been finished, would Perceval's initiation into courtly love have been more than a single lesson in his apprenticeship in chivalry? And would the moral of Gawain's adventures not have been that a roving eye leads a knight into many pitfalls?

Perhaps, though, this question as to whether Chrétien gave love or chivalry priority is void of importance or even meaning. He was less interested, I fancy, in proposing solutions or norms of conduct than in investigating a variety of problems and conditions involving love and the knightly life. Prompted by his sources, he asked himself questions ("what would happen if . . .?", "what should a knight do when . . .?") and worked through situations, offering, but not insisting on, solutions. So he examined with a steady eye the power and changing face of love: unsullied in *Erec* and leading to ideal marriage, a self-abasing passion seeking fulfilment in precarious adultery (*Lancelot*) or in scarcely more secure wedlock (*Yvain*). Moral convictions he certainly had, but he did not let them obtrude. For him with his schoolman's training the debate held greater delights than the declaration of preconceived truths. He was a man of intellect rather than of high emotion.

Although he presents us with some delightful portraits, and no doubt developed a sympathy for some of his characters (Enide and Lunete, for instance, or the charmingly gallant Gawain), one feels that he enjoyed manipulating and toying with them, and with his public too. It is hard not to sense a certain detachment from both character and situation that may often carry more than a hint of irony. Moreover, it is by no means always easy to see when he is keeping a straight face or when the shadow of a smile is playing round his lips. There may be little humour in *Erec*, but surely it is not altogether absent from *Cligés*, or from *Yvain*, still less from *Lancelot*. But how far does it go? What, for instance, are we to make of the element of sacred parody in both *Cligés* and *Lancelot*? Did Chrétien intend us to connive with him, as in some shared joke? One is loath to believe that he worked on these analogies out of a pure sense of fun; yet with him one can be sure of very little. His humour has certainly been too much neglected in the past: one so often senses its presence, ready to edge us away now and again from too close an association with the characters and their dilemmas. But perhaps Chrétien, the expert entertainer, knowing well enough that the tastes of his public were as many and varied as their degrees of sophistication or ability to take a debating point or sly allusion, deliberately cultivated levels of ambiguity, so that people could take away what they wished to find. Not one, maybe, but several meanings lie within each of his romances.

We are left with the impression of a strikingly superior and many-sided talent. Chrétien has bequeathed to us a brilliant portrait of the society that gave him his livelihood. Much of his detail is drawn from the life; yet there is much too that represents the ideal of the chivalric and courtly ethic. It was an ideal which, I believe, held for him a great sentimental attraction: this was society as he would like to see it, a society of delicate manners, impeccably courteous, generous, honourable. But at the same time he was a man of sound sense and clear vision, aware of things as they were. So he flaunted the high ideal, while constantly hinting that this was but a poet's dream. We can take it or leave it: it is up to us. But for himself, he remains at heart the realist, a quizzical spectator of life, more observer than moralist.

Chrétien had the qualities to be a great writer in any age. A few centuries later and he might have been a novelist or a man of the theatre. As it was it fell to him to bring the verse romance to its full flowering and to establish as its chief concern the rich Matter of Britain. Without him we might today scarcely have heard of King Arthur and his brave company. Certainly our literary heritage would have been vastly the poorer.

1986   D. D. R. OWEN

SELECT BIBLIOGRAPHY

ARTHURIAN ROMANCE

Arthurian Literature in the Middle Ages, ed. R. S. Loomis. Oxford, 1959.

Arthurian Romance: Seven Essays, ed. D. D. R. Owen. Edinburgh & London, 1970.

Bibliographical Bulletin of the International Arthurian Society, published annually since 1949.

Faral, Edmond. *La Légende arthurienne. Études et documents.* 3 vols. Paris, 1929.

Flutre, Louis-Fernand. *Table des noms propres avec toutes leurs variantes figurant dans les romans du moyen âge écrits en français ou en provençal* . . . . Poitiers, 1962.

Frappier, Jean. *Le Roman breton. Des origines à Chrétien de Troyes.* Paris ("Cours de Sorbonne"), 1950.

Geoffrey of Monmouth. *The History of the Kings of Britain*, translated by Lewis Thorpe. Harmondsworth (Penguin), 5th edn., 1979.

Green, D. H. *Irony in the Medieval Romance.* Cambridge U.P., 1979.

Hanning, Robert W. *The Individual in Twelfth-Century Romance.* Yale U.P., 1977.

Köhler, Erich. *Ideal und Wirklichkeit in der höfischen Epik. Studien zur Form der frühen Artus und Graldichtung.* 2nd edn., Tübingen, 1970.

Loomis, Roger Sherman. *The Development of Arthurian Romance.* London, 1963.

The Mabinogion: ed. John Rhŷs & J. Gwenogvryn Evans, *The Text of the Mabinogion and other Welsh Tales from the Red Book of Hergest*, Oxford, 1887; ed. J. Gwenogvryn Evans, *The White Book Mabinogion*, Pwllheli, 1907; English translation by Gwyn Jones & Thomas Jones, London (Everyman's Library), 1949.

Morris, Rosemary. *The Character of King Arthur in Medieval Literature.* Cambridge & Totowa, NJ, 1982.

Owen, D. D. R. "Arthurian Legend" in *European Writers. The Middle Ages and the Renaissance*, ed. William T. H. Jackson, Vol. 1, New York, 1983, pp. 137–60.

Schmolke-Hasselmann, Beate. *Der arturische Versroman von Chrestien bis Froissart: zur Geschichte einer Gattung.* Tübingen, 1979.

Vinaver, Eugène. *The Rise of Romance*. Oxford, 1971.
West, G. D. *An Index of Proper Names in French Arthurian Verse Romances* 1150–1300. Toronto, 1969.

CHRÉTIEN DE TROYES

A. BIBLIOGRAPHY

Kelly, Douglas. *Chrétien de Troyes: An Analytic Bibliography*. London, 1976.

B. EDITIONS

Christian von Troyes. Sämtliche Werke, ed. Wendelin Foerster, 5 vols. Halle, 1884–99, 1932.

Philomena, ed. C. de Boer. Paris, 1909.

Erec et Enide: ed. Wendelin Foerster, *C. von T. Sämtliche Werke*, Vol. III, 1890; and in Romanische Bibliothek XIII, Halle, 1896, 1909, 1934; ed. Mario Roques, Paris (CFMA), 1955.

Cligés: ed. Wendelin Foerster, *C. von T. Sämtliche Werke*, Vol. I, 1884; and in Romanische Bibliothek I, Halle, 1888, 1901, 1910, 1921; ed. Alexandre Micha, Paris (CFMA), 1957.

Lancelot (Le Chevalier de la Charrette): ed. Wendelin Foerster, *C. von T. Sämtliche Werke*, Vol. IV (with *Guillaume d'Angleterre*), 1899; ed. Mario Roques, Paris (CFMA), 1958; ed. and translated by William W. Kibler, New York, 1981.

Yvain (Le Chevalier au Lion): ed. Wendelin Foerster, *C. von T. Sämtliche Werke*, Vol. II, 1899; and in Romanische Bibliothek V, Halle, 1891, 1902, 1906, 1912; ed. T. B. W. Reid (Foerster's 1912 text), Manchester, 1942; ed. Mario Roques, Paris (CFMA), 1964.

Conte du Graal (Perceval): ed. Alfons Hilka in *C. von T. Sämtliche Werke*, ed. Foerster, Vol. V, 1932; ed. William Roach, Genève/ Lille (TLF), 2nd edn., 1959; ed. Félix Lecoy, Paris (CFMA), 2 vols., 1972–5.

C. GENERAL STUDIES

Bezzola, Reto R. *Le Sens de l'aventure et de l'amour (Chrétien de Troyes)*. Paris, 1947.

Brand, Wolfgang. *Chrétien de Troyes: zur Dichtungstechnik seiner Romane*. München, 1972.

Cohen, Gustave. *Un grand romancier d'amour et d'aventure au XII*ᵉ *siècle: Chrétien de Troyes et son œuvre*. Paris, n. éd., 1948.

Colby, Alice M. *The Portrait in Twelfth-Century French Literature. An Example of the Stylistic Originality of Chrétien de Troyes.* Geneva, 1965.

Foerster, Wendelin. *Wörterbuch zu Kristian von Troyes' sämtlichen Werken.* 4th edn. revised by Hermann Breuer, Tübingen, 1966.

Frappier, Jean. *Chrétien de Troyes.* Paris, 1957.

Hofer, Stefan. *Chrétien de Troyes. Leben und Werke des altfranzösischen Epikers.* Graz/Köln, 1954.

Lacy, Norris J. *The Craft of Chrétien de Troyes: An Essay on Narrative Art.* Leiden, 1980.

Loomis, Roger Sherman. *Arthurian Tradition and Chrétien de Troyes.* Columbia U.P., 1949.

Noble, Peter S. *Love and Marriage in Chrétien de Troyes.* Cardiff, 1982.

Owen, D. D. R. "Chrétien de Troyes" in *European Writers . . .* (see above), Vol. I, pp. 185–209.

Topsfield, L. T. *Chrétien de Troyes. A Study of the Arthurian Romances.* Cambridge U.P., 1981.

Zaddy, Z. P. *Chrétien Studies.* Glasgow U.P., 1972.

D. EREC ET ENIDE

Burgess, Glyn S. *Chrétien de Troyes: Erec et Enide.* London, 1984.

Luttrell, C. *The Creation of the First Arthurian Romance. A Quest.* London, 1974.

Maddox, Donald. *Structure and Sacring: The Systematic Kingdom in Chrétien's "Erec et Enide".* Lexington, Ky., 1978.

E. CLIGÉS

Frappier, Jean. *Le Roman breton: Cligès.* Paris ("Cours de Sorbonne"), 1951.

Freeman, Michelle A. *The Poetics of "Translatio Studii" and "Conjointure": Chrétien de Troyes's "Cligés".* Lexington, Ky., 1979.

Haidu, Peter. *Aesthetic Distance in Chrétien de Troyes: Irony and Comedy in "Cligés" and "Perceval".* Genève, 1968.

Polak, Lucie. *Chrétien de Troyes: Cligés.* London, 1982.

F. LANCELOT

Cross, T. P. & Nitze, W. A. *Lancelot and Guenevere. A Study on the Origins of Courtly Love*. Chicago, 1930.

Kelly, F. Douglas. *Sens and Conjointure in the Chevalier de la Charrette*. The Hague/Paris, 1966.

Ribard, Jacques. *Chrétien de Troyes: Le Chevalier de la Charrette. Essai d'interprétation symbolique*. Paris, 1972.

G. YVAIN

Frappier, Jean. *Étude sur Yvain ou le Chevalier au Lion de Chrétien de Troyes*. Paris, 1969.

Hunt, Tony. *Chrétien de Troyes: Yvain (Le Chevalier au Lion)*. London, 1986.

Owein, or Chwedyl Iarlles y Ffynnawn, ed. R. L Thomson. Dublin, 1968.

H. PERCEVAL

Frappier, Jean. *Chrétien de Troyes et le mythe du Graal. Étude sur Perceval ou le Conte du Graal*. Paris, 1972.

Kellermann, Wilhelm. *Aufbaustil und Weltbild Chrestiens von Troyes im Percevalroman*. Halle, 1936.

Le Rider, Paule. *Le Chevalier dans le Conte du Graal de Chrétien de Troyes*. Paris, 1978.

Marx, Jean. *La Légende arthurienne et le Graal*. Paris, 1952.

Owen, D. D. R. *The Evolution of the Grail Legend*. Edinburgh & London, 1968.

Pickens, Rupert T. *The Welsh Knight: Paradoxicality in Chrétien's "Conte del Graal"*. Lexington, Ky., 1977.

Pollmann, Leo. *Chrétien de Troyes und der Conte del Graal*. Tübingen, 1965.

NOTE ON THE TRANSLATIONS

In making these translations, I have kept in mind the needs of students: primarily of those using them as an aid to reading Chrétien in the original Old French, but also of others anxious to know what he says while postponing the pleasure of discovering how he says it. My renderings therefore incline towards the literal; and a particular example of this is my retention of Chrétien's frequent switches of tense between past and present, except where a change seemed too offensive for even the tolerant ear. If further excuse were needed for maintaining this common practice of Old French, I would suggest that, as used by Chrétien, it often has the effect of varying the focus and hence the dramatic tension of the narrative.

For Chrétien as for us, the adventures he relates took place in a remote legendary past. However, apart from an occasional reference to a custom or some other feature of life in those distant days, he has presented his characters and events in the terms of his own twelfth-century world. The time-gap for him was legendary and could be bridged; but the space between us and him is historical and, in a re-telling of his stories, can at best be narrowed. The problem for the translator is the extent to which he should avoid a more archaic and hence rarer term or expression in favour of a loose modern equivalent. Should one, for instance, render Old French *cortois* by "courteous", or by the more accurate "courtly", which embraces a far wider range of qualities appropriate to those living in a medieval court society? Then there are the *damoiseles* and *puceles* who throng the romances. Here, a *damoisele* is a usually young and unmarried lady of high birth; and a *pucele*, though the word has rather wider currency, is in most contexts much the same. To keep the difference in nomenclature, I have normally used the words "damsel" and "maiden" respectively, reserving the flat approximations "young lady" and "girl" as occasional variants. In general I have introduced no archaisms for their own sake, but have on the other hand made no attempt to disguise artificially the historical gap. The short glossary is intended to provide easy reference for some key or less familiar terms. Paragraph divisions are my own. An asterisk (*) in the text indicates an explanatory note, see pp. 499–526, although its position may not necessarily correspond exactly with the line number references.

For the first four romances I have used as my models the Foerster texts, the more recent editions by Roques and Micha being based on a manuscript copied by the individualistic and hence unreliable scribe Guiot. His text was also used by Hilka and Lecoy in their editions of *Perceval*, so for the same reason I have preferred that of Roach. Hence, the numerals at the beginning of each paragraph indicate the line in the Foerster or Roach text at which that section begins. Such use as I have made of major variants I have recorded in the notes. There too may be found information designed to clarify some points raised by the texts; but also, and perhaps more important, attention is drawn to questions that are still open to debate and investigation. For Chrétien is a writer to be not merely read but explored; and if this translation should help those through whose hands it passes to get to know him better or enjoy him more, its purpose will have been served.

EREC AND ENIDE

*As the popular saying goes, there are certain things we despise whose worth is far greater than we think. So a man does well to make the most of such understanding as he possesses; for anyone who neglects to do so may easily leave something unsaid that could in the future give much pleasure. Therefore CHRÉTIEN DE TROYES says it is right for everybody always to devote his thoughts and efforts to telling and teaching what is good; and from a tale of adventure he fashions a very elegant composition, giving manifest proof that there is no wisdom in not freely making one's knowledge available so far as God's grace allows. The tale, which the professional story-tellers habitually fragment and corrupt in the presence of kings and counts, is about Erec, son of Lac. Now I shall begin this story, which will henceforth always be remembered as long as Christendom endures. That is CHRÉTIEN's boast.

27 One springtide, on Easter Day, King Arthur held at his stronghold of Cardigan a court more lavish than had ever been seen; for it was attended by many good, bold, brave and proud knights and rich ladies and maidens, fair and noble daughters of kings. Now before that court disbanded, the king told his knights he wished to hunt the white stag* and renew the worthy observance of that custom. My lord Gawain was far from happy to hear his declaration. "Sire," he says, "this hunt will bring you no thanks or gratitude. For a long time we've all well known what the custom of the white stag is: whoever can kill this white stag must by right kiss the fairest of the maidens in your court, come what may. This could lead to very great trouble, for here there are no fewer than five hundred high-born damsels, attractive and intelligent daughters of kings, all with knights as lovers – bold, valiant men, each of whom would wish to claim, rightly or wrongly, that the one he favours is the most attractive and beautiful." The king replies: "I am aware of this; but I shall not give up my intention on that account, for when a king has spoken, his word should not be retracted. Tomorrow morning we shall all derive great enjoyment from going to hunt the white stag in the forest where adventures abound. It will be a truly marvellous hunt." Thus the matter is arranged for daybreak the following morning.

69 The next day, as soon as it grows light, the king gets up and
dresses, putting on a short tunic for riding in the forest. He has the
knights wakened and the horses made ready for the hunt. Without
more ado they are all mounted and on their way, equipped with
bows and arrows. Behind them mounts the queen accompanied by
an attendant maiden, a king's daughter riding a white palfrey.
Spurring hard after them comes a knight named Erec, who was of
the Round Table* and enjoyed a very high reputation at court.
While he had been there, no knight had earned more praise; and he
was so handsome that to seek a man more so in any land would
have been fruitless. For all his handsomeness, valour and fine
bearing, he was not yet twenty-five years old. Never was greater
prowess seen in any man of his age. What could I say of his virtues?
Mounted on his steed and wearing an ermine mantle, he came
galloping on his way. He had on a coat of splendid flowered silk
made in Constantinople, and the hose he wore were of brocade,
superbly made and cut. He had spurs of gold, and his feet were firm
in the stirrups; but with him he had brought no arms with the sole
exception of his sword. Riding hard, he caught up with the queen at
a street-corner. "My lady," he says, "if it pleased you, I would join
you on this ride: *I came here for no other reason than to keep you
company." And the queen thanked him: "My good friend, I assure
you that I much enjoy your company, for I can't have better."

115 Then they come at a fast gallop straight to the forest. Those who
had gone ahead had already started the stag. Some sound their
horns, others halloo; the baying dogs pursue the stag, running after
it at full stretch, barking as they go; the archers' arrows fly thick
and fast. On a Spanish hunter, the king was leading them all in the
chase.

125 Queen Guenevere stayed in the woods listening for the dogs
with Erec and her maiden, who was very courtly and beautiful, at
her side. But the party hunting the stag had gone so far ahead of
them that they could hear nothing of the horns, huntsmen or dogs.
To listen with straining ears for the sound of a horn being blown or
a hound baying somewhere, they had all three stopped in a clearing
beside the road; but they had not been there long when they saw an
armed knight approaching on a charger, gripping his lance and
with his shield slung at his neck. The queen spied him from afar. At
his right side rode a maiden of noble bearing; and on the road

ahead of them came a dwarf mounted on a nag and with a scourge, knotted at the end, in his hand. Queen Guenevere sees this handsome, able-looking knight and wishes to know who they both are, he and his maiden. She bids her own maiden go quickly to speak with him. "My damsel," says the queen, "go and tell the knight travelling there to come to me and bring his maiden with him."

159 The girl rides at an amble straight towards the knight. The dwarf comes towards her, scourge in hand. "Stop there young lady!" says the dwarf, a villainous fellow. "What are you looking for over here? You won't go any further this way!"—"Dwarf," says she, "let me pass! I wish to speak with that knight, for I'm sent by the queen." The dwarf, ill-begotten rogue that he was, stopped in the middle of the road. "You've no business here," he says. "Back you go! It's not right for you to speak to such a good knight." The maiden moved forward, wanting to force her way past; for seeing how small the dwarf was, she was quite contemptuous of him. When he saw her come up to him, the dwarf raised the scourge with the intention of hitting her across the face, which she protected with her arm. Taking aim again, he struck her directly on her bare hand, dealing such a blow on its back that it made the hand quite blue. Like it or not, the girl had no choice but to retreat. Weeping, she returned, her eyes filling with tears that streamed down her face. The queen, seeing her maiden injured, is at a loss for grief and anger. "Ah Erec, my friend," she says, "I'm very sorry to see my maiden so badly hurt by that dwarf. The knight is really base to allow such a monster to strike so lovely a creature. Erec, good friend, go over to the knight and tell him to come to me without fail: I want to meet him and his lady friend."

205 Erec spurs his horse and gallops at full speed straight in the direction of the knight. The rascally dwarf sees him coming and goes to meet him. "Stand back, fellow!" he says. "I don't know what brings you here. I advise you to go away again."—"Be off with you, you tiresome dwarf! You're being too malicious and provocative. Let me go on!"—"That you won't!"—"Yes I shall!"—"You'll not!" Erec thrusts him aside. But the dwarf's viciousness was unequalled, and he gave him a great stroke across the neck with his scourge, so that Erec's neck and face were striped from its lash: the lines made by the thongs could be seen from one side to the other. He was well aware that he would be unable to

have the satisfaction of striking the dwarf, since he saw the knight was armed and very grim and arrogant, and he was afraid he would be speedily killed, should he strike his dwarf in front of him. There being no valour in foolishness, Erec showed enough good sense to leave it at that and go back.

234 "My lady," he says, "now matters are worse: that scoundrel of a dwarf has so wounded me that he's cut my face to ribbons. I didn't strike or touch him; but I'm not to be blamed for that, as I was quite without armour. I was afraid of the armed knight, coarse and overbearing as he is: he wouldn't have found it amusing, but as a matter of pride would promptly have killed me. Yet this I promise you: I shall avenge my disgrace, if I can, or else increase it. But my arms are too far away for me to have them now when I need them, for I left them at Cardigan this morning when I set out. If I went to fetch them, I'd be unlikely ever to find the knight again, because he went off at great speed. I must follow him at once, closely or at a distance, until I can find arms to hire or borrow. If I do find anyone to lend me arms, that knight will immediately find me ready to do battle. And you may be quite sure that we shall fight together until either he defeats me or I him; and if possible I'll be on my way back the day after tomorrow. Then you'll see me home again either happy or miserable, I don't know which. My lady, I mustn't delay any longer, but go after that knight. I'm leaving. God be with you." And the queen likewise commends him to God, more than five hundred times, that He might keep him from harm.

275 Erec leaves the queen and follows the knight without pausing, whilst the queen stays in the wood, where the king had come up with the stag and, outstripping all the others at the death, had taken and killed it. They all headed back and went bearing the stag until they came to Cardigan. After supper, when all the knights were in high spirits in the castle, the king, as he was entitled to do having taken the stag, said he would bestow the kiss in observance of the custom of the stag. There was a great stir throughout the court: one says to the other that this will not happen without protests backed by sword or ashen lance. Each man wants to contend by deeds of arms that his own beloved is the most beautiful in the hall. This is all very ominous talk. When my lord Gawain heard of it, you may be sure he was not in the least pleased. He mentioned it to the king. "Sire," he says, "your knights here are much alarmed. They're all

talking of this kiss and say unanimously that it will never be given without brawling and a fight." The king's reply is sensible: "Gawain, my good nephew, advise me how to keep my honour and my rights, for I have no wish for quarrelling."

311 A large number of the best nobles in the court hurry to the council. King Yder,* the first to be summoned, came, and then King Cadoalant, who was very wise and valiant. Kay and Girflet came, so too did King Amauguin, and with them gather many of the other lords. The discussion had already begun when the queen arrived. She told them of what had happened to her in the forest, how she had seen the armed knight and the vicious little dwarf who with his scourge had struck her maiden on the bare hand and had similarly dealt Erec a terrible blow on the face, and how Erec had followed the knight to increase his disgrace or avenge it, saying he should be back in two days' time if he could. "My lord," says the queen to the king, "listen to me a moment. If these lords approve what I say, put off this kiss until the day after tomorrow when Erec returns." There is no one who does not agree with her, and the king himself gives his assent.

342 Erec continues to follow the armed knight and the dwarf who had struck him until they come to a fine, strong and very well situated fortress. They go straight in through the gate. Inside the fortress were knights and a large number of beautiful maidens, all in very high spirits. Some were in the streets feeding sparrow-hawks and moulting falcons, some were bringing out tercels and mewed tawny goshawks. Elsewhere, others play at different dice games or chess or backgammon. There in front of the stables are the grooms, rubbing down and currying the horses. As soon as they see in the distance the knight, whom they recognise, coming with his dwarf and maiden, they go three by three to meet him. They all greet and welcome him, but make no move towards Erec, who is unknown to them. Erec continues to follow at the knight's pace through the fortress until he sees him enter his lodging. He was quite overjoyed to have seen him lodged.

373 He went on a little and saw a vavasour of mature years reclining on some steps. Though his dwelling was extremely modest, he was a handsome man, white-haired, with frank features and an air of noble breeding. There he sat all alone, apparently deep in thought. Erec took him for a worthy man who would readily give him

lodging. He goes through the gate into the courtyard. The vavasour runs towards him; and before Erec has uttered a word, he greets him. "Good sir," he says, "welcome! If you care to lodge with me, here is the house at your disposal." Erec answers: "I thank you. I came here for no other reason, since I need somewhere to spend the night."

393 Erec dismounts from his horse, and the gentleman himself takes it, leading it by the rein. He does his guest great honour. The vavasour calls his wife and very lovely daughter, who were at work in a sewing-room on some task or other. The lady came out with her daughter, who was dressed in a fine white shift, widely cut and pleated.* Over it she wore a white gown, nothing more or less; but the gown was so old it was in holes at the elbows. If the dress on the outside was poor, the body beneath was fair.

411 The maiden was extremely attractive; for Nature,* who had created her, had put all her care into the work and had herself marvelled times without number that just this once she had contrived to make so lovely a person; and afterwards, try as she might, she was never able to reproduce her original model. Nature bears witness that never was so exquisite a creature seen in the whole world. I tell you truly that the hair of the blonde Iseut did not shine so fair that she could stand comparison with her.* Her brow and face were more pure and white than the lily. Her features were tinted with a fresh rosy hue wondrously painted by Nature upon the whiteness. Her eyes shone with such radiance that they seemed like two stars. Never was God able to form finer nose, mouth and eyes. What could I say of her beauty? It was truly such as was made to be gazed upon, for in it one might have looked at oneself as in a mirror.

442 She had come out of the sewing-room. At the sight of the knight, whom she had never seen before, she drew back a little as she did not recognise him, and blushed in her embarrassment. Erec, for his part, was astonished to see such great beauty in her. Then the vavasour said to her: "Dear sweet daughter, take this horse and stable it with those of mine. Take off its saddle and bridle and give it oats and hay. Tend and curry it so it's well groomed."

459 The girl takes the horse, undoes its breast-strap and removes its bridle and saddle. Now the horse is in excellent hands: she looks after it with expert care. She puts a halter over its head, rubs it well

down, curries and grooms it, then tethers it to the manger and puts before it a good supply of hay and fresh, sweet oats. Then she went back to her father, who said to her: "Dear sweet daughter, take this gentleman's hand and lead him upstairs, showing him every honour." The maiden, who had no lack of courtesy, did not delay in taking him by the hand and leading him upstairs. The lady had gone ahead and made the house ready. She had spread quilts and coverlets on the couches, on which the three of them sat down, Erec at his host's side and the girl opposite, with the fire burning brightly before them. The vavasour had no house- or chamber-maid, but was waited on by a single man-servant, who was in the kitchen hurriedly getting meat and birds ready for supper. He was good at quickly preparing meat in sauce and grilled birds. When he had provided the meal as instructed, he brought them two basins of water. Tables and cloths were soon ready and laid with bread and wine. They sat down to supper and had as much as they wished of whatever they needed.

501 When they had eaten at their leisure and left the tables, Erec addressed his host, the master of the house. "Tell me, good host," he says, "why your daughter, who is so very beautiful and clever, is wearing such a poor, mean dress."—"My good friend," says the vavasour, "many suffer through poverty, and so do I. I'm very sorry to see her so poorly dressed, but I haven't the means to do better. I've been continually at war for so long that I've lost, mortgaged or sold all my land.* Despite that, she would have been well dressed had I allowed her to take everything people wished to give her. Even the lord of this castle would have clothed her in finery and met her every wish, for she's his niece, and he is a count; and there's no nobleman in this country, however rich or powerful, who wouldn't gladly have taken her as his wife, had I approved. But I'm waiting for a still better opportunity and for God to bestow higher honour on her and chance to bring some king or count here to take her away. Is there under heaven any king or count who would be ashamed of my daughter, whose amazing beauty is so great that her equal is not to be found? Very beautiful she is, but her intelligence is far superior to her beauty. Never did God create anyone so wise or noble-hearted. With my daughter beside me I don't care a marble for the whole world. She's my delight and my pleasure, my cheer and my comfort, she's my wealth and my treasure. I love nothing so much as her."

547 When Erec had listened to the whole of his host's story, he asked him to tell him where such a chivalric company as was in the fortress had come from; for even the meanest and smallest of the streets and houses was full of knights, ladies and squires. The vavasour replied: "Good friend, these are the nobles from the surrounding country; and all of them, young and grey-haired alike, have come for a festival to be held in this town tomorrow. That's why the lodgings are so full. There will be a mighty hubbub tomorrow when they're all assembled; for there will be placed on a silver perch in front of all the people a splendid sparrow-hawk of five or six moultings, the best imaginable. Whoever wishes to obtain this hawk will need to have a mistress who is beautiful, sensible and above reproach. If there's a knight so bold as to wish to defend the merit and reputation of the one he claims to be most beautiful, he must have his mistress take the hawk from the perch in front of everybody, unless someone dares to stop her. This is the custom they observe and the reason for their gathering here each year."

581 Erec next enquires of him: "My good host, if you don't mind, tell me, if you know, the identity of a knight wearing arms blazoned with azure and gold who passed by here a little while ago with an elegant maiden very close by his side and a hunchbacked dwarf ahead of them." Then the host replied: "He's the one who will have the sparrow-hawk without any knight opposing him. I don't expect anyone to come forward: there will be no blows or wounds. He's already had it unchallenged for two years, and if he gets it this year too he'll have won it for good. Every year from now on it will be his to keep without contest or dispute."

601 Erec's answer is prompt: "I have no love for that knight! You may be sure that if I had arms I would challenge him for the hawk. Good host, I beg you to show me the courtesy and favour of kindly advising me how to equip myself with a set of arms, old or new, unsightly or handsome, I don't mind what." His reply is generous: "You mustn't worry about that! I have a good, fine set that I shall be glad to lend you. I have in the house the triple-woven hauberk, chosen from among five hundred; and I have excellent costly greaves, polished, splendid and light. The helmet is fine and bright, the shield fresh and new. In fact I'll lend you everything: horse, sword and lance – there will be nothing to find fault with."—"I

thank you, good kind sir! But I ask for no better sword than the one I've brought with me and for no horse other than my own: that will serve my needs well, if you lend me everything else. It will be a very great kindness, I'm sure. I wish, though, to ask one more favour of you, which I shall repay, if God grant that I come out of the contest with the full honours." The other replies generously: "Don't be afraid to ask for what you wish, whatever it may be! Everything I have is yours."

639 Then Erec says he wants to lay claim to the sparrow-hawk on behalf of his daughter; for there will certainly be no maiden with a hundredth part of her beauty, and if he takes her with him, he will have good and proper reason to claim, and show, that she should carry off the hawk. He added: "Sir, you don't know what guest you have lodged or what his rank and family are. I'm the son of a rich and mighty king. My father's name is King Lac. The Britons call me Erec, and I belong to King Arthur's court, having been with him a full three years. I don't know if ever anything of my father's renown or my own has reached these parts; but I promise and assure you that if you equip me with arms and grant me your daughter tomorrow for the winning of the sparrow-hawk, then, if God gives me the victory, I'll take her away to my own land. I'll give her a crown to wear, and she shall be queen of three cities."—"Ah, good sir, is this true? Are you Erec, Lac's son?"—"I am indeed," says he.

669 At this the host was overjoyed and said: "We've certainly heard tell of you in this country. Now I love and esteem you far more, for you're very valiant and bold. You'll never meet with a refusal from me: I bestow my lovely daughter on you as your very own." Then he took her by the hand, saying: "Here, I give her to you." Erec received her with delight: now all his needs are fulfilled. Everyone in the house rejoices greatly: the father is full of joy, and for joy the mother weeps. The maiden sat quite quiet;* but she too was very joyful and happy at being betrothed to him, valiant and courtly as he was; and she was sure he would be king and she herself honoured and crowned a rich queen.

691 They had stayed up late into the night. The beds were made with white sheets and soft mattresses. Then, their conversation ended, they all went happily to bed. That night Erec slept little. In the morning at the break of dawn he rises promptly and quickly, and his host with him. They both go to the church to have the Mass of

the Holy Spirit sung by a hermit, not forgetting to make an offering. When they have heard mass, they each bow to the altar and return to the house. Erec, very impatient for the contest, asks for the arms and is given them. He is armed by the maiden herself—there was no need for magic or charms!* She laces on his iron greaves and binds them with a deerhide thong. She dresses him in a well-meshed hauberk and laces on the ventail. On his head she places the burnished helmet, arming him splendidly from top to toe. At his side she fastens his sword, then orders his horse to be fetched, and that is done. He leaps on to it straight from the ground.* The maiden brings the shield and sturdy lance, and he takes the shield she offers him and hangs it from his neck by the strap. The lance in turn she places in his hand, and he grasps it by the haft.

727   Then he addressed the courteous vavasour. "If you please, good sir," he says, "have your daughter get ready. I wish to take her to the sparrow-hawk, as you've agreed I should." Immediately, without the least delay, the vavasour had a bay palfrey saddled. The harness is not worth a mention in view of the great poverty afflicting the vavasour. The saddle and bridle were put on. Without waiting to be asked, the maiden mounts, bare-headed and without a cloak. Erec has no wish to lose any more time, but sets straight off with his host's daughter close beside him* and the gentleman with his wife both following behind.

747   Erec rides with lance erect and the graceful maiden at his side. In the streets they are gazed at by everybody, great and small; and all the people are amazed and enquire of one another: "Who is he, that knight? He must be very bold and proud to take with him that lovely girl. He won't waste his efforts. He can certainly claim with justice that she's the most beautiful." One says to the other: "Truly, she should have the sparrow-hawk." Some were praising the maiden, and there were many of them saying: "God, who can that knight be who is escorting the beautiful maiden?"—"I don't know."—"Nor I," they all say. "But his polished helmet suits him well, and so do that hauberk and shield and the sharp steel sword. He sits superbly on that horse and really looks the valiant vassal. He's splendidly built and shapely in arms, legs and feet." Everybody is intent on gazing at them; but they do not linger or pause until they come before the sparrow-hawk. Once there, they stood to one side and awaited the knight.

778 Now they see him coming, with his dwarf and maiden beside him. He had heard the news of the arrival of a knight wanting to obtain the sparrow-hawk, but did not believe there was any knight in the world so bold as to dare fight with him: he was confident he would defeat and overthrow him. Well known to all the people, he was welcomed and escorted by everyone, who followed him in a noisy crowd. Knights, retainers, ladies and maidens run after him helter-skelter. The knight leads them all, with his own maiden and dwarf beside him. With great arrogance he rides swiftly towards the sparrow-hawk; but round it there was such a great throng of rough common folk that it was impossible to touch or approach it from any side. The count, arriving on the scene, goes up to the mob and threatens them with a switch he holds in his hand. The people retreat.

805 Moving forward, the knight says quietly to his maiden: "My damsel, this bird, which is so superb and well moulted, should be yours as rightful tribute to your own outstanding beauty and charm; and so indeed it shall be as long as I live. Step forward, my sweet love, and take the sparrow-hawk from the perch." The girl went to stretch out her hand; but Erec, contemptuous of her presumption, hurries to challenge her. "Damsel," he says, "draw back! Amuse yourself with some other bird, for you have no right to this one. Whoever may be offended, this sparrow-hawk will never be yours, for it is claimed by someone better than you, far more beautiful and more courtly." The other knight takes this ill; but he is held in small regard by Erec, who has his own maiden come forward. "My fair one," he says, "step up and take the bird from the perch, for it is right and proper that you should have it. Come forward, damsel! I pride myself that I shall certainly make good my claim if anyone dares to come and oppose me; for there's not a single lady to rival you, any more than the moon does the sun, in either beauty or worth, in grace or honour."

837 The other knight could no longer suffer hearing him so vehemently offering to do battle. "Say, fellow," he says, "who are you to have denied me the sparrow-hawk?" Erec boldly answers him: "I'm a knight from another land, come to obtain this hawk; for it is only right, whoever may find it irksome, that this damsel should have it."—"Be off!" says the other. "That will never be. Madness has brought you here. If you want the hawk, you'll have to pay very

dearly for it."—"Pay for it, fellow? And how?"—"You'll have to fight with me, unless you concede it to me."—"Now you've spoken nonsense," says Erec. "These, it's plain to me, are empty threats, for I've no great fear of you."—"Then I defy you outright, since a combat is inevitable." Erec replies: "In God's hands be it! I never wanted anything more." You will soon hear the sound of their blows.

863 The jousting-place was spacious and clear, with the people ranged on all sides. The knights draw more than a furlong apart, then spur their horses into the charge. Thrusting at each other with the heads of their lances, they strike with such force that their shields are pierced and shattered. The lances splinter and shiver, and the saddle-bows are hacked to pieces at the back. They have to leave their stirrups, and both topple to the ground, their horses making off across the field. Quickly they have jumped to their feet again. Not having missed with their lances, they draw their swords from the scabbards and ferociously put each other to the test, exchanging great blows with their blades, their dented helmets ringing loud. The sword-play is fierce, with mighty strokes given and received, for they do not hold back at all. Whatever they strike they shatter, cutting through shields, piercing hauberks, their blades reddened with crimson blood. The fight lasts long, and they rain so many blows on one another that they grow weary and falter.

890 With both of the maidens weeping, each knight sees his own in tears, raising her hands to God and praying Him to give the honours in the combat to the one exerting himself on her behalf. "Ah, vassal!" says the knight, "let's break off for a little and have a short rest, for these blows we're dealing are too weak. We ought to be striking better ones; for it's very nearly evening, and it's a great shame and disgrace that this contest lasts so long. Look at that attractive girl weeping and calling on God on your behalf, and mine doing the same for me. We should strive to the utmost with our steel blades for the sake of those we love." Erec replies: "You've spoken well." Then they rest a little.

911 Erec looks towards his beloved as she utters heartfelt prayers for him. No sooner has he seen her than great strength has surged back into him. Her love and beauty have restored his great fighting spirit. He remembers the queen to whom he had given his solemn promise

that he would avenge his disgrace or else make it even greater. "Ah, wretch that I am!" he says. "What am I waiting for? I've still not taken the slightest revenge for the wrong this fellow permitted when his dwarf struck me in the woods." With his wrath rekindled, he calls angrily to the knight. "Vassal!" he says, "I summon you back to the duel. We've taken too long a rest: let's continue the fight!" The other replies: "That suits me." Then they come to grips once more.

933 They were both expert at fencing: at that first assault, the knight would have wounded Erec had he not well parried the blow; yet he did strike him so hard above the shield at his temple that he hacked off a piece of the helmet. The sword grazes the bright coif as it comes down, splitting the shield to the boss and slicing away more than a span from the side of his hauberk. This was very nearly fatal for him! The cold steel cut through to the flesh on his thigh. God protected him on that occasion: had the blow not glanced off, it would have sliced him through the body. But Erec is not at all dismayed: he pays the knight back with interest and, attacking him with great courage, strikes him just by the shoulder. It is such a blow he has dealt him that the shield cannot withstand it, and the hauberk does not save him from the sword penetrating to the bone. He has made the crimson blood stream down to his waist-band.

961 Both vassals fight ferociously, with nothing to choose between them, since neither can gain so much as a foot of ground from the other. They have so rent apart their hauberks and hacked their shields to pieces that there is truly not enough of them left to serve as protection; so they are quite exposed to each other's blows. Both of them lose a great amount of blood, and each grows very weak. The knight strikes Erec and Erec him, dealing so violent a blow on his helmet that he quite stuns him. He rains the blows down, giving him three strokes in quick succession, completely shattering the helmet and cutting through the coif underneath. The sword reaches right to the skull and severs a bone in his head, but without touching his brain. He slumps and staggers; and as he does so, Erec thrusts at him so that he falls over on his right side. Erec seizes him by the helmet and forcibly tugs it from his head. Unlacing his ventail, he disarms both head and face.

989 When he recalls the outrage done him in the woods by his dwarf, Erec would have cut off his head had he not cried out for mercy.

"Ah, vassal!" he says, "you've defeated me. Have mercy! Don't kill me now you've overcome and captured me: that would never bring you fame or credit. If you struck me any more now, you'd be guilty of very base conduct. Take my sword: I surrender it to you." Erec, however, does not take it, but says: "It's lucky for you if I don't kill you!"—"Ah, mercy, noble knight! What's my crime, then, or the wrong that earns your mortal hatred? I've never seen you before, as far as I know, and have never been guilty of bringing you any harm or shame." Erec replies: "Indeed you have!"—"Ah, sir, say what it was then. To the best of my memory, I've never seen you before; and if I've wronged you at all, I'll be in your hands."

1013 Then Erec said: "Vassal, I'm the man who was in the forest yesterday with Queen Guenevere, where you allowed your obnoxious dwarf to strike my lady's maiden: it's a very shocking thing to strike a woman. Then he hit me afterwards: that dwarf really took me for a base fellow. You showed the very height of insolence when you saw such an outrage and permitted it, happy that such a misshapen creature should strike the maiden and me. For a crime like that you've earned my hatred, so great is the offence you committed. So you must declare yourself my prisoner and at once, without any delay, go straight to my lady; for you'll certainly find her at Cardigan, if you go there. You'll manage to get there tonight, because it's less than seven leagues from here, I think. You must surrender yourself, your maiden and your dwarf into her hands to do whatever she orders. And tell her I send her word that tomorrow I'll come in high spirits bringing a maiden so lovely, wise and prudent that she has no equal anywhere: you can tell her that truthfully enough! And now I want to know your name."

1045 Then, like it or not, the other told him: "Sir, my name is Yder, son of Nut. This morning I didn't believe a single man could overcome me by force of arms. Now I've found someone better than I, and have good proof of it. You're a very valiant knight. Here! I pledge you my word that straight away, without more ado, I'll go to give myself up to the queen. But tell me what your own name is: don't keep it from me. Who shall I say is sending me? I'm all ready for the road."—"I'll tell you," he replies, "I'll never hide my name from you: it's Erec. Go now, and tell her I've sent you to her."—"I'll go, then. And I will, I assure you, put my dwarf and my maiden along with myself entirely at her disposal: have no fears

about that. I'll also give her the news of you and your maiden."
Then Erec accepted his pledge. All were present at the agreement:
the count and the people round about, the maidens and the nobles.
Some were glad, some depressed, some sorry, others pleased. For
the sake of the maiden in the white shift, that noble, open-hearted
girl, the poor vavasour's daughter, the majority rejoiced; and for
Yder there grieved his maiden and those devoted to him.

1081 Yder, obliged to carry out his promise, had no wish to stay
there any longer. At once he mounts his horse, and (why should I
spin out the story?) he leads off his dwarf and maiden through
woodland and over plain. They followed the direct road until they
came to Cardigan. In the gallery outside the main hall was my lord
Gawain along with Kay the seneschal; and it seems a great number
of lords had come there with them. They spotted those who were
approaching, the first to see them being the seneschal, who said to
my lord Gawain: "Sir, I feel in my heart that the vassal on the road
there is the one the queen said caused her such trouble yesterday. It
seems to me there are three of them: I can see the dwarf and the
maiden."—"True enough," says Sir Gawain; "there's a maiden
and a dwarf coming with the knight and heading straight towards
us. The knight is fully armed, but his shield is not in one piece. If the
queen saw him, I think she'd recognise him. Just go and call her,
seneschal!"

1112 He went off at once and found her in one of the chambers. "My
lady," he says, "you remember perhaps the dwarf who angered you
yesterday by injuring your maiden?"—"Yes, I remember him well,
seneschal. Do you have news of him? Why have you mentioned
him?"—"Because, my lady, I've seen a knight travelling armed on a
grey horse; and unless my eyes have deceived me, there's a maiden
with him, and I fancy he's accompanied by the dwarf carrying the
scourge with which Erec was lashed." Then the queen rose and
said: "Let's go at once, seneschal, to see if that is the fellow! If it is
he, you may be sure I shall confirm it for you as soon as I see him."
And Kay said: "I'll point him out to you. Come up to the gallery
where your knights are. It was from there we saw him coming; and
my lord Gawain himself awaits you there. Let's go there, my lady,
for we've waited here too long."

1141 The queen then went up and came to the windows to stand
there beside my lord Gawain. She clearly recognised the knight.

"Ah, my lords," she says, "that's the man! He's had a very dangerous time and has been in a fight. I don't know if Erec has avenged
his affront or if he has defeated Erec; but his shield has taken many
blows, and his hauberk is covered with blood – there's more of it
red than shining."—"That's true," says my lord Gawain. "I'm
quite certain, my lady, that you're entirely right. His hauberk is
bloodstained and very battered and damaged: you can tell he's had
a fight. We can be absolutely sure that it's been a fierce contest.
We'll soon hear from him a tale that will spell joy or grief for us:
either Erec is sending him here to you as a captive at your mercy, or
else he's coming here in his audacity foolishly to boast to us that
he's defeated Erec or slain him. I don't believe he's bringing any
other news." The queen says: "That's what I think."—"It's very
likely," they all agree.

1171 Thereupon Yder comes in through the gate to bring them the
news. Everybody went down from the gallery to meet him. Making
for the main mounting-place, Yder there got off his horse; and
Gawain took the damsel and helped her down from her palfrey.
The dwarf dismounts elsewhere. More than a hundred knights
were present. When all three had dismounted, they were led before
the king. On seeing the queen, Yder bowed down at her feet,
greeting her first of all and then the king and his knights. He said:
"My lady, I'm sent here as your prisoner by a noble man, a valiant
and gallant knight, the one who yesterday felt the knots of my
dwarf's scourge across his face. He has overcome and vanquished
me in armed combat. Here, my lady, I bring you the dwarf, come to
throw himself on your mercy. I bring and surrender to you myself,
my maiden and my dwarf, for you to do with us whatever you
please." The queen is silent no longer, but asks him for news of
Erec. "Pray tell me," she says, "do you know when Erec will
come?"—"Tomorrow, my lady; and he will bring with him a
maiden more beautiful than any I have ever known." Once he had
delivered his message, the queen, with ungrudging good sense, said
to him courteously: "My friend, since you have thrown yourself on
my mercy, your captivity will be the less arduous: I've no wish to do
you any harm. But tell me, so help you God: what is your name?"
And he said to her: "My lady, I'm called Yder, the son of Nut." It
was the truth he told her.

1215 Then the queen arose; and going before the king, she said:
"Sire, did you hear? You've done well to wait for Erec, that valiant

knight. I gave you very good advice yesterday when I suggested you should wait for him. This shows it's good to take advice." The king replies: "It's no lie, but a very true saying that he who takes advice is no fool. It was fortunate yesterday that we heeded your suggestion. But if you have any love for me, release this knight from his captivity on condition that from now on he shall belong to my company and my court; and if he does not, then the worse for him." The king had made his pronouncement, and at once the queen gave the knight his liberty, but on condition that he should remain constantly at the court. He needed little urging, but agreed to stay there; and from then on he was a member of the court and company, which he had not been before. Then pages were alerted and hurried to disarm him.

1244 Now we must return to our account of Erec, who was still at the jousting-place where he had fought the combat. Never, I think, was there such rejoicing on Saint Samson's Isle where Tristan overcame the fierce Morholt* as there was here for Erec. Tall and short, thin and fat, all were full of praise for him. Everyone commends his chivalry, and there is no knight but says: "God, what a vassal! He has no equal under Heaven." They follow him to his lodging, singing his praises and talking much of him. The count himself, rejoicing more than any, embraces him with the words: "Sir, if it pleased you, it would be right and proper for you to take your lodging in my house, since you're the son of King Lac. You would do me great honour by accepting my hospitality, for I regard you as my lord. Good sir, I beg you, please stay with me." Erec replies: "If you don't mind, I shall not tonight desert my host, who has done me very great honour by giving me his daughter. What do you say, sir? Isn't this, then, a magnificent and very precious gift?"—"Yes indeed, sir!" says the count. "It is a very fine, splendid gift. The maiden is beautiful and wise and is of extremely high birth: her mother, you know, is my sister. I'm certainly highly delighted when you deign to take my niece. Once again I beg you to come and stay with me tonight." Erec replies: "Don't press me: I wouldn't do that on any account!" The other, seeing his request was futile, said: "As you please, sir! We need say no more about it now; but I and all my knights will be with you tonight to entertain you and keep you company." Hearing this, Erec thanked him and came to his host's house, with the count beside him.

1295 Ladies and knights were there; and the vavasour was very
happy at Erec's arrival. More than twenty pages hurried to remove
his arms with all speed. Anyone present in that house might have
witnessed a scene of great joy. First Erec took his seat, then the
others sit down in due order on couches, covered seats and benches.
Beside Erec sat the count and the bright-faced maiden, who was
feeding a small plover's wing to the sparrow-hawk on her wrist, for
which the contest had been fought. That day she had won much
honour, joy and dignity. Her heart was full of gladness for the bird
and for her lord: her joy could not have been greater, and she
clearly showed it, making no secret of her happiness, so that
everybody was fully aware of it and could see it. All those in the
house were jubilant for love of the maiden.

1320 Erec addressed the vavasour with these words: "Good host,
good friend, good sir! You've done me great honour, but will be
well rewarded for it. Tomorrow I shall take your daughter away
with me to the king's court. There my intention will be to take her
as my wife; and if you don't mind waiting a little, I shall send for
you before long. I'll have you taken into the land that belongs to my
father and will later be mine (it's far from here, by no means close at
hand); and there I shall give you two excellent, very rich and
splendid strongholds. You shall be lord of Roadan, which was built
in the time of Adam, and of another fortress close by which is not a
whit less valuable. The people call it Montrevel, and my father
owns no better castle. Then before the third day has passed I'll have
sent you much gold and silver, dappled and grey furs, and very
precious silken materials for clothes for you and your wife, my dear
lady. Tomorrow at daybreak I shall take your daughter to court in
the gown and dress she wears now. My wish is that my lady the
queen should array her in her finest robe of velvet and scarlet
cloth."

1353 In the house was a girl who was very prudent, intelligent and
talented. She was seated on a bench beside the maiden in the white
shift and was her first cousin, the niece of the lord count. Hearing
that Erec wished to take her cousin to the queen's court so very
poorly dressed, the girl spoke about it to the count. "Sir," she says,
"it would be very shameful for you more than anyone else if this
knight took your niece with him wearing such poor clothes." And
the count replies: "Please, sweet niece, give her the dress you think

best among those you have." Erec heard the girl and said: "Sir, don't speak of that! Of one thing you may be sure: on no account would I wish her to have any other dress until the queen gives her one." When the damsel heard him, she responded: "Ah, good sir, since you wish to take my cousin away like this in her white shift and smock, I'd like to offer her another gift as you're quite against her having any of my dresses. I have three excellent palfreys (no king or count ever owned better), one sorrel, one dappled and one black with white feet. I give my word that there's not one in a hundred better than the dappled. The birds flying through the air don't go faster than that palfrey; and it's not too mettlesome, but just right for a girl: a child can ride it, for it's not nervous or stubborn, it doesn't bite or kick and isn't temperamental. Anyone who looks for a better doesn't know what he's after. Nobody who rides it is uncomfortable, but goes as easily and gently as if he were in a boat." Then Erec said: "My sweet friend, I've no objection to her accepting this gift: on the contrary, it pleases me, and I don't wish her to turn it down."

1407 At once the girl calls a trusty servant of hers and tells him: "Go, friend, saddle my dappled palfrey and bring it here quickly." He does what she bids, putting the saddle and bridle on the horse and doing his best to prepare it properly; and then he mounts that well-maned palfrey.—So now the palfrey has arrived. When Erec saw it, he did not spare his praise, so fine and handsome it looked. Then he ordered a servant to go and tether it beside his charger in the stable. With that, the company dispersed, having spent a most happy evening. The count goes to his own dwelling, leaving Erec with the vavasour and saying he will escort him when he leaves in the morning. They slept the whole night through.

1430 In the morning when dawn has broken, Erec prepares for the journey. He orders his horse to be saddled, then wakes his lovely sweetheart, who dresses and makes herself ready. The vavasour and his wife rise; and there is no knight or lady who does not prepare to escort the maiden and the knight. They have all mounted, and the count with them. Erec rides next to the count with, at his side, his sweet love, who has not forgotten her sparrow-hawk, with which she plays, having taken no other riches with her. They are escorted on their way in high spirits. When the time came to part, the count wanted to send with Erec a party of his knights so they might do him honour by accompanying him; but he said he would take none of them, nor asked for company other than the maiden's. Then he said: "God be with you!" The escort had come a long way with them. The count kisses Erec and his niece and commends them to God's goodness. Her father and mother also kiss her again and again. They do not hold back their tears: at the parting her mother weeps, as do the maiden and her father too. Such is love, such is human nature and family devotion. They wept for the devotion and tenderness and affection they felt for their child; yet they knew well that their daughter was going to a place whence great honour would come to them. They wept for love and devotion when they parted from their daughter: their tears had no other cause. They were sure that in the end this would bring them honour. Many were the tears shed at the parting. Weeping, they commend one another to God; then, without lingering further, they leave.

1479 Erec parts from his host, extremely anxious to get to the king's court. He was delighted with his adventure, which had brought him great happiness; for now he had a sweetheart of extraordinary beauty who was wise, courtly and noble-hearted.* He could not look at her enough. The more he gazes, the more she pleases him. He cannot help kissing her. He delights in drawing close and keeping his eyes fixed on her. His gaze lingers over her fair hair, her laughing eyes and pure brow, her nose, face and mouth; and he is touched to the heart by a great tenderness. He gazes at everything down to her hips: the chin and white throat, the waist and sides, arms and hands. But no less intent than the knight, the maiden vies in gazing at him with fond eye and true heart. For no reward would they have stopped looking at one another! They were a perfect match in courtliness, beauty and great nobility of character; and they were so much of a kind and equal in conduct and bearing that no one wishing to tell the truth could have chosen the better or fairer or wiser of them. They were of very similar disposition and admirably suited to one another. Each steals the other's heart. Never did the sacrament of marriage bring together two so hand-some figures.

1517 Together they rode along until, about midday, they approached the fortress of Cardigan, where they were both awaited. The leading nobles of the court had gone to the upper windows to watch for them. Queen Guenevere hurried there, and the king himself came, and so did Kay and Perceval of Wales,* followed by my lord Gawain and Tor, the son of King Arés, together with Lucan the cup-bearer: many fine knights were there. They spotted Erec coming, bringing his beloved with him, and all recognised him easily the moment they saw him. The queen is overjoyed and the whole court delighted at his coming, for they are united in their love for him. On his arrival in front of the hall, the king goes down to meet him, and the queen in turn; and all greet him in God's name. They warmly welcome him and his maiden and praise and applaud her great beauty. Then the king himself took her and helped her down from her palfrey, showing very great courtesy and being in the best of spirits at that time. He did the maiden much honour, leading her by the hand up into the great stone hall.

1552 After them, Erec and the queen went up hand in hand; and he said to her: "My lady, I bring you my maiden and sweetheart, dressed in poor attire. Just as she was given to me, I have brought her to you. She's the daughter of a poor vavasour. Poverty degrades many a worthy man. Her father is of fine, courtly character, though endowed with little wealth; and her mother is a most noble lady, for she has a brother who is a rich count. I should not refuse to marry the maiden on grounds of beauty or lineage. It's because of poverty she has worn out this white shift so that both sleeves are torn at the elbow. Yet, had I wished, she would have had plenty of good dresses, for a girl, her cousin, wanted to give her a robe of ermine and spotted or grey silk; but on no account did I wish her to wear any other dress until you had seen her. Now think about it, my dear lady! As you well see, she's in great need of a fine, becoming dress." And the queen immediately replies: "You've acted quite properly. It's right that she should have one of my robes, and I shall at once give her an excellent one: beautiful and brand-new."

1587 Without more ado, the queen takes her off to her private apartment and orders that the new tunic be quickly brought along with the greenish-purple mantle embroidered with little crosses that had been made for herself. The person she had sent brought her the mantle and the tunic, which had white ermine trimmings down to the sleeves. At the wrists and neck-band there was, without a word of a lie, more than half a mark's weight of beaten gold;

and set everywhere in the gold were very precious stones of indigo, green, blue and dark brown hues. The tunic was very rich, but I fancy the mantle was worth every bit as much. As yet no fastening had been put on it, for it was, like the tunic, absolutely brand-new. The mantle was of fine, excellent quality: at the neck were two sable-skins, and in the tassels was more than an ounce of gold; on one side was a hyacinth, and on the other a ruby that shone more brightly than a burning candle. The lining was of white ermine: none finer or more splendid was ever to be seen or found. The purple cloth was superbly worked with little crosses, all different, in indigo, vermilion, violet, white and green, blue and yellow. The queen asked for a pair of bands, four ells long, made of silk thread and gold. These beautiful, well-matched fastenings are handed to her. She at once had them attached quickly to the mantle by a man who was a true expert at the work.

1631   When there was nothing more to be done to the mantle, that noble, distinguished lady embraced the maiden in the white shift, with the generous words: "My young lady, you must change that shift for this tunic, which is worth more than a hundred silver marks: that's a favour I should like to do you. Then put this mantle on over it! I shall give you more on another occasion." She did not refuse it, but took the dress with thanks. Two maids led her into a room apart, where she took off her shift, not having the slightest regard for it any more, with the request that it be given in charity for the love of God. Then she puts on the tunic, fastening a belt of gold brocade tightly round her waist; and after that she dons the mantle. Her expression was now far from dejected, for the dress suited her so well that it made her look much more beautiful than ever.

1655   The two maids bound her fair hair with a golden thread; but her locks shone brighter than the thread, though it was of very fine gold. On her head the girls place a circlet made of flowers of many different colours. They do their utmost to adorn her in such a fashion that no room for improvement could be found. One of them placed round her neck a ribbon to which were attached two small brooches of enamelled gold. Now she was so graceful and lovely that her equal, I think, could not have been found in any land, seek and search as one might, so excellently had Nature fashioned her.

1673   Then she left the room and came to the queen, who welcomed her very warmly, liking and greatly approving of her because of her beauty and fine manners. Taking each other by the hand, they came before the king, who, on seeing them, rose to his feet to receive them. As they entered the hall, so many knights rose to greet them that I cannot name one tenth, or thirteenth, or fifteenth of them; but I can tell you the names of some of the best nobles among those of the Round Table, who were the finest in the world.

1691   Before all the good knights, Gawain should come first, Erec the son of Lac second, and Lancelot of the Lake third.* Gornemant of Gohort was fourth, and fifth was the Handsome Coward. Sixth was the Ugly Brave, seventh Meliant of Liz, eighth Mauduit the Wise and ninth Dodinel the Wild. Let Gandelu come tenth for his many good qualities. I shall tell you the others in no particular sequence, because I find it difficult to put them in order. Eslit was there with Briien and Yvain son of Urien. Yvain of Loenel was also there and Yvain the Bastard. Beside Yvain of Cavaliot was Garravain of Estrangot. After the Knight with the Horn was the Youth with the Golden Ring. And Tristan who never laughed sat beside Bliobleheris, and next to Brun of Piciez was his brother Grus the Wrathful. The Armourer, who preferred war to peace, was seated next, and after him Karadués the Short-Armed, a knight of very cheerful disposition; and Caveron of Robendic and King Quenedic's son, the Youth of Quintareus and Yder of the Dolorous Mount, Gaheriet and Kay of Estraus, Amauguin and Gales the Bald, Grain, Gornevain and Carahés, and Tor the son of King Arés, Girflet the son of Do, and Taulas who never tired of arms; and a young man of great merit, Loholt, King Arthur's son; and Sagremor the Impetuous should not be forgotten, nor Bedoiier the Marshal who was an expert at chess and backgammon, nor Bravaïn, nor King Lot, nor Galegantin of Wales, nor Gronosis, well versed in evil, who was Kay the Seneschal's son, nor Labigodés the Courtly, nor Count Cadorcaniois, nor Letron of Prepelesant, whose manners were so polished, nor Breon the son of Canodan, nor the Count of Honolan who had such a fine head of fair hair and was the one who received the ill-fated king's horn and never had regard for the truth.

1751   When the lovely stranger maiden saw all the ranks of knights who were gazing steadily at her, she bowed her head low: it was not surprising that, in her embarrassment, her face turned scarlet; but her confusion was so becoming that it made her look more beauti-

ful still. When the king saw her embarrassment, he would not have
her leave him. Gently he took her by the hand and seated her beside
him on his right. The queen sat down on the king's left and said to
him: "Sire, I truly believe that a man who can win by deeds of arms
such a beautiful wife in another land is entitled to come to a royal
court. We did well to wait for Erec. Now you can bestow the kiss on
the fairest in the court. I doubt if anyone would stand in your way
or anybody but a liar ever claim that this is not the most attractive
of the maidens present here or in the whole world." The king
replies: "That's no falsehood. Upon her, unless any challenge me, I
shall bestow the honour of the white stag."

1780 Then he addressed the knights: "My lords, what do you say?
What is your view? In face and body and whatever features are
proper to a maiden, this one is the most charming and beautiful, I
think, to be found this side of where earth and sky meet. I say that it
is right and proper that she should receive the honour of the stag.
And you, my lords, what have you to say? Is there any objection
you can raise? If any man wishes to contest this, let him speak his
thoughts here and now. I am king and must not lie or be a party to
any baseness, deception or high-handedness. I must safeguard right
and reason. It's the business of a true king to uphold the law, truth,
good faith and justice.* I would not wish in any way to commit
disloyalty or wrong any more against the weak than the strong. It is
not right that any should have a complaint against me, and I do not
wish the traditional custom to lapse which my family habitually
observes. You would doubtless be unhappy if I wished to introduce
for you customs and laws other than those kept by my father the
king. Whatever may become of me, I must safeguard and uphold
the practice of my father Pendragon, the just king and emperor.
Now give me your full opinions! Let no one hesitate to say truly if
this maiden is not the fairest in my household and should not
rightly receive the kiss of the white stag: I wish to hear the truth."

1821 They all cry out with one voice: "Sire, by the Lord and His
cross! you may well kiss her in all justice, for she is the fairest one
there is. In this maiden there is more beauty than there is brightness
in the sun. You are free to give her the kiss: we agree to it unanimously." When the king hears that they are all content, he will not
delay in kissing her, but turns towards her and embraces her. The
maiden was not foolish and truly wanted the king to kiss her: it

would have been unbecoming of her to take it amiss. In the sight of all the nobles the king kissed her in courtly fashion with the words: "My sweet friend, I give you my love in all honesty. I shall love you will all my heart without baseness or impropriety." Those were the circumstances in which the king observed the rightful tradition associated at his court with the white stag. So ends the first part of the story.*

1845   When the kiss of the stag was taken according to the custom of the country, Erec, in his courtly, open-hearted way, thought about his poor host, not wanting to break his word over the promise he had given him. He kept his pledge to the letter; for he immediately sent him five plump, well-rested pack-horses laden with robes and clothing, buckrams and scarlets, half-pound ingots of gold and silver, vair, grey and sable furs, purple materials and precious eastern cloths. When the pack-animals were laden with everything to meet a gentleman's needs, he sent with them ten men from his own retinue, some knights, some attendants, asking them urgently to greet his host for him and show him and his wife equally great honour, as if to himself in person. Then, having presented them with the pack-horses they brought and with the gold and silver and bezants and all the other goods in the chests, they were to escort the lady and the vavasour with much honour to his kingdom of Further Wales.* He had promised them two strongholds, the finest, best sited and with the least to fear from war, that were in the whole of his land. One was called Montrevel, and the other's name was Roadan. When they came to his kingdom Erec's men were to make over to them these two strongholds, together with their incomes and jurisdictions, as he had promised them.

1887   The men carried out Erec's instructions in full. The messengers were not inclined to linger, but in excellent time presented his host with everything: the gold and silver, the pack-animals, the robes and the money, of which there was a large supply. They escorted him and his wife into Erec's kingdom, plying them with their service. They reached the country in three days and handed over to them the keeps of the fortresses, with King Lac's full agreement. He received them with great joy and honour, showing them affection for the sake of his son Erec. He transferred to them the ownership of the strongholds and had them installed, with knights and townsmen swearing to show them the love due to their liege lords. When this was done and the arrangements were made, the messengers returned to their lord Erec, who received them in a happy mood. He asked them for news of the vavasour and his wife, of his father and of his kingdom; and what they told him was good and auspicious.

1915 Shortly after this the time became imminent when he was to celebrate his marriage. The delay was very painful to him, and he found the waiting hard to bear. He went to ask the king's permission, if he had no objection, to hold the wedding at his court. The king granted him this favour and sent throughout his realm for all the kings and counts who held their lands from him, saying none of them should be so bold as to fail to appear at Pentecost. No one dares stay away and not come promptly to court at the king's summons. Now listen, and I shall tell you who these counts and kings were.*

1934 Count Brandes of Gloucester came with a very splendid retinue and a string of a hundred spare horses. Then came Menagormon, who was Count of Clivelon; and he of the High Mountain came with a very fine company. The Count of Treverain came with a hundred of his knights, followed by Count Godegrain bringing no fewer. With those I have mentioned came Maheloas, a great baron, lord of the Isle of Glass, an island where thunder is not heard, no lightning strikes or tempest blows, no toads or snakes stay, and it is never too hot or too cold. Graislemier of Fine Posterne brought twenty companions; and his brother Guingomar, lord of the Isle of Avalon, came. We have heard of the latter that he was Morgan the Fay's lover,* and that was certainly true. David of Tintagel came, who never suffered grief or sorrow. Guergesin, the Duke of High Wood, came very richly equipped.

1963 There were many counts and dukes, but even more kings. Garras of Cork, a most proud king, arrived with five hundred knights dressed in cloaks, hose and tunics all of brocade and light silk. On a Cappadocian horse came Aguisel, the King of Scotland, bringing with him both his sons, Cadret and Coi, two much-feared knights. With those I have named came King Ban of Gomeret, all those with him being youths without beards or moustaches: his was a very merry company, two hundred strong, and none of them, whoever it might be, without a falcon or tercel, a merlin or sparrow-hawk or a splendid goshawk, tawny or moulted. Kerrin, the old King of Riel, brought no young men with him: on the contrary, he had three hundred companions of whom the youngest was seven score years old. Their heads were hoary and white and their beards hung to their waists, so aged were they: King Arthur held them in great affection. The lord of the dwarfs came next, Bilis, King of Antipodes. This king of whom I speak was a dwarf and was the full brother of Brien. Bilis was the smallest of all dwarfs, and Brien his brother was half a foot or a full palm taller than any knight in the kingdom. To show off his wealth and grandeur, Bilis brought in his company two kings, Grigoras and Glecidalan, who were dwarfs and held their land from him: people saw them as prodigies. Having come to court, they were very well liked. All three were honoured and served at court as kings, for they were extremely noble gentlemen. In short, when King Arthur saw his lords assembled, he was exceedingly happy at heart. Then, to increase the joy, he ordered a hundred young men to take the ritual bath, since he wished to knight them all.* There was not one of them who did not receive a variegated robe of precious Alexandrian brocade, each taking the one he wanted according to his choice and preference. They all had matching arms and swift, lively horses, the worst of which was worth a hundred pounds.

2025 When Erec took his wife, he had to call her by her proper name; for otherwise, unless she is called by her true name, she is not a married woman. As yet her name was not known to anyone.* Then for the first time it did become known: Enide was the name with which she had been christened. The Archbishop of Canterbury, who had come to court, duly gave them his blessing. When the whole court was assembled, there was not a minstrel of those parts at all skilled in any entertainment who was absent. There was great revelry in the hall, with each contributing what he was good at: one leaps, another does acrobatics and another performs magic tricks; one tells tales, one sings, others play on the harp or rote, on the fiddle, the vielle, the flute or the pipes. Maidens dance to songs and music, all competing in the merry-making. There is nothing that can bring joy and prompt gladness in a man's heart that was absent from the wedding that day. The sound rings out from timbrels and tabors, bagpipes, fifes and pan-pipes, trumpets and flageolets. What else should I speak of? No gate, large or small, was closed: exits and entrances were all wide open, and neither poor nor rich were turned away. King Arthur was not miserly: to the

bakers and cooks and cup-bearers he gave orders to supply liberally
to everyone as much as he wanted, bread, wine and venison. No
one asked to be served with anything whatsoever who did not get as
much of it as he wished.

2069 There was high revelry in the great hall. But I pass over all the
rest to let you hear of the joy and delights of the marriage chamber
and bed. That night when the union was to be consummated,
bishops and archbishops were in attendance. At that first union,
Iseut was not spirited away or Brangien substituted in her place.*
The queen took charge of the preparations and the bedding of the
couple, for both of them were very dear to her. *The hunted hart,
panting for thirst, does not so long for the spring or the hungry
sparrow-hawk come so readily to the call that these two were not
still more eager to come naked into each other's arms. That night
they indeed made good all the time they had lost. With the chamber
cleared for them, they give each part of the body its due. The eyes,
which blaze the trail of love and send their messages to the heart,
gaze with delight, much pleased with all they see. After the message
from the eyes comes that sweetness, far better still, from the kisses
inviting love. Both of them sample this sweetness, and their hearts
within drink their fill of it, hardly able to desist: kissing was their
first play. Then the love they shared made the maiden more bold.
Afraid of nothing and whatever the hurt, she suffered all. Before
she rose, she had lost the name of maiden: in the morning she was a
new lady.

2109 That day made the minstrels happy, for they were all paid to
their satisfaction. Everything they had had on credit was given
them outright together with many fine gifts, robes of vair, ermine
and rabbit fur, of fine woollen cloth, scarlet or silken material. Each
was given what he wanted, whether a horse or money, according to
his skills and deserts. Thus the wedding festivities and the court
were held with great revelry and splendour for almost a fortnight.
For the sake of the pomp and ceremony and to honour Erec the
more, King Arthur had all the nobles stay for a fortnight. When the
third week began, they all jointly arranged a tournament. My lord
Gawain came forward on the one hand to sponsor it between
Evroic and Tenebroc;* and Meliz and Meliadoc guaranteed it for
their part. With that the court broke up.

2135 A month after Pentecost the tournament assembles and opens
in the plain below Tenebroc. Many a pennon flew there, vermilion,

blue, white, and many a wimple and sleeve that had been given as
love-tokens. Many a lance was carried there painted in silver and
red, others in gold and blue, and many more of different kinds,
some banded and some spotted. That day one saw there many a
gold-trimmed helmet laced and many of steel, green, yellow, vermilion, gleaming in the sun. And there were so many coats of arms
and bright hauberks, swords carried at the left side, so many good
shields, fresh and new, resplendent in silver and red, others blue
with gold bosses, so many fine horses, dark with white patches,
sorrel, tawny, white, black or bay. All come together at full speed.
The field is completely covered with arms. The ranks shudder on
both sides, and from the clash there rises a loud din, with a great
cracking of the lances. Lances break and shields are holed, the
hauberks are torn and rent, saddles are emptied and riders tumble,
the horses sweat and lather. All draw their swords on those who
clatter to the ground. Some dash up to accept their surrender,
others in their defence.

2171   Astride a white horse, Erec came to the front of the rank quite
alone to joust, if he could find an opponent. From the other side the
Haughty Knight of the Heath spurs against him, mounted on an
Irish horse that carries him along at a furious pace. Erec strikes him
on the shield protecting his breast with such force that he knocks
him off his steed, then leaves him on the field and spurs on. Next
Raindurant, son of the old woman of Tergalo, comes against him,
decked out in fine blue silk: a most valiant knight, he. They make
for each other and exchange mighty blows on the shields at their
necks. At the length of his lance, Erec topples him on to the hard
ground. Turning about, he met the King of the Red City, whose
valour and prowess were great. They take their reins by the knots
and their shields by the straps. Both had excellent arms, fine,
strong, swift horses and good, fresh, new shields. They struck each
other with such violence that both their lances shattered. Never
was such a clash seen as they crashed together with shields, arms
and horses. Girth, reins and breast-strap could not prevent the king
from falling to the ground; so he flew off his steed without leaving
saddle or stirrups, and even carrying the reins of his bridle away
with him in his hand. All those who saw this joust were quite
amazed and said that anyone who pits himself against so good a
knight has to pay too high a price.

2215 Erec's main concern was not with capturing horses or riders, but to joust and do well so as to show off his prowess. He makes the rank in front of him tremble, his valour putting new heart into those on his side. To discourage his opponents all the more he did take some horses and riders.* I must mention my lord Gawain, who performed excellently indeed. In the fight he felled Guincel and captured Gaudin of the Mountain. Capturing knights and winning horses, my lord Gawain did extremely well. Girflet the son of Do and Yvain and Sagremor the Impetuous dealt with their adversaries so well that they forced them back to the gates, taking and unhorsing many.

2235 Before the gate of the fortress the combat was begun by those inside against those outside. There Sagremor, a very valiant knight, was felled. He was taken and being held captive when Erec spurs to the rescue. He splinters his lance against one of the captors, striking him so hard on the breast that he is knocked out of the saddle. Then he draws his sword and falls on them, denting and crushing their helmets. They flee and leave the way clear, for even the boldest of them fears him. So many blows and thrusts did he launch at them that he rescued Sagremor from their clutches and drove them speedily back into the fortress. Then the evening drew to a close. Erec performed so well that day that he was the best in the contest; but he did much better on the following day. He took so many knights with his own hands and emptied so many saddles that only those who had seen it could believe it. Everyone on both sides said that by his lance and shield he had become victor in the tournament.

2263 Now Erec's fame was such that people spoke of him alone. Nor was there anyone of such charm: in his looks he resembled Absalom, by his tongue Solomon and a lion in his pride; and in his giving and spending he was the equal of King Alexander. On his return from the tournament, Erec went to speak with the king. He went to seek his leave to be allowed to go to his own land; but he first thanked him warmly in frank, thoughtful and courtly fashion for the honour he had done him, being most deeply grateful for it. Then he asked permission to leave, wishing to go to his country and take his wife with him. The king could not refuse him this, but he would have wished him not to go away. He gives him leave and begs him to return as soon as possible; for in the whole of his court there was no better or more gallant knight except for Gawain his beloved nephew, whom no one could match. But next to him he valued Erec most and was more fond of him than of any other knight.

2293 Erec wished to delay no longer. As soon as he had the king's leave, he told his wife to get ready and retained as his escort sixty excellent knights, mounted and with vair and grey furs. Once he was ready for his journey, he spent little more time at court. He asks leave of the queen and commends the knights to God. The queen grants him his leave. At the hour when the bell sounds for prime he left the royal palace. Before them all he mounted his horse, and his wife mounted the dappled one she brought from her own country; and then his whole company mounted. What with knights and attendants, they were a good seven score in the party. They spent four long days on the journey, passing across hills and slopes, forests, plains and rivers before coming on the fifth day to Carnant, where King Lac resided in a very charming stronghold. Nobody ever saw one better situated: it was well endowed with forests, meadows, vineyards and cultivated ground, streams and orchards, ladies and knights, noble, cheerful youths, courteous, well-mannered clerks who spent their income freely, lovely attractive maidens and townsfolk of substance.

2329 Before Erec came to the castle, he sent two knights on ahead to announce his arrival to the king. Having heard the news, the king at once had clerks, knights and maidens mount and ordered the horns to be sounded and the streets draped with hangings and silken cloths, to welcome his son with great joy. Then he himself mounted. There were fully fourscore clerks there, well-mannered, honourable men in grey mantles trimmed with sable. A good five-hundred knights were present, riding bay, sorrel and white-flecked horses. And there were so many townsfolk and ladies that no one could tell their number. They hurried on at the gallop until the king and his son saw and recognised one another. They both dismount to kiss and greet each other and for a long time do not move from the spot where they met. There are mutual greetings all round. The king is overjoyed to have Erec there, but from time to time leaves him to turn to Enide. He is in total bliss, hugging and kissing them both and not knowing which of them pleases him better. Joyfully they come to the castle; and to greet Erec's arrival all the bells peal loud. Every street is strewn with reeds, wild mint and rushes and decked over with draperies and hangings of flowered silk and velvet. There was much rejoicing, with all the people gathering to see their new lord. No one ever beheld greater happiness than was shown by young and grey-haired alike.

2374 First they came to the church, where they were devoutly received in procession. Erec knelt in front of the altar of the crucifix, whilst two nobles led his wife before the image of Our Lady. When she had finished her prayer, she drew back a little and crossed herself with her right hand as a well-mannered lady should. Then, leaving the church, they came to the royal palace, where the high festivities began. That day Erec received many gifts from the knights and townspeople: a palfrey of northern stock from one, a gold cup from another; this one presents him with a tawny goshawk, another with a tracking-dog, one with a greyhound, another with a sparrow-hawk; from one he has a swift Spanish charger, from others a shield, a pennon, a sword or a helmet. Never was a king seen with greater pleasure in his kingdom or more joyfully received, everybody striving to do him some service. Yet they showed even greater delight with Enide than with him because of the great beauty they saw in her and still more for her open, noble character.

2406 She was seated in a room on a coverlet of brocade imported from Thessaly. There were many lovely ladies around her; but just as the bright gem outshines the dark pebble and the rose the poppy, so Enide was more beautiful than any lady or maiden to be found in the whole world, however widely one might search. She was so charming, honourable, sensibly spoken and welcoming, pleasant and friendly in her manner. No one was ever so alert as to detect in her any folly, vice or baseness. She was so versed in good manners that she had her share of all the virtues any lady can possess, of generosity and of wisdom. Everybody loved her for her innate nobility; and whoever could do her some service derived pride and personal satisfaction from doing so. Not an ill word was spoken of her, for there was nothing anyone could say against her.

2432 In neither the realm nor the empire was there a lady of such fine character. But Erec was so deeply in love with her that he no longer took any interest in arms or attended tournaments: he no longer cared to joust, but spent his time playing the lover to his wife.* He treated her as his sweetheart and mistress. He set his heart and mind only on embracing and kissing her, seeking no other pastime. His companions were sorry about this and often complained among themselves that he showed her far too much love. It was often after midday that he rose from her side; but he was contented, whoever else was unhappy. He very seldom went far from her; but never on that account did he give his knights less in the way of arms, dress or money. There was nowhere any tournament to which he did not send them richly equipped and accoutred. Whatever the cost to him he gave them well-rested chargers for the tourney and joust. All the nobles declared it a great shame and pity when a man as gallant as he used to be did not wish to bear arms. He was blamed so much by everyone, knights and serving-men alike, that Enide heard them saying to one another that her husband was turning recreant in the matter of arms and chivalry and that his way of life had greatly changed. This worried her, but she did not dare show it; for if she told her husband, he would promptly take offence.

2473 The matter was kept from him until one morning when they lay in bed, where they had been taking great pleasure. They were lying mouth to mouth in close embrace like true lovers, he sleeping and she awake. She began thinking of the things that many people throughout the country were saying about her husband; and when she came to recall them, she could not help weeping. She was so sad and grief-stricken that she unfortunately chanced to utter words for which she afterwards felt much remorse, though she intended no harm. She began to look her husband up and down, gazing at his shapely body and clear features. Then she weeps so abundantly that her tears fall on her husband's breast; and she says: "Alas, what a misfortune that I ever left my country! What did I come here to find? The earth ought to swallow me up when the very best knight, the boldest, most resolute, noblest and most courtly ever to be numbered among counts and kings has on my account utterly given up his whole practice of chivalry. So I've truly brought shame upon him, which I would not have wished at any price."* Then she said to him: "How disastrous for you!" With that she fell silent and said no more.

2509 Erec was not sleeping soundly and heard her clearly in his sleep. At her words he woke and was very surprised to see her weeping so. He questioned her: "Tell me, my dear fair love, why you're weeping like this. What has caused you grief or sadness? I'd really like to know. Tell me, my sweet love, and be sure not to keep from me why you said it was disastrous for me. You said it about me and no one else. I heard your words plainly." Then Enide was quite dismayed, in great fear and agitation. "My lord," she says, "I don't know at all what you're talking about."—"Lady, why are you trying to get out of it? Concealing it won't do you any good. You've been crying, that's plain to see; and you don't cry for nothing. And in my sleep I heard the words you spoke."—"Ah! good husband, you never heard anything: I think you were dreaming."—"Now you treat me to lies: I hear you openly lying to me! But you'll repent too late, unless you admit the truth to me."

2540 "My lord, as you're tormenting me, I'll tell you the truth and not hide it from you any longer; but I'm very afraid it will annoy you. Everyone in this land, the dark, the fair and the red-haired, say it's a great pity for you to put aside your arms: your reputation has suffered from it. They all used to say until recently that no one knew of a better or more valiant knight in all the world: you had no equal anywhere. Now old and young, little and tall all go about mocking you and calling you a recreant. Do you think, then, that I'm not pained to hear you insulted? I'm very grieved that this is said, and grieved even more to have the blame put on me. I'm being blamed for it, and that hurts me. And the reason they all give is that I've so ensnared and caught you that, as a result, you're quite losing your merit and have no further ambition. You must change your attitude so as to efface this blame and regain your former reputation; for I've heard too much of this reproach, without ever daring to disclose it to you. Time and again when I think of it, I can only weep in anguish. Just now I was so miserable about it that I wasn't able to prevent myself saying how disastrous it was for you."—"Lady," he says, "you were right, and those who blame me for it are right.* Get ready at once, and prepare yourself to go riding! Get up from here, put on your most beautiful dress, and have your finest palfrey saddled!"*

2584 Now Enide is extremely alarmed: she gets up very sad and thoughtful, rebuking and scolding herself for the foolish thing she said; but having made her bed she must lie in it. "Ah!" she says, "wretched idiot that I am! Life was too easy for me, as there was nothing I lacked. God! Why then was I so bold as to say such a stupid thing? God! Did my husband not love me too much, then? Alas, his love for me was indeed too great. Now I'm to be banished! But what grieves me more is that I shall not see my husband, who loved me so ardently that nothing and no one was so dear to him. The best man ever to be born had devoted himself so entirely to me that nothing else mattered to him. I didn't lack for anything, so very fortunate was I. But I was too carried away by my presumption: that presumption of mine will suffer now I've said such an insolent thing – and it's quite right that I should have it suffer. No one knows what good is unless he samples evil."

2611 The lady continued to lament until she had finished dressing herself in the finest gown she had. But she took no pleasure in anything: rather it brought her great unhappiness. Then she had a maid call one of her squires whom she ordered to saddle her splendid northern palfrey: no count or king ever had a better one. As soon as he was bidden, he asked for no delay, but saddled the dappled palfrey.

2624 Erec then called another squire and ordered him to bring all he needed to arm himself. Next he went upstairs into a gallery and had a Limoges carpet spread on the floor in front of him. The man to whom he had given the order hurried to fetch the arms and put them on the carpet. Erec sat down opposite them on the figure of a leopard that was portrayed on the carpet. He prepares and makes himself ready for the arming. First he had laced on a pair of greaves of polished steel. Then he donned a hauberk so fine that not a link in it could be severed. It was a magnificent hauberk, for neither outside nor inside was there enough iron to make a needle, and it was quite rust-proof; for it was all finely worked in silver with tiny triple-woven links, and it was so skilfully fashioned that I can assure you that no one wearing it would be more tired or uncomfortable than if he had put on a silk tunic over his shirt. The servants and knights all began to wonder why he was being armed, but no one dared ask. When they had put on his hauberk, a page laced on his head a helmet circled by a golden band that shone more brightly than a mirror. After that he takes and girds on the sword and orders the Gascon bay to be brought ready saddled.

2664 Then he called a page. "Page," he says, "make haste and run to the room by the keep where my wife is, and tell her she's keeping me waiting here too long. She's been too slow getting ready! Tell her to come and mount quickly, because I'm waiting for her." He went there to find her dressed ready, weeping and showing her grief; and he said to her at once: "Lady, why are you delaying so? My lord is waiting for you out there, fully armed. He would have mounted some time ago, had you been ready." Enide was astonished, wondering what her husband's intention was; but she behaved sensibly by putting on as cheerful a face as possible when she came before him. She came up to him in the middle of the courtyard, with King Lac running behind her. Knights hurry along, competing to get there first. There is nobody, young or old, who does not go to see and ask if he will take any of them with him: each man presents himself and volunteers. But he assures them and swears that he will take no companion, with the single exception of his wife, saying he will definitely go alone.

2696 At this this king is very alarmed. "Dear son," he says, "what are you wanting to do? You ought to tell me your purpose and hide nothing from me. Tell me where you're wanting to go, seeing that, ask as they might, you're unwilling for any squires or knights to accompany you. If you've undertaken a single combat with some knight, that's no reason for your not taking with you a number of your knights to make a fine, imposing show. The son of a king ought not to travel alone. Dear son, have your pack-horses loaded, and take thirty or forty or even more of your knights; and have silver and gold carried with you, and whatever is needed for a man of rank."

2716 In the end, Erec replies with a full explanation of his plans for the journey. "Sire," he says, "it can't be otherwise: I shall take no spare horse and have no use for gold or silver, squire or attendant; and I ask for no company other than my wife's alone. But I beg you that, whatever happens, if I should die and she return, you'll love and cherish her for love of me and because I ask it; and give her half of your land without dispute or strife for her to hold freely all her life." The king hears what his son asks of him and says: "Dear son, I agree. But I'm extremely sad to see you going away without any company. If I had my way, you'd never leave like this."—"Sire, this is how it must be. I go now and commend you to God. But bear my companions in mind, and give them horses and arms and whatever a knight requires."

2742 The king cannot hold back his tears when he is parted from his son. The bystanders weep, for their part. Ladies and knights shed

tears and showed very great grief for him. There is not one person
who does not lament, and many swoon on the spot. Weeping, they
kiss and embrace him, almost out of their minds with sorrow. I
think their mourning would not have been greater had they seen
him slain or wounded. Then, to comfort them, Erec said: "My
lords, why do you weep so much? I'm not captured or maimed.
You gain nothing from this grief. Though I'm going away, I shall
return when it pleases God and I'm able to. My lords and ladies,
I commend you all to God. So now please give me leave, for
you detain me too long. To see you weeping hurts me deeply and
makes me extremely sad." He commends them to God, and they
him.

2765 They parted in great distress. Erec rides off taking his wife he
knows not where, as chance decrees. "Go on," he says, "at a good
speed; and take care, if you see anything at all, not to be so rash as
to speak to me about it or anything else. Beware of talking to me
about it unless I address you first. Ride on ahead at a good pace, and
you'll be quite safe."—"Very well, my lord," she says. She went on
ahead and was silent. They do not exchange a word; but Enide is
very unhappy and laments softly to herself, quietly so he cannot
hear. "Alas," she says, "God has raised me to a position of such
great joy, but has now in a short time cast me down. Fortune,
who had taken me to her, has now quickly withdrawn her hand.
That would not worry me if, alas, I dared speak to my husband.
But what has mortally deceived me is that my lord has conceived
a hatred for me. He has come to hate me: I see that plainly when
he won't speak to me; and I don't have the courage to dare to look
in his direction."

2795 As she was lamenting in this way, out of the woods came a
knight who lived by robbery. He had two companions with him,
and all three were armed. They cast very covetous eyes on the
palfrey Enide is riding. "Sirs," he says to his companions, "do you
know what news I have for you? If we don't now get some good
pickings, we're cowardly good-for-nothings and right out of luck.
A very beautiful lady is coming this way – I don't know whether
she's a lady or a maiden, but she's superbly dressed. Her palfrey, the
saddle and cover, breast-cloth and straps are worth a thousand
pounds in Chartres coin. I want the palfrey, and you can have all
the rest of the booty: that's all I want for my share. The knight

won't get away with the lady, so help me God! I intend to launch
such an attack on him that he'll pay a heavy price. I saw him first, so
it's right for me to go and have the first fight."

2823 The others agree to this, and he dashes off, crouching right
under his shield, while the remaining two stay at a distance. At that
time it was the usual custom that two knights should not engage a
single one in the same attack; so if they had assaulted him, it would
have appeared as a treacherous act towards him. Enide saw the
robbers and was seized by great fear. "God," she says, "what can I
say? Now my lord will be killed or captured, for there are three of
them, and he's alone. One knight against three isn't fair odds. That
one's going to strike him from behind, taking my husband
unawares. God, shall I then be such a coward as not to dare tell
him? I'll never be so cowardly! I'll tell him straight away!" At once
she turns towards him and calls: "Dear husband, what are you
thinking of? Here come three knights after you, galloping hard at
you. I'm afraid they'll do you some harm."—"What's that?" says
Erec. "What do you say? You really don't respect me much! You've
been far too bold in disobeying my command and doing what I
forbade. You'll be pardoned this time; but should it happen again,
you'd never be forgiven."

2857 Then, turning his shield and lance, he hurls himself towards the
knight. The man sees him coming and shouts out at him. On
hearing this, Erec challenges him. They both spur on and come to
grips, holding their lances at full stretch; but he missed Erec, whilst
Erec, skilfully pressing his attack, dealt him a damaging blow. He
strikes him so furiously on the shield that he splits it from top to
bottom. Nor does the hauberk protect him: Erec pierces and rips it
at the breast, plunging his lance a foot and a half into his body. As
he pulled back, he withdrew his weapon, and the man fell. With the
blade having drunk deep in his body, he had to die.

2875 One of the other two rushes forward, leaving his companion
behind, and spurs towards Erec uttering threats. Grasping his
shield tightly, Erec boldly attacks him as the man holds his own in
front of his chest. They strike each other on their emblazoned
shields, and on the one hand the knight's lance flies in two pieces,
whilst Erec thrusts a quarter of his own through his breast. This
man will not cause him any more effort! Erec topples him unconscious from his charger, then gallops at an angle against the other

man, who, seeing him coming, turned to flee: in his fear he dared not wait for him, but hurries to take cover in the forest. But flight avails him nothing. Erec follows on his heels, calling aloud: "Vassal, vassal, turn round! Get ready to defend yourself so that I don't strike you as you're running away. It's no use fleeing." But the man has no inclination to turn round, and continues his flight at top speed. Erec chases and catches him. He strikes him squarely on his painted shield and knocks him down on the other side of his mount.

2904 He has no more concern for those three: he has killed one, wounded the second, and has soundly dealt with the third by knocking him to the ground off his charger. He took the horses of all three, tying them together by the bridles. Their coats were all different: the first was milk-white, the second a handsome black, and the third dappled all over. He returned to his road, where Enide awaited him. Ordering her to lead and drive the three horses ahead, he harshly threatens her, saying she must never again be so bold as to utter a single word without his permission. She replies: "I never will, good husband, if that's what pleases you." Then they ride off, and she remains silent.

2925 They had not gone a league when five more knights approached them in a valley, each with lances in rest, shields held close at their necks and polished helmets laced: they were on the lookout for plunder. Now they see the lady coming leading the three horses, with Erec following behind. No sooner had they seen them than they shared out all their equipment in their talk as if they already had their hands on it. Covetousness is an evil thing. But matters did not turn out as they had hoped, for a stout defence was put up. Things fall far short of a fool's expectations, and some go without what they think they can take; and so it was with them in this attack. One said he would have the maiden or die in the attempt; the second said the dappled steed would be his, for he wanted nothing more from all the booty; the third said he would have the black one. "And the white one for me!" said the fourth. The fifth was no coward, for he said he would have the knight's charger and his arms. He wanted to win them in single combat, and so would be the first to attack him, if they would give him leave; and they did willingly give him permission.

2959 Then he leaves them and gallops forward, having a good, agile horse. Erec saw him but pretended he had not yet noticed him.

When Enide caught sight of them, her blood ran cold in her great fear and dismay. "Alas," she says, "I don't know what to say or do; for my lord severely threatens me and says he'll make me suffer if I speak to him about anything. But if my husband were killed now, there would be no comfort for me: I'd be broken and forlorn. God, my lord doesn't see them! What am I waiting for, then, wicked fool that I am? I'm too miserly with my words not to have told him a while ago. I know well these people approaching are bent on some wicked deed. But God! how shall I tell him? He'll kill me! Then let him kill me! I'll not hold back from telling him."

2983 Then she softly calls to him: "My lord!"—"What is it?" he says. "What are you wanting to say?"—"Forgive me, my lord. I want to tell you that five knights have broken out of that thicket, and I'm very afraid of them. My impression and belief is that they want to fight with you. Four have stayed behind, and the fifth is making for you as quickly as his horse can carry him. I'm afraid he'll strike you at any moment! The four that have stayed back aren't very far from here, though, and will soon come to his rescue if he needs them." Erec replied: "It was unlucky for you to think of disobeying my instructions after I'd forbidden you to do it. Still, I knew well enough how little regard you had for me! This is a misdirected service, for I'm not at all grateful to you – on the contrary, you may be sure I hate you all the more for it. I've told you once and I'll tell you again. Still, I'll forgive you on this occasion, but another time take care never to look at me, for you'd be acting very foolishly. I've no liking for your words!"

3011 Then he gallops across the field towards the knight, and they come to grips. Each attacks and falls upon the other. Erec strikes his opponent so hard that his shield flies from his neck and his collar-bone snaps; his stirrups break, and he falls. I have no fear of him getting up again, so badly hurt and injured was he! One of the others made for Erec, and they clash violently together. With a swift thrust, Erec plants the sharp, well-forged head of his lance into his throat below the chin, slicing through bones and nerves; the blade comes out at the back of his neck, and the warm, crimson blood streams from the wound on both sides. His soul departs and his heart is stilled. The third dashes out of his hiding-place on the other side of a ford and comes straight through the water. Erec spurs forward and encounters him before he is quite out of the ford, giving him such a blow that he knocks both him and his charger flat. The steed lay on his body long enough to drown him in the water, then with some difficulty struggled to its feet.

3041 So he has defeated three of them. The two others agreed together that they would leave the field to him without further combat. They go fleeing along the river with Erec hard on their heels. He strikes one of them on the spine, knocking him forward on to the saddle-bow. He put all his strength into that blow, breaking his lance against the man's body, so that he fell head-first. Erec makes him pay dearly for the lance he shattered against him. He drew his sword from the scabbard. Foolishly the man got up; and Erec dealt him three such mighty blows that he made the sword drink of his blood. He severs his shoulder from the trunk, so that he falls to the ground.

3060 With his sword he attacked the other, who was making off at top speed without company or escort. When he sees Erec in pursuit, he is so afraid that he does not know what to do: he does not dare wait, but cannot evade him. He has to abandon his horse as he has no more faith in it: throwing down his shield and lance, he slips off its back to the ground. When he let himself fall to the ground, Erec gave up his intention to attack him; but he bent down for the lance, not leaving it there because of his own having been broken. He goes off, taking the lance away and not leaving the horses behind: he takes all five and leads them off. Enide had difficulty when it came to leading them, the five he gives her with the other three. He orders her to set off promptly and keep from speaking to him, if she wishes to avoid harm and trouble. She says not a word in reply, but remains silent. And so they leave, leading with them all eight horses.

3086 They rode until night without finding any town or refuge. When night fell, they sheltered under a laburnum tree on a heath. Erec tells the lady to sleep, and he will keep watch. She replies that she will not do so, as that is not right and she does not wish to: he shall sleep, since he is more weary. Erec gladly agrees. He placed his shield at his head; and the lady takes her cloak and spreads it over him from head to foot. He slept, and she kept watch, not falling asleep all night long, but holding the horses with their bridles in her hand until the morning. And she blamed and cursed herself a great deal for the words she had spoken, saying she acted wrongly and had not suffered half as much as she deserved. "Alas," she says, "how disastrous were my presumption and audacity! I might have understood without question that there's no knight known who is equal to or better than my husband. I did know it, and now I know it better, for I've seen with my own eyes that he doesn't fear three, or five, armed men. A plague on my tongue for having spoken the presumptuous, insolent words for which I suffer such personal shame!" So she lamented throughout the night until day broke next morning.

3121   Erec rises early; and they resume their journey, she in front and he behind. At about midday a squire came towards them along a small valley. With him were two lads carrying cakes and wine and rich cheeses to Count Galoain's meadows for the men mowing his hay. The squire was very shrewd: when he saw Erec and Enide coming from the direction of the forest, he realised they had passed the night in the woods and had not eaten or drunk; for within a day's journey in any direction there was no castle, town, keep or fortified house, abbey, hospice or hostelry. Then he had a very generous thought. He went to meet them and greeted them politely with the words: "My lord, it's my belief that you had a hard time last night. I know you've had no sleep and spent the night in this forest. Let me offer you some of this white cake, if you would care to eat a little. I don't say this to curry favour, for I seek or ask nothing from you. These cakes are made of good wheat; and I have excellent wine and rich cheeses, a white cloth and fine goblets. If you'd like to take lunch, you need not go elsewhere. On the green grass under these hornbeam trees you may take off your armour and rest a little. Take my advice and dismount." Erec got down on to his feet and said: "My kind friend, I thank you and will eat. I don't wish to go any further."

3165   The squire tended them well: he helped the lady off her mount, and the lads who had come with him held the horses. Then they go to sit in the shade. The squire relieves Erec of his helmet, unlacing the ventail in front of his face. Then, spreading the cloth before them on the lush grass, he hands them the cake and wine and cuts the cheese, having removed the rind. Hungry as they were, they were glad to eat and drink some of the wine. The squire was not neglectful in their service. When they had eaten and drunk, Erec showed courtly generosity. "Good friend," he says, "as recompense I make you the gift of one of my horses. Take the one you most fancy! And I beg you, if you don't mind, to return to the castle and prepare me excellent lodgings there." He replies that he will gladly do whatever he pleases. Then he goes to the horses, unties them, takes the dappled one because that seems to him the best one, and thanks him for it. He mounted by the left stirrup and, leaving the couple there, came at top speed to the stronghold and obtained well-appointed quarters. Then here he is back with them. "Mount quickly now, sir," he says, "for you have good, fine lodgings." Erec mounted, and then the lady. The stronghold was quite close; and they soon arrived at their lodging-place, to be joyfully received. The host welcomed them very warmly, gladly and willingly providing in good measure for their every need.

3209 When the squire had done them as much honour as he could, he came and remounted his horse, taking it past the count's galleries to the stables. The count and three other nobles had come there and were leaning out. Seeing his squire sitting on the dappled charger, the count asked him whose it was. He replied that it was his. The count was quite amazed. "How's that?" he says. "Where did you get it?"—"A knight I think highly of gave it me, sir," he says. "I've brought him here into the castle, and he's lodged with one of the townsmen. This knight is very courtly and the most handsome man I've ever seen. Even if I'd sworn and undertaken to do so, I could never describe to you all or even half of his good looks." The count replies: "I certainly believe he's no more handsome than I am."—"Truly, sir," says the squire, "you are very handsome and good-looking: there's no knight in the land and a native of these parts than whom you're not more handsome. Yet of this man I dare claim that he's far more handsome than you, except that he's bruised and knocked black and blue by his hauberk. In the forest he fought alone against eight knights and has taken away their eight chargers. And with him comes a lady who is so beautiful that no woman ever had half her beauty." When the count hears this news, he thinks he would like to go and see if it is true or false. "I never heard such a thing," he says. "So take me to his lodgings, because I want to know for certain if you're lying to me or telling the truth." He replies: "Willingly, sir. This path is the way: it's not far from here."—"I'm very anxious to see them," says the count. Then he comes down; and the squire gets off his horse and helps the

count to mount, before running ahead to tell Erec that the count
was coming to see him.

3264 Erec was most handsomely lodged in his usual style. There
were many tapers burning and a host of candles. The count arrived
with no more than just three companions. Erec, extremely polite as
always, rose to meet him. "Welcome, sir!" he said; and the count
returned his greeting. They sit down side by side on a soft white
couch and introduce themselves. The count offers, proposes and
begs him to consent to his paying his expenses. But Erec does not
deign to accept, saying he himself has ample resources and has no
need to call on his. They talk a great deal on many subjects; but the
count keeps casting glances in the other direction, having caught
sight of the lady. Seeing how beautiful she was, he was thinking
only of her. He looked at her as much as he could. She so pleased
him and roused his desire that her beauty fired him with love.

3292 Very slyly he asked Erec's permission to speak with her. "Sir,"
says he, "I ask your leave, if you don't mind, since I should like to sit
beside that lady as a matter of courtesy and pleasure. I came with
the good intention of seeing you both, and you should see no harm
in that: above all else, I wish to offer the lady my service. You can be
sure that for the love of you I would do whatever pleased her." Erec
was not at all jealous and suspected no wrong or deception in that.
"Sir," he says, "I have no objection. Feel free to sit and talk with
her. Don't think I mind at all: I gladly give you permission."

3310 The lady was sitting two lances' length away from him; and the
count took his seat close beside her on a low stool. The lady, who
was very courteous and considerate, turned towards him. "Ah,"
said he, "how sad I am to see you travelling in such a lowly fashion!
It gives me much grief and sorrow. But if you would believe me, you
might have honour and benefit, and it would profit you extremely
well. Your beauty merits high honour and distinction. If it pleased
and appealed to you, I would make you my mistress: you would be
my dear love and lady over all my land. When I'm prepared to make
proposals of love, you shouldn't turn me down. I'm aware and can
tell that your husband doesn't love and appreciate you. You'd be
partnered with a good lord, should you stay with me."—"Sir, your
efforts are in vain!" says Enide. "That's impossible. Oh, better that
I wasn't yet born or was burnt in a fire of thorns and my ashes
scattered, than that I should be in any way false to my lord or have

any thought of wickedness or betrayal! You've committed a very great fault in making such a proposal to me. In no way shall I consent to it."

3345 The count grows heated. "Would you disdain to love me, lady?" he says. "You're too proud. Would you do nothing I want, for all my flattery and begging? It's true that the more one begs and flatters a woman, the more haughty she becomes; but if anyone shames and insults her, he often finds her more amenable. I give you my solemn assurance that, if you don't do what I wish, swords will soon be drawn here. Rightly or wrongly, I'll have your husband slain on the spot, before your very eyes."—"Ah, sir," says Enide, "you can do better than what you suggest. You'd be very wicked and treacherous to kill him like that. Please calm yourself, for I'll do what you wish. You may consider me yours: I am yours, and wish to be. What I said to you was not spoken out of pride, but to find out and be certain whether I could discover in you signs that you loved me with all your heart. But I would on no account have you commit a treacherous act. My husband isn't on his guard against you: if you killed him like that, you would behave very treacherously, and the blame for it would fall on me. Everyone in the land would say it had been done on my advice. Do nothing until the morning when my husband is about to rise. Then you'll be better able to harm him without any blame or reproach."

3384 Her inner thoughts are different from the words she speaks. "My lord," she says, "believe me! You needn't be afraid. Just send your knights and servants here tomorrow and have me forcibly seized. My husband, who is very proud and courageous, will attempt to defend me. Either in earnest or in jest, have him taken and beaten up, or have his head lopped off. I've led this life too long: to tell the truth, I have no liking for my husband's company. I'd certainly rather feel you lying naked beside me in bed. As we've come to this, you can be sure of my love." The count replies: "Good for you, lady! You were certainly born under a lucky star, and will be kept with high honour."—"My lord," she says, "I well believe it; but I should like to have your assurance that you'll treat me tenderly, otherwise I'd not entrust myself to you." The count, overjoyed, replies: "Here, lady: I pledge you my loyal word as a count that I shall fulfil all your desires. Don't worry about that: there's nothing you'll want that you won't get."

3415   Then she accepted his pledged word; but it means little to her and she sets small store by it except as a way of saving her lord. When she puts her mind to it, she knows well how to infatuate a fool. It is far better that she should lie to him than have her husband cut to pieces. The count got up from her side, commending her to God a hundred times; but he will profit little from the faith he had pledged her.

3426   Erec knew nothing of the fact that they were discussing his death; but God may well come to his help, and I think He will. Now Erec is in great danger, yet has no thought of being on his guard. The count's intentions are very evil, thinking as he is of taking away his wife and killing him when he is defenceless. Perfidiously he takes his leave, saying: "I commend you to God." Erec replies: "And I do you, sir." So the two separate, with a good deal of the night already gone. In a room apart two beds were made up on the floor. Erec goes to lie down in one, while in the other Enide lies grieving, in great distress. That night she did not sleep a wink, but watched over her husband; for from what she had seen of the count, she could tell he was full of wickedness. She is quite sure that if he has her husband in his power, he will not fail to have him harshly treated: he would be sure to be killed. Thinking of him, she finds no consolation. The whole night she has to stay on watch; but before daybreak, if she can manage it and her husband is prepared to believe her, they will be ready to take the road.

3459   Erec slept long and in safety all night until dawn was very close. Then Enide saw plainly, with some alarm, that she might wait too long. As a good, loyal wife, she was tender-hearted towards her husband, harbouring no deceit or disloyalty. She rises and gets ready; then, coming to her lord, she wakes him. "Ah my lord," she says, "forgive me! Get up quickly, for you're utterly betrayed, without cause or doing any wrong. The count is a proven traitor. If they can find you here, you'll never make your escape, but will be torn limb from limb. He desires me and hates you. But if it please God, who is capable of all good, you'll not be killed or captured. He would have slain you last evening, had I not agreed to become his mistress and wife. You'll soon see him coming here: he wants to seize and keep me and kill you, if he finds you." Now Erec hears sure evidence from his wife of her loyalty towards him. "Lady," he says, "have our horses saddled quickly and hurry to call our host and tell him to come here. Treason has been brewing for some time."

3493 The horses are soon saddled, and the lady has called the host. Erec dressed and armed himself. His host came to him, asking: "My lord, what is your hurry in getting up at this hour before daylight or the sun has appeared?" Erec replies that he has a very great distance to go and a long day's journey to make, and that for this reason he has prepared for the road, having it much on his mind. Then he said: "Sir, you've not yet made any reckoning of my expenses. You've treated me honourably and with kindness, and that merits a good reward. In settlement, take seven chargers I've brought here with me. Keep them, and be satisfied with them: I can't increase my offer to you by even the value of a halter." The townsman was delighted with this gift and, bowing low at his feet, expressed his great thanks and gratitude.

3516 Then Erec mounts and takes his leave, and they set out again on their way. He still keeps warning Enide not to be so bold, should she see anything, as to speak to him of it. Meanwhile, a hundred well-armed knights enter the house; but they were fooled, not finding Erec there. The count then discovered for certain that the lady had tricked him. He followed the horses' tracks, and they all set off on their trail. The count makes dire threats against Erec and says that, if he can catch him, nothing at all will stop him from taking off his head at once. "A curse on anyone," he says, "who spares his efforts to spur on fast! Whoever can give me the head of the knight I hate so much will have served and pleased me well." Then they press on at a furious pace, inflamed with hatred for the man who had never set eyes on them or harmed them in word or deed.

3543 They rode on until they spotted him at the edge of a forest, seeing him before he had quite gone into it. Not a single one of them halted then, but they vie with each other in their headlong gallop. Enide hears the clanging and din of their arms and horses and sees the valley full of them. As soon as she saw them coming, she could not help speaking. "Ah, my lord!" she says, "Oh how this count must hate you to bring such an army against you! Ride faster, my lord, until we get into this forest! We could probably soon give them the slip, for they're still a long way behind. If you go on at this pace, you can't avoid being killed, because you're not an equal match for them." Erec replies: "You've little regard for me and treat my words with utter contempt. However kindly I may ask you, I can't teach you your lesson. But if God in His mercy lets me escape from here, your own words will cost you dearly, unless I should change my mind."

3571 At once he turns round and sees the seneschal approaching on a strong, fast horse, spearheading the attack four bowshots ahead of the rest. He had not lent out his arms, for he was finely equipped with them. Reckoning the strength of the band, Erec sees there are a good hundred of them. He thinks he must stop the one who is so hard on his heels. They make for one another, striking great blows on the shields with their sharp, pointed lance-heads. Erec drove the steel of his stout lance through the other's body: neither his shield nor his hauberk gave as much protection as a piece of fine, blue silk.

3589 Here now comes the count at a gallop! He, as the story says, was a good strong knight; but he was foolish in having with him only his shield and lance. He had such faith in his own prowess that he did not want any other armour. With great boldness, he dashed more than ten furlongs ahead of all his men. When Erec saw him away from his troop, he turned towards him. The count is not afraid of him, and they clash fiercely together. First the count strikes him on the breast with such force that he would have lost his stirrups had he not been firmly set in them. He splits the wood of Erec's shield so that the lance-tip comes out on the other side. But the hauberk was of very fine quality and saved him from death, without a single link breaking. The count was strong: his lance shatters. Erec strikes him so viciously on the yellow-painted shield that he runs more than a yard of his lance through his belly, knocking him unconscious from his steed. That done, he turned and, without waiting any longer in that place, headed back to go spurring hard straight for the forest.

3620 Now Erec is back in the forest; and the others stopped over those who lay in the middle of the field. Vehemently they declare and swear that they will pursue him at full gallop for two or three days rather than fail to capture or kill him. The count hears what they say. He was badly wounded in the belly, but raised himself up slightly and opened his eyes a little. He recognised clearly that he had started out on a wicked enterprise. He has his knights draw back. "My lords," he says, "I tell you all that not a single one of you, whether strong or weak, high or low, is to be so bold as to dare take a step further. Go back quickly, all of you! I've acted despicably and regret my villainy. The lady who deceived me is very prudent, sensible and courtly. Her beauty fired me with love: out of desire for her I wanted to slay her husband and keep her by force. For that I really should suffer the harm that's come upon me. For my action was wicked, disloyal, treacherous and insane! Never was there a better knight born of mother than this one. He'll suffer no further harm through me, if I can prevent it. I order you all to go back!" They return disconsolate, carrying the seneschal away dead in his reversed shield. The count lived a long time afterwards, for he was not mortally wounded. That is how Erec was saved.

3663 Erec rides off at a gallop with his wife ahead of him along a road between two hedges. With both of them spurring on, they rode on their way until they came into a meadow that had been mown. Emerging from the hedged enclosure, they found a drawbridge in front of a high keep encircled by a wall and a wide, deep moat. Quickly they pass over the bridge. But they had gone a very short distance when the lord of the place saw them from up in his tower. I can tell you truly about this man that he was very small of body but bold and great of heart.* When he saw Erec cross over, he came down from the tower and had a saddle displaying gold lions placed on a great sorrel steed. He then orders to be brought to him a shield and a stout, sturdy lance, a sharp, polished sword and his bright, shining helmet, since he has seen passing in front of his lists an armed knight against whom he wishes to pit his strength in combat to the point of exhaustion, or until the other, tiring first, gives up. His orders are obeyed: the horse is brought out, already saddled and bridled, led by a squire, whilst another brings the arms. The knight rode out through the gate as quickly as he could, quite alone and without companions.

3703 Erec is making his way along a hillside when here comes the knight swooping down over the hill astride a very powerful horse so mettlesome that it crushed the stones beneath its hooves more finely than a millstone grinds wheat; and brightly blazing sparks flew in all directions, giving the impression that all its four feet were on fire. Enide, hearing the noise and tumult, almost fell unconscious from her palfrey in a faint. There was no vein in her body in which the blood did not run cold, and her whole face turned pale and white as if she were dead. She is in great dismay and despair at not daring to tell her husband, who keeps threatening and scolding her and ordering her to keep quiet. She is torn painfully between the two alternatives, not knowing which to choose: speech or silence. She deliberates on it and keeps preparing to speak, so that her tongue moves; but the voice will not come out, for she clenches her teeth with fear and shuts the speech in. Thus she controls herself and holds herself in check, closing her mouth and clenching her teeth so that the words do not pour forth.

3738 Having wrestled desperately with herself, she said: "I know very well that I'll suffer a terrible deprivation if I lose my husband here. Shall I then tell him quite openly? No. – Why not? – I wouldn't dare, because I'd anger my lord. And if my lord's anger is aroused, he'll leave me among this scrub, alone, wretched and helpless. Then I'll be even more unfortunate. – Unfortunate? What does that matter to me? I'll never lack grief or sorrow as long as I live unless my husband gets clean away from here without being mortally injured. But if I don't let him know quickly, this knight galloping up will have killed him before he looks round, for he seems very ill-intentioned. I believe I've waited too long – yet he's strictly forbidden me to do it. But telling me not to won't stop me. I can see my lord is so deep in thought that he's sunk in oblivion; so it's quite right of me to tell him." She did tell him. He threatens her, but has no mind to harm her, for he perceives and truly understands that she loves him above all else, and his love for her cannot be greater.

3770 He turns against the knight, who is calling him to combat. They meet at the foot of the hill, where they confront and defy each other. With all their strength they engage one another with the heads of their lances. The shields hanging at their necks are of less use to them than two strips of bark. The straps break and the boards are split, and the links of the hauberks burst apart. Each thrusts the tip of his lance into the other as far as his entrails, and their steeds are knocked to the ground; for these knights were very strong. Though grievously injured, they were not mortally wounded. Swiftly they got up and recovered their lances, which were not damaged or broken. They threw them away on the field; then they draw their swords from the scabbards and set to furiously. Each wounds and injures the other as they give one another no quarter. They strike such mighty blows on the helmets that they throw off fiery sparks as the swords rebound. The shields split and splinter, their hauberks are torn and rent. In four places the sword-strokes cut to the bare flesh, so that they grow weak and tired; and had both swords stayed whole for very long, they would never have drawn back, nor would the combat have finished before one of them met his death.

3807 Enide, who was watching them, almost went out of her mind with grief. To see her in her great anguish wringing her hands and rending her tresses with tears streaming from her eyes was to witness a loyal lady; and anyone seeing her would have been a scoundrel not to take great pity on her. Each deals the other great blows. From nine in the morning until after three the fight raged so fiercely that nobody could have been at all sure who would get the upper hand. Erec, striving with all his might, embeds his sword in his opponent's helmet as far as the coif of the hauberk, making him stagger; but he did well to keep himself from falling. And he attacked Erec in turn, striking him so hard on the rim of his shield that, as he pulled out his fine, precious sword, it shattered. Seeing his sword broken, he angrily threw away the piece left in his hand just as far as he could. He was afraid and had to retreat; for a knight without his sword cannot put up much of a fight in a combat or assault.

3839 Erec pursues him; and he begs him for God's sake not to kill him. "Mercy, noble knight!" he says. "Don't be harsh or cruel to me. Now my sword has failed me, you have the strength and power to slay me or take me alive, for I've no means of defence." Erec replies: "Since you plead with me, I want you to say outright if you're beaten and vanquished. You'll not be attacked any further by me if you place yourself in my power." He hesitates to say this. When Erec sees him delay, he makes a further pass at him to give him another fright, running at him with his drawn sword. In his alarm, the man cried: "Have mercy, sir! Consider me vanquished, since there's nothing else for it." Erec replies: "I need more: you'll not get off as easily as that. Tell me your name and condition, and I in turn will tell you mine."

3864 "Very well, sir," he says. "I am king of this land. My liegemen are Irish, and there's none of them who is not my tributary. And my name is Guivret the Little. I'm very rich and powerful, for in this country there's no lord whose lands border mine in any direction who goes against my authority and doesn't do everything I wish. I have no neighbour who doesn't fear me, however proud and confident he may be. But from now on I should very much like to be your close friend." Erec replies: "For my part, I pride myself in being a very noble man. My name is Erec, son of King Lac. My father is king of Further Wales and possesses many rich cities, fine halls and strong castles: no king or emperor has more, save only for King Arthur. I certainly make exception of him, for he's without an equal."

3888 Guivret is very astonished at this, and says: "Sir, this is very wonderful news. Nothing has ever given me such joy as making your acquaintance. You can put your trust in me! And if you'd be happy to stay in my land and my residence, I shall have you treated with great honour. As long as you wish to stay here, I'll be yours to command. We both have need of a doctor; and there's a manor-house of mine not far from here – less than eight leagues, or seven, away; and I should like to take you there with me and have our wounds tended." Erec replies: "I'm grateful to you for what I've heard you say. I shall not go there, thank you; but there is one request I make of you: that, should I ever be in need and you get to hear that I could do with your help, you would not then forget me."—"Sir," he says, "I pledge you that so long as I live you shall never need my help, without my going at once to your assistance with whatever resources I can muster."—"There's nothing more I would ask of you," says Erec. "You've promised me a great deal. If your deeds are as good as your words, you are my lord and my friend." They kiss and embrace each other. Never after such a hard combat was there so affectionate a parting; for out of love and generosity each cut long, broad strips from his shirt-tails and bound up the other's wounds. Having bandaged one another, they commended each other to God.

3929 Thus they parted. Guivret returns alone; and Erec has resumed his journey, badly needing plaster to dress his wounds. He continued on his way until he came to a plain beside a tall forest full of stags, hinds, does, roe-deer and other wild animals and all kinds of game. That day King Arthur and the queen and the best of his lords had come there: the king wished to stay three or four days in the forest for his pleasure and sport, and had ordered tents, pavilions

and awnings to be brought. Into the king's tent had gone my lord
Gawain, tired out after a long ride. Outside the tent stood a
hornbeam, and there he had left one of his shields and his ashen
lance. He had hitched his horse Gringalet,* still saddled and
bridled, to a branch by its rein. The horse was still there when Kay
the seneschal arrived.* He came up very quickly and, as if to amuse
himself, took the charger and mounted it without anyone stopping
him. Then he took the lance and shield which were under the tree
close by.

3965 Kay went galloping on Gringalet down a little valley until it
happened by chance that Erec met him. Erec recognised the seneschal and the arms and horse, but Kay did not recognise him, for
there were no distinguishing marks to be seen on his arms: he had
received so many blows from sword and lance on his shield that all
the paintwork had come off. And the lady, not wanting him to see
and recognise her, very shrewdly drew her wimple over her face as
if to shield it from sunburn and the dust. Kay advanced at a trot and
at once seized Erec's rein without any greeting. Before he would let
him move, he arrogantly asked: "Knight! I want to know who you
are and where you come from."—"You're a fool to hold me back,"
says Erec. "You'll not know that in a hurry!" He replies: "Don't be
offended, because I ask for your good. I can see you're obviously
wounded and injured. Tonight you'll be well lodged if you care to
come with me: I shall see that you're well cared for, honoured and
made comfortable, for you're in need of rest. King Arthur and the
queen are lodged in tents and pavilions not far away in a small
wood. I advise you in good faith to come with me and see the queen
and the king, who will be delighted to welcome you and will show
you great honour."

4009 Erec replies: "Your advice is good; but I wouldn't go there for
anything. You don't know what my business is; and I still have
further to travel. Let me go, for I'm staying too long, and there's still
a good deal of daylight left." Kay replies: "You speak foolishly
when you decline to come, and may well regret it. However reluctantly, you'll both go there, you and your wife, just as the priest
goes to the synod: willy-nilly. Tonight you'll be badly served,
believe me, if you go there as strangers. Come quickly, I'm taking
you!" Erec treated this with great scorn. "Fellow," says he, "you're
acting stupidly to drag me after you by force. You've laid hands on

me without any challenge; and I tell you that's an offence, for I thought I was quite safe and wasn't in the least on my guard against you." Then he put his hand to his sword with the words: "Vassal, let go of my bridle! Get away! I consider you arrogant and provocative. You may be sure I shall strike you if you go on dragging me after you. Let me go at once!"

4039 With that Kay releases him, draws back more than a furlong across the field, then turns about and, like a man bent on great wickedness, challenges him. They charge at each other; but Erec, since his opponent had no armour, was chivalrous enough to turn his lance butt-first, with the head at the back. He still gave him such a blow high on the widest part of his shield that he knocked it against his forehead and pinned his arm to his chest, sending him full length to the ground. Then, going to the charger, he takes it and hands it by the bridle to Enide. He was about to take it away; but the other, with his very smooth tongue, begs him to be good enough to return it to him. He eloquently cajoles and wheedles him. "Vassal," says he, "so help me God, this horse is not my property: it belongs in fact to the knight distinguished by the greatest prowess in the world, the bold lord Gawain. On his behalf I tell you to send him his steed, to your own honour. You will be acting very nobly and wisely, and I'll be your messenger." Erec replies: "Vassal, take the horse and lead it off! As it's my lord Gawain's, it's not right for me to take it away."

4073 Kay takes the horse and remounts. He comes to the king's tent and tells him the truth, without keeping anything back. Then the king called Gawain. "Good nephew Gawain," said the king, "if ever you were civil and courteous, go after him now and ask him in a friendly manner who he is and what is his business. And should you be able to use your influence on him and bring him back with you, then spare no effort to do so." Gawain mounts his Gringalet and is followed by two pages. They soon caught up with Erec, but did not recognise him. Gawain greets him, and he Gawain. After this exchange of greetings, my lord Gawain said to him in his very frank and open way: "Sir," he says, "King Arthur sends me this way to meet you. The queen and king send their greetings and beg you urgently to come and spend some pleasant time with them – it may be to your advantage and can do you no harm, and they are not far from here." Erec replies: "I'm very grateful to both the king and the queen, and to you, who seem to me both good-natured and of courteous manners. I'm not at all in the best of health, but have a deep wound in my body; yet I still won't leave my route to take lodging. You need wait no longer, thank you, but should go back."

4110 Gawain was a man of great sense. He draws back and whispers in the ear of one of the pages that he must go quickly to tell the king that he should at once take steps to strike and dismantle his tents, then come three or four leagues ahead of them and erect the linen pavilions in the middle of their road. He should spend the night there, if he wishes to get to know and entertain truly the best knight he might ever expect to see, but who, for one reason or another, is unwilling to go out of his way to take lodging. The lad goes away and delivers his message. The king immediately has his tents struck. They are taken down and loaded on to pack-horses; then they leave. The king mounts Aubagu, and then the queen mounted a white northern palfrey. Meanwhile my lord Gawain continues to delay Erec, who said to him: "I went much further yesterday than I shall go today. You're annoying me, sir. Let me go! You've disrupted a good deal of my day's journey." Then my lord Gawain says to him: "I should like to go a little further with you, if you don't mind; for there's still a long time before night."

4143 They spent so much time in talking that all the tents were erected ahead of them. And Erec sees them: he is to be given shelter, as he well realises. "Ah, Gawain!" he says. "Ah, your cleverness has outwitted me. You've very cunningly held me back. As it's turned out this way, I shall tell you my name at once: it would serve me no purpose to keep it secret. I am Erec, who in the past was your companion and friend." Hearing him, Gawain goes to embrace him. Raising his helmet, he unlaces his ventail. He hugs and embraces him for joy, and Erec returns his embraces.

4160 Gawain then leaves him, saying: "Sir, this news will indeed be most welcome to my lord. My lady and lord will be highly delighted, and I'm going ahead to tell them; but first I must embrace and warmly greet and welcome my lady Enide, your wife. My lady the queen is most anxious to see her: I heard her speak of it only yesterday." Then he goes up to Enide and asks her how she is and whether she is in good health and spirits. She replies courteously: "Sir, I should have no pain or grief, were I not very concerned for my husband; for I'm afraid he has hardly a limb without a wound."

Gawain replies: "I'm extremely worried: this shows clearly in his face, which is pale and colourless. I could well have wept myself on seeing him so pale and wan; but joy drives out grief, and I was so overjoyed to see him that I forgot all my sadness. Now come along at a gentle pace. I'll go ahead at top speed to tell the queen and king that you're following behind me. I'm sure they will both be quite delighted to know."

4193 Then he leaves and comes to the king's tent. "Sire," he says, "now is the time for rejoicing for you and my lady, for here comes Erec with his wife!" The king jumps to his feet for joy. "I am indeed most happy," he says. "I could not hear any news that could cheer me so much!" The queen and all the others rejoice and hurry helter-skelter from the tents, and even the king leaves his. They met Erec very close at hand. When Erec sees the king coming, he at once dismounts, as does Enide for her part. The king embraces and greets them, and the queen too kisses and embraces them tenderly. There is no one who does not show his joy. Right there on the spot they took off Erec's armour. Then, when they have seen his wounds, their joy turns to grief. The king sighs very deeply and has an ointment brought which Morgan, his sister, had made. This salve that Morgan had given Arthur was so effective that no wound that was treated with it, whether on a nerve or on a joint, did not fail to be quite healed and cured within a week, provided that the salve was applied once a day. They brought this ointment to the king, and it gave Erec great relief.

4229 When they had bathed and dried his wounds and bandaged them again, the king leads him and Enide into his own royal tent, saying that for love of him he intends to prolong his stay in the forest for a full fortnight, until he is quite fit and well again. Erec thanks the king for this, but says: "Good sire, I have no wound that pains me enough for me to want to abandon my journey. No one could keep me here. Tomorrow, and I shall delay no longer, I wish to leave early, as soon as I see the sun rise." The king shook his head and said: "This is most unfortunate that you are not willing to stay, for I know you're in great pain. Be sensible and stay. It will be very sad and a great pity if you die in these forests. My dear good friend, do stay until you are quite recovered." Erec replies: "Enough of this! I'm so set on making this journey that I shall definitely not stay." Hearing that nothing would make him stay at his request, the king leaves the matter there and orders supper to be quickly prepared and the tables to be laid. The servants busy themselves with this. It was a Saturday night, and they ate fish and fruit: pike and perch, salmon and trout, and then raw and cooked pears.* After supper they soon had the beds prepared. The king felt great affection for Erec: he had him put into a bed alone, not wanting anyone to lie beside him who might touch his wounds. That night he was well quartered. In another bed beside his lay Enide together with the queen, under an ermine bedspread; and they slept very soundly until day broke next morning.

4279   Next day as soon as dawn comes, Erec gets up, dresses, orders his horses to be saddled and has his arms brought. Pages run to fetch them. The king and all the knights still urge him to stay; but their entreaties are to no avail, for he would not stay on any account. Then you could have seen them all weeping and grieving as deeply as if they already saw him dead. He arms himself, and Enide rises. All the knights are sad, thinking they will never see them again. They all leave their tents and follow them, sending for their own horses so that they can lead and escort them. Erec said to them: "Don't be offended, but you're not to come a single step with me. I'm most grateful to you, but stay!" His horse was brought to him, and he mounts without waiting. Taking his shield and lance, he commends them all to God, and they commend him in turn. Enide mounts, and they depart.

4306   They entered a forest and continued on until six o'clock in the morning. Through the forest they rode until, in the distance, they heard a maiden calling out in great distress. On hearing the cry, Erec realised it was the voice of someone grief-stricken and in need of help. He at once calls Enide. "Lady," he says, "there's a maiden going through this wood crying aloud. It seems to me she needs help and assistance. I intend to hurry in that direction to find out what her trouble is. You dismount here while I go over there. And wait while I'm away."—"Gladly, my lord," she says. He leaves her alone and rides off until he finds the maiden, who was going through the woods crying aloud for her lover, whom two giants had seized and were leading away, cruelly maltreating him.

4334   The maiden went wringing her hands and tearing her hair and her tender, flushed face. Erec sees her and, in great astonishment, begs her to tell him why she is weeping and crying so. The girl weeps and sobs; and between her sighs she says: "Good sir, it's no wonder I'm lamenting, for I wish I were dead. I have no love or regard for my life, since my lover is being led away captive by two wicked, cruel giants who are his mortal enemies. God, what shall I do, pitiful wretch that I am, for the best knight alive, the noblest and most distinguished of all? Now he's in mortal danger. This very day they will villainously put him to a most shameful death. Noble knight, I implore you in God's name to rescue my lover, if you're at all able to do so. You'll not need to gallop far, for they're still quite near at hand."—"Damsel, I shall go after them," says Erec, "since you beg me to; and rest assured that I'll do everything in my power. Either I shall be captured with him or I'll return him to you free, provided the giants spare his life until I can find him. I fully intend to try my strength against them."—"Noble knight," said the maiden, "I shall always be your humble servant if you restore my lover to me. May God go with you! And please hurry!"—"Which way are they heading?"—"This way, sir: here's the path with the tracks." Then Erec left at the gallop, telling her to wait for him there. The maiden commends him to God, beseeching Him in her prayers to give him, through His authority, the strength to overcome those who are her lover's enemies.

4379 Erec goes following the tracks, spurring hard after the giants. He followed them until, in his pursuit, he spotted them before they were quite out of the woods; and he saw the knight, stripped stark naked, on a nag, his hands and feet bound as though he had been caught stealing. The giants had no lances, shields or sharpened swords, but only clubs; and they each held a scourge, with which they were beating him so cruelly that they had already cut the skin on his back to the bone. His blood ran down his side and flanks so that the nag was covered in gore down to its belly. Erec came after them on his own, extremely sad and distressed to see them treating the knight so very spitefully.

4403 On a heath between two woods he caught up with them and asked: "Sirs, for what crime are you treating this man so harshly, leading him off like a robber? You're handling him too cruelly and taking him away as if he'd been caught thieving. It's a shocking thing to strip a knight naked, then truss him up and beat him so savagely. I ask you in all honesty and courtesy to hand him over to me; I've no wish to get him from you by force."—"Vassal," they

say, "what business is this of yours? It's utterly foolish of you to
demand anything of us. If you don't like it, try to do something
about it!" Erec replies: "Indeed I don't like it, and you'll not lead
him away without a tussle. As you've left it up to me, let whoever
can get him keep him! Stand back! I challenge you. You'll not take
him any further before blows have been exchanged."—"Vassal,"
they say, "you're quite mad to want to fight with us. If there were
four of you, you'd stand no more chance against us than a lamb
against two wolves."—"I don't know about that," replies Erec. "If
the sky falls and the earth melts, many a lark will be caught. Some
boast much who are worth little. On guard! I'm coming at you!"

4438 The giants were strong and fierce, and in their clenched fists
they held their great iron-shod clubs. Erec rode at them lance in
rest, not fearing either despite their threats and arrogance. He
strikes the first in the eye and right through the middle of the brain,
so that the blood and brains spurt out of the back of his neck; and
this one falls dead, his heart stilled. When the other saw him dead,
he was worried, and rightly so. Furiously he went to avenge him.
He raised the club in both hands with the intention of striking Erec
on his unprotected head; but he saw the blow coming and took it
on his shield. Yet the giant still caught him such a blow that he
stunned him and nearly pitched him off his charger on to the
ground. Erec protects himself with his shield, and the giant makes
to deliver another blow, intending to strike him again straight on
the head; but Erec, with his drawn sword, presses home an attack
that does the giant a poor turn, striking him so hard on the nape of
the neck that he splits him down to the saddle-bow. He spreads his
entrails on the ground, and the body, cleft in two,* falls full length.

4473 The knight weeps for joy, calling on God and praising Him for
having sent him aid. Erec at once untied him, had him dress and
equip himself, mount one of the horses and lead the other along.
Then he asks who he is and receives the reply: "Noble knight, you
are my rightful lord. I want to take you as my lord, as it is only
reasonable I should, since you've saved my life, which otherwise
would have been driven with great torment and suffering from my
body. What chance, dear kind lord, sent you to me, in God's name,
to deliver me by your valour from the hands of my enemies? Sir, I
wish to pay you homage: I shall always, from now on, go with you
and serve you as my lord." Erec, seeing his desire to do him what

service he wished in any way he could, said: "Friend, I don't wish to accept your service; but you should know that I came here to your aid at the request of your sweetheart, whom I found grieving in this wood. She is lamenting and distressed on your account, her heart full of sorrow. I want to hand you over to her as a gift. Then, having reunited you with her, I shall resume my journey alone; for you shall not go with me, as I don't wish for your company. But I would like to know your name."—"My lord," he says, "as you desire: since you wish to know my name, it should not be kept from you. It is Cadoc of Tabriol: that, I assure you, is how I am known. But since I have to part from you, I should like to know, if possible, who you are and from what land, where I may seek and find you in the future, after I've left here."

4522 "Friend, that I shall never tell you," says Erec. "So say no more about it. But if you do want to know and to do me honour in some respect, then go quickly without delay to my lord King Arthur, who is devoting all his energies to a stag hunt in this part of the forest. It's my belief that he's less than five short leagues away. Go to him quickly and tell him you're sent to him as a gift by him whom last evening he welcomed and lodged in his tent. And be sure not to conceal from him the peril from which I saved your life and your person. I'm well loved at the court: if you present yourself in my name, you'll do me a service and honour. There you may ask who I am; but you'll not find out otherwise."—"My lord," says Cadoc, "I shall do just as you bid. You need have no fear that I'll not go there very willingly. I'll give a very good account to the king of the facts of the fight as you undertook it on my behalf."

4551 Conversing thus, they went on their way until they came to the maiden where Erec had left her. When the girl saw the return of her lover, whom she never expected to see again, she was full of joy. Erec took him by the hand and presented him to her, saying: "Forget your grief, damsel! Here you see your lover glad and happy." She very sensibly replies: "My lord, you must really have won us both, me and him. Together we must be yours, to serve and honour you. But who could repay this debt, or even half of it?" Erec replies: "My sweet friend, I ask no reward from you. Now I commend you both to God, for I think I've lingered here too long." Then he turns his horse about and goes off as fast as he can. Cadoc of Tabriol leaves in the other direction with his maiden. He soon gave his news to King Arthur and the queen.

4578 Erec continues to ride on at great speed to where Enide was awaiting him, grief-stricken and totally convinced he had quite abandoned her; and for his part, he was very afraid lest someone, finding her alone, had made off with her. So he made all haste to get back. But the heat of the day and his armour caused him such discomfort that his wounds opened, and all the bandages burst. His wounds continued to bleed as he came straight to where Enide was awaiting him. She saw him and was overjoyed, but did not notice or realise the pain he was suffering; for his whole body was bathed in blood, and his heart was almost failing him. As he was coming down a hill, he suddenly collapsed on to his horse's neck. When he went to raise himself, he lost his seat in the saddle and fell unconscious as if he were dead.

4606 Then, when Enide saw him fall, what a show of grief there was! In her anxiety at seeing him, she runs towards him and, without attempting to hide her anguish, cries aloud and wrings her hands; and there is no part of her dress at her breast that is not rent. She begins to tear her hair and scratch at her tender face.* "Oh God," she says, "fair sweet Lord, why do You let me go on living? Death, kill me now with all haste!" With this, she swoons on the body; and when she comes to, she blames herself. "Ah," she says, "wretched Enide! I'm my husband's murderer. I've killed him by what I said. My lord would still be alive had I not, like an insolent fool, spoken the words that prompted him to set out on this journey. Silence never harmed anyone, but speech often does damage: that's something I've put to the test and proved in many ways."

4632 She sat down in front of her husband and took his head on her knees. Then she began to lament again. "Ah," says she, "how disastrous for you, my lord who had no equal! For in you beauty was reflected, prowess demonstrated, whilst knowledge had given you its heart, and liberality, without which nobody counts for much, had crowned you. But what did I say? I acted very wrongly in uttering the word responsible for my lord's death, that fatal poisoned word for which I am to blame: I recognise and admit that no one bears any guilt in the matter but I. The fault is mine alone." Then she again falls to the earth in a faint and, when she gets up again, cries out all the more: "God, what am I to do? Why do I live so long? Why does Death hold back, and why does he wait and not carry me off without delay? Death treats me with far too much contempt! Since he doesn't deign to slay me, I must take my own vengeance for my crime. So I shall die in spite of Death, as he's unwilling to assist me! I can't die from just wishing to, and lamenting won't help me achieve my end. It's only right that the sword girt at my lord's side should avenge his death. I shall no longer merely yearn or pray or wish for mine."

4668 She draws the sword from the scabbard and begins to gaze at it. God, who is full of mercy, caused her to pause a little. While she turns over in her mind her grief and misfortune, there suddenly arrives at great speed a count with a large number of knights, having heard the lady's loud cries from a long way off. God had no wish to forget her; for she would have killed herself there and then had not these people taken her unawares, seized the sword from her and thrust it back into the scabbard. Then the count dismounted and began to ask her about the knight and whether she was his wife or his mistress. "Both the one and the other, sir," she says.* "My grief is so great I can tell you no more. I'm sorry not to be dead."

4690 The count does his best to comfort her. "Lady," he says, "I beg you in God's name to have mercy on yourself! It's right and proper for you to grieve; but there's no cause for you to despair, for you may still prosper. Don't sink into apathy, but console yourself and be sensible! God will soon make you happy. Your very great beauty ensures a good future for you; for I shall take you as my wife and make you a countess and lady of rank. That should give you real comfort. And I shall have the corpse removed and interred with great honour. So stop this sorrowing, for you're behaving foolishly." She replies: "Go away, sir! For God's sake leave me alone! You can achieve nothing here: nothing anyone might say or do could make me happy again."

4713 At that the count drew back and said: "Let's quickly make a bier to take away this corpse, and we'll bring the lady with us straight to the castle of Limors, and there the body will be buried. Then I want to marry the lady, though she may well not like it; because I never saw one so beautiful or whom I desired so much. I'm delighted to have found her. Quickly now, let's make a bier fit for a knight without more ado: don't stint your care and effort!" Some draw their swords and have soon cut two poles and bound sticks across them. They laid Erec face upwards on the litter, then hitched two horses to it. Enide rides beside it, continuing to vent her grief. She often swoons and falls back; but the knights keep a tight hold on her, supporting her in their arms, raising her up and comforting her.

4737 They carry the body to Limors and come into the count's main hall. The whole population, ladies, knights and townsfolk, follow them up to it. On a dais in the middle of the hall they placed the body, lying full length with his lance and shield beside him. The hall fills, the crowd is dense. Everyone is anxious to find out the cause of this mourning and what strange event has occurred. Meanwhile the count privately seeks the advice of his barons. "My lords," he says, "I wish to take this lady quickly as my wife. We can easily tell from her beauty and prudence that she comes of a very good family. Her fair appearance and noble bearing show that the rule of a kingdom or empire might fitly be bestowed on her. I shall never be demeaned through her; on the contrary, I expect to benefit considerably. Have my chaplain called, and go to fetch the lady! I'll give her half of my entire land as her dowry, if she will do as I wish." Then they sent for the chaplain as the count had ordered; and the lady too they brought and bestowed her on him by force, for she adamantly refused him. Nevertheless, the count married her according to his wishes.* And as soon as he had wed her, the chief steward had the tables set in the great hall and the food prepared; for it was already time for supper.

4777 After vespers that day in May, Enide was in great despair, her grief as bitter as ever. And the count put some pressure on her by both entreaty and threat to be reconciled and consoled; and against her wishes he made her sit in a fine chair. Like it or not, she was seated there, and the table was placed in front of her. Opposite sat the count, almost beside himself with rage at his inability to comfort her. "Lady," he says, "you must end and forget this grief. You may fully trust me to see you have honour and riches. You can be absolutely sure that grieving doesn't bring a dead man back to life, for no one ever saw that happen. Remember from what poverty you come to the prospect of great wealth. You were poor: now you'll be rich. Fortune is not mean to you in giving you such honour that now you will have the title of countess. It's true your husband is dead: do you think I'm surprised if you feel grief and sorrow for him? Not at all. But I give you some advice, the best I can offer. Now I've married you, you should be very glad. Take care not to anger me! Now eat, as I bid you!" She replies: "Sir, I don't care to. Indeed, as long as I live I shall not eat or drink if I don't first see my lord eat, who lies on that dais."—"Lady, that cannot happen. You make people take you for an idiot when you say such very stupid things. If you have to be asked again, you'll get what you deserve!"

4822 She would not answer him a single word, for his threat left her unmoved. Then the count strikes her in the face. She cries out; and the nobles present rebuke the count. "Stop, lord!" they say to him. "You should be quite ashamed of yourself to have struck this lady because she doesn't eat. You've done a very base thing. If this lady is unhappy because she sees her husband dead, no one should say she's wrong."—"Be quiet, all of you!" says the count. "The lady is mine and I'm hers, and I'll do as I like with her." Then she could not keep silent, but swears she will never be his. And the count raises his hand and strikes again, at which she cries aloud. "Ah, villain!" she says. "I don't care what you say or do to me! I'm not afraid of your blows and threats. Beat me and hit me as much as you like! I'll never find you so violent that I'll do anything at all for you, even if with your own hands you should tear my eyes out on the spot or flay me alive."

4851 In the middle of these arguments and disputes, Erec recovered consciousness like a man waking from sleep. It was no wonder if he was startled to see the people around him; but when he heard his wife's voice, he was troubled and filled with grief. Getting down from the dais, he quickly draws the sword. Anger and his love for his wife give him courage. He runs over to where he sees her and strikes the count on the head, beating out his brains and knocking in his forehead without any word or challenge, so that his blood and brains go flying. The knights leap up from the tables, all thinking this is a devil come in here amongst them. None, young or old, remains there, for they were all terrified. They rush helter-skelter to make their escape. They quickly emptied the hall, the weak and the strong alike, all shouting: "Flee, flee! Here comes the dead man!" There is a vast throng at the door, everybody struggling to get away speedily, pushing and shoving one another, with the person at the back of the crowd wanting to get to the very front. So they all go fleeing, with nobody daring to wait for anyone else.

4884 Erec ran to get his shield. He hangs it at his neck by the strap, and Enide takes the lance; and so they came out into the courtyard.

There is no one so bold as to go there; for they did not believe it was a man chasing them like this, but a devil or demon who had got into the yard. They all flee, and Erec pursues them; then he finds, out in the courtyard, a lad who was going to lead to the watering-place his own charger, with its bridle and saddle on. This was a lucky chance for him. Erec rushes towards the horse, and in terror the boy abandons it at once. Erec climbs up between the saddle-bows; then Enide, with the help of the stirrup, jumps on to the steed's neck as Erec, who told her to mount, ordered and instructed her. The horse carries them both off; and finding the gate open, they ride away with nobody stopping them. In the fortress there was much lamentation over the slain count; but there is no one, however valiant, who takes up the pursuit to avenge him.

4914 The count was slain at his meal. Then Erec, carrying his wife away, embraces and kisses and comforts her.* Taking her in his arms, he clasps her to his heart and says: "Sweet sister, I've put you completely to the proof! Don't be at all fearful, for now I love you more than ever, and I'm again wholly certain that you love me perfectly. From now on I wish to be entirely yours to command, as I was before. And if you've ever spoken ill to me, you have my forgiveness and pardon for both the offence and what you said." Then he kisses and embraces her anew. Now Enide is not ill at ease when her husband hugs and kisses her and reassures her of his love. They ride very fast through the night, and it is a great pleasure for them to have the bright moon lighting their way.

4937 The news travelled very quickly, for nothing else goes with such speed. The report reached the ears of Guivret the Small that a knight wounded in combat had been found dead in the forest, and that with him was so beautiful a lady that the fair Iseut would have seemed her servant-girl, and her lamentations were remarkable to hear. Count Oringle of Limors had found them both and had the body removed; and he wanted to marry the lady, but she was refusing him. When Guivret heard this report, he was far from pleased; for straight away he thought of Erec. He was moved to have the idea of going to look for the lady and having the body, if it were his, buried with high honour. He had a thousand men-at-arms and knights assemble to take the castle. If the count would not readily surrender to him the body and the lady, he would set fire and flames to everything.

4963 By the bright moonlight he led his men towards Limors with
helmets laced, hauberks on and shields hanging at their necks. So,
all armed, they advanced; and it was almost midnight when Erec
spotted them. Now he expects to be trapped or killed or captured
without hope of release. He has Enide get off the horse beside a
hedge. It is no wonder he is alarmed. "Stay here, lady," he says,
"next to this hedge for a little while until these people have gone by.
I don't want them to see you, for I don't know what people they are,
nor what they're after. Perhaps we have nothing to fear from them;
but I don't see anywhere a way for us to escape if they wanted to
cause us any trouble. I don't know if I shall come to any harm, but
I'll not be stopped by fear from going to meet them. And if any of
them should attack me, I'll not fail to joust with him. Yet I'm in
great pain and very weary: it's not surprising I complain. I intend to
ride straight up to them; and you must stay here without making a
sound. Take care until they're well past you that none of them sees
you."

4996 Here now, with lance outstretched, comes Guivret, who had
seen him from far off. They did not recognise each other, for the
moon had been hidden and obscured by a dark cloud. Erec was
weak and exhausted, and the other had to some extent recovered
from the wounds and blows. Now Erec will be very foolish if he
does not have himself quickly recognised. He goes out away from
the hedge; and Guivret spurs towards him without speaking to him
at all, and without Erec saying a word to him. He thought he could
do more than he was capable of: whoever tries to run faster than he
is able has to give up or take a rest. They joust with each other, but
the contest is unequal, for one was weak, the other strong. Guivret
strikes him with such vigour that he knocks him over the horse's
crupper down to the ground.

5019 Enide, who was in hiding, seeing her husband on the ground,
thinks herself lost and in desperate straits. Jumping out from the
hedge, she runs to her lord's assistance. If she grieved before, she is
in greater anguish now. She came up to Guivret and, seizing him by
the rein, said to him: "A curse on you, knight! For you've attacked
a man who is alone, without strength, in pain and almost mortally
wounded so unjustly that you couldn't give a reason for it. Had
there been no one here but you, alone and without help, this attack
would have turned out badly for you, if only my husband had been

fit. Now show your generosity and good manners by honourably stopping this fight you've begun; for your reputation wouldn't be increased if you had killed or captured a knight who, as you see, hasn't the strength to rise; for he has taken so many blows in combat that he's covered all over with wounds." He replies: "Have no fear, lady! I can see you love your husband loyally and commend you for it. You needn't be at all nervous of me or my company. But tell me openly your husband's name, for it will only be to your advantage. Whoever he is, tell me his name, and then he'll go away safely, a free man. There's no reason for you or him to be afraid, because you're both quite safe."

5057 When Enide hears his assurances, she answers him briefly in a word: "His name is Erec: I shouldn't lie, for I can tell you're a noble-hearted and generous man." Guivret, overjoyed, dismounts and goes to fall at Erec's feet, where he was lying on the ground. "My lord, I was on my way to look for you," he says, "and heading straight for Limors, where I expected to find you dead. I'd been reliably told and informed that Count Oringle had taken a mortally wounded knight to Limors and wrongfully wanted to marry a lady he'd found with him, but who would have nothing to do with him; and I was coming urgently to help and rescue her. Had he been unwilling freely to hand over the lady and yourself, I'd have held a poor opinion of myself if I left him a foot of land. You may be sure that I should not have undertaken this had I not loved you dearly. I'm Guivret, your friend. But if I've done you any harm through not recognising you, you really should forgive me for that." At this Erec sat up, for he could do no more, and said: "Get up, my friend! You shall be absolved of this wrong, since you didn't recognise me!"

5091 Guivret rises, and Erec tells him how he killed the count while he was eating at table, and how he had recovered his charger outside a stable, how squires and men-at-arms had fled across the yard crying: "Flee, flee! The dead man's chasing us!" He told how he was almost trapped and how he escaped down through the stronghold carrying his wife on the horse's neck: he told him everything that happened. Then Guivret, for his part, said to him: "My lord, I've a castle close by, very well sited in a healthy place. I should like to take you there tomorrow for your comfort and benefit, and we'll have your wounds tended. I have two charming, gay sisters who are very good at healing wounds: they'll soon have you properly cured. Tonight we'll have our army bivouac here in these fields until morning, because I think a little rest tonight will do you a lot of good. I suggest we lodge here." Erec replies: "I agree."

5120   There they stayed and made their quarters. They were not slow to prepare their camp, but found little they could use, for their numbers were by no means small. People go along the hedgerows finding places to sleep. Guivret had his tent erected and firewood kindled to burn up brightly. He has candles taken from the chests and lit inside the tent. Now Enide is not grieving, for things have turned out very well for her. She disarms and undresses her husband, then bathes, dries and bandages his wounds again, not allowing anyone else to touch him. Now Erec has nothing to reproach her for, since, having thoroughly put her to the proof, he has come to feel great love for her.

5139   Then Guivret, who makes much of them, had a long, high bed made with quilted coverlets that he had and grass and reeds, which they found in plenty. There they laid Erec and covered him up. Next Guivret opened a chest and took out two pasties. "My friend," says he, "now try a little of these cold pasties. And you shall drink wine mixed with water: I've six full barrels of good wine, but it's not healthy for you on its own as you're injured and wounded. My dear good friend, now try to eat, for it will do you good. And my lady your wife will eat too: she's suffered a great deal for you; but you've taken full revenge for that and have made your escape. Now eat, dear friend, and I shall eat as well!" Guivret then sat down beside him, and so did Enide, who was very pleased by everything Guivret did. Both urge him to eat and give him wine mixed with water, for undiluted it is too strong and intoxicating. Erec ate like a sick man and drank little, as much as he dared. But he rested in great comfort and slept all night long, for they kept any noise or din from his ears.

5171   In the early morning they awoke and got ready again to mount and ride. Erec was very fond of his horse and did not care to ride any other. They gave Enide a mule, for she had lost her palfrey; but she was not very nervous and gave the impression of never thinking about it. She had a fine, easy-going mule, which carried her very comfortably. And she was most relieved that Erec was not at all worried, but told them he would make a good recovery. Before nine in the morning they arrived at Penevric, a strong castle well and beautifully situated. Guivret's two sisters were residing there, for it was a most pleasant place. Guivret took Erec to a delightful, airy room well away from people. At his request, his sisters went to great pains to cure Erec, who put his trust in them, such was the confidence they inspired in him. First they took away the dead flesh, then put on ointment and lint, doing their utmost to restore him to health. They were very skilful, often bathing his wounds and applying more ointment. Each day they had him eat and drink four times or more, allowing him no garlic or pepper. But whoever might go in and out, Énide, whom he most cared for, was constantly at his side.

5210 Guivret often came in to ask and find out if there was anything he would like. He was well looked after and served, and nothing that he needed was grudged him; but gladly and willingly the maidens took such great trouble to cure him that within a fortnight he felt no discomfort or pain. Then to bring his colour back, they began to give him baths: there was nothing they needed to be taught, for they knew well how to manage. When he was able to come and go, Guivret had two robes made of different kinds of silk, one trimmed with ermine, one with vair. One was of a deep blue Eastern material, the other of fine, striped stuff sent to him from Scotland as a present by a cousin of his. Enide had the blue robe trimmed with ermine, which was very costly, Erec the striped one with the vair, which was no less valuable.

5236 Now Erec was strong and fit, healed and recovered. Now Enide is very happy. Now joy and gladness is hers; and at night they sleep together. Now she has all she desires, and her great beauty returns; for she had been very pale and wan, so seriously had her deep grief affected her. Now she was embraced and kissed, and enjoyed all good things; now to her great delight they lie naked together in one bed, exchanging embraces and kisses – nothing gives them such pleasure. They have suffered so much hardship and distress, he for her and she for him, that now they have done their penance. They each compete in trying to please the other more: I must say nothing of the rest. Now they have reinforced their love and forgotten their great anguish, which they hardly remember any more.

5260 It is now time to be on their way. So they sought leave from Guivret, in whom they had found a true friend, for he had honoured and served them in every way he could. In taking leave,

Erec said to him: "Sir, now I wish to wait no longer to go to my own land. Have everything I need fetched and made ready. I'd like to set out early tomorrow, at daybreak. I've stayed with you so long that I feel strong and vigorous. May it please God to let me live long enough to meet you again in circumstances where I'm able to serve and honour you in return. I don't intend to stay anywhere, unless I'm captured or detained, until I come to the court of King Arthur, whom I hope to see at Robais or Carlisle." Guivret at once replies: "You shall not leave alone, my lord, for I'll go with you and bring companions with us, if you're happy with that." Erec agrees to this proposal, saying he would like to make the journey just as he wishes. That night they make their preparations for the road, not wanting to stay there longer: they have everything arranged and made ready.

5294　In the early morning when they wake, the horses are saddled. Erec goes to the maidens' rooms to take his leave before he departs; and Enide runs after him, highly delighted that they are ready to travel. They took their leave of the girls; and in saying farewell, Erec, with his usual courtesy, thanks them for his health and life and assures them of his service. Then he took the hand of the one nearest to him, whereupon Enide took that of the other; and all hand in hand they left the room and went up into the main hall. Guivret calls on them to mount at once, without delay. Enide thinks the time will never come for them to be in the saddle. A very good-tempered palfrey,* easy-going, handsome and well-built, was brought out to the mounting-block for her.

5318　It was an excellent palfrey, of fine appearance, worth no less than her own one which had been left at Limors. That was dappled, this one sorrel; but the head was of a different colour: it was divided in such a way that one cheek was completely white and the other as black as a jackdaw; and between the two was a line separating the white from the black that was greener than a vine leaf. I can tell you truly of the straps, the breast-cloth and the saddle that they were richly and finely worked. The entire breast-cloth and straps were full of gold and emeralds. The saddle, in a different style, was covered with a precious purple cloth.* The saddle-bows were of ivory, and carved on them was the story of how Aeneas came from Troy, how in Carthage Dido joyfully received him into her bed, how Aeneas deceived her and she killed herself for him,

how then Aeneas conquered Laurentum and the whole of Lombardy, of which he was king for the rest of his life. It was of delicate
workmanship and finely carved, decorated all over with pure gold.
An expert craftsman who made it spent more than seven years in its
carving, without undertaking any other work. I do not know if he
sold it, but he should have been handsomely rewarded for it. Now
that Enide was honoured with the gift of this palfrey, she was
amply compensated for the loss of her own. The palfrey with all its
rich trappings was given to her, and she mounted it joyfully. Then
the lords and squires mounted quickly. For their pleasure and sport
Guivret had brought with them many tawny and mewed goshawks, many tercels and sparrow-hawks, many tracking-dogs and
greyhounds.

5367 From morning until evening they rode straight on more than
thirty Welsh leagues, then came before the outer towers of a fine,
strong, powerful fortress encircled by a new wall; and beneath it
there ran all round a very deep, broad watercourse that rushed
tempestuously along. As he eyes it, Erec stops to seek information,
if anyone could give him the facts, as to who was the lord of this
stronghold. "My friend," he says to his good companion, "could
you tell me the name of this castle and whose it is? Tell me if it
belongs to a count or a king. As you've brought me this way, tell
me, if you know."—"My lord," he says, "I know very well and will
tell you the truth. The castle's name is Brandigant; and it's so
splendid and strong that it fears no king or emperor. If France and
the whole of England and all who live between here and Liège were
laying siege to it, they'd never take it in their lifetime. For the island
on which the stronghold is situated is more than four leagues
across, and within its perimeter grows everything a powerful fortress needs: fruit, wheat and wine are found there, and there's no
lack of woods or streams. It fears attacks from no quarter, and
nothing could starve it out. King Evrain had it fortified and has held
it uncontested all his days and will keep it his whole life long. He
didn't fortify it, though, because he was in fear of anyone, but
because the castle is more attractive that way. For if there were no
walls or towers but just the river that runs round it, it would still be
so strong and secure that it wouldn't fear the entire world."

5415 "God!" said Erec, "what great might! Let's go to see the
fortress. And we'll take lodging in the castle, for I should like to

stop there."—"Sir," came the worried reply, "if you don't mind, we shouldn't stay there. There's a dangerous passage inside the stronghold."—"Dangerous?" says Erec. "Are you sure? Whatever it is, tell us, for I'm very keen to know."—"My lord," he says, "I'd be afraid you would come to harm. I know there's so much boldness and ability in your character that if I told you what I know of the adventure, which is so perilous and grim, you'd wish to go there. I've often heard tell of it; and seven years or more have passed since anyone returned from the castle who went to seek the adventure there, though proud and courageous knights have come from many lands. Sir, don't take it as a joke, but you'll never learn of it from me until you've pledged by the love you promised me that the adventure, from which nobody emerges other than shamed or dead, will not be undertaken by you."

5447 Now Erec hears what suits him. Begging Guivret not to be annoyed, he said: "Ah, dear good friend, agree, if you don't mind, to our taking lodging in the castle. It's time to find quarters for the night, and that's why I hope you have no objection; for if we come by any honour here, that should be very welcome to you. As for the adventure, I appeal to you just to tell me its name, and I'll let you off the rest."—"My lord," he says, "I can't be silent and not tell you what you want. The name is very fine to say, but it's extremely hard to achieve, for no one may escape from it alive. The adventure, I assure you, is called 'the Joy of the Court'."*—"God, in joy there's nothing but good!" says Erec. "This is what I'm looking for. Don't go discouraging me, dear good friend, from this or anything else; but let's have our lodgings arranged, because much good may come to us from it. Nothing could keep me back from going in quest of the Joy."—"Sir," says the other, "may God hear your prayer to find joy and return without trouble! I see clearly that we must go there. Since there's nothing else for it, let's go! Our lodging is secured, for I've heard it said and reported that no truly worthy knight can enter this stronghold, wishing to take lodging there, without being received by King Evrain. The king is so noble and generous that he has proclaimed to his townsfolk that, as they value their lives, no worthy man arriving from outside shall be sheltered in their houses, in order that he himself may honour all gentlemen wishing to stay there."

5493 So they go up to the fortress, passing the lists and the bridge; *and when they had gone by the lists, the crowds of folk who had flocked into the streets see the very handsome Erec and firmly believe from appearances that all the others belong to him. Everybody gazes at him in amazement, and the town is full of commotion and uproar as they discuss and talk of him. Even the maidens singing at their dance stop and pause in their song; and every one of them looks at him, crossing herself for his great beauty and showing remarkable pity for him. One whispers to the other: "Alas! This knight passing by is bound for the Joy of the Court. He will suffer before he comes back from it! No one ever came from another land to seek the Joy of the Court without finding there shame and harm and leaving his head as a forfeit." And then, so he may hear, they say aloud: "May God protect you, knight, from misfortune; for you're exceedingly handsome, and your beauty is much to be pitied, because tomorrow we shall see it effaced. Your death is fixed for tomorrow: tomorrow you'll die without reprieve, unless God guards and defends you." Erec hears plainly and understands what they are saying about him throughout the town: more than two thousand were lamenting for him, but nothing can dismay him. On he goes without lingering, politely saluting one and all, men and women alike; and they all salute him, many sweating with anxiety, more fearful than he himself of his being shamed and dishonoured. The mere sight of his bearing, his great handsomeness and general appearance has so won everybody's heart that they all, knights, ladies and maidens, dread that he will come to harm.

5542 King Evrain hears the news that some people were coming to his court bringing a large company and that it seemed from their equipment that their lord was a count or king. King Evrain came into the street to meet them with a greeting. "Welcome," he says, "to this company, to both its lord and all its members! Welcome, my lords, and do dismount!" They dismounted; and there were many to receive and take their horses. King Evrain's behaviour was faultless when he saw Enide coming: he at once greets her and runs to help her dismount. By her delicate white hand he leads her up into the great hall as courtesy requires, showing her all the honour he can: he was well versed in such behaviour, without any foolishness or unworthy thought. He had a room made fragrant with incense, myrrh and aloes. When they entered, they all complimented King Evrain on its fine appearance. They went into the room hand in hand as the king directed them, showing his great joy at their presence. *But why should I describe to you the paintings and silken draperies with which the room was decorated? I should waste my time in idle talk, and I do not want to waste it, but rather hurry on a little; for he who goes quickly along the direct route passes the man who makes a detour; so I do not wish to dwell on that.

5580 The king ordered supper to be prepared when the time came; but I have no intention of lingering over that, if I can find a more direct road. That night they had in abundance whatever the heart desires and craves: birds, venison, fruit and a variety of wines. But good cheer surpasses everything, for the sweetest of all dishes is the cheerful expression and the happy face. They were very richly served, until Erec suddenly stopped eating and drinking and began to speak of what was closest to his heart: he remembered the Joy and raised the subject, which was taken up by King Evrain.

5599 "Sire," he says, "it's high time now to speak my thoughts and say why I've come here. I've kept from mentioning it for too long and can't hide it any longer. I ask for the Joy of the Court, for I covet nothing else so much. Grant it me, whatever it may be, if it is in your control."—"Indeed, my good friend," says the king, "I hear you speak great nonsense. This is a very perilous thing and has brought many a worthy man to grief. You yourself will in the end be killed and destroyed, if you're not prepared to take my advice. But if you would take my word, I'd advise you to give up asking for something so terrible, which you would never manage to achieve. Say no more of it! Not another word! It wouldn't be very sensible of you not to heed my advice. I'm not at all astonished that you seek honour and esteem; but I shall have a heavy heart to see you in difficulties and physically injured. And I assure you I've seen many worthy men fail utterly, having asked for this Joy. They never got any benefit from it, but are all dead and perished. Tomorrow, before evening comes, you may expect a similar reward. If you do wish to strive for the Joy, then you shall, though it makes me very sad. It's something you're free to change your mind about and renounce, if you're concerned for your own good. This is why I say to you that I'd be acting treacherously and wrongly towards you if I didn't tell you the whole truth."

5642 Erec hears and concedes that the king gives him good advice; but the greater the marvel and the more difficult the adventure, the more he longs and strives for it. He said: "Sire, I can tell you that I find you a worthy and loyal man, and I cannot lay any blame on you; but I wish to avail myself of this favour, whatever the future may hold for me. The die is cast; for I shall never give up anything I've undertaken without doing my utmost before quitting the field."—"I just knew it," said the king. "You're acting against my wishes. You shall have the Joy you seek; but I'm in great despair, for I'm very afraid that things will turn out badly for you. But now you may be assured of having whatever you desire. If your efforts have a happy result, you'll have won such great honour that no man ever won greater; and my wish is that God may grant you a joyful outcome."

5669 They discussed this all night until the beds were prepared and they retired to rest. In the morning when it grew light, Erec, who was on the watch for it, saw the bright dawn and the sun, and quickly rose and dressed. Enide is greatly distressed at this and is very sad and sorrowful, having spent the night in torment from the worry and fear she felt for her husband who intends to put himself in such grave peril. Nevertheless he gets himself ready, for no one can deflect him from his purpose. When he rose, the king sent him arms to equip himself with and which he put to good use. Erec did not refuse them, for his own were worn and damaged and battered. He gladly took them and had himself armed with them in the hall. Once armed, he goes down to the bottom of the stairs and finds his horse saddled and the king mounted. Everyone in the court and the lodging-places was preparing to mount. In the whole fortress there is nobody, man or woman, erect or deformed, tall or short, weak or strong, who is able to go but stays behind.

5702 When they move off there is a great hubbub and noise in all the streets, for great and humble folk alike were crying: "Alas, alas, knight! You are betrayed by Joy, the one you expect to achieve; but you're going in quest of your grief and death." And every single one says: "This Joy – God's curse on it! For through it so many worthy men have been slain. This very day it will doubtless bring greater harm than ever before." Erec listens and hears clearly what is being said of him up and down: "Alas, alas! How disastrous for you, handsome, noble, able knight! It would indeed be unjust that your life should end so soon and that by some unhappy chance you should be wounded or injured." He plainly hears the words that are spoken, but nevertheless passes on with his head unbowed and giving no signs of cowardice. Whoever may speak, he is very impatient to see and know for certain why they are all in such dread, distress and torment. The king leads him out of the fortress into a nearby garden; and all the people follow, praying God to grant him a joyful outcome to this trial. But I must not pass on, for fear of tiring and wearying my tongue, without telling you the true facts about the garden according to the story.

5739 Round the garden there was no wall or fence except of air; yet by magic the garden was enclosed on every side by air so that nothing could enter it, any more than if it were ringed about by iron, unless it flew in over the top. And all summer and winter it had flowers and ripe fruit. Now the nature of the fruit was such that it could be eaten inside, but to take it out was impossible; for if anyone did want to carry any out, he would never get back to the gate or ever leave the garden until he had put the fruit back in its place. And there is no bird that flies under heaven and gives pleasure to man that does not sing there for his enjoyment and delight, with a number of each species to be heard there. And in its whole length and breadth the earth bears no spice or root useful for making medicine that has not been planted there and is not to be found in abundance.

5765 The throng of people, King Evrain and all the others, went in through a narrow entrance. Erec went riding through the garden lance in rest, taking great pleasure in the sound of the birds singing there, since for him they denoted his Joy, the thing he most longed for. But he saw an awesome thing that might have terrified the boldest warrior among all those we know, be it Thiebaut the Slav or Ospinel or Fernagu;* for in front of them on sharpened stakes there were bright, shining helmets, each with a man's head beneath its rim. But at the end of the stakes was one which carried nothing as yet except only a horn. He does not know the meaning of this, but, without hesitating on that account, asks the king, who was by his right side, what this might be.

5791 The king explains, saying to him: "My friend, do you want to know the meaning of what you see here? You ought to be most alarmed if you're at all concerned for your safety, for that single stake on its own where you see the horn hanging has waited a long time; but we don't know for whom, whether it awaits you or someone else. Take care your head isn't put there, for the stake stands there for that purpose. I had given you fair warning before you came here. I don't expect you ever to get out, but to be slain and cut to pieces; for we now suppose that the stake is waiting for your head. And should it happen that it is put there, as it promises to be, then as soon as your head is fixed on it, another stake will be set up next to it to wait for the coming in turn of I know not whom. I shall tell you no more of the horn but that no one has ever been able to sound it. Yet if any man can sound it, his reputation and honour will thereby increase and surpass that of all those in the land, and he will have gained such respect that everyone will come to honour him and regard him as the best of them all. Now that's all there is to tell of this matter. Have your people withdraw, for the Joy will shortly arrive – and, I fancy, make you sorry!"

5827 With that, King Evrain leaves him; and he bends down to Enide, who was in great distress at his side. And yet she kept silent; for grief expressed in words does not really hurt unless it is also heartfelt. Then, well knowing her heart, he said to her: "Dear sweet sister, noble, loyal and prudent lady, I know just what you're thinking. I can well see you're very afraid, but you don't yet know of what. You're alarmed over nothing, though, until you've seen my shield hacked to pieces and me wounded in the body and seen the blood spread over the links of my bright hauberk, my helmet broken and dented, and myself recreant and weary, no longer able to defend myself and having to hope and beg for mercy against my wishes. Then is the time for you to lament, but you've begun too soon. Sweet lady, you don't yet know what is to happen, nor do I. Your dismay is pointless. But know for a fact that if I possessed no courage except what your love gives me, I should certainly not fear to face in single combat any man alive. I'm foolish, though, to boast – not that I say this out of arrogance, but only because I want to comfort you. So be comforted and stop worrying! I can't wait here any longer, and you may come no further with me; for according to the king's orders, I mustn't take you any further." Then he kisses her and commends her to God, and she him. But she is extremely unhappy not to be able to follow and escort him until she sees with her own eyes the nature of the adventure and how he will fare; but because she must stay and cannot follow any further, she remains behind, grieving and distressed.

5878 Then he went off along a path, alone and with no one for
    company, until he came across a silver bed covered with a gold-
    embroidered cloth in the shade of a sycamore. And on the bed was a
    maiden with an attractive figure, lovely face and as much beauty as
    one could wish: there she was sitting all alone. I have no wish to
    describe her further; but if one could feast one's eyes on her
    adornment and her beauty, one might truly say that never did
    Lavinia of Laurentum,* who was so very fair and attractive, pos-
    sess a quarter of her beauty. Erec, wishing to see her more closely,
    proceeds in her direction. Meanwhile the people go to sit under the
    trees in the garden.

5898 Then suddenly here comes a knight wearing crimson armour
    who was remarkably tall; and had he not been over-tall, there
    would have been no man under heaven more handsome than he.
    But he was a foot taller, as everybody confirmed, than any knight
    known. Before Erec had seen him, he called out: "Vassal, vassal!
    You're mad, so help me, to approach my damsel. I scarcely think
    you're worthy to presume to go up to her. By my head, you'll soon
    pay very dearly for your folly! Stand back!" Then Erec stops and
    looks at him. The other stood still too. Neither made a move
    towards the other until Erec, in response, had finished speaking his
    mind to him. "My friend," he says, "one can utter foolish words
    just as readily as good sense. Threaten as much as you please, but I
    shall be the one to keep silent, for there's no wisdom in threats. Do
    you know why? A man may think he has won the game, who then
    loses it. Therefore he is a plain fool who presumes and threatens too
    much. For one who flees there are many who chase: but I don't fear
    you so much as to run away. I'm still waiting. I'm equipped to
    defend myself should anyone want to attack me and I had reluc-
    tantly to do so, being unable to get out of the situation other-
    wise."—"You certainly won't," says he, "so help me God! I
    promise you you'll not lack a fight, for I challenge and defy you!"

5938 Then you may be sure that the reins were no longer held in.
    They did not have small lances, but they were big and massive and
    had not been planed down, so they were all the stronger and more
    rigid. They strike one another so violently on the shields with the
    sharp heads of these lances that each one goes six feet through the
    shining shield; but neither touches the other's flesh, and neither
    lance was broken. Each man withdrew his lance as quickly as he

could; then they come together again to renew the proper joust. They clash with one another, striking with such ferocity that both lances are shattered and the horses fall beneath them; but the men seated on the horses suffer no harm at all. They were quick to get up, being strong and agile. They are on foot in the middle of the garden and at once fall on each other with their green swords of Vienne steel dealing great, murderous blows on their bright, gleaming helmets, so that they completely shatter them, and they see sparks in their eyes. They cannot struggle and strive with greater effort to injure and harm each other. Fiercely they set upon one another with gilded pommels as well as blades.

5974 They have battered so hard on teeth, cheeks, nose-pieces, fists, arms and much more besides, on temples, napes of necks and throats that they ache in every bone. They are in great pain and very weary; yet still they do not give up, but keep increasing their efforts. The sweat and the blood that drips down with it get in their eyes so that they can scarcely see a thing; and very often they missed their blows like men who could not see to aim their swords at each other. The one can scarcely hurt the other more, yet they did not in the least hold back from exerting all their strength. Because their eyes are blinded so they completely lose their sight, they let their shields drop to the ground and furiously seize one another. Each pulls and tugs at the other so that they fall to their knees. In this way they struggle together for a long time until three o'clock passes. Then the tall knight grows so tired that he is quite unable to draw his breath. Erec has him at his mercy; and having, by dragging and pulling, snapped all the laces on his helmet, he forces him down at his feet. He falls over on his back and has not the strength to get up again.

6008 However reluctantly, he has to concede with the words: "You've vanquished me, and I can't deny it; but it goes much against the grain. However, you may be of such standing and repute that I shall derive only satisfaction from it; and I'd beg to know, if at all possible, your true name, so that I could draw some comfort, if I've been beaten by a better man than I. I shall be glad of that, I assure you. But should I have happened to be defeated by a worse man than I, then I can only be extremely sad about it."—"You wish to know my name, my friend?" says Erec. "Then I shall tell you and not leave here before I have. But it will be on condition that you tell me at once why you're in this garden. I want to know the whole story, both your name and what the Joy is; for I'm very anxious to hear the truth from beginning to end."—"Sir," says he, "I'll not hesitate to tell you all you wish."

6036 Erec withholds his name from him no longer. "Did you ever hear speak", he asks, "of King Lac and his son Erec?"—"Yes, indeed, sir: I knew him well, for I was at his father's court for many a day before I was knighted; and, had he had his wish, I would not have left his company on any account."—"Then you must know me well, if you were once with me at the court of my father the king."—"By my faith! So things have turned out well for me. Now let me tell you who has kept me so long in this garden. I'll tell the truth, however reluctantly, since you've asked me to. That maiden sitting over there loved me from childhood and I her, and this was a source of pleasure for us both. Our love grew and developed until she asked me a favour,* but without naming it. Who would deny his sweetheart anything? There is no lover who doesn't completely carry out his mistress's every desire without any omission or deception, so far as he's at all able. I agreed to her wish. And when I'd agreed, she wanted me to go further and swear to it – had she wanted still more, I'd have done more. Still, she took me at my word. I made her the pledge, but without knowing what.

6069 "In time I was knighted. King Evrain, whose nephew I am, dubbed me in the presence of many worthy men in this very garden where we are. My damsel sitting there immediately took me up on my word, saying I'd pledged her never to leave this place until some knight should come and vanquish me in armed combat. It was right that I should stay rather than break my oath, even though I should never have pledged it. Since I saw the good in her, I should not give any indication or impression to this person who is dearest to me that I was displeased with anything; for had she noticed it, she would quickly have withdrawn her heart from me – and I would not have wished that on any account, whatever might happen. In this way my damsel intended me to stay here for a long while; she thought the day would never arrive when a knight able to overcome me would come into this garden. So she believed that, unhindered, she could keep me imprisoned with her all the days of my life. And I should commit an offence if, by holding back in any way, I didn't defeat all those I had it in my power to beat: it would have been despicable to get out of it that way. And I dare assert that I have no

friend however close against whom I would have made any pretence. I've never wearied of arms or given up fighting. You've
certainly seen the helmets of those I have defeated or slain; but the
fault's not mine, if one takes the reasonable view. I couldn't help it,
if I did not wish to be a false, disloyal perjurer.

6115 "Now I've told you the truth, and you may be sure that the
honour you have won is not small. You've brought great joy to the
court of my uncle and friends, for now I shall be released from here;
and because all those at court will derive joy from it, those who
awaited that joy called it 'Joy of the Court'.* They've long waited
for it, until now it will be granted them by you through your having
fought for it. You've really checkmated and spirited away my
reputation and chivalry. Now it's only right that I should tell you
my name, as you wish to know it. I'm called Mabonagrain. But I'm
not known or remembered by that name in any land where I've
been seen, except in this country alone; for never before my knight-
ing did I tell or divulge my name. My lord, you know the truth
about everything you enquired of me. But I still have to tell you that
in this garden is a horn, which I presume you've seen. I may not go
out of here until you've sounded that horn; but then you'll have
liberated me, and then the Joy will begin. Whoever hears and
harkens to it will let nothing prevent him, having heard the horn's
call, from coming straightway to court. Get up, sir! Go quickly! Go
and happily take the horn, for you've no cause to wait. So do what
you have to!"

6156 Erec immediately got up. The other rises with him, and
together they come to the horn. Erec takes and sounds it, blowing
with all his might, so that its call reaches far. Enide was overjoyed
when she heard the sound, and Guivret too was delighted. The king
is glad and so are his people: there is not one of them other than
very content and pleased at this. Nobody there stops or pauses in
the rejoicing and singing. That day Erec could pride himself that
never was such joy expressed: it could not be described or told by
mortal tongue; but briefly and in few words I will tell you the gist of
it. The news of how things have turned out flies through the
country. Then no one was deterred from coming to the court.
The whole population hurries there, some on foot, some riding
at the gallop, without waiting for each other. Then those who were
in the garden set about removing Erec's armour, all competing to

sing a song about the Joy; and the ladies composed a lay they called the "Lay of Joy", though it is not widely known. Erec had his fill of joy and was served with it to his heart's content.

6192 But the girl sitting on the silver bed was far from happy. The joy she witnessed brought her no pleasure – but many people have to look in silence at what saddens them. Enide behaved with great courtesy: seeing her brooding and sitting alone on the bed, she thought she would go to speak with her and tell her about her affairs and who she was, and ask that she, if possible, should tell her about herself in return, if she did not mind too much. Enide intended to go there alone, not wanting to take anybody with her. But a number of the most distinguished and beautiful of the ladies and maidens followed her out of affection and to keep her company, and also to comfort the girl who is exceedingly pained by the joy, because it seemed to her that now her lover would no longer be with her as much as he had been, since he intended to leave the garden. Whoever may be displeased, he cannot help going out of it, for the time and the moment have come. So the tears streamed from her eyes and down her face. She was much more grief-stricken and miserable than I am telling you, but she did still raise herself up. Yet none of those trying to comfort her means enough to her for her to stop her lamenting.

6230 Enide greets her politely. For a long time she could not utter a word in reply, made speechless by the sighs and sobs that greatly afflict and distress her. After a long while the damsel did return her greeting. Then, having spent some time examining and gazing at her, she fancied she had seen and known her before. However, not being entirely certain, she did not hesitate to enquire where she came from and from what country, and where her husband's birthplace was – she asks who they both are. Enide replies briefly and tells her the truth. "I", she says, "am the niece of the count who governs Lalut, daughter of his own sister. I was born and bred in Lalut."

6252 The girl is so cheered by this that, forgetting now her grief, she cannot help laughing before she hears her say any more. Her heart jumps for joy, and she can no longer hide her delight: she runs up to kiss and embrace her, saying: "I am your cousin!* I assure you this is the absolute truth; and you are the niece of my father, for your own and he are brothers. But I suppose you don't know and haven't heard how I came to this land. Your uncle the count was at war, and knights of many regions came in his service. So, dear cousin, it happened that with them in his hire there came the nephew of the king of Brandigan: he was almost a year with my father. That, I think, was fully twelve years ago, and I was still a little child. He was very handsome and good-looking. There we made together such pacts as suited us. I never had a wish he did not share, until he began to love me and pledged and swore to me that he would always be my lover and would bring me here. That pleased me and him as well. He could not wait, and I was impatient for the time he would bring me here with him; so we both came, without anybody knowing but ourselves. At that time both you and I were young and childish. I've told you the facts: now you tell me, as I've informed you, the truth about your lover and how he won you."

6294 —"Dear cousin, he married me with my father's full knowledge and to my mother's great joy. All our relatives knew and were glad about it, as they should have been. Even the count was happy with it. For he's so excellent a knight that no better can be found, and his honour and valour need no demonstrating. He comes too of a very noble line, and no one, I think, is his equal. He loves me dearly, and I him more: our love cannot be greater. Never yet have I been half-hearted in my love for him, nor should I be. Is my husband, then, not a king's son? Did he not, then, take me when I was poor and naked? Through him I've come by such honour that never was so much afforded to any helpless girl. And, if you like, I'll tell you without a word of a lie how I rose to such heights: that's something I'll never be slow to tell." Then she told her and revealed, not wishing to hide anything, how Erec came to Lalut. She recounted to her the whole story in great detail, without omitting anything. But for my part I shall not tell it to you, for anyone who tells a thing twice spins out his tale tediously.

6327 While they were speaking together, one lady stole away on her own and reported all this to the lords to heighten and increase their joy. Those who heard these things all rejoiced together. And when Mabonagrain learned of it, he was delighted for his mistress that she had found consolation. And the lady who had hurried to give them the news suddenly brought them great joy. The king himself was happy: having been very joyful before, he is now far more so and shows Erec great honour. Enide leads away her cousin, who is more beautiful, more attractive and fairer than was Helen. Now Erec and Mabonagrain run together to meet them, as do Guivret and King Evrain; and all the others come running up to greet and honour them, with no one loitering or hanging back. Mabonagrain makes much of Enide and she equally of him. For their part, both Erec and Guivret rejoice over the maiden and rejoice with her, as they kiss and embrace one another.

6358   They speak of going back to the castle, for they have been too long in the garden. Having prepared to depart, they leave in jubilation, exchanging kisses as they go. They all follow the king out. But before they arrived at the castle, the nobles from all the surrounding region had assembled, and everybody who learned of the Joy came there, if they could. A vast crowd had gathered. Everyone, high and low, poor and rich, struggle to see Erec, each jostling in front of his neighbour, greeting him, bowing to him, and all endlessly saying: "May God save him through whom joy and gladness burst forth in our court! God save the most blessed man He ever brought into being!"

6379   So they lead him to the court, striving to show their joy at the urging of their hearts. The sound of rotes, harps and vielles rings out, of fiddles, psalteries and symphonias and every kind of music that one could name or mention. But I shall give you only a brief account of it, without lingering over it too long. The king honours him as best he can, as do all the others, whole-heartedly. There is no one but offers his service most gladly. The Joy continued for three whole days before Erec was able to leave. On the fourth he was unwilling to stay longer, beg him as they might. Many people were there to escort him, and there was a huge throng at the leave-taking. He could not have returned the farewells individually in half a day, had he wished to reply to each one. He salutes and embraces the nobles, but all the others he commends to God in a single word of farewell. Enide is not silent either as she takes her leave of the nobles, saluting each of them by name, as they do her with one accord. On leaving, she kisses and embraces her cousin very tenderly. Now they have gone, and the Joy is at an end.

6411   They go on their way, and the others return. Erec and Guivret waste no time but journey on happily, arriving in nine days at Robais, where they were told the king was. The previous day he had been bled privately in his apartments, having with him only five hundred nobles of his household. Never before at any time of the year had the king been found with so little company, and he was very distressed to have so few people at his court. Then there comes running a messenger they had sent on ahead to announce their arrival to the king. He came right up before the company, where he found the king and all his people; and with a polite greeting he said: "Sire, I am a messenger from Erec and Guivret the Little." Then he informed him that they were on their way to his court to see him. The king replies: "They shall be welcome as valiant and gallant lords! I know none better than those two anywhere, and my court will be much enhanced by them." Then he sent for the queen and told her the news. The others saddle up to go to meet the lords. They were in such a hurry to mount that they did not put their spurs on.

6444 I should like to tell you and relate briefly how the company of common people, serving-lads, cooks and cup-bearers, had already come into the town to prepare the quarters. The main party was following and had already drawn so near that they had entered the town. Now came the meeting, the exchanged greetings and the kisses. They come to the lodgings and make themselves comfortable, taking off their boots and changing, arraying themselves in their splendid robes. When they had finished dressing in their' finery, they left for the court. They come to court: the king sees them, and so does the queen, who is beside herself with impatience to see Erec and Enide. The king has them sit beside him. He kisses Erec and then Guivret, puts both his arms round Enide's neck and kisses her in turn, showing his great joy. The queen for her part is not backward in embracing Erec and Enide. She was so above herself for joy that you might have used her for hawking. They all do their best to make much of each other. Then the king bids them be quiet and questions Erec, asking news of his adventures.

6474 When the chattering had stopped, Erec began his story, telling him of his adventures without forgetting anything. Do you now expect me to tell you what prompted him to set out? Not I; for you well know the truth about that and the rest, as I have revealed it to you. It would be a labour for me to tell it again, because it is not a short story for anyone to begin afresh, tricking out the words as he spoke them in his account: about the three knights he vanquished, then the five, and then the count who tried to bring him such great shame, and after that the two giants. All in order, one after the other, he told him of his adventures to the point where he stove in the forehead of Count Oringle of Limors. "You've come through many perils, my dear good friend," said the king. "Now stay in this country at my court as you usually do."—"Sire, as you wish it, I shall very gladly stay for three or four whole years; but ask Guivret to stay as well, and I make the same request of him." The king bids him stay, and he agrees to remain. Thus they both stay, the king keeping them with him, cherishing and honouring them.

6510 Erec stayed at court with Guivret and Enide, the three of them together, until the death of his father the king, who was old and had reached a great age. At once the messengers set out – noblemen, the most distinguished in his land, who went looking for him until, after their searches and enquiries, they found him in Tintagel twenty days before Christmas and told him the truth about what had happened to his old, white-haired father, now dead and gone. Erec's sorrow was far greater than he showed to the people; but grief is not becoming in a king, and it is not seemly for a king to show sorrow. There in Tintagel where he was he had vigils for the dead and masses sung, made vows, and fulfilled them as he had promised, in the religious houses and churches.

6533 He well performed all his proper duties: he selected more than a hundred and sixty-nine wretched paupers and gave them brand-new clothes; to the poor clerks and priests he gave, as was right, black capes with fur linings underneath. For God's sake he did much good to one and all: to those in need he gave more than a bushel of money. Having distributed his wealth, he proceeded to act with great wisdom in accepting his land back from the king; and then he begged him to crown him at his court. The king said he should prepare himself quickly; for they shall both be crowned, he together with his wife, at the coming Christmas-tide.* He said: "We have to go from here to Nantes in Brittany. There you shall bear the tokens of kingship, a crown on your head and a sceptre in your hand: this favour and this honour I bestow on you." Erec thanked the king for this, saying it is a splendid gift.

6559 At Christmas the king gathers all his nobles together, summoning them individually and ordering them to come to Nantes: he summoned them all; none stayed behind. For his part, Erec summoned many of his own followers; and more than he sent for came, to serve and honour him. I cannot tell or report to you who each of them was or what he was called; but whoever may have come or stayed away, neither the father nor the mother of my lady Enide was forgotten. He was the first to be summoned and came to court with much pomp like a great lord and castellan. He had a company not of chaplains or silly, doltish folk, but of excellent knights and splendidly equipped people. Each day they covered a good distance, riding joyfully and making a fine show until they came to the city of Nantes. Without stopping anywhere on the way, they went into the great hall where the king was with his people. Erec and Enide see them: you may be sure it made them very happy, and they go to meet them with all haste. They greet and embrace them, speak with them very tenderly and are as happy as is to be expected.

6594 When they had made much of each other, all four took one another by the hand and went up before the king, immediately greeting him and the queen too, who was seated at his side. Erec held his host by the hand, saying: "Sire, here you see my good host and firm friend, who showed me such great honour that he made me master in his own house. Before he knew anything about me, he lodged me extremely well, placing at my disposal whatever he had; and he even gave me his daughter without the advice or counsel of anyone else."—"And this lady with him," says the king, "who is she, my friend?" Erec hides nothing from him. "Sire," says he, "I can tell you that this lady is my wife's mother."—"Her mother, is she?"—"Yes indeed, sire."—"Then I can truly say to you that the flower that buds from such a graft should be very beautiful and attractive, and the fruit from it all the better to pick; for the product of excellence has a sweet fragrance. Enide is beautiful, and it is right and proper she should be so; for her mother is a most beautiful lady, and in her father one sees a handsome knight. She does not fail to live up to them in any respect, for she closely follows and takes after them both in many ways."

6628 Now the king pauses and is silent after bidding them to be seated. They do not disobey his command, but sit down at once. Enide is now overjoyed to see her father and mother, for it had been a long time since she had set eyes on them. Great joy has welled up inside her: she was highly pleased and delighted and showed it as plainly as she could; but she was unable to display it so clearly that her joy was not actually greater.

6641 I wish to say no more of this here, for my heart draws me towards the court, now completely assembled. There were counts, dukes and kings from many different countries: Normans, Bretons, Scots, Irish; there were very powerful nobles from England and Cornwall, and from Wales to Anjou, in Maine or Poitou there was no knight of great importance and no attractive lady of high birth of whom the best and most engaging were not in the court at Nantes as summoned by the king. Now hear, if it is your wish, of the great joy and grandeur, the pomp and splendour displayed at court.

6660 Before three o'clock had struck, King Arthur had dubbed four hundred knights and more, all sons of counts and kings. To each of them he gave three horses and two pairs of robes to enhance the appearance of his court. The king displayed great opulence and liberality: he did not give cloaks made of serge or rabbit fur or brown cloth, but of velvet and ermine, whole vair furs and flowered silk, bordered with hard, stiff gold braid. Alexander, for all his conquests, who subjugated the whole world and was so liberal and wealthy, was poor and mean compared with him. Caesar, the Emperor of Rome, and all the kings named in stories and epic songs did not distribute as much at a single festival as King Arthur gave on the day he crowned Erec; nor would Caesar and Alexander have dared spend as much as was paid out at that court. The cloaks were pulled out of the chests and spread about throughout all the halls; and anyone who wished chose freely from them. In the middle of the court on a carpet were thirty bushels of bright sterlings; for at that time sterlings had been the currency throughout the whole of Britain since the days of Merlin. There everybody helped himself, each taking as much as he wished to his lodging that night. At nine o'clock in the morning of Christmas Day they all assembled again at court. Erec is quite carried away with the great joy that awaits him. The tongue or lips of no man, however expert, could describe a third or quarter or a fifth of the splendours displayed at his coronation. So it is a foolish undertaking of mine to attempt its description; but as I must do so, come what may, I shall not fail to tell part of it as best I can.

6713 The king had two thrones of gleaming ivory, new and well made, that were identical in design and form. The man who made them was a very skilful and subtle craftsman; for he made them both so alike in height, breadth and decoration that, however you might scrutinise them to tell one from the other, you would never be able to find anything in the one that was not in the other. There was nothing about them of wood, but everything was of gold or of fine ivory. They were well carved with great delicacy; for, on each, one side had the form of a leopard and the other of a crocodile. A knight, Bruiant of the Isles, had given them as a present to King Arthur and the queen. King Arthur took his seat on one and had Erec sit on the other, wearing a garment of watered fabric.

6736 In the story we read the account of this robe; and so that no one accuses me of lying, I give as my authority Macrobius,* who devoted himself to describing it. Macrobius is my model for the description, as I found it in the book, of the cloth's workmanship and what was depicted on it. Four fairies had made it with great artistry and craft. One of them represented there Geometry, how she surveys and measures the extent of the sky and the earth without anything being overlooked, their depth and height, length and breadth; and she surveys the sea to gauge its width and depth, and so measures the whole world. That was the work done by the first. The second devoted herself to portraying Arithmetic, striving hard to show well how she cleverly counts time's days and hours, each single drop of the sea, then every grain of sand and all the stars in order, knowing the full truth about them, and how many leaves there are in the woods: she was never deceived by numbers and, when she wishes to apply herself properly, will never get anything wrong—such is the talent of Arithmetic. The third portrayal was of Music, with whom all pleasure is in harmony: song and descant, the sounds of strings, harp, rote and vielle. This work was fine and good, for before her were ranged all the instruments and delights.

6777 The fourth, who next showed her handiwork, applied herself to an excellent design, for she represented the best of the arts. Her subject was Astronomy, who accomplishes so many marvels, consulting with the stars, moon and sun. Nowhere else does she get her inspiration for anything she has to do, and from them gains good, sound advice. All the information she seeks from them about whatever was or will be they reliably provide for her without lying or deceit. This was the matter portrayed on the cloth of which Erec's robe was made, worked and woven as it was with gold thread. The lining sewn into it was made of the skins of grotesque beasts whose heads are quite white and whose necks are the colour of blackberries, whilst their backs are scarlet, their bellies green and their tails dark blue. These beasts come from India and are called barbioletes.* They eat nothing but spices, cinnamon and fresh cloves. What could I tell you of the cloak? It was extremely rich, fine and handsome, and had four stones in the tassels: two chrysolites on one side and, on the other, two amethysts mounted in gold.

6810 Enide had still not come to the great hall by this time. When the king sees she is late, he orders Gawain to go quickly and bring her and the queen. Gawain wasted no time in hurrying there together with King Cadoalant and the bountiful King of Galloway. Guivret the Little accompanies them, followed by Yder the son of Nut. So many of the other nobles hurried up to escort the two ladies that they could well have destroyed an army; for there were over a thousand present. The queen had put her best efforts into dressing Enide in her finery. They brought her into the great hall with the courtly Gawain on one side and, on the other, the generous King of Galloway, who was very fond of her for the sake of Erec, who was his nephew. When the ladies came into the hall, King Arthur hurried forward to meet them and courteously seated Enide beside Erec, very anxious to do her great honour. He at once orders two massive, pure gold crowns to be fetched from his treasury. No sooner had he given the command than, without any delay, the crowns were brought before him, gleaming with carbuncles, of which there were four in each. Moonlight is as nothing compared with the brilliance of just the smallest of the carbuncles. All those in the great hall were so completely dazzled by the radiance they emitted that for a long time they could see nothing; even the king was affected, yet he was very delighted to see them bright and beautiful. He had one taken by two maidens and the other held by two noblemen.

6856 Then he commanded the bishops and priors and the abbots of the religious orders to step forward and anoint the new king according to the Christian rites. All the prelates, some young, some grey-haired, stepped forward immediately, for a large number of bishops and abbots had come to court. The Bishop of Nantes himself, a very worthy and saintly man, performed the anointing of the new king in a very fitting and holy manner and placed the crown on his head. King Arthur had a sceptre brought, which was much admired. Let me describe the sceptre to you: it was clearer than a pane of glass, made entirely of a single emerald, and fully as thick as a man's fist. I dare tell you quite truthfully that in the whole world there is no kind of fish or wild beast or man or bird that flies that was not worked and carved on it, each in its true likeness. The sceptre was handed to the king, who gazed at it in wonder and then, without further delay, placed it in Erec's right hand: he was now properly king. Then he crowned Enide in her turn.

6888 Now the bells were rung for mass; and they go to the main church to hear mass and the service. To pray, they went to the cathedral. You might have seen Queen Enide's father and her mother Carsenefide weeping for joy. That indeed was her mother's name, and her father's was Liconal. Both were most happy. When they came to the cathedral, the procession moved out of the church to meet them, bearing relics and treasures. Crosses, liturgical books, censers and reliquaries together with their relics, of which the church had many, were brought out to meet them; and there was no lack of chanting. Never were seen together at one mass so many kings, counts, dukes and nobles: the crowd was so vast and dense that the church was quite full. No low-born man could go in, but only ladies and knights. A large number were left outside the church door, so many were thronging there without being able to enter.

6918 When they had heard the mass through, they returned to the great hall. Everything there was already fully prepared, with tables set and laid with cloths: there were five hundred tables and more. But I have no wish to persuade you of something that seems untrue. It would seem too gross a lie if I told you that five hundred tables were set up next to each other in a single hall, and that is not what I mean to say: rather that there were five halls filled with them, so that one could only make one's way with difficulty between the tables. At each table there was truly either a king or a duke or a count; and fully a hundred knights sat at every one. A thousand knights served the bread, a thousand the wine, a thousand the dishes, all dressed in new ermine tunics. A great variety of dishes was served: although I did not see them, I could still give you an account of them; but I must turn to something other than describing the food – they all had a great deal without stint and were served joyfully and very generously to their hearts' content.

6947 When that celebration was over, the king dismissed the gathering of kings, dukes and counts, who were very numerous, and of the others, including the ordinary folk who had come to the festivities. With great liberality he gave them horses, arms and silver, cloths and brocades of many sorts because of his most generous character and for the sake of Erec, whom he loved so much. Here the story comes to its end.   6958

CLIGÉS

The author of the story of Erec and Enide, who translated into French Ovid's commands and the Art of Love, composed the Shoulder Bite, the tales of King Mark and the fair-haired Iseut, and of the metamorphosis of the hoopoe, the swallow and the nightingale, begins a new story about a young man who lived in Greece and was a kinsman of King Arthur. But before I tell you anything of him, you shall hear of the life of his father, where he came from and of what family. He was of such a noble, spirited temperament that, in order to win a reputation and renown, he went from Greece to England, which at that time was called Britain. This story that I wish to tell and pass on to you we find written down in one of the books in the library of my Lord Saint Peter at Beauvais. That was the source of the tale which CHRÉTIEN turned into this romance. The book that is the authority for the truth of this story is very ancient, which makes it all the more worthy of belief. Through the books we possess we learn of the deeds of the people of past times and of the world as it used to be. Our books have taught us how Greece ranked first in chivalry and learning; then chivalry passed to Rome along with the fund of transcendent learning that has now come to France.* God grant it may be kept here and find such a pleasing home that the honour now arrived may never depart from France! The others had received it from God on loan; for no longer do people speak at all of the Greeks and Romans – there is no more talk of them, and their glowing embers are dead.

45 CHRÉTIEN begins his story as it is told in the history dealing with an emperor, mighty in wealth and honour, who ruled over Greece and Constantinople. There was an empress too, of great nobility, by whom the emperor had two children. But already before the birth of the second the first was so grown up that he might, had he wished, have become a knight and governed the whole empire. The name of the elder was Alexander, and the younger was called Alis. Their father's name was Alexander and their mother's Tantalis. Of the empress Tantalis, the emperor and Alis I shall say no more now, but will tell you about Alexander, who was so brave and proud that he did not deign to be knighted in his own country. He had heard tell of King Arthur, who reigned at that time, and of the barons

93

continually in his company, making his court feared and renowned throughout the world. Regardless of the outcome for him and whatever might result, nothing at all can prevent him from wanting to go to Britain; but before setting out for Britain or Cornwall, he is obliged to have his father's leave.

81   To seek and obtain his leave, handsome, valiant Alexander goes to speak with the emperor to tell him of his desire and what he wishes to do and undertake. "Dear father," he says, "in order to learn the ways of honour and win distinction and fame, I dare to ask you a favour that I hope you will grant me. And should you agree, then don't keep me waiting for it." The emperor sees in this no harm whatsoever: he should be eager and anxious for his son's honour above all else. In increasing the honour of his son, he would think he acted very well. – Think? He would in fact do so. "Dear son," he says, "I grant your wish; so tell me what you want from me."

102 Now the young man has done his work well; and when the request he had so set his heart on was granted, he was very happy. "Sire," says he, "do you wish to know what you have agreed to? I should like to have a large supply of your gold and silver and, from among your men, companions of my choice; for I wish to leave your empire and go to offer my service to the king who rules over Britain, so that he may make me a knight. I promise you I shall never wear armour on my face or a helmet on my head any day of my life until King Arthur girds on my sword, if he condescends to; for I wish to receive arms from no one else." The emperor replies without hesitation: "Dear son, for God's sake don't say that! This country, along with mighty Constantinople, is entirely yours. You can't call me mean when I'm prepared to make you such a fine gift. Before long I shall have you crowned, and tomorrow you shall be knighted. All Greece will be in your hands, and you shall accept from your barons, as is your right, their oaths and their homage. There's no wisdom in refusing this."

135 The young man hears his father's promise and wish to dub him the following day after Mass, but says he will show himself base or noble in a country other than his own. "If you wish to satisfy the request I've made of you, then give me vair and grey furs, good horses and silk cloths; for before I become a knight, I wish to serve King Arthur. I'm not yet sufficiently competent to be able to bear

arms. No one could dissuade me by entreaty or flattery from going to that foreign land to see the king and barons who enjoy such great fame for their courtliness and prowess. Many high-born men lose through laziness the high reputation they might have if they travelled about the world. It seems to me that repose and reputation don't go well together; for a man of substance who remains idle gains no renown at all.* To a base man prowess is heavy to bear, and to a man of valour baseness is a burden: that's how distinct and opposed the two things are. And a man is a slave to his wealth if he goes on keeping and increasing it. Dear father, so long as I have the opportunity to win renown, if I'm capable of it, it's to that I intend to devote my efforts and energy."

169 At this the emperor doubtless feels both joy and grief. He is joyful on hearing that his son is bent on prowess, and on the other hand sad because he is leaving him. But on account of the promise he has made, whatever grief it may cause him, he has to grant what he wants; for an emperor must not lie. "Dear son," he says, "since I see you are intent on honour, I must not fail to do as you wish. You may have from my treasury two boatloads of gold and silver; but take care to be very generous and courtly and to conduct yourself well." Now the young man is very happy to have his father promise him so much, to the extent of putting his treasure at his disposal while exhorting and instructing him to give and spend liberally for the reasons he mentions: "Dear son," he says, "generosity, believe me, is the mistress and queen that gives lustre to every virtue, as is not hard to prove. Where could one find a man, however powerful and rich, who isn't blamed if he is mean? And who, though not appreciated for his many other qualities, doesn't earn praise by his generosity? Liberality on its own makes a worthy man; and that can't be achieved by high birth, courtliness, wisdom, nobility, wealth, strength, chivalry, boldness, authority, beauty or anything else. But just as the rose is more lovely than any other flower when it opens fresh and new, so where liberality appears it surpasses all other virtues and increases five hundred times the qualities it finds in a worthy, upright man. There's so much to be said about liberality that I couldn't tell the half of it."*

218 The young man was successful in obtaining everything he sought and asked for, as his father provided him with whatever he wished. The empress was very sad when she heard of the journey on

which her son was to embark. But whoever might grieve or sorrow, accuse him of youthful folly or blame him for it or try to dissuade him, the youth ordered his ships to be made ready as soon as possible, having no wish to stay any longer in his own country. On his orders the ships were loaded that very night with wine, meat and biscuits.

235 The ships took on their cargoes in the port; and the following day Alexander came to the shore in high spirits together with his companions, who were happy to be making the journey. They are escorted by the emperor and the grieving empress. At the port they find the sailors in the ships close by the cliff. The sea is calm and smooth, the wind light and the weather clear. Having parted from his father and taken leave of the empress, whose sorrow was heartfelt, Alexander is the first to board his ship from the small boat; and his companions lose no time, but compete to embark with him in fours, threes and twos. At once the sail is hoisted and the ship's anchor raised. Those on land, unhappy to see the young man leave, follow him with their eyes as far as they can see; and to keep them in sight longer and more clearly, they all climb a high hill by the shore and from there gaze at the cause of their sadness as long as he is in view. It is truly the source of their grief they are watching, since they are very sad for the young man: may God lead him to port without hindrance or peril!

270 They were at sea for the whole of April and part of May. Without great danger or alarms they arrived at the port of Southampton. One day between three o'clock and vespers they entered port and dropped anchor. The young men, unused to suffering discomfort and hardship, had been so long on the uncongenial sea that the strongest and healthiest of them had quite lost their colour and grown weak and feeble. Nevertheless, they show great joy at having come through the sea crossing and arrived where they wished to be. Because of their extremely sick state they spend that night at Southampton, but in the best of spirits, and make enquiries as to whether the king is in England. They are told he is in Winchester and that they can get there very quickly, so long as they are prepared to set out early in the morning and take the direct road. This news delights them; and at daybreak the next morning the youths wake early, dress and equip themselves. Once ready, they left Southampton and, following the direct route, came to

Winchester where the king was staying. Before six o'clock in the morning the Greeks had arrived at court.

306 They dismount at the foot of the steps; and their squires and horses remain in the courtyard below while the youths go up into the presence of the best king who ever was or ever may be in the world. And when the king sees them coming, their appearance greatly pleases and delights him. But before approaching him, they unfasten their cloaks from their necks so as not to be considered ignorant. In this way, with their cloaks removed, they went before the king. All the nobles fell silent, very pleased at the sight of these handsome, well-mannered young men and not doubting they were all sons of counts or kings. So indeed they were: all of a most attractive age, good-looking and well built; and the clothes they wore were all of the same cloth and cut, of identical design and colour. There were twelve of them apart from their lord, of whom I will merely tell you that none was better than he. But it was modestly and without presumption that he stood before the king without his cloak, very handsome and of fine physique as he was. He knelt before him; and all the others knelt as a mark of honour beside their lord.

339 Alexander, his tongue well schooled in wise and eloquent speech, salutes the king. "King," he says, "unless accounts of your fame are false, since God created the first man there never was born a God-fearing king of your might. King, your widespread fame has brought me to your court to serve and honour you; and, if you approve my service, I should like to stay here until I'm made a new knight by your hand and no other; for unless it is through you, I shall never be called knight. If you appreciate my service enough to wish to knight me, then keep me with you, noble king, and also my companions here." The king immediately replies: "My friend, I turn neither you nor your company away, but bid you all welcome. For you seem, and I think you are, the sons of high-born men. Where are you from?"—"We come from Greece."—"From Greece?"—"Yes indeed."—"Who is your father?"—"The emperor, sire, I assure you."—"And what is your name, my good friend?"—"Alexander was the name given me when I received the salt and holy oil and Christianity at my baptism."—"Alexander, my dear good friend, I will retain you with me very willingly, and I'm most pleased and delighted to do so, for you have done me great

honour in coming to my court. I am most anxious for you to be honoured here as noble, wise and well-conducted vassals. But you've been on your knees too long: I bid you rise, and be from now on members of my court and my confidants, for you have found a good haven."

385 At that the Greeks rise to their feet, happy that the king has so kindly made them welcome. Alexander is well off, for he lacks nothing he wants; and in court there is no noble, however high his rank, who does not receive him kindly and welcome him. He is not foolish and does not give himself airs or behave in a self-important, swaggering manner. He makes the acquaintance of my lord Gawain and of the others, one by one, becoming very popular with each of them; and my lord Gawain is even so fond of him that he calls him his friend and companion.

399 The Greeks had taken the best lodging they could have with one of the citizens of the town. Alexander had brought great wealth from Constantinople, being anxious above all to heed the emperor's entreaties and advice to have his heart set on generous giving and spending. To this he devotes much attention and effort, living very well in his lodgings and giving and spending liberally as befits his wealth and his heart dictates. The whole court wonders where his resources have come from; for he gives to all and sundry valuable horses he had brought from his own country. Alexander has made such great efforts and excellently performed his service to such good effect that he gains the great love and esteem of the king as well as of the nobles and the queen.

422 At that time King Arthur wished to cross into Brittany. He summoned all his lords together to advise him, asking to whom he can entrust England until his return, to hold it in peace and security. On their unanimous advice, I believe, it was placed in the charge of Count Angrés of Windsor;* for it was their opinion that there was no more trustworthy lord in all the king's territory. The following day, with the land placed under the count's control, King Arthur set out, together with the queen and her maidens. In Brittany they hear that the king is coming with his lords; and the Bretons rejoice greatly at the news.

441 Aboard the ship in which the king made the crossing there was no young man or maiden other than Alexander and, accompanying the queen, Soredamors,* who was scornful of love. She had never

heard tell of a man, however handsome, valiant, noble or highly born, whom she might condescend to love. Yet the damsel was so charming and beautiful that she really should have learnt something of love, had she wished to turn her attention to it; but she was never willing to give it a thought. Now Love will make her suffer, intending to take full vengeance for the great arrogance and reluctance she has always displayed towards him. Love has taken good aim and, with his arrow, pierced her to the heart. She often turns pale and frequently perspires, being forced to love despite herself. She can hardly restrain herself from gazing at Alexander, but has to be on her guard against my lord Gawain, her brother. She pays dearly to make amends for her great pride and disdain.

470 Love has warmed for her a bath which she finds very hot and scalding. Now she likes it and now it is painful for her, now she wants it and now rejects it. She accuses her eyes of treason, saying: "My eyes, you have betrayed me! Through you my heart, which used to be so faithful, has come to hate me. Now I'm distressed at what I see. Distressed? But no – rather it pleases me. And if I do see anything that distresses me, are not my eyes under my control? I should really have lost my authority and should have a poor opinion of myself if I cannot rule my eyes and make them look elsewhere. In that way I can easily guard against Love, who wishes to control me. What the eye doesn't see, the heart doesn't grieve over: if I don't see him, he means nothing to me. He asks or requests nothing from me. If he loved me, he would have made some approach; so as he does not love or have any regard for me, shall I love him when he doesn't love me? If his beauty lures my eyes and my eyes respond to the lure, should I say I love him because of that? No, for that would be a lie. So he has no claim on me, and I have no more or less of a claim on him. One cannot love with one's eyes. And what crime, then, have my eyes committed against me, if they look where I wish? What wrong are they guilty of in that? Should I blame them for it? No. Whom then? Myself, who am in charge of them. My eyes gaze at nothing unless it suits and pleases my heart; and my heart should not wish for anything that might grieve me, but it is its wish that makes me suffer. – Suffer? Then I am indeed foolish when through it I'm wanting something that upsets me. I should, if I can, banish any desire that brings me pain. – If I can? Foolish girl, what have I said? I should not be able to do much at all,

if I had no control over myself. Does Love think he can put me on the right road, when he usually leads others astray? He had better guide others, for I'm not at all dependent on him, nor ever will be nor ever was; nor shall I ever cherish his friendship."

524   So she argues with herself, one moment loving, hating the next. She is in such a quandary that she does not know what it is better to do. She thinks she is defending herself against Love; but defence avails her nothing. God, if she only knew how Alexander, for his part, is thinking of her! Love shares equally between them what he has to distribute. He treats them very fairly and justly, since each loves and desires the other. This love of theirs would have been right and true if only they each knew the wishes of the other; but he does not know what she wants, and she is unaware of the cause of his distress.

541   The queen sees and notes how they both keep losing their colour and turning pale, sighing and trembling; but she does not know the reason, unless it is the sea they are on. She might perhaps have realised it, had not the sea deceived her; but she is duped and tricked by the sea, so that on it she is blinded to the love; for they are on the sea, and from love and its bitterness comes the pain they feel.* Of the three involved, the queen can only blame the sea; for to her the two say it is the fault of the third, and by the third the two excuse themselves, though they are the guilty parties. A person free of blame and guilt often pays for another's sin. So the queen roundly accuses and rebukes the sea; but she is wrong to lay the blame there, for the sea is innocent in the matter. Soredamors suffered a great deal before the ship arrived in port. As for the king, it goes without saying that the Bretons welcomed him joyfully and gladly served him as their liege-lord. I do not wish to speak further of King Arthur at this point: rather you will hear me tell how Love torments the two lovers on whom he has launched his attack.

575   Alexander loves and desires the girl, who sighs for love of him; but this he does not and will not know until he has endured much pain and grief. On account of his love, he serves the queen and her maids-in-waiting, but without addressing or speaking to the one he thinks most of. If she dared press the claim she thinks she has on him, he would gladly have told her the truth; but she neither dares nor should do so. The fact that they see each other without having the courage to say or do anything further is a great hardship for

them, increasing and kindling their love. But it is the way of all lovers happily to feast their eyes by gazing, if they can do no better; and they think that, because they derive pleasure from what gives rise to their love and causes it to grow, it should be good for them. Yet it harms them, just as someone who moves up close beside the fire burns himself more than the person who draws back. Their love keeps growing and increasing; but each feels embarrassed before the other, and they both conceal and disguise their feelings so that no flame or smoke appears from the coal under the ashes. That does not make the heat less: on the contrary, it lasts longer below than above the ash. Both are in very great torment; but to prevent anyone from being aware of their trouble or noticing it, each has to deceive everybody by putting on a false appearance. At night, however, they both lament bitterly to themselves.

616 I shall tell you first how Alexander gives vent to his grief and despair. Love puts in his mind the image of the one on whose account he feels such hurt, since she has wounded his heart and allows him no rest in his bed; for he takes such delight in recalling the beauty and manner of her he entertains no hope of ever obtaining gratification. "I may well think myself a fool," he says. "A fool? I am indeed a fool, when I don't dare say what I think, because that would bring me misfortune. I've turned my thoughts to folly. But isn't it better for me to think it than to have myself called a fool? What I want will never become known. So shall I hide what troubles me and never seek help or a remedy for my grief? A man's a fool who feels he's sick without looking for a way to recover his health, if he can find one anywhere. But many think they're acting in their own interest and seeking what they want, when they're actually bringing about their own suffering. And why should someone go to ask advice if he doesn't think he will find health? He'd be wasting his effort. I feel my own sickness is so serious that I'll never be cured of it by any medicine or potion, herb or root. Not every illness has its remedy, and mine is so deep-seated that it can't be treated. – Can't be? I think I've lied. If, as soon as I first felt this sickness, I had dared disclose or mention it, I might have consulted a doctor who would have completely cured me. But it's very difficult for me to discuss it; and perhaps he wouldn't care to attend to it or be willing to take a fee for that.

661 "It's no wonder, then, that I'm afraid; for I'm very ill, and yet I don't know from what sickness I'm suffering or what is the cause of

this pain. – I don't know? But yes, I think I do know. Love has brought this sickness on me. – What? Can Love do harm, then? But is he not gentle and good-natured? I thought there was nothing but good in Love, but I've found him very cruel. No one knows the tricks Love plays unless he has experienced them. Anybody who joins up with him is a fool, for he always likes to harm his followers. I swear his is not a fair game. It's dangerous to play with him, for his game will do me harm. – What shall I do, then? Withdraw? I think I'd be sensible to do so, but I don't know how to. If Love uses warnings and threats in order to teach and instruct me, ought I to disregard my master? Only a fool scorns his master. I should obey and observe the lesson Love teaches me, for I might soon reap great benefit from it.

689 "But he frightens me by belabouring me so. – You're complaining, when there's no trace of a blow or wound? Aren't you mistaken, then? – No, for he has gravely wounded me to the extent of shooting his arrow right to my heart and hasn't yet pulled it out again. – How, then, has he shot you with it in the body without the wound showing on the outside? Tell me: I should like to know. Where has he shot you? – Through the eye. – Through the eye? Without putting it out? – He hasn't hurt me at all in the eye, but causes me such pain in the heart. – Well, explain to me how the arrow has passed through the eye without its being wounded or damaged. If the dart goes in through the eye, why is the heart hurt in the breast, but not the eye as well, which has been struck first? – I can readily explain that: the eye is not concerned with comprehending anything and is totally incapable of doing so; but it is the mirror for the heart, and through this mirror there passes, without damaging or breaking it, the fire that sets the heart ablaze. For is not the heart placed in the breast just like the lighted candle placed inside the lantern? If you take the candle away, no light will come out; but as long as the candle lasts, the lantern is not dark, and the flame shining inside does not damage or harm it. It's the same with a glass window: however strong or unflawed it may be, the sun's ray passes through it, but without breaking it at all; and never will glass be so bright that one can see any better by its own brilliance without another light striking through it.

732 "You may be sure the same is true of the eyes as of the glass and the lantern. For through the eyes comes the light by which the heart

views itself and sees the outside world, whatever it may be. It sees many different objects, some green, others violet, one scarlet, another blue, finding fault here, praising there, having a low opinion of one, prizing another. But something may seem attractive to the heart when it looks at it through the mirror which may deceive it if it's not wary. My own mirror has betrayed me badly, for in it my heart saw a ray of light that has afflicted me by lodging within it, causing my heart to fail me. I'm ill-treated by my friend who thus forgets me for my enemy. I can charge him with felony, because he has wronged me gravely. I thought I had three friends, my heart and my two eyes; but it seems to me they hate me. Where shall I ever find a friend, when these three are my enemies, belonging to me yet causing my ruin? My servants are playing too much on my trust in acting simply according to their wishes without caring about mine. Now I understand very clearly from those who have despoiled me how the love of a good lord is corrupted through his sheltering a wicked servant. A man with a wicked servant in his company is bound to regret it, whatever happens, sooner or later.

770   "Now I shall tell you how the arrow which has been allotted and assigned to me is made and fashioned. But I'm very afraid I shall fail in the attempt; for it is so magnificently made that my failure would not be surprising. Yet I shall do my best to give my impression of it. The nock at the shaft-end and the feathers are so close together, if one examines them closely, that they are separated by no more than the width of a narrow parting in the hair. The nock, though, is so polished and straight that in it there is, without question, no room for improvement. The feathers are coloured as if they were of gold or gilt. But there is no question of gilding; for these feathers, I know, were more shining than that. The feathers are the fair tresses I saw at sea the other day. That is the arrow that inspires my love. God, what a very precious possession! If anyone could have such a treasure, why should he desire any other riches his whole life long? For myself, I could swear I'd wish for nothing more; for I wouldn't give up even the feathers and the nock for Antioch itself.

801   "And since I value these two things so highly, who could estimate the value of the rest? That is so beautiful and charming, so costly and precious, that I still long and yearn to gaze upon that brow which God has made so bright that it would not pale beside any mirror or emerald or topaz. But all this is as nothing if one

looks at the brilliance of the eyes; for to all those who see them they seem like two burning candles. And whose tongue is resourceful enough to describe the form of her delicate nose and radiant face, where the hue of the rose suffuses that of the lily so that it masks it a little to heighten the face's colouring? Or who could speak of the dainty, smiling mouth, which God shaped so that no one might see it without thinking it was laughing? And what of the teeth in the mouth? They are set so close to one another that they seem to be joined together; and to make them more attractive still, Nature added some small touches so that, seeing the mouth open, nobody would say the teeth were not of ivory or silver. There is so much to tell and recall in portraying every detail of the chin and ears that it would not be very surprising if I omitted something. Of the throat I say only that crystal is cloudy beside it. Beneath the tresses the neck is four times as white as ivory. Between the dress's neckband and the brooch fastening it at the breast I saw the bare bosom exposed, whiter than freshly fallen snow. My pain would have been quite soothed had I seen the whole of the arrow. I would very gladly tell of the appearance of the shaft, if I knew it; but I didn't see it, and it's not my fault if I can't give a description of something I haven't seen. On that occasion Love showed me only the nock and the feathers; for the arrow was placed in its quiver, that is the tunic and shift the maiden wore.

858   "That, I swear, is the sickness that is killing me; that is the dart and that the shining ray at which I am growing shamefully angry. I'm very churlish to get annoyed. My commitment to Love will never be broken by any provocation or hostility towards him on my part. Now let Love do what he will with me, as he should with one who belongs to him, for I'm content and wish it so and never want this sickness to leave me. I'd rather have it always hold me in its grip like this than recover my health from anyone, unless that health comes from the same source as my illness."

873   Bitterly though Alexander complains, the maiden's lament is no less impassioned. All night she is in such great anguish that she neither sleeps nor rests. Love has incited within her a furious conflict that greatly troubles her spirit and so torments and plagues her that the whole night long she weeps and laments, tosses and turns and almost faints away. Then, having suffered agonies, sobbing and gasping, shaking and sighing, she looked into her heart to

see who and what manner of man this was on whose account Love was tormenting her. After cheering herself up by thinking of something that pleases her, she stretches and turns over again and decides everything she has just been thinking is foolish.

896   She then begins another line of thought, saying: "Silly girl! What is it to me if this young man has a noble character and is sensible, courtly and valiant? That's all to his honour and advantage. And what do I care if he's handsome? Let his handsomeness go away with him! That it will do, in spite of me; and I'd never wish to take any of it away from him. – Take it away? No indeed! I'd certainly not do that. If he had the wisdom of Solomon, and Nature had endowed him with so much beauty that she could never put more into a human body, and if God had placed in my hands the power to undo it all, I should still not wish to spite him; but, if I could, I'd gladly make him more wise and handsome. So I honestly don't hate him: but does that make me his lover? No: no more than anyone else's. Why, then, do I think more about him, if he's no more pleasing to me than any other? I don't know: I'm completely confused; for never before have I thought so much about any man alive; and if I had my way, I'd see him all the time and would never want to take my eyes off him, such is my delight when I see him.

926   "Is this love? Yes, I believe so. I should never call for him so often if I didn't love him more than any other. So I love him: let's agree on that. Well, shall I not follow my desire? Yes, provided that doesn't displease him. This desire is wicked; but Love has so overpowered me that I'm mad and out of my mind. I've no defence against this, so I shall have to suffer his attack. For a long time I've guarded against him so sensibly and was never prepared to do anything on his behalf; but now I'm too obliging towards him. And what gratitude should he show for that, when he can get no loving service or goodwill out of me? He has tamed my pride by force, so I must be at his disposal. Now I want to love. Now I have a master, and Love will teach me. And what? – How I should serve him. But I'm very well informed about that and am so expert in his service that no one could find fault with me, and there's nothing more of it I need to learn. Love's wish, and mine too, is that I should be prudent and without pride, good-natured, welcoming and friendly to all for the sake of a single man. Should I love them all for the sake of one? I should behave pleasantly towards everyone, but Love doesn't teach

me to be a close friend to everybody. Love teaches me only what is good.

962 "It's not for nothing that I'm known by the name of Sore-damors. I should love and should be loved, as I intend to prove through my name, if I can find the reason there. There is signifi-cance in the fact that in the first part of my name is the colour of gold, for the best are those whose hair is most golden. I therefore think my name the best, as it begins with that colour that is matched by the finest gold. And the ending makes me think of love. Therefore whoever calls me by my right name rehearses for me the colour of love. One of its halves gilds the other with a shining surface of fair gold; for the meaning of Soredamors is 'gilded over with love'. So Love has highly honoured me by gilding me over with himself. A gilding of gold is not so fine as that with which I shine; and I shall devote all my care to being a gilding for him, without ever complaining about it.

988 "Now I love and always shall. Whom? – That's a fine question indeed! The one whom Love commands me to, for no other shall ever have my love. But what does that matter, since he'll not know it unless I tell him myself? What shall I do, if I don't make an approach to him? Anyone who longs for something should cer-tainly request and ask for it. – What? Should I then put my request to him? – No. – Why not? – It never happened that a woman acted so wrongly as to propose love to a man, unless she were strangely out of her mind. I really would be proved a fool if anything passed my lips for which I might be reproached. If he should learn it from my mouth, I think this would give him a lower opinion of me, and he would often blame me for having made the first advances. May love never fall so low that I should approach him first and have him look down on me for it!

1012 "Ah, God! How will he learn of it, since I shall not reveal it to him? As yet, I've hardly suffered enough to make me so upset. I'll wait until he notices, if ever he does notice. I truly believe he'll find out, if he has ever had experience of love or learned of it by word of mouth. – Learned of it? Now I've spoken nonsense. Love's charms are not such that anyone can learn of them by hearsay, without having had personal experience of them. I know this well from my own case; for I was never able to get to know anything of them from false blandishments or other talk, and I've had a good deal of experience of that and been flattered on many occasions; but I've always kept myself at a distance. He, though, makes me pay a heavy price, for now I know more about these things than an ox about ploughing. But there's one thing that makes me despair: that this man, perhaps, has never loved; and if he doesn't love and never has, then I've sown in the sea, where seeds cannot grow. So there's nothing to do but wait and suffer until I see if I can lead him on by signs and spoken hints. I shall do this until he's sure of my love, if he dares to obtain it. Now there's no more to be said about it except that I love him and am his: even if he doesn't love me, I shall love him."

1047 Thus both he and she lament, hiding their feelings from one another: they suffer by day and still more by night. I suppose they remained in Brittany in this distress for a long time until the end of the summer came. At the very beginning of October, messengers came from London and Canterbury by way of Dover, bringing the king news that filled him with dismay. The messengers told him he risks staying in Brittany too long; for the man to whom he had entrusted his land is intending to rebel against him, having already summoned a great army of his own men and his friends and established himself in London in order to hold that city against the king whenever he might arrive.

1067 On hearing the news, the king, angry and incensed, calls together all his lords. To goad them better into bringing the traitor to grief, he says that all the blame for his trouble and strife is theirs, for it was on their advice that he placed his lands in the hands of that criminal who is worse than Ganelon.* There is not one of them who does not admit that the king is absolutely right, for that was the advice they gave him; but they say the man will be utterly destroyed, and he may be quite sure that no castle or city will afford him protection against their hauling him out by force. Thus they all reassure the king, solemnly pledging and swearing to deliver the traitor to him or never again hold a fief. And the king proclaims throughout Brittany that no one fit to bear arms in battle shall fail to come at once to follow him.

1093 The whole of Brittany is on the move, and never was there seen such an army as King Arthur assembled. When the ships set sail it seemed the whole world was at sea, for the waves were so covered by ships that nothing of them could be seen. This will be a real war!

From the commotion on the sea it seems the whole of Brittany is under way. Already the ships have made the crossing, and the assembled host is quartered along the coast. Alexander had the idea of going to beg the king to knight him; for if he is ever to win renown, he will win it in this war. Fired by a determination to put his plan into effect, he took his companions with him, and they went to the king's tent.

1115 The king was seated in front of his tent; and when he saw the Greeks coming, he called them into his presence. "Sirs," he says, "don't keep from me the reason for your coming here." Alexander spoke for them all, telling him of his desire. "I've come", he said, "to beg you, as I should entreat my lord, on behalf of my companions and myself, to confer knighthood on us." The king replies: "Very gladly, and there shall be no delay in doing it, since you've requested it of me." Then the king orders equipment to be brought for thirteen knights. The king's bidding is done. Then each asks for his own equipment, which is given to one and all, fine arms and a good horse. They all took their own gear. That for each of the twelve, arms, robes and horse, was of equal value; but Alexander's own outfit, should anyone wish to value or sell it, was worth exactly as much as all the other twelve. At the sea's edge they undressed, washed and bathed themselves.* Not wishing or consenting that any other bath be heated for them, they made the sea serve as bath and tub.

1147 These events are known to the queen, who does not dislike Alexander: on the contrary, she is very fond of him, praises and thinks highly of him, and wishes to do him a real favour, which is far greater than she realises. She rummages through all her chests and empties them until she takes out a white silk shirt, splendidly made and of very fine, delicate quality, sewn with nothing but gold or, at the least, silver thread. From time to time Soredamors had taken a hand in the stitching; and in places, on the two sleeves and the collar, she had worked in beside the gold a hair from her own head,* as a test to see if she could ever find a man who would examine it so closely as to tell the one from the other; for the hair was just as bright and golden as the gold itself, or more so. The queen takes the shirt and has it sent to Alexander.

1171 Ah God! How great Alexander's joy would have been had he known what the queen was sending him! And she, too, who had

worked her hair into it would have been very joyful had she known
that her beloved was to have and wear it. She would have been able
to take great comfort from that; for she would not have cared so
much for the rest of her hairs as for the one Alexander had. But they
are both unaware of this; and it is a great pity they do not know.
The queen's messenger came to the port where the young men were
bathing and, finding the youth in the sea, presented him with the
shirt. He is delighted with it, especially as it has come from the
queen. But had he known the rest, he would have cherished it far
more and would not in exchange have accepted the whole world;
rather he would have treated it, I think, as a holy relic and adored it
day and night.

1197 Alexander waits no longer, but dresses himself at once. When
he was dressed and equipped, he returned to the king's tent along
with all his companions. The queen, it seems, had come to sit in the
tent, wishing to see the new knights arrive. One might think them
handsome; but the fine figure of Alexander was the most handsome
of them all. Now they are knights; and I shall say no more of them,
but speak of the king and the army which came to London. Most of
the people joined with him, but he also had a large number against
him. Count Angrés gathers together on his own side as many as he
could win over by promises and gifts. Once he had mustered his
men, he fled secretly at night since, as he was hated by many, he was
afraid of being betrayed. But before he made off, he plundered
London of all the foodstuffs, gold and silver he could, and distributed everything among his men. The king is given the news of
the traitor's flight together with his entire force, and told that he has
taken from the city so much wealth and provisions that the townspeople are impoverished, made destitute and ruined. And in
response the king declares that he will never take a ransom for the
traitor, but will hang him, if he can catch or lay hands on him.

1236 At once the whole army moved off and came as far as Windsor.
In those days, whatever it may be like now, the castle was far from
easy to take from anyone who wished to defend it; for the traitor, as
soon as he planned his treachery, fortified it with triple walls and
moats, and had the walls buttressed behind with heavy logs, so that
catapults could not bring them down. He had spent a great deal
on the fortifications, taking all June, July and August to build
walls and palisades, moats and drawbridges, ditches, barriers and

barricades, iron portcullises and a great keep of dressed stone.
Never was a gate closed there from fear or against an assault. The
castle stood on a high hill, with the Thames flowing beneath. The
army encamped on the river bank, and that day they were fully
occupied in preparing their quarters and erecting the tents.

1261 The army has pitched camp beside the Thames, and the whole
meadow is covered with green and scarlet tents. The sun strikes
down on the colours, making the riverbank blaze with them for a
full league and more. The men from the castle had come to amuse
themselves by the waterside, with just their lances in their hands
and their shields held against their chests, but otherwise unarmed.
By coming without their armour, they showed those outside the
castle that they had little fear of them. On the other bank, Alexander noticed these knights duelling with each other in front of
them. He would like to come to grips with them, and so calls to his
companions by name, one after the other. First there was Cornix,
who was very dear to him, then the bold Licorides, then Nabunal of
Mycene, Acorionde of Athens, Ferolin of Salonica and Calcedor
from Africa, Parmenides and Francagel, mighty Torin and Pinabel,
Nerius and Neriolis. "Sirs," he says, "I should like to go and try
conclusions with shield and lance against those people who've
come to joust in front of us. I can see they have a poor opinion and
think little of us, or so it seems when they've come to joust here,
unarmed, under our very noses. We're newly dubbed and haven't
yet favoured any knight or quintain with our attentions. We've
kept our first lances intact far too long. What were our shields made
for? They're still not holed or broken. They're useless things to
have except in a fight or attack. Let's cross by the ford and set about
them!" They all say: "We'll not fail you!" And each adds: "So help
me God, anyone who lets you down now is no friend of yours!"

1311 They immediately gird on their swords, secure their saddles
and tighten their girths, mount and take their shields. Having hung
the shields at their necks and grasped the lances painted with their
individual colours, they all gallop as one to the ford; and those on
the other side lower their lances and charge to strike at them. But
they knew how to give as good as they got, and without sparing or
avoiding them or yielding as much as a foot against them, each
strikes his opponent so hard that there is not a knight good enough
to stay in the saddle. They did not mistake the Greeks for mere lads

or cowards or idiots! Their first blows were not wasted, for they unhorsed thirteen of their enemies. The news of the great blows they dealt reached the army. There would soon have been a fine set-to had the others dared to wait for them. The men in the army rush for their arms, then dash into the water with a great clamour; and the others turn to flight, thinking that is no place for them to linger. And the Greeks go after them, keeping them company with blows from lances and swords, lopping off plenty of heads, but without any of their own number being wounded. That day they gave a good account of themselves; but Alexander took the main credit, capturing four knights by himself, trussing them up and leading them away. And the dead lie on the sand, for there were many decapitated, others wounded or maimed.

1349 Alexander courteously presents to the queen the gift of his first spoils as a knight, not wanting the king to have them in his power, for he would quickly have them hanged.* The queen has them taken and held prisoner on a charge of treason. Throughout the army they talk of the Greeks, and everyone says that Alexander is very courtly and sensible not to have surrendered the knights he had captured to the king, for he would have burned or hanged them. But the king does not find that amusing and sends at once for the queen, telling her to come and speak with him and not keep custody of his traitors; for she must either hand them over or displease him by keeping them. The queen came to the king, and they duly had their discussion about the traitors. All the Greeks had remained in the queen's tent with her maidens, the twelve talking a great deal with them, but Alexander not saying a word. Sore-damors, who had sat down close to him, noticed this. With chin in hand, he appears lost in thought.

1380 They sat for a long time like this until Soredamors saw at his arm and at his neck the hair she had used in her stitching. She drew a little closer to him, having now found an opportunity to speak with him; but first she wonders how to open a conversation with him and what word she should begin with, whether she should call him by his name. So she turns it over in her mind. "What shall I say first?" she asks. "Shall I address him by name, or call him friend? – Friend? Not I. – What, then? – Call him by name! God! 'Friend', though, is such a beautiful, sweet word to utter. If I dared call him friend! – Dared? What stops me? – The fact that I think that would be lying. – Lying? I don't know what will come of it, but if I lie, I'll be sorry. So it's best to admit I wouldn't want to lie. God! Yet he'd tell no lie if he called me his sweet friend! And would I be lying about him? We both ought to speak the truth. But if I do lie, the fault will be his. And why is his name so hard for me to say that I want to use a second name for him? It seems to me to have too many letters, and I'd stop in the middle. But if I called him friend, that's a name I could say very quickly. Because I'm afraid of not getting through the other, I'd gladly shed my blood for his name to be 'my sweet friend'."

1419 She remains immersed in these thoughts until the queen returns from the king who had summoned her. Alexander sees her coming and goes to meet her, asking what the king orders to be done with his prisoners and what their fate is to be. "My friend," she says, "he requires me to hand them over to him at his discretion and let him bring them to justice. He's very angry that I've not already surrendered them to him; so send them to him I must, for I see no way out of it." Thus they spent that day; and on the next the good, loyal knights gathered before the royal tent to pronounce legal judgment as to the punishment and torture by which the four traitors should die. Some say they should be flayed, others that they should be hanged or burned. And the king himself maintains that a traitor should be drawn apart.* Then he orders them to be fetched. When they are brought, he has them bound and says they are to be drawn all round the castle in full view of those inside.

1449 After this sentence had been passed, the king addresses Alexander, calling him his dear friend. "My friend," he says, "yesterday I saw you attacking and defending splendidly, and I wish to reward you for it. I increase your company by five hundred Welsh knights and a thousand men-at-arms from my own land. When I've brought my war to an end I shall, in addition to what I've given you, have you crowned king of the best kingdom in Wales. There I shall give you towns and castles, cities and halls until such time as you inherit the land held by your father, of which you are to be emperor." Alexander expresses to the king his deep gratitude for this gift, and his companions add their own thanks for it. All the nobles in the court say that Alexander fully deserves the honour the king confers on him.

1473 No sooner does Alexander see his men, his companions and men-at-arms that the king is pleased to give him, than bugles and trumpets are duly sounded throughout the army. All without exception take up arms: good men and bad, those from Wales and Brittany, Scotland and Cornwall, for indeed the army was greatly reinforced from all quarters.

1484 The level of the Thames was low as there had been no rain all summer, and the drought was such that the fish in it had died, the boats were stranded in the port, and it was possible to ford the river at its widest point. The army crossed the Thames, part occupying the valley and part climbing on to the higher ground. Those in the fortress observe them and watch the arrival outside of this amazing army, which is making its preparations to destroy and seize the castle, while they for their part make ready to defend it. But before any attack is launched, the king has the traitors drawn round the castle by four horses, through the valleys and over the hills and fallow ground. Count Angrés is furious at the sight of those he held dear being dragged round his castle; and the rest are very dismayed, but despite their alarm they have no wish to surrender. They need to defend themselves, for the king openly displays to all his anger and wrath, and they see plainly that if he captured them he would put them shamefully to death.

1515 When the four had been drawn, and their limbs were strewn over the field, then the assault began. But all the attackers' efforts are in vain, for however much they hurl and shoot their missiles, they can achieve nothing. Nevertheless they try their hardest, casting and shooting great numbers of javelins, bolts and darts. On all sides there is a great din from the crossbows and catapults, and arrows and round stones fly as thick and fast as rain mixed with hail. They struggle like this all day, some defending, some attacking, until night separates them. And on his side, the king has a proclamation made telling the army of the gift he will bestow on the man responsible for the taking of the castle: he will give him an extremely valuable cup of gold weighing fifteen marks, the most costly in his treasury. The cup will be very fine and rich and, to tell the ungarbled truth, should be admired more for its workmanship than the material. The craftsmanship of the cup is excellent; yet, if the truth be told, the stones on its sides are worth more than either the workmanship or the gold. If the man who has the castle taken is a foot-soldier, he shall have the cup; if it is taken by a knight, then whatever reward he may ask as well as the cup, he shall have it, provided it can be found in the world.

1553 When this proclamation was made, Alexander had not neglected his custom of going each evening to see the queen. That evening too he had gone, and he and the queen had sat down side by side. Nearest to them, on her own, sat Soredamors, gazing at him with such pleasure that she would not have wished to be in paradise. The queen held Alexander's right hand and examined the gold thread, which was growing very tarnished; but though that was losing its colour, the hair was becoming even more beautiful. Then she happened to remember that Soredamors had done that stitching, and the thought made her laugh. Alexander noticed this and asked her to say, if it could be told, what made her laugh. The queen hesitates to speak and, looking towards Soredamors, calls her over. She was happy to come and kneel before her. Alexander was delighted to see her draw so close he could have touched her. But he is not bold enough even to dare look at her; instead, he is so disconcerted that he almost becomes speechless. And she for her part is so overcome that she has no use for her eyes, but gazes down at the ground without looking anywhere else. The queen is very surprised to see her pale at one moment, crimson the next; and she makes a mental note of the behaviour and expression of each of them individually and both together. She notices and is convinced that these changes of colour are the effects of love; but, not wishing to distress them, she gives no sign of taking note of anything she sees.

1602 This she did very effectively, not giving anything away by her expression, but simply saying to the maiden: "My damsel, look at this and say honestly where that shirt was stitched that this knight is wearing, and whether you were involved or put anything of your own into it." The girl is embarrassed to say, and yet does tell her willingly; for she is very keen that the truth shall be heard by the one who, hearing her relate and describe the making of the shirt, is so overjoyed that at the sight of the hair there he can scarcely refrain from worshipping and doing obeisance to it. The presence with him of his companions and the queen caused him much trouble and vexation; for because of them he refrains from raising it to his eyes and mouth as he would have been eager to do, had he not thought he would be seen. He is happy to possess that much of his beloved, but neither believes nor expects he will ever obtain anything more of her: his desire makes him timid. Nevertheless, when he does have the opportunity, he kisses it more than a hundred thousand times; and having left the queen, he thought himself very fortunate. The whole night he treats it with great joy, taking good care that nobody sees him. When he is lying in his bed, he takes a vain delight and consolation in what gives him no true satisfaction, embracing the shirt all night long; and when he gazes at the hair, he thinks he is lord of the whole world. Love truly makes a fool of a wise man when he rejoices over one hair and in it takes such pleasure and delight. But he will see that delight replaced before the bright dawn and sunrise.

1648 The traitors are in council, discussing their course of action and their prospects: it is certain that they will be able to hold out in the castle for a long time, if they apply themselves to its defence. But they know the king to be so fierce in his determination that he will not in all his life go away without taking it; and then they are doomed to die. And if they surrender the castle to him, they need expect no mercy on that account. Thus both choices are grim for them, as they see death in either case, and find no comfort there. But their deliberations produce a plan: before daybreak they will secretly leave the castle and find the army disarmed and the knights still lying in their beds asleep. Before they are awake, dressed and equipped, they will have carried out such slaughter that for ever after people will tell of that night's battle. All the traitors approve this proposal in desperation, having little hope of saving their lives. Come what may, despair gives them courage for the battle, since they see no remedy other than death or imprisonment; and that is no healthy remedy. Nor is it any use trying to flee, for they see nowhere they could find safety if they do so, since the water and their enemies surround them, and they are in the middle.

1687 They spend no longer in council, but arm and equip themselves at once, then go out through an old postern-gate to the north-west, the direction where they expected the men of the army to be the least on the alert. Out they went in serried ranks, dividing their men into five companies, each containing fully two thousand foot-soldiers well equipped for battle and one thousand knights. That night neither stars nor moon had shown their rays in the sky; but before they reached the tents, the moon began to rise. And I believe it rose earlier than usual to do them damage, and that God, wishing to harm them, lit the dark night,* having no love for their army but rather hating them for their sin with which they were tainted. For God hates traitors and treason more than any other wrong. So He commanded the moon to shine in order to bring them to grief.

1713 The moon does them a great disservice as it shines on their gleaming shields, and they are put at a great disadvantage too by their helmets, which reflect the moonlight; for the sentries on lookout duty for the army see them and raise the cry throughout the camp: "Up, knights, up! Get up quickly! Get your arms and put them on! Here come the traitors at us!" The whole army rushes to arms, with men struggling hard to put on their armour, as they had to in such an emergency; and not a single one of them moved off until they were all comfortably in their armour and mounted on their horses. While they are arming, the others are making haste in their eagerness for battle, hoping, by finding them without their arms, to take them by surprise; and they have the companies into which they had divided their men approach from five directions. One kept close to the woods, the second followed the river, the third went into the forest, the fourth was in a valley; and the fifth company spurs ahead by a cutting in a rock, thinking they could rush on unhindered among the tents. But they did not find that route and passage safe, for the royal troops oppose them, hurling fierce challenges at them and rebuking them for their treason. They make for each other with the tips of their lances, which are splintered and broken; then they go dashing together with their swords, felling each other face down, sending one another sprawling, and rushing upon each other at least as fiercely as lions that devour all they can catch fall upon their prey.

1757 In this first assault the slaughter on both sides was truly heavy. But help comes to the traitors, who put up a very fierce defence and sell their lives dearly. When they can hold out no longer, they see their companies coming to their rescue from four sides. Then the king's men swoop down on them, riding as hard as they can, and deal such blows on their shields that, as well as the wounded, they bring down more than five hundred of them. The Greeks do not spare them, and Alexander is not idle, striving to give a good account of himself. In the thickest of the fight he goes to strike a rogue so hard that his shield and hauberk were not worth a button to him as he was flung to the ground. Having finished with him, he offers his services to another without wasting or squandering them, for he serves him so savagely that he drives his soul from his body, and its lodging-place is left untenanted. After these two he meets with a third, dealing a very noble, dashing knight such a blow through his flanks that the blood spurts out on the other side and the soul he breathes forth takes leave of his body. Many he slays and many others he wounds, hurling himself like a flying thunderbolt at all those he attacks. For the ones he strikes with lance or sword neither coat of mail nor shield offers any protection. His companions too spread blood and brains around most generously and are free in handing out their blows; and the king's men massacre so many that they break them up and scatter them like a confused rabble.

1802 So many corpses lay about the ploughed land and so long had the fight gone on that well before daybreak their forces were mangled to such an extent that the line of dead stretched for five leagues down the river. Count Angrés abandons his banner in the fight and steals away, taking with him seven of his companions. He retreated towards his castle by a path so well hidden that he thinks no one can see him; but Alexander notices him and, seeing him fleeing from the battle, thinks he will go to engage him and his men, provided he can slip away without anyone missing him. But before he came to the valley, he saw some thirty knights coming behind him down a track, six of them Greeks and the other twenty-four Welsh. They thought they would follow him at a distance in case he might need them in an emergency. When Alexander caught sight of them, he stopped to wait for them, observing the direction taken by the men retreating to the castle, until he saw them enter it.

1832 Then there came to him the idea of a bold, though very dangerous, exploit and a quite wonderful stratagem. And having worked it out in his mind, he went back to his companions to tell them. "Sirs," he says, "if you wish to have my affection, agree freely to what I want, whether it's foolish or sensible." They promised not to oppose him, whatever he wished to do. "Let's change our insignia", he says, "by taking the shields and lances of the traitors we've killed. Like that we can go to the castle, and the traitors inside will think we're some of them; and, whatever may come of it, the gates will be opened to us. And do you know what we'll do for them in exchange? God willing, we'll take them, dead or alive. And if any of you goes back on his promise, you may be sure I'll never show him true affection so long as I live."

1859 They all agree to his wish. They go and take the shields from the slain and, equipped with them, move on. Then the people in the castle, having climbed up to the battlements of the keep and clearly recognised the shields, think they belong to their men, oblivious to the trick lurking beneath those shields. The gate-keeper opens the gate for them and lets them in. By not saying anything to them, he is duped and deceived; and none of them utters a word, but they pass on in silence, without speaking, making a show of grief by trailing their lances after them and bending low under their shields so that they appear to be in great distress. They go wherever they wish until they are past the three walls. Up there they find a large number of men-at-arms and knights with the count: I cannot tell you how many there were, but they were all unarmed except for just those eight who had returned from the battle; and even they were preparing to take off their armour. But they could have been in too much of a hurry, for those who have come up there to confront them drop their pretence, give their chargers their head, brace themselves in the stirrups and, without waiting to challenge them, charge to the attack, striking dead thirty-one of them. The traitors are filled with dismay and shout: "Treason! We're betrayed!" But the attackers show no alarm, for they test their swords well on those they find unarmed; and of those they did find armed, they even cast such a spell on three that they left only five alive.

1904 Count Angrés dashes forward and in the sight of all deals Calcedor such a blow on his golden shield that he hurls him dead to the ground. Alexander is very grieved to see his companion slain: he almost goes mad, and his blood boils with rage, but his strength and courage are doubled, and he goes to strike the count with such fury that he shatters his lance; for if he could, he would dearly like to avenge the death of his friend. But the count was a very powerful man and an excellent, brave knight, as good as any in the world had he not been a criminal and traitor. He returns the blow so strongly that he bends his lance until it splits and shivers; but the shield does not break, and neither man yields before the other any more than a rock would do, for both were very strong. But the fact that the count was in the wrong does him great harm and damage. They set furiously one upon the other, drawing their swords after breaking their lances.

1933 There would have been no escape had these two craftsmen been prepared to continue their combat: one or other would finally have had to meet a prompt end. But the count does not dare stay there when he sees his men, who had been caught unarmed, slain around him, with the others pursuing them furiously, hacking, slashing, carving them and spilling their brains, branding the count as a traitor. When he hears himself accused of treason, he goes to take refuge in his keep, and his men flee with him. Then their enemies chase them in hard and fierce pursuit, not letting any of all those they catch escape them, killing and despatching so many that no more than seven, I think, found refuge.

1955 Having arrived in the keep, they stopped at the entrance, for those at their backs had followed them so closely that their men would also have got inside had the way been open. The traitors put up a stout defence, expecting help from their own people, who were arming down in the town. But on the advice of Nabunal, a very wise Greek, the approach was blocked so that they could not come in time, since they had waited far too long through cowardice and slackness. There was only a single entrance to this upper stronghold; and if they stop this opening, they will have no fear of being set upon by any force that would pose a threat to them. Nabunal calls on twenty of them to go to that gate; for men who, given the strength and power, would do them some harm might soon force their way in to attack and engage them. Twenty should go to close that gate, with ten making a frontal assault on the keep to prevent the count from securing himself inside.

1984 Nabunal's advice is taken: ten remain to fight at the entrance to the keep, and twenty go to the gate. They almost left it too late, for they see approaching on foot a band of men eager and burning for the fight, including many cross-bowmen and an assortment of soldiers with a variety of arms. Some carried halberds, others Danish axes, lances, Turkish swords, bolts, darts and javelins. They would have had to pay a very heavy price had these people fallen on them, but they did not arrive in time. Thanks to Nabunal's sensible advice, the Greeks got there first and forced them to remain outside. When they see they are shut out, they stay there quietly, realising they could achieve nothing by attacking. Then there begins such a great weeping and wailing of women, small children, old men and youths that those in the castle would not have been able to hear heaven's thunder itself. The Greeks are overjoyed, for now they are quite sure that the count has no chance of escaping without being captured. Four of them quickly climb on to the battlements just to keep watch in case those outside use some ruse or trickery to surprise them inside the castle. The other sixteen go to join the ten in their fight.

2026 It was now broad daylight, and the ten had already managed to break into the keep. The count, armed with an axe, had taken his stand beside a post, where he puts up a fierce defence, cleaving through anyone he reaches; and his men are in position close to him, not sparing in this extremity their efforts to wreak their vengeance. Alexander's men lament the fact that, having recently numbered twenty-six, they are now no more than thirteen. Alexander almost goes out of his mind when he sees his company weakened by such damage and loss. But he does not neglect to take vengeance: he finds just beside him a long, heavy pole, and with it strikes one rogue so hard that neither his shield nor his hauberk was worth a button in saving him from being felled to the ground. After him he goes for the count, raises the pole and takes good aim, then deals him such a blow with that massive stave that the axe falls from his hands; and he was so stunned and dazed that, had he not leaned against the wall, he would not have stayed on his feet.

2057 With this blow the fight ends. Alexander leaps at the count, who does not move as he seizes him. Nothing more need be said of the others, for they were easily captured when they saw their lord taken. They are all made prisoners with the count and led away in great shame, as they had deserved.

2066 The beseigers outside knew nothing of all this; but that morning when the battle was over they had found their comrades' shields among the corpses, and the Greeks mistakenly made a great lament for their lord. On account of his shield, which they recognised, they all give vent to their grief and anguish, swooning on his shield and saying they have lived too long. Cornix and Nerius, then Torin and Acorionde fall in a swoon and, when they come to, regret they still live. From their eyes the tears stream down on to their breasts; life and joy mean nothing to them, and Parmenides most of all tore and rent his hair. These five could not grieve more bitterly for their lord. But their distress is groundless: thinking it is their lord, they bear away another in his place. They sorrow too over the other shields, which lead them to think that these are their companions' bodies;* so they swoon and are in anguish over them. But all the shields deceive them, for of their company only one, Neriolis, was slain. Him they might properly have borne away, had they known the truth. But their grief for the others is as great as for him; so they took them all and carried them off. In all but one case they were mistaken; but like the dreamer who takes an illusion for the truth, so they were persuaded by the shields that this illusion was true: by the shields they have been deceived.

2108 They move off with the bodies and come to their tents, where there were many grieving people; but, hearing the lamentations of the Greeks, all the rest gathered, crowding together because of their sorrow. Now Soredamors, hearing the cry and mourning over her beloved, is quite convinced she is unlucky ever to have been born. This grief and anguish makes her lose her senses and her colour; and she is particularly troubled and hurt because she dares not give open expression to her distress, but keeps her own grief hidden in her heart. Had anyone taken any notice, he could have seen from her expression and outward appearance what agony she was in; but everybody was so preoccupied with the venting of his own sorrow that he had no concern for others. Each one lamented from personal grief, for they find the river-bank covered with their own relatives and friends who have been slaughtered and hacked down. Each man lamented his own loss, which for him is intimate and bitter. There is a son weeping over a father, and here a father over a son, one swoons over a cousin, another over a nephew; thus fathers, brothers, relatives are lamenting on all sides. But in greatest evidence is the grief expressed by the Greeks; yet they could be anticipating great joy, for that grief, the bitterest in the whole army, will soon turn to gladness.

2147 The Greeks outside are plunged in great mourning, whilst those within think hard how they can give them the news which may bring them great joy. They disarm and bind their prisoners, who beg and entreat them to strike off their heads at once. But this they neither wish nor deign to do, saying that they shall keep them until they are handed over to the king, who will pay them what they have earned, so that they shall have their deserts in full. When they had disarmed them all, they took them up on to the battlements to show them to their own people below. This kindness was by no means to their liking, for when they saw their lord captive and bound, they were not at all happy. Alexander, from up on the wall, swears by God and all the saints that he will not leave a single one of them alive, but will kill them all without more ado, unless they all go and surrender to the king before he can seize them himself. "I order you", he says, "to go confidently to my lord and put yourselves at his mercy. None of you has deserved death, except for the count you see here; and you shall never lose life or limb if you cast yourselves on his mercy. If you don't save yourselves from death by simply calling for clemency, then you may have very little hope for your lives and bodies. Go out completely unarmed before my lord the king, and tell him on my behalf that Alexander sends you. You'll not be wasting your time, for the king my lord is so kind and good-hearted that he will forgive you for all the anger and wrath you have caused him. If, though, you wish to act otherwise, you're doomed to die, for I'll never take pity on you."

2193 Without exception they take this advice and go unhesitatingly to the king's tent where they all fall at his feet. The story they told him is soon known throughout the army. The king mounts, then all follow suit and ride at the gallop to the castle without wasting more time.

2201 Alexander goes out of the castle to meet the delighted king, to whom he hands over the count. The king did not delay in bringing him to justice there and then. But he praises and esteems Alexander highly; and all the others make much of him, lavishing on him their congratulations and praise. There is no one who does not express his joy. Their jubilation drives out the grief they showed earlier. But no joy can be compared with that of the Greeks. The king has him presented with the very precious cup weighing fifteen marks, giving him the firm assurance that he has no so treasured possession, apart from the crown and the queen, that he will not make it over to him, should he but ask for it. Alexander dares not take up this offer by saying what he desires, though he knows well he would not be refused should he ask him for his beloved. But he is so afraid of displeasing her who would, in fact, have been overjoyed that he would rather grieve without her than possess her against her will. So he asks to be given a little time, not wishing to put his request until he is sure of her own attitude. However, he asks for no delay or respite in taking possession of the golden cup: he receives it, then courteously begs my lord Gawain to accept this cup from him, which he did, but with great reluctance. When Soredamors learned the truth about Alexander, she was highly pleased and delighted. Now she knows he is alive, she is so joyful that it seems to her she will never be unhappy again; but she feels he is too long in making his customary visit. Eventually she will have what she wants, for they both share a single preoccupation.

2249 Alexander was most impatient to be able to feast his eyes on just one sweet glance from her. He would long since have wished to go to the queen's tent had he not been detained elsewhere. He was very unhappy at having to wait; but just as soon as he could he did go to the queen in her tent. The queen received him, knowing a good deal of what he was thinking without his having told her, for she had read his mind well. When he enters the tent she greets him and, knowing what brings him, makes a great fuss of him. Anxious to do him a favour, she calls Soredamors to her side; so the three of them conversed together on their own some way from the others. The queen, who had no doubt that both he and she were in love with the other, was the first to speak. She is certain of this in her own mind and knows that Soredamors could not have a better lover. Sitting between the pair, she began by addressing to them some appropriate and timely words.

2279 "Alexander," says the queen, "love is worse than hate, for it grieves and torments its devotee. Lovers don't know what they are doing when they conceal their feelings from one another. Love is a very difficult business, and anyone who doesn't begin boldly by laying its foundations can scarcely achieve success in it. They say nothing is so hard to cross as the threshold. I want to teach you about love, for I'm well aware that love is tormenting you, and that's why I'm giving you this lesson. And take care not to hide anything from me, for I've clearly seen from the behaviour of both of you that of your two hearts you have made one. So don't keep anything at all from me! You're each behaving very foolishly in not speaking your thoughts, for by concealing them you're putting each other to death and will be the murderers of love. Now I advise you never to pursue force or lust in love. Bear each other company in marriage and honour.* Like that, in my opinion, your love is likely to last long. I'm prepared to give you the assurance that, if this is your desire, I will arrange the marriage."

2311 When the queen had spoken her mind, Alexander did the same. "My lady," he says, "I don't defend myself against any of your reproaches, but admit to all you say. I wish never to be free of love or to fail to devote my constant attention to it. What you've said to me gives me great pleasure and delight, and I thank you. Since you know what is in my mind, I see no point in concealing it from you any longer. Had I dared, I would have confessed it long ago, because hiding it has been very painful for me; but it may be that this maiden would not on any account wish me to be hers and herself to be mine. But should she grant me no part in her, I still pledge myself to her." At this the girl gave a start; and she does not decline the gift. She betrays in her words and attitude what her heart desires; for tremblingly she gives herself to him, saying that she herself, her will, her heart and her body are without exception entirely at the queen's command, and she will do whatever she wishes.

2340 The queen embraces them both and presents each to the other. Laughing, she says: "Alexander, I make over to you the body of your sweetheart – I know you are not lacking her heart. Whoever may pull a sour face or grimace, I give you each to the other: each of you take what is hers or his!" She has what is hers, and he what is his; he has her totally and she the whole of him. At Windsor that very day, with the consent and agreement of my lord Gawain and the king, the marriage was celebrated. No one, I think, could describe so much of the magnificence, the feasting, the joy and the entertainment at this wedding that there was not even more of it. Because it might displease a number of people, I do not intend to use and waste more words, but to apply myself to a more profitable subject.

2361 At Windsor in a single day Alexander had as much honour and joy as he could wish. Three joys and three honours were his: one was the castle he captured, another King Arthur's promise that, when his war was over, he would give him the best kingdom in Wales; and that day he did make him king in his hall. The greatest joy was the third: that his sweetheart was queen on the chessboard where he was king. Before five months had passed, Soredamors found herself bearing human seed and fruit, which she carried to its full term. The seed remained in germ until the fruit was fully developed. No more beautiful child was ever created before or since; and they called this child Cligés.

2383 So Cligés was born, in whose memory this story was turned into the vernacular tongue. You will hear me tell a long tale of him and of his knightly valour on reaching an age to establish a reputation. But in the meantime it happened in Greece that the life of the emperor who held Constantinople drew to its end. He died, as die he must, not being able to pass the natural span. But before his death he summoned together all the leading nobles of his land to have them begin a search for Alexander his son, who was staying very happily in Britain. The messengers leave Greece and put to sea, where they are struck by a tempest that brings disaster on their ship and company. They were all drowned at sea except for one renegade rogue who was more devoted to Alis the younger son than to Alexander the elder. Having escaped from the sea, he made his way back to Greece and reported that they had all been shipwrecked as they were returning bringing their lord from Britain, and that he was himself the only one to survive the perils of the storm. His lying account was believed; and without any objection or opposition they take Alis and crown him, investing him with the empire of Greece.

2419 But it was not very long before reliable news reached Alexander that Alis was emperor. He took leave of Arthur, being quite unwilling to abandon his land to his brother without a fight. The king does nothing to hinder him: on the contrary he tells him to take with him such a great host of Welshmen, Scots and Cornishmen that his brother, on seeing the army assembled, will not dare to oppose him. Had he wished, Alexander might have taken a great force with him; but he has no desire to bring destruction on his own people, provided that his brother is prepared to respond by agreeing to his conditions. With him he took forty knights and Soredamors and his son, not wishing to leave behind these two, who had a great claim on his love. At Shoreham they took leave of the entire court and put to sea. The wind was favourable, and their ship sped far faster than a fleeing stag. Within the month, it seems, they made harbour before Athens, a very rich and powerful city. The emperor was actually in residence in the city, where many of the chief nobles of the region were assembled. As soon as they had landed, Alexander sent one of his trusted friends into the city to find out if he might be received or if they would contest his claim to be their rightful lord.

2457 This mission was entrusted to a wise, courtly knight called Acorionde, a man with a wealth of possessions and eloquence and of good standing in the country, being a native of Athens. His ancestors had traditionally always exercised very high authority in the city. Having learned that the emperor was in the town, he goes to challenge his right to the crown on behalf of his brother Alexander and in no way condones his having illegally usurped it. Going straight to the palace, he finds a warm welcome from many people, yet does not reply or say a word to anyone who greets him, but waits to hear their wishes and feelings regarding their rightful lord. He goes directly to the emperor, but does not salute or bow to him or call him emperor. "Alis," he says, "I bring you news from Alexander, who is out there in the harbour. Listen to your brother's message: he demands from you what is his and seeks nothing unreasonable. Constantinople, which you are holding, should be and shall be his. It would not be right or proper if there were dissension between you two. Take my advice: come to an agreement with him and pass the crown peacefully to him, for in justice you should surrender it to him."

2495 Alis replies: "My dear good friend, you've acted foolishly in bringing me this message. You've brought me no comfort, for I well know my brother is dead. If he were alive and I knew it, that would be a great consolation to me; but I'll not believe it until I see him. He died some time ago to my sorrow, and I believe nothing of what you say. And if he is alive, why doesn't he come? He has no reason to fear I shall not give him plenty of land. He's foolish to stay away from me; and if he serves me, it will never be to his disadvantage. But no one shall hold the crown and empire in opposition to me." The other hears that the emperor's reply is unacceptable; and he does not fail to speak his mind out of fear. "Alis," he replies, "may God confound me if matters rest here! In your brother's name I defy you, and in his name I duly summon all those I see here to abandon you and join him. It is right that they should rally to him and take him as their lord. Now show who is loyal!"

2525 With that he leaves the court, and for his part the emperor calls on those he trusts most, asking their advice on his brother's defiance and wishing to know if he can trust them not to lend support or aid to his brother in this conflict. In this way he tries to discover the attitude of each of them. But he does not find a single one to support him in the dispute; instead they tell him to remember the war Polynices waged against his own brother Eteocles and

how each died at the hands of the other.* "The same may happen
to you if you intend to wage a war; and the land will be laid waste."
Therefore they advise the making of a peace that is just and reasonable without excessive demands being made on either side. Thus
Alis gathers that if he does not make a fair agreement with his
brother, all the nobles will turn against him. So he says he will make
proper arrangements for any pact they wish, though stipulating
that, however things turn out, the crown shall remain with him.

2555 To conclude a firm and stable peace, Alis, through one of his
marshals, summons Alexander to come to him and take over the
whole land, provided only that he do him the honour of allowing
him the name of emperor and leaving him the crown. In this way, if
he is willing, the two of them may reach agreement. When this
proposal was put to Alexander, he and his men mounted and came
to Athens, where they were received with joy. But Alexander is
unwilling for his brother to rule over the empire and have the
crown unless he gives him his solemn word never to take a wife, and
that after him Cligés shall be emperor of Constantinople. On this
the brothers agreed. Alexander stipulated the conditions, and Alis
agreed and pledged him never in his lifetime to take a wife in
marriage. They are reconciled and remain friends. The nobles show
their great joy; and they recognise Alis as emperor; but all matters,
important and trivial, are referred to Alexander, and whatever he
orders and decrees is carried out, little being done except through
him. Alis retains nothing but the name, being called emperor; but
the other is served and loved, and anyone who does not serve him
out of love must do so from fear. By himself and through others he
rules the whole land as he wishes.

2595 But he whom they call Death spares no man, weak or strong,
but kills and slays them all. Alexander had to die, for he was taken
captive by a sickness for which he could find no cure. But before
Death seized him, he sent for his son and said to him: "Dear son
Cligés, you will never know the extent of your prowess and ability
if you don't first put yourself to the test with the men of Britain and
France at King Arthur's court. Should you chance to go there,
conduct yourself and behave in such a way that your identity is not
known until you've measured yourself against the flower of that
court. I advise you to believe what I say; and if you have the chance,
don't fail to match yourself against your uncle, my lord Gawain. I
beg you not to forget this."

2619 After making this plea, he did not live very long. Soredamors's
grief was such that she could not live on after him but died of a
broken heart at the same time.* Both Alis and Cligés mourned
them as they should, but then they ceased their grieving; for all
sorrow must pass and everything be brought to a close. It is wrong
to persist in mourning, for no good can come of it. So the grief came
to an end; and for a long time afterwards the emperor, wishing to
keep faith, refrained from taking a wife. But there is no court in the
whole world free from bad advice; and through believing false
counsels the nobles often go astray and do not uphold loyalty.

2640 His vassals often approach the emperor with advice, urging
him to take a wife. They so urge and pester him and every day press
him so hard that, with their constant harrying, they made him
break his pledge and agree to their wish. But he says that the lady
who is to be mistress of Constantinople must be very attractive,
beautiful and wise, rich and noble. Then his counsellors tell him
they wish to get ready to go to the land of Germany to seek the
emperor's daughter.* They advise him to choose her, for the
emperor of Germany is extremely rich and powerful, and his
daughter is so charming that never has there been in all Christendom a maiden of her beauty. The emperor agrees to everything;
and they set out on their journey as a well-equipped party and ride
by daily stages until, at Regensburg, they found the emperor. They
requested him to give them, on their emperor's behalf, his eldest
daughter.

2669 The emperor was delighted with this message and happily
granted them his daughter, for in this he does not debase himself at
all or diminish his honour in the least. But he says he had promised
to give her to the Duke of Saxony, and they would not manage to
take her away unless the emperor came bringing powerful forces,
so that the duke would not be able to do him any harm or harass
him on the homeward journey.

2681 When the messengers have heard the emperor's reply, they
take their leave and depart. Returning to their lord, they gave him
the answer. Then the emperor chose from among his men knights
experienced in arms, the best he could find; and with them he takes
his nephew on whose account he had made the vow never to have a
wife in his lifetime. But he will not keep this vow if he can reach
Cologne. One day he leaves Greece behind and heads for Germany;

for he will not fail to take a wife whatever the blame or reproach, though his honour will suffer for it. He continues to Cologne, where the emperor was holding his court for a German festival. When the company of the Greeks reached Cologne, there were so many Greeks and Germans there that more than sixty thousand of them had to be lodged outside the town.

2707 There was a great throng of people, and the joy shown by the two emperors, who were delighted to meet each other, was immense. The nobles assembled in the great hall, which was very long; and the emperor immediately sent for his charming daughter. The maiden did not delay, but came at once into the hall; and she was as beautiful and shapely as if God Himself had fashioned her for the pleasure of seeking to make people marvel. Never did God who created her endow with speech a man who could tell so much about beauty that hers was not still greater.

2725 The maiden's name was Fenice,* and not without reason; for just as the phoenix bird is the most beautiful of all and there can be only one at any time, so Fenice, I think, was peerless in beauty. It was a miracle and a wonder that Nature was never able to create her like again. Since my words would be inadequate, I shall give no description of her arms, her body, her head or her hands. For if I had a thousand years to live and my talents doubled every day, I should use up all my time before I could tell the truth about her. I am sure that if I made the attempt I should exhaust all my skill and squander my efforts, and it would be a waste of time. The maiden hurried to come into the great hall with her head and face uncovered; and the radiance of her beauty lights the hall more brilliantly than four carbuncles would have done. Cligés stood, uncloaked, before the emperor his uncle. It was a rather dull day, but the maiden and he were both so fair that their beauty gave forth a ray which brightened the hall just like the sun, shining clear and red in the morning.

2761 To tell the beauty of Cligés I wish to give a description that I shall make very brief. He was in the flower of youth, being by now almost fifteen years old. He was more handsome and charming than Narcissus,* who saw his reflection in the spring beneath the elm-tree and, on seeing it, fell so much in love with it that they say it caused his death, as he was unable to possess it. Whereas he had much beauty, if little sense, Cligés had far more, just as pure gold surpasses copper, and more again than I describe. His hair was like fine gold and his face like a freshly opened rose. He had a well-formed nose and attractive mouth and was of a stature as fine as Nature could contrive; for into him she put together everything she shares out among other individuals. With him Nature was so lavish that she put it all into one package and gave him just as much as she could. Such was Cligés, endowed with good sense and beauty, generosity and strength; he had the wood as well as the bark. He knew more of swordsmanship and archery than Tristan, King Mark's nephew, and more than he of birds and dogs. No good quality was lacking in Cligés.

2793 The handsome Cligés stood before his uncle; and those who did not know him were eager to look at him, whilst the others, who did not know the maiden, all gazed at her with equal eagerness and amazement. But love turns Cligés's eyes surreptitiously towards her; and then he turns them away again so discreetly that their movement to and fro could cause no one to think him imprudent. He gives her very tender glances, but without noticing that the maiden repays him in kind: out of genuine love, not flattery, she lends him her eyes and receives his own. This seems to her a very good exchange, and it would have appeared to her much better still, had she known something about him. But she knows only that he is handsome to look at, and that if she were ever to love anyone for the beauty she saw in him, it would be wrong for her to bestow her heart elsewhere. She fixed her eyes and heart on him, and in return he promised his own. – Promised? Rather gave outright. – Gave? No: to be sure I am lying, for nobody can give his heart away. I must put it differently.

2823 I shall not follow those who say there are two hearts united in one body, for it neither is true nor seems to be that there should be two hearts together in a single body; and even if they could come together, it would not appear true. But if you care to listen, I could explain to you how two hearts are united as one without actually coming together. They are joined as one only in that the desire of each passes from the one to the other so that they have one common wish; and because they share a single desire, there are those in the habit of saying that each person possesses both hearts. But one heart is not in two places: the desire may well be one, yet each still has his own heart, just as many different men may sing a song or ditty in unison. By this analogy I prove to you that it is not by having two hearts that one person can know another's desire or that the other knows whatever the first loves and hates; no more can a body possess more than one heart than can those voices joining together so they seem like one belong to a single person.

2855 But it is fruitless for me to dwell on this, for another matter presses. I must go on now to speak of the maiden and Cligés, and you will hear of the Duke of Saxony, who has sent to Cologne one of his nephews, a very young man. He informs the emperor that his uncle the duke sends him word that he need expect no truce or peace from him unless he sends him his daughter, and that the man who is intending to take her away with him should not be over-confident on the road; for he will not find it clear but rather defended very strongly against him, unless she is surrendered to him.

2871 The young man delivered his message well, without a trace of pride or arrogance; but he finds no one replying to him, neither knight nor emperor. When he saw everyone remaining silent and that they did so out of scorn, he left the court defiantly; but as he did so, his youth and immaturity led him to challenge Cligés to a joust. They mount their horses for the jousting in equal numbers, there being three hundred of them on either side. The entire hall is cleared and emptied, with not a soul remaining, not a knight and not a damsel, as they all go up to the balconies, battlements and windows to see and watch those about to joust. Even that maiden whom Love had overcome and subjected to his will went up to sit very gladly at a window, since from there she can see the one who has smuggled away her heart; and she has no wish to recover it from him, for she will never love any other. But she does not know his name, nor who he is, nor of what family; and as it is not proper for her to ask, she is impatient to hear something that may cheer her heart.

2905 Through the window she gazes at the shields gleaming with gold and at the men who carry them at their necks as they enjoy their jousting. But she has fixed her thoughts and gaze entirely in one direction, having no other concern: she is intent on watching Cligés, following him with her eyes wherever he goes. And he for his part strives to joust in full view on her account, so that she may at least hear of his valour and skill; for it will be only right that she should praise him for his prowess.

2920 He makes for the duke's nephew, who was breaking many a lance and playing havoc with the Greeks. But Cligés, very annoyed at this, braces himself firmly in the stirrups and goes to strike him at full gallop so that despite himself his opponent vacated the saddle-bows. There was a great commotion when he got up again. The young man gets to his feet and mounts, intending to take good vengeance for his shame. But a man may think that, having the opportunity, he can avenge his shame, when he only increases it. The youth makes headlong for Cligés, who lowers his lance against him and thrusts with such force that he again knocks him to the ground. Now his shame is doubled, and everybody on his side is perturbed, realising they will never come out of the fight with honour; for not one of them is valiant enough to keep his seat in the saddle in the face of an assault by Cligés. So the people from Germany and Greece are delighted at the sight of their men seeing off the Saxons, who retreat in confusion. They pursue them with mockery until they catch up with them at a river, where they make many of them take a plunge and a bath. Cligés unhorsed the duke's nephew into the deepest part of the ford, and with them so many others that to their shame and chagrin they make off grieving and dejected.

2956 Cligés returned jubilantly, having won the chief honour on two counts, and came directly to a gate next to the apartment where the maiden was. And as he went through the gate, she exacted as toll a tender glance, which he paid her as their eyes met. Thus each of them vanquished the other. But there is no German from north or south who has the power of speech and does not say: "God! who is this paragon of handsomeness? God! how does he come to have won so quickly such a high honour?" So one or another keeps asking: "Who is this young man? Who is he?" Eventually the truth becomes known throughout the city: his own name and that of his father, and the solemn agreement the emperor had made with him.

2978 There was so much talk of this on every hand that it even reached the ears of the one whose heart rejoiced because she now cannot say that Love has made a fool of her, nor has she any cause for complaint, since he has made her love the most handsome, courtly and gallant man to be found anywhere. Yet she is compelled to accept someone who cannot please her; and she suffers misery and distress, not knowing from whom she can seek advice about the one she desires, but is left to her own thoughts and nightly broodings. These two circumstances so afflict her that they cause her to grow pale and wan, so that people see plainly from her loss of colour that her desires are unfulfilled; for she plays, laughs and enjoys herself less than usual, though she conceals the reason and dissembles well should anyone ask her what the matter is. Her governess, her childhood nurse, was named Thessala;* and she was very skilled in magic. She was called Thessala because she had been born in Thessaly, where devilish enchantments are traditionally taught and practised. The women of that country work charms and spells.

3011 Seeing the girl who is in Love's power grown pale and wan, Thessala spoke to her privately: "God!" she says, "are you bewitched, my dear sweet young lady, for your face to be so pallid? I'm very puzzled to know what's wrong with you. Tell me, if you know, where this pain hurts you most. For if anyone is to cure you, you can count on me, because I'll be able to bring you back to health all right. I know how to cure the dropsy, I can cure gout, quinsy and asthma; I know so much about the urine and the pulse that you'd be wrong to have any other doctor. And, if I dare say so, I know more well-tested, genuine spells and charms than Medea ever knew.* I've never before said anything about this to you, although I've brought you up until now. But don't blame me for it, for I'd never have spoken to you about it if I didn't see quite clearly that you're suffering from a sickness for which you need my help. Be sensible, my young lady, and tell me what your illness is before it gets a greater hold on you. The emperor put me in charge of you to take care of you; and I've seen to that so well that I've kept you in the best of health. Now I'll have wasted my effort unless I cure you of this illness. Be sure not to hide from me whether this is sickness or something else."

3050 The maiden dares not openly disclose her whole desire, being very afraid that she would blame and discourage her. But since she listens and hears how much she boasts and prides herself on being an expert on spells, charms and potions, she will tell her the reason why her face is pale and drained of colour; but first she will make her promise always to keep her secret and never to oppose her wishes.

3063 "Nurse," she says, "I truly believed I didn't feel ill, but it won't be long before I'll think I do. Just to have it on my mind hurts me greatly and dismays me. But how does anyone who doesn't experience it know what is sickness and what is well-being? Mine is different from all other illnesses, for to tell you the truth, it pleases me greatly and yet I suffer from it, and I find delight in my discomfort. And if what pleases can be a sickness, then my trouble is what I want, and my suffering my health. So I don't know why I should complain, for I'm aware of no source for my illness unless it comes from my wishes. My desire is perhaps a sickness; but I feel so well in my desire that it makes me suffer sweetly, and I find so much joy in my trouble that I'm pleasantly ill. Tell me, nurse Thessala: is this sickness, then, not hypocritical to seem pleasant to me and yet torment me so? I don't know how to tell whether it is an illness or not. Nurse, tell me its name, its nature and what kind of a thing it is. But you may be sure I'd rather not be cured at all, for my distress is very dear to me."

3095 Thessala, who was very knowledgeable about love and all its ways, knows and understands from what she says that love is at the root of her torment. Because she describes it as being sweet, it is certain she is in love; for all illnesses are bitter with the sole exception of the one that comes from loving, but that one transforms its bitterness into a pleasant sweetness, then often changes back again. But Thessala, knowing well what the matter is, replies to her: "There's nothing to be afraid of: I'll readily tell you both the nature of your sickness and its name. You said to me, I think, that the pain you feel seems joy and health to you: that's the symptom of love-sickness, for in it there is both joy and pain. So you're in love, as I prove to you, for I find no sweetness in any illness except in love alone. Apart from that, every single illness is always vile and repulsive, but love is sweet and gentle. I'm quite sure you're in love, but I don't think the worse of you for that. I'll think it wrong of you, though, if out of childishness or folly you hide your feelings from me."—"Nurse, it's no use appealing to me before I know for a fact that you'll never on any account speak of this to any living soul."—"Indeed, young lady, the winds will tell of it sooner than I do, without your permission. And what's more, I'll give you my word to act in your interest so you'll be quite sure of achieving your joy through me."

3137 —"In that case, nurse, you'd have cured me. But the emperor is giving me in marriage; and that brings me much grief and sorrow, because the one who attracts me is the nephew of the one I must accept – and if that man has his joy of me, then mine is altogether lost along with all hope of ever achieving it. I'd rather be torn limb from limb than have people in referring to us recall the love of Iseut and Tristan,* about whom such nonsense is talked that I'm ashamed to speak of it. I couldn't reconcile myself to the life Iseut led. With her, love was too debased, for her body was made over to two men, whilst her heart belonged entirely to one. In this way she spent her whole life without ever rejecting either one. This love was unreasonable, but mine is firm and constant, nor will my body or my heart ever be shared under any circumstances. Never will my body be prostituted between two owners. Let him who has the heart have the body: I reject all others.

3165 "But I can't conceive how the one to whom my heart yields itself up can have my body, when my father gives me to another, and I daren't go against his wishes. Then, when he's master of my body, if he treats it in a way I wouldn't want, it's not right for me to take someone else. But nor can he take a wife without breaking his sworn word; for unless he wrongs Cligés, he is to have the empire after his death. If, though, you were skilful enough to prevent the man I'm given and pledged to from having any share in me, you would have done me a very welcome service. Nurse, please do your best to stop him from breaking that undertaking never to take a wife which he pledged to Cligés's father on the conditions he had laid down. His vow will be broken, for he's about to marry me. But I don't have such a low opinion of Cligés that I'd not rather be buried alive than have him lose through me a pennyworth of his rightful inheritance. May there never be born to me a child who causes him to be disinherited. Now, nurse, do what you can to put me always in your debt."

3196 Then her nurse promises her that she will weave so many spells and make so many potions and charms that she need never be wary or afraid of this emperor once he has taken the drink she will provide for him. They will both lie together; but however great their intimacy, she may feel just as safe as if there were a wall between them. "But don't mind if he just has his pleasure of you in his dreams; for when he's fast asleep he will enjoy you in his slumbers and will be quite convinced he has his joy while awake, and won't think any of it is a dream or a hallucination or illusion. In this way he'll take his pleasure of you, for in his sleep he will suppose he's awake."

3217 The maiden welcomes, applauds and appreciates this kind service. Her nurse gives her great hope with this promise, which she undertakes to keep. In this way, whatever her impatience, she expects to attain her joy. For if Cligés knows she loves him and on his account is living in such a way as to keep her virginity and thus preserve his inheritance for him, he will never be so churlish as not to be touched to some extent, provided he has a noble nature and is as he should be. The maiden believes her nurse and puts great trust and confidence in her. They mutually promise and swear that this plan shall be kept so secret that no one will ever get to know of it. Thus their discussion ends. Then, in the morning, the emperor sends for his daughter, who comes at his bidding. What more should I tell? The two emperors have together expedited their arrangements to the point where the marriage is celebrated and in the great hall the rejoicing begins. But I do not wish to waste time in describing every detail, so I shall return to the subject of Thessala, who is busy preparing and mixing her potions.

3251 Thessala pounds her concoction, putting in an abundance of spices to sweeten and temper it. She beats and mixes it well, then strains it until it is quite clear and not sour or bitter, for the spices in it make it sweet and fragrant. When this potion was prepared, the day had drawn to a close, and the tables were set up for supper and the cloths laid. But I pass over the supper. Thessala has to be on the lookout for some means or intermediary to deliver her drink. They were all seated at the meal and had had more than six courses, with Cligés serving his uncle. Seeing him do this, Thessala thinks he is wasting his service, since he is assisting at his own disinheritance; and this annoys and troubles her greatly. Then in her well-intentioned way, she hits on the idea of having the potion served by the one to whom it will bring joy and benefit.

3277 Thessala sent for Cligés, who went to her at once and asked her to tell him why she had summoned him. "My friend," she says, "I want to treat the emperor at this meal to a drink that will delight him; and I want him to take no other tonight, either at supper or when he goes to bed. I think it should please him very well, for he never tasted so good a drink, nor was ever any so costly. And I warn you, take good care that no one else drinks any, because there's very little of it. And I also advise you not to let him know where it came from; but say you came across it by chance among the presents and, having tried it yourself and smelt the aroma of the choice spices filling the air and seeing how clear it was, you poured the wine into his cup. If he happens to ask, you may be sure that will satisfy him. But don't let anything I've said put dark suspicions in your mind, for the drink is clean and healthy and full of wholesome spices; and I fancy it will perhaps do you some good one day."

3309 When he hears it will be to his advantage, he takes the potion and goes back, for he is unaware that there is any harm in it. In a crystal cup he placed it before the emperor. Taking the cup, the emperor, who has great confidence in his nephew, drinks a great draught of the potion; and at once he feels its strength passing down from his head to his heart, from which it rises to his head again, surging through him from top to toe, penetrating every part of him, but harmlessly. When the time came to clear the tables, the emperor had taken so much of the drink he had enjoyed that he will never be free of its influence: each night in his sleep he will be intoxicated by it, and it will have such an effect on him that he will think he is awake when sleeping.

3329 Now the emperor has been tricked. When the time came to retire, many bishops and abbots were present to bless the marriage-bed with the sign of the cross. The emperor, as he should, lay with his wife that night. – As he should? That is not true, for he neither kissed nor fondled her, though they lay together in one bed. At first the maiden trembles in great fear and trepidation lest the potion does not work. But it has so bewitched him that he will never desire her or any other woman except in his sleep. But then he will have as much pleasure of her as is possible in a dream, and that dream he will believe to be true. Nevertheless she is afraid of him and at first draws away from him, whilst he is unable to approach her, for he cannot help falling asleep at once. Then he sleeps and dreams, thinking he is awake, doing his very utmost to cajole the girl; and she shows great reluctance, protecting her virginity. He entreats her, tenderly calling her his sweetheart, thinking he holds her, though he does not. But he finds great enjoyment in nothing at all, embracing nothing and kissing nothing, holding nothing and caressing nothing, seeing and speaking to nothing, struggling and striving with nothing. The potion was very skilfully prepared for it to produce such an effect on him. All his great efforts are in vain, for he truly thinks and flatters himself that he has taken the fortress. That is his firm belief as he tires and ceases his striving that was all for nothing.

3371 As I have told you once and for all, he never took any other pleasure. He will always have to carry on in this manner, provided he can take her back with him. But before he can have her safe, I think he will be faced with great difficulties; for when he is on his way back, the duke to whom she had originally been given will not be wasting his time. The duke has assembled a strong force and garrisoned all the frontiers, while at court he has his spies informing him each day of the whole situation there, the preparations, how long the visitors will stay, and when they will leave and by what routes and passes they will return. The emperor did not wait long after the marriage, but left Cologne in good spirits; and the German emperor escorted him with a very large company out of fear and apprehension for the Duke of Saxony's force.

3395 The two emperors journey without a halt as far as Regensburg; and one evening they were encamped in the meadows beside the Danube. The Greeks were in their tents in the fields by the Black Forest, and opposite them were encamped the Saxons, keeping them under observation. The duke's nephew stood alone on a vantage point to watch for an opportunity for some gain at the expense of those on the other side or to do them some harm. From where he stood on watch he saw Cligés and three other young men riding for their pleasure and carrying lances and shields to amuse themselves at jousting. Now the duke's nephew would like to inflict some damage and injury on them if at all possible. He sets out with five companions; and they took cover in a valley beside the woodland, so that the Greeks did not see them until they emerged from the valley. Then the duke's nephew makes an assault, striking Cligés and wounding him slightly near the spine. Cligés bends and leans forward so that the lance passes him, but just grazes him a little.

3425 When Cligés feels he is wounded, he makes for the youth and strikes him with such violence that he drives his lance straight into his heart, felling him dead. Then all the Saxons take flight in panic and disperse into the forest. And Cligés, unaware of the trap, acts boldly but foolishly in leaving his companions and pursuing them in the direction of the duke's forces, where the whole army was already preparing to launch an attack on the Greeks. He goes chasing them all alone, without support. The young Saxons, quite dismayed at having lost their lord, come running to the duke and tell him, weeping, of the loss of his nephew. The duke does not make light of this, but swears by God and all His saints that he will find no joy or good fortune in all his life as long as he knows his nephew's slayer to be alive; and he says that the man who brings him his head will win his firm friendship and give him great comfort. Then one knight boasted that, if Cligés waits for him, he will be the man to make this gift of his head.

3458 Cligés continues his pursuit of the youths until he falls among the Saxons and is seen by the one who claimed he would come with his head. Without delay the man sets off, Cligés having turned back to distance himself from his enemies and come at the gallop to the place where he had left his companions; but he found none of them there, as they had returned to the tents to tell of their adventure. The emperor had the Greeks and Germans mount their horses together. Throughout the army the nobles quickly arm and mount. And the Saxon knight continued to spur hard after Cligés, fully armed and with his helmet laced. When Cligés saw this man, who was determined never to be counted a faint-hearted recreant, approaching, he hurled abuse at him. But first the knight, unable to hide his feelings, insolently called him a lad. "Lad," he says, "you shall pay here your forfeit for my lord whom you killed. If I don't take your head away with me, then I'll not think myself worth a counterfeit bezant. I want to give it as a present to the duke: that's the only forfeit I'll take, and that much I'll give him for his nephew, so he'll have done well in the exchange." Cligés hears his stupid, coarse insults. "Fellow," he says, "be on your guard now; for I challenge you for my head, and you'll not get it without my permission."

3497 With that they attack each other. The Saxon misses, and Cligés strikes with such force that he knocks him and his charger down in a heap. The horse falls backwards on to him so heavily that it snaps one of his legs. Cligés dismounts on the green grass and disarms him. Having done so, he puts the armour on himself and cuts off his head with the man's own sword. Having decapitated him, he stuck his head on the tip of his lance, saying he will serve it up to the duke, to whom the man had promised the gift of his own head, if he could meet him in combat. Cligés had scarcely put the helmet on his head and taken up the shield (not his own, but that of the man who had fought with him) and, having done that, remounted on the other's charger, letting his own stray off to the dismay of the Greeks, when he saw more than a hundred banners and large, strong companies of Greeks and Germans combined. Now the violent, bitter clashes between the Saxons and Greeks will soon begin. As soon as Cligés sees these companies approaching, he heads straight towards the Saxons, with the others hotly pursuing him, not recognising him because of the arms he bears. His uncle is distressed to see the head he is carrying; and his fear is not to be wondered at.

3536 The whole army sets off after him; and Cligés has them chase him to provoke the fight until the Saxons see him coming. But the arms he is equipped with mislead them all. He has them fooled and duped; for the duke and all the others, seeing him coming lance in rest, say: "Here comes our knight! He's bringing Cligés's head on the point of the lance he's holding, and the Greeks are on his heels. To horse, now, and go to his rescue!" Then they all give their horses their head; and Cligés spurs towards the Saxons, bent low and crouching behind his shield, stretching out the lance with the head on its tip. Though lion-hearted, he was no stronger than any other man. On both sides they think, the Saxons and the Greeks and Germans alike, that he is dead; and while the former rejoice, the others grieve. But before long the truth will be known; for Cligés keeps silent no longer. With a shout he dashes at a Saxon, striking him on the breast with his ashen lance that still carries the head, so that he loses his stirrups. Then he calls aloud: "Strike, my lords! I am Cligés whom you're seeking. Come on, you bold and noble knights! Let no one show cowardice, for the first joust is ours. This is no dish for a coward to taste!"

3571 The emperor was overjoyed to hear his nephew Cligés calling and urging them on: that gave him great delight and comfort. And the duke is horrified, for now he knows he is betrayed, unless his forces are the stronger. He has his men tightly close their ranks; and the Greeks in close formation do not keep their distance, for at once they spur and gallop ahead. On both sides they thrust their lances forward, striking and receiving blows as they must in such an encounter. In the first clashes shields are pierced and lances shattered, girths cut and stirrups broken, with the chargers of those fallen on the field remaining riderless. But whatever all the others do, Cligés and the duke charge at each other with lances outstretched; and each strikes the other on his shield with such force that the lances fly in splinters, strong and well-made though they were. Cligés, an expert horseman, stays upright in his saddle without being shaken or thrown off balance. The duke, losing his seat, quits the saddle-bows despite himself. Cligés thinks he will lead him away captive and tries his hardest to do so; but he has not the strength, for the surrounding Saxons rescue him by force of arms. Nevertheless Cligés leaves the fight uninjured and with booty, for he leads off the duke's charger, which was whiter than wool and to a gentleman was worth the fortune of Octavian of Rome: it was an Arab steed. The Greeks and Germans are jubilant when they see Cligés on its back, for they had noticed the value and quality of the Arab horse. But they were not on their guard against a subterfuge, nor will they be aware of it before they have suffered great loss.

3621   A spy came to the duke with news that caused him great joy. "Duke," says the spy, "in all the Greeks' tents there's no one left able to defend himself. Now, if you take my advice, you can have the emperor's daughter seized while you see the Greeks preoccupied with fighting in the battle. Give me a hundred of your knights, and I'll give them the one you love. I'll lead them so skilfully by an old byway that they'll not be seen or met by any German from north or south before they're able to seize the girl in her tent and take her away quite freely and unopposed." The duke is delighted at this. With the spy he sent a hundred or more able knights; and he guided them so well that they led the maiden away captive without using much force, so easily did they manage to abduct her. When they had her well away from the tents, they sent her on with twelve of their number, whom they escorted only a short way. These twelve take the girl off, while the others give the duke the news of their success.

3652   The duke, having just what he desired, at once makes a truce with the Greeks until the following day. With the truce agreed on both sides, the duke's men withdrew and the Greeks went back, each to his own tent. But without anybody noticing, Cligés remained alone on a look-out point until he saw the twelve coming swiftly at the gallop with their captive. In his thirst for glory, Cligés immediately dashes after them, for he supposes and feels in his heart that they are not making off for nothing. As soon as he sees them, he gallops after them; and when they catch sight of him, a foolish idea comes to them. Each of them says: "The duke is following us: let's wait a little for him. He has left the army on his own and is hurrying to catch up with us quickly." This is what every one of them believes. They all want to go to meet him, but each wishes to go by himself. Cligés has to ride down a deep valley between two mountains. He would never have been able to recognise their insignia had they not come to meet him or waited for him.

3683 Six come towards him, but it will be an unfortunate encounter for them. The others stay with the maiden, leading her gently along at a walk or amble, while the six go spurring at speed along the valley. The one with the fastest horse led the rest, shouting: "God save you, Duke of Saxony! Duke, we've got your sweetheart back. Now the Greeks won't take her off, for she'll soon be handed back to you." When Cligés heard these words that the man came shouting, his heart was far from glad: it was rather a wonder he did not go out of his mind. Never was any wild beast, be it leopard or tiger or lion, so enraged and furious to see its young taken or so eager for the fight as was Cligés, for whom life means little if he fails his beloved. He would rather die than not win her back. In his mortification his anger mounts and inspires him with great boldness.

3709 He goads and spurs on the Arab steed and delivers such a violent attack against the Saxon on his painted shield that, without a lie, he gives his heart the feel of his lance. This one has given Cligés confidence. He spurred and urged his Arab mount on for more than a furlong before he came to the second of them, for they were all approaching in single file. One gave him no cause to fear the next, since he jousts with each individually, encountering them one by one, with none of them being helped by the one after. He attacks the second who was intending, like the first, to tell him exultantly of his own misfortune. But Cligés is not interested in his story or in hearing what he has to say: he plunges his lance into his body, from which the blood spurts as he withdraws it, thus depriving him of both soul and speech. After these two he confronts the third, who expects to find him friendly and to cheer him with what actually distresses him. This one comes spurring up to him; but before he has a chance to say a word, Cligés has run a fathom of his lance through his body. At the fourth in turn he strikes such a blow that he leaves him unconscious on the field. After the fourth he assails the fifth, and after the fifth the sixth. None of them provides any resistance, but he leaves them all silent and mute, having less fear for these others and attacking them more boldly. For these six he had no further concern.

3749 Having taken care of those, he goes to make a gift of shame and disaster to the remainder, who are leading off the maiden. Once he has caught up with them he attacks them like a famished, ravening wolf leaping on its prey. Now he feels blessed by Fortune when he can openly display his chivalry and bravery before the one who gives him life. Now it will be death to him if he does not free her, and she too is at death's door in her great distress for him, not knowing he is so close to her. Lance in rest, Cligés has made an assault that pleases him well, striking one Saxon and then another to fell them to the ground in a single charge, but shattering his ashen lance. And they fall in such agony that, being wounded in the body, they have no strength to get up again to cause him any hurt or harm. In their rage, the other four go to strike Cligés all at once, but he is neither rocked nor shaken, and they fail to unsaddle him. Quickly he draws from its sheath his sword of sharpened steel and, so that she who waits in anticipation of his love may be grateful to him, gallops against a Saxon to give him such a blow with his sharp sword that he strikes his head and half his neck from his trunk: he showed no more pity than that.

3787 Fenice, who is watching and sees him, does not know that this is Cligés. She would have liked it to be he, but because of the peril of the situation, she says she would not wish it so: in both respects she is a good friend to him, for she fears his death and desires his honour. Then, with his sword, Cligés assaults the three, who give him a fierce fight, holing and splitting his shield; but they are powerless to lay hands on him or to break the meshes of his hauberk. And nothing of theirs that Cligés strikes withstands his blow, but he cuts it quite through and shatters it, as he whirls about faster than the top sent spinning and driven by the whip. Prowess and the love that holds him ensnared make him bold and valiant. He pressed the Saxons so hard that he killed and slew all but those he maimed or overcame. But one of them he allowed to escape, because they were on an equal footing and through him the duke might learn of his loss and grieve for it. But before the man left him, he begged Cligés to tell him his name; and he went back and told it to the duke, who was utterly enraged.

3817 Hearing now of his misfortune, the duke was overcome by grief and sorrow. Cligés, meanwhile, brings back Fenice, racked and tormented by his love for her. But if he makes no declaration to her now, Love will be his lasting enemy, and hers too if she also remains silent and does not say where her pleasure lies; for now they have the chance to tell each other in private what their feelings are. But they are so afraid of being rejected that they dare not open their hearts to one another. He fears she will refuse him; and she would also have spoken out but for her fear of being rejected. Yet, had they realised it, they both reveal their thoughts through their eyes. The looks in their eyes are eloquent, but with their tongues they are so cowardly that they dare not make any reference to the love that holds them in its sway.

3839 It is not surprising that she is afraid to take the first step, for a maiden should be a demure, timid creature. But why this waiting and hesitancy from him, who is always bold on her behalf, yet so cowardly when he confronts her alone? God! what is the reason for this fear that makes him afraid of a weak, timid, simple and quiet girl on her own? I seem here to be seeing the hounds fleeing before the hare and the fish chasing the beaver, the lamb the wolf, the pigeon the eagle; it is as if the labourer runs away from the mattock with which he toils for his livelihood, as if the falcon flees from the duck, the gerfalcon from the heron, the great pike from the minnow, and as though the stag hunts the lion, with everything turned topsy-turvy.* But I feel I would like to give some explanation for the fact that true lovers come to lack the sense and courage to say what they are thinking when the circumstances are favourable and the opportunity and time are theirs.

3865 You who make a study of Love and faithfully uphold the customs and practices of his court and who have never broken his law,* whatever the result for you, tell me if one can see any source of amorous attraction without trembling and turning pale. No one will ever contradict me on this point without my confounding him. For whoever does not not grow pale and tremble and does not lose his wits and faculties is trying to obtain and achieve by theft what is not rightly his due. A servant who does not fear his master should not stay in his retinue or service. Not to respect his master is not to fear him, and whoever does not respect him does not love him, but does his best to deceive him and steal his property. A servant should shake with fear when his master calls or summons him. And whoever commits himself to Love takes him as his lord and master, so it is right that he should hold him in reverence and fear and honour him a great deal if he really wishes to belong to his court. Love without fear and trepidation is fire without flame and heat, day without sun, comb without honey, summer without flowers, winter without frost, sky without moon, a book without letters. That is how I would put my refutation, for where fear is lacking there is no question of love. He who wishes to love must fear, otherwise he is unable to love. But let him fear only her whom he loves, and for her sake let him always be bold. So Cligés commits no fault or error if he fears his beloved. But he would still not have refrained from promptly speaking and requesting her love, whatever her reaction, were she not his uncle's wife. This causes his wound to fester and bring him all the more agony and pain because he dares not express his wish.

3915 So they return to their own people, speaking, if at all, of nothing that really matters to them. Each mounted on a white horse, they rode quickly towards the camp, which was plunged in great sorrow. The whole army is distraught with grief, not, though, relying on any true report, for they say Cligés is dead, and that is the cause of their great and bitter grieving; and for Fenice too they are in distress, thinking they will never recover her. So for the one and the other the entire army is in deep sorrow. But they will not be long in coming, and the whole situation will change. For now they are already back at the camp to turn the grief into joy. Joy returns and sorrow flees: everyone comes to meet them, until all of the army is gathered round. The two emperors, hearing the news about Cligés and the maiden, go together to welcome them with the utmost joy. But each is anxious to hear how Cligés had found and recovered the empress. Cligés tells them, and those who hear him are amazed and full of praise for his prowess and valour.

3946 But elsewhere the duke is furious; and he swears, asserts and proposes that, if Cligés dares, the two of them should meet in single combat, which he will arrange on the condition that, if Cligés is the victor, the emperor may leave in safety, free to take the maiden with him; and if he slays or overcomes Cligés, who has done him much harm, then there shall be no truce or peace, but it will be for each to do the best he can. The duke follows this matter through and, by an interpreter of his who knew both Greek and German, informs the two emperors of his wish to hold the combat on these terms.

3963 The emissary delivered his message in both languages so that all understood it well. It put the whole army in a state of agitation and uproar, with everyone saying that, please God, Cligés should not undertake the combat. Both emperors, too, are extremely alarmed at it. But Cligés falls at their feet, begging them not to worry but, if ever he did anything to please them, to grant him this combat as reward and recompense; and if it is refused him, he will never again serve his uncle a single day to his profit and honour. The emperor, who had a proper affection for his nephew, raised him by the hand and said: "Dear nephew, I'm sad to find you so eager to fight that I expect joy to be followed by sorrow. You've made me happy, and I can't deny it; but it's very distressing for me to agree to send you to the combat, for in my view you're not yet old enough. Yet you have, I know, such a proud heart that I dare not on any account deny you anything you care to ask: you can be sure that your request will suffice for it to be done; but if my pleading were of any avail, you would never take this burden upon yourself."—"Sire, your words are in vain," says Cligés; "for may God confound me if I would take the whole world in return for not fighting this duel. I see no reason to ask you for a long respite or delay." The emperor weeps for pity, whilst Cligés weeps for joy to be granted the combat: many tears were shed there. But there was no waiting or postponement: before six o'clock in the morning, by way of his own messenger, the combat was confirmed with the duke as he had proposed it.

4011 The duke, believing and feeling quite confident that Cligés will have no defence against death and defeat at his hands, has himself quickly armed. Cligés, impatient for the duel, feels no concern about his ability to put up a good defence against him. He asks the emperor for arms, with the request that he dub him knight. Graciously the emperor gives him arms, and he receives them, his heart burning for the combat for which he is so keen and eager. He makes great haste to don his armour. Once he is armed from top to toe, the emperor goes sorrowfully to gird on the sword at his side. Cligés, fully armed, mounts the white Arab steed. At his neck he hangs by the straps a shield made from an elephant tusk so that it could not break or split and carrying no paint or colour. His armour was completely white; and the steed and harness too were whiter than any snow.

4037 Cligés and the duke are armed. Together they arranged to meet halfway; and on either side their men will be pledged and sworn to carry no swords or lances at all, and none will be so bold for the duration of the combat as to dare move for any reason any more than he would dare to pluck out his own eye. On these conditions they came together, each of them full of impatience, for both expect to obtain the glory and joy of victory. But before a blow is struck, the empress, racked with anxiety for Cligés, has herself escorted to the place. She is fully determined that, should he die there, so will she: no comforting will serve to keep her from accepting death with him, for without him life holds no pleasure for her.

4059 When they had all, high and low, young and old, come to the place of combat and the guards had been posted, they both took up their lances and charged each other with such a will that each broke his lance and was unhorsed, unable to keep in the saddle. But they were not wounded at all and quickly got to their feet again to set to at once. With their swords they play such a tune on their clanging helmets that their supporters are astounded; and to the onlookers their helmets seem to catch fire and blaze; and as the swords rebound, bright sparks fly off as from the smoking iron that the smith hammers on the anvil after taking it from the forge. Both these valiant men are generous with the many blows they strike, each showing himself very willing to repay promptly what he borrows; and neither of them is reluctant or slow to hand over to the other capital and interest without counting or reckoning it up. But the duke is extremely annoyed and burns with anger at not having overcome and slain Cligés in the first assaults. He deals him such an amazingly hard and mighty blow that he is brought to one knee at his feet.

4095 The emperor was greatly alarmed at the blow that knocked Cligés down and was in no way less dismayed than if he himself had been under the shield. Then Fenice was so frightened that, come what might, she could not restrain herself from crying at the top of her voice: "God help him!" But she called out only these words, for

at once her voice failed her and she fell in a swoon, arms outstretched like a cross, hurting herself a little on the face. Two noble
lords raised her up and supported her on her feet until she
recovered consciousness. But no one who saw her had any idea,
despite her appearance, why she had fainted. Nobody at all blamed
her for it, but everyone praised her, since they all believed she
would have done the same for them had they been in his place; but
in that they were quite wrong. When Fenice cried out, Cligés heard
very plainly. Her voice restored his strength and courage; and,
quickly jumping up again, he came angrily back at the duke and so
attacked and assailed him that the duke was dismayed by it. For he
finds him more belligerent, strong, nimble and aggressive, or so it
seems to him, than he had been when they first came together.
Then, intimidated by his assault, he said to him: "Young man, so
help me God, I find you very brave and valiant. If it weren't for my
nephew, whom I'll never forget, I would gladly make peace with
you, abandon the dispute in your favour, and take no further
interest in it."

4139 —"Duke," says Cligés, "what is it you want? Must one not
surrender his right when he's unable to recover it? When necessary,
one has to choose the better of two evils. Your nephew was foolish
to lose his temper and pick a quarrel with me. You may be sure I'll
deal just the same with you if I can, unless I find you making a
proper peace with me." The duke, to whom it seems that Cligés's
strength continues to grow, thinks it much better to give up in mid-
course, before he is completely worn out; yet he does not admit the
truth openly to him, but says: "Young man, I can see you're noble
and honest and very courageous; but you're extremely young, and
so I think – in fact I know – that if I defeat and kill you, I should gain
no fame and credit from that and would never come across any
gentleman in whose hearing it would be proper for me to say that I
had fought with you; for that would bring you honour and shame
to me. But if you know the meaning of honour, then it will always
be a great honour for you to have held your own against me in just
two bouts. Now I'm inclined and resolved to resign this dispute to
you and not fight with you any further."

4173 —"Duke," says Cligés, "this won't do. You shall declare this
aloud so that everyone can hear, and it shall never be said and
spread about that you did me a favour rather than that I had mercy

on you. In the hearing of all those here, you must repeat what you've said, if you want to be reconciled with me." The duke repeats his words in the hearing of them all; and in this way they made peace and were reconciled. But however the agreement was concluded, Cligés had the honour and the glory, and the Greeks were overjoyed. The Saxons, however, could not laugh, for they all clearly saw their lord exhausted and defeated; and it goes without saying that, had he been able to do anything about it, this pact would never have been concluded, and, had he found it possible, he would rather have driven Cligés's soul from his body.

4194 The duke returns to Saxony in grief, sorrow and shame, for there are no two of his men who do not consider him an abject, craven, failure. The Saxons, covered in shame, returned to Saxony. Then the Greeks wait no longer but, very happy and jubilant, resume the journey back to Constantinople, for Cligés, through his prowess, has opened up the way for them. The Emperor of Germany follows and escorts them no further. Having taken leave of the Greek people and of his daughter and Cligés and then of the emperor, he has remained in Germany. And the emperor of the Greeks leaves, very happy and in high spirits.

4214 The valiant, courtly Cligés calls to mind his father's bidding. If his uncle the emperor will grant him leave, he will go and request him urgently to be allowed to go to Britain to speak with his great-uncle the king, for he wishes to see him and make his acquaintance. He goes to present himself before the emperor and begs him, if he is agreeable, to let him go to Britain to see his uncle and his friends. Very civilly he puts his request; but his uncle, having listened attentively to what he asked and had to say, refused it. "Dear nephew," he says, "I'm not pleased that you wish to leave me. I'll never give you leave and my consent for this without regret. For I'm very happy and content that you should be my associate and, with me, lord over my whole empire."

4237 Now Cligés hears something not to his taste when his uncle rejects his plea and request. He said: "My dear lord, it is not for me, nor am I valiant and wise enough, to accept a partnership with you or anyone else in the duties of emperor. I'm too youthful and ignorant. One rubs gold on the touchstone to see if it is pure. The fact of the matter is that I also wish to put myself to the test and proof where I think I can find the touchstone. In Britain, if I am valiant, I can put myself to the test and to the true, fine touchstone and there prove my prowess. In Britain are the worthy men illustrious for their honour and prowess; and whoever wishes to win honour should associate himself with them, for that's where honour lies, and one profits from keeping the company of a worthy man. This is why I ask you to grant me leave; and you may be quite sure that, if you don't send me there and accord me this favour, I shall go without your leave."—"Dear nephew, rather than that, I give it you, since I see you so disposed that I couldn't keep you back by force or pleading. Now may God give you the inclination and desire to return before long. Since neither begging nor prohibition nor force would be of any use, I wish you to take away with you more than a bushel of gold and silver, and for your recreation I'll give you horses of your choice." He had scarcely finished speaking when Cligés bowed to him. Everything the emperor promised and intended for him was immediately put before him.

4283 Cligés took all the wealth and companions he wished and found to his liking; and for his own personal use he took four different horses: one white, one sorrel, one tawny and one black. But I almost passed over something that must not be omitted. Cligés goes to ask and take his leave of his beloved Fenice, wishing to bid her farewell in God's name. He comes before her and falls to his·knees, weeping so bitterly that he moistens with his tears his whole tunic and its ermine trimming; and he turns his eyes to the ground, afraid to look at her directly, as if he has offended and wronged her in some way for which he seems ashamed. And Fenice, eyeing him timidly and nervously, is unaware of what brings him. With some difficulty she said to him: "My friend, good sir, please rise! Sit beside me; stop weeping and tell me what you wish."—"My lady, what can I say and what should I leave unsaid? I ask you to give me leave."—"Leave? To do what?"—"My lady, I must go away to Britain."—"Tell me, then, for what purpose, before I give you leave."—"My lady, my father on his deathbed, when he passed away, begged me not to fail on any account to travel to Britain as soon as I was made a knight; and I wouldn't wish for anything to go against his bidding. I'll not find it too fatiguing to go there from here. It's a very long way to Greece; and if I went to Greece, the journey from Constantinople to Britain would be too long for me. But it is right that I should take my leave of you, as of one to whom I am entirely devoted."

4328 At their parting many sighs and sobs were suppressed and disguised, so that there was never anyone with his eyes so wide open or his hearing so sharp that he was able to tell positively from what he heard or saw that there was any love between these two. Cligés, however much it grieves him, parts from her as soon as he has the opportunity and leaves deep in thought, whilst the emperor and many another remain pensive. But Fenice broods more deeply than them all, finding no bottom or bounds to the thoughts that fill her mind, so thick and fast do they press upon her and multiply. Pensively she came to Greece, where she was held in high honour as lady and empress. But her heart and mind are set on Cligés, wherever he goes, and she would never have her heart return to her, unless it is brought back by him who is dying of that malady with which he has gravely afflicted her. Should he get well, she will recover; and he will never pay the price it exacts without her paying it as well.

4354 Her sickness shows in her complexion, for it has become very pale and faded. The fresh, clear, pure colour with which Nature had endowed her has quite fled from her face. Again and again she weeps and sighs, caring little for her empire and the wealth that is hers. She always holds in her memory the moment when Cligés left, and the leave he took of her, how he lost his colour and turned pale, his tearful expression; for he came weeping before her as if to worship her, humbly and meekly, on his knees. All this is pleasant and sweet for her to recall and turn over in her mind. Afterwards, as a relish, she places on her tongue instead of a spice a sweet phrase which, in the sense in which she understood it, she would not wish for the whole of Greece its speaker to have uttered with any lack of sincerity; for she lives on no other titbit, and nothing else gives her pleasure. This single phrase sustains and nourishes her and relieves her of all her suffering. She has no wish to feed on any other dish or take any other drink; for when their moment of parting came, Cligés said he was entirely devoted to her.

4386 These words she finds so sweet and delicious that from the tongue they touch her heart; and she places them both in her heart and on her lips to be all the more assured of them. She does not dare to store this treasure under any other lock, nor could she keep it anywhere else as safe as in her heart. In no circumstances will she ever take it out, so afraid is she of thieves and robbers; but her fear is baseless, and those birds of prey need cause her no alarm, because this is no movable possession but is more like a building that cannot be demolished by flood or fire and will always stay in one place. But, in her uncertainty about it, she devotes all her care and efforts to seeking an explanation that will give her confidence, envisaging matters in various ways.

4408 She herself puts both the positive and the negative case as she conducts this disputation:* "With what purpose did Cligés say to me 'I am entirely devoted to you', unless Love made him say it? What power can I have over him to justify his thinking of me so highly as to treat me as his lady? Is his beauty not greater than mine, and is he not of far higher rank than I? I see nothing but Love that could grant me this favour. By my own case I, who am unable to escape Love's clutches, will prove that, if he did not love me, he would never declare himself wholly mine, any more than I should be, or should say I was, wholly his, had Love not consigned me to him. There is no way that Cligés, for his part, ought to say he was wholly mine unless Love holds him in his bonds. For if he does not love me, he is not afraid of me. Perhaps Love, who hands me entirely over to him, gives him completely to me in return. Yet what really alarms me is that it is a well-worn phrase, and I may myself easily be under an illusion, for there are people who, just to flatter, say even to strangers: 'I and all I have are entirely yours', and they are greater prattlers than jays. So I don't know what to think, for it's a real possibility that he said it to flatter me.

4442 "But I saw him change colour and weep quite pitifully. To my mind his tears and embarrassed, glum expression were not the product of deception: there was no shamming or trickery there. His eyes didn't lie to me when I saw the tears run down from them: I could see all the marks of love there, if I know anything about it. Yes, and so much so that I thought it and have learned and remembered it to my cost, for it has proved very disastrous for me. – Disastrous? Yes, in all conscience: I'm in dire straits when I don't see him who has so flattered and cajoled me that he has robbed me of my heart. Because of his cajoling blandishments my heart has left its home and is no longer willing to stay with me, finding the lodging and accommodation I offer so hateful. So he has truly treated me badly by having my heart in his power. Some one who robs me and seizes what is mine doesn't love me, I'm sure of that! –

I'm sure? Why, then, did he weep? – Why? It wasn't without reason, for he had very good cause to. I should really not think myself responsible for it, since one is extremely distressed to part from people one knows and loves. When he left those he knows, I'm not surprised if he was sad and depressed and wept.

4476 "But the person who gave him this advice to go and stay in Britain couldn't have struck me more deeply to the heart. To lose one's heart is to be cut to the quick. Anyone who deserves it should come to grief, but I have never deserved it. Ah, wretch that I am! Why, then, has Cligés dealt me a mortal blow for no offence? But I charge him in vain, for I have no case against him. I'm sure that Cligés would not at any time have deserted me had his heart been the same as mine. I don't believe it is like mine. And if mine attached itself to his never to leave it, then his will never go away without mine; for mine follows his secretly, such is the attachment they have formed. But, to tell the truth, they are very different and opposite. How are they opposite and different? His is the lord and mine the servant, and the servant, like it or not, must do what his lord desires and leave aside everything else. But how does that concern me? He is hardly concerned with my heart and my service.

4504 "I'm very unhappy with this distribution that makes the one the lord of both. Why should mine not be just as capable on its own as his, so that they would be equal in power? My heart is captive, since it can't move unless his moves; and if his travels or tarries, mine always prepares to follow after it. God! why are our bodies not close enough for me somehow to retrieve my heart! – Retrieve? Wicked fool! Like that I should remove it from its happiness and might well kill it. Let it stay there! I have no wish to move it, but rather that it remain with its lord until he feels sorry for it; for he's more likely to have mercy on his servant there than here, because they're in a foreign land. If it's skilled at using flattery in his service, as is the way to serve at court, then it will be rich before it returns.

4529 "Whoever wishes to enjoy his lord's favour and sit at his right hand, as is the common practice nowadays, should pick the feather off his head, even when there's none there. There is, however, a very serious drawback in this: having smoothed him down on the outside, he'll never be honourable enough, should the lord be wicked and base within, to tell him so, but will rather give him to understand and believe that none could rival him in prowess and

wisdom, leaving him thinking he tells the truth. A man has little
knowledge of himself when he accepts someone else's assurance
about a quality he doesn't possess. For even if he's a perverse
scoundrel, wicked and as cowardly as a hare, stingy, stupid and
deformed, base in thought and deed, some person who'll pull a face
at him behind his back still applauds and praises him to his face; but
he only praises him in this way in his hearing when he speaks of him
to someone else, acting as if the man doesn't hear a word of their
conversation; if, however, he really thought he couldn't hear, he
would never say anything that might give him pleasure. And should
his lord choose to lie, he's quite ready to agree with him and affirm
whatever he says to be the truth: for that he'll never be at a loss for
words. Whoever frequents courts and the nobility must use lies in
performing his service. It's necessary for my heart to do the same if
it wants to find favour with its lord: let it be a wheedler and a
flatterer. But Cligés is so knightly, so handsome, open and loyal
that my heart, however highly it praises him, will never be deceitful
or false, for in him there is no room for improvement. Therefore I
wish my heart to serve him; for, as the popular proverb goes: 'Only
the worthless frequent good men without growing better in their
company.'"

4575 Thus love torments Fenice; but for her this torment is a delight
of which she can never tire. Cligés, meanwhile, has crossed the sea
and come to Wallingford, living there in luxury, splendidly lodged
and lavish in his spending. But his thoughts are always with Fenice,
who is never out of his mind for a moment. In the course of his stay
there his men, on his instructions, asked around and made enquiries until they obtained the information that King Arthur's barons
and the king in person had arranged a tournament in the plain
outside Oxford, which was close to Wallingford. The tourney thus
arranged was to last for four days. But in the meantime Cligés will
have plenty of time to get himself ready, should he lack anything,
since there was a full fortnight and more before the tournament.

4600 He has three of his squires go quickly to London, telling them
to buy three different sets of arms, one black, one crimson and the
third green; and he orders that on the way back each set shall be
covered with new cloth so that, should anyone meet them on the
road, he would not know the hue of the arms they are bringing. The
squires set out at once and come to London, where they find

available everything they are seeking. Having quickly completed
their business, they soon returned, getting back as speedily as they
could. They show the arms they have brought to Cligés, who is full
of praise for them. He had them hidden secretly away together with
those given him on the Danube by the emperor when he dubbed
him knight. If anyone should choose to ask me at this point the
reason for his having them stored away, I should be reluctant to
give him an answer; for it will all be told you in the story once every
high nobleman in the land come in pursuit of glory is mounted on
his horse.

4629   On the proposed and appointed day, the distinguished nobles
assemble. King Arthur, with all the men he had chosen from among
his best, established himself in the vicinity of Oxford, whilst most
of the knights arrived near Wallingford. Do not expect me to drag
out my story by telling you that this or that king or count or such
and such a person was there. When the time came for the nobles to
come to grips, an outstanding knight from among King Arthur's
companions, following the custom of those days, came forward
alone from between two ranks to get the tournament under way.
But no one dares to present himself as his opponent in the joust, and
every single man holds back. Then there are some who ask: "Why
are those knights waiting, with none of them coming out from their
ranks? One of them will soon make the first move." And the
response of the others is: "Don't you see, then, what an adversary
their side has sent against us? Anyone who didn't know may be sure
that this man is a pillar of strength to be ranked among the four best
known."—"Who is he, then?"—"Why, don't you see? He's
Sagremor the Impetuous. That's certainly who it is, without any
doubt."

4662   The listening Cligés hears this. Mounted on Morel, he was
wearing armour darker than a ripe blackberry, for he was armed
entirely in black. He breaks from the ranks of the others, spurring
Morel to a furious gallop; and nobody who sees him does not say to
his neighbour: "This man rides well with his lance in rest. Here's a
very skilful knight, bearing his arms in quite the proper fashion and
with his shield very well positioned at his neck. But he may well be
thought a fool to have undertaken to joust against one of the very
best men known in the entire land. But who is he? Where was he
born? Who knows him?"—"Not I."—"Nor I. But he's not been

out in the snow at all: his armour is blacker than the cowl of any monk or priest." As remarks like these are exchanged, the contestants give their horses their heads without wasting more time, for they are burning with fierce impatience to engage in the joust. Cligés strikes his opponent so that he pins his shield to his arm and the arm to his body. Sagremor falls full length; and Cligés goes quite properly to have him declare himself his prisoner, which Sagremor does.

4694 Now at once the tourney begins, and there is a general rush to join in combat. Cligés has hurled himself into the fray and goes about looking for an opponent to joust with. He comes up against no knight without capturing or felling him. He takes the chief honour of either side, for wherever he turns to joust, he brings the whole tourney to a standstill. And whoever makes to joust with him is not lacking in high prowess: indeed he gains more honour in facing up to him than in capturing any other knight; and should Cligés lead him away as his prisoner, he is very highly regarded for the mere fact that he dared to face him in a joust. Cligés wins the honour and glory of the entire tournament. When evening came, he returned to his lodging secretly so that no one should strike up a conversation with him about anything. And lest anybody should try to discover the lodging where the black arms were, he shuts them away in a room to avoid their being found or seen; and at the street-door he has the green arms displayed so as to be noticed by the passers-by. If anyone asks or makes enquiries for him, he will not know where he is staying as he sees no sign of the black shield he is seeking.

4727 That is how Cligés stays in the town, hiding himself by this stratagem. And the men who were his prisoners went from one end of the town to the other asking for the black knight; but no one was able to give them any information. King Arthur himself has him sought up and down. But everybody says: "We haven't seen him since we left the tourney, and don't know what became of him." More than twenty young men sent there by the king search for him; but Cligés has kept so well out of the way that they find no trace of him. King Arthur crosses himself when the news is given him that no one great or small can be found who can tell where he is staying any more than if he were in Caesarea or Toledo or Crete. "Upon my word," he says, "I don't know what to say; but this seems a great wonder to me. Perhaps it was a ghost that came among us. He has overthrown many knights today; and he has accepted the pledges of some of the best, who won't find his door, or his native district or land within the year and so will each have broken faith with him." So the king expressed his opinion, which he might as well have left unspoken.

4759 That night all the nobles talked a great deal of the black knight and discussed nothing else. The next day they took up their arms again without being called or asked to do so. Lancelot of the Lake, who is not at all faint-hearted, was the first to spring forward to open the jousting.* Lancelot is awaiting the encounter when here comes Cligés at speed, greener than the meadow grass, riding a fallow steed that carries its mane to the right. Everybody, long-haired or bald, watches in astonishment as Cligés spurs his tawny mount on; and on all sides they say: "This man is in every respect much nobler and more skilful than the one yesterday with the black arms, just as the pine is more beautiful than the hornbeam and the laurel than the elder. But we still haven't discovered who the man yesterday was. Still, we'll find out who this one is before the day's over. Let anyone who knows him tell us." Each one says: "I don't know him and never saw him before as far as I'm aware. But he's more handsome than that knight yesterday, and more so than Lancelot of the Lake. If his armour were a sack and Lancelot's of silver and gold, he would still be the more handsome." So they all side with Cligés.

4792 Then the combatants, spurring as hard as they can, ride against each other at full tilt. Cligés gives his adversary such a blow on his golden shield with its painted lion that he hurls him down from his saddle. Then he went up to him to take his pledge. Being unable to defend himself, Lancelot surrendered as his prisoner. With that the din began, with the noise and cracking of lances. Those on Cligés's side place all their faith in him; for no one who suffers his aggressive blows is strong enough to avoid being felled from his horse to the ground. That day Cligés performed so well and unhorsed and captured so many men that he pleased his party twice as much and won double the praise he received on the previous day. When evening came, he returned to his quarters as fast as he could and quickly had the scarlet shield and other equipment brought out, ordering the arms he had worn that day to be hidden away. His host concealed them well. That night he was again the object of a long search by the knights he had captured, but they hear no news of him. In their lodgings, most of those who speak of him do so with admiration and praise.

4824 Next day the knights, fit and full of vigour, resume their arms. From the ranks on the Oxford side there comes forward a highly reputed warrior called Perceval the Welshman. As soon as Cligés saw him make his move and, hearing him called Perceval, learned his true identity, he was very anxious to match himself against him. At once he left the ranks on a sorrel Spanish charger, bearing his scarlet arms. Then everybody gazes at him with even greater amazement than before; and they say that never have they seen a knight of such fine appearance. And the contestants do not delay but immediately spur forward, each pressing on to give each other mighty blows on their shields, bending their short, massive lances almost double. Watched by all the spectators, Cligés gives Perceval such a blow that he knocks him down from his horse and has him surrender as his prisoner without a long contest or much argument. Once Perceval had given his pledge, the tournament began with a general engagement.

4854 Cligés clashes with no knight whom he fails to bring to the ground. That day he was not to be seen out of the combat even for an hour. Each man strikes at him in turn as against a tower: they do not strike two or three at a time, for that was not the accepted custom of the day. He made an anvil of his shield, as they all forge and hammer upon it, splitting and breaking it to pieces; but no one strikes it without paying the price of being deprived by Cligés of his stirrups and saddle. And no one not wishing to lie could say when the tourney broke up that the knight with the red shield had not been the outright victor that day. Then all the best and most courtly people would have liked to make his acquaintance, but had no early opportunity; for when he saw the sun set, he left secretly, had his scarlet shield and all his other equipment removed and those white arms in which he had been dubbed knight brought; and these arms and his charger were put outside the door.

4882 But now the realisation dawns on most of the participants and they say and recognise that they have been overcome and eliminated from the tourney by one single man who, however, disguises himself each day by changing his horse and arms and thus appears other than he is: now they have noticed it for the first time. And my lord Gawain said that never had he seen such a jouster; and as he would like to make his acquaintance and learn his name, he says that the next day he will be the first at the knights' encounter. Yet he does not boast at all, but says he fully expects the other to have the advantage and glory from the fight with lances, though he would not perhaps better him at sword-play, since no one had ever been found to master him at that. Now tomorrow he would like to pit himself against this stranger knight who each day takes different arms and changes his horse and trappings. If he goes on like this, regularly shedding his plumage and putting on new, he will soon have had many moultings!

4911 Such are his words and reflections; and the following day he sees Cligés return whiter than a lily, grasping his shield by the straps and mounted on the fresh white Arab steed as he had arranged the night before. The valiant, illustrious Gawain is hardly at rest on the field of combat, but spurs and gallops on, making every endeavour to engage in a fine joust, if he can find an opponent. Shortly they will both be on the field, because Cligés had no wish to hold back once he had heard people muttering the words: "That's Gawain who is no weakling either on foot or on horseback: he's the one nobody can match." Hearing these words, Cligés rushes towards him in the middle of the field. Each advances towards the other, and they clash together charging more swiftly than the stag that hears the barking of the dogs which come baying after it. The lances thrust at the shields, dealing such resounding blows that they split, shatter and break off right at the butt, whilst the saddle-bows give way at the back, and girths and breast-straps burst. Together they come to the ground and draw their naked swords. The people have gathered round to watch the combat. King Arthur came before them all to separate and reconcile them. But they had badly rent and torn the links from their shining hauberks, pierced and hacked their shields to pieces and burst their helmets before there was any talk of peace.

4951 When the king had watched them for as long as it pleased him, along with many of the others who said they did not rate the white knight in the slightest respect inferior in arms to my lord Gawain, they still could not tell which of them was the better and which the worse, or which would have vanquished the other had they been given the chance to fight the combat to a finish. But it was not the king's wish or pleasure to have them do more than they had already done. He comes forward to separate them with the words: "Stand back! Let no more blows be struck, but make peace and be friends! Gawain, dear nephew, I ask this of you; for no gentleman should prolong a fight or combat without any dispute or bad blood being involved. But should that knight be willing to come to my court with us for his entertainment, it wouldn't be to his harm or disadvantage. Invite him to, nephew!"—"Gladly, sire!" Cligés has no thought of declining, but agrees to go there when the tourney is over. For now he has amply done his father's bidding. And the king says he has no liking for a tournament that goes on too long, and they may as well stop at once. Since the king wishes and orders it, the knights disperse.

4986 Cligés sends for all his equipment, since he is to follow the king. He comes to the court as soon as he can, having first made himself quite ready and dressed in the French fashion. On his entry into the court, everyone comes running up to him, none of them holding back, but all showing the greatest possible joy and jubilation on his account; and all those he had captured in the tournament address him as lord. But he will not accept this from anyone, declaring them completely released from their pledges, if they firmly believe it was he who had captured them. And there was not a single man who did not say: "It was you: we're sure of that! We value your acquaintance highly and owe you great affection and respect, and should call you lord, for none of us is your equal. Just as the sun puts out the lesser stars so that their light does not appear in the heavens where the sun's rays appear, so are our deeds of valour extinguished and eclipsed by yours; yet ours used to be highly renowned throughout the world." Cligés does not know what to reply to them, since it seems to him that they all join in praising him more than they should. He is pleased by this, but also abashed, and the blood rises in his face so that they can see he is quite embarrassed.

5022 They escort him into the middle of the hall and lead him before the king, desisting from their compliments and words of praise. It was already time to eat, and those whose duty it was hurried to set the tables. In the great hall they put up the tables, some taking the towels and the others holding the basins and offering water to those who come. Having all washed, they took their seats, with the king taking Cligés by the hand and, very anxious if possible to learn all about him this very day, having him sit opposite him. There is no need to tell of the meal, for the courses were as copious as if an ox could be had for a penny.

5041 When they had had all the courses, the king remained silent no longer. "My friend," he says, "I should like to know if it was through pride that you did not condescend to come to my court on your arrival in this country, and why you kept so apart from people and changed your arms. Let me know, too, your name and what family you come from." Cligés replies: "I'll not hide it from you." He told and revealed to the king everything he wished to know. Then, once the king has heard everything, he embraces him joyfully, and there is no one who does not make much of him. My lord Gawain, having learned the truth, embraces and welcomes him with more affection than all the rest, and everybody else behaves warmly towards him, whilst all who speak of him say how handsome and valiant he is. The king loves and honours him more than any other of his nephews.*

5063 Cligés stays with the king until summer returns, having travelled throughout Britain, France and Normandy and performed many knightly exploits, through which he truly proved his worth. But the love whose wound afflicts him gets no better and allows him no relief. His heart's desire keeps him continually brooding on a single thing: his thoughts turn back to Fenice, who from afar torments his heart. He is seized by the wish to go back, for he has deprived himself too long of the sight of the most longed-for lady that anyone could ever desire, and he wants to put an end to this privation. He prepares for the journey to Greece and, having taken his leave, sets out. I suppose my lord Gawain and the king were very grieved not to be able to keep him any longer.

5086 Anxious to make his way to the one he loves and yearns for, he presses on over land and sea, finding the road very long, so impatient is he to see her who has stolen and taken away his heart. But she gives him fair return and payment and makes good restitution for her larceny, giving him back her own, cash down, for she is no less in love. He, though, is by no means sure of this, never having had a contract or agreement about it; so he is in great torment. And she, for her part, is in anguish too, being afflicted and tortured by her own love; for since that moment when she lost sight of him, nothing she might see can bring her pleasure or satisfaction; and she does not even know if he is alive, which fills her heart with great grief. But Cligés draws nearer each day, fortunate in having fair winds and no gales; and joyfully and in high spirits he made port before Constantinople. The news reached the city; and it was welcome to the emperor, and to the empress a hundred times more so — let no one doubt that!

5115 Cligés has returned with his company to Greece, straight to the port of Constantinople. All the most powerful and noble men come to the harbour to meet him. The emperor, having gone there ahead of them all with the empress at his side, runs when they meet to embrace and greet him in front of them all. And when Fenice greets him, each changes colour on account of the other; and it is a wonder as they come close together that they do not embrace and exchange such kisses as are the delight of Love. But that would have been madness and folly. Folk run up from every direction in their pleasure at seeing him; and all of them, either on foot or on horseback, lead him through the town to the imperial palace. This is no place to speak of the rejoicing there or of the honour and service shown him; but every man strove to do whatever he supposed would please and gratify him. His uncle then makes over to him all he possesses, except for the crown, anxious for him to help himself to anything he would like to have from him, whether land or treasure. But he is not concerned for silver and gold when he does not dare reveal his thoughts to her through whom he finds no rest. Yet he has every chance and opportunity to speak them, were he not afraid of being rejected; because all day long he can see her and sit beside her in complete privacy without being denied or forbidden, since nobody sees or thinks there is any harm in that.

5157 One day, a long time after his return, he came alone into the room of her who was not his enemy; and you may be sure the door was not slammed in his face! He sat, half reclining, by her side; and all the others had drawn away so that there was no one seated near them able to hear their conversation. Fenice first raised with him the subject of Britain, enquiring after the character and manners of my lord Gawain before venturing to broach the topic that filled her with apprehension: she asked him if he was in love with any lady or maiden in that land. To that Cligés was by no means hesitant or slow with his reply, but was swift to respond to her enquiry. "Lady," he says, "I was in love over there, but not with anyone who came from there. In Britain my body was without its heart just like bark without the wood. After I set out from Germany, I don't know what became of my heart, except that it followed you here: my heart was here and my body there. I was not absent from Greece, for my heart had come here, and that's why I've returned. Yet it doesn't come back or return to me, and I can't recover it: I neither wish nor am able to do so. And how have you fared since you came to this country? How have you enjoyed yourself here? Do you like the people and the land? I shouldn't ask you more than whether the country is to your liking."

5198 —"It didn't please me before, but now I feel a growing joy and satisfaction. You may be sure I wouldn't wish to lose this for Pavia or Piacenza, for I can't separate my heart from it and shall never force it away. There's nothing left of me but the bark, for I live and exist without a heart. I've never been to Britain, yet my heart has been to Britain without me on some business, but I don't know what."—"My lady, when was your heart there? Tell me when it went there, at what time and season, if this is something you can properly tell me or anyone else. Was it there when I was?"—"Yes, but you weren't aware of it. It was there just as long as you were, and it left with you."—"God! I never knew of its presence or saw it. Had I seen it there, my lady, I'd certainly have kept it good company."—"You would have comforted me greatly – and so indeed you should have done, for I would have been very kind to your heart had it chosen to come where it knew I was."—"My lady, it did in fact come to you."—"To me? It came as no exile, then, for mine also went to you."

5230 —"In that case, my lady, both our hearts are here with us, then, according to you, because my own is entirely yours."—"And you, my friend, have mine too, so we're in perfect accord. And you can rest assured that your uncle, so help me God, has never had a share in me, since I was unwilling and he had no opportunity. He has still never known me as Adam knew his wife. I'm wrongly called 'lady', though I'm sure that anyone who does call me 'lady' doesn't know I am a virgin. Not even your uncle has any idea, for, having drunk the sleeping potion, he thinks he's awake when he's sleeping, and it seems to him he has his pleasure of me just as he wishes, as if I'm lying in his arms; but I have kept him at bay.

5250 "My heart is yours and yours my body, and no one will ever learn base behaviour from my example; for when my heart gave itself up to you, it presented you with the body and promised it to you so that no other shall have any share in it. I was so deeply wounded by love for you that I never thought I should recover, any more than that the sea might dry up. If I love you and you love me, you shall never be called Tristan nor I Iseut, for then this would be no honourable love. But I promise you that you'll never have any pleasure of me other than you now have unless you contrive a way for me to be taken by stealth from your uncle and my union with him, so that he can never find me again or be able to blame either you or me or know what to do about it. Tonight you must think about this, and tomorrow you'll be able to tell me the best ideas you have; and I too shall give it some thought. Early tomorrow when I am up, come to speak with me; then we'll exchange ideas and put into effect the one we prefer."

5281 When Cligés hears what she wants, he agrees to it all, saying that will be an excellent course. He leaves her happy, and happy he goes away. And that night each lies awake in bed and takes great delight in thinking how it seems best to act. The next day, as soon as they had got up, they met again to discuss matters in private, as they had to do. Cligés speaks first and tells of his thoughts during the night. "My lady," he says, "it's my considered opinion that we could do no better than go to Britain: my idea is to take you there. So don't stand in the way of this, for the joy with which Helen was received in Troy when Paris had brought her there was never so great that you and I would not inspire greater joy still throughout the land of my great-uncle the king. And if this isn't to your liking, tell me what you think yourself; for whatever happens, I'm ready to fall in with your ideas."

5309 She replies: "I'll tell you, then. I shall never go away with you like that; because then, once we had left, people throughout the world would speak of us as of the fair-haired Iseut and Tristan; and on every side one and all would heap blame on our enjoyment of our love. Nobody would, or is likely to, believe the truth of the matter. For who would believe of your uncle that I ran away and escaped from him so freely with my virginity intact? People would consider me quite brazen and shameless and you a fool. But it's well to observe and remember Saint Paul's bidding: if anyone does not wish to remain chaste, Saint Paul instructs him to act so prudently that he attracts no gossip, blame or reproach.* It is good to stop evil tongues, and I think I can well succeed in this, if you have no objections. For I should like to pretend I'm dead – that's my plan. Soon I'll sham sickness, and you must think about providing my burial place. Take very good care that both the tomb and the coffin are made in such a way that I don't die or suffocate; and let no one notice anything when you want to take me out of it at night. And find some hiding-place for me where nobody but you can see me; and let no one but you, to whom I entrust and give myself, supply any of my needs or requirements.

5349 "Never in all my life do I wish to be served by any other man. You will be my lord and my servant, and I'll be happy however you treat me; and I shall never be mistress of any empire unless you are its lord. A mean, dark, squalid place when you're with me will seem to me brighter than any of these halls. If I have you and can see you, I shall have all wealth at my command, and the whole world will be mine. And if the affair is conducted sensibly, no harm will ever be seen and no one be able to find fault with it; for it will be supposed throughout the empire that I'm rotting in the ground. Thessala, who brought me up, my governess in whom I have great faith, will help me loyally, for she is wise, and I have every confidence in her."

5370 Hearing his beloved's words, Cligés replies: "My lady, if it's feasible and you believe your governess is likely to give you sound advice, it remains only to make the preparations and act with speed; but unless we go about it sensibly, we're irredeemably lost. In this city there's a craftsman wonderfully skilled at carving and sculpting: there's no land where he's not known for the works he has executed, carved and modelled. His name is John, and he's a serf of mine. There's no work, however unusual, at which anyone could vie with him, should he wish to apply himself to it, for compared with him they're all as much novices as a nurseling. Men in Antioch and Rome have learnt all their skills from copying his works; nor is there known any more loyal man. But now I intend to put him to the test; and if I find him trustworthy, I'll give him and all his descendants their liberty. And I shall not fail to tell him of our plan, provided he swears and gives me his word to help me faithfully in this and never give me away."

5401 She replies: "So be it." Taking his leave, Cligés left the room and went away. Then she sends for Thessala, her governess, whom she had brought from her native land. Thessala came immediately, without waiting or delaying, but without knowing why she summons her. She asks in confidence what is her wish and pleasure. Fenice neither conceals nor withholds any detail of her thoughts. "Nurse," she says, "I'm quite sure that nothing I tell you will be allowed by you to go any further, for I've formed a very sound opinion of you and found you most prudent. You've done so much for me that I love you for it. I come to you with all my troubles and seek advice from no other quarter. You know very well how I lie awake and what my thoughts and wishes are. My eyes can see one thing alone that pleases me, but I shall derive no good or comfort from it without first paying a very heavy price. Yet I have found my equal, for if I desire him, he wants me too, and if I am distressed, he feels distress in turn at my grief and anguish. Now I must disclose to you a plan and decision we two alone have formed and agreed on."

5436 Then she told and explained to her how she wishes to feign sickness, saying she will make so much of her complaints that she will in the end be taken for dead; and that night Cligés will steal her away, and they will be together for evermore. It seems to her that in no other way could she survive. But if she were sure that she would be willing to help her, this affair would be carried through just as they would wish. "But my joy and good fortune are so far away and long in coming." At that, her governess assures her that in this matter she will help her in every way, and she should have no fear or alarm. And she says that as soon as she gets to work, her efforts will be such that no one who sees Fenice will ever fail to be convinced that her soul has left her body. That will be after she has served her with a drink that will leave her cold, drained of colour, pale and stiff, without speech or breath; yet she will be thoroughly alive and healthy, without sensations of any kind and unharmed by anything in either the tomb or the coffin throughout a day and an entire night.

5467 Having heard this, Fenice said in reply: "Nurse, I put myself in your hands and leave the responsibility for my care entirely to you. I am yours: think of my interests. And tell the people I see here that every one of them must go away. I'm ill, and they disturb me." She tells them politely: "Sirs, my lady's not well, and she would like you all to go away, because you're talking too much and too loud, and the noise is bad for her. She will have no rest or comfort so long as you're in this room. Never before, as far as I can recall, has she had any sickness of which I've heard her complain so much – that's how much worse and more severe her illness is. Please go away, if you don't mind." They all leave in a hurry once she has asked them to.

5488   Then Cligés sent for John to come quickly to his quarters; and in private he said to him: "John, you don't know what I have to tell you. You are my serf, and I'm your lord; and I can give or sell you, take over your person and your possessions as my own property. But if I could trust you for a project I have in mind, you and your direct descendants would be free for all time." John, very anxious to have his liberty, replies immediately. "My lord," he says, "there's nothing whatever you wish, that I wouldn't do, if by that I could see myself a free man and my wife and children with their liberty. Give me your orders, and they will never be for anything so difficult as to cause me distress or affliction or trouble me in any way. Besides, even if it were unwillingly, I'll be obliged to do it and leave aside all my own affairs."—"True, John; but this is something I'm afraid to mention, unless you give me your pledged word and an absolute assurance that you'll help me faithfully and never betray me in the matter."—"Willingly, my lord," says John. "Have no doubt on that score; for I swear and pledge that never as long as I live will I say anything that I think may harm or offend you."

5525   —"Ah, John, were I to die for it, there's no man I'd dare tell of the matter on which I want to ask your advice – I'd sooner have my eye plucked out. I'd rather you killed me than told anyone else. But I find you so loyal and discreet that I'll tell you what I have in mind. I'm sure you'll do just as I wish both by helping me and by keeping quiet about it."—"Indeed my lord, so help me God!" Cligés proceeds to tell him openly all about the situation. And when he had disclosed to him the facts (of which you are aware, having heard me tell them), John says he guarantees him he will put all his efforts into making a good job of constructing the tomb. He then says he would like to take him to see a house of his; and, if he cares to go with him to where he works and paints and carves entirely alone and with no one else, he will show him something he has made that has never been seen before by either his wife or any child of his. He will show him the most beautiful and attractive place he has ever seen. Cligés replies: "Let's go there, then!"

5555   In a remote spot below the city John had laboured with great ingenuity to build a tower.* He took Cligés there with him, leading him through the apartments that were decorated with beautiful, finely painted pictures. He shows him the rooms and the fireplaces and leads him everywhere, up and down. Cligés looks over this isolated house that no one inhabits or frequents. He passes from room to room until he thinks he has seen everything; and he is very pleased with the tower, saying it is extremely beautiful: it will suit the young lady well for as long as she lives, for nobody will ever know that is where she is. "No indeed, my lord: they'll never know! But do you suppose you've seen all of my tower and amenities? There are still more hidden places that no one could find. And if you chose to put it to the test by searching as thoroughly as possible, however you might hunt, you're not so crafty and clever as to find more apartments here unless I point them out and show them to you. You may be sure there's no lack of baths here or of anything else a lady needs that I can think of or comes to my mind. The lady will have every comfort here. This tower, as you'll see, widens out below ground level, and you'll not be able to find a door or entrance anywhere. So ingeniously and skilfully is the door made from hard stone that you'll never find the join."

5595 —"This is an amazing story," says Cligés. "Lead on, and I'll follow, for I'm anxious to see all this." Then John set off, leading Cligés by the hand up to a smooth, polished door that was painted and coloured all over. John stopped at the wall and held Cligés by the right hand. "My lord," says he, "there's no one who could see a door or window in this wall, so do you suppose it's possible to get through it in any way without damaging it and breaking it down?" Cligés replies that he does not think so and will never believe it without seeing it. Then John says he shall see it, and he will open the door in the wall for him. John, whose work this was, unlocks and opens the door in the wall without doing it any harm or damage; and, one behind the other, they go down a spiral stair to a vaulted apartment where John worked at his craft when he chose to make something. "My lord," he says, "of all the men God has created none but us two have ever been where we are now; and yet the place is well fitted out, as you'll see very shortly. I suggest this as your retreat and that your sweetheart be hidden here. A lodging such as this is suitable for such a guest, for it contains bedrooms and bathrooms with hot water for the baths piped in under the ground. If anyone wanted to find a comfortable place to hide his sweetheart away, he would have to go far to find anywhere so delightful. When you've been all over it, you'll find it very suitable."

5638 John then showed him everything, the fine rooms and painted vaulting, and pointed out many of his works, which pleased him greatly. Then, when they had seen the entire tower, Cligés said: "John, my friend, I free you and all your descendants and am entirely in your hands. I want my beloved to be quite alone in here, with no one knowing of it except only for myself and you and her." John replies: "I thank you! Now we've been here long enough and have nothing more to do, so let's go back."—"You're right," replies Cligés. "Let's go!" And they go away and leave the tower. On their return to the city, they hear the people confiding in each other: "Don't you know the astonishing news about my lady the empress? May the Holy Spirit restore her health to that noble, wise lady, for she lies very gravely ill!"

5663 On hearing these whisperings, Cligés rushed to the court; but there was no joy or pleasure there, because everyone was sad and depressed on account of the empress, who is dissembling, for the sickness of which she complains is causing her no suffering or hurt. She has told everybody that she does not wish anyone to come into her room so long as her illness, which causes her pain in her heart and head, has such a strong hold on her, except for the emperor and his nephew, since she does not wish to stop them from entering – though she will not care if the emperor her husband does not come! For Cligés she has to subject herself to great anguish and danger; but she is distressed that he does not appear, as he is the only one she wants to see. Cligés will be before her very soon to tell her what he has seen and discovered. He does come to her with his news, but stayed there a very short time; for Fenice, to make people believe she was annoyed by what pleased her, called aloud: "Go away! Go away! You vex and annoy me too much; for I'm suffering so severely from my illness that I'll never get up cured of it." Cligés is very content with this and goes away, putting on an expression of grief, a more woeful air than ever you saw. Outwardly he appears extremely sad, but inside his heart is glad in anticipation of its joy.

5699 The empress, without being sick, complains and pretends to be ill; and believing her, the emperor grieves continually and has doctors fetched for her. But she is unwilling for anyone to see her and will not let herself be touched. The emperor is understandably depressed when she says there will only ever be one doctor who can easily restore her to health when he so wishes. He will make her die or live. She relies entirely on him for her health and her life. They think she refers to God;* but she means something quite different, having Cligés alone in mind: he is her god who is able to cure her or bring about her death.

5719 In this way the empress makes sure that she comes under the eye of no doctor; and the better to deceive the emperor, she refuses to eat or drink, until she grows quite pale and livid. Her governess attends her. With remarkable shrewdness she scoured the town secretly, without anyone knowing, until she discovered a woman suffering from an incurable, fatal illness. In order to refine her hoax she kept returning to see her, promising to cure her of her ailment; and every day she took with her a urinal to examine her urine, until she saw that no medicine could ever help her and that she would die that very day. She brought back this urine and kept it carefully until the emperor got up, when she at once went before him and said: "Sire, if it please you, send for all your doctors; for my lady, who is suffering greatly from this illness, has passed water and wishes the doctors to see it, provided they don't come into her presence."

5749 The doctors came into the hall. Then, seeing the urine foul and pale, each gave his opinion. Finally they agree that she will never recover or even last until three o'clock, or if she does live so long, God will then take up her soul to Himself. This they whispered privately among themselves. The emperor then asked and entreated them to speak the truth. They reply that they have no confidence at all in her recovery, and that she cannot last beyond three o'clock without giving up the ghost. When the emperor heard this verdict, he barely kept from falling to the ground in a swoon, as did many of the others who heard it. Never were people plunged into such mourning as that which then filled the whole palace.

5770 I pass over the account of the grief, and you shall hear how Thessala is busy mixing and brewing the potion. She mixed and pounded it, for she had long ago provided herself with everything she knew she needed for the potion. Shortly before three o'clock she gives Fenice this potion to drink. No sooner had she taken it than her sight grew dim and her face turned as pale and white as if she had lost her blood; and she would not have moved a hand or foot had she been flayed alive, nor does she stir or utter a word; yet she hears and is well aware of the emperor's grieving and the crying that fills the hall. The city is full of the cries of weeping people, who say: "God! What distress and misfortune vile Death has brought on us! Greedy, grasping Death! Death is worse than any insatiable wolf. Never before have you managed to take such a cruel bite out of the world. Death, what have you done? May God confound you for having extinguished perfect beauty! You have slain the best and most saintly creature, had she lived, whom God ever took pains to form. God's patience is too great when He allows you the power to destroy what He has created. Now God should show His wrath and withdraw the authority vested in you, for you have committed an act of extreme arrogance, pride and outrage." Thus all the people show their anger, wringing their hands and beating their palms together; and the clerics present read their psalms and pray for the good lady, asking God to have mercy on her soul.

5815 Amidst the tears and cries, as the book tells, three venerable physicians arrived from Salerno,* where they had spent a long time. The great mourning caused them to stop and ask for information as to the reason for the crying and weeping and why the people are suffering torment and affliction. They receive the grief-stricken reply: "God! sirs, don't you know? The whole world would be distraught along with us if it knew of the deep grief and sorrow, the affliction and great loss that has befallen us this very day. God! Where have you come from, then, that you don't know what has just happened in this city? We'll tell you the truth, for we wish you to join with us in the grief we feel. Do you not know how today grim Death, who desires and covets everything, lying everywhere in wait for all that's best, has committed a typically quite senseless act? God had illumined the world with a single radiance, a single light. But Death can't break from his usual practice: he always does his utmost to annihilate the best he can find. Now, wishing to show his power, he has carried off in one person more goodness than he's left behind. Had he taken away the whole world, he would have done no worse, so long as he had left alive and well this prey with which he's made off. Death has robbed and cheated us of beauty, courtliness, wisdom and every aspect of goodness a lady could possess, destroying all these virtues in the person of my lady the empress: that's how Death has laid us low."

5862 —"Ah God," say the doctors, "it's clear You hate this city, since we didn't arrive earlier! Had we come yesterday, Death would have had good cause to boast if he'd seized anything from us by force."—"Sirs, my lady would on no account have let you see her or try to treat her. There were many good doctors available, but my lady never agreed to any one of them seeing her to attend to her illness. No, truly: she would have none of it." Then they remembered the case of Solomon and how his wife hated him so much that she deceived him by shamming death.* This woman, perhaps, has done the same. But if they could talk their way into examining her, they would not lie for any living soul should they discover some trickery, but would divulge the whole truth of the matter.

5885 They set out at once for the court, where the clamour and crying was so great that one could not have heard God's thunder peal. The chief and most learned of them went up to the coffin without anyone saying to him "Hands off!" or pulling him back. He places his hand on her breast and side and feels that, without any doubt, she still has all her breath in her body: he can tell and is quite convinced of that. Before him he sees the emperor, stricken and overcome by grief, and calls aloud to him: "Emperor, take comfort! I can see and am certain that this lady isn't dead. Forget your sorrow and be consoled! If I don't restore her to you alive, you may put me to death or hang me!"

5905 At once all the hubbub throughout the hall is stilled and dies away. Then the emperor told the doctor that he might now give the orders and instructions and that he would henceforth be entirely his should he bring the empress back to life, and he would accept him as his lord and master; but if he has lied to him in any way, he will be hanged like a thief. And the doctor replied: "I agree; and may you never have mercy on me if I don't have her speaking to you here. Without hesitation or second thoughts have this great hall cleared for me so that nobody at all stays behind. I must investigate in private the illness from which the lady is suffering. Only these two doctors, who are my colleagues, are to stay with me in here, and all the others must leave." John, Cligés and Thessala would have objected to this; but all those present could have put a bad interpretation on it, had they offered any opposition. Therefore they keep quiet, approve what they hear the others approving, and go outside.

5934 The three doctors ripped open the lady's shroud without using any knife or scissors, then said to her: "Lady, don't be afraid or alarmed, but speak in complete safety. We're absolutely certain that you are quite healthy and well. Now be sensible and co-operative and don't despair of anything; for if you seek our help, we'll all three guarantee to give you all the help we can, whether for good or ill. We shall be very loyal to you both in keeping the secret and in the aid we give. Don't let us have to keep asking! Since we place our ability and service at your disposal, you ought not to refuse." In this way they expect to dupe and deceive her, but it is no use; for she has no concern for or interest in the service they promise her: they are quite wasting their time. Then, when the physicians see they will get nowhere with her by either coaxing or begging, they take her out of the coffin and strike and beat her; but their efforts are futile, for they get no word out of her like that.

5966 They proceed to threaten and terrify her by saying that if she does not speak, she will much regret it before the day is out, because they will do such astonishing things to her that the like was never inflicted on the body of any wretched woman. "We know well enough that you're alive and don't deign to speak to us. We're quite sure you are shamming and deceiving the emperor. Don't be afraid of us! But if anyone has annoyed you, before we hurt you any more, admit to your folly, for you're acting in a very disreputable fashion; and then we'll help you, whether your purpose is sensible or foolish." They can achieve nothing: it is all to no avail. Then they renew their attack with their lashes on her back, down which the weals appear; and they beat her tender flesh so hard that they make the blood flow from it.

5989 When they have scourged her with their lashes until they have torn her flesh and the blood runs down as it flows from the wounds, they cannot even then achieve their ends or extract a sigh or a word; and she neither stirs nor moves. They then say they need to obtain fire and lead, which they will melt and pour into the palms of her hands, before they will get her to talk. They ask for and procure materials for a fire and some lead, then light the fire and melt the lead. In this way the wicked scoundrels torture and torment the lady, taking the heated lead boiling from the fire and pouring it into her palms. And, still not satisfied even when the lead has passed clean through her palms, the vile rogues declare that, if she does not speak quickly, they will put her there and then on a grill until she is completely roasted. She remains silent and shows no opposition as

they tear and wound her flesh. They were on the point of putting
her on the fire to be roasted and grilled when more than a thousand
ladies, who were outside the great hall, come to the door and,
through a small chink, see the torment and ill-treatment these men
are inflicting on the lady as they martyr her over the coals and
flame. They bring axes and mallets to smash and break down the
door. There was a great din as they violently set to on the door,
breaking and shattering it. If they can now get at the doctors, they
will not have to wait long to get their full deserts!

6033 All together the ladies burst into the hall; and in the crowd is
Thessala, anxious only to reach her mistress. She finds her by the
fire, quite naked, badly injured and in a sorry state. Placing her back
in the coffin, she covers her over with the shroud. And the ladies go
to mete out their deserts to the three doctors: they had no thought
of sending for or awaiting the emperor or seneschal, but flung them
down from the windows into the courtyard, shattering the necks,
ribs, arms and legs of all three – no ladies ever did a better job!

6051 Now the three doctors have received their grisly fee, paid them
by the ladies. But Cligés is extremely alarmed and full of grief to
hear of the terrible anguish and martyrdom suffered by his sweetheart on his account. He almost goes out of his mind, being much
afraid, and with good reason, that she has been killed and brought
to her end by the torture to which she has been subjected by the
three docotors who are now dead: this fear causes him despair and
anguish. Then Thessala came, bringing a very precious ointment
with which she tenderly anointed the lady's body and wounds. In
the place where she was laid away again, the ladies wrapped her
once more in a white Syrian cloth, but leaving the face uncovered.
The whole night long their cries continue without abatement or
end. Throughout the entire city, high and low, poor and rich are
frantic with grief, giving the impression that each strives to outdo
the rest in mourning and has no intention of ceasing. All night the
grieving is intense.

6080 Next day John came to the court. He is sent for by the emperor,
who puts to him this strict request: "John, if you ever created a
masterpiece, now show and apply your skill in the construction of a
sepulchre to surpass all others in beauty and craftsmanship." And
John, who had already done this, says he has a superb and richly
sculptured one prepared; but it was never his intention when he

began to make it that anything but a holy relic should be placed in it. "Now let the empress be enclosed there as in a reliquary, for she, I think, is a very holy person."—"You are right," says the emperor. "She shall be buried outside my lord Saint Peter's church where the other bodies are interred; for before she died she begged me urgently that I should have her laid there. Set to now and erect your sepulchre, as is only right and proper, in the finest position in the cemetery." John replies: "Gladly, sire."

6109   John goes away at once and makes the tomb quite ready, using all his experience. He put inside a feather bed because of the hardness of the stone and especially on account of the cold; and so that it should smell fragrant to Fenice, he spread flowers and leaves over it; but he did that more particularly so that nobody would see the mattress he had placed in the grave. Already the service in the main and parish churches was over, and the bells were tolling continuously as is proper for a death. The order is given for the body to be borne away to be placed in the tomb which John, with such care, has made so rich and imposing.

6128   No one, small or great, remains in all Constantinople; but they follow the body in tears, cursing and reproaching Death. Knights and young men swoon, the ladies and maidens beat their chests and breasts as they rail at Death: "O Death," they all say, "why did you not take a ransom for my lady? Your gain was little indeed, but the loss to us is great." Cligés certainly mourns for his part and to such effect that he is more overcome and distraught than all the others, and it is a wonder he does not kill himself; but that he puts off until the time and moment arrives for him to exhume Fenice and hold her and know whether she is alive or not. At the graveside stand the noblemen who lower the body into place; but they do not do John's work of putting the sepulchre in position; moreover, they could not see in, but all fell in a swoon, so John had plenty of time to do as he pleased. He positioned the sepulchre entirely by himself, sealing it well and closing it tightly. After that anyone who could remove or unfasten any part of John's work without forcing or breaking it might well have prided himself on his feat.

6163   Fenice is in the tomb until the dark night has fallen; but she is guarded by thirty knights in the brilliant light of ten candles. The knights were wearied and exhausted by the strain they had suffered, so that night they ate and drank until every one of them fell asleep. At nightfall Cligés steals away from the court and all the people without any knight or servant ever knowing what became of him. He comes straight to John, who gives him all the advice he can and provides him with arms, which he will never need to use. Once armed, they both go spurring to the cemetery. But it was completely enclosed by a high wall; and the knights, who were fast asleep having secured the gate on the inside, thought they were safe from any intruder.

6188   Cligés can see no way to get in, since he cannot enter through the gate; nevertheless he must go in, for Love prompts and urges him on. Tackling the wall, he climbs up, being very strong and agile. Inside was a garden full of trees, one of which was planted close to the wall and reached across to it. Now Cligés has what he was wanting, for by this tree he let himself down. The first thing he did was to go and open the gate for John. Seeing the knights asleep, they extinguish all the lights so there is no illumination at all. Then John at once uncovers the grave and opens the sepulchre without damaging it in any way. Cligés climbs into the grave and lifts out his beloved, who is very limp and appears dead. He embraces, kisses and hugs her, not knowing whether to rejoice or grieve, as she does not move or stir. As quickly as he can, John has closed the sepulchre again so that there is nothing to show that anyone has touched it.

6218   They made for the tower just as fast as they could. When they had put her in the tower, in the underground rooms, they stripped off her shroud. And Cligés, knowing nothing of the potion that was in her system depriving her of the power of speech and movement,* consequently thinks she is dead; so he is in despair and distress, overcome by sighs and tears. But soon the time will come when the potion loses its strength. Then Fenice, hearing his laments, strives and struggles hard to be able to console him with either a word or a glance. Her heart almost breaks to hear him venting his grief. "Ah, Death," he says, "how base you are to spare and reprieve vile, despicable creatures! You allow those to survive and live on. Death! are you insane or drunk to slay my sweetheart but not me? This is a wonder I see: my beloved is dead, and I live on! Ah, sweet love, why is it that your lover is alive and sees you dead? Now it could be rightly said that you have died in my service and that I have slain you and put you to death. Beloved, I then am that death which has killed you. Is this not wrong? For I have taken from you my own life and kept your own: were they not mine then, sweet love – your health and your life? And so was not my own yours? For I loved no other but you, and we were both as one. Now I have done my duty by keeping your soul in my body, while mine has left yours; and the one should keep company with the other, wherever it might be, and nothing should part them."

6266 At that she heaves a sigh and faintly whispers: "My love, my love! I'm not quite dead, but nearly. I care no longer for my life! I intended to play out a farce and a pretence; but now I've good reason to be sorry, for Death has no interest in my farce. It will be a wonder if I come out of this alive, for the doctors have gravely wounded me, tearing my flesh to ribbons. Yet if it were possible for my nurse to be here with me, she would make me quite well, if hard effort could do it."—"Sweetheart, don't worry then!" says Cligés, "for this very night I'll bring her in here to you."—"Let John go instead, my love."

6285 John goes and, having sought until he found her, explains to her how he wants her to come along, without being kept back by any pretext, since Fenice and Cligés summon her to a tower, where they are waiting for her, because Fenice is in a very serious state. So she must come equipped with ointments and medicines; and she may be sure she will have very little time to live unless she hurries to her aid. Thessala runs at once to take ointment, plaster and a medicine she had made, then rejoins John. They leave the city secretly and come straight to the tower. When Fenice sees her governess, she supposes she is quite cured, so much does she love her and believe and trust in her. Cligés embraces and greets her with the words: "Welcome, nurse, for I have much love and respect for you. Nurse, in God's name, what's your opinion of this young lady's illness? What do you think? Will she recover?"—"Yes, my lord; don't doubt that I shall cure her completely. Within a fortnight I'll make her so well that never at any time has she been more healthy or in better spirits."

6317 Thessala puts her mind to healing her; and John goes to provide the tower with everything necessary for that. Cligés comes and goes to and from the tower boldly and quite openly, as he has put a goshawk there to moult and says he goes to see it; and no one can tell that he goes there for any reason other than the hawk alone. He spends much time there by day and night, having John guard the tower so that nobody he does not want can enter. Fenice has no ill to complain of, for Thessala has quite cured her. If Cligés were now Duke of Almeria, Morocco or Tudela, he would not have thought that worth a hawthorn berry compared with the joy that is his. Indeed, Love did not debase himself by pairing these two, for each of them feels as they embrace and kiss each other that the whole world must be a better place because of their joy and contentment. Now ask me no further about this: but there is nothing that one of them wishes in which the other does not acquiesce. Thus they share a single desire, as if the two of them were but one.

6347   For the whole of that year and a good deal of the next, two months and more I think, Fenice was in the tower. When summer came round again, when the blossom and leaves burst on the trees and the little birds rejoice, voicing their happiness in their own tongue, it chanced that one morning Fenice heard the nightingale sing. Cligés, with one arm round her waist and the other about her neck, was holding her tenderly and she him in the same fashion, when she said to him: "My dear sweet love, a garden where I could enjoy myself would be very good for me. I've not seen the moon or sun shine for more than a full fifteen months. If it were possible, I would love to go out there into the daylight, for I'm cooped up in this tower. If there were a garden close by where I could go for my pleasure, I should often derive great benefit from that." Then Cligés promises her to ask John's advice as soon as he sees him; and the chance came at once, for here is John coming in as he often used to do. Cligés spoke to him about Fenice's wish. "Everything she asks for", says John, "is all provided and ready. This tower is well appointed with whatever she wishes and requires." Then Fenice shows her delight and asks John to take her there. He is at her service, he says. With that John goes and opens a door made in a way I am quite incapable of telling or describing. No one but John would have been able to make it, nor could anyone have told there was a door or window there, so well was it hidden and concealed as long as the door was not open.

6393   When Fenice saw the door open and the sun streaming in as she had not seen it for a long time, all her blood ran quick with joy; and she says that she asks for nothing more now that she can leave her refuge, nor does she wish to have any other lodging. She went through the door into the garden, which was much to her liking and fancy. In the middle of the garden was a grafted tree laden with blossom and leaves and spreading out at the top. The branches were trained so that they all hung downwards and almost touched the ground, except for the top of the trunk from which they sprang and which rose straight up. This spot is all that Fenice desires. Beneath the tree the sward is very pleasant and fine, and however high the sun is at noon when it is hottest, not one of its rays can penetrate, so well had John been able to arrange it by guiding and training the branches. There Fenice goes for her pleasure, making her bed there in the daytime; and there they indulge their joy and delight. The garden is enclosed all round by a high wall connected to the tower, so that nothing at all can enter without going up by the tower.

6425 Now Fenice enjoys great comfort: there is nothing that displeases her, and she lacks nothing she wants, when she is free to embrace her lover beneath the blossom and the leaves. At the time of the year when people go hawking with sparrowhawk and pointer, hunting the lark and wheatear and stalking the quail and partridge, it happened that a knight from Thrace, a noble, spirited young man with a good reputation for his chivalry, had gone hawking one day in the close vicinity of the tower. Bertrand was the knight's name. His sparrowhawk had flown off, having failed to take a lark. Now Bertrand will think himself most unfortunate if he loses his hawk. He noticed it come down and alight in a garden below the tower; and he was very pleased to see this, thinking now he would not lose it. He goes at once to clamber up the wall and manages to get over it. Beneath the grafted tree he saw Fenice and Cligés, both naked, sleeping in a close embrace. "God!" says he, "what's happened to me? Isn't this Cligés? Yes, it certainly is. And isn't that the empress with him? No: but she looks like her, for one person never so resembled another. Her nose, mouth and brow are just like those of my lady the empress. Nature never managed to make two creatures more alike. I can see no feature in this woman that I might not have seen in my lady. If she were alive, I should really say it was she."

6466 Just then a pear breaks off and drops close to Fenice's ear. She gives a start, wakes and, seeing Bertrand, cries aloud: "My love, my love, we're lost! See, Bertrand's here! If he escapes you, we're caught in a terrible trap: he'll say he's seen us." Then Bertrand realises it is the empress beyond any doubt. He needs to get away, since Cligés had brought his sword into the garden with him and had put it in front of the bed. He jumps up, seizing the sword; and Bertrand takes to his heels and climbs the wall as fast as he can. And he is almost over it when Cligés comes after him and, quickly raising the sword, strikes him so hard that he slices off his leg below the knee as if it were a fennel stalk. Nevertheless Bertrand has got away, though maimed and in a bad state; and his men on the other side take him, almost out of their minds with grief and anger to see him in this desperate condition, and ask him to tell them who it was who had done this to him. "Don't question me now," he says, "but mount me on my horse! This affair will never be reported except before the emperor. The man who has done this to me shouldn't be unafraid – indeed he won't be, because mortal danger is not far away from him!"

6503   Then they have put him on his palfrey and, in high alarm, lead him, grieving as they go, through the city. More than twenty thousand people go after them, following them to the court; and one after the other the whole populace runs up, each trying to get there first. Already Bertrand has placed his case and complaint before the emperor in the hearing of all. But they take him for a spinner of tales when he claims to have seen the empress stark naked. The city is in a ferment of excitement over it; some think when they hear this news it is pure nonsense, others advise and urge the emperor to go to the tower. There is a great hubbub and din from the people who follow in his wake; but in the tower they find nothing, as Fenice and Cligés have fled and taken with them Thessala, who comforts and reassures them. She says that if they happen to see people following them, coming to arrest them, they need have no fear, since they would never get nearer with a view to doing them any harm or mischief than a man could fire a strong crossbow with a windlass.

6534   In the tower, the emperor has John found and summoned. He orders him to be bound and fettered, saying he will have him hanged or burnt and his ashes scattered to the wind. Because of the shame he has suffered, John will have his reward, though an unprofitable one, for having hidden in his tower his own nephew with his wife. "Upon my word, what you say is true," says John. "I'll never lie, but stick to the truth; and if I've done anything wrong, it's only right I should be arrested. But my excuse for this is that a serf should refuse to do nothing that his rightful lord commands. It's very well known that I am his, and so is this tower."—"It is not, John: on the contrary, it's yours."—"Mine, sire? Certainly, after him; but I myself am not my own, nor do I have anything that is mine except in so far as he allows it to me. And if you wanted to go so far as to say that my lord has wronged you, I'm ready to come to his defence without his ordering it. But I'm given courage to speak my mind and my opinions, just as I have formed them and worked them out, because I know well that I must die. Let that be as it may! For if I die for my lord, I'll not die with dishonour; because the facts are widely known about the oath and undertaking you pledged to your brother that after you Cligés, who is now going into exile, would be emperor – and, please God, he still will be. And your action is open to reproach, for you should not have taken a wife, yet all the same you took her, wronging Cligés though he did you no offence at all. And if I'm put to death by you and so die unjustly for his sake, he will, if he lives, avenge my death. Now do the best you can because, if I die, you'll die too!"

6587 Hearing John utter these defiant words, the emperor sweats with rage. "John," he says, "you shall have a reprieve until they find your lord, who has behaved badly towards me though I was very fond of him and had no intention of cheating him in this; but you'll be held in prison. If you know what has become of him, I order you to tell me at once."—"I tell you, sire? How could I commit such a great crime? Were the life to be dragged from my body, I'd certainly not disclose to you my lord's whereabouts if I knew them, and the more so since, so help me God! I don't know any more than you where they've gone. But your jealousy is pointless. I'm not so afraid of your anger as not to tell you straight, in the hearing of everyone, how you've been deceived, even if I'm never believed. You were duped and deceived by a drink you took on your wedding night. Never since then, unless you were asleep and it happened in a dream, have you had your joy of her; but the night made you dream, and the dream was as pleasing to you as if it was while you were awake that she held you in her arms, though you had no other benefit from it. Her heart was so set on Cligés that she feigned death for his sake; and his trust in me was such that he confided in me and put her in my house, of which he was the rightful master. You shouldn't blame me: I should deserve to be burnt or hanged were I to betray my lord and refuse to do what he wished."

6631 When the emperor heard the reference to the potion he enjoyed drinking, with which Thessala deceived him, he then realised and understood for the first time that he had never had his pleasure of his wife, unless it had happened in a dream: but that was an illusory joy. And he says that if he does not exact vengeance for the shame and disgrace the traitor has brought upon him by seducing his wife, he will never in his life be happy again. "Quickly now!" he says. "Let there remain no castle or city as far as Pavia and from here to Germany that is not searched for him. Whoever brings both of them back captive will be more dear to me than any other man. Now do your best and search high and low, near and far!" Then they set out with great urgency and spent the whole day in the search; but among them are friends of the fugitives who, should they find them, would rather lead them to some hiding-place than bring them back again. Throughout that whole fortnight they carried out an arduous hunt for them. But Thessala, who is guiding them, leads them so safely by her arts and magic that they feel no dread or fear at all the emperor's might. And though they spend the nights in no town or city, they have everything they want or desire just as readily as they are used to, or more so; for Thessala seeks out, obtains and brings to them whatever they wish. Now they are no longer followed or hunted by anyone, because everybody has headed back for home.

6672 Cligés, however, is not idle. He went to his great-uncle King Arthur, having sought until he found him; and to him he made his protest and complaint about his uncle the emperor who, to disinherit him, had disloyally taken a wife he should not have had, since he had pledged to his father that never in his life would he marry. The king says he will go with a fleet before Constantinople and will fill a thousand ships with knights and three thousand with men-at-arms, so that no city, borough or town and no castle, however strong or lofty, will be able to withstand their assaults. And Cligés did not forget to thank the king then for the aid he offers him. The king has all the high nobles of his land sought and summoned; and he has ships, galleys, transport vessels and barks found and equipped. He has a hundred ships filled and loaded with shields, lances, bucklers and knights' armour. The king makes such massive preparations for war that not even Caesar's or Alexander's matched them. At his summons there gathered all England, Flanders, Normandy, France and Brittany and all the men as far as the Spanish passes.*

6706 They were just on the point of crossing the sea when messengers arrived from Greece to put off the voyage and stop the departure of the king and his troops. With the messengers who came was the very trustworthy John, for he would never verify or report anything that was untrue or he was not certain of. The messengers were important men from Greece in search of Cligés; and they looked and asked for him until they found him at the king's court. They said to him: "God save you, lord, in the name of all those of your empire! Greece is made over and Constantinople given to you by virtue of the right you have to them. Though you do not know it, your uncle has died of the grief he suffered because he could not find you. His grief was so great that he went out of his mind and never drank or ate again, but died a madman. Good lord, come back now! For all your barons summon you: they want you urgently and call for you, wishing to make you emperor." There were some who were happy at this situation and others who would gladly have left their homes and would have been delighted had the army left for Greece; but the journey is completely abandoned, for the king sends his men away, and the army disbands and its members return home. Cligés, anxious to return to Greece and in no mind to linger, makes his preparations in haste. Having made ready and taken leave of the king and all his friends, he then set out, taking Fenice with him.

6748 They do not stop until they are in Greece, where the people receive them with great joy as is fitting for their rightful lord; and they give him his beloved as his wife and crown them both together. Of his sweetheart he has made his wife; but he calls her his sweetheart and his lady, so that in this way she does not lose his love as his sweetheart; and she loves him too just as one should a lover.* And each day their love grew stronger; and he never doubted her or found fault with her at all. *Nor was she ever kept shut away as has since been the case with those ladies who succeeded her; for never again has there been an emperor who was not afraid of being deceived by his wife, once he had heard tell how Fenice deceived Alis, first by the potion he drank and then by that other ruse. For

this reason the empress, whoever she might be and however rich
and noble, is guarded in Constantinople as in a prison; for the
emperor does not trust her so long as he remembers this other lady,
but always has her kept in a room, more out of fear than in case of
sunburn. And no male will ever accompany her unless he is a
eunuch from childhood: with them there is no fear or anxiety that
Love will ensnare them in his bonds.

Here ends the work of Chrétien.   6784

LANCELOT
(THE KNIGHT OF THE CART)

Since my lady of Champagne* wishes me to undertake the writing of a romance, I shall very gladly do so as one who (and I utter no word of flattery) is entirely at her disposal for the performance of any task in the world. But another might set about it with the intention of flattering and might say, and I would bear him out, that this is the lady who surpasses all others alive by as much as the warm wind that blows in May and April surpasses the other winds. I am not one, I swear, who would wish to flatter his lady. Shall I say the countess is worth as many queens as a gem is worth pearls and sards? Certainly not: I shall not mention it; yet it is true, whether I like it or not. But I will go so far as to say that her bidding is more important for this work than any inspiration or effort I might put into it. CHRÉTIEN begins his book about the Knight of the Cart. Its subject-matter and treatment* are supplied and given to him by the countess, and he puts his mind to it without contributing anything beyond his effort and application. Now he starts his account.

31 King Arthur, one Ascension Day, had left Caerleon and held a most magnificent court at Camelot* with all the splendour appropriate to the day. After their meal, the king did not leave those in his company. In the hall there were many nobles; and the queen was there too and with her, I believe, numerous beautiful courtly ladies conversing easily in French. Kay, who had waited at the tables, was eating with those who had served with him; and as he was sitting there at his meal, all of a sudden here is a knight arriving at court well equipped and fully armed. And, thus arrayed, the knight went right up to the king where he sat among his nobles. He gave him no greeting, but said: "King Arthur, I hold in captivity knights, ladies and maidens from your land and your household. However, I give you this news of them not because I intend to return them to you: on the contrary, I wish to tell and inform you that you lack the strength and resources to be able to get them back. And you may be sure you'll die without ever being in a position to help them." The king replies that he must put up with this, if he can do nothing about it, though he is deeply grieved on that account.

66 The knight then makes as if he wishes to leave and turns away, not staying before the king, but going as far as the hall door. Yet he does not go down the steps, but stops there, with the words: "King, if there is in your court so much as one knight whom you trust enough to dare hand over to him the queen, to be taken after me into those woods where I'm heading, I'll promise to wait for him there; and, if he can win her from me and manage to bring her back, I'll return to you all the prisoners held captive in my land." Many in the palace heard this, and it set the court in a turmoil.

84 Kay, hearing this news as he was eating with the servants, leaves his meal and comes straight to the king and, with every appearance of anger, addresses him thus: "King, I've given you very long, faithful and loyal service. Now I take my leave and shall go away, for I'll not serve you any further. I have no intention or desire to serve you from now on." The king is saddened by what he hears; and as soon as he is able to reply, he at once says to him: "Do you mean this, or are you joking?" And Kay replies: "My good lord king, I've no mind to joke now, but am quite definitely taking my leave. I don't ask from you any other reward or wages for my service. That's what I'm determined to do now: to be off, without delay."—"Is it out of anger or defiance that you want to leave?" asked the king. "Seneschal, stay at court as usual, and you may be sure that I have nothing in this world I would not give you without hesitation just to keep you here."—"Sire," says Kay, "it's no use: I'd not accept a bushel a day of the purest gold." Imagine the king's great despair as he then goes off to the queen. "My lady," says he, "you've no idea what the seneschal wants from me! He's asking for his leave and saying he won't be at my court any longer – I don't know why. What he refuses to do for me he'll readily do if you ask him. Go to him, my dear lady! Since he doesn't deign to stay for me, beg him to do so for your sake, even if it means falling at his feet; for I'd never be happy again without his company."

130 The king sends the queen away to the seneschal, and off she goes to him. Finding him with the others, she went up to him and said: "Kay, you may be quite sure that I'm extremely upset at what I've heard about you. I've been told, to my sorrow, that you want to leave the king's service. Where did you get this idea? What is your motive? I don't now think of you at all as sensible and courtly, as I used to. I want to beg you to stay. Stay, I beseech you!"—"My

lady," he says, "I thank you; but I wouldn't remain here." Again the queen pleads with him, joined by the whole company of knights. And Kay tells her her efforts will be quite fruitless. Then the queen falls full length at his feet.* Kay begs her to rise, but she refuses: she will never get up again until he agrees to do as she wishes. Kay then promised her to stay, provided the king will first agree to what he will propose and that she will herself consent to it. "Kay," says she, "whatever it is, both I and he will agree to it. Now come along, and we'll tell him you will stay on this condition." Kay goes with the queen, and they come before the king. "My lord," says the queen, "I've kept Kay here after a great deal of trouble; but I bring him to you on the understanding that you will do what he proposes." The king sighed with joy, saying that whatever his request to him may be, he will do as he wishes.

173 "Sire," says Kay, "this, then, is what I want and the nature of the favour you've promised me; and I think myself very fortunate that I shall have it, thanks to you: you've agreed, sire, to hand over to me my lady here, and we shall go after the knight who is waiting for us in the forest." This saddens the king, yet he makes her over to him, for he never went back on his word; but the distress and grief it caused him were clearly evident on his face. The queen too was extremely dejected; and everyone throughout the building says that what Kay had asked and sought was arrogant, outrageous and absurd. Then the king took the queen by the hand with the words: "My lady, it is inevitable that you must go away with Kay." And Kay says: "Hand her over to me now; and have no fear at all, for I'll bring her back, quite happy and unharmed, without fail."

198 The king entrusts her to him, and he leads her away. Everybody follows them out, all very troubled, without exception. You may be sure the seneschal was fully armed; and his horse was brought into the middle of the courtyard, and beside it a palfrey fit for a queen. The queen comes to this palfrey, which was neither fiery nor impetuous. Miserable and depressed, the queen sighs as she mounts. Then, softly so that no one might hear her, she said: *"Oh! If only you knew, you would never, I think, allow me to be led away a single step without opposition!" She thought she had said that very quietly; but Count Guinable, who was close to her when she mounted, did hear. When they left, every man and woman watching grieved as bitterly as if she lay dead in her coffin, not believing she would ever come back again in her lifetime.

222   The seneschal in his recklessness leads her to where the other knight awaits him. But no one was sufficiently concerned to take the trouble to follow him until my lord Gawain said openly to his uncle the king: "Sire, you've done an extremely silly thing which astonishes me. But if you take my advice, while they're still close at hand you and I and anyone else who wants to come will follow them. Nothing could keep me from going after them immediately: it would not do at all if we didn't follow them at least until we knew what will happen to the queen and how Kay will acquit himself."—"Ah, good nephew," said the king, "now that's a very chivalrous suggestion. And since this is what you're set on doing, order our horses to be brought out, bridled and saddled, so that it only remains to set out."

247   At once the horses are brought and saddled with all their trappings. The king is the first to mount, followed by my lord Gawain and all the others, just as fast as they can. Anxious to be in the company, everybody sets out as he pleases, some of them armed and many without arms. My lord Gawain was armed and had two chargers led along by two squires. Then as they approached the forest they saw Kay's horse running out; and they recognised it and saw that both reins of the bridle were snapped. The horse came riderless, with its stirrup-leathers blood-stained and the cantle of its saddle broken and battered. This upsets them all, and they exchange winks and nudges. My lord Gawain was riding well ahead of the whole company; and before long he saw a knight approaching at a walk on a horse that was weary to the point of exhaustion, breathing hard and lathered with sweat.

276   First the knight greeted my lord Gawain, and then Sir Gawain him. And, recognising Sir Gawain, the knight said to him: "My lord, you see clearly that my horse is bathed in sweat and in such a state that it's no more use; and I suppose these two chargers are yours. So I would beg you now to give me either of them as a loan or gift, on the understanding that I'd return your service and favour." To this he replies: "Choose whichever of the two you prefer." The knight, in his pressing need, did not stop to pick out the better or more handsome or bigger one, but very quickly leapt on to the one he found nearest to him and at once galloped off on it. Then the one he had abandoned fell dead; for that day he had driven and worked it very hard and worn it out.

301 Without a pause the knight goes spurring through the forest with my lord Gawain following, pursuing him furiously until he comes down to the bottom of a hill. Having gone some distance, Gawain came upon the charger he had given the knight; but it was dead, and round it he saw the ground much trampled by horses and many signs of the shattering of shields and lances. To all appearances a great fight between several knights had taken place there, and he was very sorry and disappointed not to have been present. He did not linger there, but passed swiftly on until he happened to catch sight again of the knight, alone and on foot, fully armed, with his helmet laced, his shield at his neck and his sword girt. He had caught up with a cart.

323 In those days the cart was put to the same use as pillories are now; and in every fair-sized town where now one finds over three thousand of them, there was at that time just one; and that, like the pillories, was used for all those guilty of treason and murder, for those defeated in judicial combat, and for thieves who had stolen the property of others or engaged in violent highway robbery. Anyone caught committing a crime was put in the cart and led through all the streets, thereafter losing all his legal rights and never again being heard or honoured or welcomed in any court. It was at that time that, because of the carts' sinister nature, the saying originated: "Whenever you see a cart in your path, cross yourself and turn your thoughts to God, so that it does not bring you bad luck."

347 The knight, on foot and without his lance, comes up behind the cart; and, seeing a dwarf on the shafts holding a long switch in his hand like a carter, he says to him: "Dwarf! Tell me in God's name if you've seen my lady the queen pass this way." The boorish, vulgar dwarf was not prepared to give him any news of her, saying instead: "If you want to get into this cart I'm driving, you'll be able to find out by tomorrow what has happened to the queen." With that he went on his way without waiting even a moment for him. Before he climbs in the knight hesitates merely for two steps; but it was unfortunate for him that he did so and unfortunate that his fear of shame stopped him from jumping in at once, for he will rue the consequences.

369 But Reason,* who is at odds with Love, tells him to avoid getting in, warning and instructing him to do and engage in nothing that

might bring him shame or reproach. Reason, who dares tell him this, is not in the heart but the mouth; but Love, who bids and urges him to climb quickly into the cart, is enclosed within his heart. It being Love's wish, he jumps in regardless of the shame, since Love commands and wills it. My lord Gawain hurriedly gallops after the cart; and, when he finds the knight sitting in it, he is astonished. Then he asked the dwarf: "Give me news of the queen, if you have any." And the dwarf said: "If you hate yourself as much as this knight sitting here, get in with him if you like, and I'll take you after her." When my lord Gawain heard that, he thought it sheer madness and refused to climb in, for it would be a very bad exchange to swap a horse for a cart. "But go wherever you wish, and I shall go along with you."

399 Then they set off, the one on horseback, the other two riding on the cart, and together they follow the same road. Late that evening they come to a stronghold which was, I assure you, very splendid and fine. They all three went in through the gate. The people were amazed at the knight being carried by the dwarf in his cart; but rather than discuss it quietly among themselves, all of them, great and small, old men and children, shout abuse at him, filling the streets with their clamour, so that the knight hears a great deal of slander and abuse at his expense. They all ask: "What punishment is this knight going to suffer? Will he be flayed or hanged, drowned or burnt in a fire of thorns? Say, dwarf – you who're driving him: what's the crime he was caught committing? Is he convicted of theft? Is he a murderer, or the loser in a judicial fight?"

422 The dwarf kept silent, not uttering a single word. He drives the knight to his lodging-place, with Gawain continuing to follow the dwarf towards a keep near the town and on the same level. On the other side were meadows, and the tower was sited close to them on a high, dark rock that fell precipitously away. Gawain, on horseback, follows the cart into the keep.* In the hall they met an elegantly dressed damsel, more beautiful than any other in the land; and coming with her they see two lovely, attractive maidens. As soon as they saw my lord Gawain, they greeted him with every sign of joy, then asked about the knight: "Dwarf, what wrong has this knight done, for you to be driving him like a cripple?" He was not prepared to give them any explanation, but had the knight get down from the cart, then made off without their knowing where.

My lord Gawain dismounts, whereupon men-servants come forward and disarm them both. The damsel had two mantles brought, trimmed with vair, and these they put on. When it was time for supper, the food was handsomely served. The damsel sat beside my lord Gawain at the meal. They would on no account have wished to change their lodging to look for better; for all that evening the damsel showed them great honour and provided them with good and pleasant company.

463 When they had sat up for a long while, two high, long beds were made up in the middle of the hall; and alongside them was a further one, finer and more luxurious than the others; for, as the tale affirms, it offered every comfort that could be desired in a bed. When the appropriate moment came to retire, the damsel took both her guests for whom she had provided lodging and, showing them the two handsome long, wide beds, said: "These two beds out here are prepared for your own use. But in that further one nobody lies who has not merited it: it was not set up to be used by you." The knight who arrived on the cart, scornful and contemptuous of the damsel's prohibition, at once replies to her: "Tell me on what grounds this bed is forbidden." She answers without reflection, her mind quite made up. "It's not for you", she says, "to ask or want to know. Once a knight has been in a cart, he suffers shame on earth, and it's not right for him to concern himself with the matter you've asked me about, and still less for him to lie there, for he might quickly pay for it. It certainly hasn't been decked out so richly for you to lie on! If you even thought of doing so, you'd pay a very heavy price."—"You'll see," he says, "all in good time."—"I'll see?"—"Yes indeed."—"That's as may be."—"By my head," says the knight, "I don't know who's going to pay for it! Whoever may be vexed or annoyed, I intend to lie and rest comfortably on this bed."

507 Then he at once undressed on the bed, which was long and raised half an ell above the other two and was covered with a yellow velvet cloth, a coverlet starred with gold. The furs were not at all of vair worn bald but of sable, and the coverlet over him was quite fit for the use of a king. The mattress was not made of thatch or pea-straw or old matting. At midnight, down like a thunderbolt from the rafters shot a lance, point downwards, and almost pinned the knight through the body to the coverlet and white sheets and to

the bed where he lay. On the lance there was a pennon that was all ablaze. The coverlet, sheets and mattress all caught fire together; and the head of the lance grazed the knight's side so that it removed a little of his skin but without really wounding him. Then the knight sat up, put out the fire and, taking the lance, hurled it into the middle of the hall, though without leaving his bed to do so: in fact he lay down again and slept as soundly as before.

539 Very early in the morning, as day broke, the damsel of the tower had preparations for mass made for them and saw that they were wakened and got up. When mass had been sung for them, the knight (the one who had sat in the cart) seated himself by the windows overlooking the meadowland and, deep in thought, gazed at the fields below. The maiden had come to the next window, where my lord Gawain had chatted with her for a while in private,* though I do not know what was said or the subject of their conversation. But they were still leaning on the window ledge when they saw a litter being carried along down in the meadows beside the river with a knight lying on it* and beside it three damsels, mourning bitterly. Behind the litter they saw a procession coming with, at its head, a tall knight leading a beautiful lady on his left. The knight at the window recognised her as the queen. For as long as he could he continued to gaze at her intently and with great pleasure. Then, when he could no longer see her, he wanted to let himself fall and drop to the ground below; and he was already half-way out when my lord Gawain saw him and, pulling him back, said to him: "Calm yourself, sir, I beg you! For God's sake, don't ever again think of doing such a crazy thing! It's very wrong of you to find your life repugnant."—"No, he's right," says the damsel; "for won't the news of his calamity become common knowledge? Since he's been in a cart, he really should want to be killed, because he'd be better dead than alive! From now on his life is shameful, despicable and wretched."

587 Then the knights asked for their armour and donned it, whereupon the damsel acted in a courtly, handsome and generous manner. For, having heaped mockery and ridicule on the knight, she gave him a horse and lance as a token of good-will and reconciliation. The knights took their leave of the damsel in a courtly, polite fashion; and, bidding her farewell, they left in the direction they had seen the procession take. And so they rode out of the strong-

hold without anyone speaking to them and quickly went past the place where they had seen the queen. They did not catch up with the company, since it was proceeding at a rapid pace. From the meadows they passed into an enclosed area of woodland and found a paved road. Through the forest they travelled until possibly six in the morning, when they came across a damsel at a crossroads.

612 Having both greeted her, they ask her urgently to tell them, if she knows, where the queen has been taken. Her reply is reasonable: "In return for a promise on your part I could easily direct you and put you on the right road; and I would tell you the name of the land and that of the knight who is abducting her. But anyone who wished to enter that land would have very great trials to undergo and would suffer great tribulations before he arrived there." My lord Gawain says to her: "So help me God, young lady, I give you my firm promise to place my every effort at your service whenever it pleases you, provided you tell me the truth." And the knight who had been in the cart did not say he promises her his entire effort, but declares instead, as one to whom love gives strength and power and courage in every situation, that he promises to do anything she desires, without hesitation or fear, and subjects himself completely to her will. "In that case I shall tell you," she says. Then the maiden gives them this information:* "I assure you, my lords, that Meleagant, a tall, strapping knight who is the King of Gorre's son, has seized her and taken her into the kingdom from which no stranger returns, but is forced to stay in that land in servitude and exile."

648 Then they ask her further: "Damsel, where is that land? How can we find the road there?" She replies: "You'll soon know. But you may be sure you'll find many obstacles and perilous passages on the way; for it's not easy to get in without the permission of its ruler, whose name is King Bademagu. However, it is possible to enter by two highly dangerous roads and two most treacherous crossings: one is called the Water Bridge, because the bridge runs under the water, of which there is as much below it to the bottom as there is above, neither more nor less, the bridge being precisely halfway up; and it is only a foot and a half wide and of the same thickness. This is no palatable choice to make, and yet it is the less dangerous (and there are numerous hazards besides that I won't mention). The other bridge is worse and far more perilous; and it

has never been crossed by any man, for it's like a sharp sword, which is why everybody calls it the Sword Bridge. I've told you the truth as far as I can give it you."

680 They then put another request to her: "If you're prepared to, young lady, please direct us to these two roads." And the damsel replies: "Here's the direct route to the underwater bridge, and the one over there goes straight to the Sword Bridge." Then, for his part, the knight who had been a passenger in the cart says: "My lord, I'm happy to leave the choice to you: pick one of these two roads and let me have the other – you take the one you prefer."—"Upon my word," says my lord Gawain, "both the one passage and the other are extremely dangerous and difficult: I can't make a sensible choice and scarcely know which to pick. But it's not right for me to hesitate when you've offered me the choice: I'll take on the underwater bridge."—"Then it's up to me to go without any fuss to the Sword Bridge," says the other; "and I agree to that." With that, all three go their separate ways, having courteously commended each other to God. And when the girl sees them leaving, she says: "Each of you owes me a favour to be paid as I wish and whenever I want to accept it. Take care not to forget that!"—"We certainly won't, dear friend," say both of the knights.

714 Thereupon each sets off on his own, the one from the cart deep in thought like a man without strength or defence against love's domination.* And his thoughts are such that he becomes oblivious of himself, unaware of whether or not he exists, not remembering his name, not knowing if he is armed or not or where he is going or where he comes from; he remembers no single being save one, and on her account he has put the others from his mind. He is so intent on her alone that he neither sees nor hears anything. And his horse carries him on very swiftly, following no roundabout road, but the best and most direct; and it presses on until it has carried him by chance on to a heath. On this heath was a ford, on the other side of which was an armed knight who guarded it; and with him he had a damsel, who had come on a palfrey. It was already late in the afternoon, yet the knight had still not given up or tired of his reverie. The horse, which was very thirsty, saw the ford quite clearly and, when it did so, galloped towards the water.

745 The man on the other side shouted: "Knight, I guard the ford and forbid you to use it!" Prevented by his thoughts, the knight

neither heeded nor heard him; and the horse continued its swift dash towards the water. The other shouts to him to act wisely by getting well away from the ford, for that is not the way to cross; and he swears by the heart within his breast to strike him if he sets foot in it. But the knight hears nothing of this; so he calls out to him a third time: "Knight, don't enter the ford against my wishes when I forbid it; for, by my head, I'll strike you as soon as I see you in that ford!" He is so deep in thought that he does not hear him. The horse jumps quickly into the ford, goes out from the side and eagerly begins to drink. The guardian says he will pay for this and neither his shield nor the hauberk on his back will ever save him. Then he sets his horse off at a canter and from a canter urges it into a full gallop, and gives the knight such a blow that he knocks him down flat into the middle of the ford which he had forbidden him to cross and sends his lance and the shield at his neck flying.

777 When he feels the water, the knight starts, then jumps to his feet quite bemused like someone waking from sleep; and he listens and looks around, wondering who it can be who has struck him. Then, seeing the other knight, he says to him: "Fellow, tell me why you've struck me when I didn't know of your presence and hadn't wronged you in any way."—"Upon my word you had," says the other. "Didn't you treat me with contempt when I warned you three times against using the ford, telling you at the very top of my voice? You must have heard my challenge at least two or three times, yet went in against my wishes; and I told you plainly I'd strike you as soon as I saw you in the ford." To that the knight replies: "A curse on anyone, myself included, who ever saw or heard you! It's quite possible I was deep in thought when you forbade me to use the ford. But you may be sure it would be unlucky for you that you did so if I could get at least one of my hands on your bridle." The other replies: "What would happen then? You can hold me by the bridle here and now, if you dare take it. I don't care a handful of ashes about your arrogant threats." He replies: "That's all I want. Whatever may come of it, I'd like to get my hands on you now."

813 Thereupon the guardian knight advances into the middle of the ford, and the other takes him by the rein with his left hand and by the thigh with his right, then tugs and pulls and clings on so hard that he cries out, for it seems to him he is pulling his leg right out of

his body. So he begs him to let go, and says: "Knight, if you're happy to fight me on equal terms, then take your shield and horse and lance, and joust with me." He replies: "I swear I won't, for I think you'd make off as soon as you got out of my clutches." When the other heard that, he was quite ashamed and retorted: "Knight, just mount your horse without worrying, and I promise you faithfully to neither retreat nor run away. What you've said to me is shameful and I find it offensive." He answers him once more: "You'll give me your solemn pledge first: I want you to swear to me that you will neither flee nor withdraw and that you won't touch or approach me until you see me mounted; and I'll have done you a very good turn by letting you go when I have you in my grasp." Having no choice, the man gave his word. And when the knight had received his pledge, he retrieved his shield and lance, which had continued to float away in the ford and were already a long way downstream; and then he returned to get his horse. When he had it and was mounted, he took his shield by the straps and set the lance in its rest. Then each spurs against the other as hard as their horses can carry them.

856 The knight responsible for defending the ford launches the first attack on the other, striking him so hard that his lance shatters completely. The latter then gives him such a blow that he knocks him into the ford to land flat in mid-stream so that the water closes over him. Then he draws back and dismounts, confident that he could drive before him and put to rout a hundred like him. He draws his steel sword from its sheath; and the other jumps up and draws his own fine, flashing blade. Then they come together in hand-to-hand combat, thrusting forward and protecting themselves with the shields which gleam with gold. Without pause or respite they use their swords to good effect, courageously exchanging many stout blows until the combat has lasted so long that the knight of the cart feels great shame in his heart, saying he will do scant justice to the expedition he has undertaken when he has needed so long to defeat a single knight. If yesterday he had found a hundred of his sort in a valley, he does not believe or imagine they would have found any defence against him; so he is very grieved and angry to have now grown so much weaker that he is not making his blows tell and is wasting time. Then he rushes at him and presses him so hard that he gives way before him and flees,

surrendering the ford and crossing to him, though extremely loath to do so. But the knight from the cart continues to chase him until he falls forward on to his hands, then runs up to him, swearing by everything in sight that it was unlucky for him that he knocked him into the ford and brought him out of his reverie.

898 The damsel whom the knight had brought with him, on hearing these threats, is very frightened and begs him for her sake to spare his life. He tells her that indeed he will not, nor can he have mercy on her account, since he has acted so shamefully towards him. He then makes for him with drawn sword; and in terror the knight says: "For God's sake and my own do grant it, the mercy I ask of you!" He replies: "As God may be my aid, no one ever did me such wrong that if he asked me for mercy in God's name I did not then have mercy on him once, for God's sake, as is right. And I'll do the same for you, since I should not refuse it to you when you've asked it of me. But first you'll pledge me to give yourself up to me as my prisoner wherever I wish and when I summon you." This he pledged him most reluctantly. In turn, the damsel says: "Sir knight, in your kindness, now he has sought your mercy and you've granted it to him, if ever you released anyone from captivity, then release this captive for me! Absolve him from surrendering himself prisoner for my sake on condition that, when the opportunity arises, I shall do you any favour you please to the best of my ability." Then, having accepted her assurance expressed in these terms, he made the knight over to her freed from his obligation. She feels embarrassed and anxious in this situation, thinking he may ravish her, for she would not have wished that.* But he departs forthwith, the knight and maiden commending him to God and asking his leave, which he gives them.

941 Then he goes on his way until, late in the evening, he met a damsel coming his way who was exceedingly beautiful and attractive, elegantly dressed and adorned. This damsel greets him discreetly and politely, and he replies: "May God keep you healthy and happy, young lady!" Then she said to him: "My home, sir, is all ready for your lodging, if you're prepared to accept it. But you'll be given hospitality on condition that you sleep with me: those are the terms of my offer." Many people would have thanked her five hundred times for this favour; yet it leaves him quite miserable, and he gives her a very different reply: "I thank you, damsel, for your

offer of hospitality and am most grateful for it. But, if you were agreeable, I could well do without the sleeping arrangement."—"By my eyes," says the maiden, "my offer depends on that!" Then, as there is nothing else for it, he agrees to her condition. It pains him deeply to consent; and whilst just that alone hurts him, he will feel gravely distressed when he goes to bed. And the damsel, who takes him with her, will suffer much anguish and sorrow. She may perhaps feel such love for him that she will not want to free him from his obligation. As soon as he had met her wishes and granted what she desired, she led him into a castle bailey fairer than any this side of Thessaly, being totally enclosed by a high wall and a deep moat. Inside there was no man other than the one she was bringing there.

983 For her residence here she had had many handsome rooms built and a very large, spacious hall. Riding beside a river they came to the lodging-quarters, a drawbridge having been lowered to let them cross. They went over the bridge and found the hall, which was roofed with tiles, open. Entering through the door that stood open for them, they saw a banqueting table covered with a broad, white cloth, on which the meal had been set and the burning candles placed in their holders, and the silver-gilt goblets stood together with two pots, one full of mulberry wine and the other of strong white wine. Beside the table on one end of a bench they found two basins filled with warm water for washing their hands, and on the other they saw a beautiful white, finely worked towel for drying them. They neither found nor saw any serving-lad, attendant or squire inside.

1010 The knight removes the shield from his neck and hangs it on a hook, then takes his lance and puts it up on a rack. Then he at once jumps down from his horse and the damsel from hers. The knight was very pleased that she did not want to wait for him to help her down. As soon as she has dismounted, without any pause or delay she runs to a room to fetch for him a short mantle of fine woollen cloth, which she puts on him. The hall was by no means dark, though the stars were already shining: there were so many great twisted candles burning inside that it was brilliantly illuminated. Once she had placed the mantle on his shoulders, she said to him: "My friend, here's the water and towel: no one is offering or passing it to you because, you notice, there's nobody in here but me. When you wish and would like to, do wash your hands and sit down: as you can see, the time and the food call for it." He washes, and willingly and gladly takes his seat, whilst she sits down beside him; and they eat and drink together until the time comes to leave the table.

1043 When they had risen from the meal, the maiden said to the knight: "Sir, if it's no trouble to you, go and amuse yourself outside; but please only stay there until you think I may be in bed. Don't be vexed or displeased, for then you can come straight in, if you want to keep the promise you made me." He replies: "I'll keep my promise to you and come back when I think it's time." Then he goes out and stays in the courtyard a very long while until he has to go back in; for he must keep his pledge. He makes his way back into the hall, but without finding his would-be mistress, for she is not there. Failing to find or see her, he said: "Wherever she may be, I'll look for her until I find her."

1066 He wastes no more time before going to search for her on account of the promise he had made her.* On entering one room, he hears a maiden crying out; and it was none other than the one with whom he was supposed to go to bed. Then he sees the door of another room standing open; and going across there, he sees before his very eyes a knight who, having thrown her on her back, is holding her, with her clothing removed, across the bed. Feeling sure he would come to her rescue, she screamed out: "Help! Help, sir knight who are my guest! If you don't get this man off me, I'll find no one else to remove him; and if you don't help me quickly, he'll rape me in front of you. It's you who should lie with me as you promised to, so is this man to have his will of me by force while you stand there watching? Noble knight, do your best and rescue me quickly!"

1092 He sees the man brutally holding the damsel stripped to the navel and is very ashamed and distressed to see his naked body touching hers, though without any feeling of jealousy or any risk of his ever being cuckolded by him. At the entrance, however, were doorkeepers: two fully armed knights holding drawn swords. Behind them stood four men-at-arms, each holding an axe fully capable of cutting through a cow's spine as easily as through a root of juniper or broom. Our knight stops at the door, saying: "God, what can I do? I've set out on no less a task than going to Queen

Guenevere's assistance. I shouldn't have the heart of a hare when I'm on this quest for her. If Cowardice lends me his heart and I do his bidding, I'll not achieve my goal. If I stop here, I'm disgraced. Now I'm thoroughly ashamed of having mentioned stopping. I'm very sad and downhearted; and I'm full of shame now and so sorry that I wish I'd die for having stayed here so long. May God never have mercy on me, and I don't say it out of pride, if I wouldn't far rather die with honour than live in shame. What honour would I gain from it if the way were clear for me and these people gave me leave to pass through without opposition? In that case, without a word of a lie, the worst man living would get through too. And I can hear this wretched maiden calling for help again and again, reminding me of my promise and blaming me most bitterly."

1138 He at once goes to the doorway and pushes his head and neck through; and looking up towards the lintel he sees two swords coming down. He draws back. And the knights were unable to check their strokes, which they had launched with such force that they drove their swords into the floor and smashed them both to pieces. When he sees they are broken, he has less regard for the axes and fears and dreads them less. Hurling himself among the men-at-arms, he strikes first one and then another with his elbows. At these two nearest him he lunges with his elbows and arms to such effect that he flattens both of them. The third having missed him, he is attacked by the fourth, who strikes him so that he cuts his mantle and shirt, and badly grazes the white flesh by his shoulder, causing the blood to run down from it. But instead of showing any hesitation or complaining about his wound, he presses on harder still, finally seizing by the forelock the man who was violating his hostess. He is intent on keeping his promise and pledge to her before he leaves. Whether the man likes it or not, he drags him up.

1169 Then the one who had missed him comes at him as fast as he can, raising his weapon again, quite expecting to cleave his head down to the teeth with his axe. But defending himself cleverly, he thrusts the knight forward so that he receives the axeman's stroke at the point where the shoulder joins his neck, with the result that they are split apart. Quickly wrenching the axe from the other's grasp, our knight takes it and lets go of the man he has been holding; for he must look to his defence, since the knights along with the three others with axes are bearing down on him. They attack him very viciously; and he jumps nimbly between the bed and the wall, saying: "Come on now, all of you! If there were thirty-seven of you, now I've got this much cover you'll have a good fight on your hands. I'll never be overcome by you!" Then the maiden, who is watching, says: "By my eyes, you've nothing to worry about from now on when I'm here." Immediately she calls off the knights and men-at-arms, whereupon they go out promptly and without objection. And the damsel continues: "Sir, you've defended me well against all my household. Now come along where I take you." They go into the hall hand in hand. But he was not at all pleased, for he could well have done without her.

1207 In the middle of the hall a bed had been set up on which the sheets were by no means dirty, but white and fine and broad. The bedding did not consist of chopped straw or rough mattresses. Over the bed was spread a coverlet made of two cloths of flowered silk. The damsel lies down, but without taking off her chemise. Then the knight had great trouble taking off his hose and undoing the knots. He could not help sweating with apprehension; nevertheless, in the midst of this anguish, his pledge has the upper hand and gets the better of him. Is this, then, a matter of force? — Virtually it is. He is being forced to go and lie with the damsel: his pledge summons and calls him to do so. He takes his time to lie down, but without removing his shirt any more than she had taken off her chemise. He takes great care not to touch her, but instead draws away from her and lies with his back turned, saying no more than would a lay-brother, to whom speech is forbidden when he lies in bed. Not once does he turn his eyes towards her or anywhere else.

1235 He cannot show her any sign of affection. Why not? — Because he does not feel it in his heart, though she is extremely beautiful and attractive; but he does not find pleasing or desirable what everyone else considers beautiful and attractive. The knight has only one heart; and that no longer belongs to him, but is entrusted to someone else, so that he cannot lend it out elsewhere. Love, who rules over all hearts, has it remain in just one place. All hearts? — No: only those he values. And the person Love deigns to rule should value himself all the more. Love valued the heart of this man so highly that he held it more than all others in his sway, affording him such great pride that I would not blame him at all if he rejects what Love forbids him and concentrates on what he desires.

1255 The maiden sees clearly and is aware that he dislikes her company and would gladly be rid of it and that, as he does not try to touch her, he would never ask anything more from her. So she said: "If you don't mind, sir, I shall leave. I'll go to bed in my own room, and you'll be more comfortable. I don't think you're very happy to have the pleasure of my company: but don't think badly of it if I tell you what I think. Now rest for the remainder of the night; for you've kept your promise to me so well that I can't properly ask a single thing more of you. So now I should like to commend you to God and then leave." With that she gets up. The knight is not at all sorry, but gladly lets her go, as one who is the true lover of someone else: of this the damsel sees clear evidence. So she came to her room and, having retired to bed naked, said to herself: "Since I met my first knight, I've never known a single one whom I would have thought worth a third of an Angevin penny when compared with this one. For my guess and belief is that he's bound on such a great mission that never did a knight dare to undertake one so perilous and fraught with difficulty. May God grant him success in it!" Thereupon she fell asleep and lay in bed until daylight appeared.

1293 As soon as dawn breaks she wakes and gets up. For his part, the knight wakes, dresses and gets ready, arming himself without waiting for help. Then the damsel comes to find him already dressed. "May this be a good day for you," she says when she sees him. "And for you too, damsel," comes the knight's reply. Then he says he is impatient to have his horse brought out for him. The maiden has it fetched for him and says: "Sir, I would accompany you for a fair distance on your road if you dared to take me with you and would escort me according to the convention and customs established in the kingdom of Logres* before our day." At that period the customs and rights decreed that a knight, finding a damsel or girl alone, if he wished to keep his good reputation, would no more treat her with less than total honour than he would cut his own throat; and should he rape her, he would be disgraced for ever in all courts. But if she had an escort, then another person wishing to fight a combat with him for her and win her by force of arms would be able to have his will of her without incurring any shame or reproach. That is why the damsel said that should he dare and be willing to escort her according to this custom, so that no other could do her any harm, then she would go with him. He tells her: "No one will ever cause you any trouble, I assure you, without first doing so to me."—"Then I wish to come," she says.

1338 She has her palfrey saddled, her order being promptly obeyed. The palfrey was led out for her, and the horse for the knight. They both mount without a squire and set off at a very fast pace. She speaks to him; but he pays no attention to anything she says to him, greatly disliking her talk and chatter: he enjoys meditating, and talk disturbs him. Again and again Love reopens the wound he has dealt him. Yet he never applied a plaster to it for its healing or relief, since he has no inclination or wish to look for a plaster or a doctor unless his wound grows worse. But that lady he would gladly seek . . .*

1356 Keeping to the right route, they follow roads and tracks until they come close to a spring, which was in the middle of a meadow and had a stone slab beside it. There on this slab was a comb of gilded ivory, forgotten by someone, I know not whom. Never since the time of Ysoré* had anyone, wise or foolish, ever seen such a splendid one. In the teeth of the comb there was almost a handful of hair, left by the lady who had used it.

1369 When the damsel notices the spring and sees the slab, not wanting the knight to see them, she turned on to another road. And he, indulging and delighting in his own most pleasant thoughts, is by no means quick to notice that she is diverting him from his route. However, when he has noticed, he fears he has been tricked, thinking she has turned aside and is going out of the way to avoid some peril. "Stop, damsel!" he says. "You're going wrong: come this way! I don't believe anyone ever went the right way by leaving this road." – "We'll do better by going this way, sir: I'm sure of it," says the maiden. And he replies: "I don't know what you have in mind, damsel; but you can see plainly enough that this is the proper beaten track. Having started out along it, I'll not go off in any other direction. So please come along, for I'm going to keep to this road."

1396 Then they proceed until they come near to the slab and see the comb. "Truly never, as far as I can remember," says the knight, "have I set eyes on such a fine comb as this one I see here."—"Give it me," says the maiden.—"Gladly, damsel," he says, then bends down and picks it up. As he holds it, he looks at it for a long time and gazes at the hair. Then she begins to laugh. Seeing this, he begs her to tell him the reason for her laughter. She replies: "Say no more about it: it will be some time before I tell you that!"—"Why?" says he.—"Because I don't want to." Hearing this, he calls upon her on the assumption that lovers should on no account ever break faith with one another: "Damsel, if you feel true love for anyone or anything, I request, implore and beg you by that love not to keep the reason from me any longer."—"Your appeal", she says, "is certainly very pressing; so I'll tell you without a word of a lie. If I was ever sure of anything, that comb was the queen's – I know it. And believe me about one thing: those very beautiful bright, shining hairs that you see left between the teeth came from the queen's head. They never grew in any other meadow!" The knight said: "There are many queens and kings, I swear. So who is it you mean?" Then she said: "Upon my word, good sir, King Arthur's wife."

1436 Hearing that, he had not enough strength to stop himself collapsing, but was forced to lean forward on the saddle-bow. When the damsel saw this, she was amazed and alarmed, thinking he would fall. Do not blame her for being afraid, because she thought he had fainted. So, more or less, he had, having come so close to doing so; for he felt such a pain in his heart that for a long while he had lost his colour and power of speech. The maiden dismounted and ran as fast as she could to support and help him, since not for anything would she have wanted to see him fall to the ground. When he saw her, he felt ashamed and said to her: "What's your purpose in coming up to me here?" Do not suppose the damsel would admit to him the true reason, for he would have been ashamed and distressed if she confessed the truth, and it would hurt and offend him. So, taking care not to tell the truth, she said with extreme tact: "I came, sir, to get the comb: that's why I dismounted, for I was so anxious to have it I couldn't wait to get my hands on it." He is happy for her to have the comb and gives it to her, having removed the hairs so gently that he does not break a single one.

1472 Never will the eye of man see anything receive such reverence;* for he begins to adore them, putting them fully a hundred thousand times to his eyes and mouth, to his brow and his face, with every show of joy. They are his great treasure and delight. He places them against his breast, between his shirt and flesh, next to his heart. He would not exchange them for a cartload of emeralds or carbuncles.

Now he is confident that he will never suffer from boils or any other illness. He scorns potions of crushed pearl, pleurisy cures or theriac, or even the protection of Saint Martin and Saint James, having no need of their help, such is the faith he places in those hairs. But what were the hairs like? I shall be taken for a liar and a fool if I tell the truth about them. When the Saint Denis fair is at its height and stocked at its fullest, the plain fact is that the knight would not have wished for all the wealth there rather than his discovery of the hairs. And if you want the truth from me, gold refined a hundred thousand times and melted down again as often would, when placed against the hairs and seen beside them, be darker than the night compared with the brightest summer day there has been all this year.

1507 But why should I spin out the tale? The maiden very quickly mounts again, taking the comb with her, whilst he delights and revels in the hair which he keeps next to his breast. After the plain they come to a forest and take a short cut. Eventually their road narrows so they are forced to go in single file, as it would be quite impossible to take two horses abreast there. The maiden rides very quickly straight along this road ahead of her guest. Then, where it was at its narrowest, they see a knight approaching. As soon as she set eyes on him, the maiden recognised him and said: "Sir knight, do you see the man coming towards us fully armed and ready for a fight? He thinks he can certainly take me straight off with him without opposition: I'm sure that's what he has in mind. He loves me and is foolish to do so; and for a very long time he has been wooing me both in person and through his messengers. But my love's not for him because I couldn't love him on any account. So help me God, I'd rather kill myself than love him under any circumstances. I know well that at this moment he's as overjoyed and delighted as if he already had me for himself. But now I'll see what you can do, and now it will be revealed if you're gallant or not. Now I'll see and it will become clear whether having you as my escort will save me. If you can protect me, then I shall say in all truth that you're a valiant and very worthy man." And he replies: "Go on! Go on!", which was as much as to say: "That doesn't worry me; for you've no cause to be alarmed about anything you've told me."

1553 As they went along talking of these things, the knight, who was on his own, was not slow to advance in their direction. He headed for the two of them at the gallop, eager to make good speed because he thought his efforts would not be wasted and counted himself lucky to see the one he loved most. As soon as he gets near her, he greets her from his heart with the words: "May the one I most desire, but who gives me the least joy and the greatest pain, be welcome, wherever she comes from!" It is not proper for her to be so mean with her speech as not to return his greeting, with her tongue at least. The knight much appreciated the maiden's greeting, which did not sully her mouth or cost her anything. And had he at that moment been jousting and come through an entire tournament, he would not have been so proud of himself or have considered he had won as much honour or credit.

1579   Because of his increased conceit and self-esteem he grasped her bridle-rein, saying: "Now I'll take you away: I've been sailing a very good, straight course and come to an excellent port. Now I'm released from all my troubles: after the perils of the sea I've reached harbour, after great distress high delight, after severe pain sound health. Now I have all I desire, since I find you in circumstances that allow me to make off with you at once without suffering dishonour." And she says: "You've no business here, for this knight is escorting me."—"And a poor escort indeed it is," says he, "for I'm about to take you off! I fancy this knight would have eaten a bushel of salt before he could protect you from me: I don't believe I've ever seen one from whom I couldn't win you. And since I conveniently find you here, though it may well vex and displease him, I'll take you away under his very nose, despite all his best efforts."

1605   The other does not in the least lose his temper on hearing all his arrogant words but, without any insults or boasts, makes to defend her against him, saying: "Don't be hasty, sir, or waste your words; but moderate your speech a little. Your right to her will never be denied when you have it. You'll well understand that the maiden has come here under my escort. Let go of her! You've held her back too long; and anyway she's not concerned with you." The knight says he is prepared to be burnt if he does not take her away in spite of him. Then the other says: "It wouldn't do for me to let you go off with her. You may be sure I'd sooner fight for her. But if we really did want to fight, we couldn't possibly do so on this track. Let's rather go to a main road or into a meadow or on a heath." The knight replies that he asks nothing better and says: "I certainly agree fully to that: you're absolutely right, for this track is too narrow. Indeed, my horse would be so restricted that I'm afraid he'd break his leg before I could turn him round."

1635 He does then turn about with great difficulty, but without harming his horse or doing it any injury, and says: "I'm really very annoyed that we haven't come to grips in some open place in front of other men, for I'd have liked people to see which of us gives the better account of himself. But come now, and we'll look for a spot: we'll find a big, wide, open piece of ground close by." Then they go on until they come to a meadow. In this meadow were maidens, knights and damsels playing at various games, for it was a beautiful place. It was not just frivolous amusements they were engaged in, but backgammon and chess or, in other cases, dice games of different types. Most were playing at these games: the others were indulging in their own pastimes – dances, rounds and jigs, or were singing, tumbling, leaping or trying their strength at wrestling.

1661 A rather elderly knight, mounted on a Spanish sorrel, was on the other side of the meadow. His trappings and saddle were of gold, and his hair was greying. He had placed one hand elegantly on his hip and was watching the games and dancing, dressed in his shirt because of the fine weather and with a short mantle of fine cloth completely trimmed with vair about his shoulders. On the opposite side, beside a path, were as many as twenty-three armed men on good Irish steeds. As soon as the three arrive among them, they all cease their merry-making, and the meadows are filled with their cries: "See! Look at that knight who was driven in the cart! Let nobody keep playing any longer while he's here! A curse on anyone who tries to play on and on anyone who deigns to do so while he's about!"

1685 Meanwhile here is the man who loved the maiden and already claimed her as his own approaching the elderly knight and saying: "Sir, I'm overjoyed; and let anyone who wants to listen hear this: God has given me the one I've always most desired; and His gift wouldn't have been as great had He made me a crowned king, nor would I have been so grateful to Him or have gained so substantially, for this is a fine, handsome prize."—"I'm not sure it's yours yet," says the knight to his son, who promptly replies: "You're not sure? Can't you see, then? In God's name, sir, never doubt it when you can see I've got her: I met her on her way through that forest

I've just left. I think God brought her there for me, and I've taken
her as my own."—"I don't yet know if that man I see following you
consents to this: I think he's coming to claim her from you." While
these words were being exchanged, the dancing was stopped on
account of the knight they saw; and out of ill-will and contempt for
him they ceased their games and merriment.

1716 Our knight continued to advance quickly on the heels of the
maiden and said: "Give up this damsel, knight, for you've no right
to her! If you dare, I'll defend her against you here and now." Then
the old knight said: "Didn't I know it? Dear son, don't keep that
maiden any longer: just let her go."* This was not at all to his
liking: on the contrary, he swears never to give her up, saying:
"May God never grant me joy if I surrender her to him! I hold her
and shall keep her as my own property. The shoulder-strap and all
the arm fastenings of my shield will be burst, and I shall have no
more faith in my body or in my arms, my sword or my lance before I
give up my beloved to him." His father replies: "I'll not let you
fight, whatever you may say. You have too much confidence in
your own valour. Just do as I order you!" Arrogantly he retorts:
"What? Am I a child to be scared? I'm quite prepared to boast that
of the many knights in all the lands the sea encircles there's not one
so excellent that I'd give her up to him and whom I wouldn't expect
to bring to submission in a trice."

1750 His father says: "My dear son, I've no doubt that's what you
believe, so confident are you in your strength; but I don't want you
to take on this knight now or at all today." He replies: "It would be
shameful for me to follow your advice. A curse on anyone who
believes it and gives up on your account, and on me if it stops me
putting up a good fight! It's true that a man does poor deals with
those close to him: I'd do better to bargain elsewhere, for you're out
to cheat me. I'm certain I'd be better off among strangers. No one
who didn't know me would thwart my wishes, whereas you go
against them and frustrate them. I've all the more incentive because
you've found fault with me; for as you know, to decry what a man
or woman wants to do is to fan the flames of that desire. But may
God never bring me joy if I give up at all on your account: on the
contrary, I'll fight in spite of you."—"By the faith I owe the apostle
Saint Peter," says his father, "it's obvious to me now that I would
get nowhere by pleading. All my advice to you is wasted; but before

long I shall find a way of persuading you that, like it or not, you'll have to do just what I want, for I'll have the upper hand."

1784 With that he calls all the knights to him and orders them to seize his recalcitrant son, saying: "I'll have him bound rather than let him fight. You're all my vassals to a man and owe me your devotion and loyalty: by everything you hold from me, I both order and entreat you. He seems to me extremely foolish and acting most arrogantly to go against my wishes." They say they will seize him and that once they have him he will never want to fight and will have to give up the maiden despite his reluctance. Then, all together, they go and take hold of him by the arms and neck. "Now, then, don't you think you're a fool?" says his father. "So admit the truth: now you don't have the strength or ability to fight or joust, however much it may hurt and annoy and irk you. It will be sensible of you to agree to what I want and what suits me. Do you know what I have in mind? So as to lessen your disappointment, if you like, let's follow that knight together today and tomorrow, through the woods and over the plain, each of us riding at an easy pace. We might quite soon find his conduct and behaviour to be such that I would let you test yourself against him and have your wish in fighting him."

1822 The son then grudgingly agreed to this out of necessity. For lack of a better alternative he says he will give in to him, provided they both follow the knight. And when the people in the meadow see this turn of events, they all say: "Did you see that? The man who was in the cart has done so well for himself here that he's abducting my lord's son's mistress, and my lord is allowing it. We can truthfully say he must think there's some merit in him, when he lets him take her off. So a hundred curses on anyone who stops playing from now on because of him. Let's return to our sport!" Then they resume their games, with rounds and dancing.

1841 At once the knight leaves without staying any longer in the meadow;* and the maiden does not stay behind, but is taken with him. They both press ahead, with the father and son following them at a distance across the mown meadows. Having ridden until mid-afternoon, they find a church, very pleasantly situated and with a walled cemetery beside the fenced precinct. It was not base or foolish of the knight to enter the church, on foot, to pray to God; and the damsel held his horse for him until he returned. Once he had made his prayer and was just leaving, he saw an aged monk approaching him; and when they met, he courteously asked to be told what this place was, as he did not know. On being informed there was a cemetery there, he said to him: "As God is your help, take me in there!"—"Gladly, sir!" And he leads him to it. The knight follows the monk in and sees the most splendid tombs that might be found this side of Dombes or even of Pamplona; and on each one was an inscription carrying the names of those who were to lie in the tombs. He himself began to read the inscriptions and came upon: "Here will lie Gawain, here Louis and here Yvain." After these three, he read many another name of some of the outstanding, most respected and finest knights of that or any other land.

1883 Among these other tombs he found one of marble, apparently quite new and richer and more handsome than all the rest. Calling the monk, the knight said: "What is the purpose of these tombs here?" He answered: "You've already seen the inscriptions; and if you've understood them, you know what they say and what the tombs signify."—"And tell me what that large one there is for." The hermit replies: "I'll tell you all about it. It's a sarcophagus that surpasses all others ever made. Neither I nor anyone else ever saw one so rich or finely sculpted. It's beautiful on the outside and even more so within. But don't concern yourself with that because, as you'll never see inside it, that would do you no good; for it would take seven big, strong men to remove the lid if anyone wanted to open that tomb, covered with a slab as it is. And you may be sure it's a fact that to lift it would require seven men stronger than you or I. And it carries an inscription saying that whoever raises this slab alone and unaided will release all the men and women who are imprisoned in that land which no serf or nobleman can leave unless he is a native of those parts: no one has as yet come back from there. Foreigners are held prisoner there, whilst the inhabitants come and go in and out as they please."

1922 At once the knight goes to seize the slab, which he raises without the slightest difficulty, more easily than ten men would have done using all their strength. The monk was so astounded that he almost collapsed at the sight of this wonder, for he was not expecting to see anything like it in all his life. He said: "Now, sir, I would dearly like to know your name. Will you tell me it?"—"Not

I," says the knight, "upon my word!"—"I'm indeed sorry for that," he says. "But if you did tell me, you would show much courtesy and might benefit greatly from it. Who are you, and where do you come from?"—"I'm a knight, as you see, and a native of the kingdom of Logres: I hope that's enough to satisfy you. And now, for your part, please tell me who is to lie in this tomb."—"That man, sir, who will deliver all those trapped in the kingdom from which none escapes." When he had told him everything, the knight commended him to God and all His saints; and then he returned to the damsel, having been unable to do so before. The old, grey-haired monk escorts him from the church, and they come to the road. And as the maiden mounts, the monk informs her of everything the knight had done inside, begging her to tell him his name if she knows it, until she admits to him that she does not know. But she does dare tell him one thing for certain, namely that there is no knight to equal him anywhere as far as the four winds blow.

1967 With that the maiden leaves him and hurries after the knight. Immediately those following them arrive and find the monk, whom they see alone in front of the church. The elderly, shirted knight addressed him: "Tell us, sir, have you seen a knight escorting a damsel?" He replies: "It won't be hard for me to give you precise information about them, for they've only just left here. And the knight was inside there and performed a most amazing feat by raising, on his own and without any trouble at all, the slab on the great marble tomb. He's on his way to rescue the queen; and without a doubt he will rescue her, along with all the other people. You yourselves are well aware of this, having often read the inscription on the slab. Truly, no knight to match this one was ever born of man and woman or took his seat in a saddle."

1993 Then the father said to his son: "What about that, son? Isn't he then very valiant to have performed such a feat? Now you really understand who was in the wrong and know well enough whether it was you or I. Not for the town of Amiens would I have wanted you to fight him; yet you put up a stubborn resistance before you could be dissuaded. Now we can return, since it would be most foolish of us to follow him any further." He replies: "I agree to that: it would be no use for us to follow him. Let's go back, as that's what you want." They were very sensible to return. But the maiden continues travelling close beside the knight, wanting him to pay some attention to her. She wishes to learn from him his name and by turns demands and begs him to tell her, until in sheer annoyance he answers her: "Haven't I told you I'm from King Arthur's realm? By my faith in God and His might, you shall not know my name!" Then she asks him for his leave to go, and she will turn back; and he grants it gladly.

2023 Thereupon the maiden left; and he rode on by himself until it was very late. After vespers, about the hour of compline, as he continued on his way he saw a knight coming from the woods where he had been hunting. He was approaching with his helmet laced and with such game as God had granted him lashed to his big grey hunter. This vavasour came riding at speed to meet the knight and offered him hospitality. "Sir," he says, "it will shortly be night: it's high time to find lodging and right for you to do so. I've a house of mine close by and will take you there. No one ever gave you better hospitality than I shall provide to the best of my ability: if you consent, I'll be delighted."—"And I'm very happy for my part," says he. The vavasour immediately sends his son on ahead to prepare the lodging suitably and have a meal ready quickly. Without waiting, the young man at once obeys him very willingly and gladly and sets off at high speed. Then the others proceeded on their way, without wishing to hurry, until they arrived at the house.

2057 The vavasour's wife was a very gracious lady; and he had five sons (three still youths and two already knighted) whom he loved dearly, and also two beautiful and attractive daughters who were still unmarried. They were not natives of the country, but were captives there, having been held prisoner for a very long time, though they were born in the kingdom of Logres.* The vavasour leads the knight into his courtyard, and the lady runs to meet them, whilst his sons and daughters dash up, all doing their utmost to serve him. They greet him and help him dismount. Neither the sisters nor the five brothers pay much attention to their father, in the full knowledge that their actions have his approval. They do him much honour with their warm welcome. And when they had taken off his armour, one of his host's two daughters put her own mantle on him, unfastening it from her neck and placing it round his. However well he was served at supper, I have no wish to speak of that; but when the meal was over, they showed no reluctance at all to talk of many matters.

2088 First the vavasour began to enquire of his guest who he was and from what land, but without directly asking his name. Unhesitatingly he replies: "I come from the kingdom of Logres and was never before in this country." When the vavasour hears him, he, his wife and his children are all quite amazed, and there is not one of them who is not very upset. They began to say to him: "How unlucky for you, good fair sir! What a great misfortune for you! For now you'll be in servitude and exile just like us."—"And where do you come from, then?" he asks. "We're from your country, sir. In this land there are many of your countrymen in servitude. A curse on the custom and on those too who uphold it! For no foreigners come here without being compelled to stay, detained in this land: anybody who wishes may enter it, but will then have to stay here. It's all over for you yourself: I'm sure you'll never leave."—"Yes I shall," says he, "if I can." Then the vavasour retorts: "What? Do you think you'll get out?"—"Yes, if it's God's will; and I shall do my level best to do so."—"In that case, there's no doubt that all the others would be free to leave; for once one escapes fairly from this imprisonment, all the others may legitimately leave unhindered."

2128 The vavasour then recalls that he had been told and assured that a knight of great goodness was coming forcibly to enter the country to seek the queen, who was being held by Meleagant, the king's son. He reflects: "Indeed, it's my firm belief this is he; so I'll put it to him." Then he said to him: "Sir, don't hide from me any of your business, on the understanding that I'll give you the best advice I know. I myself shall profit if you can succeed in it. Divulge the truth to me for your benefit and my own. I'm convinced you've come into this country among these heathen folk who are worse than Saracens in order to look for the queen." The knight replies: "I didn't come here for anything else. I don't know where my lady is shut away, but I'm intent on rescuing her and badly need advice. So give me some, if you can."—"Sir," he says, "you've undertaken an extremely difficult journey. The road you are on leads straight to the Sword Bridge. You should take my advice: if you would believe me, you'd take a safer route to the Sword Bridge, and I would have you led there." The knight, anxious to go the shortest way, asks him: "Is it as direct as this road here?"—"No," he says. "On the contrary, it's longer, though safer." Then he says: "I'm not interested in that; but give me advice about this one!"

2170 —"I'm prepared to do so," he says; "but I doubt if it will be at
all to your advantage if you go this other way. Tomorrow you'll
reach a narrow place where you may quickly come to grief. It's
called the Stony Passage. So do you want me to tell you what a
terrible place that passage is? Only a single horse can pass through:
two men couldn't go abreast there, and the passage is well guarded
and defended. It will certainly not be surrendered to you on your
arrival: you'll take many sword- and lance-blows there and will
deal plenty before you get through." When he had given his whole
account, a knight, one of the vavasour's sons, stepped forward,
saying: "Sir, if you don't mind, I shall go with this noble knight." At
that, one of the youths stands up with the words: "I'll go as well."
And their father very willingly gives them both leave to go. Now the
knight will not set off on his own; and, delighted with their company, he thanks them for it.

2199 Then the conversation ends, and they conduct the knight to his
bed, where he falls into a welcome sleep. As soon as he could see
daylight he got up; and those who were to go with him saw him and
rose at once. The knights armed themselves and, having taken their
leave, set out, with the youth taking the lead. Together they go on
their way until, just at the hour of prime, they come to the Stony
Passage. In the middle of it was a wooden tower where there was
always a man posted. Before they came close, the man in the tower
saw them and shouted at the top of his voice: "Here comes an
enemy! Here comes an enemy!" At that you could see a knight
emerge from the tower, mounted and clad in new-looking armour
and flanked by men-at-arms carrying sharp axes. When the other
knight approaches the passage, its guardian hurls blame and abuse
at him concerning the cart, saying: "Vassal, it was very bold of you,
arrant fool that you are, to enter this country. No man who'd been
in a cart should ever come here, and may God never grant you any
joy of it!"

2232 Thereupon they spur at each other as hard as their horses can
go. And the one whose job it was to guard the pass at once breaks
his lance, dropping both pieces. The other's blow just misses the
rim of his shield and catches him in the neck, hurling him down on
his back across the stones. Then the men-at-arms leap forward with
their axes, but deliberately miss him, not wishing to harm either
him or his horse; and it is clear to the knight that they are not

wanting to injure him at all and mean him no harm. So he does not bother to draw his sword, but passes on without opposition, and his companions follow him, saying to each other: "No one ever saw so good a knight, and there is none to compare with him. Hasn't he performed an amazing feat in forcing his way through here?" And the one who is knighted says to the other: "Good brother, hurry off, for God's sake, and go to my father and tell him what has happened." The young man asserts and vows he will never go to him, or ever leave this knight until he has dubbed him and made him a knight. But let his brother go with the message if he is so set on it.

2267 Then all three go on together until perhaps just after mid-afternoon, when they come across a man who asks them who they are. They reply: "We are knights going about our business." Then the man said to the knight: "Sir, I should like then to offer lodging to you and your companions as well." This he says to the one who seems to him lord and master of the others; but he answers: "I couldn't possibly take lodging at this time; for a man is a good-for-nothing if he lingers and rests at his ease once he has undertaken a great task. And I'm engaged in such an enterprise that it will be some time before I take my lodging." To this the man replies: "My house is not close by, but some distance ahead. You can be assured of coming there to take your lodging at the proper hour, for it will be late when you arrive."—"In that case," says he, "I will go there."

2292 Then the man who is guiding them sets off in front, and the others follow along the road. Having gone a good distance, they met a squire coming their way at full gallop on a nag as plump and round as an apple. This squire says to the man: "Sir, sir, come as quickly as you can! For the people from Logres have risen in force against the inhabitants of this land and have already started to make war and begun hostilities and fighting; and they say a knight who has fought in many parts has invaded this country, and, wherever he wants to go, no one can deny him passage or stop his progress, like it or not. And all of those in this land say he will deliver every one of them and subdue our own people. So I advise you to hurry now!" Then the man puts his horse to the gallop; and the others, who had also heard this, were quite delighted, for they will want to help their own men. The vavasour's son says: "Listen, sir, to what this squire says! Let's go and help our people who are in a fight with those on the other side!" And the man rides on, not waiting for them but heading rapidly for a strong fortress built on a hill. He gallops up to the entrance with the others spurring behind him.

2330   The bailey was surrounded by a high wall and a moat. *No sooner had they gone in than a gate was lowered at their heels so that they would not be able to get out again that way. They say: "Come on, come on, for we'll not halt here!" They follow the man at a rapid pace until they reach the other exit, which was not barred to them; but the moment he had passed through, a portcullis was dropped just behind him. At this, the others were very distressed, seeing themselves shut in and thinking they were bewitched. But the one of whom I have more to tell you had on his finger a ring whose stone had the power to prevent him remaining under any spell once he had looked at it. He holds the ring before his eyes and gazes at the stone, saying: "Lady, lady, so help me God, I'm now in great need of you to come to my help!" That lady was a fairy who had given him the ring and brought him up as a child; and he had every confidence that, wherever he might be, she would help and rescue him. But his appeal and the stone in the ring provide clear evidence for him that there is no enchantment, so he knows without a doubt that they are shut in and imprisoned. Then they come to a narrow, low postern gate with its door barred. All together they draw their swords, with which each man strikes to such effect that they cut through the bar.

2373   Once outside the stronghold, they see the great battle has begun and is raging fiercely down across the meadows, with fully a thousand knights at least on either side, without counting the lowly foot-soldiers. When they came down into the meadows, the vavasour's son spoke with temperate good sense: "Sir, before we arrive there, I think we'd be sensible to have someone go and get information about the position of our people. I don't know which direction they're coming from; but I'll go there, if you wish."—"I'd like you to," he says. "Go there quickly and be sure to come back soon!" Quickly he goes there and promptly returns, and says: "We're very lucky, for I've definitely seen that these are our people over here."

2394   The knight immediately makes for the battle; and, meeting a knight coming his way, he jousts with him and strikes him so hard in the eye that he knocks him down dead. Then the young man dismounts, takes the knight's horse and the armour he was wearing, and arms himself well and with skill. Having donned the armour, he mounts without delay and takes the shield and big, stout, painted lance; and at his side he girds a sharp, bright, flashing sword. Into the battle he goes, following his brother and his lord, who has acquitted himself splendidly in the affray for some time, breaking, cleaving and shattering shields, helmets and hauberks. Neither wood nor iron saved those he struck hard from being badly wounded or from flying dead off their horses: by himself he performed so admirably that he vanquished them all. And those who had come with him did very well too.

2421 However, the people from Logres are amazed, since they do not know him; and they ask the vavasour's sons about him. Many of them ask insistently until they are told: "Sirs, this is the man who will deliver us all from exile and the dire misfortune in which we've languished for a long time; and we should do him great honour when, to free us from imprisonment, he has come through so many perilous places and will pass through many more. He has much to do and has accomplished much." There is no one who is not filled with joy. On hearing this news, their people are greatly cheered. With the spreading of the news until it was told to everybody, they all heard it and knew the facts. From the joy they feel they gain the strength and vigour to slay many of the others; and they wreak greater havoc on them, it seems to me, through the sole inspiration of the achievements of a single knight than by the efforts of all the rest together. And had it not been so near nightfall, their opponents would all have gone away utterly defeated. But when night came it was so dark that they had to break off the engagement.

2451 Once they had disengaged, all the captives alost fought to gather round the knight, seizing his bridle from all sides and calling out to him: "Welcome, good sir!" And each said: "By my faith, sir, you shall lodge with me! By God, sir, and in His name, don't take lodging with anyone but me!" What one says, all say; for everybody, young and old alike, wishes to give him lodging. Everyone says: "You'll be better off in my house than in anybody else's!" They all address this offer to him and compete with each other to take him, all wanting him for themselves and very nearly coming to blows over him. Then he tells them their squabbling is foolish and quite in vain. "Stop this stubborn behaviour, for it does neither me nor you any service. It's not good for us to quarrel among ourselves: on the contrary, we should be helping each other. You ought not to be arguing between yourselves about giving me shelter, but be concerned with lodging me somewhere for your common benefit and with me on my proper route." Yet they each continue to say: "That will be in my house."—"No, in mine!"

2484 —"You're still not talking sense," says the knight. "To my mind the wisest of you is a fool, judging by the way I hear you quarrelling. You should help me on my way, and you're wanting to turn me aside. If you'd all taken it in turns, one after the other as you chose, to do me as much honour and service as it's possible to do a man, then, by all the saints invoked in Rome, once I had accepted your kindness, I'd never be more grateful than I am for your good intentions. As God may grant me joy and health, the intention cheers me as much as if you'd each already done me great honour and kindness. So let the word stand for the deed." In this way he subdues and calms them all.

2504 They lead him to a well-to-do knight's house on his road, and all do their utmost to serve him. Everybody afforded him a most joyous welcome, honouring and serving him all night until bedtime, for he was very dear to them all. When, in the morning, it was time to part, they each wanted to go with him, volunteering and offering their company. But he has no wish or desire for anyone to accompany him other than just those two he had brought there; and them alone he took with him. That day they rode from morning to evening without coming across any adventure. Making a very good pace, they emerged quite late from a forest; and as they did so they saw the house of a knight; and sitting by the gate they noticed his wife, a lady of fine appearance. As soon as she caught sight of them, she rose to her feet to meet them. With a very happy smile she greets them, saying: "Welcome! I should like you to accept my hospitality: this is your lodging, so please dismount."—"Thank you, my lady: since you ask us, we will do so and accept your hospitality for the night."

2537 They dismount, whereupon the lady has the horses led away, for she has an excellent household. She calls her sons and daughters: courteous, handsome youths and knights and beautiful daughters. Some she orders to unsaddle the horses and tend them well. No one would have dared refuse her: on the contrary, they were very glad to obey. She had the knights disarmed, with the daughters eager to oblige. Once disarmed, they are given three short mantles to put on, then are at once led to their very fine quarters. The master, however, was not there, but in the woods accompanied by two of his sons. But he arrived before long; and his extremely courteous household hurries out through the gate to meet him. They quickly unload and untie the game he brings, then give him the news: "Sir, sir, you don't know it, but you have three knights as guests."—"God be praised!" says he. The knight and his two sons treat their guests most warmly. The rest of the household was not idle, with even the least of them ready to do whatever was necessary. Some run to speed the preparations for the meal, others to light the candles, which they burn in profusion. They fetch a towel and basins and pour the water for washing their hands. They are far from mean with everything. Having all washed, they take their seats. Nothing to be seen in there was disagreeable or unpleasant.

2580 With the first course came a bonus in the form of a knight outside the gate, looking more arrogant than a bull, which is a very haughty beast. He was sitting, armed from head to toe, on a charger and was held in the stirrup by one leg, whilst to give himself an air of jaunty elegance, he had thrown the other over his charger's neck and mane. Here he is, arriving in this fashion, without anyone noticing him until he came in front of them with the words: "I want to know which of you it is who is so foolish and arrogant and utterly brainless as to come into this country with the idea of crossing the Sword Bridge. He's come to expend all his energy for nothing and has just wasted his time." Undismayed, the knight answers him quite confidently: "I'm the one who wants to cross the bridge."—"You? You? How did you dare think of it? Before undertaking such a thing, you should consider how you might finish and end up; and you should remember the cart into which you climbed. I don't know if you're ashamed at having been carried in it; but no one in his right mind would have embarked on such a great enterprise having been taxed with this reprehensible act."

2615 He does not deign to utter a word in reply to what he hears the man say to him; but the master of the house and all the others are extremely astonished at it, and with good reason. "Oh, God, what a great misfortune!" each of them says to himself. "A curse on the time when the cart was first invented and made! For it's a very vile and loathsome thing. Ah, God, what was he accused of? And why was he put in a cart? For what sin? For what crime? This will always be held against him in future. If he were cleared of this blame, no knight could be found within the furthest bounds of the whole world who, however well tried in prowess, would be comparable in merit to this one. And if every knight were gathered together, one would see none as handsome or noble, if the truth were told." This was the common opinion.

2638 Then the newcomer resumed his arrogant talk, saying: "Listen to this, you knight who are making for the Sword Bridge: if you like, you can cross the water very easily and smoothly. I'll have you ferried over in a boat in no time. But when I have you on the other side, I'll exact a toll from you: if I feel like it, I'll take off your head; otherwise you'll keep it at my discretion." He replies that he is not looking for trouble, and that he will never put his head to this risk, even if things turn out badly for him. The other at once replies: "Since you don't want to do this, you'll have to come out here and fight me man to man to the shame and grief of one or other of us." To humour him, he answers: "If I could refuse, I'd gladly get out of it; but I'd certainly rather fight here than have to do something worse."

2664 Before leaving the table where they were sitting, he told the youths serving him to saddle his horse quickly for him and take his arms and bring them. They put every effort into doing this speedily: some work hard at arming him, others bring his horse. And you may be sure that as, astride his horse, he rode off at a walk completely armed and holding his shield by the straps, there seemed no case for excluding him from the tally of the handsome and the good. The horse really looked as if it belonged to him, so well did it suit him, as did the shield strapped to his arm; and the laced helmet he wore on his head fitted him so well that you would never suppose it to be borrowed or on loan – on the contrary, it would have been so much to your liking that you would have said he was born and grew up like that. I hope you will take my word for this.

2691 Outside the gate where the combat was to be held was a heath ideally suited for the contest. As soon as the two see each other they spur as hard as they can to clash violently together, exchanging such blows with their lances that they both bend and buckle before flying into splinters. With their swords they hack at shields, helmets and hauberks. The wood is split and the metal fractured so that they wound each other in numerous places. Angrily they pay one another with blows exchanged as if in a deal. But very often their swords are deflected on to the horses' cruppers and slake their thirst in their blood, of which they drink their fill, being driven right into their flanks until they fell both of them dead.* Then, when the combatants have fallen to the ground, each attacks the other on foot; and had they shared a mortal hatred, they could certainly not have set upon one another more ferociously with their swords. They rain down their blows more thick and fast than the dice-player stakes his coins when he keeps playing on and on, doubling up at every losing throw. But this was a very different game, consisting not of losing throws but of blows and hard, savage, fierce combat.

2724 Everyone had come out of the house: the master, lady, daughters and sons. No man or woman, no member of the household or stranger was left behind there, but all had come and lined up on the broad heathland to watch the fight. The knight of the cart blames and accuses himself of cowardice when he sees his host watching; and he notices the others too, who are all there looking on. His heart quite quivers with anger; for it seems to him that he should long ago have vanquished his opponent. Then he strikes him with a sword-blow very close to his head and hurls himself at him like a tempest, pressing and harrying him until he forces him to give ground, pushing him back and driving him so hard that he can scarcely draw breath and puts up very little resistance. And then the knight recalls how he had very basely reproached him about the cart; so he makes a pass at him with such dire effect that no lace or strap remains unbroken round his neck-band, and he knocks down the ventail and sends the helmet flying from his head. He assails and bears so hard upon him that he has to beg for mercy. Just like the lark, which cannot withstand the merlin, having nowhere to escape as it is outflown and outsoared by it, so he, to his great shame, goes to him asking and begging for mercy since there is nothing better he can do.

2765 When the other hears him calling for mercy, he does not touch or strike him, but says, "Do you wish for mercy?"—"What a very clever thing to say!" says he. "Any fool might ask that. I never wished for anything as much as I do for mercy at this moment." Then the other says: "You'd have to climb into a cart. Whatever story you could think of to tell me would be to no avail unless you got in the cart, because your tongue's been foolish enough to have scurrilously blamed me for doing so." The knight replies to him: "May it never please God that I get in it!"—"No?" says he. "Then you'll die where you are."—"You can easily kill me, sir; but in God's name I beg and ask your mercy, provided only I don't have to climb into a cart. There's no condition, however hard and strict, that I wouldn't accept, apart from this one. I'd rather be killed a hundred times over than suffer such a fate. There's nothing you can propose, however unpleasant, that I won't do to have your mercy and pardon."

2793 While he is asking him for mercy, here across the heath there suddenly comes a maiden, bare-headed and without a cloak, riding at an amble on a tawny mule. She held a whip with which she kept lashing the mule; and in fact no horse at full gallop could have gone as fast as that mule was ambling. The maiden said to the knight of the cart: "May God fill your heart, sir knight, with joy for the one who delights you most!" Pleased to hear this greeting, he responds: "May God bless you, maiden, and give you joy and health!" Then she said what her purpose was: "Sir knight," she says, "I've come a long way to you here, and in urgent need, to ask a favour for which you will earn as great a reward as I can grant you—and I do believe you'll find my help useful some time." He replies to her: "Tell me what you want; and if it's something I have it will be yours at once, provided it's nothing too difficult to grant." She says: "It's the head of that knight you've defeated; for indeed you've never come across a more wicked or faithless man. You'll not be doing anything at all sinful or wrong, but rather something charitable and good, for he's the most faithless person who ever was or ever will be." Then, when the defeated man hears that she wants him killed, he says: "Don't believe her, for she hates me! Instead I beg you to show me mercy in the name of God who is both son and father and who took as His mother her who was His daughter and hand-maiden!"—"Ah, knight," says the maiden, "don't believe that traitor! May God grant you all the joy and honour you can desire and give you every success in what you have undertaken!"

2844 Now the knight is in such a dilemma that he hesitates and dwells on the question as to whether he shall give the man's head to the girl who is calling on him to cut it off, or whether he shall show kindness and take pity on him. He wants to do what both girl and man ask. Generosity and Pity bid him do what each wants, for he was generous and compassionate. But if the girl carries off the head, then Pity is defeated and slain; and if she does not take it as her own, then Generosity is vanquished. This is the bondage and plight in which he is held by Pity and Generosity, tormented and afflicted by each. The maiden wants him to meet her request and give her the head, and on the other hand the man is making his plea in the name of pity and magnanimity; and since he has sought mercy from him, shall he not then have it? Yes! For it had never happened that any man, however great an enemy, having been overcome by him and forced to plead for mercy – never yet had it happened, even once, that he denied that man mercy, though it would have been quite fruitless for him to seek for anything more. So he will not refuse it, as that is his way, to this man who is asking and begging him for it. And the girl who wants the head: will she have it? Yes, if possible.

2880 "Knight," he says, "you must fight me once more; and if you want to defend your head, I'll have mercy on you to the extent that I'll let you take back your helmet and have time to re-arm your body and head as best you can. But you may be sure that you'll die if I defeat you this time." He replies: "I ask for nothing better and seek no further concession from you."—"And I'll give you this further great advantage", says the other, "by fighting you without moving from the stance I've taken here." His opponent makes ready, and at once they return furiously to the fight. But then our knight overcame him again and more speedily than the first time. The maiden immediately calls out: "Don't spare him, knight, whatever he may say to you! He would certainly not have spared you, having once defeated you. You may be sure that if you believe him he'll trick you again. Noble knight, cut off the head of the most perfidious man in this empire and kingdom, and give it to me! You really should give it me, since I intend to reward you for it. If he has his way, the day will surely come when he will once again deceive you with his words." The man, seeing his end is near, cries to him for mercy at the top of his voice; but neither his calls nor anything he can find to say to him is of any avail. For the other seizes him by the helmet, bursting all its laces, and knocks from his head the ventail and bright coif. He redoubles his cries: "Mercy, in God's name! Mercy, noble knight!" He replies: "As I hope for salvation, I shall never have pity on you, having let you off on one occasion."—"Ah," says he, "you'd do wrong if you believe my enemy and kill me like this!" She, on the other hand, intent on his death, urges him to cut his head off quickly and no longer to believe what he says.

2936 He strikes. His head flies on to the heath, and his body falls. This pleases and contents the maiden. The knight picks up the head by the hair and hands it to the girl to her great delight. She says: "May your heart find great joy in whatever it most desires, just like that which my own heart now feels regarding my fondest wish. My only source of unhappiness was that he lived so long. I have a reward waiting for you which you shall get at a very opportune time. From this service you've done me you will reap great benefit, I assure you. Now I shall go: may God be with you and keep you from harm." The maiden leaves immediately, with each commending the other to God. But all those who had seen the fight on the heath are overjoyed. They happily disarm the knight at once and honour him in every way they can. Without more ado they wash their hands again, wishing to resume their seats at the meal. Now they are in a happier mood than usual, and they eat in very high spirits. When they had spent a long time over their food, the vavasour said to his guest sitting beside him: "Sir, some time ago we came here from the kingdom of Logres, where we were born. So we should like you to enjoy honour, fortune and happiness in this country; for we would profit with you, and it would be to the advantage of many others if you gained honour and fortune in this land and from this undertaking." He replies: "May God hear your wishes!"

2979 When the vavasour had said what he had to and ceased speaking, one of his sons went further, saying: "Sir, we ought to serve you to the very best of our ability and in action rather than promises: if you need our service, we shouldn't wait for you to ask for it. Don't worry, sir, about your horse, if it's been killed. We have fine, strong horses here. I want you to take whatever you need of ours, and you shall leave with the very best we have in place of your own." He replies: "I'll be very glad to." With that they have the beds prepared and retire for the night. In the morning they rise at daybreak and dress. Once ready, they leave. Their behaviour at their departure is impeccable, as they take leave of the lady and the lord and all the others. But so that I omit nothing, let me tell you one detail: the knight was unwilling to mount the borrowed horse standing ready for him at the door. Instead, I must tell you that he had it mounted by one of the two knights who had come with him, while he got on to the latter's horse, for that is what pleased and suited him. With each astride his mount and with the leave and permission of their host, who had served and honoured them as best he could, all three took to the road. They make their way straight ahead until, as the day draws to a close, they come to the Sword Bridge late in the afternoon, towards evening.

3021 At the end of that very dangerous bridge* they get off their horses to see the treacherous water thundering swiftly past, black and turbid, as horrid and terrifying as if it were the Devil's river, and so perilous and deep that there is nothing in the whole world which, having fallen into it, would not vanish as into the salt sea. The bridge across it was quite different from all others: there never was nor will be one like it. If anyone asks me the truth, never did so terrible a bridge or foot-crossing exist. This bridge over the cold water consisted of a polished, gleaming sword; but it was a strong, stout sword as long as two lances. At each end was a tree-trunk to which the sword was nailed. No one needed to fear falling off on account of its breaking or bending, for it was so well made that it could bear a great weight.

3046 The two knights who were with the third were, however, very disturbed by the fact that they believed there were two lions or leopards tied to a stone slab at the opposite end of the bridge. The water, the bridge and the lions make them so terrified that they tremble with fear and say: "Good sir, take heed of what you see, for you have every need to. This bridge is wickedly made and formed: an evil structure. If you don't change your mind in time, it will be too late to repent. One must act cautiously in all the many cases of this kind. Now suppose you've got across – but that can't possibly happen, any more than that one could restrain the winds and forbid them to blow, or command the birds not to sing so that they were afraid to continue, or return to one's mother's womb and be born again (but that would be impossible), or empty the sea – can you suppose and imagine that those two raging lions chained on the other side wouldn't kill you, suck the blood from your veins, eat your flesh and then gnaw your bones? I have very strong nerves just to dare see and look at them. If you don't take care, you may be sure they'll kill you: without showing you any mercy, they'll have broken and rent apart your limbs in no time. But now take pity on yourself and stay here with us! You'd be wronging yourself if you knowingly exposed yourself to the risk of such certain death."

3092 With a laugh he replies to them: "My thanks and gratitude to you, sirs, for being so concerned on my account: you're prompted by love and your natural honesty. I'm sure that in no circumstances would you wish any harm to come to me. But I have such faith and belief in God that He will protect me at all times. I'm not afraid of this bridge or this water any more than of this solid ground. No, I intend to get ready to attempt the crossing. I'd rather die than turn back!" They find nothing more to say, but each of them shows his pity in a wealth of tears and sighs. Then he prepares as best he can for the crossing of the torrent by doing a quite astonishing thing: he removes the armour from his feet and hands. He will hardly be fit and unscathed when he reaches the other side! Having stripped off his foot- and leg-armour along with the socks, he will cling tightly with his bare hands and feet to the sword, which was sharper than a scythe. He was little worried if he wounded himself in his hands and feet: he would prefer to injure himself than to fall off the bridge and take a bath in the water, from which he would never emerge.

3124 In the way that suited him he crosses over very painfully and in great distress, wounding himself on hands, knees and feet. But Love, who guides and leads him on, gives him complete comfort and relief, so that all his suffering is pleasant to him. With his hands, feet and knees he manages to reach the further side. Then he thinks back and remembers the two lions he thought he had seen when he was on the other bank; and he looks and sees there not so much as a lizard or anything at all to do him harm. Holding his hand up to his face, he gazes at his ring and thus proves, when he finds there neither of the two lions he believed he had seen, that he has been bewitched and deceived, there being no living creature present. And those on the other bank, seeing he has made the crossing in that way, are rightly overjoyed, though they do not know of his injuries. He considers himself very fortunate not to have suffered greater harm.

3150 With his shirt he wipes away the oozing blood from all round his wounds. Then before him he sees a keep so strong that he had never set eyes on one of such strength. The keep could not have been finer. Leaning at a window was King Bademagu, who was very perceptive and keen on every point of honour and good conduct, and anxious above all to preserve and exercise loyalty in all things. Leaning beside him was his son, who constantly strove to do the opposite, since he favoured disloyalty and never tired or wearied of baseness, treachery and wickedness. From their vantage point they had watched the knight cross the bridge with great difficulty and pain. Meleagant's face has changed colour with anger and rage; for he well knows that now his possession of the queen will be challenged. But he was such an able knight that he feared no man however strong or fierce. There would have been no finer knight had he not been treacherous and disloyal; but he had a heart of wood, quite devoid of gentleness and pity. The king was made happy and glad by the cause of his son's anger and grief. He knew for certain that the man who had crossed the bridge was far superior to all others; for none would ever have dared make the crossing in whom there lurked any latent wickedness, which brings more shame to its possessors than merit brings honour to good men. Therefore worthy behaviour cannot achieve as much as can wickedness and sloth. This is true – never doubt it – that it is easier to do evil than good.

3195 I could tell you much about these two things, except that that would delay me. But to pick up my narrative again, I turn to another matter; and you shall hear how the king speaks to his son and takes him to task. "My son," he says, "it was by chance that you and I came here to lean by this window; and in doing so we've been rewarded by witnessing the boldest deed that was ever so much as thought of. Tell me now if you don't think well of the man who has performed such a marvellous feat. Come to an agreement and be reconciled with him, and hand the queen over to him! You'll never gain from a conflict with him, but are likely to suffer greatly for it. Show yourself sensible and chivalrous by sending him the queen before he sees you. Do him honour in your land by giving him what he's come to seek before he asks for it. You know very well that he's in search of Queen Guenevere. Don't give the impression of being obstinate or foolish or arrogant. If he's alone in your land, you ought to offer him your company; for one worthy man should not keep aloof from another, but associate with him, honour him and treat him with deference. One gains honour by dispensing it; and you can be certain that honour will be yours if you do honour and service to the man who is fully the best knight in the world." He replies: "May God confound me if there aren't others as good or better!" The king blundered in disregarding him, for Meleagant has just as high an opinion of himself.

3238 Meleagant adds: "Perhaps you want me to join my hands and feet in homage as his vassal and hold my land from him? So help me God, I'd rather become his vassal than give the queen up to him! God forbid that I surrender her to him in that way! She'll certainly never be given up by me, but denied and defended in the face of all those foolish enough to dare to come and seek her." Then the king repeats his advice: "My son, it would be very courtly of you to abandon this obstinate attitude. I advise and beg you to keep the peace. You're well aware that the honour will go to this knight if he wins the queen from you in combat. He would certainly rather have her through combat than through kindness, because that will enhance his reputation. In my opinion he's seeking her not in order for her to be handed to him peacefully, but in the hope of winning her in combat. Therefore you'd be wise to deprive him of that fight. I'm very sorry to see you acting foolishly; but if you do scorn my advice, you'll suffer for it. It will be the worse for you, and your misfortune may come quickly; for the knight has nothing to fear except from you alone. I offer him peace and security on behalf of all my men and myself. I have never committed any disloyalty, treason or treachery and shall not begin now for you any more than for any stranger. I don't want to put you under any delusion: I guarantee the knight that he'll never need anything in the way of arms or a horse that shall not be his, since he has acted so courageously as to come as far as this. He will be safely guarded and protected from all men except yourself alone. Of this I want to assure you: that if he can defend himself against you, he'll have no one else to fear."

3288 —"Just now", says Meleagant, "I'm bound to hear you out in silence, while you say what you please. But I'm not interested in what you say. I'm not like a hermit, so merciful and charitable, and I don't intend to be so honourable as to give him what I most love. His task won't be performed so promptly or speedily: on the contrary, things will go very differently from what the two of you think. We'll not fall out if you help him against me. What do I care if he enjoys peace and a truce with you and all your men? My heart doesn't miss a beat on that account: rather, so help me God, I'm delighted he only has me to deal with; and I don't want you to do anything for me that could be criticised as disloyalty or treason. You be as moral a man as you like, but let me be cruel."—"What? Won't you behave in any other way?"—"Not at all," says he.—"Then I say no more about it. Now do the best you can, for I'm leaving you and going to speak to the knight. I want to offer and give him my help and advice in every respect, for I'm entirely on his side."

3319 The king then went down and had his horse fetched. A great charger is brought for him, and he mounts it by the stirrup. With him he takes some of his men, having just three knights and two men-at-arms accompany him. They ride on downhill without stopping until they reach the narrow bridge, where they see the knight staunching his wounds and wiping away the blood. The king intends to have him as his guest for a long time in order to heal his wounds; but he might as well be aiming at having the sea drained. Hurriedly the king dismounts; and at once the seriously injured man gets up to meet him, not that he recognises him; and he gives no more sign of the great pain in his feet and hands than if he were completely well. Seeing the effort he is making, the king quickly runs forward to greet him with the words: "Sir, I'm most amazed that you have forced your way into this country among us. But be welcome here! For no one will ever undertake this again; and it has never happened, nor will it, that any man showed such courage as to brave a peril like this. And rest assured that I feel all the greater affection for you because you've accomplished what no one would have dared think of, still less do. You will find me very kind, loyal and courteous towards you. I'm the king of this land and offer you freely all my advice and service; and I have a very good idea of the object of your quest: I believe you are seeking the queen."—"Sire," he says, "your supposition is correct: no other purpose brings me here."

3364 —"My friend," says the king, "you'll have to suffer hardship
before you obtain her. And you're very badly hurt: I can see your
wounds and the blood. You'll not find the man who brought her
here so generous as to give her up to you without a fight. But you
must rest and have your wounds treated until they are quite healed.
I'll give you some of the three Marys' ointment,* and better if it
could be found, for I'm very concerned for your comfort and
recovery. The queen is so closely confined that no mortal man can
touch her, not even my son who brought her here with him and is
very annoyed at this: no one has ever been so furious and enraged
as he is. I, though, am very well disposed towards you and, so help
me God, will be delighted to give you anything you need. My son,
who won't thank me for it, will never have such fine arms that I
don't give you equally fine ones, together with the kind of horse you
need. And I take you under my protection against all men, no
matter whom this displeases. You'll not have anyone to fear except
that man alone who brought the queen here. No man ever threatened another as I threatened him; and in my anger I very nearly
drove him from my land because he doesn't surrender her to you.
He may be my son, but let that not worry you, for unless he defeats
you in combat, he'll never be able to do you a scrap of harm, if I
have my way."

3405 —"Thank you, sire!" says he. "But I'm frittering away time
here that I don't want to waste. I'm not suffering from anything and
have no wound that causes me any discomfort. Take me to find
him; for with such arms as I have I'm ready to enjoy myself straight
away by giving and receiving blows."—"My friend, it would be
better for you to wait a fortnight or three weeks until your wounds
have healed, for it would do you good to rest for at least two weeks;
and I could on no account allow or contemplate that you should
fight in front of me with arms and equipment like that." He replies:
"With your agreement, no other arms but these would be used, for
I'd gladly fight the combat with these and wouldn't ask for there to
be one hour or one second of respite, postponement or delay. But
for you I'll go so far now as to wait until tomorrow; then it will be
futile for anyone to raise the matter, because I'll not wait any
longer." The king then assured him he would be entirely at his
disposal and has him shown to his lodging; and he urgently
requires those who take him to go to great pains to serve him,
which they do to the very best of their ability.

3439 Then the king, who would dearly like to make peace if he could, went back to his son and spoke to him in terms showing his desire for peace and reconciliation saying: "Dear son, come to an agreement with this knight without fighting! He has not come here for amusement or to go hunting with the bow or hounds, but rather in pursuit of honour and to further his reputation and fame; and, as I've seen, he's badly in need of rest. Had he taken my advice he wouldn't, either this month or next, be hankering after the combat he's so keen on now. Are you afraid of incurring dishonour if you surrender the queen to him? Never fear that, because there can be no blame in it for you: on the contrary, it's wrong to keep something to which one has no reasonable right. He would have very gladly fought the duel here and now, though his hands and feet are not undamaged – quite the reverse, they're gashed and injured."—"You're foolish to be alarmed," says Meleagant to his father. "By the faith I owe Saint Peter, I'll never trust your advice in this matter. Indeed, I ought to be dragged apart by horses if I believed it. If he's seeking honour, so am I; if he's wanting to make his reputation, I'm wanting to make mine; and if he really wants the fight, then I want it a hundred times more."—"I see clearly you're determined to act like a fool," says the king, "and so you shall. Tomorrow you'll try your strength against this knight, since that's what you want."—"May nothing worse ever happen to me than that!" says Meleagant. "I would much rather the combat were today than tomorrow. Just see how much more dejected I'm looking than usual! My eyes are quite dull now and my face very woebegone. Never until I fight shall I know joy, satisfaction or contentment or any kind of pleasure."

3491 The king hears that his advice and pleading are of no avail whatsoever; so very reluctantly he leaves his son, then selects a very strong, fine horse and splendid arms and sends them to the one on whom they are not wasted, along with a surgeon who was a trustworthy and good Christian man: there was no more loyal person in the world, and he knew more about the healing of wounds than all the doctors of Montpellier.* That night, on the king's instructions, he treated the knight to the best of his ability. Already the news had spread to the knights and maidens, the ladies and the lords of all the surrounding region; and from the entire area strangers and friends came riding at top speed throughout the night until it was bright daylight. At daybreak there was such a motley throng of people in front of the keep that one could not move a step. The king, deeply regretting the combat, rises early and comes yet again to his son, whose helmet, made in Poitiers, was already laced on his head. There is no possibility of a postponement or of peace being made: despite the king's insistent urging, there is no chance of his granting it.

3526 It is in the square in front of the keep, where all the people have assembled, that the combat will be held, according to the king's wishes and orders. He sends at once for the stranger knight, who is brought into the square filled with the people from the realm of Logres; for just as folk normally go to church to hear the organ on regular feast-days, at Pentecost or Christmas, so they had all flocked together there. All the foreign maidens from King Arthur's realm had fasted for three days and gone barefoot in hair-shirts so that God might give the knight who was to fight for the captives strength and power against his adversary. And equally the natives of this country were, for their part, praying for their lord, that God might grant him the victory and honour in the combat. Very early, before the bell rang for prime, both contestants had been brought into the middle of the square, fully armed on two iron-clad horses. Meleagant cut a very handsome figure, open-featured and well-built; and his close-meshed hauberk, helmet and shield that hung at his neck became him admirably. But everyone was attracted to the other, even those who would have liked to see him shamed; and they all say that Meleagant is worthless compared with him.

3566 As soon as they were both in the centre of the square, the king arrives to restrain them as far as he can and tries hard to make peace; but he fails to win over his son to it. He said to them: "At least hold your horses on the rein until I've climbed up into the keep. It won't be too great a favour to wait that long for me." Then, deeply troubled, he leaves them and comes straight to where he knows the queen to be, she having begged him the previous night to put her in a position from which she would have an unobstructed view of the combat. Having granted her this favour, he went to look for her and bring her there; for he was anxious to do all he could to honour and serve her. He placed her at one window, while he reclined at another on her right-hand side; and with the two of them was a large number of both knights and prudent ladies and maidens, who were natives of that country. There were also many captives there, very intent on their prayers and intercessions. All the prisoners, male and female, were praying for their lord, since they put their faith in God and in him for their rescue and deliverance.

3600 Then the contestants lose no time in having all the people stand back. Knocking their shields free of their elbows, they thrust their arms into the straps, then spur at each other to drive their lances two arms' length through the opposing shields, shivering and shattering them to pieces like flying sparks. The horses meet so violently head on, clashing together breast to breast, shields and helmets colliding, that the crash they make sounds like a great thunderclap. No breast-strap, girth, stirrup, rein or saddle-strap remains unbroken. The saddle-bows, very strong as they are, break in pieces. And it is no shame to the knights to fall to the ground after all this has given way. Very swiftly they jump back to their feet and make for each other without any exchange of pleasantries but more fiercely than two wild boars. Not bothering with threats, they deal each other mighty blows with their steel swords, displaying their great mutual hatred. Time and again they catch helmets and shining hauberks so savagely that pieces of metal fly, and the blood spurts after them. They fight an outstanding combat, stunning and mangling each other with wicked, heavy blows. They vie in launching at one another many fierce, hard, long attacks, so that the spectators were unable to tell who was winning or losing.

3638 Inevitably, however, the one who had crossed the bridge was greatly weakened by his wounded hands. The people who support him are extremely alarmed as they see his blows growing more feeble, and they fear he may get the worst of it. By now they had the impression that he was being beaten and Meleagant having the upper hand; and all around they were discussing it with bated breath. But at the windows of the keep is a very astute maiden, who thinks and says to herself that the knight has certainly not undertaken the combat for her, or for the other ordinary folk gathered in the square, and that he would not have engaged in it except on behalf of the queen. And she thinks that if he knew her to be placed at the window watching and seeing him, this would increase his strength and courage. Had she known his name, she would very gladly have told him to look around him a little. Then she comes to the queen and says: "My lady, for God's sake and for your benefit and ours too, I would ask you to tell me, if you know it, the name of that knight, so that it might be of some help to him."—"Young lady," says the queen, "you've put to me a question in which I detect no animosity or treachery, but only goodwill. The knight's name, I believe, is Lancelot of the Lake."*—"God, how my heart is lifted, cheered and gladdened!" says the maiden. Then she jumps forward and calls to him at the top of her voice, so that all the people hear it: "Lancelot! Turn round and see whose attention is fixed on you!"

3685 When Lancelot heard his name called, he lost no time in turning round. Having done so, he sees, seated up in a gallery in the tower, the one he most desired to see in the entire world. From the instant he spotted her, he did not turn away or divert his face and eyes from her, but defended himself behind his back. Meleagant continued to press him as hard as he could, happy in the thought that he now has no more protection against him. At this the natives of the country are delighted and the foreigners so distraught that they cannot stay on their feet, and many, quite overwhelmed, cannot help dropping to the ground on their knees or lying prostrate: thus both joy and grief are felt. Then the maiden shouted once more from the window: "Oh, Lancelot! How can you behave so foolishly? You used to be the soul of all excellence and prowess; and I really don't believe that God ever created a knight who could equal you in valour or merit. Now we see you in such straits that you're dealing your blows behind you and fighting with your back turned. Work your way round over here so you can keep your eyes on this tower, for it's well worth looking at!"

3722 Lancelot feels so ashamed and mortified that he hates himself for having, as he well knows, had the worst of the combat for a long time in the sight of every man and woman there. Then he jumps back and moves round, forcing Meleagant to go between him and the keep. Meleagant tries hard to get back on the other side; but Lancelot rushes at him and, when he attempts to reverse his position, charges him so heavily with his body and shield that he makes him spin right round two or three times, however much it annoyed him. Then he grows in strength and courage, being greatly helped by Love and by the fact that he had never hated anything so much as that man who is fighting him. Love and mortal hate, so great that its like was never felt before, make him so fierce and spirited that

Meleagant by no means treats this as a game, but is very afraid of him, since he had never come across or known so doughty a knight, nor had any ever done him as much harm or injury as this one. He is prepared to draw well back from him, to dodge and flinch, avoiding his detested blows. Lancelot hurls no threats at him, but with his onslaught drives him towards the tower where the queen is leaning out. In front of her he repaid her with his service up to the point where he came so close to her that he had to halt because, had he gone another step forward, he would not have seen her.

3763 In this way Lancelot repeatedly drove him to and fro wherever he fancied, continually pausing in front of the queen his lady, who had kindled within him the flame on account of which he keeps gazing at her in this way. And this flame fired him so much against Meleagant that he managed to drive and chase him wherever he wished. He drives him like a man who is blind or on crutches, whether he likes it or not. The king sees his son in such a plight that he cannot help or defend himself. Then he is sorry for him and pities him and will come to his assistance if he can; but if he wishes to proceed correctly, he must ask the queen's permission. Then he broached the subject with her: "My lady, I have shown you great love, service and honour since I've had you in my power. I never thought of anything, provided I saw it as being in your honour, which I failed to do. Now give me my reward! For I should like to ask you a favour, which you should not grant me except out of love. I see clearly that my son has undoubtedly the worst of this combat. I'm not saying this at all because it distresses me, provided that Lancelot, who has it in his power to kill him, doesn't do so. And you should not want this, though not indeed because he has not wronged both you and him; but, if you please, I urgently beg you for my sake to ask him to stop striking him. In this way, if you were agreeable, you could repay me for my service."—"Dear sir, I'm ready to do this at your request," says the queen. "If I nursed a mortal hatred against your son, whom I certainly don't love, nevertheless you have served me so well that, since this is your pleasure, I'm quite happy for him to desist."

3813 These words were not uttered in private, but in the hearing of Lancelot and Meleagant. One who loves is very obedient; and gladly and with alacrity, if he is the perfect lover, he does whatever might please his beloved. So this indeed Lancelot had to do, loving as he did more than Pyramus,* if any man ever was able to love more than he. Lancelot heard what was said; and, once the last word had passed her lips (when she had said "Since it's your wish for him to desist, I'm quite happy"), Lancelot would not then have touched him for anything, nor would he have moved, even if the other should kill him. He neither touches him nor stirs. But Meleagant, on hearing he has been reduced to the point where a plea has to be made for him, strikes at him as much as he can, out of his mind with rage and shame. Then the king, to remonstrate with him, went down from the keep and, intervening in the combat, said at once to his son: "What? Is it then proper for you to strike him when he's not touching you? You're far too cruel and vicious, and your valour now is totally misplaced. We also know quite certainly that he has the better of you." Then Meleagant, nonplussed in his shame, says to the king: "Perhaps you've gone blind! It seems to me you can't see a thing. Anybody who doubts that I've got the upper hand over him is blind."—"Find someone to believe that!" says the king. "All these people know well enough whether you're telling the truth or lying. We're quite sure of the facts of the matter."

3856 Then the king told his lords to restrain his son for him. They lose no time, and his order is quickly obeyed, as they pull Meleagant back. But no great force was needed to restrain Lancelot; for the other might have done him great harm before he would have touched him. Then the king says to his son: "So help me God, now you'll have to make peace and surrender the queen! You must abandon this whole dispute and give up your claim."—"Now you've spoken utter nonsense! This is useless talk I'm hearing from you! Be off with you, and let us fight without interfering!" But the king says he will intervene, because he is sure Lancelot would kill him if they were allowed to fight on. "He'd kill me? On the contrary, I'd very soon win and make an end of him, if you didn't bother us but let us fight." Then the king says: "Whatever you say, God help me! will do you no good."—"Why not?" he asks.—"Because that's not what I want. I'll not heed your foolish talk and your bragging just to see you killed. A man really is stupid to wish for his own death as you do, though you don't know it. I'm well aware you hate me for wanting to protect you. God will never let me see and witness your death, if I can help it, for it would cause me too much grief."

3893 He talks and remonstrates with him until finally they reach a peaceful agreement. The terms are that he would surrender the queen to Lancelot on condition that he, without any prevarication, would fight with Meleagant once more whenever he called upon him to do so, within a year from the day he summoned him. Lancelot does not mind this. All the people hurry up as peace is made and determine that the combat will be held at the court of King Arthur, who holds Britain and Cornwall: there they decide it shall be. It is necessary for the queen to consent and for Lancelot to agree that if Meleagant should bring him to submission, she will come back again with him and nobody shall restrain her. To this the queen assents and Lancelot agrees. Thus they were brought to terms, parted and disarmed.

3917 It was the custom in that country that, once one person left it, all the others would leave. They were all blessing Lancelot: as you can well understand, that was a time for great joy, such as was certainly shown. All the foreign folk gather together, rejoicing over Lancelot and saying so that he could hear: "Truly, sir, we were quite elated as soon as we heard you named, for we were absolutely certain that now we should all be set free." There was a huge crowd present at this happy scene, with everyone striving and struggling to be able to touch him, and those able to get closest being more delighted than they could say. There was an abundance of joy and grief there; for those released from captivity have given themselves over to unrestrained joy,* whilst Meleagant and his supporters have nothing to cheer them, but are brooding, dejected and miserable. The king goes from the square, not leaving Lancelot there but taking him with him. Lancelot begs him to lead him to the queen. "I'm quite prepared to," says the king, "for it seems to me a good idea. And I'll show you Kay the seneschal at the same time, if you like." Lancelot almost falls at his feet, he is so overjoyed. At once the king led him into the hall where the queen had come to wait for him.

3955 Seeing the king holding Lancelot by the hand, the queen rose before him, but with a show of anger, lowering her head and not uttering a word. "My lady," says the king, "here is Lancelot come to see you: this must please and suit you very well."—"Me, sir? He can't please me. I'm not interested in seeing him!"—"Come, my lady!" says the king in his open, courtly way. "What has now put

you in this mood? This is not at all the way to treat a man who has
served you so well that he has often put his life in mortal danger for
you in the course of this journey, and has rescued and saved you
from my son Meleagant, who was furious to have to give you
up."—"Truly, sir, he's wasted his time; and I'm not at all grateful
to him for it – that I'll never deny." Here now is Lancelot quite
bemused. Very humbly, in the manner of a true lover, he replies to
her: "This indeed grieves me, my lady; and I dare not ask the
reason." Lancelot would have expressed his great desolation had
the queen listened to him; but, to his hurt and dismay, without a
single word in response she went away into one of the rooms.
Lancelot accompanies her with his eyes and heart as far as the door;
but for his eyes it was a short journey as the room was very close by,
and they would dearly have liked to go in after her, had it been
possible. His heart, with its greater seniority and authority and
being far more powerful, did pass through after her while his eyes,
full of tears, remained outside with his body.

3999 The king then whispered to him in confidence: "Lancelot, I'm
most surprised, and wonder what can be the reason and motive for
the queen's refusal to see you and unwillingness to talk with you. If
ever it is her custom to speak to you, she shouldn't be reticent or
disregard what you say now, after what you've done for her. Tell
me now, if you know, for what reason or misdeed of yours she has
behaved like this towards you."—"Sire, I was not expecting that
just now. But she's not happy to see me or hear what I have to say,
and that greatly distresses and grieves me."—"It's certainly wrong
of her," says the king; "for you've even risked death on her behalf.
Come now, my dear good friend! We'll go and speak to the seneschal."—"I'll be very glad to," says he. They both proceed to the
seneschal. When Lancelot came to him, the seneschal's first words
to him were: "How you've shamed me!"—"I? In what way?" says
Lancelot. "What shame have I done you? Tell me!"—"Very great
shame; because you've succeeded in doing what I was unable to,
and have accomplished what I found impossible."

4031 With that the king leaves them together and goes out of the
room alone. Lancelot enquires of the seneschal whether he has
suffered a great deal. "Yes," he says, "and I still do. I've never been
in greater pain than now and would have been dead long ago but
for the king who has just left: he's shown me, out of sympathy, such

kindness and friendship that never, when he knew of anything I needed, did he once fail to have it provided for me the moment I wanted it. But for every kindness he showed me, his son Meleagant on the other hand, full of malicious trickery as he is, treacherously summoned the doctors and instructed them to treat my wounds with ointments that would kill me. Thus I had both a father and a stepfather;* for whenever the king, who would dearly have wished to see me quickly cured, had a beneficial plaster applied to my wounds, his son, intent on my death, treacherously had it promptly removed and replaced by a harmful ointment. I know for certain, though, that the king was unaware of this: he would in no way have allowed such murderous, wicked behaviour. But you don't know how generously he has behaved towards my lady: never since the time that Noah built the ark has any border tower been kept under such close guard that he has not protected her better still, not letting her so much as be seen, other than in public or in his own presence, by his son, who is very distressed at this. Thanks to the king's kindness, he treats her, and has done up to now, with every form of consideration she could propose. Nobody made suggestions about this other than she, for she determined how things were to be; and the king respected her all the more for the integrity he recognised in her. But is it true, as I'm told, that she's so very angry with you that she has totally refused in public to speak to you?"

4087 —"You've been told the absolute truth," says Lancelot. "But for God's sake, can you tell me why she hates me?" He replies that he does not know, but on the contrary is completely dumbfounded. "Let it be as she commands, then," says Lancelot, at a loss for any better course to take, then adds: "I must take my leave and go to look for my lord Gawain, who has entered this land and promised me to go straight to the underwater bridge." With that, he left the room, came before the king and asked his leave to make that journey. The king readily gives his permission; but those he had delivered and released from their captivity ask him what they shall do. He says: "Everyone who would like to accompany me may come; and those who wish to stay with the queen should do so: it's not right that they should come with me." All those who wish then go with him, more happy and joyful than they normally are. There remain with the queen maidens rejoicing openly as well as many ladies and knights. However, not a single one of those who stay behind would not have preferred to return to their own country than to remain there; but the queen keeps them back because my lord Gawain is coming; and she says she will not leave before she has news of him.

4125 The news has spread everywhere that the queen is quite free, and that all the captives are released and may legitimately leave whenever they please and see fit. The people of the land ask each other about the facts, and where folk gather together there is talk of nothing else. And they are very angry that the dangerous passages have been done away with and so anyone who wishes may come and go, and things are not as usual. But when the natives of the country who had not been present at the combat learned of Lancelot's performance in it, they all made off in the direction they knew he had taken; for they thought the king would be pleased if they caught Lancelot and took him back to him. His own men had all removed their arms and were therefore caught off guard when the men of the country arrived fully armed. It was no wonder they seized the unarmed Lancelot. They turn back with him captive, his feet tied together under his horse. His men say: "Sirs, this is wrong of you, for we're under the king's safe-conduct. We're all under his protection." The others say: "We don't know about that; but as we've taken you captive, you must come like this to court."

4158 The rumour, which quickly flies and spreads about, reaches the king claiming that his men have taken Lancelot and slain him. On hearing this, the king is very troubled and swears by far more than his head that those who have killed him shall die for it and never find any protection for themselves; for, if he can catch and seize them, no other fate will be theirs but to be hanged, burnt or drowned. And if they try to deny what they have done, he will on no account believe them, for they have filled his heart with too great a grief and committed so shameful an act that he would deserve reproach if it were not avenged; but vengeance will certainly be his.

4175 This rumour circulated until it reached the queen as she was sitting at table. On hearing the news of Lancelot, she almost killed herself there and then: it was false but, believing it to be true, she is so utterly dismayed that she is nearly speechless. However, for the benefit of the people there, she says aloud: "Indeed, I'm very sorry about his death; and my sadness is justified, since he entered this country for my sake, and so I should feel grieved." Then she says to herself, softly so that no one can hear, that she need never again be urged to drink or eat, if it is true that that man is dead whose life gave purpose to her own. She at once rises from the table in great distress, voicing her grief so that no one listening can overhear. She is so bent on killing herself that again and again she seizes herself by the throat. First, however, she confesses to herself, repents and says her *mea culpa*, and bitterly blames and accuses herself of the sin she had committed against him who, she knew, had always been hers and would still be, were he alive. She is so grief-stricken at the thought of her cruelty that she loses much of her beauty. Her cruelty, her wickedness weakened her and drained her colour more than her loss of sleep and fasting. She invokes together her misdeeds, and they all return to confront her.

4214 As she ponders them, she says again and again: "Alas, what was I thinking of, when my lover came before me and I should have made much of him, not even to be prepared to listen to him! Was I not foolish to deny him my glances and my words? Foolish? Rather, so help me God, I behaved with criminal cruelty. Yet I didn't mean it seriously; but that's how he took it, and he hasn't forgiven me for it. No one but I gave him his death-blow, I'm sure. When he came before me laughing and expecting me to be happy to see him and full of joy on his account and then I wouldn't see him, wasn't that a mortal blow? By refusing to speak to him, I then robbed him at the same time of his heart and his life. These two blows, it seems to me, have killed him: he wasn't the victim of any other kind of marauder. God! Shall I ever make reparation for this murder, this sin? No indeed: every river and the sea will dry up first! Alas, what a consolation and great comfort it would have been for me had I held him once in my arms before he died! And how? Certainly, with both of us naked for my greater pleasure. Since he is dead, I'm very wicked not to bring about my own death. But why? Should it then harm my lover for me to live on after his death, when I take delight in nothing but the pangs I suffer on his account? If I find pleasure in that after his death, the tribulations I now covet would have been most sweet to me were he alive. A woman is wrong to prefer death to enduring sorrow for her lover. It's indeed very pleasing to me to go on mourning him for a long time. I'd rather live and suffer these blows than die in order to find rest."

4263 For two days the queen mourned in this fashion without either eating or drinking, until people thought she was dead. There are many who are more prompt to bring bad news than good; and the report reaches Lancelot that his lady and beloved is dead. Do not doubt his distress at this: one and all may be sure that he was extremely sad and grief-stricken. If you want to hear and know the facts, he was truly so dejected that he held his life cheap. He wished to kill himself without delay, but first he uttered a brief lament. Tying a running noose with one end of a belt he wore round his waist, he says to himself through his tears: "Ah, Death, what an ambush you have now sprung on me to make me unwell though I'm in good health! I am unwell, yet feel no sickness except from the grief that weighs down on my heart. This grief is a sickness, in fact a mortal one. I'm very content it should be so, and please God I shall die of it. – What? If that doesn't please the Lord God, can I not die in some other way? Yes I shall, if only He will let me pull this noose tight round my throat: in that way I'm confident I can compel Death to slay me despite himself. Death, who has never coveted any but those who don't care for him, doesn't want to come, but my belt will bring him here as my prisoner; and once he's in my power, he'll do as I wish. That's so, but he'll be too slow to come, such is my anxiety to have him."

4302   Then he does not hesitate or delay, but puts his head into the noose until it lies round his neck; and so as to be sure of harming himself, he ties the end of the belt tightly to the saddle-bow without anyone noticing. Then he lets himself slip to the ground, wanting to have himself dragged by his horse until he expires: he does not deign to live a moment longer. When those who were riding with him see him fallen to the ground, they think he has fainted, for none of them notices the noose tied round his neck. At once they take him in their arms and lift him up. Then they found the noose through which, by placing it about his neck, he had become his own enemy. They are very quick to cut it. But the noose had hurt his throat so badly that for some time he was unable to speak, for the veins in his neck and throat were nearly ruptured: after that, even if he had badly wanted to, he was unable to do himself any damage. In his annoyance at being watched over, he was almost blazing with mortification, because he would very gladly have killed himself had no one been keeping an eye on him.

4335   Being unable to harm himself, he says: "Ah, base, vile Death! In God's name, Death, why did you lack the power and strength to take my life before my lady's? Perhaps you didn't wish or deign to do it because you'd have been doing a good deed! You spared me out of treachery, for you'll never be credited with any other motive. Oh, what service and what kindness, and how opportunely performed! A curse on anybody who thanks you or is grateful to you for this service! I don't know who hates me more: Life, who wants to keep me, or Death, who will not slay me. In this way I'm destroyed by the one and the other. But, so help me God, it is just that I live on against my wishes, for I should have killed myself as soon as my lady the queen gave me an indication of her hatred. And she didn't do that without some reason: no, she had a very proper motive, but I don't know what it was. Had I known, then before her soul went into God's presence, I would already have made as full amends as she wished, provided she'd had mercy on me. God, what could this crime have been? I think she perhaps knew I climbed into the cart. I don't know what she might have blamed me for except that. That was my undoing. If this was why she hated me, God! why did this misdeed count against me? A person who held me blameworthy for that never truly knew Love; for no one could name anything prompted by Love which would lend itself to reproach. On the contrary, whatever one may do for one's mistress is itself an act of love and courtliness.

4379 "But I didn't do it for my 'mistress'. I don't know, alas, what I should call her. I don't know if I should say 'mistress' or not: I don't care to use this name for her. But this much I think I know of love: that, if she loved me, she should not have despised me but have called me her true love, in view of the fact that it seemed to me an honour to do whatever Love wills, even to climb into a cart. She should have counted that an act of love; and there lies certain proof that in this way Love puts his followers to the test and recognises those who are truly his. But this service was not welcome to my lady, as I discovered from her attitude to me. Yet her lover did for her sake what has brought him shame and the reproaches and blame of many; and they've made what I'm blamed for a subject of ridicule and have changed my sweetness into bitterness. For I swear it is the habit of those who know nothing of love to wash even honour in shame. To immerse honour in shame is not, however, to wash, but to soil it. Those, in fact, who maltreat him in this way are ignorant of Love; and a person who does not fear his command greatly alienates himself from him. Undoubtedly, whoever does what Love bids is much the better for it, and everything he does is forgivable, whilst he who dares not do it is a coward."

4415   Thus Lancelot laments; and his men beside him grieve as they look after and support him. Meanwhile there comes the news that the queen is not dead. Lancelot takes comfort at once; and if before his great grief at her death had been deep and intense, his present joy at her being alive was a full hundred thousand times greater. When they came to within six or seven leagues of the stronghold where King Bademagu was, he was given news of Lancelot which delighted him: he heard with pleasure that he was alive and approaching, hale and hearty. With utmost courtesy he went to tell the queen; and she replies: "My dear sir, seeing that you tell me, I believe it; but had he been dead, I assure you that I should never have been happy again. My joy would have quite left me, if a knight in my service had met and suffered death."

4441   At that the king leaves her; and the queen is very impatient for the arrival of her lover and her joy. She is no longer disposed to pick any quarrel with him. However rumour, which does not rest but never ceases to fly about, once more reaches the queen, reporting that Lancelot would have killed himself for her, given the opportunity. She is glad of this and quite believes it, though she would not have wished that for anything, since it would have been a very heavy blow for her. Meanwhile, here is Lancelot arriving in great haste. As soon as the king sees him, he runs to kiss and embrace him, feeling as if he is going to fly, so light is he made by his joy. But this joy is shortlived on account of those who captured and bound Lancelot. The king says they were unlucky to have come, for death and destruction await them all. Their reply to him was that they believed that was what he wished. "It displeases me, but suited you," says the king. "And he's not the one affected by it: you've brought no shame on him but only on me, who was giving him safe-conduct. However you look at it, the shame is mine. But you'll never escape from me to treat it as a laughing matter." When Lancelot hears him fly into a rage, he does his very best to make and restore peace, which eventually he does. Then the king takes him to see the queen.

4478   This time the queen did not drop her eyes towards the ground, but went gaily to meet him, honoured him as best she could and had him sit beside her. Then, quite at their ease, they talked of whatever they chose; and they were not short of topics, for Love gave them a plentiful supply. When Lancelot sees things going well for him, since nothing he says fails to please the queen greatly, he says to her in confidence: "My lady, I wonder very much why, when you saw me yesterday, you behaved as you did and never uttered a word to me. You almost dealt me a mortal blow, and I was not so bold as to dare question you about it as I'm asking you now. My lady, I'm now ready to make amends, once you've told me of the crime which has brought me such great distress." Then the queen explains to him: "What? Were you not then ashamed and afraid of the cart? You showed great reluctance to climb in when you hesitated for the space of two steps. That indeed was why I refused either to address or to look at you."—"May God save me", says Lancelot, "from doing such a wrong a second time; and may God never have mercy on me if you were not absolutely right! My lady, accept my apology here and now, in God's name; and tell me, for His sake, if you might ever pardon me for it."—"My friend, you are completely and totally forgiven," says the queen. "I give you my pardon very willingly."

4519 —"My lady," he says, "I thank you. But I can't say to you here everything I would wish to. I'd like to speak with you at greater leisure, if possible." Then the queen indicates to him a window with her eyes, not her finger, and says: "Come and talk to me at that window tonight, when everyone inside is asleep: you can reach it through a garden. You'll not be able to get or stay in there: I shall be inside and you outside and unable to enter; and I shall not be able to reach you except with my mouth or hand. But if you wish, I'll be there until the morning for love of you. We can't come together, because opposite me in my room lies Kay the seneschal, suffering from the wounds with which he's covered; and as for the door, it's not left open but is shut tight and well guarded. When you come, make sure that no lookout spots you."—"My lady," says he, "if I can help it, I'll not be seen by any spy who might think or speak evil of it." So, after this discussion, they separate very happily.

4551 Lancelot leaves the room so happy that he does not remember any of all his troubles. But for him the night is too long in coming, and what he has to bear with makes his day last longer than a hundred others or an entire year. He would have gone very gladly to the tryst, had night fallen. Eventually black, dark night, having won its struggle with the day, drew over it its covering and wrapped it in its cloak. Seeing the daylight fade, he pretends to be weary and exhausted and says that, having lost much sleep, he needs to rest. You, who have done as much yourselves, can understand and supply the reason for his shamming tiredness and going to bed with an eye to the people in his house; but he found little attraction in his bed and would not have rested there for anything, nor could he or would he dare, or even wish to have the courage and ability to do so. Very soon he quietly left it and was by no means sorry that there was no moon or star shining, and in the house no candle, lamp or lantern burning.

4582   Out he went, taking such care that nobody noticed him: on the contrary, they expected him to be fast asleep in his bed all night. With no companion or escort, he goes quickly towards the garden without meeting a soul; and it is lucky for him that a piece of the garden wall has recently fallen down. He passes swiftly through this breach and continues up to the window; and there he stands quietly without so much as a cough or a sneeze until the queen has come, wearing a pure white smock. Over it she had put on no tunic or jacket, but wore a short mantle of fine cloth and marmot fur. When Lancelot sees the queen leaning at the window with its massive iron bars, he offers her, as pledge, a tender greeting. Promptly she gives another in return; for they were full of desire, he for her and she for him. The conversation they exchange contains nothing base or tedious. They draw towards each other until they can hold one another's hand.

4612   Their inability to come close together makes them extremely sad, to the point of accusing the iron grille. Lancelot, however, boasts that, if the queen approves, he will go inside with her: the bars would never keep him out. To this the queen replies: "Can't you see how stiff this iron is to bend and tough to break? You couldn't wrench or tug or pull them hard enough to tear out a single one."—"My lady," he says, "don't worry! I really don't think iron bars could stop me. Your restraint alone can keep me from joining you without difficulty. If you give me your permission to do so, the way is quite open to me; but without your ready consent, it's so full of obstacles for me that I couldn't possibly get past."—"Certainly," she says, "I do want that: my wishes don't stand in your way.

But you must wait until I'm back in my bed, in case you're unlucky enough to make a noise. For there would be no pleasures or enjoyment if the seneschal, who sleeps here, were wakened by your noise. So it's only proper for me to go back, because there's no good construction he could put on it if he saw me standing here."—"Go then, my lady," he says. "But don't have any fear of my making a noise. I think I can pull away the bars so softly and effortlessly that I'll not wake anyone."

4651 With that the queen withdraws, and he makes ready and prepares to force the window. He takes hold of the bars, which he pulls and tugs until he bends them all and drags them from their sockets. But the iron was so sharp that he split the tip of his little finger to the nerve and cut the end joint of his second finger right through. However, with his mind on another matter, he feels neither the wounds nor the blood that drips down from them. The window is by no means low, nevertheless Lancelot passes through quickly and easily. After finding Kay asleep in his bed, he comes to that of the queen, to whom he bows in adoration, for no holy relic inspires him with such faith.* The queen holds out her arms to him and embraces him, hugging him to her breast, then draws him into her bed beside her, showing him all the endearments of which she is capable, prompted by the love in her heart.

4679 The warmth of her welcome is motivated by love; and if he was very dear to her, his love for her was a hundred thousand times as great, for love in all other hearts was non-existent compared with that in his own: in his heart love was wholly rooted and so totally present that there was but a meagre supply for all other hearts. Now Lancelot has all he desires, when the queen welcomes his company and intimacy, with him holding her in his arms and she embracing him. He finds her love-making so sweet and splendid as they kiss and fondle that they truly come to experience such joy and wonderment that its equal was never heard or known; but of that I shall keep silent, since it should not be told in a story. The supreme and most exquisite of their joys was that which the tale conceals from us and leaves untold.

4703 All that night Lancelot experienced great joy and pleasure. But, to his deep regret, day comes and he rises from his beloved's side. When he did so he was a true martyr: so distressed was he at the parting that when it came he endured terrible martyrdom. His heart is ceaselessly drawn back to where the queen remains; and he has no power to take it away, for it finds in the queen such pleasure that it has no wish to leave her: the body goes, but the heart stays behind. He goes straight back to the window; but enough of himself remains behind for the sheets to be soiled and stained with the blood that dripped from his fingers. Lancelot leaves in very great distress, full of sighs and tears. No time has been set for them to meet again; and much as that grieves him, it cannot be. Reluctantly he goes out through the window by which he had entered most willingly. His fingers were by no means unscathed, for he had injured them badly; yet he straightened the bars and put them back in place so that from neither in front nor behind nor from one side or the other did it seem that any of them had been removed or pulled away or bent. As he left, he bowed before the room, behaving just as though he were before an altar, then went away in deep anguish.

4738 Without meeting anyone who knew him, he came to his lodging. He lies down naked in his bed without waking a soul; and then for the first time he notices with astonishment that his fingers are injured. However, he is not at all alarmed at that, since he has no doubt that he hurt himself in pulling from the wall the bars at the window. He was not vexed on that account, because he would rather have had both arms pulled off than have failed to get through. Had he, though, hurt and so seriously injured himself in another place, he would have been highly distressed and upset.

4755 In the morning, the queen had fallen into a gentle sleep in her curtained room, without noticing how her sheets were blood-stained,* but supposing them to be perfectly white and immaculate as they should be. Meleagant, as soon as he was dressed and ready, went to the room where the queen was lying, to find her aroused. Then, seeing the sheets stained and spotted with fresh blood, he nudged his companions and, as if noticing something amiss, looked across at Kay the seneschal's bed, where he saw that his sheets were blood-stained; for, you understand, his wounds had opened during the night. Then he said: "Now, my lady, I've found the kind of evidence I wanted! It's very true that it is sheer folly for anyone to attempt to keep an eye on a woman: he wastes his efforts and his pains, since the man who keeps a watch on her loses her sooner than the one who pays her no attention. In having you kept under surveillance on my account, my father has mounted a splendid guard! He's kept you from me all right; but in spite of him Kay the seneschal had his eyes on you last night and has done just as he pleased with you, as will be clearly proved."—"How?" she asks.—"I've found blood on your sheets as evidence, since I'm compelled to say. I know it and have proof by finding on your sheets and his the blood that ran from his wounds: that's conclusive evidence."

4795 Then for the first time the queen saw the bloody sheets on both of the beds. She was amazed and blushed scarlet for shame, then said: "As the Lord God is my protector, this blood I see on my sheets was never put there by Kay; but my nose bled during the night – I suppose it came from my nose." And she thinks she is speaking the truth. "By my head," says Meleagant, "there's nothing at all in what you say. It's no use prevaricating, because you've been caught in the act, and the truth will be fully proved." Then, to the guards who were there, he said: "Sirs, don't go away; and make sure the sheets aren't taken off the bed before I get back! I want the king to do me justice once he's seen how things are."

4816 He then looked for him until he found him. Falling at his feet, he says: "Sire, come and see something you don't suspect. Come to see the queen, and you'll witness a truly amazing thing that I've found out and seen for myself. But before you go there, I beg you not to deprive me of justice and my rights. You're well aware to what risks I've exposed myself for the queen in the face of your hostility as shown by your having her guarded from me. This morning I went to look at her in her bed, and I saw enough to convince me that Kay lies with her every night. For God's sake, sire, don't take it amiss if I'm upset and complain about this, because it's extremely humiliating for me to be hated and despised by her while Kay enjoys sexual relations with her."—"Silence!" says the king. "I don't believe it."—"Then come, sire, and see the sheets and what Kay has done to them. As you don't take my word for it but think I'm lying to you, I'll show you the sheets and bedspread stained with the blood from Kay's wounds."—"Let's go, then, and I'll look," says the king, "for I want to see it. My eyes will teach me the truth of the matter."

4849 The king goes immediately to the room, to find the queen just getting up. He sees the blood-stained sheets on her bed and also on

Kay's and says: "Lady, things are serious if what my son has told me is true." She replies: "So help me God, such a wicked lie was never told, even in a dream! I'm sure Kay the seneschal is so courtly and loyal that he's not to be mistrusted; and I don't put my body up for sale or offer it for the taking in the market-place. Indeed, Kay is not a man to make such a shocking request of me; and I've never been disposed to do that or ever will be."—"Sire," says Meleagant to his father, "I'll be most grateful to you to have Kay pay for his outrage so that the queen may be put to shame. Justice is your business and responsibility, and I claim and beg it from you. Kay has betrayed his lord King Arthur, who had placed such confidence in him that he had entrusted to him the one he loves most in the world."

4878 "Sire, permit me to reply now," says Kay, "and I shall clear my name. May God, when I leave this world, never grant my soul pardon if ever I lay with my lady! Indeed, I would rather be dead than be responsible for attempting such a vile wrong against my lord; and may God never grant me better health than I have now but rather may I be struck dead on the spot, if ever that thought entered my mind! But this much I know: that my wounds bled profusely during the night, and that has made my sheets blood-stained. This is why your son suspects me, but without any justification whatsoever." Then Meleagant answers him: "So help me God, the devils and living demons have betrayed you! Last night you grew too overheated, and no doubt your wounds opened because you over-exerted yourself. Excuses will do you no good: the blood in both places is proof – we can see it plainly, and it's quite obvious. It's right that someone who is caught red-handed should pay the penalty. No knight of your eminence ever acted so disgracefully, and you are shamed for it."—"My lord, sire," says Kay to the king, "I shall defend my lady and myself against your son's accusations. He causes me trouble and vexation, but is harrying me quite wrongfully."—"You can do without a combat", says the king, "for you're not fit enough."—"Sire, if you will allow it, I shall fight him sick as I am and demonstrate that I'm guiltless of the charge he lays against me."

4922 The queen, however, had sent secretly for Lancelot; and she tells the king she will have a knight to defend the seneschal against Meleagant, if he dare face him, in this affair. At once Meleagant said: "I don't draw the line for you at any knight, even if he were a giant, against whom I'd not do battle until one of us was left vanquished." Thereupon Lancelot entered, and with him such a great crowd of knights that they filled the entire hall. As soon as he had arrived, the queen tells of the situation in the hearing of all, young and greybeards alike. She said: "Lancelot, I've been taxed here by Meleagant with this shameful act. He has put me under suspicion in the eyes of all those who hear him say it, unless you make him retract his words. Last night, he claimed, Kay lay with me; for he's seen my sheets and his stained with blood. And he says Kay stands convicted, unless he can defend himself against him or unless some other is prepared to help him by undertaking the combat."

4950 —"There's no need for you to plead in your defence", says Lancelot, "so long as I am present. May it not please God that either you or he should be suspected of such a thing! I'm ready to take on the combat to refute, if it is in my power, the charge that he ever thought of such a thing. I shall defend him to the best of my ability and undertake the combat on his behalf." Meleagant sprang forward with the words: "As God is my saviour, I'm happy with that: it suits me very well, and let no one suppose I object." Then Lancelot said: "My lord king, I have some knowledge of trials, laws, disputes and judgments: with such allegations no combat should be fought without oaths being taken." Unhesitatingly Meleagant quickly replies: "Let oaths be taken, then, and the holy relics be brought at once, for I'm quite sure I'm in the right." Lancelot retorts: "No one, so help me God, who has known Kay the seneschal has ever suspected him of such an act."

4977 They at once ask for their horses and order their arms to be brought, which are promptly fetched: attendants help them on with them, and they are armed. Next the relics are produced. Meleagant steps forward with Lancelot beside him, and they both kneel. Meleagant stretches out his hand to them and swears outright: "So help me God and this saint, Kay the seneschal last night kept company with the queen in her bed and took his full pleasure with her."—"And I charge you with perjury," says Lancelot, "and swear for my part that he did not lie with her or touch her. And may God, if it please Him, take vengeance on him who has lied and make the truth plain. But I will take one further oath and swear that, no matter whom it may displease or vex, if today I may be enabled by the sufficient aid of God and these relics here to get the better of Meleagant, then I shall never have mercy on him." The king felt no joy at all when he heard this oath.

5007 When the oaths had been taken, their horses, which were handsome and excellent in every respect, were brought out for them. Each mounts his own, and they ride at one another as fast as their steeds can carry them. Then, when their horses are at full gallop, the valiant knights strike each other so hard that nothing at all is left of their lances beyond their fists. The one brings the other to the ground; but they look far from finished, for they get up at once and do each other what harm they can with the blades of their naked swords. The blazing sparks fly up towards the heavens from their helmets. So furiously do they attack each other with the swords bared in their hands that, in the cut and thrust, they clash and exchange blows without allowing themselves enough rest to be able to recover their breath. The king, very unhappy and worried at this, called to the queen, who had gone up to lean from the balcony in the keep, and asked her in the name of God the Creator to let them be separated. "I'm happy with whatever pleases you," says the queen, quite sincerely. "You'll not offend me at all."

5039 Lancelot heard clearly what the queen replied to the king's request, whereupon he made no further attempt to fight, but quit the fray immediately. Meleagant, having no mind to pause, strikes and hacks at him; but the king thrusts himself between them and holds back his son, who says and swears that he has no wish to make peace – he wants to fight and is not interested in a truce. Then the king tells him: "Be quiet and have the sense to take my advice. You'll certainly suffer no shame or harm if you take my word, but will be acting as you should. Don't you remember you arranged for a combat against him at King Arthur's court? And can you have any doubt that it would be a greater honour for you to succeed there than anywhere else?" The king, having said this to try and calm him, does quieten him down and so separates them.

5064 Lancelot, very anxious to find my lord Gawain, then comes to seek and request leave from the king and afterwards from the queen. With their permission he makes his way speedily towards the underwater bridge, with a very large band of knights following along behind; but of those making the journey he would have been glad to have many stay where they were. They cover a very good distance each day until they are approaching the underwater bridge but still a league short of it. Before they came close enough to the bridge to be able to see it, a dwarf on a great hunter came to meet them holding a whip for driving and goading on his mount. At once he asked, as he had been instructed: "Which of you is Lancelot? Don't keep it from me – I'm on your side. Just tell me in confidence, because I'm asking it for your own great profit." Lancelot answers for himself, saying: "I'm the very man you're looking and asking for."—"Ah, noble knight," says the dwarf, "leave these people and trust in me. Come along with me on your own, for I want to take you to an excellent place. Let no one follow you on any account, but let them wait for you at this spot, because we'll be back shortly."

5099 Suspecting nothing wrong, he has his entire company stay behind and follows the dwarf, who has betrayed him. His men awaiting him there may have to do so for a very long time, because the people who have seized and captured him have no intention of handing him back. And when he fails to show up or return, his men are so distressed that they do not know what they can do. They all say the dwarf has betrayed them and are much concerned. To search for him would be futile; yet sorrowfully they do begin to look, though without knowing where they might find him or in what direction to seek him. Then they discuss the matter together. The most sensible and wisest of them agree, it seems, that they should go to the nearby passage of the underwater bridge and after that search for Lancelot with the advice of my lord Gawain, should they find him in wood or plain. They all entirely agree on this plan, without any dissent.

5125 They set off for the underwater bridge, and as soon as they reach it they see my lord Gawain, * who had slipped and fallen from the bridge into the very deep water. One moment he surfaces and the next he sinks, now they see him and now lose sight of him. They leap forward and manage to catch him with branches, poles and hooks. He only had his hauberk on his back; and on his head was set his helmet, which was worth a good ten others; and he wore his iron greaves that were rusty from his sweat, for he had endured many hardships and suffered and overcome many perils and assaults. His lance, shield and horse remained on the other bank.

Those who have pulled him from the water do not think he is alive, for he has taken in a great deal of it, and until he has disgorged it, they hear no word from him. But once his speech and voice were regained and the passage to his heart cleared so that he could be heard and understood, just as soon as he was able to utter a word, he spoke, asking those present at once about the queen and whether they had any news of her. And those who answered him said that she never leaves the company of King Bademagu, who does her great service and honour.

5161 "Has anyone come to seek her in this land since she arrived?" asks my lord Gawain. "Yes," they reply.—"Who?"—"Lancelot of the Lake," they say, "who crossed the Sword Bridge and rescued and delivered her along with all the rest of us. But a stunted, hunchbacked, grimacing dwarf has betrayed us and basely tricked us by abducting Lancelot from us; and we don't know what he's done with him."—"When was that?" asks my lord Gawain.—"The dwarf did this to us today, my lord, very near here, as Lancelot was coming with us to find you."—"And how has he conducted himself since he entered this country?" Then they set about telling him, giving him a thorough account without forgetting a single detail; and as for the queen, they inform him that she is waiting for him and says that certainly nothing would induce her to leave the country before seeing him or hearing credible news of him. My lord Gawain replies to them: "When we leave this bridge, shall we go in search of Lancelot?" Every single one of them advises that they should rather go first to the queen, and the king will have a search made for him, because they think that his son Meleagant, who really hates him, has had him treacherously taken captive. Wherever he may be, if the king knows, he will have him handed over: they can confidently expect that.

5199 They all agreed to this plan and at once took to the road, travelling until they approached the court where the queen and the king were. With them was Kay the seneschal; and there too was that perfidious man, full to the brim with treachery, who has caused all those now on their way to worry desperately about Lancelot. They feel themselves utterly thwarted and betrayed, and in great distress display their bitter grief. This is uncivil news to bring the queen such grief; nevertheless she takes it as cheerfully as she can. For the sake of my lord Gawain she has to bear it to some extent, and so she does. Even so, she does not hide her grief so well as not to show it a little. She has to express both joy and grief: her heart is faint for Lancelot, and towards my lord Gawain she makes a show of being overjoyed. No one who hears the news of the loss of Lancelot is not full of sorow and dismay at it.

5225 To have my lord Gawain arrive and to make his acquaintance would have been a joy and delight for the king; but he is so sad and depressed by the betrayal of Lancelot that he is dejected and dumbfounded. Then the queen calls him, begging him to have him sought up hill and down dale throughout his land without delay or respite. So do my lord Gawain and Kay: there is not a single person who fails to make the same request and appeal. "Leave this to me", says the king, "and say no more about it, for I've already been prepared for some time to do that. This search will indeed be carried out with no need for begging or asking." Everybody bows and pays him reverence. Then the king sends at once throughout his realm his messengers, trusty, prudent servants who asked for news of Lancelot over the whole country. Everywhere they sought for some word of him, but without learning anything of the truth. They find out nothing and so return to where the knights are staying, Gawain, Kay and the rest, who declare that they will go to seek him fully armed and lance in rest: they will never send anyone else on the quest.

5257 One day, after their meal, they were all arming themselves in the hall, having reached the point where it only remained for them to set out, when a youth entered and passed among them to come before the queen. There was no rosy hue to her complexion, since her grief for Lancelot, of whom she had no news, was such that she had lost all her colour. The youth greeted both her and the king, who was near to her, and then all the others in turn, together with Kay and my lord Gawain. In his hand he held a letter; and this he handed to the king, who took it. So that all could hear, he had it read out by someone who did so accurately: the reader had no difficulty in telling them what he saw written on the parchment. He says that Lancelot greets the king as his good lord and, as one entirely at his discretion and command, thanks him for the honour and service he has done him. And he may know quite definitely that he is hale and hearty with King Arthur; and he suggests the queen be advised that, if she pleases, she should come there with my lord

Gawain and Kay. The message bore credible identification marks, and they fully believed it. It made them very glad and happy: the whole court rings with joy.

5294 The next morning at daybreak they say they will start back. So when it is daylight they get ready and equip themselves and, having risen, mount and set off. The king follows and escorts them happily and with a show of great joy for a considerable distance along their way, conducting them out of his land. Having seen them across the frontier, he took leave of the queen and then of all the others together. And the queen, at the leavetaking, thanks him graciously for all the services he has done her; and, putting her arms round his neck, she offers and pledges him her own service and that of her lord: more than that she cannot promise. My lord Gawain also pledges his, as to his lord and friend; so does Kay, and all make him the same promise. With that they take to the road, and the king commends them to God. After those three he salutes all the rest; and then he turns back.

5320 The queen and the company she leads do not rest any day all that week, until the news reached the court of her approach, which delighted the king, and of his nephew's, which also filled his heart with great joy and gladness, for he supposed his prowess to be responsible for the return of the queen and Kay and all the lesser folk; but things are different from what he thinks. For them the whole town empties, with everyone going to meet them, and all who come up with them, knights and common folk alike, say: "Welcome to my lord Gawain, who has brought back the queen, freed many ladies from captivity, and restored many prisoners to us!" Gawain answered them: "Sirs, you praise me without reason. Don't trouble to say this any more, for I've had nothing to do with it. This honour you do me brings me shame, for I didn't arrive in time, but too late, and failed through my tardiness. Lancelot, however, got there in time and achieved such great honour that no knight ever won greater."—"Where is he then, dear good sir, since we don't see him anywhere here?"—"Where?" is Gawain's prompt rejoinder. "At my lord the king's court. – Isn't he there, then?"—"No indeed, nor in the whole of this territory. We've had no news of him since my lady was abducted."

5358 Then for the first time my lord Gawain realised that the missive which betrayed and deceived them was forged. They have been duped by that letter. Then they are all moved to grief once more: they come lamenting to court, and the king immediately asks to be told what has happened. There were plenty of people to tell him how Lancelot had performed, how through him the queen and all the captives have been recovered, and how and by what deception the dwarf stole and inveigled him from them. This business is not to the king's liking, but greatly grieves and vexes him. His spirits, however, are raised by his great joy on account of the queen, so that his grief gives way to joy: when he has the one he most desires, he feels little sorrow for anything else.

5379 While the queen was out of the country, it seems, the ladies and damsels, who were in low spirits, conferred together and decided they would like to be married in the very near future; and as a result of their discussion they arranged a contest and tournament, with the lady of Noauz issuing a challenge to the lady of Pomelegloi. They will have nothing to do with those who perform badly in it; but they declare they will willingly accept those who do well. So they had it proclaimed and announced throughout all the neighbouring lands as well as the distant ones, having the date of the contest promulgated very well in advance to ensure a better attendance.

5400 Now before the appointed day, the queen arrived; and as soon as they learnt that the queen had come, most of them travelled to the court and came before the king to ply him with their requests to do them a favour and grant them their wish. Before he knew what they had in mind, he agreed to do whatever they wanted. They then told him they would like him to permit the queen to come and see their tourney; and he, unaccustomed to refusing anything, said he was willing, if she wished to do so. Delighted at this, they go to the queen and say at once: "Lady, don't deprive us of what the king has granted us!" She asked them: "What is that? Don't keep it from me!" Then they tell her: "If you wish to attend our tourney, he has no desire to prevent you and has no objection." So she says that, since he gives his permission, she will go to it. At that the damsels send word throughout the kingdom, proclaiming that they were to bring the queen along on the day announced for the jousting.

5435 The news spread everywhere, far and near, in this direction and that, travelling so far and wide that it reached the realm from which no one used to return, although now whoever wished was free to enter and leave without any prohibition. In that realm the news was told and passed on and spread until it came to the ears of a seneschal of the perfidious Meleagant, the traitor – may he burn in hellfire! He had in his keeping Lancelot, whom his enemy Meleagant in his bitter hatred had made over to him to hold captive. Lancelot learned about the tourney, its time and date; and after he heard of it his eyes were never without tears or his heart glad.

5456 The lady of the house saw Lancelot miserable and pensive and spoke to him in private. "Sir, in God's name and for your soul's sake, tell me truly", says the lady, "why you are so changed. You neither drink nor eat, and I don't see you joking or laughing. It's safe for you to tell me what's on your mind and what troubles you."—"Ah, my lady, in God's name don't be surprised that I'm miserable, for I'm truly very despondent when I can't be where all the good in the world will be: at the tourney where the earth trembles beneath all the people gathering there. Nevertheless, if it pleased you and God granted you the courtesy to let me go there, you could be quite certain that I would act properly towards you and return to be your prisoner."—"Indeed," she says, "I'd do that very willingly if I didn't see it leading to my undoing and my ruin. But I'm so terrified of my lord, the vile Meleagant, that I wouldn't dare do it, for he would utterly destroy my husband. It's no wonder I'm afraid of him in view of his wickedness, which you well know."

5488 —"My lady, if you're frightened that I wouldn't return to my captivity with you immediately after the contest, I'll take an oath that I shall never break, swearing that nothing will ever keep me from returning to your custody straight after the tournament."—"Upon my word, then," says she, "I'll allow it on one condition."—"What's that, my lady?" She replies: "That you swear to me, sir, to come back and also promise me that I shall have your love."—"My lady, I grant you all I have, and swear to return."—"Now," says the lady with a laugh, "there's nothing there that I can depend on. I'm well aware that you've bestowed on someone else the gift of the love I've asked of you. Even so, I'm not too proud to take as much of it as I can get. I'll cling on to what I can and accept your oath that you will behave properly towards me by returning into my charge."

5515 Lancelot meets her wish by swearing for her by holy Church that he will come back without fail. With that the lady gives him her

husband's scarlet arms together with his horse, which was wonderfully handsome, strong and bold. He mounted, then set forth,
armed with a splendid set of brand-new arms, and journeyed until
he came to Noauz. Choosing to joust on the Noauz side, he took
lodgings outside the town. Never did so noble a man have any like
these, for they were extremely cramped and mean; but he had no
wish to stay anywhere he might be recognised. There were numerous fine, outstanding knights gathered in the fortress; but there
were a lot more outside, for so many had come because of the queen
that not a fifth of them could be lodged within the walls: out of
every eight there, fully seven would not have attended had it not
been for the queen's presence. The nobles were quartered for a
good five leagues round about in tents, lodges and pavilions. There
was also an amazing number of elegant ladies and damsels.

5546 Lancelot had set his shield outside the door of his lodging and,
in order to relax, had taken off his armour and was lying on a bed
that was not at all to his liking, being narrow, with a thin mattress,
and covered with a coarse hemp cloth. On this bed Lancelot was
reclining, completely disarmed. As he lay there so uncomfortably,
suddenly there appeared a fellow in his shirt-sleeves, a herald-
at-arms, who had left his coat and shoes as a pledge at the tavern
and came rushing in, barefoot and in a general state of undress. He
found the shield in front of the door and inspected it, but was quite
unable to recognise it or tell who owned it or was to bear it. Seeing
the door of the house open, he goes in and sees Lancelot lying on the
bed. As soon as he set eyes on him, he recognised him and crossed
himself at the sight. Then Lancelot gave him strict instructions not
to mention him wherever he might go; because if he did say he
knew about him, it would be better for him to have his eyes plucked
out or his neck broken. "My lord," says the herald, "I've always
much admired and esteemed you, and so long as I live, nothing will
induce me to do anything to make you annoyed with me." With
that he dashes out of the house and goes off shouting at the top of
his voice: "Now the one who will take their measure has arrived!
The one who will take their measure has arrived!" The fellow
shouts this everywhere, and people rush up from all directions
asking him the meaning of his call. He is not so rash as to say, but
instead goes off shouting the same thing. That, in fact, was the first
use of the expression "Now the one who will take their measure has

arrived!" It was from that herald, who taught us to say it, that we
learnt it.

5595 The companies have now assembled: the queen and all the
ladies, the knights and other people, along with many men-at-arms
to right and left, on all sides. In the place where the tournament was
to be held there were large wooden stands for the use of the queen,
the ladies and the maidens: such fine, long, well-constructed stands
had never before been seen. Following the queen, all the ladies
gathered there, wanting to see the contest and who would perform
better or worse. Knights arrived in tens, twenties and thirties,
eighty here, ninety or a hundred there, now more, now twice as
many, so that, with such a large crowd assembled around and in
front of the stands, they begin the combat. As they gather, some
armed, some unarmed, the lances are like a great forest; for so
many are brought by those wanting to join in the sport that there is
nothing but lances, banners and standards to be seen. The jousters
move into position to find plenty of companions who have also
come for the jousting; and the others, for their part, prepare to
engage in different knightly contests. The meadows and ploughed
and fallow land are so full that it is impossible to estimate the
number of the knights, so many were there. At that first encounter,
though, Lancelot made no appearance. However, when he came
across the meadow and the herald saw his arrival, he could not
refrain from shouting: "Here's the one who will take their measure! Here's the one who will take their measure!" They ask him:
"Who is that?" But he refuses to tell them anything.

5641 When Lancelot joined in the tourney, he alone was worth
twenty of the best. And he begins to do so well that no one can take
his eyes off him, wherever he is. On the Pomelegloi side there was a
bold, valiant knight, whose horse was spirited and swifter than a
wild stag. He was the King of Ireland's son and performed well and
handsomely; but everybody was four times as pleased with the
unknown knight. They all ask frantically: "Who is this man who is
fighting so well?" The queen drew to one side a prudent, sensible
girl and said: "Maiden, you must take a message and convey it
quickly and in few words. Get down from this stand and go for me
to that knight bearing the scarlet shield, then tell him privately that
I bid him do 'his worst'." She goes there promptly and carefully
carries out the queen's wishes. She makes her way to the knight;

and, coming up close to him, says with polite tact out of the hearing of any man or woman nearby: "Sir, the instructions I bring you from my lady the queen are to do 'your worst'." Hearing this, he replies: "Very willingly!" in the manner of someone who is entirely hers.

5677 Then he rides against a knight as fast as his horse can carry him, but misses when he should have struck him; and thereafter until evening fell he did nothing but the worst he could, since that was the queen's pleasure. His opponent did not miss in his attack, but struck him to his great discomfiture. At that he took flight without ever again turning his charger's head towards any knight; nor would he, for as much as his life was worth, do anything in which he did not see his great shame, disgrace and dishonour, pretending to be afraid of all those who come and go. And the knights who greatly respected him earlier now make him the object of their jokes and ridicule. Then the herald who had been saying: "He'll defeat them all in turn!" is most miserable and upset, for he hears their gibes and taunts as they shout: "Say no more now, friend! This one won't take our measure any more: he's been measuring so much that he's broken that yardstick of his which you praised so much for us." Many say: "What does this mean? Not long ago he was so valiant, yet now he's such a cowardly wretch that he daren't face any knight. Perhaps he did so well at first because he'd never before taken part in armed combat; so when he arrived he was so brave that no knight, however expert, could stand up to him, for he struck like a madman. Now he's learnt so much about the business of arms that he'll never want to bear them again as long as he lives. His heart can't stand it any longer, for he's the world's greatest coward."

5720 As she watches him, the queen is delighted and well pleased, for she is quite sure, though she keeps it to herself, that this is certainly Lancelot. Thus all day long until evening he let himself be thought a coward. But when night approached, they dispersed; and as they parted there was much talk about those who had performed best. The King of Ireland's son thinks it cannot be contradicted or denied that the chief credit and merit belong to him; but he is seriously mistaken, since many were as good as he. Even the red knight so pleased the fairest and most beautiful of the ladies and maidens that they had had no eyes that day for any other so much as for him; for they had plainly seen how he had at first performed valiantly and boldly, before then becoming so cowardly that he did not dare face any knight, but the very worst could have felled and captured him had he wished.

5746 However, they were all prepared, knights and ladies alike, to return to the tourney on the morrow; and the damsels would take as husbands those who won honour that day: this they declare and confirm. They then return to their lodgings. Once they were back, people in various places began to ask: "Where is the worst, the most worthless and despicable of knights? What's become of him? Where has he hidden himself? Where is he to be found? Where shall we look for him? Perhaps we'll never see him again; for he's been driven away by cowardice, with which he's so loaded himself down that he's the most craven creature in the world. And he's not wrong, for a coward enjoys a hundred thousand times more comfort than an intrepid fighter. Cowardice is very easy-going, and that's why he's given her the kiss of peace and accepted from her all he possesses. Certainly Prowess has never debased herself to the extent of lodging within him or placing herself at his side; but Cowardice has entirely sheltered in him, finding a host who will do her such honour and service that for the sake of her honour he loses his own." The scandal-mongers spend the whole night in such slanderous talk. But one man often speaks ill of another when he is far worse than the one he blames and disparages. Everyone, then, spoke his mind about him.

5783 When day broke, all the people made ready again and returned to the tourney. The queen was back in the stand with the ladies and maidens; and with them too were numerous knights without their arms who had been captured or who had taken the cross,* and who interpreted for them the armorial bearings of their favourite knights. They say among themselves: "Do you see the one now with the golden band across the red shield? That's Governal of Roberdic. And can you see that next one with an eagle and a dragon painted side by side on his shield? That's the son of the King of Aragon, who has come to this country to win honour and renown. And can you see the one beside him who is spurring so hard and jousting so well, the one with part of his shield green with a leopard painted on it and the other half azure? That's the much-loved Ignaures,* the popular lover. Then that one bearing the shield with the pheasants painted beak to beak is Coguillant of Mautirec. And do you see, to his side, those two on dappled horses and with sable lions on their golden shields? One is called Semiramis and the other is his companion, which is why their shields have the same decoration. Do you see too the one whose shield is painted with a gate from which a stag seems to be emerging? I swear that's King Yder." Such were the explanations given in the stands.

5824 "That shield was made in Limoges and brought here by Pilades, who always wants to be in the fight: he's a real glutton for it. That other one, along with the horse's breast-band and straps, was made in Toulouse and brought by Kay of Estraus. That one came from Lyons on the Rhône, and there's none so fine under heaven; and it was presented for some outstanding service to Taulas of the Desert, who bears it and defends himself splendidly with it. That other one is of English workmanship, made in London: you see those two swallows on it that seem about to fly off; but they don't move and instead take many blows from weapons of Poitou steel. It's young Thoas who carries that."

5843 In this way they distinguish and describe the arms of those they recognise; but they see no sign there of the one they had held in such contempt, so they assume he has slipped away, as he has not joined in the jousting. When the queen sees nothing of him, she has a mind to send someone to search the lists until he is found. She knows of no one better she can send to look for him than the girl who went to him on her behalf the previous day. She summons her at once, saying to her: "Go, damsel, and mount your palfrey! I'm sending you to the same knight as yesterday, so search for him until you find him. Don't delay on any account! Then tell him once more that now again he must do 'his worst'; and when you've given him these instructions, pay attention to how he replies." The girl wastes no time at all; for the previous evening she had taken good care to note the direction in which he left, since she was convinced she would be sent to him again. She made her way through the lists until she spotted the knight. At once she goes to advise him to do "his worst" once more if he wishes to enjoy the queen's love and favour: this is her bidding. He replies: "My thanks to her, since she commands it!" Thereupon the girl left him.

5879 Then a shout goes up from grooms, men-at-arms and squires: "Here's an amazing thing! The one who wore the scarlet armour

yesterday is back again. But what can he want? There's really no
such base, despicable renegade as he on this earth. He's so firmly in
the grip of cowardice that there's nothing he can do about it." The
maiden makes her way back to the queen who, after pressing her
very closely, obtained that answer which brought her great joy,
since she now knows without any doubt that this is he to whom she
belongs entirely, whilst he is totally hers. She tells the maiden to
hurry back and tell him that she orders and begs him to do "the very
best" he can; and she replies that she will go at once and not linger.
She went down from the stand to where her groom was waiting for
her in charge of her palfrey. Then she mounts and rides until she
finds the knight, to whom she goes at once with the words: "Now,
sir, my lady bids you do 'the very best' you can." He answers: "Tell
her then that there's nothing I'm loath to do, if she approves; for
whatever pleases her is a pleasure for me."

5914   Then the girl was not slow to return with her message, confidently expecting it to gladden and delight the queen. She made for
the stands as directly as she could; and the queen rose and went to
meet her, not going all the way down, but waiting for her at the top
of the steps. The girl arrives, very happy to be able to bring her her
message. She makes her way up the steps; and once she reached her,
she said: "My lady, I never saw as courteous a knight, so perfectly
willing is he to obey your every command. For, if you ask me, he
accepts the good and bad alike with equanimity."—"Indeed," she
says, "that may well be." Then she returns to the window to watch
the knights.

5938   Without more ado, Lancelot catches up his shield by the straps,
inflamed with the desire to show off all his prowess. He points his
horse's head and has it gallop between two ranks. All those duped,
deluded men who spent a large part of the day and night mocking
him will be confounded before very long, having for some time had
their fun, amusement and sport at his expense. The King of Ireland's son, holding his shield strapped to his arm, spurs furiously
against him from the opposite side. They clash with each other so
hard that the Irish king's son has no further interest in the joust, for
his lance breaks and shatters, having struck against not moss, but
very hard, dry boards. In that encounter Lancelot taught him a
lesson by pinning the shield to his arm and his arm to his side and
knocking him off his horse to the ground. Immediately knights dart

out from both sides, spurring and pricking hard, some coming to his rescue, some to add to his trouble. Some men, hoping to help their lords, empty the saddles of many of their opponents in the joust and general melee. Gawain, however, who was there with all the others, never took up arms all that day; for he was so happy watching the valorous deeds performed by the knight with the red-painted armour that those achieved by the others seemed to him to be eclipsed and to fade to nothing in comparison. And the herald so recovered his spirits that he shouted at the top of his voice in the hearing of all: "Now here's the one who will take their measure! From now on you'll see what he can do. Now he'll show his mettle!"

5986 Then this knight guides his horse and makes a tilt at a very smart knight, whom he strikes so hard that he knocks him to the ground a hundred feet or more from his horse. He begins to perform so well with both sword and lance that there is none of those not bearing arms who does not enjoy watching him. Even many of those who do bear them also take pleasure and delight in the spectacle; for it is great entertainment to watch him bringing down and toppling horses along with their riders. He hardly engages any knight who can keep his saddle, and he gives the horses he wins to anybody who wants them. Then those who had earlier made fun of him say: "We're ashamed and mortified. We were very wrong to despise and vilify him. He's certainly worth a thousand of such as abound on this field, for he has defeated and surpassed all the knights in the world: there's none to take him on." And the damsels, feasting their eyes on him, said he is preventing them from marrying. For they did not dare to place so much faith in their beauty, riches, power or distinction as to suppose that this very valiant knight would deign to choose any of them for her beauty or wealth; and despite that, most of them make vows pledging that unless they do marry this man, they will not be wed or bestowed on any lord or husband this year.

6027 Then the queen, hearing their extravagant talk, laughs and chuckles to herself, being sure that the object of all their desire would not take the best or most beautiful or attractive of them for all the gold of Arabia, if it were set before him. They share one common wish, each wanting him for herself. One is jealous of the next as though she were already his wife, since in their eyes he is so skilful that they do not suppose or believe that any mortal man, please them as he might, could do what he did. He performed so well that when the tourney disbanded, those on both sides said that, without a word of a lie, the knight bearing the scarlet shield had had no equal there. They all said so, and it was true. But when they dispersed, he dropped his shield along with his lance and trappings where he saw the crowd was thickest, and then set off at a great pace and so furtively that no one present in the whole gathering noticed. He took to the road and made good speed straight to the place he had come from, so that he might keep his oath.

6060 When the tournament breaks up everybody searches and asks for him, but without finding him, since, not wanting to be recognised, he has taken flight. The knights are extremely sorry and upset, but would have been overjoyed to have him with them. And if the knights were sad to have him abandon them like that, the damsels, when they learned of it, suffered far greater grief, declaring by Saint John that they would not marry that year. Not having the one they love, they dismiss all the rest; and so the tourney disbanded without a single one of them getting a husband out of it. Lancelot does not linger, but returns quickly to his imprisonment.

6079 The seneschal arrived back two or three days before Lancelot and asked where he was. Then the lady, who had given Lancelot his splendid, well-tended scarlet arms as well as his harness and his horse, told the seneschal the truth about how she had sent him to where the jousting had taken place at the tournament of Noauz. "Really, wife," says the seneschal, "you couldn't have done worse! I think very great harm will come to me from that because my lord Meleagant will treat me more harshly than would the law of salvage if I'd been shipwrecked.* I'll be ruined and destroyed as soon as he knows, for he'll never have pity on me."—"Good husband, don't worry," says the lady, "and don't be so afraid, for there's no need. Nothing can keep him away, because he swore to me on holy relics that he would return just as soon as he could."

6105 The seneschal mounts at once and, coming to his lord, tells him what happened in this whole affair, but reassures him greatly by telling him how his wife extracted from him an oath to return to his imprisonment. "He'll never break it," says Meleagant: "that I know. Nevertheless, I'm very disturbed by what your wife has done. On no account would I have wanted him to be in the tourney.

But go back now and, once he has returned, take care that he's so closely confined that he can't escape from his prison or have any freedom of action. Then send me word of it at once."—"Your orders will be carried out," says the seneschal, then leaves. And he found Lancelot back in captivity at his court.

6128 A messenger, despatched by the seneschal, hurries back to Meleagant by the shortest route to inform him of Lancelot's return. *On hearing this, he takes masons and carpenters who, like it or not, did as he told them. He sent for the finest ones in the country and instructed them to build him a tower and to do their utmost to have it ready quickly. The stone was transported by sea; for over beside Gorre there runs a large, broad arm of the sea, in the middle of which was an island well known to Meleagant. There he ordered the stone and timber for the tower's construction to be shipped. In less than fifty-seven days the tower was entirely completed, high and massive, on solid foundations. When it was ready he had Lancelot brought there by night and, having him shut in the tower, ordered the doors to be walled up; and he had all the masons swear that no word of that tower would ever be divulged by them. He wanted it sealed like that, without any door or entry remaining other than one small window. There Lancelot had to stay; and, on the orders and instructions of the treacherous villain, he was given through this small window mean helpings of poor food at certain fixed times.

6167 Now Meleagant has done just what he wants; and so he sets straight off for King Arthur's court. There he is, then, newly arrived. When he came before the king, brimming over with impetuous arrogance, he began to hold forth: "King, I've made arrangements for a combat at your court in your presence; but I see no sign of Lancelot, who undertook to fight against me. Nevertheless, I duly offer myself for combat in the hearing of all whom I see present here. So if he's here, let him come forward, prepared to make a pact to meet me in your court one year from today. I don't know if you've ever been told how and in what circumstances this combat was agreed on; but I see knights present here who were there when we made our pact and could readily tell you, if they were prepared to reveal the truth of the matter. But should he wish to deny it, I'll not hire anyone to substitute for me, but prove my point man to man."

6194 The queen, who at the time was seated beside the king, draws him towards her with the words: "Do you know, sir, who this man is? It's Meleagant, who abducted me when I was being escorted by Kay the seneschal, on whom he inflicted a good deal of shame and injury." The king answered her: "My lady, I've heard all about that and know very well that he's the man who held my people in captivity." The queen says no more, but the king addresses Meleagant in these terms: "My friend," he says, "so help me God, we've had no news of Lancelot and are very worried about him."—"Sir king," says Meleagant, "Lancelot told me I should find him here without fail; and I'm only to issue this challenge to combat in your court. So I wish all the lords here to bear me witness that I call for it a year from today according to the arrangement we made when we agreed on the duel."

6221 Hearing this and much distressed at his words, my lord Gawain gets to his feet and says: "Sire, there's no trace of Lancelot in the whole of this land, but we'll have him sought; and, please God, he'll be found before the year is out, unless he's dead or a prisoner. Then, if he doesn't come, grant me the duel, and I shall fight it: I'll take up arms for Lancelot on that day, unless he arrives earlier."—"Ah, for God's sake, dear lord king," says Meleagant, "grant him that! He wants it, and I request it of you, for I know no knight in the world against whom I'd so gladly try my strength except only for Lancelot. But you may be quite sure that, should I not fight one of them, there's no compensation or ransom I'd accept other than one of these two." The king says he agrees to this unless Lancelot arrives in time.

6246 At this Meleagant leaves the king's court and journeys without pause until he finds his father King Bademagu. In order to appear in his eyes impressively valorous, he began by putting on an air of wonderfully high spirits. On that day the king was holding very joyful court in his city of Bath. It was his birthday, and so it was held with lavish splendour, and innumerable people of every sort had joined him. The whole palace was thronging with knights and maidens, and one of them was Meleagant's sister: I will tell you later my thoughts and reasons for mentioning her; but to give them at this point would be irrelevant, and I have no wish to distort, corrupt or labour my subject-matter but want to treat it in a direct, straightforward manner. So now I will tell you how Meleagant on his arrival and in the hearing of all, large and small, spoke to his father at the top of his voice. "Father," says he, "as God is my saviour, please tell me truly now if a man should not rejoice greatly and is not of very high merit when he inspires fear at King Arthur's court through his feats of arms?" His father, without listening further to his question, replies. "Son," he says, "all good men ought to honour, serve and associate with one so deserving."

6288 Then he cajoles and entreats him, asking not to be kept in ignorance of his reason for mentioning this, what he is seeking, what he wants, and whence he has come. "Sire," says Meleagant then, "I don't know whether you remember the arrangements and agreements that were announced and set out when you made peace between Lancelot and me. Then it was stipulated, I believe, and we were told in the presence of many people that we must both be available in one year's time at Arthur's court. I went there at the proper time, equipped and ready for what I'd gone there to do. There I performed everything required of me: I sought and asked for Lancelot, against whom I was to pit myself. But I couldn't see or find him: he'd fled and got out of the way. So I left on this condition: Gawain pledged me his word that, if Lancelot's no longer alive or doesn't come by the time fixed, I have his full assurance and promise that there will be no postponement, but he himself will undertake the combat against me on Lancelot's behalf. It's well known that Arthur has no knight so highly praised as he; but before the elder-trees blossom I shall see, if we come to blows, whether his deeds match his reputation – and the sooner the better, as far as I'm concerned!"

6324 —"Son," says his father, "now you're really making a fool of yourself! Anyone who didn't know your stupidity before knows it now from your own words. It's a fact that a good heart shows humility, but one that's foolish and arrogant will never be rid of its folly. I tell you, son, that your character is so extremely hard and arid that there's nothing gentle or friendly in it. Your heart is utterly pitiless, and you're altogether consumed by folly. That's why I find you contemptible, and that's what will lay you very low. If you are valiant, there will be plenty who will bear witness to it when necessary. A worthy man has no need to praise his own mettle in order to advertise his deed, for the deed speaks its own praise. Your vaunting doesn't help you to increase one whit in merit: rather I esteem you less for it. Son, I'm teaching you a lesson. But what's the use? Whatever you tell a fool counts for little; for a man merely wears himself out in trying to strip a fool of his folly, and virtue that one teaches and expounds is worthless unless put into practice, but is gone and lost in no time."

6354 How desperately upset and furious Meleagant was! I can tell you truthfully that you never saw any man born of woman as enraged as he was; and because of his anger the bond between them was broken there and then, because far from ingratiating himself with his father, he said to him: "Is this some fantasy, or are you dreaming when you say I'm out of my mind to tell you of my situation? I believed I'd come to you as to my lord, as to my father. But that doesn't seem to be the case, for I fancy you insult me more foully than you've a right to do; and you can't give me any reason for having started this."—"I can, plenty!"—"What, then?"—"Because in you I can see nothing but stupidity and madness. I know very well what you have in mind, and it will yet get you into great trouble. A curse on anyone who will ever believe that the courteous Lancelot, who is honoured by all but you, has fled through fear of you! But perhaps he's in his grave or shut away in some prison whose door is so stoutly barred that he can't leave without permission. That would indeed be a terribly grievous thing for me, if he were dead or injured. It would certainly be a great loss if so sincere, handsome, valiant and pleasant a person had met such an untimely end. But, please God, that's not the case."

6394 With that, Bademagu falls silent. But every word he had spoken had been overheard and noted by a maiden who was a daughter of his; and you should know that it was she whom I mentioned earlier in my story, and that she is not now happy to hear such things told of Lancelot. It strikes her that he is being kept hidden, since no one has found any scent or trace of him. "May God", she says, "turn His sight from me if I ever rest again until I have some certain and definite news of him!" Immediately, without delay, discreetly and without fuss, she hurries off to mount a handsome mule that was very comfortable to ride. But for my part I assure you that she has no idea which way to turn when she leaves the court: she neither knows nor asks, but takes the first road she finds and rides at high speed she knows not where, but as chance leads her, unaccompanied by knight or squire.

6420   She makes great haste, very eager to achieve the object of her quest. She pursues her search relentlessly, but it will not be over at all quickly: she must not rest or stay long in one place, if she wants properly to accomplish what she has decided to do, namely to release Lancelot from his prison if she can find him and manage it. But I fancy that before she does find him she will have searched through many lands, and will have traversed and scoured many a one before she hears any news of him. But what would be the use of my telling either of the places where she lodged or of her daily travels? She did, though, take so many roads up hill and down dale, high and low, that the entire month and more had passed without her being able to learn any more or anything beyond what she knew before, which is precisely nothing. One day, disconsolate and lost in thought, she was crossing a field when she saw far away, next to the shore beside an arm of the sea, a tower, but without any house, hut or dwelling within a league of it. Meleagant had had it built and had shut Lancelot inside; but she knew nothing of that. Then, as soon as she had seen it, she fixed her gaze on it so intently that she did not avert it or turn it elsewhere. And her heart confidently assures her that this is what she has sought so long. But now she has reached her goal, since Fortune, having tried her so sorely, has brought her along the right road.

6459   The maiden goes towards the tower and has come so close that she can touch it. She walks round it, alert and listening very attentively, doubtless to see if she could hear anything that might bring her joy. She looks and gazes up and down, sees how strong, tall and wide the tower is, and wonders in amazement how it is possible that she can see in it no door or window except for a single small, narrow one. On the high, sheer tower there was no ladder or stair, which convinces her that it has been so made intentionally and that Lancelot is inside. However, before any food passes her lips she will discover whether that is true or not. Then she wants to call out his name. She was intending to call: "Lancelot!" But before she utters a word, she is deterred by hearing a voice from the tower making an amazingly bitter lament, asking for nothing but death. It longs for death and wishes to die, so afflicted is it and full of grief. Despising its life and its very self, it goes on, feebly and in its low, hoarse tone to say: "Ah, Fortune, how cruelly your wheel has now turned for me! You've turned it round to my great cost, for recently

I was raised up but now I'm back down; then things were going well for me, now they go badly; now you weep for me, then you smiled on me. Alas, poor wretch, why did you trust in her, when she has deserted you so soon! Truly she has taken but a short time to cast you down so low from such a height. Fortune, you were very wrong to mock me: but what do you care? It means nothing to you, whatever happens. Ah, sacred Cross! Ah, Holy Spirit! How I'm ruined and undone! How utterly spent I am!

6504   "Ah, Gawain, you who are so worthy a man and unequalled in goodness, I'm indeed greatly astonished that you don't come to my rescue. Truly you're leaving it much too late and are not behaving in a courtly way. The man you used to love so much really deserves your help. I can certainly say without question that there would have been no corner or out-of-the-way place either on this side of the sea or beyond it where I wouldn't have sought you for at least seven or ten years before finding you, had I known you to be imprisoned. But why am I so worked up? You're not concerned enough to want to take this trouble. It's a very true saying that one can scarcely find a friend any more. In one's need one can easily discover who is a good friend. Alas, it's over a year ago that I was imprisoned here in this tower! Gawain, I really take it amiss that you've left me here! But perhaps you know nothing of this, and I may be blaming you unfairly. Indeed it's true, and I concede it, that it was outrageous and very wrong of me to believe that, because I'm confident that not for everything beneath the heavens would you and your friends have failed to come and get me out of this plight and trouble if you knew the facts of the situation; and you should do it out of love and companionship – I say it for no other reason. But that's out of the question: it can't happen! Ah, may the man be cursed by God and Saint Sylvester who has so shamefully shut me away; and may God destroy him! That's Meleagant, the most wicked man alive, who, out of envy, has done his very worst to me."

6550   With that, the man who is wearing himself out with grief says no more and falls silent. But the girl standing in a quandary below, having heard all he had said and knowing now that she has reached her goal, waited no longer but sensibly called to him at the very top of her voice: "Lancelot! My friend up there, speak to someone who loves you well!" But the man inside did not hear her. Then she strains harder and harder until, feeble as he was, he half heard her and wondered with surprise who it could be who had called him. He hears the voice and his name being called, but without knowing by whom: he thinks it is a ghost. He looks all around him, doing his best to see if he can spot someone; but he sees nothing apart from the tower and himself. "God," he says, "what's that I hear? I can hear someone speaking and can't see a thing! I swear this is utterly amazing, yet I'm not asleep but wide awake. Perhaps if it happened to me in a dream I might think it wasn't true; but I'm awake, and that's what worries me." Then with some effort he gets up and totters, one step at a time, across to the little opening. When he gets there, he presses himself against it, taking up its full height and width. Peering out to look as best he could, he did then see the one who had shouted to him.

6586 When he saw her he did not recognise her; but she knew him at once and said: "Lancelot, I've come a long way to look for you. Now, thank God, it's turned out that I've found you! I'm the one who asked you a favour when you were on your way to the Sword Bridge, and you were very pleased to grant it when I asked you for it: that was the defeated knight's head, which I had you cut off because I hadn't the slightest affection for him. It's on account of that favour and that service that I've subjected myself to this hardship: that's why I'll get you out of here." – "Thank you, maiden," the prisoner then replies. "The service I did you will be well repaid if I'm freed from here. *If you're able to get me out, I can truly assure and promise you to be yours for ever more, so help me Saint Paul the Apostle! And, as I may see God face to face, there will never come a day when I fail to do whatever it pleases you to command. And there's nothing you could think of asking for which, provided I have it, would not be yours without delay."

6617 —"Never fear, my friend, that you'll not be freed from here all right! Today you will be released and at liberty. I wouldn't for a thousand pounds fail to have you out of here before another day dawns. Then I shall take you to a fine retreat where you will rest with every comfort. There will be nothing I have that pleases you which, if you would like it, you'll not have. Don't fear for anything; but first I must somewhere hereabouts obtain some tool, if I can find one, with which you can enlarge this opening at least sufficiently for you to be able to get out."—"May God grant that you find it!" says he in full agreement. "And I've plenty of rope in here, which the scoundrels have given me to haul up my food – hard barley bread and dirty water, which sickens my heart and body." Then Bademagu's daughter, after a search, procures a strong, massive, sharp pickaxe, which she proceeds to give him. With it he batters and hammers, strikes and gouges, despite the pain it causes him, until he gets out quite freely. Now he is greatly relieved and, you may be sure, overjoyed to be let out of prison and be able to leave that place where he has been cooped up so long. Now he is at large in the open air; and you need have no doubt that not for all the gold scattered throughout the world, even if it were put in a single heap and given and paid out to him, would he have wished to be back there.

6657 Here now is Lancelot at liberty, but so faint that he staggered in his weak and feeble state. The girl sets him in front of her on her mule gently enough not to hurt him, and then they make off at high speed. However, the maiden deliberately leaves the high-road so as not to be seen and rides by hidden ways; for if she travelled openly, it was possible that someone who recognised them might very soon do them some harm, and she would not have wanted that. So she avoids the risky ways in coming to a retreat where she often goes to stay because of its beauty and charm. There Lancelot arrived; and no sooner had he come and was undressed than the maiden gently lays him on a splendid high couch, then bathes him and tends him so excellently that I could not describe or tell the half of it. She cossets and massages him as tenderly as she would her father: she completely restores and revives him, cures him and makes a new man of him. Now he is no less fair than an angel, and now he is more nimble and sprightly than anyone you ever saw. Being no longer mangy and starving but strong and handsome, he left his bed. And when he did so the maiden, having found for him the finest robe she could, presented him with it; and he, more lively than a bird in flight, happily put it on.

6700 He kisses and embraces the maiden, then says affectionately: "My dear, I give thanks to God and yourself alone for my being healed and fit. You are responsible for my escaping from imprisonment, and for that you may take and keep my heart, my body, my service and my wealth – whatever you wish. You've done so much for me that I am yours. But it's a long time since I was at the court of my lord King Arthur, who has shown me such great honour; and there's a great deal I should do there. So now, my sweet, generous friend, I would beg your leave in love's name to depart. Then, if it please you, I would very gladly go there."—"Lancelot, my good, kind, dear friend," says the maiden, "I'm very willing, because I'm concerned for your honour and welfare here, there and everywhere." Then she gives him a wonderful horse of hers, the finest ever seen, and he leaps on to it without calling on the stirrups:* he was mounted before she was aware of it. Then they warmly commend each other to God the ever truthful.

6729 Lancelot took to the road so happy that, had I sworn to do so, I could never, however hard I tried, tell of the joy he shows at having thus escaped from the trap he was in. But now he repeats over and over again that it was unlucky for that degenerate traitor that he held him captive and has now been tricked and duped: "And I've got out in spite of him!" Then he swears by the heart and body of Him who created the whole world that there are no riches from Babylon to Ghent for which he would let Meleagant escape, if he had him in his grasp and got the upper hand over him; for he has done him too much harm and shame. But, as things are turning out, he will soon have him where he wants him; for this very Meleagant, whom he threatens and is already running to earth, had that day arrived at court without anyone having summoned him; and once there, he asked for my lord Gawain until he found him. Then the wicked proven traitor asks him about Lancelot, whether he has been seen again or found, just as though he knew nothing of him! Nor did he: he did not know the truth, though he really thought he did.

6762 Gawain then told him truthfully that he had not seen him again, nor had he been back. "Since that's how it is and I don't find him here," says Meleagant, "then come and keep your pact with me, because I shall not wait for you any longer." Gawain says: "If it please God, in whom I trust, I shall certainly keep my agreement with you very shortly. I do intend to settle my debt to you. But if it comes to throwing dice and I throw more points than you, then, so help me God and the holy Faith, I shall scoop all the stakes and go on until I do." *Then, without further delay, Gawain orders a carpet to be put down and spread before him. The squires, on hearing his command, did not hide or lie low, but set about doing as he asks without grumbling or fuss. They bring the carpet and place it where he ordered; then the one who had sent for it sits down upon it and asks to be armed by the young men standing, lightly attired, before him. There were two of them, whether his cousins or nephews I do not know; and they were certainly accomplished and well trained. They arm him so thoroughly well that there is no fault on earth that can be criticised and no mistake to be found in anything they did there. When they have armed him, one of them goes to fetch a Spanish charger so fine that it could run more swiftly across country, through woods, up hill and down dale, than ever the excellent Bucephalus did.* On this horse you are hearing of mounted Gawain, the most famous and highly skilled knight ever blessed by the sign of the cross.

6807 He was just about to take up his shield when, quite unexpectedly, he saw Lancelot dismount before him. He stared at him in sheer amazement, so sudden was his arrival; and, unless I tell a lie, his astonishment was as great as if he had just dropped from the heavens in front of him. But then, when he sees that it really is he, nothing at all he might have had in mind to do prevents him from dismounting, holding out his arms towards him and embracing and kissing him in greeting. Now he is overjoyed and relieved at having found his companion. I shall here tell you the strict truth, and do not doubt me: Gawain would not have wished to be chosen as king there and then, had it meant losing him. The king soon knows, and all the others too, that, whoever may be displeased, Lancelot, for whom they had so long been on the lookout, has returned quite safe and sound. So they all rejoice together; and the court, which has been yearning for him for a long time, gathers to celebrate his arrival. There is nobody, however aged or youthful, who does not rejoice. Joy shatters and dispels the grief that was there before: sorrow takes flight, and joy appears and raises their spirits high.

6842 And the queen: is she not there amid all this rejoicing? – Indeed she is, and right in the forefront. – Really? – In God's name, where else would she be? Never before had she been so jubilant as she is now on his return. – Would she not have gone up to him? – Indeed she has: she is so close to him that her body virtually came within an ace of following her heart. – Where, then, is her heart? – It was kissing and making much of Lancelot. – Why, then, was her body hiding? Why is her joy not complete? Is it, then, mingled with anger or hatred? – Certainly not in the least; but it is possible that the king or some of the others there, who have their eyes on everything, would have quickly become aware of the whole situation if she had been prepared to follow the promptings of her heart under the public gaze. And had Reason not rid her of this foolish thought and mad impulse, they would have seen just what her feelings were, and that would have been the height of folly. So Reason shuts away and shackles her foolish heart and rash thoughts and has to some extent brought her to her senses and postponed the outcome until he sees and spies out a favourable and more private occasion where they might fare better than they would at present.

6876 The king does Lancelot great honour; and after his very warm welcome he said: "My friend, it is indeed some time since I heard news of anyone which delighted me as much as this concerning you. But I'm quite baffled to know in what land or country you've spent so long. I've had you sought high and low all winter and summer without anybody being able to find you."—"Indeed my good lord," says Lancelot, "I can tell you in a few words just what became of me. Meleagant, the wicked traitor, has held me imprisoned since the time the captives were released from his land; and he has had me live a life of great shame in a tower beside the sea. There he had me put and locked away and there I would still be leading a grim existence, were it not for a friend of mine, a maiden for whom I once performed a slight service. She has generously repaid me such a very small favour, doing me high honour and an extremely good turn. But to the man for whom I have no love at all, who has contrived to think up and do me this shameful, wicked deed, I wish to pay his due at once, without delay. He's come to ask for it and shall have it. He'll not have to wait to collect it, for the amount is all ready, loan and interest; but God forbid that he get any satisfaction from it!"

6914 Then Gawain speaks to Lancelot. "My friend," says he, "if I, your debtor, make this payment for you, it will be an exceedingly small favour. Moreover, I'm already mounted and prepared, as you see. My dear, good friend, don't deny me this favour I ask and desire!" The other says he would rather let one eye, or even both, be plucked from his head than be persuaded by him to allow that. He swears it will never happen. The debt is his, and he will repay it; for he has pledged Meleagant with his own hand. Gawain sees clearly that nothing he can say to him will make any difference, so, stripping his hauberk from his back, he removes it and promptly disarms. Lancelot dons his own arms without hesitation or delay, being very anxious and impatient to discharge and repay his debt. Meleagant, who is astonished beyond measure at the marvel he sees before his very eyes, will enjoy no further good fortune, but will receive his settlement. He almost loses his wits and very nearly goes out of his mind.

6942 "Indeed," he says, "I was a fool not to go and check before coming here if I still held imprisoned in my tower that man who has now played a trick on me. Ah, God, but why should I have gone there? How and for what reason should I have believed that he could have escaped from there? Isn't the wall strongly enough constructed and the tower stout and high enough? And there was no opening or crevice through which he could pass except with outside help. Perhaps his presence there was made known. Supposing the wall had become dilapidated and caved in and collapsed, would he not too have been destroyed, killed, crushed and dismembered? Yes, so help me God, if it had fallen down, he would inevitably have been killed. But I do believe that before that wall fails without being knocked down by force, the sea and all its water will dry up so that no drop remains and the world will come to an end. No, there's some other reason, not that: he had help to get out and escaped in no other way. I've been foiled by some plot. However it happened, he's got out. But if I'd taken proper precautions earlier, it would never have happened so, and he wouldn't ever have come to court. But my repentance has come too late: the rustic, who is not in the habit of lying, has a very sound saying that it's too late to shut the stable door once the horse is out. I know well enough that I'll now have deep shame and humiliation inflicted on me unless I'm to endure great hardship and suffering. What suffering and what hardship? Anyway, so help me God in whom I place my trust, for as long as I can last out I'll give him plenty of trouble!"

6987 So he goes bolstering up his courage, not asking any more than that they shall be pitted against each other on the field. And there will not be long to wait, I think, for Lancelot goes to attack him, confident that he will quickly overcome him. But before they set upon one another, the king tells them both to go down on to the heath beside the keep, the most beautiful this side of Ireland; and this they do. They went and were very soon down there. The king and all the men and women go there in great milling throngs. They all go off, and nobody stays behind, with many making for the windows: the queen, and beautiful ladies and maidens with her.

7005 On the heath was a sycamore as splendid as any there could be: it spread very wide over a large area, and all round was a border of fine thick, fresh grass that was not withered at any time of the year. Beneath that lovely, handsome sycamore, which was planted in the time of Abel, there gushes a clear, very fast-flowing spring. Its pebbled bed is extremely beautiful, bright as silver; and I believe the channel through which it runs is made of pure, unblemished and refined gold. It flows down across the heath through a valley between two woods. There, where the king sees nothing he finds disagreeable, he is pleased to take his seat. He has the people draw well back; then Lancelot rushes impetuously at Meleagant as at someone he hates bitterly. But before striking him, he called fiercely to him in a loud voice: "Take your stand: I challenge you! And you may be absolutely certain that I'll not spare you at all!"

7032 With that he digs his spurs into his horse and pulls back a little, the length of a bowshot. Then they charge one another with their horses at full gallop and at once strike each other on their sturdy shields, holing and piercing them; but at that encounter neither is wounded nor has his flesh touched. Without pause they ride past each other, then turn again, racing their horses at top speed, to deal more great blows on their good, stout shields. They are both vigorous, valiant and noble knights, their horses strong and swift. With the mighty blows they strike against the shields at their necks, the lances pass straight through without breaking or shattering and force their way right to their naked flesh. So violently do they assault one another that they are both hurled to the ground, no breast-strap, girth or stirrup saving them from falling backwards from their saddles, which are left without their occupants. Their horses run loose over hills and valleys, one of them kicking out, the other biting, attempting to kill each other.

7065 Having fallen, the knights jumped up as quickly as they could and promptly drew their swords, which were engraved with lettering. Holding their shields before their faces, they proceed to do their utmost to cause each other injury with their good steel swords. Lancelot has no fear, for he knew half as much again about fencing as did his opponent, having studied it since his youth. Both strike great blows on the shields at their necks and on the helmets banded with gold, bursting and buckling them. But Lancelot presses his opponent close and gives him a great hard blow past his shield directly onto his mail-clad right arm, severing it at a stroke. Feeling the loss of his right arm, he declared that Lancelot would pay dearly for it. He will not fail at any price to make sure of that, if the chance comes his way; for so intense are his pain, his anger and his fury that he is almost beside himself and little fancies his chances, unless he can play some vicious trick on his rival. He runs towards him, trying to grapple with him. Lancelot, however, is on his guard, making with his keen sword such a notch on his tally-stick that he will not recover from it before April and May are past, for he smashes his nose-guard against his teeth, breaking off three of them in his mouth. Then Meleagant's wrath is such that he cannot speak or utter a word; and he does not deign to ask for mercy, because his foolish heart, which holds him bound too tightly in its thrall, prompts him with bad advice. Lancelot steps up, unlaces his helmet, and cuts off his head: this man will never give him the slip! He has fallen dead: that is the end of him. But I can assure you now that nobody present who saw this took any pity on him. The king and everyone there display the great joy they feel. Happy as never before, they disarm Lancelot forthwith and lead him away amid great jubilation.

7120 My lords, if I told any more, that would be going beyond my matter; and so I reach my conclusion: this is the very end of the romance. The clerk GODEFROI DE LEIGNI has brought "the Cart" to a close; but let no one find fault with him for having added his work to CHRÉTIEN'S, since he did it with the approval of CHRÉTIEN, who began it. He composed to the end of the story from the point where Lancelot was walled in. That much he has done, not wishing to add or omit anything that would be to the story's detriment. 7134

YVAIN

(THE KNIGHT WITH THE LION)

Arthur, the good King of Britain, whose noble qualities teach us that we ourselves should be honourable and courtly, held a court of truly regal splendour for that most sumptuous festival that is properly called Pentecost. The court was at Carlisle in Wales. After the meal, throughout the halls, the knights gathered where they were called by the ladies, damsels and maidens. Some related anecdotes; others spoke of love, of the torments and sorrows and of the great blessings that often come to the members of its order, which at that time was powerful and thriving. Nowadays, however, it has few adherents, since almost all have abandoned love, leaving it much debased. For those who used to love had a reputation for courtliness, integrity, generosity and honour; but now love is made a laughing-stock, because people who feel nothing of it lie by claiming to love; and they make a deceitful mockery of it when they boast of it without having the right. But let us leave those still alive to speak of those who once were! For, in my view, a courtly man who is dead is still worth more than a living churl. Therefore I am pleased to relate something worth hearing concerning the king who was of such repute that he is spoken of near and far; and I agree with the people of Britain that his name will live on for ever. And through him are remembered those fine chosen knights who devoted all their efforts to honour.

42 That day, however, they were quite astonished to find the king rise and leave their company; and some of them were very offended and did not spare their comments, having never before, on such an important feast-day, seen him retire to his room to sleep or rest. On this day, though, he came to be detained by the queen and happened to stay so long at her side that he forgot himself and fell asleep. Outside the door of his room were Dodinel and Sagremor, Kay and my lord Gawain and with them my lord Yvain;* there too was Calogrenant,* a very good-looking knight, who had begun to tell them a story that was not to his honour but to his shame. As he was telling his tale, the queen could hear him; and she got up from the king's side and came upon them so stealthily that she had

landed in their midst before anyone caught sight of her, except that
Calogrenant alone jumped to his feet to greet her.

69 Then Kay, who was extremely abusive, wickedly sarcastic and
sneering, said to him: "By God, Calogrenant, I see you're very
gallant and sprightly now, and indeed I'm delighted you are the
most courtly of us; and I know very well you think so – you're so
completely devoid of sense. So it's only right for my lady to suppose
that you possess more courtliness and gallantry than the rest of us.
Perhaps it was out of laziness that we failed to rise, or else because
we didn't deign to? I assure you, sir, that wasn't our reason, but
the fact that we didn't see my lady until you had stood up
first."—"Really, Kay, I do believe you'd burst", says the queen, "if
you couldn't empty yourself of the venom you are full of. You're
tiresome and churlish to insult your companions."—"My lady,"
says Kay, "if we don't gain from your company, take care we're not
the worse for it! I don't think I said anything that should be counted
against me, so I beg you to speak no more of it. It's neither courtly
nor sensible to quarrel over a trifle. This argument should go no
further, and no one should make any more of it. But have him carry
on with the story he'd begun to tell us, for there shouldn't be any
squabbling here."

105 At this Calogrenant speaks up in reply. "Sir," says he, "I'm not
greatly worried by the quarrel: it's of small concern or importance
to me. If you've wronged me, I'll never be harmed by that; for you,
my lord Kay, have often insulted more worthy and wiser men than
I, as indeed is your usual practice. The dung-heap will always stink,
the gad-fly sting and the bee buzz, and a pest pester and plague. But,
if my lady doesn't press me, I'll tell no more of my story today; and I
beg her kindly to refrain from asking me to do anything I don't wish
to."—"My lady," says Kay, "everybody here will be grateful if you
do insist, as they will be glad to hear it. Don't do anything for my
sake; but by the faith you owe the king, your lord and mine, you'll
do well to tell him to go on."—"Calogrenant," says the queen,
"take no notice of the attack of my lord Kay the seneschal! He's so
used to uttering abuse that no one can talk him out of it. I would
beg you urgently not to harbour any resentment on his account or
to refrain because of him from telling us something we'd like to
hear. So, if you want to enjoy my affection, begin again from the
beginning!"—"Really, my lady, I find what you ask me to do very

irksome: I'd rather have one of my eyes plucked out than tell any more of my tale today, were I not afraid of annoying you. But I shall do as you please, however much it may hurt me. Listen, then, as this is what you wish!

150 "Lend me your hearts and your ears! For things one hears are lost unless they are understood by the heart. There are people who don't understand what they hear and yet commend it: they have nothing but the power of hearing. So long as the heart understands nothing of the words, they reach the ears like the blowing wind; but rather than stopping and lingering there, they very swiftly pass on, unless the heart is alert enough to be ready to receive them. The ears are the route and channel by which the voice reaches the heart, and the heart receives in the breast the voice that penetrates to it through the ear. Whoever, then, should wish to understand me now must lend his heart and ears; for I have no intention to speak of a fantasy, a fiction or a lie such as many others have served up to you, but shall instead tell you of what I've seen.

175 "It happened some seven years ago that, as solitary as a country-man, I was travelling in quest of adventures, fully equipped with arms as a knight should be, when on the right hand I found a way leading through a dense forest. It was a very difficult track, full of briars and thorns. Not without trouble and hardship I made my way by this path. Almost the whole day I rode on like that until I came out of the forest, which was in Broceliande.* I emerged from the forest on to a heath and saw a wooden tower half a Welsh league away: if it was as far as that, it was no further. I headed in that direction at more than a walking pace and saw the bailey and the deep, broad moat all round it. And standing on the bridge, with a moulted goshawk on his wrist, was the owner of the fortress. I had scarcely greeted him when he came up to take my stirrup and bade me dismount. I dismounted, there being no alternative, since I needed a lodging-place. Immediately, more than a hundred times in succession, he said to me that blessed was the road by which I had arrived there. With that, passing over the bridge and through the gate, we entered the courtyard. In the middle of the courtyard of this vavasour, to whom may God grant as much joy and honour as he bestowed on me that night, there hung a gong in which I think there was no iron or wood or anything but copper. The vavasour struck three times on the gong with a hammer that hung on a post.

Those who were upstairs in the building heard the sound of its clanging and dashed from the house and down into the yard, some taking charge of my horse, which the good vavasour was holding.

226 "I then saw a beautiful and attractive maiden coming towards me and looked at her with some attention: she was slender, tall and erect. She showed her skill in disarming me, which she did efficiently and well, and dressed me in a precious mantle of fine, peacock-blue cloth and trimmed with miniver. Then everyone left us alone, nobody staying either with me or with her; and that suited me well, for I wished to see no other. And she took me to sit on the prettiest lawn in the world, enclosed all around by a wall. There I found her so refined in behaviour and well informed in conversation, such delightful company and so well mannered, that to be there was a great pleasure for me, and I would never have wished to leave on any account. But that night the vavasour thwarted my wishes by coming to look for me when supper-time came round. Unable to linger there any longer, I at once did as he asked. Of the supper I will simply tell you that it was entirely to my liking once the maiden, when she sat down to it, was placed opposite me. After supper the vavasour admitted to me that he did not know how long it was since he had given lodging to a knight journeying in search of adventure, though he had been host to many. Afterwards he begged me to repay him by returning if possible by way of his home; and I replied: 'Gladly, sir!' since it would have been shameful to refuse him – not to grant that request would have been a poor return to my host.

269 "I was very well lodged that night; and as soon as daylight appeared my horse was saddled, as I had urgently asked the night before that it should be; so my request was properly carried out. I commended my good host and his dear daughter to the Holy Spirit, took leave of everyone, and left as quickly as I could. I had not put my lodging-place far behind me when, in a clearing, I came upon some wild, unruly bulls, all fighting together with such a din and displaying such haughty ferocity that, to tell you the truth, I drew back in fear; for there is no animal fiercer or more rampant than a bull. Sitting on a tree-stump with a great club in his hand I saw a churl,* who looked like a Moor and was immensely huge and hideous: the great ugliness of the creature was quite indescribable.

294 "On approaching this fellow I saw he had a head larger than that of a pack-horse or any other beast. His hair was tufted and his

forehead, which was more than two spans wide, was bald. He had great mossy ears like an elephant's, heavy eyebrows and a flat face with owl's eyes and a nose like a cat's, a mouth split like a wolf's, the sharp yellow teeth of a wild boar, a black beard and tangled moustache, a chin that ran into his chest, and a long spine that was twisted and humped. He leant on his club wearing a most odd garment containing no linen or wool: instead he had, fastened at his neck, the recently flayed hides of two bulls or oxen. The instant he saw me approach him, the churl leapt to his feet. Whether he wanted to touch me I don't know, nor what his intention was, but I prepared to defend myself until I saw him standing up quite still and quiet, having climbed on to a tree-trunk. He was a full seventeen feet tall. He looked at me without uttering a word, any more than a beast would have done. Then I assumed he was witless and unable to talk.

327   "At all events, I plucked up my courage to say to him: 'Pray tell me if you are a good creature or not!' And he replied: 'I'm a man!'—'What sort of man are you?'—'Such as you see: I'm never any different.'—'What are you doing here?'—'I stay here looking after these animals in this wood.'—'Looking after them? By Saint Peter of Rome, they don't pay heed to any man. I don't believe a wild beast can possibly be looked after in any plain or woodland or anywhere else unless it is tethered or penned in.'—'I look after these and control them so well that they'll never leave this spot.'—'You do? How then? Tell me the truth of the matter.'—'There's not a one that dares to move when they see me coming. For when I get hold of one of them with these hard, strong fists of mine, I force it down by its two horns so that the rest all shake with fear and gather all round me as if to call for mercy. But if anyone except me got among them, he couldn't reckon on not getting killed on the spot. That's how I'm master of my beasts. Now it's your turn to tell me what kind of a man you are and what you're looking for.'—'I am, as you see, a knight looking for something I'm unable to find: I've sought long and can find nothing.'—'And what would you want to find?'—'Some adventure, to put my prowess and courage to the proof. Now I beg and enquire and ask of you to give me advice regarding some adventure or marvel, if you know of any.'

367   "—'You'll not get any of that,' says he. 'I don't know anything about "adventure" and never heard tell of it.* But if you wanted to

go to a spring not far from here, you wouldn't get back again easily
if you followed the proper custom there. Close by you'll find a path
that will take you there. Keep going straight ahead if you don't
want to waste your efforts, because you could easily go wrong, for
there are lots of other tracks. You'll see the spring boiling, although
it's colder than marble. It's in the shade of the loveliest tree that
Nature ever managed to create. It keeps its leaves the whole year
round and doesn't shed them however hard the winter; and there's
an iron basin hanging on a chain long enough to reach the spring.
Beside the spring you'll find a large slab such as you'll see: I can't tell
you what it's made of, for I never saw another like it. And on the
other side you'll find a chapel – small, but very pretty. *If you'll
take some water in the basin and spill it on the slab, you'll see such a
tempest get up that no animal will stay in this wood, not a roebuck
or fallow deer, not a stag or swine – even the birds will get out. For
you'll see so many thunderbolts flying, such a wind blow and trees
torn to pieces, such rain, thunder and lightning that, if you can get
free of it without a deal of bother and trouble, you'll be luckier than
any other knight who ever came there.' I left the fellow then, once
he had clearly pointed out the way.

410   "It was perhaps after nine in the morning and possibly almost
midday when I saw the tree and the chapel. As regards the tree I'm
sure, and that's the truth of the matter, that it was the finest pine
that ever grew on earth. And I don't believe it would ever rain so
hard that one drop of water would get through: instead it would all
run over it. Hanging from the tree I saw the basin of the purest gold
that was ever as yet for sale in any fair. As for the spring, you may
take my word that it was boiling like hot water. The slab was of
emerald, bored out like a cask; and underneath were four rubies
that shone more bright and crimson than the morning sun when it
appears in the east. I shall not knowingly tell you a word of a lie. I
wished to see the marvel of the tempest and thunderstorm, which,
as I discovered, was unwise; for I would gladly have changed my
mind, had I been able to, the moment I had sprinkled water from
the basin into the hollowed-out slab. But I'm afraid I poured too
much, because then I saw the heavens in such a commotion that
from more than fourteen directions the lightning flashed in my eyes
and the clouds hurled down snow, rain and hail pell-mell. It was
such appallingly violent weather that a hundred times I expected to

be killed by the thunderbolts falling all around me and by the shattering of the trees.

449 "You may be sure that I was quite terrified until the weather grew calm again. But God brought me relief in that the storm was soon over, and all the winds died away: they did not dare blow against God's wishes. And when I saw the air clear and serene, I was completely relieved and joyful; for joy, in so far as I have ever experienced it, quickly erases the memory of great trouble. As soon as the storm was past, I saw, if anyone is prepared to believe me, so many birds gathered on the pine that there was not a branch or leaf to be seen that was not completely covered by birds, which made the tree still more beautiful.* And all these birds sang together in harmony, though each sang a different song so that I never heard the song of one being sung by another. Their joy gladdened me, and I listened until they had brought their service to its very end; for never before had I heard so lovely a paean, nor do I believe any man will hear one, unless he goes to hear that one that gave me such pleasure and delight that it quite turned my head.

478 "I stayed there until I heard some knights coming, as I supposed – I'd have thought as many as ten, such was the noise and clatter made by a single approaching knight. Seeing him coming quite alone, I at once tightened the girths of my horse and lost no time in mounting. And the man came on in a hostile manner, faster than an eagle and looking as fierce as a lion. Then at the top of his voice he began to shout a challenge at me. 'Vassal,' he said, 'without issuing any challenge you've done me an injury and harm. If there were any dispute between us, you should have challenged me or at least sought justice before launching an attack on me. But sir vassal, if I can manage it the mischief of this obvious damage will rebound on you! The evidence is all around me in my flattened wood. The victim of an assault is entitled to make a complaint; and I'm within my rights to complain, since you've driven me from my house with thunderbolts and rain. You've carried out an injurious act against me, and a curse on anyone who approves that! For you've committed against my woods and my stronghold an aggression against which neither men nor arms nor walls would have availed me anything. There was no man at all who was safe there in any fortress of solid stone or wood. Be on your guard then, for from now on you'll get no truce or peace from me!'

517 "After this summons we clashed together, holding our shields on our arms, each covering himself with his own. The knight had a good horse and a stout lance and was certainly a full head taller than I. Thus I was at a complete disadvantage, since I was shorter than he and his horse bigger than mine. I'm telling the full truth, you understand, as some excuse for my shame. Without holding back, I dealt him the hardest blow I could strike, catching him on the top of his shield; and into it I put my full strength, so that my lance flew in pieces. His own remained intact, since it was by no means light but, on the contrary, thicker I would say than any knight's lance, for I never saw one more massive. And the knight struck me so violently that he knocked me down over the horse's crupper flat on the ground, leaving me ashamed and dispirited, and never looked at me again. He took my horse and abandoned me, then set off back the way he had come; and I, at a loss to know what to do, remained brooding and indignant.

548 "I sat down beside the spring for a little while and rested, not daring to follow the knight for fear of acting foolishly. And even if I had had the courage to follow him, I didn't know what had become of him. In the end I took it into my head to keep my promise to my host and return by way of his home. This idea pleased me, and that is what I did. In order to travel more easily I left all my arms and went back full of shame. When I came to his dwelling that night, I found my host exactly the same as before, just as good-humoured and courtly. I never gained the slightest impression that either his daughter or he was less glad to see me or did me less honour than they had done the previous night. Everyone in that house earned my gratitude by showing me great honour, saying that, as far as they knew or had heard tell, no man had ever escaped from the place I had come from and avoided being killed or captured. That's how I went, and that's how I came back; and on my return I thought myself a fool. So I've foolishly told you what I never wished to tell at all."

581 —"By my head," said my lord Yvain, "you are my first cousin, and I should love you dearly. But I must say you are foolish to have concealed this from me for so long. If I've called you foolish, I beg you not to be offended. For if I'm able and have the chance, I shall go to avenge your shame."—"It's obvious that it's after dinner," says Kay, unable to hold his tongue. "There are more words in a

potful of wine than in a barrel of beer. They say a cat makes merry when it's drunk. After a meal everyone sets out to slay Nureddin without stirring; and you'll be off to take vengeance on Forré!* Are your saddle-pads ready stuffed, your iron greaves polished and your banners unfurled? By God, quickly now my lord Yvain! Will you set out tonight or tomorrow? Let us know, good sir, when you're going to this ordeal, for we'd like to escort you. There's no provost or magistrate who won't be glad to be your escort. And I beg you, whatever happens, not to go without taking leave of us. And if you have a bad dream during the night, then stay at home!"

612 —"Are you out of your mind, then, my lord Kay," says the queen, "for your tongue to keep wagging? Shame on that tongue of yours and all the bitter medicine it dispenses! Your tongue must surely hate you, for it says the very worst things it knows to everyone, whoever it may be. A curse on any tongue that never tires of speaking ill! The way yours behaves makes you hated everywhere: it can't be more active in betraying you. I tell you, if it were mine I'd charge it with treason. Anybody who can't be reformed should be bound like a madman in front of the choir-screen in church."—"Truly, my lady," says my lord Yvain, "his taunts don't bother me. My lord Kay shows such wisdom, ability and merit in every court that he'll never be deaf or dumb. He's good at replying to ill-mannered talk with sense and courtesy and never did otherwise – you know well enough if I'm lying! But I have no wish to quarrel or begin any nonsense; for it's not the one who deals the first blow who begins the fight, but the one who returns it. A man who picks a quarrel with his companion would do better to do so with a stranger. I don't want to be like the watchdog that bristles and shows its teeth when another dog snarls at it."

649 While they were talking in this way, the king came out of the room where he had been for a long time, having slept until now. And seeing him, all the nobles sprang to their feet to greet him. He had them all be seated again and himself sat beside the queen. Then the queen at once tells him Calogrenant's story word for word, relating it to him ably and well. The king heard it with pleasure, then swore three full oaths by the soul of his father Utherpendragon and by those of his son and his mother that, before a fortnight had passed, he would go to see that spring along with the storm and the marvels, arriving there on the eve of my lord Saint John the

Baptist's feast and pitching his camp there that night. He says that all those who wish are to go with him. The entire court thought all the better of the king because of his plan, for the lords and young knights were very keen to go there. But whoever may have been happy and jubilant, my lord Yvain was sorry about it, for his intention was to go there on his own; so he was miserable and aggrieved that the king should be going. The only reason for his displeasure was that he was well aware that my lord Kay would certainly have the combat rather than he, as it would not be refused him should he ask for it. Or perhaps my lord Gawain himself would be the first to request it. If either of these two asks for it, it will never be denied him.

691 However, he will not wait for them, as he has no wish for their company. Instead, he determines to go on his own, whether to his joy or his grief; and whoever might stay at home, he wishes to be in Broceliande in two days' time and, if he can, to search until he finds the narrow, wooded path (so very anxious is he), and also the heath and stronghold, the cheer and delightful company of the damsel who is so attractive and beautiful and, together with his daughter, that worthy man who does his utmost to show honour, being so open-hearted and noble. Then he will see the bulls in the clearing and the enormous churl looking after them. He is full of impatience to see this fellow who is so hideous, huge and fearsome, deformed and black as a smith. Then if possible he will see the slab and the spring and basin and the birds on the pine tree, and he will make it rain and blow. He has, though, no intention of boasting of this; and, if he has his way, no one will know about it before it has brought him great shame or great honour: then let the facts be known!

723 My lord Yvain steals from the court without joining up with anybody,* but going alone to his lodging. Finding all his household and ordering his horse to be saddled, he calls a squire of his from whom he concealed nothing. "Now then," he says, "follow me outside and bring my arms! I shall shortly go out through that gate on my palfrey. Be sure not to take long, for I have very far to travel. Have my horse well shod and bring it quickly after me, and then you'll take my palfrey back. But I order you to take good care not to say anything of this if anybody asks you about me. Otherwise, if you rely on me for anything, you need never do so again."—"My

lord," says he, "all will be well, for no one will ever hear about it from me. Go ahead, and I'll follow you."

747 At once my lord Yvain mounts. He will avenge, if he can, his cousin's shame before he returns. The squire runs for the arms and for the horse, which he mounts without more delay, since it had no shoes or nails missing. He followed his master's tracks until he saw him dismounted, as he had been waiting for him for a little while in a secluded spot off the road. Bringing him all his armour and equipment, he accoutred him in it. My lord Yvain wasted no time once he was armed, but travelled on day after day over mountains and through valleys and extensive forests and outlandish, wild places, passing through many dangerous spots and many perils and difficulties until he came directly to the dark path that was full of thorns: he was then safe from the possibility of losing his way. Whoever may have to pay for it, he will not stop before seeing the pine shading the spring, and the slab and the tempest of rain, snow, hail and wind.

777 That night, you may be sure, he was lodged as he wished to be; for he found the vavasour far kinder and more honourable than he had been led to believe, and as for the maiden, in her he saw a hundred times more intelligence and beauty than Calogrenant had described; for it is impossible to tell all the virtues of a good lady and a worthy man. When the latter devotes himself to doing great good, no full account can be given, because no tongue could tell all the honourable actions of which such a gentleman is capable. My lord Yvain had that night excellent lodging which quite delighted him. Then the next day he came to the clearing and saw the bulls and the churl, who told him the way to take. But he crossed himself more than a hundred times out of amazement that Nature was able to form such an ugly, loathsome creature. Then he journeyed to the spring and saw all that he wished. Without stopping to sit down, he poured a basinful of the water straight on to the slab. And at once there came the wind and the rain and the kind of weather that was to be expected. And when God restored the calm, the birds gathered on the pine and rejoiced wonderfully above the perilous spring.

811 Before their joy had subsided the knight arrived, more blazing with rage than live coals, and making as great a din as if he were hunting a rutting stag. And the moment they saw each other they

rushed together, both seemingly full of mortal hatred. They each had a stout, strong lance; and they exchange such hard blows that both of the shields at their necks are pierced, the hauberks are rent, the lances shatter and shiver, and the splinters from them fly aloft. They attack one another with their swords and, in this sword-play, have cut the straps from their shields, which themselves are hacked from top to bottom so that the pieces hang down and they cannot use them for protection or defence; for they have so carved them to bits that they strike each other with their gleaming swords directly on their sides, arms and hips. Savagely they put each other to the test, never changing their position any more than would two blocks of stone. Never were two knights so intent on hastening each other's death. They have no inclination to waste their blows, but launch them as best they can.

842 Their helmets are dented and give way, and the links fly from their hauberks with the result that they draw much blood from each other; for the hauberks are so heated by their own bodies that each gives scarcely more protection than a surplice. They jab at one another's faces with their swords, and it is amazing how long such a fierce, hard combat lasts. Yet they are both so stout-hearted that neither on any account would yield a foot of ground to the other without being mortally wounded. And they behaved with great gallantry in that they never struck or injured the horses at all, something they neither wished nor deigned to do; but they stayed mounted the whole time without ever setting foot on the ground, which made the combat all the more splendid. In the end, my lord Yvain shatters the helmet of the knight, who was stunned and dazed; and never having suffered such a savage blow before, he was terrified. For under the coif it had split his head down to the brain, so that the links of the shining hauberk were stained with brains and blood, which caused him such intense pain that his heart almost failed him. If he then fled, he had good reason, since he felt himself mortally wounded and any further resistance would have been quite useless.

876 As soon as he comes to this conclusion he makes off as fast as he can in the direction of his castle, where the bridge was lowered and the gate opened wide for him. And my lord Yvain spurs impetuously after him, as hard as he can go. As a gerfalcon, swooping from a distance, hotly pursues a crane and comes so close to it that

it thinks it can seize it, but misses, so does the one flee and the other press him so closely as almost to have him in his arms, but cannot quite reach him; and yet he is so near that he hears him groaning for the distress he is in. He still, however, flees as best he can; and the other pursues him with all his might, afraid he would have wasted his effort unless he takes him dead or alive, remembering as he does the taunting words Kay had spoken to him. He will not have carried out the promise he had made to his cousin nor be in the least believed unless he takes back some clear evidence. He spurred after him right to the gate of his stronghold; and both went in, without finding any man or woman in the streets through which they passed. Then they both came headlong to the door of the great hall.

907 The doorway was very high and wide;* yet the way in was so narrow that two men or two horses could not enter together or meet in the door without getting in each other's way and having great difficulty; for it was constructed just like the trap lying in wait for the rat as it goes on its nefarious business. At the top of that waits the hidden blade, which is set off by being released and snapping down to strike and catch whatever makes contact with the trigger, however lightly it touches it. Similarly, under this gate were two catches holding up a portcullis of iron ground to a sharp edge. If anything trod on these devices, the gate fell down and anyone underneath hit by it would be caught and completely mangled. The passage, precisely in the middle, was as narrow as a footpath.

932 The knight very knowingly dashed through by the proper way, whilst my lord Yvain imprudently rushed after him at a great pace and came so close to catching him that he held him by the back saddle-bow. He was very lucky to be leaning forward, otherwise he would have been sliced right through; for the horse stepped on the wood that supported the iron gate. Down comes the gate like a devil out of Hell, catching the saddle and the horse behind it, slicing it clean through the middle. But, thank God, it did not touch my lord Yvain except that it grazed so closely down his back that it cut off both spurs level with his heels; and to his great consternation he fell down, which allowed the mortally wounded man to escape him. Beyond, there was another gate just like the first. The retreating knight fled through that gate, which fell behind him.

961 So my lord Yvain was caught, remaining anxious and disconcerted, shut up in the hall with its decorated ceiling studded with

gilded nails and its walls finely painted in rich colours. But nothing caused him so much sorrow as the fact that he did not know which way the other had gone. While he was in this plight he heard the small door of a little adjoining room open, and through it alone came a very attractive and beautiful damsel, closing the door behind her. When she found my lord Yvain, she was at first very startled. "Really, sir knight," she says, "I'm afraid you've got yourself into trouble. If you're seen in here you'll be hacked to pieces, because my lord is mortally wounded, and I'm sure you have caused his death. My lady is in such a state of grief along with her people lamenting around her that they're almost killing themselves with sorrow. And they are certain you're in here, though they're so overcome by anguish that they can't do anything about it now. If they wish to kill or capture you, they can't fail to do so when they do come to set about you."

993 My lord Yvain replies to her: "Please God they'll never kill me, nor shall I be captured by them."—"No," says she, "for I shall do all I can for you. There's no valour in a man who fears too much, so I think you're a worthy man not to be extremely terrified. You may be sure too that, if I could, I would serve and honour you because you, indeed, did the same for me. My lady once sent me on an errand to the king's court. Perhaps I wasn't as prudent, courtly or well behaved as a maiden should be; but there was not a single knight there who deigned to speak a word to me except you alone who stand here. But you, thanks to your great kindness, honoured and served me there. For that honour you did me there I shall reward you here. I've recognised you and know your name very well: you're King Urien's son, and your name is my lord Yvain. Now you may be absolutely sure that, if you're prepared to believe me, you'll never be captured or injured. You shall take this little ring of mine and, if you will, return it to me when I've rescued you."

1026 She then handed him the small ring, telling him it had the same property as the bark on wood, which covers it so that nothing of it is seen. But it must be held so that the stone is enclosed in the palm: then whoever wears it on his finger has no fear of anything, since nobody, however wide open he keeps his eyes, will ever be able to see him any more than the wood which is covered by the bark that grows on it. This is to my lord Yvain's liking; and when she had told him of it, she took him to sit on a couch covered by a quilt so costly that the Duke of Austria never had its equal. Then she said to him that, if he wished, she would bring him something to eat; and he said he would appreciate that. The damsel runs quickly into her room and is very promptly back, bringing a roast capon, a cake, a cloth, and a full pot of choice wine covered with a shining goblet. She invited him to eat; and he, who needed this, ate and drank very gladly.

1055 By the time he had finished his food and drink, the knights inside were on the move looking for him, wishing to avenge their lord, who had already been laid on his bier. Then the girl said to him: "My friend, can you hear them all seeking you already? There's a very loud din and uproar; but whoever may come or go, don't move, whatever the noise, for you'll never be found if you don't stir from this couch. You'll soon see this hall full of very troublesome, hostile people expecting to find you here; and I think they'll bear the corpse through here for burial and will start to hunt for you under the benches and beds. It would be amusing entertainment for a man who wasn't afraid to watch such blind people; for they will all be so blinded, confused and deluded that they'll all go mad with rage. That's all I have to tell you now, and I daren't stay any longer. But praise be to God who has given me the occasion and opportunity to do something to please you, for I longed to do so!"

1086 Then she went away again; and when she had left, all the people gathered, having come to the gates from both directions, carrying sticks and swords. So there was a vast crowd and throng of cruel, malevolent folk; and in front of the gate they saw the half of the horse that had been sliced in two. Then they thought that once the gates were opened they would be quite sure of finding inside the man they were seeking in order to kill him. They then had those gates raised which had caused the death of many a man. However, no catch or trap was set for the passage this time, but they all came in abreast. And they found the other half of the slain horse on the threshold; but they did not have between them an eye to catch sight of my lord Yvain, whom they would have been delighted to kill. And he watched them beside themselves with rage and fury.

1111 Then they said: "How can this be? For in here there's no door or window through which any living creature could escape, unless it were a flying bird, or a squirrel or marmot or some animal just as small or smaller, because the windows are barred, and the gates were closed as soon as my lord went out. The person is here, dead or alive, since he's not stayed outside: far more than half the saddle is in here, as is plain to see; but of him we can't see a trace, apart from the spurs that were cut off and fell from his feet. Now let's hunt through all these corners and stop this idle prattling! For I believe he's still in here; or else we're all bewitched, or demons have stolen him from us." And so all of them, seething with rage, searched for him throughout the hall, beating on the walls and the beds and benches. But that couch on which he had lain down escaped and was spared the blows, being neither struck nor touched, though they beat vigorously all round it and, with their sticks, made a violent onslaught on everything inside, like a blind man groping about to find something.

1144 As they went rummaging around under beds and stools, there entered one of the most beautiful ladies ever seen by mortal eye. Never was there talk or mention of so lovely a Christian lady, but she was so crazed with grief as to be close to taking her own life. From time to time she would cry out at the top of her voice and then fall down in a faint. Then, when she had got up again, she would begin to rend her clothes and tear her hair. She tugs at her hair and rips her clothing, swooning again at every step; and nothing can comfort her as she sees her husband borne away before her, dead on the bier: for that she thinks she will never be consoled, and that was why she cried aloud. The holy water and the cross and candles led the procession along with the ladies from a convent and the gospels and censers and the clerks officiating for the granting of the final absolution, on which the unfortunate soul is intent.

1173 My lord Yvain heard the cries and indescribable grief: no one could give an account of it, and never was its like described in a book. Then the procession passed by, but a great throng gathered round the bier in the middle of the hall; for from the dead man's wound the warm blood ran again, clear and crimson; and that was positive proof that the man who had fought the combat, defeating and slaying him, was certainly still present.* They then searched and sought, hunted and rummaged everywhere until they were bathed in sweat from the anguish and agitation on account of the crimson blood dripping before their eyes. And my lord Yvain was well beaten and prodded where he lay, but did not budge at all because of that. The people grow more and more frantic owing to the opening of the wounds; and they wonder in astonishment why they are bleeding and do not know where to lay the blame. Every single one of them says: "The man who slew him is among us, and we can't see him: this is a marvel and the work of the Devil!"

1203 It all caused the lady to grieve so intensely that she came near to death and cried out as if demented: "Oh, God! Will no one then find the murderer, the traitor who has slain my good lord? Good? Certainly: the finest of all good men! True God, the fault will be Yours if You allow him to escape like this. There is no other I should blame but You, since You hide him from my sight. Never was such an outrage witnessed or such grave wrong as You do me in not even letting me see that man who is so close to me. When I can't see him, I really must say that some spirit or demon has intruded here among us and put me totally under a spell. Or else he's a coward and afraid of me. He is indeed a coward to fear me. It's great cowardice that prevents him from daring to show himself before me. Ah, spirit, you craven thing! Why are you cowardly towards me when you showed great boldness towards my husband? You futile, paltry creature, if only I had you now in my power! If I could just lay my hands on you now! But how could it come about that you slew my husband, unless you did it treacherously? My lord would certainly never have been overcome by you if he had seen you. For in the world there was not his equal known to God or man, and none of his like remain. Had you been mortal, you would not indeed have dared to confront my lord, for no man could vie with him."

1243 Then the lady wrestles and fights with herself alone, and thus she herself works her own injury. And with her, for their part, her people are as grief-stricken as they could be. They bear away the body and bury it. Then, having toiled at their search until they are all tired of looking, everyone gives up out of weariness; for they can see no one who seems in the least suspect. The nuns and priests, having already completed the service, had returned from the church and gone over to the tomb. But the damsel from the room was not concerned with all that. Remembering my lord Yvain, she promptly came to him and said: "My lord, these people have been after you in very great force. They've been threshing around in here a great deal and ransacking every nook and cranny more thoroughly than a hound on the scent of a partridge or quail. You must really have been afraid."—"Upon my word," he says, "you're right! More than I thought I ever would be. Yet if it were possible, I'd be very glad to look out through some opening or window to see the procession and the body." Yet his interest was in neither the body nor the procession, for he would have liked to have them all burned, even if it had cost him a thousand marks. A thousand marks? Yes: indeed three thousand. But he said it on account of the lady of that town, whom he wished to see.

1282 The damsel placed him by a small window, repaying him as best she could for the honour he had shown her. Through this window my lord Yvain spies the beautiful lady, who is saying: "My lord, may God have mercy on your soul just as truly as, I believe, no knight ever sat in saddle who approached your worth in any way! My dear good husband, no knight has ever rivalled you in honour or in courtliness. Liberality was your mistress and Boldness your companion. May your soul rest in the company of the saints, my dear lord." Then she beats herself and tears her clothes wherever her hands can reach. My lord Yvain restrained himself only with very great difficulty from running, come what might, to restrain those hands of hers.

1305 However, the damsel, courtly and good-natured as she is, begs, advises, bids and instructs him to beware of doing anything foolish, saying: "You're very well off here. Don't move for anything until this mourning has died down; and let these people disperse, as they will do quite soon. If you act my way, following my advice, it may be to your very great advantage. You can remain sitting here and watch the people inside and out going on their way without any of them seeing you, which puts you in a very good position. But be sure not to speak out rashly; and if you have foolish thoughts, take care not to utter them. The wise man conceals his foolish ideas and, if he can, puts the good ones into effect. So, like a wise man, beware of putting your head at risk, for they wouldn't put it up for ransom! Take good care of yourself and bear my advice in mind; and rest quietly until I get back, because I daren't remain here any longer. I might, perhaps, stay so long that I should come under suspicion because of not being seen with the others in the crowd; and then I'd be in serious trouble."

1339 With that she leaves, and he remains behind, not knowing how to behave. He is perturbed to see them burying the corpse when he can get nothing as evidence that he overcame and slew him and which he would be able to display openly. If he has no conclusive evidence, then he is utterly shamed. Kay is so extremely malicious and spiteful, so full of mockery and abuse that he would never be left in peace by him: he would always go on insulting him and hurling taunts and mockery at him as he did the other day. Those taunts are still fresh and rankling in his heart. But new-found Love, with his sugar and honeycomb, has brought him fresh sweetness, having hunted through his lands and fastened on his prey. His heart is carried away by her who is his enemy, and he loves the person who most hates him.* The lady, without knowing it, has fully avenged her husband's death. For it she has taken a greater revenge than she would have found possible had not Love avenged her by attacking him so gently and, through his eyes, striking him to the heart.

1369 The effect of this thrust lasts longer than that of one from any lance or sword. A sword-blow is cured and heals very quickly once a doctor attends to it: Love's wound, though, grows worse the nearer it is to its doctor. My lord Yvain's wound is such that he will never recover from it, for Love has dedicated himself entirely to him. Love goes round examining the places he used to frequent and then abandons them, unwilling to have any lodging or host but this one; and he acts worthily in withdrawing from a poor place in order to devote himself entirely to Yvain. Not wishing any part of himself to remain elsewhere, he scours all the mean lodging-places. It is disgraceful that Love's way is at times to behave so badly as to take shelter in the basest place he finds just as readily as in the very best of all. But now he is well off: here he will be treated honourably and find it good to stay. Such is the proper behaviour for Love, who is such a noble being that it is amazing how he dares to incur the shame of falling as low as he does. He is like a man who spreads his balm in ashes and dust, hating honour and preferring blame, blending sugar with gall and mixing soot with honey. Now, however, Love has not acted like that, but has instead lodged in a noble place, for which he is beyond reproach.

1406 When the dead man had been buried, all the people went away. There remained behind no cleric, knight, servant or lady other than the one who makes no secret of her grief. She, however, stays there quite alone, often clutching at her throat, wringing her hands and slapping her palms, and reading her psalms from a psalter illuminated with gold lettering. My lord Yvain is still at the window gazing at her; and the longer he observes her, the more he loves and is attracted by her. He would have liked her to stop weeping and reading and wished he might have the opportunity of speaking to her. Love, who has caught him at the window, has filled him with this desire; but he despairs of having what he wishes, for he cannot suppose or believe that what he wants can come about.

1428 He says: "I may well think myself stupid to want what I shall never have. Having mortally wounded her husband, do I think I can be reconciled with her? That's no sensible idea, I swear, for at this moment she hates me more than any living thing, and justly so. – I was right to say 'at this moment', because a woman has more than a thousand fancies. Perhaps she will change again from her present frame of mind: or rather she will change it, with no 'perhaps', so I'm foolish to despair of it. God grant she change before long! I must be in her power for ever more, since Love wishes it. Anyone who doesn't make Love welcome when he seeks his company commits a crime and treason; and I declare to any who is prepared to hear that such a person deserves neither success nor happiness. But I'll not be a loser on that account, though instead I'll be loving my enemy; for I shouldn't hate her unless I want to betray Love. I should love whatever Love wishes. And should she call me her lover? Yes indeed, because I do love her. And I call her my enemy as she hates me, and rightly, since I slew the object of her love. Am I her enemy for that reason? Certainly not – rather her friend, for I was never set on loving anyone so much.

1462 "I am much grieved for her hair, which surpasses gold, so very brightly does it shine; and to see her tear and cut it racks and torments me with grief. And the tears that fall from her eyes can never be dried. All this is repugnant to me. Despite their being full of tears that flow on without ceasing, there never existed such lovely eyes. I'm grieved to see her weep, and nothing distresses me as much as the way she wounds her face, for it couldn't have deserved such treatment. Never have I seen one so shapely or so freshly complexioned. It has hurt me very deeply too to watch her clutching at her throat. Indeed she can't keep from doing herself the greatest harm in her power; yet no crystal or mirror is so bright or smooth. God! Why does she commit such great folly, and why does

she not do herself less injury? Why does she wring her lovely hands
and beat and tear her breast? For would it not be truly wonderful to
look at her if she were happy, when she is now so lovely in her grief?
Yes indeed, I can certainly vouch for that. Never before has Nature
succeeded in achieving such an extreme of beauty, for here she has
doubtless passed the bounds of all her previous work. How, then,
could this have come about? Where might such great beauty have
come from? God surely made her with His bare hand in order to
astound Nature. Should she wish to make a copy of her, she might
spend all her time without ever being able to achieve it. Not even
God, I think, if He might want to attempt it, could ever manage to
create another like her, however hard He might try."

1507 Thus my lord Yvain represents to himself the lady who is
torturing herself with grief. And I do not believe it could ever
happen again that any man who was imprisoned (as is my lord
Yvain, and fearing for his head) would be so madly in love with
someone to whom he will never himself make an approach nor, in
all likelihood, have another do so for him. There at the window he
stood until he saw the lady go away again and both the portcullises
had been lowered. Anybody else would have been distressed at this,
preferring escape to continued imprisonment: to him it makes no
difference whether they are closed or opened. He would certainly
not go away were they opened for him, even if the lady gave him
leave and freely pardoned him the death of her husband so that he
might depart in safety. For he is held back by Love and Shame, who
confront him on either hand. If he goes away, it is to his shame, for
no one would ever believe he had acquitted himself to such effect;
and on the other hand, he has such longing at least to see the
beautiful lady, even if she may afford him nothing else, that he is
not worried by his imprisonment and would rather die than go
away.

1541 However, the damsel returns with a view to keeping him
company, cheering and entertaining him and fetching and bringing
to him whatever he might wish or require. Finding him brooding
and languid from the love that had taken possession of him, she
said to him: "My lord Yvain, what sort of a time have you had
today?"—"One", he says, "that has given me much pleasure."—"Pleasure? In God's name, are you telling me the truth?
What? Is it possible, then, for someone to have a good time when he

sees he's being hunted down to be killed, unless he wants his own
death and is anxious for it?"—"Truly, my sweet friend," he says, "I
wouldn't at all wish to die. Nevertheless, as God is my witness,
what I saw pleased me greatly, pleases me still and will always
please me."—"Now let's say no more about all that," says she, "for
I'm well enough aware what these words of yours imply. I'm not so
naïve or foolish that I can't see through what people say. But now
follow me, because I shall take prompt steps to release you from
your imprisonment. I'll certainly get you to safety, if you wish it,
either tonight or tomorrow. Come now: I'll lead on!" And he
replies: "You may rest assured that I shall not ever leave furtively or
by stealth: when the people are all gathered outside in the streets,
that's when I shall go out, more honourably than by night." With
that, he follows her into the little room. The damsel, a shrewd girl,
was anxious to serve him, and provided him on credit with everything he needed. And when the opportunity came she bore in mind
what he had told her about being very pleased at what he saw while
those who wanted to kill him were seeking him throughout the hall.

1589 The damsel was in such good favour with her lady that she was
not afraid to say anything to her, whatever might come of it; for she
was her confidante and companion. Why, then, should she be
fearful of comforting her lady and reminding her about her
honour? On the first occasion, she said to her in private: "My lady,
I'm quite astonished to see you acting foolishly. Do you think you
can get your husband back now by mourning him?"—"Not at
all," she replies, "but if I had my way, I should be dead of
grief."—"Why?"—"So as to follow him."—"Follow him? May
God forbid it and give you again as good a husband, as He has the
power to do!"—"You never told such a lie, for He couldn't give
me as good a one again!"—"He'll give you a better one if you're
prepared to take him, and I'll prove it."—"Off with you! Say no
more! I'll certainly never find one."

1613 —"You will, my lady, if it suits you. But now, if you please, tell
me who will defend your land when King Arthur comes; because
next week he's due to arrive at the slab and spring. You've already
been informed of this in the letter sent you by the Dameisele
Sauvage. Ah! what a good turn that was! Now you ought to be
making arrangements for the defence of your spring, and you never
stop weeping! If it pleased you, my lady, you ought not to delay; for

indeed, as you well know, those knights of yours are not together worth a single chambermaid. Neither shield nor lance will be taken up even by the one with the highest opinion of himself. You've plenty of good-for-nothing people, but none of them will be so bold as to dare mount a horse. And the king's coming with such a great army that he'll seize everything without any opposition." The lady knows well enough and accepts that she is giving her sincere advice. But she has an irrational streak that other ladies have and almost all show by refusing to admit their folly and rejecting what they really want. "Be off," she says, "and leave me in peace! If I ever hear you mention this again, you'll do well to take to your heels! I find all this talk of yours most exasperating."—"Very well, my lady!" she says. "It's obvious you're a woman, who gets angry on hearing anyone giving her good advice on how to act!"

1653 Then she went away and left her; and the lady reflected that she had been very much in the wrong. She would dearly have liked to know how she could have proved that it was possible to find a knight better than her husband ever was. She would have gladly heard her explain, yet has forbidden her to do so. She was preoccupied with this desire until the damsel returned and, ignoring her injunction, immediately said to her: "My lady, is it fitting at this time for you to pine away with grief like this? For God's sake, do control yourself and stop it, for shame if nothing else! It's not fitting for such a great lady to continue to mourn for so long. Remember your honour and your very noble birth! Do you suppose that all noble qualities died with your husband? There are a hundred as good and a hundred better men still living throughout the world."—"If you're not lying, may God confound me! Still, just name me a single one with such a reputation for excellence as my husband enjoyed all his life."—"But then you'd be annoyed with me, fly into a rage, and despise me for it."—"No I won't, I assure you."

1686 —"May it be for your own future good, if you should find it agreeable, and may God grant that you do! I see no reason to keep quiet, as no one is listening or overhearing us. You'll consider me quite presumptuous, but I think I shall speak my mind. When two knights have come together in armed combat and one has defeated the other, which do you think the more worthy? For my part, I give the honour to the victor. And what would you do?"—"It seems to me you're setting a trap for me and wanting to catch me out in what I say."—"On my word, you may rest assured that I'm telling the simple truth and demonstrating to you that of necessity the man who overcame your husband is more worthy than he was: he defeated him and boldly pursued him all the way in here, so that he shut him up inside his house."—"Now," she answers, "I hear the greatest nonsense ever uttered. Go away, possessed as you are by an evil spirit! Be off, you foolish, tiresome girl! Never say such an absurd thing again, and never again come before me to discuss him!"—"Indeed, my lady, I well knew I'd never have your approval, and I told you as much beforehand. But you agreed not to take offence or be at all angry with me. You've not kept your agreement with me very well, so I'm now in the position of being given a piece of your mind and have lost the advantage of keeping quiet."

1727 With that she returns to the room where my lord Yvain is resting very comfortably in her care, though he sees nothing to please him when he cannot look at the lady and does not suspect or know anything of the damsel's proposals to her. But all night long the lady had a lively argument with herself in her great anxiety to protect her spring. And she begins to repent of having blamed and insulted the damsel and treated her with contempt, for she is quite certain and convinced that she never raised his case for reward or profit or for any love she felt for him; moreover, the girl loves her more than him and would never give advice that would bring her shame or trouble, being too loyal a friend of hers.

1749 See now how the lady has changed already: she thinks that the one she had abused is unlikely ever again to love her devotedly, whilst the man she had rejected she has fairly pardoned through rational and logical argument, since he had committed no crime against her. She puts the case just as though he had come into her presence, beginning her argument as follows. "Well now," she says, "can you deny that my husband was slain by you?"—"That", says he, "I cannot do, but fully admit it."—"Tell me, then: why did you do it? To harm me? Out of hatred or spite?"—"May my death not be delayed if ever I did it to cause you harm!"—"Then you've done no wrong at all against me; nor were you guilty of anything towards him, for had he been able, he'd have killed you. It's therefore my opinion and belief that my judgment is truly just."

Thus she proves to herself that there is justice, good sense and reason in the belief that she has no right to hate him. So her conclusion is what she would wish, and she kindles her emotions by herself like the firewood that smokes until the flame has taken hold without anyone blowing or stirring it. And if the damsel came now, she would soon win that dispute which has involved so much argument with her and her being roundly abused.

1785 In the morning she did return and took up her plea where she had let it drop. And the lady kept her head bowed, knowing she had done wrong in insulting her; but now she would like to make amends to her and ask about the knight's name, rank and lineage. So she sensibly humbles herself and says: "I want to ask your forgiveness for the very offensive and arrogant things I foolishly said to you; and I will follow your advice. But tell me about the knight of whom you spoke to me at such length, whether you know what sort of man he is and of what family. If he's the kind of person who is suitable for me, and provided there's no reluctance on his part, I agree to make him lord of my land and my person. But it will need to be done in such a way that no one may reproach me and say: 'That's the woman who took the man who killed her husband.'"—"In God's name, my lady, that's how it will be. You shall have the noblest, most distinguished and handsome husband ever to come from Abel's line."—"What is his name?"—"My lord Yvain."—"Upon my word, this is no ill-bred man: on the contrary, he's very noble, as I well know; and he's the son of King Urien."—"Indeed, my lady, what you say is true."

1820 —"And when shall we be able to have him here?"—"Within five days."—"That would be too long, for if I had my way he would already have arrived. Let him come tonight, or tomorrow at the latest!"—"My lady, I don't think any bird could fly so far in one day. But I'll send a servant of mine who travels very fast, and he'll get all the way to King Arthur's court, I hope, at least by tomorrow evening; for he'll not be found any nearer than that."—"This is much too big a delay. The days are long. But tell him to be back here tomorrow evening and to make greater haste than usual; for if he's prepared to do his best, he can turn two days' journey into one. And it will be moonlight tonight, so let him turn the night into day! Then on his return he shall have from me whatever he wants me to give him."

1842 —"Leave this business to me, and you'll have him in your hands by the day after tomorrow at the latest. In the meantime you shall summon your men and ask their advice about the coming arrival of the king. You should take sound advice on upholding the custom of the defence of your spring; and there will never be a man, however distinguished, who will dare boast that he'll go there. Then you'll be able to say straight out that you'll need to marry: a very renowned knight is seeking your hand, but you daren't accept him unless they all approve. And this I can guarantee: I know them all to be so base that, in order to load on to someone else the burden that would be too heavy for them, they'll all fall at your feet to thank you for it, since they'll have got out of a very difficult situation. For anyone who is afraid of his shadow will gladly avoid, if he can, any meeting with lance and spear: that's a poor game for a coward!" And the lady replies: "Upon my word, that's how I wish it, and so I agree to it, having already thought things out as you've described them; and that's what we shall do. — But why are you waiting here? Go along and don't delay any longer, but set about getting him! And I for my part will summon my people." That is how their discussion finished.

1879 The damsel then pretends to send to my lord Yvain's country for him. Each day she has him bathed and well washed and groomed; and in addition she prepares for him a robe of scarlet woollen cloth lined with vair and with the chalk still on it.* There is nothing needed to fit him out that she does not lend him: a golden clasp worked with precious stones worn at the neck and the height of elegance, and a belt with a purse of costly fabric. She has really equipped him completely, then advised her lady that her messenger is back, having ably performed his task. "Is that so?" she says. "And when will my lord Yvain come?"—"He's already here."—"He's here? Then let him come quickly, discreetly and in secret while no one is with me. Make sure nobody else comes, for I'd hate to have a fourth person here."

1904 The damsel leaves at once and returns to her guest. But she does not betray in her expression the joy she feels in her heart, saying instead that her lady knew she had sheltered him in there and was very annoyed with her about it. "It's no longer any use my hiding anything. Things have gone so far regarding you that my lady knows the facts and blames and hates me a great deal; and

she's taken me much to task for it. But she's given me an assurance
that I can take you before her without any risk or harm. I don't
think she will ill-treat you at all, except that (for I shouldn't be
dishonest and lie to you) she wishes to keep you imprisoned and to
have such complete possession of your person that not even your
heart will be at liberty."—"Indeed," says he, "that suits me well
and will be no hardship at all for me. I'm very willing to be in her
prison!"—"And so you will be, by this right hand I hold you with!
Now come along, and take my advice by behaving so humbly in her
presence that she doesn't make your imprisonment hard for you.
Don't be afraid, though! I really don't think you'll have too irksome a confinement." With that the damsel leads him away, both
alarming and reassuring him as she speaks ambiguously about the
imprisonment he will suffer (for there is no lover who is not
imprisoned: she is right to call him a prisoner, since anyone who
loves is truly in prison).

1943 The damsel leads my lord Yvain by the hand to where he will be
dearly loved; and yet he fears he is in a difficult situation, and it is no
wonder he is afraid. They found the lady sitting on a scarlet quilt. I
assure you my lord Yvain was terrified to find, on entering the
room, the lady not speaking a word to him. This increased his
alarm so that he was overcome by fear, thinking he had really been
betrayed. So he stood there keeping his distance until the maiden
spoke up and said: "Five hundred curses on the head of anyone
who brings into a beautiful lady's room a knight who won't
approach her and lacks a tongue in his head and the sense to be able
to introduce himself." So saying, she grasps him by the arm and
adds: "Come over here, knight, and don't be afraid my lady is going
to bite you; but try to make peace and be reconciled with her. And
I'll join you in pleading with her to forgive you for the death of
Esclados the Red, her late husband."

1972 My lord Yvain immediately clasps his hands and, falling to his
knees, says like a true lover: "Indeed, my lady, I shall not implore
your mercy but rather thank you for whatever you wish to do with
me; for nothing could cause me displeasure."—"Nothing, sir? And
what if I kill you?"—"My lady, by your grace be it, for you'll never
hear me say anything else."—"Never," says she, "have I heard such
a thing as when you place yourself entirely and unreservedly at my
disposal without any compulsion from me."—"My lady, there's

truly no force as powerful as that which commands me to submit
totally to your will. I fear to carry out no order you may be pleased
to give me. And if I could make amends for that death for which I
bear no guilt at all, I would readily do so."

1995 —"What?" she says. "Tell me now, to be absolved of all
penalty, if you wronged me in any way when you killed my husband."—"My lady," he says, "forgive me, but when your husband
attacked me, how was I wrong to defend myself? If one man is
intent on slaying or capturing another and the latter kills him in
self-defence, tell me if he commits any offence."—"Not at all, if one
takes the just view. And I suppose it would have been futile to have
you put to death. I'd be very glad to know, too, where that force can
come from which compels you to agree unquestioningly to my
every wish. I absolve you from all your wrongs and misdeeds. But
be seated and tell me how you've been so subdued."—"My lady,"
says he, "the force comes from my heart, which is drawn to you: my
heart has imposed this desire on me."—"And what prompted your
heart, my dear good friend?"—"My eyes, lady."—"And what the
eyes?"—"The great beauty I saw in you."—"And where does the
fault of this beauty lie in that?"—"In that it makes me love, my
lady."—"Love? And whom?"—"You, my dear lady."—"Me?"
—"Yes, truly."—"In what way?"—"To the greatest possible
degree, so that my heart never wanders from you or is to be found
elsewhere; so that I can't think of anything else; so that I surrender
myself entirely to you; so that I love you more than myself; so that,
if it is your pleasure, I wish to live and die wholly for you."—"And
would you dare to undertake for me the defence of my fountain?"—"Yes certainly, my lady, against all comers."—"Then rest
assured that we are reconciled." Thus they do find speedy
reconciliation.

2038 Then the lady, having previously held her council with her
lords, says: "We shall go from here to the hall where my men are
who've given me advice and counsel, on account of the emergency
they see as existing, to the effect that they beg me to take a husband.
And in this crisis I shall do that. Here and now I give myself to you,
for I shouldn't refuse as my husband a fine knight and a king's son."
Now the damsel has completely achieved her purpose, and my lord
Yvain enjoys greater authority than any words could describe. For
the lady takes him with her into the hall, which was full of knights

and men-at-arms; and my lord Yvain was so handsome that they all
looked at him in astonishment. They all rose when they entered,
each man saluting and bowing to my lord Yvain and surmising:
"This is the one my lady will take, and a curse on any who opposes
her, for he seems a wonderfully worthy man! Indeed, the Empress
of Rome would be well married to him. Would they had now given
their hands in an exchange of pledges and were to wed today or
tomorrow!" So they all declare, one after the other.

2070 At the end of the hall was a bench, on which the lady took her
seat where they could all see her. Then my lord Yvain made as if he
wished to sit at her feet. But she raised him up, and summoned her
seneschal to speak so that his words could be heard by all. The
seneschal, who was no stammering laggard, then began. "My
lords," he says, "war is upon us. Not a day goes by without the king
preparing with all possible haste to come and lay waste our land.
Before a fortnight has passed it will be totally devastated, unless it
has a good defender. When my lady married, not quite seven years
ago, she did so on your recommendation. Her husband, to her
sorrow, is dead. Now he who held this entire land and did so most
admirably has but six feet of earth. It is a great pity his life was
short. A woman is unable to bear a shield or strike with a lance. It is
greatly to her profit and advantage to take a good husband; and
never before was her need greater. Advise her, all of you, to take a
husband before the custom lapses which has been observed in this
castle for over sixty years!" Hearing this, they unanimously declare
that it seems to them a good thing to do.

2107 They then all throw themselves at her feet, urging her to do
what she in fact wishes; thus she has herself begged to act as she
wants to until, as if against her will, she agrees to what she would
have done even if everyone opposed her, saying: "My lords, as that
is your pleasure, this knight sitting beside me has insistently begged
and sought my hand. He wishes to devote himself to my honour
and service, for which I thank him and you should thank him too. I
have in fact never known him personally, though I've heard a great
deal about him. You should know that he is no lesser man than
King Urien's son. Apart from his being of high birth, he is of such
great valour and is so courtly and intelligent that nobody should
advise me against accepting him. I suppose you've all certainly
heard of my lord Yvain: well, it is he who is seeking my hand. The

day he has it I shall have a nobler husband than is my due."
Everyone says: "If you act wisely, this day won't pass without your
having concluded the marriage; for anybody who waits a single
hour before doing what is good for him is very foolish." They
beseech her until she agrees to do what she would have done in any
case, *for Love bids her do what she asks advice and guidance
about; but she accepts him far more honourably by doing it with
her men's approval. And their urgings are not at all unwelcome to
her: rather they incite and encourage her heart to have its way. The
horse that is not going slowly presses on still harder at the touch of
the spur.

2148   In the sight of all her nobles the lady gives herself to my lord
Yvain. From the hand of one of her chaplains he has taken Laudine
of Landuc,* the lady who was the daughter of Duke Laudunet, of
whom a lay is sung. That very day without any delay he wed her,
and their marriage was celebrated. There were many mitres and
croziers present, for the lady had summoned her bishops and
abbots. There was great happiness and rejoicing, many people
attending and much wealth displayed – more than I could tell you
of, even after giving it much thought: it is better for me to say
nothing than just a little. Now, though, my lord Yvain is master,
and the dead man is completely forgotten. His slayer is married to
his wife, and they sleep together, whilst the people love and esteem
the living man more than they ever did the dead. They served him
well at his wedding celebrations, which lasted until the vigil when
the king arrived, together with his companions, at the marvellous
spring and slab.

2175   Every member of his household was present on this expedition,
not one single man staying behind. And my lord Kay said: "Now
what's happened to Yvain, then, when he was boasting after his
meal that he'd go to avenge his cousin? It's obvious that he said that
after his wine! I imagine he's run away, for he wouldn't have dared
come here for anything. His boast was highly presumptuous. A
man is very bold who dares boast of something nobody else praises
him for, whilst he has no evidence for his glorious deed but some
falsely flattering report. There's a great difference between the
coward and the hero. For the coward by the fireside indulges in fine
talk about himself, supposing everyone to be a fool and believing
they can't see through him, whilst the valiant man would be very

distressed to hear someone else telling of his knightly qualities. Nevertheless, I agree with the coward, who is quite justified in praising and boasting about himself, because he'll not find anyone else to lie for him. If he doesn't speak of it, who will? Everybody keeps quiet on the subject, even the herald, who calls the names of the valiant but ignores cowards." So said my lord Kay; then my lord Gawain spoke: "Enough, my lord Kay, if you please! Though my lord Yvain isn't here now, you don't know what keeps him away. He certainly never stooped so low as to speak as much ill of you as all the gracious things he's said."—"Sir," says Kay, "I'll say no more. From now on you won't hear me speak of him, since I see it annoys you."

2218 Then, to see the rain, the king poured a basinful of the water on to the slab under the pine tree; and at once the rain fell in torrents. It was not long at all before my lord Yvain came, without pausing, fully armed into the forest and arrived at a very fast gallop on a large, sturdy horse that was strong, mettlesome and fleet-footed. *And my lord Kay was keen to ask for the combat, however it might turn out. He always wanted to begin the combats and fighting, otherwise he would get very angry. Before all the rest he calls on the king to leave this combat to him. "Kay," says the king, "since it is your wish and you have been the first of all to make the request, it should not be denied you." Kay thanks him and then mounts. If my lord Yvain can now shame him a little, he will be delighted and very happy to do so, because he clearly recognises him by his arms. He grasped his shield by the straps, and Kay took his; then they rush upon each other.

2246 They spur their horses and lower their lances, grasping them firmly and thrusting them forward a little until they gripped them by the leather-covered butts; and as they clashed together, they put such effort into their blows that both lances shattered and split right down to their fists. My lord Yvain dealt Kay such a heavy blow that he somersaulted over the saddle and struck the ground with his helmet. Without trying to do him any further harm, my lord Yvain dismounts, taking his horse. Many were pleased at this, and a number were prompted to say: "Aha! Look at you now lying there, you who spoke of other people with contempt! Yet it's only right to pardon you for it this time, for this has never happened to you before." Then my lord Yvain came before the king, leading the horse, which he held by the bridle with the intention of handing it over to him. "Sire," he says, "now accept this horse, for I should do wrong to keep anything of yours."—"Who are you, then?" says the king. "I should never recognise you unless I heard your name or saw you without your armour." Then my lord Yvain gave his name, at which Kay was overcome with shame, dejected, mortified and crestfallen, having said that he had run away. The rest are delighted at this and overjoyed at the honour he has won.

2285 Even the king showed great joy; and my lord Gawain, who liked his company more than that of any other knight he knew, was a hundred times more joyful than anyone else. And the king begs him insistently to tell him, if he will, what he has been doing; for he is most anxious to hear, and presses him urgently to say what happened throughout his journey. So he told him everything: both the adventure and the kindness shown him by the damsel, without garbling the facts or forgetting anything. After this he invited the king and all his knights to come and lodge with him, since they would do him very great honour by staying with him; and the king replied that he would gladly spend a whole week affording him the honour and joy of his company. For this my lord Yvain thanks him, and they stay there no longer, but mount at once and leave by the direct route for the castle. Ahead of the company my lord Yvain sends a squire bearing a crane-falcon so that they should not take the lady unawares and that her people could decorate the streets for the king's arrival. When the lady hears the news of the king's approach, she is overjoyed; and nobody who learns of it fails to be delighted and to mount on horseback. The lady calls them all together and asks them to go to meet him, at which there is no grumbling or fuss, because they were all eager to do as she wished.

2329 On great Spanish horses they set out to meet the King of Britain, greeting with high ceremony King Arthur first of all and then his entire company. "Welcome", they say, "to this company full of such worthy men! Blessed be their leader, who brings us such excellent guests!" At the king's approach the town rings with all the rejoicing. Silken cloths are brought out to be hung as decorations, and carpets are spread underfoot throughout the streets as they await the king's arrival. And they make yet more preparations by covering the streets with awnings on account of the sun's heat. The church-bells, horns and trumpets make the town so resound that one could not have heard God's thunder. The maidens dance before him, flutes and pipes, tabors, cymbals and drums sound forth. Elsewhere the nimble youths leap to play their own part. They all do their utmost to express their joy, joy with which they fittingly receive the king.

2359 The lady in turn has come forth, dressed in regal attire, a brand-new ermine robe, with a diadem on her head adorned all over with rubies; nor did she wear a sad expression, but looked so gay and merry that she was, I think, more beautiful than any goddess. Around her the crowd was dense, with all crying in turn: "Welcome to the king, chief of kings and of all the lords in the world!" It is impossible for the king to reply to them all as he sees the lady coming towards him to hold his stirrup. But, not wishing to wait for this, he dismounted in great haste as soon as he saw her. Then she greets him with the words: "Welcome a hundred thousand times to the king, my lord, and a blessing on my lord Gawain, his nephew."—"All joy and good fortune, beautiful one," says the king, "to your fair body and face!" Then the king with noble courtesy clasps her in an embrace, and she throws her arms about him.

2388 I shall say nothing of her warm welcome to the others; but I have never heard of any people so warmly greeted, so honoured or well served. I could tell you much of that joy, except that I should be wasting my words. But I would just like to make a brief mention of the friendship that was struck up in private between the moon and the sun. Do you know of whom I want to tell you? The man who was chief of the knights and honoured above them all should indeed be called the sun. I refer to my lord Gawain, for chivalry gains lustre from him just as in the morning the sun casts its rays and lights up all the places where it shines. And by the moon I mean she who is uniquely endowed with good sense and courtly ways. Yet I say this not only because of her good reputation, but because her name is Lunete.

2415 The damsel's name was Lunete, and she was a charming brunette, very sensible, shrewd and intelligent. She develops a friendship with my lord Gawain, who gains a high opinion of her and loves her well; so he calls her his sweetheart, since she had saved his companion and friend from death, and is generous with his offers of service.* And she tells him and describes how difficult it had

been to persuade her mistress to take my lord Yvain as her husband, and how she kept him out of the hands of the people who
were looking for him, when they could not see him despite his being
in their midst. My lord Gawain laughed heartily at her story and
said: "My young lady, I place at your disposal such a knight as I am
when you need me and when you don't. Never exchange me for
anyone else, unless you believe you'll be better off. I am yours, and
you be my own damsel from now on!"—"I thank you, sir," says
she. That is how these two formed their relationship.

2442 The others also indulged in flirtations, for there were some
ninety ladies there, every one beautiful and attractive, noble, intelligent, prudent, sensible and a damsel of high breeding. So the men
could enjoy themselves by embracing and kissing them, talking to
them, looking at them and sitting by their side: they had at least that
satisfaction from them! Now my lord Yvain has the joy of having
the king stay with him. And the lady shows them all such honour,
individually and collectively, that there are those foolish enough to
suppose that the courtesies and civility she shows them are prompted by love. But they must be called naïve for thinking themselves
the object of love when a lady is so courteous as to approach some
wretched fellow and make him happy with a caress. A fool is
cheered by kind words and very quickly taken in by them.

2466 That whole week they had a most joyful time: the forests and
rivers offered plenty of sport for all who wished. And as for anyone
who wanted to get to know the land that had come into my lord
Yvain's possession through the lady he had married, he could enjoy
himself visiting the nearby castles within a radius of two, three or
four leagues. The king having stayed there for as long as he wished,
he made preparations for travelling once again. But throughout
that week they had all begged and put forward the strongest
possible pleas to be able to take my lord Yvain away with them.

2484 "What? Will you now be one of those", my lord Gawain said
to him, "who lose in merit because of their wives?* Shame on him,
by Saint Mary, who marries and degenerates as a result! Anyone
who has a beautiful lady for mistress or wife should grow all the
better for it; and it's not right for her to love him once his reputation
and merit have lapsed. Indeed, you'd also find yourself regretting
the loss of her love, should you degenerate; for a woman is quick to
withdraw her affection, and rightly so, if she despises a man who,

once he's lord of her realm, deteriorates in any respect. Now more than ever your worth should increase. Break the bridle and the halter, and let's go tourneying together so you don't get a reputation for jealousy!

2503 "You shouldn't now dream your time away, but do the round of the tournaments, join in combats and joust hard, whatever it may cost you. He's a great idler who stays in one place. You really must come, for I'll be in your company. Take care, my dear companion, not to be responsible for the breakdown of our comradeship, for it certainly won't lapse through me. It's amazing how people set store by a life of perpetual comfort. A pleasure postponed is all the sweeter, and a small pleasure delayed is more enjoyable than a great one sampled at once. The joy of love when it comes late is like the burning of a green log, which gives out all the more heat and keeps its ability to do so all the longer, the slower it is to kindle. One may grow accustomed to something which is then very difficult to give up and, when one wishes to, one cannot. For all that I grant you, my good friend, that if I had a mistress as lovely as yours, by my faith in God and His saints, I'd be most reluctant to abandon her and would consider myself a fool to do so. Some people, though, are good at advising others yet are incapable of advising themselves, like those preachers who are deceitful tricksters, teaching and preaching virtue without being themselves prepared to practise it."

2539 My lord Gawain made this point to him so forcibly and pressed him so hard that he consented to go if, having put it to his wife, he is able to obtain her leave. Whether it is a foolish or a sensible thing to do, he will not fail to seek her leave to return to Britain. To this end he drew aside the lady, who was unprepared for this request for leave, and said to her: "Sweet lady of mine who are my heart and soul, my treasure, my joy and well-being, grant me one thing for the sake of your honour and my own!" The lady, not knowing what he intends to ask, at once gives her consent, saying: "Dear husband, you may require of me whatever you please." My lord Yvain immediately requests her leave to escort the king and take part in tournaments to avoid being called recreant. She replies: "I grant you leave until a certain date. But you may be absolutely sure that my love for you will change to hate if you over-step the time limit I shall set you.* You can be certain I shall never break my word: if you break yours, I'll keep mine. If you wish to have my love, and if I mean anything at all to you, remember to come back at the latest a year from now, a week after Saint John's Day, today being the eighth day since his feast. You'll be checkmated as far as my love is concerned unless you are here back home with me on that day!"

2579 My lord Yvain weeps and sighs so bitterly that he scarcely manages to say: "My lady, this date is too distant. If I could be a dove whenever I wished, I should be with you very often. And I pray God that He may please not to let me stay away so long. However, a man may expect to come back very quickly without knowing what the future holds; and I don't know what will happen to me – whether I may be prevented if sickness or imprisonment keep me back. You've been unjust in not making an exception at least of physical impediment."—"My lord," she says, "I will make that exception. Nevertheless I give you full assurance that, if God protects you from death, no obstacle will stand in your way so long as you remember me. But now put on your finger this ring of mine, which I lend you; and I'll explain clearly to you the nature of its stone. No true, loyal lover can be held prisoner or lose any blood or suffer any harm provided that he wears and cherishes it and bears his love in mind: instead he becomes harder than iron. It will serve you as shield and hauberk. Never before have I been prepared to lend or give it to any knight; but I give it to you because you are dear to me." Now my lord Yvain has his leave; and when he took it they wept bitterly.

2616 The king was unwilling to stay longer despite all attempts at persuasion, but was impatient to have all their palfreys brought, ready for the road and bridled. His wish was met with all speed, the palfreys being led out for them so that it only remained to mount. I do not know what I should tell you of the manner of my lord Yvain's departure and of the kisses bestowed on him sprinkled with tears and fragrant with tenderness. And what should I tell you about the king – how he is escorted by the lady and her maidens with her and her knights too? I should spend too long in doing so. Because of the lady's tears, the king begs her to come no further but return to her dwelling. He continued his pleadings until, with great reluctance, she went back, taking her company with her.

2639 My lord Yvain parted from the lady so very unwillingly that his heart stayed behind. The king can lead away his body, but will take no part of his heart, which clings so closely to the heart of the one who is left behind that he is powerless to take it with him. When the body is without the heart, it cannot possibly survive; and if the body does live on without the heart, that is a wonder never seen by man – yet this wonder has come about, since it has remained alive without the heart it used to contain, as that was no longer willing to follow it. His heart is well off where it has stayed, and his body lives in hope of returning to the heart, creating a strange kind of heart out of hope, which is often fickle and treacherous. He will never, I think, be aware of the moment when hope will have betrayed him; for if he overstays by a single day the time that had been mutually agreed, he will find it very hard to make again a truce or peace with his lady. He will overstay it, I fancy, for my lord Gawain will not let him leave his company, going together as they do to the tournaments wherever they are held.

2672 Meanwhile the year passes; and throughout it my lord Yvain did so well that my lord Gawain was at great pains to honour him, and so kept him back so long that the whole year had passed together with a good part of the next until mid-August came round,* when the king held court at Chester. The previous evening they had returned from a tournament where my lord Yvain had been and had carried off all the honour. And the story as I know it says that the two companions were unwilling to lodge together in the town, but had their tents erected outside it and held court there, not once coming to the king's court, but the king coming to theirs; for the majority, and the best, of the knights were with them. King Arthur was sitting among them, when there occurred to Yvain a thought which took him more aback than any he had had since the moment he took leave of his lady; for he realised he had broken his pledge to her and that the time-limit had passed. He had great difficulty in holding back his tears, but shame forced him to do so. He remained deep in thought until he saw a damsel coming straight towards them at a very fast amble on a black palfrey with white feet. In front of the tent she dismounts, without anyone helping her down or going to take her horse.

2711 As soon as she spotted the king she let her mantle fall and, entering the tent uncloaked, went right up to him. She said that her lady sends greetings to the king and my lord Gawain and all the others except my lord Yvain, the disloyal traitor, liar and deceiver,

who has abandoned and duped her. "She has quite seen through his
lying talk, pretending as he did to be a true lover, though he is a
false, treacherous thief. This thief has betrayed my lady, who
suspected no wrong and had not the slightest idea he would steal
her heart. Those who truly love don't steal hearts away, though
they are called thieves by some who go about practising deceit in
love without knowing anything at all about it. The lover takes his
beloved's heart in a way that is not theft: rather he guards it from
being stolen from her by thieves in the guise of honest men. These
are hypocritical thieves and traitors, competing in the theft of
hearts to which they are indifferent; but the lover, wherever he may
go, treasures the heart and brings it back again.

2742   "Yvain, though, has dealt my lady a mortal blow, for she
believed he would keep her heart for her and, before the year was
out, return it to her. Yvain, you were indeed highly forgetful to fail
to remember that you were to return to my lady within a year. She
permitted you to be away until the festival of Saint John, and you
held her in such scorn that after that you never thought of her
again. In her room my lady has marked out every single day and all
the seasons; for a person in love is ill at ease and never able to sleep
soundly, but all night long counts up and reckons the days as they
come and go. Do you know how lovers behave? They keep account
of the time and season. Her complaint has not been premature or
made without reason. And, without making a formal accusation, I
maintain that the person who married you to my lady has betrayed
us. Yvain, my lady has no further concern for you, but instructs you
through me never to return to her and not to keep her ring any
longer. She demands through me whom you see here present that
you send it to her. Hand it over, for you're obliged to return it to
her!"

2774   Yvain cannot reply to her, having lost his senses and power of
speech. The damsel jumps forward and pulls the ring off his finger,
then commends to God the king and all the others except him,
whom she leaves in great distress. And his distress continually
increases: everything he hears afflicts him, and all he sees grieves
him. He would have wished to take flight, quite alone, in a land so
wild that nobody would know where to look for him, and where
there was no man or woman or anybody knowing anything more
of him than if he were in the pit of Hell. He hates nothing so much

as himself and does not know to whom to turn for comfort now he has caused his own death; but he would rather go out of his wits than fail to take vengeance on himself now he has robbed himself of his own joy. He leaves the company of the nobles, fearing to go out of his mind in their midst; and they did not notice this, but let him go off alone. They are well aware that he does not care about their conversation or their doings.

2802 He went away until he was far from the tents and pavilions. Then his head is assailed by so wild a delirium that he loses his senses, whereupon he tears and rends his clothes and goes fleeing across fields and ploughed land, leaving his men at a loss, wondering where he can be. They go looking for him throughout the whole neighbourhood, in the knights' lodgings, under hedges and in gardens, seeking him where he is not to be found. *He continued his rapid flight until, near a park, he came across a serving-lad holding a bow and five barbed arrows, very sharp and broad. He had enough sense to go up to this lad and take the bow and arrows he was holding, without, however, remembering anything he had done. He lies in wait for the animals in the woods, kills them, and then eats the game quite raw.

2827 He lived in the woodland like a wild madman until he found the very small, low house of a hermit, who was busy clearing his ground. When he saw this naked man, he could tell beyond doubt that he was not at all in his right mind. The fear this caused him made him shut himself up in his cottage. The good man, out of charity, took some of his bread and pure water and placed it for him outside his house on a narrow window-ledge. The other, ravenous for the bread, then seizes it and takes a bite. I doubt if he had ever tasted any so coarse and rough. The measure of grain from which the bread was made, of barley kneaded with straw and more sour than yeast, had not cost five sous; moreover it was actually mouldy and as dry as bark. But he is so driven and tormented by hunger that the bread tasted to him like porridge; for hunger is a sauce, well blended and prepared, for any food. My lord Yvain ate up all the hermit's bread, which tasted good to him, and drank from the cold water in the pot. Having eaten, he makes for the woods again in search of stags and does.

2861 Then, seeing him go off, the good man beneath his roof prays God to defend and protect him from his ever returning that way.

But there is no creature with so little sense that it does not very readily return to a place where it is kindly treated; and after that, as long as he was in the grip of that madness, not a single day passed without his bringing some wild beast to the hermit's door for him. This was the life he led from then on; and the good man looked after the skinning and set plenty of the venison to cook; and the bread and pitcher of water were always on the window-ledge to feed the madman. So to eat and drink he had venison without salt or pepper and cold spring-water. And the good man took the trouble to sell the hides and buy bread made from barley or oats or other grain, so that Yvain then had an abundant supply of bread and venison.

2887 That lasted him for a long time until one day he was found asleep in the forest by two damsels along with a lady, their mistress, in whose household they were. When they see the naked man, one of the three hurries towards him and dismounts. But she looked at him long and hard before she could see on him any sign by which she might recognise him; yet she had seen him so often that she would quickly have recognised him had he been as richly attired as often in the past. She took a long time before recognition came, but nevertheless gazed at him until, in the end, a scar he had on his face seemed to her to resemble one my lord Yvain had on his: she was quite sure of this, having seen it frequently. This scar persuades her without any doubt that it is he; but it is a great wonder to her how it has come about that she has found him thus poor and naked. She crosses herself again and again in her astonishment; yet she does not touch or wake him, but instead takes her horse, remounts and then, riding back to the others, tells them through her tears what has happened.

2918 I do not know if I should waste time by telling you of the grief she showed; but she was weeping as she said to her mistress: "My lady, I've found Yvain, the most distinguished and excellent knight in the world. But I don't know what misfortune has brought the noble man to this plight. Perhaps he has suffered some grief that makes him behave in this way, for one may well go out of one's mind with grief. And one can tell by looking that he's not at all in his right mind, because he would certainly never have come to act in such a base way unless he'd lost his wits. Would now that God had restored his sense to him as sharp as ever it was! And if only he were willing afterwards to stay and come to your aid! For in his war against you Count Alier has launched an extremely heavy attack. I'd see this war between you ended to your great honour, should God grant you such good fortune that he returned to his senses and undertook to help you in this emergency."

2946 The lady said: "Don't worry now; for indeed, if he doesn't run away, I think that with God's help we shall get all the madness and frenzy out of his head. But we must make haste! For I've remembered an ointment given me by Morgan the Wise,* who told me that there's no madness in the head it won't clear." They at once make for the castle, which was quite close – not a step more than half a league away, measured by the leagues of that country, of which, compared with our own, two make one and four two of ours. Yvain remains sleeping on his own while she goes to fetch the ointment. The lady unlocks a case of hers and takes out the box, which she entrusts to the damsel, asking her not to be too lavish with it: she must rub it only into the temples, since there is no need to apply it anywhere else; she must anoint nothing but the temples with it and take good care of the remainder, because he has nothing wrong with him anywhere but in his brain. She has her take a suit of clothes, coat and mantle, trimmed with vair and of scarlet silk. The girl takes this for him and leads with her an excellent palfrey; and she adds things of her own – a shirt, fine breeches and new, well-cut hose.

2981 With all this she hurried off and found him still asleep where she had left him. Having put her horses in an enclosure, tethered them and tied them fast, she comes with the clothing and the ointment to the sleeping man. And she is exceedingly bold, going right up to the madman so that she can touch and handle him. Taking the ointment, she rubs him with the entire contents of the box, being so anxious to cure him that she proceeds to anoint him all over, using everything up without taking any notice of her mistress' warning or even remembering it. She applies more of it than she should, but supposes she is using it to good effect. She rubs it into his temples and forehead and his whole body down to the toes. In the warm sunshine she rubbed his temples and entire body until the madness and depression left his brain. But she was foolish to anoint his body, since he had no need at all of that. Had there been ten gallons of it, I fancy she would have done the same. She runs off carrying the box and takes cover near her horses. But she does not take away the clothing, so that, if God brings about his recovery, he will see it laid ready, take it and put it on.

3016 She stays behind a large oak-tree until he had slept enough and was cured and well again, having recovered his wits and his memory. But seeing himself as naked as ivory, he is very ashamed and would have been more so had he known what had happened; yet all he does know is that he finds himself naked. He sees the new clothes in front of him and is utterly amazed, wondering how and by what chance that clothing had come there. However, he is concerned and bewildered at the sight of his naked flesh, saying he is lost and ruined if any person who recognised him has found or seen him like this. Nevertheless, he dresses and looks about the forest to see if anyone at all is coming. He thinks he will rise and stand up, but lacks the strength to walk away. He needs to find help: someone to assist him and lead him along; for his grave illness has struck him so hard that he can scarcely stand on his feet. Now the damsel has no wish to stay where she was any longer. Instead, she mounted and rode close by him, as if she did not know he was there.

3046 Then Yvain, in dire need of help regardless of its source to get him to some lodging where he might recover his strength, makes every effort to hail her. And the damsel, for her part, looks all around her as if not knowing what is the matter. With a bewildered air she goes hither and thither, not wanting to go straight up to him. He begins to call again: "Over here, young lady! Over here!" Then the damsel turned her ambling palfrey towards him. By this sham she made him think she knew nothing of him and had never seen him before, which was sensible and courtly of her. Having come up to him, she said: "Sir knight, what do you want, when you call me so urgently?"—"Ah, my good damsel," he says, "I've found myself in this woodland through some mishap or other. In God's name and by your faith in Him, I beg you as a great favour to lend or give me outright this palfrey you're leading."—"Gladly, sir! But come with me where I'm going."—"Where's that?" says he.—"Out of this wood to a castle near here."—"Tell me, then, young lady, if you have need of me."—"Yes," she says; "but I think you're not at all in a fit state. You ought to rest for at least a fortnight. Take this horse I'm leading, and we'll go to the lodging-place."

3086 Then he, who asked for nothing more, takes it and mounts. And so they go on until they come to a bridge over a swift, roaring torrent, into which the damsel flings the empty box she is carrying. By doing this she thinks she can explain away her ointment to the lady, for she will say that in crossing the bridge she accidentally let the box fall into the water: because her palfrey stumbled under her the box slipped from her hand; and she very nearly fell in after it, which would have been an even greater loss. This is the deception she will practise on her lady when she comes before her.

3104 They continued on their way together until they arrived at the castle, where the lady gladly received my lord Yvain and asked her damsel, but in private, for her box and the ointment. She told her the falsehood as she had invented it, not daring to tell her the facts of the matter. At that the lady was furious and said: "This is a most serious loss, and I'm absolutely certain it will never be made good. But as the thing has gone, I'll have to do without it. One often sets one's heart on some benefit only to find that what one desires turns out badly; and in the same way I, expecting to gain some benefit and joy from this knight, have lost my best and dearest possession. Nevertheless, it's my wish that you should serve him above all else."—"Ah, my lady, how right you are! For it would be a very bad move that turned one misfortune into two."

3131 After that, no more is said of the box. Then to the very best of their ability they tend to my lord Yvain, bathing him and washing his head, having him shaved and his hair trimmed, for one could have taken hold of a good handful of beard on his face. They satisfy his every wish: if he wants arms, they are made ready for him, and should he want a horse, he is provided with one that is fresh, big and handsome, strong and mettlesome. He rested there until, one Tuesday, Count Alier arrived at the castle with men-at-arms and knights, raising fires and plundering. The people in the castle, meanwhile, mount and equip themselves with arms. Those that have them and those who are unarmed go out and make contact with the marauders, who do not deign to make off on their account, but wait for them in a defile.

3152 My lord Yvain, having been rested until he had regained his strength, rushed at their band, striking a knight full on the shield with such violence that he felled, I think, horse and rider together in a heap; and the man never got up again, for his heart burst in his breast, and his backbone was snapped through. My lord Yvain withdrew a little, then charged again, covering himself completely with his shield and spurring forward to clear the pass. More quickly than one could count up to four, with even greater speed and despatch, one might have seen him bringing down four knights. Then those with him were inspired by him to great courage; for when he sees before his eyes a valiant man undertaking some great enterprise, a weak-hearted coward may immediately be overcome by feelings of shame and disgrace that drive his feeble heart from his body and suddenly furnish him with boldness and the heart of a hero. So these men have become valiant, and each of them stands his ground very well in the affray and the fighting. The lady had climbed to the top of her castle keep and saw the encounter and the attack to win and hold the pass; and she saw lying on the ground many wounded and slain from among her own men and the enemy, though more of the latter than of hers. For my courtly, gallant, excellent lord Yvain made them surrender just as the falcon does the teals.

3196 The men and women who had stayed in the castle watching the fighting exclaimed: "Ah, what a valiant knight! How he lays his enemies low, and how fiercely he attacks them! He hurls himself at them like the lion among fallow deer when it is driven and tormented by hunger. And all our other knights are bolder and more spirited because of him; for, were it not for him alone, not a lance would have been broken or any sword drawn to strike. When one finds a man of worth, he should be well loved and cherished. See now how this one proves himself, see how he holds firm in the rank, see how he stains his lance and naked sword with blood! See how he chases them, see how he rounds them up, rides at them, attacks them, how he draws back then turns about, spending little time on his retreat and wasting none in coming back! See, when he enters the fray, how little regard he has for his shield, letting it be quite hacked to pieces without feeling any pity for it at all! But we see him very eager to avenge those blows he is given. If lances were made for him from the entire forest of Argonne,* I don't think he would have any left tonight; for he can't have so many put into his rest that he doesn't shatter them all and call for another. And see the work he does with his sword when he draws it! Roland never cut with Durendal* such swathes through the Turks in Roncevaux or Spain! If he had in his company some equally good companions, the villain we complain of would be routed before the day is out or else be utterly put to shame where he is." And they say the woman would be fortunate who received the love of this man who is such a doughty warrior and as conspicuous among the rest as a torch among candles or the moon among the stars or the sun beside the moon. *He has so won the heart of men and women alike that they would all have wished, on account of the prowess they see him display, that he had taken their lady to wife and the land was his to govern.

3255 Such was the praise bestowed on him by every man and woman, and truthfully, because he has so set about their adversaries that they take to flight as best they can. But he pursues them closely, followed by all his companions, who feel as safe at his side as if they were enclosed by a high, thick wall of hard stone. The pursuit lasts a very long time until the fugitives become exhausted and their pursuers hack down and disembowel all their horses. The living roll over on the dead. They maim and kill one another in their vicious struggle. And the count continues his flight with my lord Yvain after him, by no means half-hearted in his pursuit. He chases him until, at the foot of a steep slope, he catches up with him very close to the entrance of a stronghold of his. There the count was captured without anybody being able to help him; and after no great parley my lord Yvain accepted his submission since, once he held him in his hands and they were on their own man to man, there was no question of his escape or evasion or self-defence: instead he pledged him that he would go and give himself up to the lady of Noroison, constitute himself her prisoner and make peace with her on her conditions. Then, when Yvain had accepted his word, he made him take off his head-armour and remove the shield from his neck; and he surrendered to him his naked sword. This honour of taking the count away captive having fallen to him, he hands him over to the man's enemies, who are not a little jubilant.

3298 Before that, however, the news that they were coming was announced in the castle. All the men and women came out to meet them, with the lady at their head. My lord Yvain, holding his prisoner by the hand, presents him to her. Then the count fulfilled her wishes and requirements to the letter and gave her guarantees in the form of his sworn oath and pledges. These pledges he gives her, vowing henceforth to keep the peace with her and to make good whatever losses she can show and prove, and rebuild as new those of her dwellings he had razed to the ground. When these matters were agreed to the lady's satisfaction, my lord Yvain asked her leave to depart. But she would not have granted it had he been prepared to take her as his mistress or marry her as his wife. However, unwilling to be followed or escorted a single step of his way, he left her immediately, deaf to all entreaties. Now he set out on his return journey, leaving very disconsolate the lady whom he had made very happy; and the greater the happiness he had brought her before, the more it grieves and distresses her when he will stay no longer. For she would have wished to honour him and, had he been willing, would have made him lord of all she possessed, or else would have paid him handsomely for his service with any sum he cared to accept. He refused, however, to listen to whatever any man or woman said on the subject; and, despite their deep regret, he parted from the knights and the lady, since they were unable to detain him any longer.

3341 *My lord Yvain was travelling immersed in his thoughts through a dense forest when, from its depths, he heard a loud, anguished cry. At that he turned in the direction from which he had heard the cry. And when he reached the spot he saw, in a clearing, a lion with a serpent holding it by the tail and scorching all its hindquarters with searing flames. My lord Yvain does not spend long looking at this extraordinary sight, but debates in his mind which of the two he will help. Then he says he will go to the aid of the lion, since one should do nothing but harm to any venomous, treacherous creature; and the serpent is venomous and so full of evil that fire is spurting from its mouth. For that reason my lord Yvain thinks he will kill it first.

3364 He advances with drawn sword, holding his shield in front of his face in order not to be harmed by the flame it was spewing from its throat, which was wider than a pot. If the lion subsequently attacks him he will not get away without a fight; but whatever happens to him afterwards, he is determined to help it now, being urged and moved by pity to bring aid and assistance to the fine, noble beast. He goes to strike the treacherous serpent with his keen sword and cuts down through it to the ground, slicing it in half. He strikes again and again with such vigour that he chops it all into pieces. But he had to sever a piece of the lion's tail, because it was held by the evil serpent's head. He cut off as much of it as was necessary: he could not take less.

3388 Having rescued the lion, he supposed he would have to fight it
and that it would attack him. Yet it never thought of doing so. Now
hear what the lion did! It acted in a noble, civilised way, putting on
a show of surrendering to him, joining its fore-feet and holding
them out to him and bowing its face towards the ground.* Then it
stood up on its two hind-feet before kneeling down, while its entire
face grew wet with tears of humility. My lord Yvain is certain the
lion is thanking him and humbling itself before him on account of
the serpent he had slain, thus saving it from death. Much pleased by
this circumstance, he wipes his sword clean of the serpent's venom
and filth, thrusts it back into the scabbard and resumes his journey.

3412 The lion stays close by his side, for never again will it leave him
but always stay with him, wishing to give him service and protection. It proceeds ahead along the road until it scents in the wind, as
it leads the way, some wild animals grazing. Then hunger and its
nature prompt it to seek out and hunt its prey to obtain its food, as
it is its instinct to do. For a little while it tracked them until it made
clear to its master that it had noticed and detected the scent and
smell of game. Then it looks round at him and stops, wanting to
serve him as he pleases; for it would not wish to go anywhere
against his will. He realises from its manner that it is showing him it
is waiting for him. He clearly perceives and realises that if he holds
back it will too, and if he follows it it will catch the game it has
scented. Then he shouts and calls to it as he would to a leash of
hounds. At once the lion puts its nose to the scent it had caught and
which had not deceived it; for it had not gone a bowshot when it
saw a roe-deer grazing on its own in a valley. It will soon catch that,
if it has its way; and so, with its first leap, it did, then drank its blood
still warm. Having killed it, it tossed it on to its back and then
carried it off until it came to its master. He was very fond of the lion
after that and, because of the great affection it showed, took it as
his companion all the days of his life.

3456 As night was already approaching, it suited him to spend it
there and to skin as much of the deer as he wanted to eat. He then
sets about preparing it, splitting the skin along the ribs and taking a
steak from the loin. He strikes fire from a flint and with it kindles
some dry firewood, then puts his steak on a roasting-spit to cook
quickly over the fire, and roasts it until it is done to a turn. But he
took no pleasure from his food, for he had no bread, wine or salt,

nor any cloth or knife or anything else. While he ate, his lion lay in front of him, never moving, but watching him the whole time until he had eaten as much of his steak as he could. The lion ate all that was left of the deer right down to the bones. And Yvain lay all night with his head on his shield, taking what rest he could that way. The lion was intelligent enough to stay awake, intent on guarding the horse as it grazed the grass, from which it derived some small nourishment.

3485 In the morning they set off again together; and the two of them, it seems, led the same kind of existence as that night for the best part of the week, until chance led them to the spring beneath the pine-tree. There my lord Yvain almost went out of his mind a second time once he had come up to the spring and its slab and chapel. *A thousand times he calls "Alas!", voicing his grief, then falls in a swoon, such is his anguish. His sword slips from its scabbard, and its point passes through the links of his hauberk and into his neck close to the cheek. There is not a link that does not open, and the sword cuts the flesh of his neck under the bright mail, making the blood run down.

3506 The lion thinks it sees its companion and master dead. Never have you heard told or described greater grief over anything than it began to display over this! It writhes about, scratches itself and cries and wants to kill itself with the sword which it supposes to have slain its good master. It pulls the sword from him with its teeth, props it up against a fallen log, and wedges it against a tree-trunk behind so that it will not slip or give way when it strikes its breast against it. Its intention was about to be realised when the knight came out of his swoon; and the lion, which was rushing full tilt to its death like an enraged boar that dashes on without heeding where, held itself back.

3526 Thus my lord Yvain swoons beside the slab. When he comes to, he reproaches himself bitterly for having overstayed the year and so incurred his lady's hatred. He says: "Why should he not kill himself, this wretch who has deprived himself of joy? What am I doing in my misery not to take my own life? How can I stay here and see my lady's possessions? Why does my soul linger in my body? What is a soul doing in so miserable a breast? Had it left it, it would not be in such torment. Truly I should hate and blame and despise myself greatly, as indeed I do. Someone who loses joy and contentment through his own misdeed and fault should have a quite mortal hatred of himself. He should hate and kill himself. And why do I, while no one is watching me, spare myself from ending my own life? Have I not, then, seen this lion suffering such great grief on my account that it was quite determined to impale itself through the breast on my sword? Should I, then, fear death, having turned my joy to grief? Joy has abandoned me. – Joy? What joy? I shall speak no more of it, for no one could tell of it, and I have asked a quite futile question. The one that was vouchsafed me was the most joyful of all joys; but it lasted far too briefly for me. And anyone who loses that through his own fault has no right to enjoy good fortune."

3563 While he was lamenting in this way there was a poor, suffering wretch in the chapel where she was shut away; and all this she saw and heard through a crack in the wall. As soon as he got up after his swoon she called to him. "God," she said, "who is that I hear? Who is it that is grieving so?" He answers her: "And who are you?"—"I", says she, "am a captive, the most miserable person alive." He replies: "Be quiet, you foolish creature! Grief like yours is joy and your misfortune happiness compared with that which I'm enduring. The more a man has discovered a life of delight and joy, the more, compared with another man, he is distraught and stupefied by grief when it comes. A weak man through practice and habit can carry a weight that someone else of greater strength would be quite incapable of bearing."—"Indeed," she says, "I know well that what you say is completely true; but that doesn't make it credible that you're worse off than I am, or persuade me of it. For it seems to me you can go wherever you wish, whilst I am imprisoned here; and it's been decreed that I'll undergo the fate of being taken from here tomorrow and suffer the death penalty."—"Oh, God!" says he. "For what crime?"—"Sir knight," she says, "may God never have mercy on my mortal soul, if I've ever deserved it! Still, I'll tell you the truth, without a word of a lie, about why I'm in prison here. I'm accused of treason, and I can't find anyone to protect me from being burned or hanged tomorrow."

3607 —"Now more than ever", says he, "I can see that my grief and anguish exceeds your distress. For you could be saved from this danger by someone or other. Isn't that a possibility?"—"Yes, except that I don't yet know by whom. There are only two men in the world who would dare take on a combat against three men in my defence."—"What? Are there three of them, for God's sake?"—"Yes, sir, on my word! There are three who accuse me of treachery."—"And who are those men who love you so much that they'd have the courage to dare fight one against three in order to defend and save you?"—"I'll tell you truly: one is my lord Gawain and the other my lord Yvain, on whose account I shall tomorrow wrongly suffer the death penalty."—"On whose account?" says he. "What's that you say?"—"So help me God, sir, it's on account of King Urien's son."—"Now I've heard you properly. But you won't die in his absence. I myself am that Yvain, because of whom you're in distress. And you, I suppose, are the one who guarded me in the hall, saving my life and my person between those two portcullises where I found myself anxious, troubled, alarmed and at a loss. I'd have been killed or captured without your kind help. Now tell me, my sweet friend, who are those people who accuse you of treason and have shut you up in this cell?"

3648 —"My lord, I'll not keep it from you any longer, but tell you since you wish to know. It's true I was not slow to help you in good faith. Through my persuasion my lady took you as her husband, following my recommendation and advice; and, by the holy Paternoster, I thought and still think I was doing it more for her benefit than for yours. I now admit that to you, as God may grant me health! I sought to serve her honour and your desire. But when it happened that you'd overstayed the year when you should have returned here to my lady, she became angry with me and felt she had been badly deceived in believing me. When this became known to the seneschal, a wicked, disloyal scoundrel who was very envious of me because in many matters my lady believed me more than him, he saw plainly that he could stir up great enmity between me and her. In open court and public view he charged me with having betrayed her for you. I had no counsel or aid except from myself alone; but I knew I'd never committed or contemplated treason against my lady. So in my alarm I replied at once, without taking advice, that I would have my case defended by one knight against three. He quite lacked the courtliness to deign not to accept this; and it wasn't at all possible for me, whatever happened, to get out of it or withdraw. So he took me at my word, and I had to guarantee to present one knight against three within a period of forty days. Since then I've visited many courts. I was at King Arthur's and found no one to advise me there or anyone who could give me any satisfactory news of you, for they had no information about you."

3698 —"And what, pray, of my noble, kindly lord Gawain? Where was he then? No helpless damsel was ever in need of his assistance without it being provided for her."—"Had I found him at court, I couldn't have made any request of him that would have been refused me. But I was told that a knight had abducted the queen,* for the king had acted senselessly in sending her off after him: I believe Kay escorted her to the knight. And my lord Gawain has undertaken a very difficult task in his quest for her. He'll never have any rest until he has found her. I've told you the complete, exact truth about what has happened to me. Tomorrow I shall die a shameful death and be burnt without fail as an act of defiance and contempt against you." He replies: "God forbid that anyone should harm you on my account! You'll not die so long as I'm alive! Tomorrow you may expect me prepared to the best of my ability to commit myself to your deliverance, as is my duty. But be careful not to tell or inform the people who I am! Make sure that, whatever happens in the combat, I'm not recognised!"

3732 "Certainly, my lord! I'll not reveal your name, even under torture. I would rather suffer death than do so, since that's what you want. Nevertheless, I implore you not to come back for my sake. I don't want you to undertake such a very terrible combat. I thank you for your promise to fight it willingly; but consider yourself completely released from it! For it's better that I die alone than that I should see them exulting over your death and mine. I'll not escape it just because they've killed you; so it's better that you remain alive than that we should both be dead."—"Now you've offended me greatly, sweet friend!" says my lord Yvain. "Perhaps you either don't want to be saved from death or despise the support my help affords you. I don't want to discuss it with you any more now; for indeed you've done so much for me that I ought not to fail you in any need you have. I know well enough that you are very dismayed. But, if it please God in whom I trust, they will all three be put to shame. That's it, then; and now I'm off to find shelter somewhere or other in this wood, for I know of no lodging close by."—"My lord," she says, "may God grant you a good lodging and a good night too, and guard you against anything that might harm you: that is my wish!"

3770 My lord Yvain leaves at once with the lion following behind. They went on until they came near to a nobleman's stronghold completely enclosed by a massive, strong, high wall. The castle feared no assault from mangonel or catapult, for it was impressively strong. However, outside the walls the ground was so completely cleared that no hut or house there remained standing. You shall know the full reason for this on another occasion, at an appropriate time. My lord Yvain keeps straight on towards the stronghold; and as many as seven young men, having lowered the bridge, dash forward to meet him. But they are terrified of the lion they see coming with him and ask him, if he does not mind, to leave his lion at the gate lest it should savage or kill them. He replies: "Don't speak of it, for I'll not go in without it! Either we shall both have lodging or I shall stay out here; for I love it as dearly as myself. Don't be afraid, though, because I'll look after it so well that you'll be able to feel quite safe." They answer: "Very well, then."

3803 With that they entered the castle and went on until they met knights and ladies and attractive damsels approaching. They greet him and help him dismount, then set to removing his armour, saying: "Welcome to our company, good sir! And God grant that you stay here until you may leave with great joy and honour!" From the highest to the lowest they do their best to give him a jubilant welcome and lead him into the castle with much rejoicing. Then, when they have expressed to him their great gladness, a grief which oppresses them causes them to forget that joy again; and they revert to weeping and wailing and tearing at their faces.

3822 Thus, for a very long time, they continue to rejoice and to weep: they rejoice in honour of their host, though against their inclination, being very apprehensive of something they expect to happen the next day; and they are convinced and certain that it will occur before midday. My lord Yvain was taken aback to find them alternating so often between their expression of grief and of joy. So he enquired of the master of the house and home: "In God's name, my good, kind, dear sir, would you be willing to tell me why you've done me such honour amid so much rejoicing and so many tears?"—"Yes, if that's your wish; but you'd be far better to want it to be concealed and not mentioned. I shall never willingly tell you anything to cause you unhappiness. Leave us to our grief, and don't take it at all to heart!"—"On no account could I possibly see you grieving without having my heart touched by it. No, I'm very anxious to be told, however unhappy it may make me."—"Then I'll tell you," says he.

3852 "A giant had done me great offence by wanting me to give him my daughter, whose beauty surpasses that of all other maidens in the world. This wicked giant, whom God confound! is called Harpin of the Mountain. There is not a day when he doesn't take everything of mine he can lay his hands on. There's no one with more cause than I for lamenting in sorrow and grief. I might well go out of my mind from grief; for I had six sons, all knights, more handsome than any I've known in the world. The giant has taken all six. He has killed two before my very eyes, and tomorrow he will slay the other four, unless I find someone who dares to fight him for the release of my sons, or unless I'm prepared to hand my daughter over to him. And he says that, once he has her, he'll pass her on to the vilest, foulest serving-lads he can find in his household, for their amusement; for he'd no longer deign to take her himself. I can expect this calamity tomorrow, unless God comes to my aid. And so, dear good sir, it's no wonder we are weeping; but for your sake we try hard, now and then, to put on a cheerful expression. For anyone who invites a worthy man into his company is a fool not to show him honour; and you seem a worthy gentleman to me. Now I've told you all there is to tell about our great distress. The giant has left us nothing in any castle or fortress except what we have in here. You yourself saw that plainly this evening, if you paid attention; for outside these walls, which are quite new, he hasn't left anything worth an egg, but has razed the entire town. When he'd carried off all he wanted he set fire to what was left. In this way he's played me many an evil trick."

3899 My lord Yvain listened to everything his host told him; and having heard it all, he chose to give this reply. "Sir," he says, "I'm very sorry and distressed about your plight. But I'm surprised if you've not sought help at good King Arthur's court. There's no man so mighty that he couldn't find at his court some men who would be prepared to try their strength against his." Then the nobleman discloses and reveals to him that he would have excellent aid had he known where to find my lord Gawain: "He wouldn't have taken it lightly, because my wife is his full sister. But a knight from a foreign land is abducting the king's wife, having gone to the court to claim her. Even so, he would never have taken her off by his own devices had it not been for Kay, who duped the king into handing over the queen to him and placing her under his protection. He was a fool, and she rash to entrust herself to him as an escort. And I'm the one to have already suffered very great harm and loss as a result; because there's no shadow of doubt that the valiant lord Gawain would have sped here for the sake of his niece and nephews, had he known what has happened. But he doesn't know, and that grieves me so much that my heart is near to breaking. Instead, he's gone off after that man on whom may God bring shame and trouble for having taken the queen away."

3940 My lord Yvain keeps sighing as he listens to this; and seized by pity he replies: "My good, kind, dear sir! I'd happily undertake the adventure with its perils if the giant and your sons came tomorrow early enough for me not to have to wait too long for them. Because tomorrow at noon I must be somewhere other than here, as I have promised."—"I give you, dear sir," says the worthy man, "a hundred thousand thanks together for your willingness." And all the people in the house said as much to him.

3957 Just then the maiden, with her graceful figure and beautiful, attractive face, emerged from a room. She came forward very modestly and sadly, without a word, so incessant was her grief; and she held her head bowed. Her mother too came beside her, since the master had sent for them, wishing to present his guest to them. They approached wrapped in their mantles to hide their tears; but he tells them to open their mantles and raise their heads, saying: "You shouldn't mind my telling you to do this, for God and good fortune have brought to us here a very well-bred gentleman, who assures me that he will fight the giant. Now waste no more time, but go and fall at his feet!"—"May God never permit me that sight!" says my lord Yvain at once. "Truly, it would not be proper on any account for the sister and niece of my lord Gawain to fall at my feet. May God forbid that I should harbour such arrogance as to let them throw themselves down at my feet! Indeed, I should never forget the shame that would bring me; but I'd be most obliged to them if they would take some consolation until tomorrow, to see if it is God's will to help them. I need no further entreaties, provided that the giant comes soon enough for me not to break my other pledge; because I wouldn't fail for anything to attend, at midday tomorrow, to the most important business I could ever undertake."

3999 He is thus unwilling to give them a firm assurance, being afraid the giant would not come early enough for him to be able to reach in time the maiden shut up in the chapel. Nevertheless, he promises them enough to make them quite hopeful. They thank him, men and women alike, placing great confidence in his valour; and they take him to be a very fine man because he is accompanied by the lion, which lies beside him as gently as any lamb. Owing to the hope they place in him, they cheer up and rejoice and show no further grief. When the time came, they took him to his bed in a brightly-lit room; and the damsel and her mother were both present when he retired to bed, for he was already very dear to them and would have been a hundred thousand times more so, had they known of his courtliness and great valour. He and the lion lay in there together to take their rest. No other people dared sleep there, but instead they fastened the door so securely that they could not then get out until daybreak the next morning.

4030 When the room was opened up, he rose and heard mass and waited until the hour of prime on account of the promise he had made them. In the hearing of all, he calls to the lord of the castle himself and says: "My lord, I've no more time to spare, but will leave, if you don't mind, because it's impossible for me to stay longer. But you may be quite certain that, had my business not been most urgent and to be performed far from here, I'd have waited some time yet for the sake of the nephews and niece of my lord Gawain, whom I love dearly." The blood of the maiden and of the lady and lord seethes and boils with fear. They are so afraid he will go away that they were ready to fall full length at his feet, when they recalled that he would not have liked or approved of that.

4054 The lord then offers to give him, if he will accept it, either some of his land or some of his wealth, provided he will wait a little longer. He replies: "God forbid that I should ever take any of this!" Then the maiden, terrified, begins to weep copiously and begs him to stay. In a distraught, anguished manner she beseeches him in the name of the glorious Queen of Heaven and of the angels and in

God's name not to leave, but to stay just a little longer – and in the name, too, of her uncle, whom he says he knows, loves and respects. Then he takes great pity on her, when he hears her invoking the name of the man he loves most, and of the Lady of Heaven and God, who is the very honey and sweetness of mercy. He heaves a sigh of distress since, for the kingdom of Tarsus, he would not wish her to whom he had given his pledge to be burnt. His life would not have long to run, or else he would live without his senses, if he were unable to get there in time. Yet on the other hand, the noble magnanimity of his friend, my lord Gawain, holds him back. So his heart almost splits in two when he is unable to stay.

4088 Even so, he still makes no move, but lingers and waits until the giant comes quickly up, bringing the knights with him. On his shoulder he carried a huge, massive stake, pointed at the front end, with which he gave them frequent prods. They were wearing no clothing worth a straw other than soiled, filthy shirts. Their feet and hands were tightly bound with cords, and they were seated on four weak, skinny, worn-out nags that limped along. They came riding along by a wood, tied tail-to-tail by a dwarf like a puffed-up toad, who went beside them, flogging them continuously with a four-knotted scourge, which he thought a valiant thing to do! He was beating them until they bled. Thus the giant and dwarf together brought them shamefully along. The giant stops at a level place in front of the gate and shouts to the worthy lord a threat to put his sons to death unless he surrenders to him his daughter, whom he will hand over as a whore to his rabble of knaves; for he does not feel enough affection or respect for her to debase himself with her. And there will be a thousand or so of them such as porters and scullions, verminous and naked, constantly with her, all with their contribution to make.

4125 The worthy man almost goes out of his mind when he hears him saying he will give his daughter over to prostitution or else his four sons will be killed on the spot before his very eyes. He is as distressed as a man who would rather be dead than alive. He often calls himself a poor wretch, sheds many tears, and sighs. Then my noble, kindly lord Yvain begins to speak to him: "My lord, that giant is very wicked and insolent to swagger out there; but may God never permit or wish him to have your daughter in his power!

He greatly demeans and degrades her. It would be an immense calamity if so lovely a creature of such high birth were handed over to serving-lads. Let's have my arms and horse! Have the bridge lowered, and let me across! One of us must be toppled: either I or he – I don't know which. If I could humble the cruel villain who is so maltreating you, so that he surrendered your sons to you and came in here to make amends for the shameful things he's said to you, then I should wish to commend you to God and go about my business."

4158 Then they go to bring out his horse and give him all his arms. They put all their efforts into arming him and soon have him well prepared. They wasted no time, or as little as possible, in his arming. When they had him well fitted out, it only remained to lower the bridge for him and let him pass. It is let down for him, and he goes out; and the lion would on no account stay behind. Then those who have remained behind commend him to the Saviour, extremely afraid for him lest that devil, that demon who had slain many good men on the field before their eyes should do the same to him in his turn. So they pray God to protect him from death and return him to them alive and well, and to allow him to slay the giant. Each one according to his wishes prays very fervently to God.

4182 Then the giant came fiercely towards him, threatening him with the words: "The man who sent you here had no love for you, by my eyes! Indeed, there's no better way in which he could get his own back on you. He's taken very good vengeance for whatever wrong you've done him!"—"You're just wasting your words!" says the other, quite unafraid. "Now do your best, and I'll do mine, for idle chatter wearies me." At once my lord Yvain, impatient to get away, rides at him. He goes to strike him on the chest, which was protected by a bearskin. And from the other side the giant rushes at him with his stake. My lord Yvain lands such a blow on his chest that he pierces the pelt and wets his lance's head in his body's blood by way of sauce. The giant catches him so hard with his stake that he makes him bend double. My lord Yvain draws the sword with which he is capable of dealing great blows. He found the giant unprotected, because he put such faith in his strength that he did not deign to wear armour. Holding his drawn sword, he attacked him and gave him such a stroke with the cutting edge, not the flat side, that he hacked from his cheek a slice fit for grilling. The

giant gave him a return blow that made him slump right forward on
to his steed's neck.

4219 The lion bristles at this blow and prepares to help its master.
Enraged, it leaps forward with great violence, seizes the hairy skin
the giant is wearing, rending it like bark; and under the pelt it tears
away a large piece from his hip, slicing through nerves and flesh.
The giant frees himself from its clutches, bellowing and roaring like
a bull, for the lion had badly wounded him. He raises the stake with
both hands in an attempt to strike with it, but misses, and the lion
jumps away; so his blow is wasted and falls harmlessly to the side of
my lord Yvain, catching neither of them. My lord Yvain raises his
arm to strike, gets in two blows and, before the giant can look
round, has severed the shoulder from his trunk with the keen edge
of his sword, whilst with the second stroke he thrust the whole
blade of the sword under his breast and through his liver. The giant
falls with death pressing him hard; and were a great oak tree to fall,
I think it would make a crash no louder than the giant did when he
toppled.

4248 That blow was what everybody on the battlements was most
anxious to see. Then it became clear who was the speediest, for they
all ran to be in at the death like hounds who have hunted their
quarry until they have caught it. Thus they all ran hard, men and
women alike competing with each other to reach the spot where he
lay on his back, mouth gaping. The lord himself runs up with all the
people from his court. His daughter comes running, her mother
too. Now the four brothers, who had suffered terribly, are overjoyed. Being quite sure that they could not detain my lord Yvain,
come what may, they beg him to return to have a pleasant and
restful time just as soon as he has completed his business wherever
he is going. He replies that he dare not make any promises, for he
cannot guess whether it will turn out well or ill for him.

4273 He did however tell the lord that he would like his four sons
and daughter to take the dwarf and go to my lord Gawain when
they knew he had returned; and he would like him to be fully
informed of how he has acquitted himself. For it is futile to do good
if one does not want people to know about it. They say: "This good
deed will not be kept secret, for that would not be right. We will
indeed do whatever you wish. But tell us what to say when we come
before him. Whose praise can we speak, when we don't know your

name?" He replies: "When you come to him, you can go as far as to say I told you my name was the Knight with the Lion.* And in addition I would beg you to tell him from me that he knows me well and I him, yet he doesn't know my identity. I ask you nothing more. Now I must leave here; and my greatest fear is that I may have stayed too long, for I'll have much to do elsewhere before midday has passed, if I can get there in time." Then he leaves without staying there any longer, having first been entreated by the lord as persuasively as possible to take his four sons with him. There was no one who would not have done his utmost to serve him, had he wished; but it did not please or suit him that anybody should accompany him. On his own, he left the place of combat to them.

4313   As soon as he sets off, he heads back towards the chapel as fast as his horse can carry him. The road was straight and easy, and he had no difficulty in keeping to it. But before he could reach the chapel, the maiden was taken out from it, and the pyre on which she was to be put was built. Clad in nothing but her smock, she was held bound beside the fire by those who were falsely accusing her of something which had never entered her head. My lord Yvain arrives, sees her by the fire into which they intend to hurl her, and was naturally greatly angered: no courtly or sensible person would have the slightest doubt about that. It did indeed make him very angry, but he has every confidence that God and Justice will side with him and help him: he places great trust in these companions and by no means hates his lion either. He goes rushing into the crowd, shouting: "Leave the damsel alone! Leave her, you wicked people! It's not right for her to be put on a fire or into a furnace; for she has committed no crime." They at once draw back on either side, leaving a path for him.

4344   He is most impatient to set his eyes on the one whom his heart sees wherever she may be; *and with his eyes he searches for her until he finds her. He puts his heart to a severe test by holding it in check and reining it in, just as someone uses a strong curb to check, with great difficulty, a strongly pulling horse. Nevertheless he gazes at her very gladly and sighs, but not deeply enough for his sighs to be noticed: instead he stifles them, though with great distress. And he feels deep pity at the sound and sight of the poor ladies whom he hears lamenting bitterly and saying: "Ah, God, how You have forgotten us! How great our plight will be now we're losing so kind a friend, a source of such help and aid to us at court! On her advice my lady clothed us in her fur-lined mantles. Now everything will be different, for there will be no one to put in a word for us. May God curse the man who takes her from us! A curse on the one who causes our loss, for we shall be sorely harmed by it! No longer will there be anybody to say or suggest: 'This mantle trimmed with vair, this gown and this surcoat, dear lady! Give them to that honest woman; for if you do send them to her they'll certainly find a good home, because she's in urgent need of them.' There will never be any talk of that again, as no one is courtly or good-hearted any more: instead, everybody makes requests for himself rather than others, and without needing to."

4385 So they voiced their regrets; and my lord Yvain was among them, plainly hearing their laments, which were neither groundless nor half-hearted. And he saw Lunete on her knees, stripped to her smock, having already made her confession, asked God's forgiveness for her sins, and said her *mea culpa*. Then he, who had been very fond of her, raises her to her feet and says: "My damsel, where are the men who blame and accuse you? They'll be challenged in combat here and now, unless they refuse it." Without yet having seen or looked at him, she replies: "My lord, God bless you for coming in my hour of desperate need! The men who are bringing the false testimony are here all prepared against me. Had you been a little later, I should soon have been cinders and ashes. You've come to defend me, and may God give you the power to do so, seeing that I'm entirely guiltless of the charge laid against me!"

4412 The seneschal and his two brothers heard these words. "Ah," they say, "woman that you are, stingy with the truth and generous with lies! He's a real fool now to take on such a heavy burden on your word. This knight is very stupid to come to die for you, for he's alone and there are three of us. But I advise him to go away again before he gets the worst of it!" In great annoyance he replies: "Let anyone who's afraid run away! I'm not so frightened of your three shields as to go off defeated without a blow. I'd be unchivalrous indeed if I now abandoned the ground and field to you while I'm quite hale and hearty. Never, so long as I'm alive and sound, will I flee before your threats. But I advise you to withdraw your charge against this damsel whom you've wrongfully slandered; for she tells me, and I believe her, and has sworn as the safety of her soul depends on it that she never committed, spoke or thought of any treason against her lady. I have complete faith in what she's told me about this and, if I can, I shall defend her, since I find the justice of her case is on my side. And, to tell the truth, God for His part favours what is just, God and justice being inseparable.* So when they come against me, I have better company and better assistance than you have."

4449 The seneschal replies in his folly that he may use whatever methods please and suit him to inflict damage upon him, provided his lion does him no harm. He answers that he never brought his lion there as his champion and has no intention that any but himself shall take part. But if his lion does attack him, then let him look to his defence against it, for he gives him no assurances on that score. The other replies: "You can say what you like; but unless you control your lion and make it keep quiet, then you've no business being here but had better be sensible and go away again. For it's well known throughout this country how the girl betrayed her mistress; so it's right that she should get her deserts in fire and flame."—"May the Holy Spirit forbid!" says he who really knows the truth. "And may God never let me move from here until I've freed her!" Then he tells the lion to draw back and lie down quietly; and it does as he wishes.

4475 The lion having withdrawn, nothing more is said or discussed between the two of them, and they move some distance apart. Together, all three then spur at him, whilst he advances towards them at walking pace, not wishing to act rashly or strain too hard at the first exchange of blows. He lets them shiver their lances and keeps his own intact, making for them a target of his shield so that each breaks his lance against it. Then he gallops away, putting a furlong between himself and them before returning rapidly to his business, since he had no long rest in mind. When he gets back, he catches the seneschal in front of his two brothers, breaks his lance on his body and carries him to the ground despite himself. The blow he dealt him was so solid that he lay unconscious for a long while without being any threat to him. Then the other two assailed him with their naked swords, both giving him hard blows, but receiving even harder ones from him, a single blow of his being worth fully two of theirs. So he defends himself against them to such effect that they gain no advantage over him until the seneschal gets up and does his best to injure him; and the others add their efforts to his until they wound him and get the upper hand.

4509 Seeing this, the lion waits no longer to come to his aid, for it thinks he needs it. Together all the ladies, who love the damsel dearly, call again and again on God, praying Him earnestly to refuse to allow at any price that this man be slain or defeated, having undertaken the contest on her behalf. The ladies aid him with their prayers, having no other weapons. And the lion helps him so effectively that at its first attack it strikes the seneschal, who was on foot, with such ferocity that it makes the meshes fly from his hauberk like chaff; and it drags him down so violently that it strips the flesh from his shoulder and down his side. It tears away everything it touches, so that his entrails are exposed. The other two suffer for this blow.

4533 Now both sides are equal on the field. The seneschal cannot escape death as he writhes and welters in the crimson flood of warm blood gushing from his body. The lion sets about the others, for in no way can my lord Yvain drive it back with blows or threats, though he tried very hard to do so. But the lion knows full well that its master does not disapprove of its help, but loves it all the more for it; so it attacks them fiercely until they quail under its blows, but on the other hand wound and injure it. When my lord Yvain sees his lion wounded, this deeply hurts the heart within his breast, and not without reason. But he tries hard to avenge it and so belabours them that he almost annihilates them so that, defenceless against him, they surrender unconditionally owing to the help afforded him by the lion, which is in a sorry state; for it has been wounded in so many places that it might well feel distressed. On the other hand, my lord Yvain himself was by no means completely unscathed, but had many wounds in his body. He is not, though, as worried about all that as he is for his suffering lion.

4566 Now he has rescued the damsel exactly as he wishes; and the lady was quite happy to forgive her for the grief she had caused her. Then the defeated men were burnt on the pyre that had been kindled for her burning, since it is right and just that someone who wrongly condemns another should die by the same death as he had demanded for him. Now Lunete is joyful and glad to be reconciled with her mistress, and they rejoiced more freely than anybody had ever done before. And one and all duly offered their services to their lord, but without recognising him. Even the lady, who possessed his heart without knowing it, begged him insistently to agree to stay and rest until he had cured his lion and himself.

4588 He then says: "My lady, it will not be today on this occasion that I shall stay – not until my mistress frees me from her displeasure and anger. Then all my hardships will be at an end."—"Indeed," she says, "I'm sorry. I don't consider the lady who bears you ill-will to be very courtly. She should not close her door against a knight of your merit, unless he had wronged her very grievously."—"My lady," he says, "however much it hurts me, all that pleases her I find agreeable. But don't question me any further! For on no account would I tell the offence or the penalty to any but those who are well aware of them."—"Does anyone know, then, other than you two?"—"Yes indeed, my lady!"—"Please tell us, good sir, at least your name. Then you will be quite free to leave."—"Quite free, my lady? That I should not be. I owe more than I could repay. Nevertheless, I shouldn't hide from you the name I've adopted. You will never hear about the Knight with the Lion without hearing about me. I wish to be known by this name."—"In God's name, good sir, how can it be that we never saw you before or heard your name mentioned?"—"That shows, my lady, that I'm not very well known." Then the lady says once more: "If you didn't object, I would again beg you to stay."—"Truly, my lady, I wouldn't dare to until I knew for certain that I had my lady's goodwill."—"Then go, good sir, and God be with you; and may He be pleased to change your sorrow and unhappiness to joy!"—"My lady," says he, "may God hear your prayer!" Then, softly under his breath, he said: "You have the casket in which my joy is locked, and, though you don't know it, you hold the key."

4635 With that he leaves in deep distress; and there is nobody who recognises him except for Lunete alone, who accompanies him for some distance. Lunete is his only escort; and he begs her urgently never to reveal who her champion was. "I won't, my lord," she says. After this he made a further request, namely that she should remember him and put in a good word for him with her lady, if she had the opportunity. She tells him to say no more, for she will never be forgetful or dilatory or lazy on that score. He thanks her a hundred times for that, then goes off deep in thought and worried about his lion, which he has to carry, since it cannot follow him. He makes for it a litter of moss and bracken in his shield; and having made its bed for it, he lays it there as gently as he can and carries it along stretched out on the inside of his shield. In this way he bears it away on his horse until he arrived at the gate of a fine, strong house. Finding it locked, he calls; and the porter has it opened so promptly that he does not need to call a second time. The man reaches out to take the rein and says to him: "Come along now, good sir! I offer you my lord's lodging, if you care to dismount."—"I'd like to accept this offer," he replies, "for I'm in great need of it, and it's time to find somewhere to spend the night."

4675 He proceeded through the gate and saw all the people of the house assembled and coming to meet him. Having greeted him and helped him to dismount, they put his shield with the lion on it down on a mounting block. Others took his horse and stabled it, and the rest duly relieved him of his arms and took care of them. The lord of the place heard the news and came into the courtyard to greet him. He was followed by his lady, his sons and all his daughters, along with great crowds of other people. Very gladly they took him to his lodging. Finding him ill, they take him to a quiet room and show great consideration by putting his lion in with him. Two maidens, daughters of the lord of the house, who were skilled in surgery, set about healing him. I do not know how many days he spent there before both he and his lion were cured and had to set off once more.

4703 Now in the meantime it happened that the lord of Noire Espine had a dispute with Death;* and Death launched such an attack on him that he was compelled to die. After his death it came about that the elder of his two daughters said she would take full possession of the land for all the days of her life, without ever giving her sister a share. The latter said she would go to King Arthur's court to seek help in establishing her claim to her land. When the other saw that her sister would in no way let her keep the whole land without opposition, she was extremely perturbed, and determined if possible to reach the court before her. Immediately she got ready and equipped herself and then, without any delay or waste of time, made her way to the court. The other took to the road after her and made all the haste she could; but she wasted her time and her journey, because the elder sister had already put her case to my lord Gawain,* and he had agreed to her request. However, the agreement between them was that, should anybody hear of this from her, he would not then bear arms for her; and to this she consented.

4737 Just then the other sister arrived at court, wearing a short mantle of fine woollen cloth and new ermine. This was two days after the queen's return with all the other captives from her imprisonment at the hands of Meleagant, while Lancelot was still treacherously held in the tower. And on that very day when the maiden came to the court, the news was received there of the wicked, cruel giant fought and slain by the Knight with the Lion, from whom greetings had been brought to my lord Gawain by his nephews; and his niece told him all about the heroic service he had done them for his sake, saying that he knew him well, though she was not aware of his identity.

4759 This report was heard by the sister who was in a state of great dismay, worry and alarm, thinking she would find no help or assistance at court, the very best man there being unavailable. For she had tried to enlist my lord Gawain in a number of ways, by her entreaties and appeals for affection's sake; but he had said: "My dear, you're appealing to me in vain, for I can't do it, since I've undertaken another affair, which I couldn't abandon." The maiden immediately leaves him and comes before the king. "Your majesty," she says, "I've come to you and your court to seek help. But I can't find any and am quite astonished that I'm unable to obtain aid. However, it would be unwise of me to go away without asking your leave. And in any case my sister should know that, if she wanted anything of mine, she could have it for love; but I'll never, if I can help it, surrender my heritage to her because of force, provided I can find aid or support."—"You speak sensibly," says the king. "While she is here now, I advise, urge and beg her to leave you your rightful portion."

4790 Then the other sister, sure of the best knight in the world, replies: "Sire! May God confound me if I allot to her from my estates any castle, town, clearing, wood, land or anything else! But if any knight, whoever it may be, dares to take arms for her with the intention of defending her claim, let him come forward immediately!"—"This isn't a fair offer of yours," says the king; "and it should be improved. If she wishes, she can have at least forty days within which to obtain someone, as is the recognised practice in all courts." And she says: "Good King, my lord, you may establish your laws as you please and see fit, and it's not up to me or my concern to go against you; so I must grant her the postponement, if she requires it." The other says she does want it, is most anxious for it and requests it. With that she commends the king to God and leaves the court thinking she will spend her whole life searching every land for the Knight with the Lion, who devotes his efforts to aiding women in need of help.*

4821 So she entered on her quest and passed through many regions without ever hearing any news of him, which caused her such grief that she fell ill. But she was very fortunate in coming to the home of a friend where she was dearly loved; and it was quite evident from her face that she was by no means well. They were at pains to keep her there, until she told them her business. Then another maiden undertook the journey she had embarked on: she took up the quest on her behalf. So she stayed behind to rest, while the other, quite alone, rode all day long at an amble until dark night came on. While the night worried her a good deal, her distress was doubled by the fact that it was raining as hard as God could make it, and she was in the very depths of the woods. The night and the woods cause her great trouble but, more than by the woods or the night, she is distressed by the rain. The track was so bad that her horse was often almost up to its girth in mud.

4850 A maiden might well be highly alarmed to be unescorted in a forest in bad weather and on a foul night so dark that she could not see the horse she was riding. That is why she called continually on God first, His Mother next, and then on all the saints of either sex: that night she offered up many prayers, asking that God might lead her to a lodging-place and release her from this forest. Thus she prayed until she heard a horn, which cheered her a great deal, for she expected to find a lodging, provided she could reach it. So she headed for the sound until she came on to a paved road; and that led her straight on in the direction from which she heard the horn-blasts; for three times the horn gave very long, loud calls. She made straight for the sound until she came to a cross standing on the right-hand side of the road. It was in that area, she thought, that the horn might be and the person who had sounded it. She spurred that way until she drew near to a bridge and saw the white walls and outer fort of a small, circular castle. So, by chance, she reaches this castle, having taken her bearings by the sound that led her there.

The call of the horn blown by a watchman mounted on the walls had guided her to it. As soon as the watchman sees her, he greets her and then comes down, takes the key to the gate and opens it for her, saying: "Welcome, maiden, whoever you are! Tonight you'll have a good lodging."—"That's all I ask for this night," says the maiden; and he takes her in.

4894 After the hardship and trouble she had endured that day, she has been very lucky with the lodging-place, because she is very comfortable there. After the meal, the host spoke to her, asking where she was going and what she was looking for. Then she replies: "I'm looking for someone whom, so far as I'm aware, I've never seen or known; but he has a lion with him, and I'm told that, if I find him, I can have every confidence in him."—"I", says he, "can vouch for that; because the day before yesterday God sent him to me when I was in desperate need. A blessing on the paths that led him to my house! For he took vengeance for me on a mortal enemy of mine, giving me the great pleasure of seeing him slain before my very eyes. Outside that gate you'll be able to see tomorrow the body of a huge giant he killed so quickly that he scarcely broke sweat."—"In God's name, sir," says the maiden, "please tell me as accurately as you can where he went and whether he spent the night anywhere."—"As God is my witness," he says, "I don't know. But tomorrow I'll certainly put you on the road by which he left."—"May God", says she, "lead me somewhere where I can get precise news of him! For if I find him, I'll be overjoyed."

4929 Thus they talked together for a long while until at last it was time for bed. Once dawn had broken, the damsel rose, much concerned to find the object of her quest. The master of the house and all his companions get up and set her on the right road for the spring beneath the pine. She made good time on her journey by the direct route for the castle until, on her arrival there, she asked the first people she found if they could guide her to the lion and the knight who had been travelling together. They said they had seen him vanquish three knights there, on that very spot. Immediately she says: "For God's sake, having told me so much about him, don't keep back anything more you can tell me!"—"No," they say, "we only know as much as we've told you. We've no idea what became of him. If the person for whose sake he came here can't give you any news of him, there's nobody here to

give you any further information. But if you wish to speak to her,
you don't have far to go, because she's gone to pray to God and
hear mass in that church and has already been so long in there that
she's had time to say many prayers."

4965 As they were talking together in this way, Lunete came out of
the church. So they said: "Look, there she is!" She went up to her,
and they exchanged greetings. Then at once the maiden asked for
the information she was seeking. Lunete said she would have one of
her palfreys saddled, as she would like to go with her and take her
to an enclosure where she had left him. The maiden thanks her
from her heart. The palfrey was not long in coming; and when it is
brought Lunete mounts. As they ride along she tells her how she
was accused and charged with treason, how the pyre on which she
was to be put was lit, and how he came to her aid just when her need
was greatest. As they talked, she escorted her and took her on to the
actual road where my lord Yvain had left her. Having accompanied
her as far as that, she said to her: "You should follow this road until
you come to some place where you will be given, if it please God
and the Holy Spirit, more precise news than I have. I well remember
that I left him either near here or at this exact spot; and since then
we've not seen each other, nor do I know what he's done since. He
did, though, badly need his wounds dressing when he left me. So I
send you this way after him, and may God grant you find him well,
and rather today than tomorrow, if it please Him. So go now! I
commend you to God, since I'll not follow you further lest my
mistress get angry with me."

5008 At once they separate, one to go back, the other going on alone
until she came across the house where my lord Yvain had stayed
until he was quite better. In front of the gate she saw a number of
people: knights, ladies and men-at-arms, and also the master of the
house. She greets them and enquires of them if they have any news
they can give her and can direct her to a knight she is seeking.
"Who's that?" they ask.—"The one who, I've heard, will never be
without a lion."—"Upon my word, maiden," says the lord, "he's
only just left us! You'll still catch up with him today if you can keep
an eye on his horse's tracks; but don't lose too much time!"—"My
lord," she says, "may God forbid! But tell me now which way to
follow him." They tell her: "Straight along this way." And they beg
her to give him their greetings; but they need not have bothered, for

she paid no attention to that, but set off at once at a hard gallop since her palfrey's amble seemed to her too slow, although it did go very fast at that gait.

5038 So she gallops through morasses and over good level roads alike until she sees the man accompanied by the lion. She is delighted and cries: "So help me God! Now I can see the one I've been pursuing so long: I've done splendidly to follow and track him. But if my hunt doesn't end in a capture, what use will it be to me if I catch up with him? Little indeed, or none at all, I swear! If I don't take him away with me, then I've been wasting my time." With these reflections, she pressed on so hard that her palfrey was all in a lather. Then she catches him and greets him. His reply is prompt: "May God keep you, fair one, and deliver you from your care and sorrow!"—"And you, my lord who, I hope, could well give me relief from it!"

5058 She then rides up by his side, saying: "My lord, I've sought you for a long time. Your most distinguished reputation has led me to wear myself out and pass through many regions in my pursuit of you. I've been looking for you until at last, thank God! I've caught up with you here. And if I've endured any hardship in my search, I'm not in the least sorry; and I don't complain or remember it. My limbs have grown quite light, for the pain left me the moment I joined you. Yet the errand is not my own: I'm sent to you by someone better than myself, a more noble, worthy woman. But if she fails to enlist your help, then your renown has betrayed her, since she expects aid from no other quarter. My damsel, who is being disinherited by a sister of hers, thinks that through you she'll be able to obtain complete satisfaction in her dispute. She doesn't want anyone else to undertake this, because nobody can convince her that any other would be able to help her. You'll have won and secured the disinherited lady's love and increased your chivalry by establishing her claim to her inheritance. She herself was seeking you to obtain the favour she hoped to have from you, and no one else would have come, had she not been prevented by an illness that forces her to keep to her bed. Now answer me, if you please, and say if you will dare to come, or if you'll fail to act in the matter!"—"Not at all!" he says. "No man can win fame by inactivity; and I'll not fail to act, but will willingly follow you, sweet friend, wherever you wish. And if the lady for whom you seek my help is in

great need of me, never despair of my doing all in my power for her.
Now may God grant me the grace and favour to establish, through
His good providence, her rightful claim!"

5107 Thus they rode on together in conversation until they
approached the fortified town of Pesme Avanture.* They had no
wish to pass by it, since the day was drawing to a close. They came
making their way up to the stronghold; and all the people who see
them approaching said to the knight: "You're ill come, sir, ill come!
You were directed to this lodging-place to suffer harm and shame:
an abbot would take his oath on that!"—"Ah," says he, "you
foolish, base folk, you totally wicked people lacking in goodness,
why have you turned on me like this?"—"Why? You'll know well
enough, if you go much further! But you'll not discover the reason
until you've been up in that fortress." My lord Yvain heads
immediately for the keep, and all the folk shout at him, saying:
"Hey, hey you wretch! Where are you off to? If ever in your life you
found anyone to do you some shame or injury, you'll have so much
done to you where you're going that you'll never be able to tell of
it!" My lord Yvain listens to this and says: "You dishonourable,
depraved people, miserable and insolent as you are, why do you
turn on me and attack me? What are you asking and what do you
want from me to mutter away at me like this?"

5142 —"There's no cause for you to get angry, friend," said a rather
elderly lady, who was very courtly and sensible; "for they mean no
harm in anything they say; but, if only you understood, they're
warning you not to go up there to find lodging, though they daren't
tell you why. They're warning and criticising you because they
want to frighten you. They usually behave in the same way to all
comers, to stop them from going in there. And the custom is that we
dare not, come what may, offer shelter in our houses to any
gentleman coming from outside. The rest is now up to you. No one
is barring your way. You can go up there if you wish, but if you take
my advice, you'll go back."—"Lady," he says, "if I followed your
advice, I'd expect it to be to my honour and advantage; but I
wouldn't know of anywhere to find lodging tonight."—"Then I'll
speak no more about it," says she, "upon my word; for it's none of
my business. Go wherever you please! Even so, I'd be quite
delighted to see you come back out of there without suffering too
much shame. But that would be impossible."—"Lady," says he,

"may God reward you for that! But my foolish heart draws me in there, and I shall follow the dictates of my heart." He makes immediately for the gate, together with his lion and the maiden. Then the porter calls out to him and says: "Come quickly! Come along! You've arrived somewhere where you'll be well kept – and a curse on your coming!"

5185 Thus the porter summons and urges him to come up, but in extremely uncivil terms. *Without replying, my lord Yvain passes in front of him and finds a great new, lofty hall, outside which was a yard enclosed by huge round, pointed stakes; and looking inside between the stakes he sees up to three hundred maidens engaged in various kinds of work. Each one was sewing as best she could with gold thread and silk. But they were in such poverty that many of them were bare-headed and ungirdled, so poor were they; and their dresses were torn at the breast and elbows, and their smocks were dirty at the neck. Their necks were thin and their faces pale from hunger and hardship. He sees them, and they him; and they all bow their heads and weep; and for a long time they give up what they are doing and are unable to take their eyes from the ground, such is their distress. When he had looked at them for a short while, my lord Yvain turns about and goes straight back to the gate.

5215 The porter jumps to bar his way, calling out: "It's no use, for you'll not get out now, good master! You'd like to be outside now; but, by my head, that gets you nowhere. First you'll have suffered such shame that you couldn't suffer more. So you didn't act sensibly in coming in here, for there's no question of your going out again!"—"I'm not wanting to, good brother," he replies. "But tell me, by your father's soul, where have those damsels come from whom I saw weaving cloths of silk and gold brocade in that yard? They're doing work that I find very pleasing; but I'm very displeased that their bodies and faces are thin, pale and pitiful. Yet it seems to me they would be very lovely and attractive, if they had things to give them pleasure."—"I'll not tell you," he says. "Find someone else to!"—"So I shall, if that's the best I can do."

5240 He then looks until he finds the gate to the yard where the damsels were working; and he goes up to them, greeting them all together. Weeping as they are, he sees the teardrops running down and falling from their eyes. He spoke to them: "May it please God to take from your hearts this grief, the source of which I don't know, and cause it to turn to joy!" One of them replies: "May God, whom you have entreated, hear your prayer! Who we are and from what land will not be kept secret from you. I suppose that's what you wish to ask."—"I came in here", he says, "for nothing else."

5256 —"It happened, sir, a long time ago that the King of the Isle of Maidens went round the courts and countries in search of new experiences and travelled about like a born fool until he rushed headlong into the danger here. It was an unlucky day when he came to this place, for we who are held captive here suffer shame and affliction which we never deserved. And you may be sure that you yourself may expect to find great shame here, unless a ransom is accepted for you! But in any case, it came about in that way that my lord arrived at this castle, where there are two devil's sons – and don't take that as a joke, for they were born of a woman and a goblin. These two were to fight with the king, who was extremely distressed as he was only eighteen years old, and they would have been able to cleave him in two like a tender lamb. Then, in his terror, the king got out of the situation as best he could by swearing that each year for the duration of the pact he would send here thirty of his maidens; and by this payment he obtained his freedom. And a condition of the oath was that this tribute should be continued throughout the lifetime of the two demons; but on the day they were overcome and defeated in combat he would be freed from this imposition and we, who are now subjected to shame, grief and hardship, should be released. Never again shall we have any cause for pleasure.

5295 "But I was very silly just now when I spoke about our release, for we shall never get out of here. We shall always go on working with our silk and will never be any better dressed for it. We shall always be poor and half-naked, continually hungry and thirsty: we shall never manage to earn enough to be able to eat any better. We have scarcely any bread: a little in the morning and less in the evening, for none of us will get from her handiwork more than fourpence of every pound earned.* With that we can't get enough food and clothes, because anyone earning twenty shillings a week is still badly off. And you may be assured of the fact that there isn't one of us who doesn't earn twenty shillings or more – enough to make a duke rich! So we're in great poverty, while the man we work for is rich on our earnings. We stay up a large part of the nights and all day to make money; for when we take a rest we're threatened with maiming, so we don't dare to rest. But why should I go on telling you this? We're so badly and shamefully treated that I can't tell you a fifth of it. But what makes us go crazy with grief is very often to see powerful knights, worthy men, killed in combat with the two demons. They pay very dearly for their lodging, just as you will tomorrow; for, like it or not, you'll have to fight single-handed and lose your reputation against those two living fiends."—"May the true God of Heaven protect me against them," says my lord Yvain, "and restore your honour and your joy, if that be His will! It's time now for me to go and see the people inside and find out what welcome they'll give me."—"Go then, my lord! And may He who bestows and dispenses all good things protect you!"

5347 He then goes on into the hall, where he finds no one, good or bad, to accost him. He and his companions passed through the house and continued until they came to a garden. They never discussed or spoke of stabling their horses. But what did that matter? For those who considered them already their own stabled them well. I do not know if that was a wise thought, for their master is still hale and hearty. The horses have oats and hay and litter up to their bellies. My lord Yvain enters the garden, followed by those in his company. He sees a gentleman reclining on a silken rug and leaning on one elbow, as a maiden in front of him was reading from a romance, about whom I know not. And a lady too had come to recline there and listen to the romance. She was the girl's mother and the gentleman her father; and they were able to take great pleasure in seeing and hearing her, since they had no other children.

5374 She herself was not yet seventeen years old, yet she was so lovely and attractive that the god of love, were he to see her, would devote all his efforts to her service and would never have her love anyone but himself. To serve her he would become a man and, shedding his divinity, would strike his own body with that dart whose wound never heals unless some perfidious doctor attends to it. It is not right for anyone to recover from it so long as no disloyalty is discovered; and if anybody should be cured in some other fashion, then he is no faithful lover. I could tell you so much about this wound that, if you were happy to listen, I should not finish my account today. There would be someone, though, who would quickly say that I was talking nonsense;* for people no longer fall in love nor do they love any more as they used to, and so they do not even want to hear about it.

5397 But now hear how, and with what kind of welcome and hospitality, my lord Yvain was given lodging. All those in the garden leapt to their feet the moment they saw him, saying: "Come over here, good sir! May you and all you love be blessed by God by word and deed!" I do not know if they are deceiving him, but they receive him with great joy and give the impression that they are delighted for him to be very comfortably lodged. Even the lord's daughter serves him and shows him great honour, as one should treat a worthy guest: she completely disarms him, and not the least of her attentions is to wash his neck and face with her own hands. The lord wishes him to be shown every honour, and her example to be followed. She takes from her chest a pleated shirt, a pair of white breeches and needle and thread for his sleeves, which she sews on as she dresses him.* God grant he does not pay too dearly for this attentiveness and service! She gives him a fine surcoat to put on over his shirt; and round his shoulders she places a fur-trimmed mantle of fine woollen cloth in excellent condition. She puts so much effort into serving him that he feels ashamed and embarrassed; but the maiden is so courteous, generous and polite that she still feels she is doing little for him. And she knows well that her mother is pleased if she omits to do nothing for him that she thinks will gratify him.

5438 That evening at table he was served with such a number of dishes that they were too abundant. The servants who brought the courses in must have been worn out by serving them. So that night they did him every honour and then put him most comfortably to bed; and once he was lying there they did not come near him again. And his lion lay, as usual, at his feet. In the morning, when God had lit His great light over the world as early as consistent with the due order He observes in all things, my lord Yvain and his maiden rose with all haste and, in a chapel, heard mass, which was promptly said for them in honour of the Holy Spirit.

5457 After mass, my lord Yvain heard terrible news, just when he thought he should leave in order to avoid harm. But he could not have his way in that. When he said: "My lord, I'm going now with your leave and if it please you," the master of the house replied: "I don't grant it you yet, my friend. I can't give it for a good reason, because in this castle a frightful, devilish custom is observed which I have to uphold. I shall now have two huge, strong servants of mine come to you here; and, rightly or wrongly, you'll have to take arms against them both. If you can defend yourself against them and overcome and slay them both, then my daughter desires you for her husband, and the ownership of this castle and all its dependencies awaits you."—"My lord," says he, "I want nothing of it. May God never grant it to me in this fashion! And let your daughter stay with you – or the Emperor of Germany would be very well off if he took her, she is so beautiful and well-mannered."

5485 —"Say no more, my good guest!" says the lord. "I'm deaf to your excuses, for you can't get out of it. Whoever can overcome these two who are about to come and attack you must have my castle, my daughter as his wife, and the whole of my lands. The combat can in no way be cancelled or put off. But I'm quite sure you're refusing my daughter out of cowardice; for in this way you think you can avoid the combat altogether. But make no mistake at all about this: you must fight this combat! No knight lodged here can possibly escape. This is an established custom and prerogative, which will last a very long time; for my daughter shall not be married until I see them slain or defeated."—"Then, though it's against my wishes, I'll have to fight them just the same. But I assure you that I should be very willing and happy not to need to. Sorry as I am, I'll fight the combat since it's inevitable."

5512 Then both the sons of the goblin arrive,* hideous and black, each carrying a jagged club of cornel-wood, which they had covered with copper and bound with brass. They were armed from their shoulders down to their knees, but their heads and faces were unprotected; and their legs, which were by no means small, were bare. As they came armed in this way, they held over their heads round shields that were strong and light for protection. The lion begins to quiver as soon as it sees them, for it well knows and can tell from the weapons they hold that they are coming to fight its master. Its coat and mane bristle, it trembles with aggressive courage and wrath and lashes the ground with its tail, wishing to save its master before they kill him.

5536 When they see it, they say: "Take your lion away from here, vassal: it's threatening us! Either you surrender to us, or else I insist that you put it somewhere where it can't go to your help or do us any harm. You must come alone to enjoy yourself with us! For the lion would very much like to help you, if it could."—"Take it away yourselves if you're afraid of it!" says my lord Yvain. "For it suits me well, and I'm quite happy for it to injure you if it can, and I'd be delighted if it helps me."—"Upon our word," they say, "that's out of the question: you shall never have its aid! Do the best you can alone, without any outside help! You must be on your own against two of us. If the lion were with you so that it joined in the fight against us, then you wouldn't be alone, but two against us two. So I assure you that you'll have to remove your lion from here at once, however much it may distress you."—"Where do you want it to be?" he says. "Where do you want me to put it?" Then they show him a small room and say: "Shut it in there!"—"I'll do that, as that's what you want."

5569 He then takes it away and shuts it up there. At once his armour is fetched for him to put on, his horse is brought out and handed over to him, and he mounts. The two champions ride at him to do him harm and put him to shame, for they are reassured about the lion now it is shut away in the room. They deal him great blows with their maces, with the shield and helmet he has affording him little help because, when they catch him on the helmet, they badly dent and break it, whilst his shield shatters and melts like ice: they make holes in it big enough to put your fists through. The pair of them fight fearsomely. And what does he do against these two demons? Burning with shame and fear, he defends himself with all his might. He strains and puts every effort into dealing massive, heavy blows: they are not short of presents from him, for he returns their kindnesses twofold.

5594 Now the lion in the room is grief-stricken and heavy-hearted, remembering the very good turn generously done it by this man who could now desperately do with its service and assistance. It would at once return this favour in more than full measure and with no deductions if only it could get out of there. It goes hunting round in all directions but can see no way of escape. It clearly hears the blows struck in the dangerous, bitter combat; and this upsets it so much that it is beside itself and out of its mind with grief. It searches about until it comes to the threshold, which was rotting next to the ground; and it scratches at it until it can squeeze and force itself in almost up to the haunches. Meanwhile, my lord

Yvain was very hard pressed and bathed in sweat, for he found the two ruffians very strong, savage and tenacious. He had suffered many blows and returned them as best he could, but without injuring them at all, for they were too well versed in duelling, and their shields were not of the sort that can be cut apart by a sword, however sharp and keen. Consequently, my lord Yvain had good reason to be very afraid of being killed. But he continues to hold his own until the lion has scratched away so much under the threshold that it has got out.

5630 If the scoundrels are not beaten now, they never will be; for they will never have a truce or peace from the lion as long as it knows they are alive. It seizes one of them and drags him to the ground like a log. Now the villains are terrified; but there is no one at the scene who does not feel joy in his heart, since the one the lion has brought down will never get up again if the other does not come to his rescue. He runs over to help him and to protect himself, for the lion would turn on him once it had killed the one it had felled; and he, for his part, was more afraid of the lion than its master. Now, though, my lord Yvain will be a fool to let him live long once he has turned his back to him and he can see his neck completely exposed, for things have turned out well for him. The rogue offered him openly his bare head and neck; and he gave him such a stroke that he sliced his head from his trunk so smoothly that he knew not a thing about it. He at once dismounts in order to rescue the other and take him from the lion, which is holding him down; but in vain, for he is in such a bad state that a doctor could never be there in time, since the lion, when it arrived and came furiously at him, wounded him badly and left him terribly mauled. Nevertheless, he pushes it back, then sees that it has shattered his entire shoulder and torn it from his body.

5670 He is not at all concerned about him now, for his club has fallen from his grasp, and he lies without stirring or moving, almost like a dead man. But he does just manage to speak and says, as best he can: "Call off your lion if you please, good sir, so that it can't touch me any more! From now on you can do whatever you want with me. A man who begs and asks for mercy should not have his plea turned down, unless he's faced by someone quite pitiless. And so as to obtain mercy, I'll not defend myself any further or get up from here: I just place myself in your hands."—"Then tell me," says he, "that you admit to being defeated and vanquished!"—"My lord," he says, "that's obvious: I'm defeated, much as I dislike it; and I concede that I'm vanquished."—"Then you need have no more fear of me; and my lion will also leave you alone."

5694　All the people then hurry to gather around him, and both the lord and the lady with them, showing their joy for him, embracing him and speaking to him of their daughter. They say to him: "Now you will be the lord and master of us all, and our daughter will be your lady, for we give her to you as your wife."—"And I", says he, "return her to you. Let the one who has her keep her! I have no wish for her; though I don't say this out of disdain. Don't be upset if I do not accept her, for I cannot and must not do so. But please hand over to me the captives you hold! The agreement, as you well know, is that they should go free."—"What you say is true," the lord replies. "I give them up and surrender them freely to you, without any further opposition. But you'll be wise to take my daughter, who is beautiful, attractive and prudent, along with all my possessions. You'll never make so rich a marriage if you don't accept this one."—"My lord," he says, "you don't know the reason that prevents me or what my situation is, and I dare not explain them to you. But when I refuse what no man entitled to devote his heart and attentions to a lovely, charming maiden would refuse, you can rest assured that I would gladly accept her if I could or ought to take this girl or any other. You may, however, be certain that I cannot, so now leave me in peace on that score, because the damsel who came here with me is waiting for me! She has kept me company, and I wish to do the same for her, whatever the outcome for me."

5737　—"Is that what you want, good sir? How, then? Never, unless I have a mind to and order it, shall I have my gate opened for you: rather you'll stay here as my prisoner. It's arrogant and improper on your part, when I beg you to accept my daughter, to disdain to have her."—"Disdain, my lord? Upon my soul I don't! But I cannot, at any price, marry a wife or remain here. I shall follow the damsel under whose conduct I am, for it cannot be otherwise. But if you like, I'll pledge you with my right hand, and do believe me, that, just as you see me now, I'll return if at all possible, and then will take your daughter whenever it suits you."—"Damn anyone", says he, "who asks you for your word, pledge or promise! If my daughter attracts you, you'll be back here quickly enough! I doubt if you'd come back any sooner because of your word or any oath you'd sworn. So go now, for I dispense you from all promises and agreements. I don't care if you're kept away by rain or wind, or by nothing at all. I don't hold my daughter so cheap that I'd force her on you. Be off to your business now! For it's all the same to me whether you go or whether you stay!"

5771 With that, my lord Yvain departs, staying no longer in the castle. He takes with him the maidens released from captivity, whom the lord has made over to him, poor and ill-dressed as they are, though now they consider themselves rich. All together, two by two, they go out of the town in front of him. *I do not believe they would have rejoiced as greatly as they did on his account for Him who created the whole world, had He come down to earth from Heaven. All those people who had heaped on him as much shame as they could now go to make peace with him and ask his forgiveness; and so they escort him on his way. He says he does not know what they mean. "I don't know," he says, "what you are talking about; and I hold nothing against any of you, for, as far as I remember, you never said anything to offend me." They are very happy with what they hear, and praise his civility highly. So, having escorted him a long way, they all commend him to God. And the damsels for their part ask his leave and depart; and, as they do so, each bows before him and in their prayers express the wish for him that God may grant him joy and health and the achievement of his desire wherever he may go in the future. He, very unhappy at lingering so long, responds with the wish that God may save them all. "Go!" he says. "And may God guide you safe and happy to your countries!"

5808 They at once set out and go on their way rejoicing greatly, while my lord Yvain takes to the road again in a different direction. He continues to travel at top speed every day of that week under the guidance of the maiden, who knew well the road and the refuge where she had left the disinherited sister in a sad and melancholy mood. However, when she heard the news of the arrival of the maiden along with the Knight with the Lion, there never was such joy as that which she felt in her heart; for now she believes that, if she wishes it, her sister will grant her a share in her inheritance. The maiden had lain ill for a long time and had recently recovered from her sickness, which had taken a great deal out of her, as her face clearly showed. She is the very first to go promptly to meet them; and she greets them and does them every conceivable honour in her power. There is no need to speak of the joy that filled the house that night; and not a word will be said of it, for it would take too long to tell.

5840 I pass over everything until, next day, they mounted and left. Then they journeyed until they saw the castle where King Arthur had been staying for a fortnight or more. There too was the damsel who was disinheriting her sister; for since going there, she had kept a very close eye on the court, awaiting the arrival of her sister, who is on her way and getting near. But that causes her little concern, as she does not believe she would have found any knight who could withstand my lord Gawain in combat; and only one day of the forty remained. Had this single day passed, she would have made good her claim in reason and in law to be free to hold the inheritance on her own. However, there is much more to happen than she supposes or believes. That night they spent outside the castle, in a small, cramped lodging where nobody knew them; for had they slept in the castle everyone would have recognised them, and they did not want that. On the following morning when dawn appeared, they went out very hastily and hid away and lay low until it was broad daylight.

5872 I do not know how many days previously my lord Gawain had gone away, without anybody at court having news of him other than the maiden for whom he was to fight. He had withdrawn some three or four leagues from the court, where he then arrived equipped in such a way that he could not be recognised from the arms he brought by people who had seen him constantly about. The damsel, whose wronging of her sister is only too apparent, presents him at court in the sight of all, desiring through him to establish her claim in the dispute in which right is not on her side; and she says to the king: "Time passes, sire. It will soon be after the hour of none, and today is the last day; so you see plainly how I'm prepared to maintain my rights. If my sister were going to return, she wouldn't have to delay much longer. God be praised that she's not coming back here. It's obvious she can't do anything more and her efforts have been fruitless. I myself have been prepared every day until this final one to make good my claim. I've totally proved my case without a combat. So now it's my right to go away and hold my inheritance in peace; for as long as I live I wouldn't be answerable for it to my sister; and she'll spend a miserable and wretched life."

5909 The king, who knew full well that the damsel was very disloyally wronging her sister, says to her: "My friend, in a royal court, I swear, one must wait until the king's judges are sitting preparatory to giving their verdict. There's no question of cheating, for in my opinion your sister will still arrive in good time." Before the king had finished what he was saying, he saw the Knight with the Lion and the damsel beside him. The two of them were coming alone, having slipped away from the lion, which had stayed where they had spent the night.

5925 The king saw the damsel and did not fail to recognise her; and he was extremely pleased and gratified to see her, since he was on her side in the dispute in his concern for justice. In his joy, he said to her just as soon as he could: "Step forward now, my fair one, and may God save you!" On hearing this, the other gives a start and, turning round, sees her and the knight she had brought to obtain justice for her. Then she turned darker than earth. The maiden was greeted very warmly by everybody; and then she went before the seated king. Once before him, she said: "May God save the king and all his company! O King, if my rights and my case can now be established by a knight, then so they will be by this knight who has followed me here, and I thank him for it. There is much he should have done elsewhere, this generous, noble knight; but he was so sorry for me that he turned his back on all his other affairs for the sake of mine. Now my lady and very dear sister, whom I love as much as my own heart, would act with courtesy and good sense if she would allow me enough of what is due to me for there to be peace between me and her, for I ask for nothing which is hers."—"Nor I," she says, "anything of yours, because you have nothing and will never have anything. However much you may preach, your preaching will make you no better off. You may wither away with grief!"

5965 At once the other replies in her very tactful way, sensible and courtly as she was. "Indeed," says she, "I'm most sad that, very small as our quarrel is, two such worthy men as these are to fight on our behalf. But I can't waive my claim, because I'd be in too great need of it. So I should be grateful to you if you would give me my rightful dues."—"Indeed," says the first, "anyone who gave in to you would be an idiot. May the infernal fire and flame consume me if I give you anything to make your life easier! The banks of the Seine would sooner come together and prime become none than I'd exempt you from the combat."—"May God and the right in which I stand, where my trust is placed and has always been until this day, give aid to the man who, in charity and the goodness of his heart, has offered himself in my service, though he doesn't know who I am, and neither of us knows the other's identity!"

5991 After this exchange of words no more is said; and they proceed to bring the knights into the middle of the courtyard. All the people hurry along, just as folk usually come running on such an occasion, wishing to see duelling and blows struck in combat. But the men intending to fight and who used to be the greatest of friends did not recognise each other at all. *So do they not love one another now? My reply to you is "yes and no", and I shall find arguments to prove the one and the other. Certainly my lord Gawain loves Yvain and declares him to be his companion, and Yvain reciprocates, wherever he is. Even here, if he recognised him, he would make much of him; and each would give his head for the other sooner than do him harm. Is this not true and total love? Yes indeed. – Their hatred, then: is not that also quite evident? Yes, because it is a certain fact that each would doubtless be glad to have broken the other's head or to have inflicted on him such disgrace that he would be the worse for it. Upon my word, to have found love and mortal hatred in the one receptacle is an absolute miracle!

6024 God! How can two so contrary things dwell together in one single lodging? It seems to me they cannot be together in one house; for one could not stay with the other in one place without there being discord and quarrelling once each knew the other's presence. But in one dwelling there are a number of apartments: a gallery and separate rooms. The situation might well be like this: perhaps Love had shut himself away in some hidden room, and Hate had gone to the gallery overlooking the street, wanting to be in full view. Now Hate is quite ready for action, for he spurs, pricks and gallops against Love as hard as he can; and Love makes no move at all. Ah, Love, where have you hidden? *Come out, and you will see what an ally your friends' enemies have brought and set against you! – The enemies are those very same men who love each other with a most sacred love; for love which is neither false nor a sham is a most precious and holy thing.

6053 Here Love is totally blind, and Hate sees nothing either; for Love, had he recognised them, should have forbidden them to lay hands on each other or do anything that might distress him. Love, then, is blind, thrown into confusion and duped because he sees, yet does not recognise, those who rightly belong entirely to him. And Hate, though he cannot say why one of them should detest the other, nevertheless intends to engage them in a wrongful combat, with each having a mortal hatred of the other. A man, you may be sure, is not loved by someone who would wish to have him put to shame and desires his death. What? Does Yvain, then, want to slay his friend my lord Gawain? Yes, and the wish is mutual. So would my lord Gawain wish to slay Yvain with his own hands or do even worse than I say? No, I swear and promise you. The one would not want to have shamed or harmed the other for all that God has made for man or for the sake of Rome's entire empire. Now I have told a grave lie; for it is very plain to see that each of them, with his lance at the ready in its rest, is intending to attack the other, wishing to do him harm and injury without holding back at all.

6088 Now tell me: when one has defeated the other, whom will the one who gets the worst of the blows have to blame? For, if they do come to attacking each other, I am very much afraid they will keep up the combat and fight until it ends in the victory of one of them. Will Yvain, if he gets the worst of it, be able to claim with justice that that man has caused him injury and shame who counts him among his friends and has never named him otherwise than as friend and companion? Or, if it should happen by chance that it is Yvain who does Gawain some injury or gets the better of him in any way, will the latter, then, have the right to complain? No, for he will not know whom to blame.

6106 As they do not recognise each other, they both take their distance; then, as they clash, their lances, which were massive and made of ash, shatter. Neither calls out anything to the other: had they exchanged words, their meeting would have been of a different kind! Then at their encounter there would have been no exchange of blows with lance or sword; and rather than seeking to injure, they would have gone to kiss and embrace one another. As it is, they do each other mutual hurt and injury. Their swords are not improved by this, nor are their helmets or shields, which are dented and split, whilst the edges of their swords are notched and blunted;

for they exchange great strokes with the edges, not the flat, of the blades, and with the pommels strike such blows on nose-pieces, necks, foreheads and cheeks that they are quite black and blue where the blood clots under the skin. Their hauberks are so rent and their shields so shattered that neither of them is unscathed. They expend such effort and energy that they are almost breathless. So heated is their encounter that every jacinth and emerald set in their helmets is ground and smashed to pieces; for they strike with their pommels so hard on each other's helmets that they are quite dazed and almost knock out one another's brains. Their eyes blaze in their heads. Their fists are large and powerful, their sinews strong and their bones hard; and they exchange vicious blows to the face with the swords they grasp and which serve them very well as they strike violently on.

6149 Having expended their energies for a long time until their helmets are battered in, the meshes completely ripped from their hauberks by the hammering of the swords, and their shields split and broken, they draw back a little way, giving the blood in their veins a rest and regaining their breath. However, they do not wait long, but dash at each other once again and more fiercely than ever. Everyone declares they have never seen two more spirited knights. "They're not fighting for fun but in deadly earnest! Their merits will never receive the reward they deserve." The two friends intent on their mutual injury hear these words and hear too the people speaking of reconciling the two sisters; but they are unable to persuade the elder one to make peace. The younger one, though, had agreed to accept what the king would say and would in no way oppose him. But the elder was so malicious that even Queen Guenevere, the knights, the king, the ladies and the townsfolk side with the younger; and everybody comes to beg the king to give her a third or a quarter of the land despite her elder sister and to separate the two knights who are of such outstanding valour, for it would be a very great shame if one of them should maim the other and deprive him of any of his honour. The king replies that he would never take the responsibility for making peace since the elder sister is such a malevolent creature that she spurns it.

6193 All this talk was heard by the two men, who continue to strike wounding blows at each other so that it seems to everyone a miracle that the combat is so even, for there is no way of telling who has the better and who the worse of it. And even the two combatants, who are purchasing honour with agony, are amazed and astounded; for their attacks are so equally matched that each of them wonders in astonishment who this is who is resisting him so fiercely. So long do they fight that the day draws on towards night. The arms of both are weary, their bodies in pain, with the hot, boiling blood gushing from them in many places and flowing down beneath their hauberks: it is no wonder if they want to rest, so great is their suffering. Then they do both take a rest, each thinking to himself that now, though he has had a long time to wait, he has met his match. Thus they rest for a long time, not daring to resume their combat. They are no longer anxious to fight, partly because of the darkness of the falling night and partly because they are very afraid of each other. These two considerations keep them apart and encourage them to remain at peace. But before they leave the field, they will have discovered each other's identity, and there will be joy and sympathy on both sides.

6229 My very valiant and courtly lord Yvain was the first to speak. But his good friend did not recognise him from his speech, being hindered by his low tone and hoarse, weak and broken voice, for the circulation of his blood was disturbed by the blows he had received. "My lord," he says, "night is approaching. I don't think we would ever be blamed or criticised if night should separate us. But for my part I admit that I fear and admire you greatly; and never in my life did I undertake a combat which has caused me so much distress or have I expected to see a knight whose acquaintance I should so dearly like to make. You're very good at landing your blows and know well how to put them to good use. No knight I've ever known was able to deal out so many blows. I'd rather not have received as many as you've paid out to me today: your strokes have quite stunned me."—"I swear", says my lord Gawain, "that you're not so dazed or faint that I'm not equally or more so. And if I for my part made your acquaintance, you wouldn't perhaps mind. If I've paid you out anything of mine, you've returned the loan in full, capital and interest; for you were more ready to return it than I was to accept it. But, however things may turn out, since you would like me to tell you the name by which I'm known, it shall never be kept from you: my name's Gawain, the son of King Lot."

6268 As soon as my lord Yvain heard this, he was utterly dumbfounded and dismayed. In his rage and anger he flung to the ground his bloodstained sword and broken shield, then dismounted from his horse, saying: "Alas! What a tragedy! We've fought this combat in appalling ignorance, through not recognising one another, for had I known who you were, I would never have fought you but, I assure you, would have admitted defeat before a blow was struck."—"What?" says my lord Gawain. "Who are you, then?"—"I'm Yvain, who loves you more than any man in the whole wide world; for you've always shown me affection and honour in every court. But in this affair I wish to make amends and honour you by declaring myself utterly vanquished."—"You'd do that for me?" asks my amiable lord Gawain. "I should indeed be extremely presumptuous if I accepted this as reparation. This honour shall certainly never fall to me: on the contrary, it shall be yours, and I leave it for you!"—"Ah, good lord, never say that again, for that could not be! I'm so weak and exhausted that I can't stay on my feet any longer."—"It's no use at all persisting!" says his friend and companion. "But I'm overcome and all in; and I'm not saying that out of flattery, for there's no complete stranger in the world to whom I wouldn't say as much rather than take any more blows." As he said this he dismounted; and each put his arms round the other's neck, and they kiss one another, with each continuing to declare himself to have been defeated.

6314 The argument continues until the king and the nobles come running from all around. They see them making much of each other and are very anxious to know the reason and who they are, to be showing each other such joy. "My lords," says the king, "tell us who has so suddenly brought you to this reconciliation and friendship, when all day there has been such hatred and hostility between you!"—"Sire," says his nephew my lord Gawain, "we'll not keep from you the misfortune and disaster that gave rise to this combat. Since you've stayed here to hear and learn about it, it will be proper for you to be told the truth. I, Gawain your nephew, didn't recognise my companion, my lord Yvain here, until, thanks to him and the will of God, he asked my name. Each of us gave his name to the other; and then, having been fighting hard, we recognised each other. We've given one another a good battering: had we fought a little longer, it would have gone badly for me. For, by my head, he'd have killed me by his prowess and also because of the wrong done by her who had sent me to fight as her champion. But I'm happier

now to have been vanquished in combat than to have been killed by
my friend."

6350 Then my lord Yvain's blood ran cold, and he said to him:
"Dear good lord, you're very wrong in saying that, so help me God!
Let the king, my lord, be in no doubt that I was definitely vanquished and defeated in this combat!"—"No, I was."—"No, I,"
they each exclaim. They both have such noble and generous
natures that they each grant and offer the victor's crown to the
other, and neither is prepared to accept it. Instead, they each put it
forcibly to the king and all the people that he has been vanquished
and forced to submit. But the king, having listened to them for a
while, puts an end to the dispute; for he was very pleased with what
he had heard and also by seeing that they had embraced one
another, although each had injured the other and wounded him in
numerous places. "My lords," he says, "there is deep affection
between you two. You show it plainly by each claiming to have
been vanquished. But now leave things to me! Then I think I can
arrange matters so well that your honour will be satisfied and the
whole world will praise me for it." With that they both agree to do
just what he wishes and proposes.

6382 The king then says he will settle the dispute fairly and in good
faith. "Where", he says, "is the damsel who has expelled her sister
from her land and has forcibly and pitilessly disinherited
her?"—"Sire," says she, "I'm here."—"You're there? Come here,
then! I've been aware for a long time that you were disinheriting
her. Her right shall no longer be denied, for you've just admitted
the truth to me. So you are now required to hand over her share to
her in full."—"Sire," she says, "if my reply was naïve and foolish,
you shouldn't take me up on it. For God's sake, sire, don't be hard
on me! You are the king and should guard against wrong and
injustice."—"That," says the king, "is why I wish to restore to your
sister her rights; for I've never had any sympathy for what is wrong.
And you heard clearly how both your knight and hers put themselves at my discretion. What I shall say will not be pleasing to you,
but your wrong has been admitted. Each knight is so anxious to
honour the other that he claims to have lost the combat. There's no
need for me to dwell on that. But since the matter has been left in my
hands, either you will carry out all my instructions blamelessly, as I
wish, or I shall say that my nephew has been defeated in the

combat. Then things would go worse for you. But I shall be reluctant to say that."

6420 He would actually not have said it on any account; but he spoke in this way to see if he could alarm her so much that she would surrender the heritage to her sister out of fear, for he could tell quite clearly that she would never hand over any of it, whatever he said to her, unless force or fear were brought to bear. Because she is alarmed and fears him, she answers: "My good lord, now I must do as you wish, though it makes me very heavy-hearted. So I shall comply, however much it hurts; and my sister will have what she wants. I offer her you yourself as surety for her portion of my inheritance, so that she may be all the more sure of it."—"Invest her with it immediately!" says the king; "and let her become your liege-woman, holding it from you! Then love her as your vassal, and she you as her liege-lady and her true sister!" Thus the king conducts the affair until the maiden is in possession of her land, for which she thanks him.

6447 The king next says to his nephew, that valiant, gallant knight, that he should let himself be disarmed; and my lord Yvain, if he wishes, should have his armour removed too, since they can now well do without it. Then the noble knights disarm and separate on equal terms. And as they were disarming, they saw the lion running up in search of its master. As soon as it sees him it begins to show great joy. Then you might have seen people retreating, with even the boldest of them taking flight! "Stay, all of you!" calls my lord Yvain. "Why are you running away? No one's chasing you. Don't be afraid that that lion you see coming will do you any harm! Please believe me when I say that he is mine and I am his: we're companions together." Then all those who had heard tell of the adventures of the lion itself and its companion knew for a fact that it was none other than this man who slew the wicked giant.

6475 My lord Gawain says to him: "Sir companion, you've really put me to shame today, so help me God! I've given you poor reward for the service you did me in killing the giant for the sake of my nephews and my niece. I've been thinking about you for a long time and have been very anxious because it was said that we two knew each other and were dear friends. I have indeed thought about it a great deal; but I myself could not think, nor had I ever heard in any land where I had been, of any knight who, to the best of my knowledge, went under the name of the Knight with the Lion." As they talked in this way, they were disarmed. Then the lion was not slow to come to where its master was sitting. When it was by him, it showed all the joy a dumb beast could. It was necessary for both the knights to be taken to a sickroom in an infirmary, since they needed a doctor and plaster to heal their wounds. The king, who loved them dearly, had them taken on ahead of him. A surgeon more skilled at healing wounds than any other was summoned for them by King Arthur; and he devoted himself to their cure until he had healed their wounds just as well and as quickly as he could.

6510 When he had cured them both, my lord Yvain, whose heart was irrevocably set on love, saw clearly that he could not go on, but would in the end die of love unless his lady took pity on him, pining away for her as he was. So he decided to leave the court on his own and go on the warpath to her spring, where he would cause such lightning, wind and rain that she would of necessity be compelled to make peace with him, or he would never stop the commotion at the spring, with the wind and the rain.

6527 As soon as my lord Yvain felt he was healed and recovered, he departed without anyone knowing; but with him he had his lion, which wanted never in its whole life to leave his company. Then they journeyed until they saw the spring, where they caused a downpour of rain. Do not think I am lying to you, but the turmoil was so fierce that no one could describe the tenth of it, for it seemed that the whole forest would crash into the abyss. The lady fears her entire town will collapse: the walls totter and the keep shakes almost to the point of falling down. The boldest man would rather be a captive in Persia in the hands of the Turks than within those walls. The people are so terrified that they execrate all their ancestors, saying: "A curse on the first man to build a house in this land and on those who founded this town! For they could not in all the world have found so detestable a place, when a single man can assault, torment and harry us."

6556 —"You must think what to do about this, my lady," says Lunete. "You'll not find anyone who will come to your help in this crisis unless he's to be discovered a very long way away. We'll certainly never feel easy in this town and won't dare go beyond the walls or the gate. If all your knights were to be assembled for this emergency, you well know that the very best of them wouldn't dare come forward; and the position is that you now have no one to defend your spring, so you'll look foolish and contemptible. It will be a real honour for you to have the person who has made such an assault on you getting away without a fight! You're indeed in trouble unless you take for yourself some other steps!"—"You're so knowledgeable," says the lady; "so tell me what measures to take, and I'll follow your advice."—"My lady, I'd certainly be happy to suggest something to you if I knew what. But you badly need a wiser person to advise you. So I daren't take a hand in it; but along with the rest I'll put up with the rain and the wind until, if it please God, I see some worthy man at your court who will take the responsibility and burden of this combat. But I don't think that will be today, and so much the worse for you!" The lady immediately replies: "Talk of something else, damsel! Forget about the people in my house, because I have no expectation whatever that any of them will ever defend the spring and the slab. But now, please God, we shall hear what your advice and ideas are; for they always say that it's in times of need that you should put your friend to the proof."

6602 —"My lady, if anyone thinks he could find the man who killed the giant and defeated the three knights, he'd do well to have him fetched. To my knowledge, though, so long as he's the object of his lady's enmity, wrath and ill-will, there's no man or woman under heaven he'd follow before being pledged and promised that person's fullest possible help to allay the hostility his lady feels towards him, which is so great that he's dying of the grief and distress it causes him." The lady says: "Before you go in search of him, I'm ready to give you my word and I'll make a vow that, if he comes to me, I'll bring about if I can, and without any pretence or deceit, the reconciliation he desires." Then Lunete replies: "My lady, have no fear that you can't, if you want to, very readily secure his reconciliation. But as for the vow, I'll still accept it, if you don't mind, before I set out."—"No, I don't mind," says the lady.

6630 Lunete, who was well versed in courtly manners, had a very precious reliquary brought out for her at once; and the lady knelt. Very civilly, Lunete trapped her into making the equivocal pledge. She administered the oath and, in doing so, omitted nothing that would be to her advantage. "Lady," she says, "raise your hand! I don't want you, in a couple of days' time, to accuse me of anything in all this, for you're doing nothing in my interest, but in yours alone. So you will please swear that in good faith you will use your best endeavours in the interest of the Knight with the Lion until he is sure of enjoying his lady's love as fully as ever in the past." Then the lady raised her right hand and said: "I declare that, exactly according to the terms you've stated, so help me God and this saint, my heart will never shrink from using my best efforts in the matter! If I have the strength and power to do it, I shall restore to him the love and favour which he used to enjoy with his lady."

6659 Now Lunete has done well; for she had desired nothing so much as what she had just achieved. Already an easy-paced palfrey had been brought out for her. Showing in her face her contentment and happiness, Lunete mounted and left, proceeding until, beneath the pine-tree, she found the man she did not expect to discover so close by: on the contrary, she imagined she would have a long search before reaching him. As soon as she saw him, she recognised him by the lion; and then, riding swiftly up to him, she dismounted on to the firm ground. My lord Yvain noticed her at a distance and recognised her at once. She returned his greeting with the words: "My lord, I'm delighted to have found you so near at hand!" To this my lord Yvain replies: "What? Were you looking for me, then?"—"Yes, my lord! And I've never been so happy since the day I was born, because I've put my lady into the position where, unless she wants to perjure herself, she'll be your wife just as she used to be, and you her husband. I dare tell you this as a fact."

6689 My lord Yvain is overjoyed at the news he is given, for he thought he would never hear it. He could not make too much of the one who had brought this about for him. He kisses her eyes and then her face and says: "Truly, my sweet friend, I shall never be able to reward you adequately for this! I fear my powers and time won't be sufficient to do you due honour and service."—"My lord," she says, "don't worry or feel any concern on that account, for you'll have plenty of ability and time to do good turns to me and to others. If I've done my duty, I deserve no more gratitude than someone who borrows another's wealth and then repays it. I still don't think I've returned to you what I owe you."—"Oh, but you have, as God is my witness, more than five hundred thousand times! Now we'll go wherever you wish. But have you told her who I am?"—"Upon my word no! And she doesn't know you by any name other than the Knight with the Lion."

6717 As they were conversing in this way, they set off promptly and continued, constantly followed by the lion, until they all three came to the stronghold. They said nothing at all to any man or woman in the town until they arrived before the lady. And the lady was full of joy as soon as she heard the news that the maiden was coming and that she was bringing the lion and the knight, whom she was very anxious to see, meet and get to know. My lord Yvain, still fully armed, fell at her feet; and Lunete, who was at his side, said to her: "My lady, raise him to his feet again and apply your efforts and strength and skill to obtaining the reconciliation and pardon that no one except yourself in the whole world can procure for him!" Then the lady has him rise and says: "I'll do all I can for him. I would very much like to be able to meet his wishes and desires."—"Indeed, my lady," says Lunete, "I should not say this if it weren't true: it's entirely in your power to do this, and far more so than I've told you. But now I shall tell you the truth of the matter, and you'll understand: you never had and never will have a friend as close as this one. God, whose will it is that between you and him there should be true and enduring peace and love, caused me to find him today so close at hand. There's nothing I need say to prove the fact other than this: my lady, forgive him for incurring your wrath, for he has no lady except you – this is your husband, my lord Yvain!"

6759 The lady starts at these words and says: "God save me, you've got me well and truly in a trap!* You'll have me love in spite of myself that man who neither loves nor respects me. Now you've done a fine thing and have just performed a most pleasing service for me! I'd rather suffer gales and storms all my life! And were it not such a vile and base thing to break one's word, he would never, try as he might, make his peace or be reconciled with me! There would always have smouldered within me, just as fire smoulders in ashes, that experience I don't want to go back over or care to bring up again now that I have to be reconciled with him."

6777 My lord Yvain hears and understands that his cause is going well and that he will be peacefully reconciled with her. He says: "Lady, one should show compassion to a sinner. I've paid for my folly, and it was only right that I should pay for it. It was foolishness that made me stay away, and I acknowledge my guilt and my crime. I've acted with very great boldness in daring to come into your presence; but if you are willing to keep me now, I shall never again wrong you in any way."—"Indeed," she says, "I am very willing, since I should perjure myself if I didn't do all I could to make peace between you and me. If that's your wish, I grant it to you."—"My lady," he says, "five hundred thanks! For, as I call on the Holy Spirit for aid, God could give me no other happiness in this mortal life!"

6799 Now my lord Yvain has found his peace; and you may well believe that he was never so happy for anything, great though his distress had been. All has ended very well for him, for he is loved and cherished by his lady, and she by him. He remembers none of his troubles, as they are driven from his mind by the joy he finds in his dearly beloved mistress. And Lunete too is very content: her pleasure is complete now that she has made a lasting peace between my excellent lord Yvain and his beloved and matchless mistress.

6814 Thus CHRÉTIEN concludes his romance of the Knight with the Lion; for I never heard any more of it told, nor will you ever hear more of it related, unless someone chooses to make some lying addition.   6818

PERCEVAL:

THE STORY OF THE GRAIL

Sow little and you reap little. And whoever wishes to have something to harvest should scatter his seed in a place where God will increase it for him a hundredfold; for in worthless ground good seed dries up and fails. CHRÉTIEN sows the seed of a romance he is beginning; and he sows it in so favourable a place that great benefit must accrue, since he does it for the most worthy man in Rome's empire. This is Count Philip of Flanders, whose merit exceeds that of Alexander, who is reputed to have been so good a man. I shall prove, though, that the count's worth is far greater than was his, for he embodied all those vices and faults of which the count is guiltless and free.

21 The count is not a man to listen to ignoble prattle or foolish talk and is unhappy to hear ill spoken of anyone, whoever it may be. The count loves true justice, loyalty and holy Church and hates all baseness; and he is more bountiful than any man known, since he gives without hypocrisy or deceit, as taught by the Gospels, which state: "Let not your left hand know of the good deeds done by your right hand." Let that be known by the one who benefits and by God, who sees all secrets and knows every inmost corner of hearts and beings.

37 Why do the Gospels say: "Hide your good deeds from your left hand"? The left hand, according to scripture, stands for vainglory, which stems from false hypocrisy. And what does the right signify?—Charity, which does not boast of its good works, but rather keeps quiet about them, so that they are known to none other than Him whose name is God and Charity: God is charity, and whoever dwells in charity, as it is written and I have read in Saint Paul's words,* dwells in God and God in him. Know then truly that the gifts bestowed by good Count Philip are given in charity, for he never consults anyone about them, but only his fine, generous heart, which prompts him to do good. Is his merit not greater than was that of Alexander, who was not concerned with charity or good works? Yes: have no doubts on that! Therefore CHRÉTIEN will not be wasting his efforts as he labours and strives, on the count's orders, to tell in rhyme the finest story ever related in a royal

court. That is the Story of the Grail, found in the book the count gave him.* Hear how he acquits himself.

69 It was at that season when trees burst into leaf and grass, woodland and meadows grow green, when in the morning the birds sing sweetly in their own tongue and every living thing is fired with joy, that the son of the widowed lady from the wild, desolate forest got up and found it no effort to saddle his hunter and take up three javelins. Thus equipped he left his mother's house, thinking he would go to see the workers she had sowing and harrowing her fields of oats with their twelve oxen and six harrows. So into the forest he goes. The heart within his breast at once thrilled with joy at the fair weather and the glad birdsong he heard, all of which gave him pleasure. Because of the sweet serenity of the weather he unbridled his hunter and let it graze freely on the fresh, verdant grass. Then, expert as he was at throwing the javelins he carried, he went casting them around him, now back, now forward, at one moment low, at the next high, until he heard five armed knights coming through the forest; and as they approached, the arms with which they were fully accoutred made a very loud din, for the branches of the oaks and hornbeams often knocked against them. The lances clashed against the shields to the clanking of all the hauberks: the woods reverberate, the iron in shields and hauberks resounds.

111 The lad hears but does not see the men, who are riding at a walking pace in his direction. In his astonishment he exclaimed: "By my soul, my lady mother spoke the truth when she told me that devils are the most hideous things in the world; and she taught me the lesson that you should cross yourself as a protection against them. But I'll ignore this advice, and indeed I'll not cross myself, but instead I'll catch the very strongest of them such a blow with one of these javelins I'm carrying that I'm sure none of the others will ever come near me." That is what the youth said to himself before he saw them. Then, when he had a clear view of them once they had emerged from the woods, and when he saw the glittering hauberks and the bright, gleaming helmets and the lances and shields, which he had never seen before, and saw the white and the scarlet shining in the sunlight and all that gold, sky-blue and silver, he was charmed and delighted and exclaimed: "Ah, God have mercy on me! These are angels I see here. Now I've really committed a great

sin and have just done very wrong to say they were devils. My mother wasn't telling stories when she told me angels were the most beautiful creatures there are, apart from God who is the most beautiful of all. I think I can see the Lord God here, because I can pick out one of them who is so fair that the others, so help me God, don't have a tenth of his beauty. Mother herself told me that we should worship God above all and do Him reverence and honour Him: so I'll worship this one and then all the angels after him." Throwing himself at once to the ground, he recited the whole of his creed and those prayers he knew which his mother had taught him.

159 Then the leader of the knights saw him and said: "Stand back! A youth who has seen us has fallen to the ground from fright. If we all go up to him together, I fancy he'd be so terrified he would die and not be able to answer any of the questions I put to him." The others stop, and he rides at full speed up to the lad, greets him, and reassures him with the words: "Don't be afraid, young man!"—"I'm not," says the lad, "by the Saviour in whom I believe! You're God, aren't you?"—"Not at all, by my faith!"—"Who are you then?"—"I'm a knight."—"I've never known a knight," says the lad, "and never seen one, nor ever heard tell of them. But you're more beautiful than God. Now if only I were just like you, formed the same and all shining!" He at once went up close to him; and the knight asked him: "Have you seen five knights and three maidens on this heath today?"

186 The lad is determined to press his enquiries for other information. He reaches his hand out to his lance, takes hold of it and says: "Dear good lord, you who are called a knight, what's this you're holding then?"—"Now I'm very well informed, it seems!" says the knight. "I supposed, my dear good friend, that I should get some news from you, and it's you who want to hear some from me! I'll tell you, though: this is my lance."*—"Do you mean", says he, "that you launch it as I throw my javelins?"—"Certainly not, lad: how stupid you are! You strike with it directly."—"One of these three javelins you see here is more useful, then; for with them I kill whatever I want: birds or beasts as the need arises. What's more, I kill them from as far away as you can shoot a bolt from a crossbow."—"That's of no interest to me, lad. But answer my question about the knights! Tell me if you know where they are. And have you seen the maidens?" The youth takes hold of the

bottom of the shield and says straight out: "What's this, and what do you do with it?"—"Lad," he replies, "this is a trick to divert me from what I'm trying to find out from you. I thought, so help me God, that you would give me information rather than get some from me, and yet you want me to supply it. At all events, I'll tell you, for I'm happy enough to humour you. What I'm carrying is called a shield."—"It's called a shield?"—"Yes indeed," says he; "and I shouldn't despise it, for it's so loyal to me that if someone hurls or throws anything at me, it gets in the way of all the blows. That's the service it renders me."

231 Then the men who had stayed back came hurrying along the road up to their lord and promptly asked him: "My lord, what did this Welshman say?"—"So help me God," says their chief, "he's a real ignoramus; for he never gives me a straight answer to anything I ask him, but instead he himself asks about everything he sees: what it's called and what it's for."—"You may be perfectly certain, my lord, that the Welsh are by nature more stupid than grazing beasts; and this one is just like a beast. It's foolish for anyone to hang about with him unless he wants to trifle and stupidly fritter away his time."—"I don't know about that," he says, "but, as God is my witness, before I take the road I'll tell him everything he wants to know and shall not leave otherwise." Then he asks him once again. "Young man," he says, "tell me, if you don't mind, about these five knights and the maidens too – whether you've met or seen them today." The youth then caught him by the hauberk and tugged at it. "Tell me now, dear sir," he says, "what's this you're wearing?"—"Don't you know then, lad?" he says.—"No, I don't."—"It's my hauberk, lad; and it's as heavy as iron because, as you can see, it's made of iron."—"I know nothing of that," says he. "But, as God's my saviour, it's very handsome. What do you do with it, and what use is it to you?"—"That's simple to explain, young man. If you tried to throw a javelin or shoot an arrow at me, you couldn't do me any harm."—"Then, sir knight, may God keep hinds and stags from having such hauberks, or else I'd never be able to kill one and would never go chasing after them!"

277 The knight then says to him once more: "God bless you lad, can you give me any news of the knights and maidens?" But he, in his rather naïve way, said to him: "Were you born like that?"—"No lad: that's impossible, for no one can be born that way."—"Who

rigged you up like this, then?"—"I'll tell you who, lad."—"Tell me, then."—"Very gladly: it's still less than five full years since I was given all this equipment by King Arthur, who dubbed me knight. But now you tell me: what became of the knights who passed this way, escorting the three maidens? Are they keeping an easy pace or making off at speed?" He replied: "Just look, sir, at the highest wood you can see lying all round that mountain. That's where the passes of Valbone are."—"And what of that, dear brother?" says he.—"My mother's harrowers are there, sowing and working her lands; and if those people went that way and they saw them, they'll tell you." They say that, if he will guide them, they will go with him as far as the men harrowing the oats.

307 The youth takes his hunter and goes to where the harrowers are harrowing the ploughed lands where the oats are sown. And when they saw their master they quite trembled with fear. Do you know why? On account of the armed knights they saw coming with him; for they are convinced that if they have spoken to him of their way of life and activities, he would want to be a knight; and his mother would go out of her wits, because they had been trying to prevent him from ever seeing a knight or learning about what they did. Then the youth said to the men who drove the oxen: "Have you seen five knights and three maidens pass this way?"—"They kept on going today through those passes," say the ox-drivers.

328 The youth then told the knight who had spent so long talking to him: "Sir, the knights and the maidens did go this way. But now give me more information about the king who makes knights and where he's usually to be found."—"Lad," he says, "I'll tell you. The king is in residence in Carlisle. He was staying there not five days ago, for I was there and saw him. And if you don't find him there, there will certainly be someone to tell you where he is: he won't have gone so far away that you'll not get information about him there. *But now please tell me what name I shall call you by."—"Sir," says he, "I'll tell you: my name's 'dear son'."—"So you're 'dear son'? I'm sure you have another name too."—"Indeed, sir, I'm called 'dear brother'."—"I can well believe you. But if you're prepared to tell me the truth, I should like to know your real name."—"Sir," he says, "I can tell you that by my proper name I'm called 'dear master'."—"So help me God, that's a fine name. Have you any more?"—"Not I, sir; and I've certainly never had any

more."—"God help me, I'm hearing the most amazing things I've ever heard or think I ever shall!" With that the knight makes off at full gallop, impatient to catch up with the others.

364 The youth then lost no time in going back home, where his mother was sad and heavy-hearted because he had been away so long. The instant she sees him, she is overjoyed and cannot conceal her delight but, showing her deep motherly love, runs towards him, calling: "Dear son, dear son!" more than a hundred times. "Dear son, I've been feeling very miserable because you were away such a long while. I've been so upset I nearly died of grief. Where have you been all this time today!"—"Where, my lady? I'll tell you without a word of a lie, because I've seen something that's made me extremely happy. Mother, haven't you always said that the angels and our Lord God are so beautiful that Nature never created anything so lovely and that there's nothing as beautiful in the world?"—"And so I still say, dear son. I say it for certain, and repeat it."—"Say no more, Mother! Haven't I just seen going through the wild forest the most beautiful things there are? To my mind they're more beautiful than God or all His angels." His mother takes him in her arms, saying: "Dear son, I put you in God's care, because I'm very afraid for you. I do believe you've seen those angels folk complain of that kill everything they come across."—"Not at all, Mother, truly I haven't! They say they're called knights."

403 At that, hearing him call them knights, his mother faints; and then, once she had come to, she said like a woman distraught: "Alas, what a plight I'm in! My dear, sweet son, I thought I could shield you so well from knighthood that you'd never hear of it and would never see a knight. You yourself, dear son, were to have been a knight, had it pleased the Lord God to spare for you your father and other kinsmen. There was no knight in all the Isles of the Sea* who was of such great merit or so feared and dreaded, dear son, as was your father. And you can pride yourself, dear son, that you are no disgrace at all to his lineage or to my own; for I myself am of knightly stock, among the finest in this land. In my day there was no family better than mine in the Isles of the Sea. But the best of them are fallen, as is commonly seen, with misfortunes overtaking worthy men who conduct themselves with great honour and valour.

432 "Wickedness, shame and sloth don't decline, for they cannot; but good men have to fall. Your father, though you don't know this, was wounded through the thigh and physically maimed.* His great land and rich treasure, which he possessed as a man of worth, all went to rack and ruin, and he lapsed into great poverty. After the death of Utherpendragon, who was king and father of good King Arthur, noble men were impoverished, disinherited and wrongfully brought to destitution. The lands were devastated and the poor people degraded, so that anyone who could flee did so. Your father owned this manor-house here in this wild forest. He was unable to flee, but had himself brought here in great haste on a litter, not knowing where else he could take refuge. You, who were small, had two very handsome brothers: you were just a tot, a mere infant scarcely more than two years old.

459 "When your two brothers were grown up, with your father's encouragement and advice they went to two royal courts to obtain their arms and horses. The elder went to the King of Escavalon and was in his service until he was dubbed knight; and the other, his junior, was with King Ban of Gomeret. On one and the same day both young men were dubbed and knighted, and also on the same day they set out to return home, wanting to delight both me and their father, who never saw them again, because they met their death in armed combat. They were both slain in combat, which has brought me great grief and distress. A strange thing happened to the elder, for the ravens and crows pecked out both his eyes, which was how people found him, dead. His father died out of grief for his son; and since his death I have lived a life of great bitterness. You were all the comfort and the only blessing I had, for nobody else of my family remained: God had left me with no other source of joy and happiness."

489 The young man pays little attention to what his mother has told him. "Give me something to eat," says he. "I don't know what you're talking to me about. I'd very much like to go to the king who makes knights; and so I shall, whoever may be sorry about it!" His mother keeps him back and delays him as long as she is able. Then she prepares and provides for him a coarse canvas shirt and breeches made in the style of the Welsh, who, it seems, have the leggings joined to the breeches. He also had a tunic with a closed hood of stag-hide. That was how his mother equipped him. She

held him back for three days and no longer, since further persuasion was useless. Then her grief was extraordinary as, kissing and embracing him, she said through her tears: "Now, dear son, I'm filled with very deep sorrow to see you leave. You'll go to the king's court and tell him to give you arms. There will be no refusal, for I'm sure he will give them to you. But when the time comes for you to attempt to bear arms, what will happen then? How will you know how to perform what you have never done yourself or seen anyone else do? Poorly for sure, I fear. You'll be bad at everything; because it's no wonder, it seems to me, if someone doesn't know what he hasn't learnt. It is surprising, though, if one doesn't pick up something that one often hears and sees.

527   "Dear son, I want to give you some sound advice, which you'll do well to listen to; and if you're prepared to remember it, it may be of great benefit to you. My son, if it please God, and as I believe, you will shortly be a knight. Should you find, near or far, any lady in need of help or maiden in distress, be prepared to help them if they ask you to, for that is a matter of the highest honour. When a man doesn't behave honourably towards ladies, his own honour must be dead. Serve ladies and maidens, and you'll be honoured everywhere. But if you pay court to any one of them, be careful not to annoy her by doing anything that might displease her. To kiss a maiden is to have much from her; and should she grant you that kiss, I forbid you to take the rest, if you're prepared to forgo it for my sake. But if she has a ring on her finger or a purse on her girdle and, out of love or at your request, she should give you that, then I'll be happy and content for you to take her ring: you have my leave to take the ring and the purse too. Dear son, there's something else I want to tell you: don't have a companion on the road or in a lodging-place for long without asking his name. You should know that in effect one knows the man by the name he has. Dear son, speak with worthy men and keep their company: a worthy man never gives bad advice to those who keep company with him.

567   "Above all else I would implore you to go to churches and minsters to pray our Lord to grant you honour in this world and let your conduct be such that you may come to a good end."—"Mother," he says, "what is a church?"—"My son, it's where divine service is held for God, who created heaven and earth and placed men and women there."—"And what is a

minster?"—"The same, son: a beautiful, very holy house where there are holy relics and treasures; and there we sacrifice the body of Jesus Christ, the holy Prophet, to whom the Jews did many shameful things. He was betrayed and wrongfully condemned, and suffered the anguish of death for the sake of men and women; for souls went to Hell when they left their bodies, and He cast them out again. And He was bound to the stake and beaten, then crucified and wore a crown of thorns. I advise you to go to church to hear masses and matins and to pray to that Lord."—"Then I'll very gladly go to churches and minsters from now on," says the young man; "and that's a promise!"

599 Thereupon, without waiting any longer, he takes his leave; and his mother is in tears. His horse was already saddled. He was equipped in the Welsh manner and fashion: he wore a pair of shoes made of untanned hide on his feet; and wherever he went he was in the habit of carrying three javelins. He wanted to take his javelins with him, but his mother had two of them taken away, because he would have looked too much like a Welshman; and she would gladly have done the same with all three, had it been possible. In his right hand he carried a riding-switch to use on his horse. His mother, who loves him dearly, weeps as she kisses him on his departure and prays God to be his guide. "Dear son," she says, "may God lead you! Wherever you go may He grant you more joy than there remains for me!" When the young man has gone as far as you can throw a small stone, he looks round and sees, back at the end of the bridge, his mother fallen and lying in a faint just as though she had dropped dead. Then he lashes his hunter on the rump with his switch; and it sets off, by no means stumbling but bearing him at a great pace through the great, dark forest. From that morning he rode on until the day drew to its close. He spent the night resting in the forest until the bright day dawned.

635 In the morning the youth rises with the birdsong, mounts, and pursues his journey until he sees a tent pitched in a beautiful meadow beside the stream running from a small spring. It was a wonderfully handsome tent: one side was scarlet and the other embroidered with golden thread, and on top was a gilded eagle. This eagle was caught by the bright, radiant sun, and all the meadows in turn gleamed in the light reflected from the tent. All around that tent, which was the fairest in the world, had been

erected leafy bowers, arbours and shelters made in the Welsh fashion. The youth made for the tent; and before he got there, he said: "Now, God, I can see your house, and I'd do wrong not to go and worship you. My mother spoke the absolute truth when she said that a church is the most beautiful thing there is and told me never to come across one without going in to worship the Creator in whom I believe. By my faith, I'll go to pray to Him to ask Him to give me something to eat today, for I could well do with that!"

667 He then reaches the tent to find it open; and, in the middle of it, he sees a bed draped with a fine silk counterpane. On the bed, all alone, lay a young girl fast asleep. Her companions were in the woods, her maidens having gone to pick fresh flowers, which they wanted to strew about in the tent, as they usually did. When the youth entered the tent, his horse gave such a loud neigh that the damsel heard it and woke with a start. And the lad, in his naïvety, said: "Maiden, I greet you as my mother taught me to. My mother's instructions to me were that I should greet maidens wherever I might come across them." The girl trembles with fear on account of the youth, who to her seems crazy; and she considers herself an utter fool to have let him find her alone. "Be on your way, lad!" she says. "Be off, before my lover sees you!"—"By my head, I'll kiss you first, whoever it may upset," says the youth, "because my mother told me to!"—"I'll certainly never kiss you if I can help it," says the maiden. "Be off lest my lover find you; for if he does, that's the end of you!"

700 The young man had strong arms; and he gave her a very gauche embrace, not knowing how else to do it. He stretched her out full length beneath him; and she put up a strong defence, doing her best to wriggle free. But her defence was to no avail, for, whether she liked it or not, the lad gave her seven kisses in a row (as the story tells) until he spotted on her finger a ring set with a brilliant emerald. "My mother also told me," says he, "that I should take the ring from your finger but do nothing else to you. Now let's have the ring! I want it."—"Indeed you'll never have my ring, you may be sure of that," says the maiden, "unless you tear it from my finger by force!" The youth seizes her by the fist, forces her finger straight and, having removed the ring from it, put it on his own finger with the words: "Bless you, maiden. Now I'll be off well rewarded – and it's much nicer kissing you than any chambermaid in all my

mother's house, for there's nothing bitter about your mouth!" She bursts into tears and says: "Don't take my little ring away, lad, because I'd get into trouble and you, I promise you, would lose your life for it, sooner or later."

734 The young man takes nothing he hears to heart; but not having had anything to eat for some time, he was in the last extremities of hunger. He discovers a small cask full of wine with a silver goblet beside it; and on a bundle of rushes he sees a new, white cloth. This he lifts, and under it finds three fine, fresh venison pies, a dish he does not find displeasing! Being quite tormented by hunger, he breaks open one of these pies in front of him and eats with gusto, then pours into the silver cup some of the far from inferior wine and takes frequent, long draughts of it. He said: "Maiden, I'll not get through these pies myself today. Come and eat, for they're excellent. There will be plenty for each of us, and that will still leave a whole one over." But she continues to weep despite his entreaties and invitation: the damsel replies not a word to him, but just weeps bitterly and vigorously wrings her hands. Then he ate as much as he wanted and drank until he had had his fill, after which he covered over again what was left and at once took his leave, commending to God the girl, to whom his farewells gave no pleasure. "God save you, my fair friend!" he says. "But for God's sake don't be upset about your ring and my taking it away; because before I die and pass away, I'll repay you for it. And now, by your leave, I'm going." Weeping, she says she will never commend him to God, because on his account she will have to suffer shame and distress greater than any wretched girl has suffered; and as long as he lives she will never be saved or helped by him; and he may know for sure that he has betrayed her.

781 So she remained weeping. Then before very long her lover returned from the woods. He saw the tracks of the young man who had resumed his journey, and this disturbed him. He then found his beloved weeping, and said to her: "My damsel, I believe from the signs I can see that there's been a knight here."—"No there hasn't, sir, I swear to you; but there has been a Welsh lad, a tiresome, uncouth and stupid one, who has drunk as much of your wine as he wanted and fancied, and who ate some of your three pies."—"And are all your tears because of that, my fair one? If he'd drunk and eaten the lot, that would have been fine by me."—"There's some-

thing more, sir," she said. "There's the question too of my ring, for he took it from me and has made off with it. I'd rather be dead than have had him take it away like that!"

804 Here now is her lover troubled and deeply worried. "By my faith," he says, "this is an outrage! But since he's taken it away, let him keep it! Yet I think there was more than that happened. If there was something more, don't hide it!"—"Sir," she said, "he kissed me."—"Kissed you?"—"Yes indeed: that's what I'm telling you. But he did it against my will."—"On the contrary, it suited you and pleased you! There was never any opposition," says he, tortured by jealousy. "Do you think I don't know you? Well I certainly do: I know you well! I'm not so one-eyed and I don't have such a squint that I can't see your falseness! You're going down a dangerous road, where there will be serious trouble in store for you. Your horse shall never have oats to eat and will never be bled until I've taken my revenge.* Whenever it loses a shoe, it will never be reshod. If it dies, you'll follow me on foot. And the clothes you wear will never be changed, but on foot and naked you shall follow me until I've taken his head off: that's the only penalty I'll ever exact from him." With that he sat down and ate.

834 The young man rode on until he saw a charcoal-burner approaching, driving a donkey in front of him. "My good man," he says, "you who are driving your donkey before you, tell me which is the most direct way to Carlisle. They say that King Arthur, whom I wish to see, makes knights there."—"Young man," he says, "in this direction there's a castle standing by the sea. My dear good friend, you'll find King Arthur both happy and miserable in that castle, if you go there."—"I'd like you to tell me, then, the reason for the king's happiness and sorrow."—"I'll tell you very readily," he says. "King Arthur and his entire army have been fighting against King Rion:* the King of the Isles was defeated, which made King Arthur happy; and he's sad on account of his companions, who dispersed to go and stay in the castles they found most attractive, and he doesn't know how they are faring – that's the reason for the king's grief."

859 The youth would not have given a penny for the charcoal-burner's information, except that he did take the road in the direction he had pointed out to him and eventually saw a fine, strong castle in a very good situation overlooking the sea. Then he

sees, riding out through its gate, an armed knight holding in his hand a golden cup. With his left hand he held his lance, his reins and his shield, and with his right the golden cup. He cut a fine figure in his arms, which were completely crimson. The youth saw how splendid these brand-new arms were and was delighted by them; and he said: "By my faith, I'll ask the king for those: if he gives them to me I'll be very happy; and a curse on whoever asks for any others!" With that he gallops towards the castle in his anxiety to reach the court, until he came close to the knight. The latter stopped him briefly to ask: "Where are you off to, young man? Tell me."—"I'm wanting", he says, "to get to the court to ask the king for those arms."—"That's a good thing to do, lad," says he. "Go there quickly now, and come back again. And you can tell this good-for-nothing king that, if he's not willing to hold his land from me, then he must give it up to me or else send someone to defend it against me, for I declare that it's mine. Here to convince you is the evidence; for just now I seized under his very eyes the cup I'm carrying here along with the wine he was drinking." – Now let him find somebody else to pass on his message, for the lad has not taken in a word of it.

900 Straight to the court he went, where the king and his knights were sitting at their meal. The hall was at ground level; and on his horse the youth enters this hall, which was paved and as long as it was broad. King Arthur was sitting deep in thought at the head of the table; and all the knights were laughing and joking together apart from him, as he brooded in silence. The youth came forward without knowing whom to greet as he did not recognise the king, until he was approached by Yvonet,* who held a knife in his hand. "Fellow!" says he. "You who are coming here with that knife in your hand, show me which is the king!" Yvonet, a very courtly man, said to him: "There he is, my friend." The lad at once went up to him and greeted him as best he knew. The king, in thought, said nothing. So he addresses him for a second time; but the king, thinking deeply, does not utter a word. "By my faith," the youth then said, "this king never made anyone a knight! How could he make a knight, when you can't get a word out of him?" At once he makes as if to go away again and turns his hunter's head; but in his awkward way he brought it so close to the king that, without a word of a lie, he sent his cloth hat flying from his head on to the table in front of him.

938 The king turns his bowed head towards the lad, comes quite out of his reverie and says: "Welcome, dear friend! I beg you not to take offence because I failed to return your greeting. I couldn't reply to you for grief and anger, because the worst enemy I have, who hates and alarms me more than any other, has here challenged me for my land; and he's so mad that he says he'll have it at his entire disposal, whether I like it or not. His name is the Red Knight from the Forest of Quinqueroi. And the queen had come to sit here before me to comfort the knights who have been wounded. That knight would scarcely have angered me by anything he said, but he seized my cup before my face and raised it up so recklessly that he spilled the whole cupful of wine over the queen. So dire and grievous was the shame of it that the queen, burning with wrath and anguish, went off into her room in a suicidal mood; and I don't think, so help me God, that she can come out of this alive." The youth does not care a chive for anything the king tells and recounts to him, nor for his grief or shame; and he is not concerned about his wife. "Make me a knight, sir king," he says, "because I want to be off!"

974 The eyes in the head of the uncultivated lad were bright and laughing. No one who see him thinks him prudent; but all who set eyes on him considered him handsome and engaging. "My friend," says the king, "dismount and give your hunter to a stable-lad, and he'll look after it and do as you require. Very soon you will be a knight, to my honour and your advantage." The young man replied: "The ones I met on the heath weren't dismounted, yet you want me to get down. By my head, I'll never dismount! But be quick about it, and then I'll leave!"—"Ah, my dear good friend," says the king, "I'll be glad to do it, to your profit and my honour."—"By the faith I owe the Creator, good lord king," says the lad, "I'll not be a knight in a hurry, unless I'm a red knight. Give me the arms of that one I met in front of the gate carrying off your golden cup!"

1001 The seneschal, who was one of the wounded, was angry at what he heard and said: "You're right, my friend. Go at once and seize those arms from him, for they're yours! It wasn't at all foolish of you to come here for that!" Hearing this, the king was enraged and said to Kay: "You're very wrong to mock this lad: that's a very grave fault in a gentleman. Although the youth is naïve, he may well be of good birth; for it's a matter of upbringing, and he has learnt under a bad master. He can still turn out a worthy vassal. It's churlish to make fun of others and to promise without giving. A worthy man shouldn't undertake to promise someone else anything at all that he cannot or does not wish to give, lest he incur the ill-will of that person who, without the promise, is his friend but who, having received his promise, is anxious for it to be made good. Therefore you may be sure that it's far better to refuse a man than to arouse his expectations. And to tell the truth, a man who makes a promise without keeping it mocks and deceives himself, and deprives himself of his friend's affection."

1033   The king spoke to Kay in these terms. Then the young man, as he was leaving, noticed a beautiful, attractive maiden and greeted her;* and she returned his greeting with a smile then, laughing, said this: "Young man, if you live long, I think and am convinced that in the whole world there will not be, nor has there been, nor will anyone hear of any knight better than you. That's what I think and feel and believe." That maiden had not laughed for more than six years, and she said this out loud so that everyone heard her. Then up jumps Kay, much annoyed by her words; and he gave her such a hard slap across her tender face that he knocked her full-length to the floor. Having struck the maiden, on turning round he found a fool standing beside a fireplace; and in his rage and anger he kicked him into the blazing fire, because the fool used to say: "This maiden will not laugh until she sees the man who will be supreme among knights." So the fool cries out and the maiden weeps; and the youth waits no longer but, without taking any advice, sets out after the Red Knight.

1067   Yvonet, who knew all the right paths and was very eager to bring news to the court, hurries away on his own, without any companion, through a garden at the side of the hall and down through a postern-gate until he comes straight to the road where the knight was waiting for some chivalric adventure to come his way. Then the youth came dashing towards him to take his arms, whilst the knight, as he waited, had set down the golden cup on a slab of dark grey stone. When the youth had come close enough to him for them to hear each other, he shouted to him: "Put them down, those arms of yours, and don't wear them any more: those are King Arthur's orders!" And the knight asks him: "Is anyone daring to come here, lad, to champion the king's right? If anybody is coming, don't keep it to yourself."—"What, sir knight? In the devil's name, are you making fun of me by not yet having taken off my armour? I tell you to get out of it at once!"—"Lad," he says, "I'm asking you if anyone is coming here on the king's behalf with the intention of fighting me."—"Sir knight, take off that armour quickly before I take it off for you, for I'll not let you keep it any longer! You can count on my hitting you if you force me to say any more about it!"

1102 At that the knight lost his temper. Raising his lance with both hands, he gave him such a blow across the shoulders with the butt end that he made him slump down over his horse's neck. Then the youth was annoyed to feel himself hurt by the blow he had received. Taking the best aim he can at his eye, he lets fly with his javelin. Without the knight's hearing or seeing or being aware of it, it strikes through his eye into his brain so that from the back of his neck there spurt forth the blood and brains. His heart fails with the pain; and he topples over to fall full length. Then the youth dismounts, lays the lance to one side and removes the shield from his neck; but he cannot deal with the helmet on his head, for he does not know how to take it off. And he wants to unbuckle his sword; but he does not know how to do that and cannot draw it from the scabbard: instead he takes hold of the sword and tugs and pulls at it.

1130 Then Yvonet, seeing the youth's embarrassment, begins to laugh. "What's all this, my friend?" says he. "What are you doing?"—"I don't know. I thought your king had given me these arms; but I'll have chopped the corpse up into steaks before I can get any of the armour off, for it sticks so tightly to the body that it seems to me the inside and outside are one, so closely do they stick together."—"Now don't worry about anything, for I'll easily get them apart, if you like," says Yvonet.—"Do it quickly, then," says the lad, "and give them to me at once!" Yvonet sets about it immediately and strips the knight down to his toes, not leaving on him his hauberk, mail leggings, the helmet on his head or any other piece of armour.

1152 However, the youth was unwilling to give up his own clothes or, whatever Yvonet might say, take a superbly made tunic of quilted silk cloth, which the knight wore under his hauberk when he was alive. Nor can Yvonet take off his feet the hide shoes he wore. He said instead: "Damn it! Are you joking? Would I change my good clothes that my mother made me the other day for those of that knight? My stout hempen shirt for his soft thin one? Would you want me to give up my waterproof tunic for this one that would never keep a drop out? May a man be throttled who will exchange at any time his own good clothes for other, bad ones!" Teaching a fool is a very painful business: despite every plea, he was determined to take nothing but the arms.

1176 Yvonet laces on the armour for him and fits the spurs to his shoes over the leggings; then he helps him into the hauberk, as fine as any there ever was, and over its cap he places the helmet, which fits him excellently. Next he teaches him how to gird on the sword so that it hangs quite slack; and then he sets his foot in the stirrup and has him mount the charger. He had never seen stirrups before and knew nothing of spurs, having only used whips and switches. Yvonet brings him the shield and lance and hands them to him. Before Yvonet went away, the youth said to him: "My friend, take my hunter away with you, for he's a very good one; and I give him to you because I have no further need of him. And take the king his cup with my greetings. Then tell the maiden Kay struck on the cheek that, if I can before I die, I intend to make things so hot for him that she'll consider herself avenged." He replies that he will return his cup to the king and deliver his message faithfully. With that they part and go their own ways.

1208 Yvonet goes through the door into the hall where the nobles are and brings the king his cup back, saying: "Rejoice now, sire, since your knight who was here sends you back your cup."—"What knight are you talking about?" asks the king, who was still very upset.—"In God's name, sire," says Yvonet, "I'm speaking of the one who left here a short time ago."—"Are you referring, then, to the young Welshman," says the king, "who asked me for the red-painted arms of that knight who has done me as many shameful deeds as he could?"—"Indeed, sire, I am speaking of him."—"And how did he get my cup? Does that man love and respect him so much that he gave it up to him of his own free will?"—"On the contrary, the young man exacted such a price for it that he killed him."—"And how did that happen, my dear friend?"—"I don't know, sire, except that I saw the knight hit him with his lance to his great annoyance, and the youth struck him back with a javelin right through the eye slit, making blood and brains spurt out at the back and knocking him full length to the ground."

1239 Then the king said to the seneschal: "Ah, Kay, what a bad deed you've done today! Through your malicious tongue with all its insults you've robbed me of that young man who has this day done me a great service."—"Sire," says Yvonet to the king, "by my head, he sent word by me to the queen's maiden, whom Kay attacked and struck out of spite and malice towards him, saying that he will avenge her, given the opportunity." The fool sitting by the fire hears what is said, then jumps to his feet and comes happily before the king, hopping and skipping for joy and saying: "Lord king, as God is my saviour, the time of our adventures is now approaching: you will often see hard and terrible ones befall us. And I assure you that Kay may be quite certain that his feet and hands and his foolish, scurrilous tongue have served him ill; for before a fortnight has passed the knight will have avenged the kick he gave me; and the buffet he gave the maiden will be well returned and paid for at a high price, because his right arm will break between the elbow and the armpit. He'll carry it in a sling for half a year, and let him carry it well there: he can't escape it any more than death."

1275 This pronouncement so riled Kay that he came close to bursting with rage and anger and handling the fool so severely in front of everybody as to kill him. Only because it would have displeased the king did he refrain from attacking him. Then the king said: "Oh, Kay! How angry you've made me today! If anyone had instructed and trained the young man in the use of arms so that he had some idea how to handle a shield and lance, he would certainly have made a good knight. But he doesn't know the slightest thing about arms or anything else, so that he couldn't even draw his sword if he needed to. Now he's sitting armed on his horse, and he'll meet some ruffian knight who won't hesitate to do him some injury to acquire his horse. He'll have killed or wounded him in no time, since he won't know how to defend himself. He's so naïve, like a dumb animal, that he'll not last long." So the king laments and deplores the loss of the youth and shows his despondency; but there is nothing he can do about it, so he falls silent.

1305 The youth goes riding on and on through the forest until he reaches a flat stretch of country by a river that was wider than a crossbow could shoot and all of whose water was channelled and restricted to its proper bed. He rides down through a meadow towards the great, roaring river. But he did not go into the water, because he saw how very dark and swift-flowing it was and far deeper than the Loire. So he follows the bank along past a huge outcrop of rock on the far side of the river, whose waters beat against its foot. On that rock, situated on a slope that ran down towards the sea, was a magnificent, strong castle. Where the river opened into a bay, the youth turned to the left and saw the castle towers springing up; for it seemed to him they were shooting up and emerging from the rock. Rising in the centre of the castle was a high, strong keep. A massive barbican faced the bay, challenging the sea, which broke against its foot. At the four corners of the wall with its hard stone blocks were four strong, handsome, low turrets. The castle was extremely well sited and excellently appointed inside. In front of the round gatehouse was a bridge over the water, built of stone, sand and lime. The bridge was strong, high and completely battlemented. In the middle of it was a tower and in front of it a drawbridge conveniently placed and constructed for its function of bridge by day and gate by night.

1351 The youth makes his way towards this bridge. On it a worthy man dressed in a robe of purple cloth was taking his ease. Here now comes the youth towards the bridge. In his hand the gentleman held a cane with an elegant air, and behind him came two serving-lads in light attire. The youth, very mindful of his mother's instructions, greeted him and added: "Sir, my mother taught me that."—"God bless you, dear brother," says the nobleman, realising from his words that he was a naïve simpleton; and he went on: "Where have you come from, dear brother?"—"Where? From King Arthur's court."—"What did you do there?"—"The king made me a knight, and good luck to him."*—"A knight? May God prosper me! I didn't suppose he would be thinking about that kind of thing at this moment: I thought that just now he had other preoccupations than making men knights. Tell me then, my good brother: those arms – who supplied you with them?"—"The king", he says, "gave them to me."—"Gave them you? How was that?" Then he tells him the facts as you have heard them in the story. It would be boring and futile to have it told a second time, for no story is improved that way.

1384 Then the worthy man asks him further how he can handle his horse. "I run him up and down just as I used to gallop the hunter I had that I brought from my mother's house."—"And as for your armour, dear friend, tell me what you can do with it."—"I can put it on and take it off all right, just like the lad who armed me with it when I'd watched him take it off the knight I'd killed. And it's so light for me to wear that it's not in the least uncomfortable."—"By my faith," says the gentleman, "that seems good to me. I'm very pleased. Now tell me, if you don't mind, what purpose brought you here."—"Sir, my mother told me that I should approach worthy men wherever I might find them, and that I should believe what they told me because people who do so profit from it." The gentleman replies: "A blessing on your mother, dear friend, for she gave you sound advice. But is there anything else you want to say?"—"Yes."—"What, then?"—"Just to ask you for lodging now – that's all."—"Very willingly," says the gentleman, "provided you do me one favour, from which you'll see great benefit come."—"What's that?" says he.—"To take your mother's advice and mine."—"By my faith," he says, "I grant you that."—"Dismount, then!" And he dismounts.

1420   One of the two lads who had come there takes his horse, and the other disarms him, so that he is left in the absurd outfit, the crude shoes and the ill-made, ill-cut, stag-hide tunic which his mother had given him. Then the worthy man had his sharp steel spurs, which the lad had brought, fitted on his own feet before mounting his horse, hanging the shield by its strap at his neck and taking the lance. He then said: "Now, my friend, learn the practice of arms, and pay attention to the manner of holding a lance and of spurring and curbing a horse!" Then, having unfurled the pennon, he tells and shows him how to hold his shield. He has him hang it a little forward until it touches the horse's neck, then lays the lance in its rest and spurs the horse, which was worth a hundred marks, for there was no more willing, faster or more powerful runner. The gentleman was very knowledgeable about shield, horse and lance, having learnt all that in his boyhood; and everything this worthy man did gave the youth great pleasure and satisfaction.

1451   When he had completed his manoeuvre well and elegantly before the young man, who had watched with close attention, he rode back to him with his lance raised and asked him: "My friend, would you be able to manage the lance and shield like that, and spur and control the horse?" And he declared emphatically that he would never wish to live a day longer or amass any wealth without knowing how to do this. "My dear good friend," says the gentleman, "what you don't know you can learn, given effort and application. Into every craft you need to put your heart and effort and practice: with these three things you can master it. And when you've never done it yourself or seen anyone else do it, there's no shame or blame attached to not knowing how to." Then the worthy man had him mount; and he began to bear his lance and shield as impeccably as if he had spent his whole life in tournaments and wars and had done the rounds of every land in search of battle and adventure; for it came naturally to him; and with nature as his teacher and his heart entirely in it, nothing can be difficult for him thus aided by the efforts of nature and his heart. Throughout he performed so well that he delighted the gentleman, who reflected that had he spent his whole life earnestly devoting himself to arms, this would still be a high standard of accomplishment.

1491   When the young man had made his circuit, he rode back to come before the worthy man with his lance raised, as he had seen him do, and said: "Have I done it well, sir? Do you think my effort, if I keep it up, will ever do any good? My eyes have never seen anything I desired so much. I'd love to know as much about it as you do."—"My friend, if your heart is set on it," says the nobleman, "you'll get the knowledge: you've no need to worry about that." The worthy man mounted three times and three times gave him instruction in arms to the best of his ability until he had taught him a great deal, then had him mount three times. The last time he said to him: "My friend, if you met a knight, what would you do if he struck you?"—"I'd strike him back!"—"And if your lance broke?"—"After that, there would be nothing for it but for me to set about him with my fists."—"You wouldn't do that, my friend."—"What should I do, then?"—"You should attack him with sword-play." Then the worthy man plants the lance upright in the ground in front of him, anxious as he is to teach and instruct him in arms so that he may know how to defend himself well with the sword when attacked and take the offensive when the opportunity comes. He then took the sword in his hand. "My friend," says he, "this is the way to defend yourself if you're attacked."—"As God is my saviour," he says, "no one knows as much about that as I do, because I trained hard at it at my mother's house, using cushions and big shields, until I was quite worn out."—"Let's go to my house straight away, then," says the gentleman: "there's nothing more I can think of; and tonight nothing will stop us enjoying Saint Julian's lodging."*

1539 Then they go off side by side; and the young man said to his host: "Sir, my mother told me that I should never be with a man or keep his company for long without getting to know his name. And if what she taught me was good sense, I'd like to know your name."—"My dear good friend," says the gentleman, "my name is Gornemant of Gohort." And so they reach the dwelling, holding each other by the hand. As they mounted the steps, a well-intentioned serving lad came up bringing a short mantle and ran to put it on the young man so that, after getting hot, he should not come to any harm by catching cold. The gentleman possessed a fine, large, richly appointed house and good servants. Then the meal was made ready: it was excellent and well and attractively prepared. The knights washed, then sat at table, with the gentleman placing the young man beside him and having him eat with him from the same dish. I shall not go into details about the courses, how many or what they were; but they ate and drank their fill: that is all I shall say about the meal.

1570 When they had left the table, the worthy man, with his great courtesy, begged the young man who had sat beside him to stay for a month. He would gladly keep him a full year, if he wished; and during that time he would teach him, if he cared to know, things that would be useful to him in time of need. To this the youth replied: "Sir, I don't know if I'm close to the house where my mother lives, but I pray God to lead me to her so that I may see her again; for I saw her fall in a faint in front of the gate at the end of the bridge, and I don't know whether she's alive or dead. I'm sure she fell fainting from the grief I caused her when I left her; and for that reason I couldn't possibly stay here for long until I know how she is. So instead, I'll leave tomorrow at daybreak." The gentleman sees that his pleas are in vain. Their conversation ends; and without further discussion they retire for the night, the beds being already made.

1597 The worthy man rose early in the morning and went to the youth's bed, where he found him still lying; and as a gift he had a shirt and breeches of fine linen brought to him as well as hose dyed with brazil-wood and a tunic of indigo silk that had been woven and made in India. He sent them for him to put on and told him: "My friend, if you take my advice you will wear these clothes you see here." The youth replies: "Good sir, you could make a far better suggestion. Aren't the clothes my mother made for me better than these? Yet you want me to put these on?"—"Young man, I swear by my head and my two eyes that these are worth far more!" The youth replies: "No, they're worth less."—"When I brought you here, my good friend, you assured me you'd do everything I told you to."—"And so I will," says the youth: "I'll never let you down in anything." He wastes no more time in putting on the clothes, abandoning those he had from his mother.

1624   Then the worthy man bent down and fitted on his right spur, it being customary for the man conferring knighthood to fasten on the spur. There were numerous other youths present, and each of them who could attend him lent a hand in his arming. Next the worthy man took the sword, girt it on him and kissed him, saying he had conferred on him with this sword the highest order created and ordained by God, namely the order of chivalry, which must be free of all baseness.

1639   He said: "Dear brother, remember now something I want to tell and beg you, should it happen that you have to fight some knight. If you get the better of him so that he can no longer defend himself or put up any opposition against you but has to ask for mercy, then be sure to have mercy on him and not kill him instead. Moreover, don't be too ready to speak: no one can be too talkative without often saying something that makes him look foolish, for the wise man's saying goes: 'Whoever talks too much does himself a bad turn.' Therefore, dear friend, I warn you against speaking too freely. I also beg you, if you find any man or woman, whether an orphan or a lady, who is in distress for any reason, you'll do well to give them your support, if you know how to and can do so. There's one further lesson I have for you that you shouldn't neglect, for it's not to be taken lightly: go willingly to church to beseech Him who has made everything to have mercy on your soul and, in this earthly life, to keep you as His Christian."

1671   The youth replied to the worthy man: "A blessing on you by all the popes in Rome, good sir, for I heard my mother say the same!"—"Now, dear brother," says the gentleman, "never say that your mother has taught you something: just say I have. But don't think we blame you for having said it up to now; however in future, if you please, I beg you to drop the habit; for if you went on saying that, people would think it foolish. So I beg you to beware of that."—"What shall I say then, my dear good sir?"—"You can say that the vavasour who fitted on your spur taught and instructed you so." Then the youth granted his request that never in all his born days will he speak of anyone but him: of that he may be sure, for his instruction seems good to him. At once the worthy man made the sign of the cross over him with his raised hand, then said: "Since you have a mind to leave, may God go with you and guide you, as you'd rather not stay."

1699   The new knight parts from his host, extremely anxious to return to his mother and to find her alive and well. He then headed into the desolate forests, with which he was more familiar than with the open country, for he was much at home in the woods. He rode until he saw a strong, well-sited fortress with nothing outside its walls but sea and stretches of water and wasteland. He hurried on towards this stronghold until he arrived before the gate. However, before he could reach the gate there was a bridge to be crossed that was so flimsy that he hardly thought it would bear him. Riding up on to that little bridge, he crossed it without meeting with any accident, misfortune or hindrance. When he came up to the gate he found it locked. He knocks on it by no means softly and shouts in hardly too low a voice! He hammered away until a thin, pale maiden came running to the windows of the hall, asking: "Who is it calling?" The youth looks in the maiden's direction, sees her and says: "My fair friend, I'm a knight begging you to let me in and grant me lodging for the night."—"Sir," she says, "that you shall have, but you'll give me small thanks for it. Nevertheless, we'll lodge you as best we can." Thereupon the maiden withdrew.

1736   Then the youth waiting at the gate is afraid he is being kept waiting too long, so he starts to call again. Four men-at-arms promptly arrived, holding axes in their hands and each girt with a good sword; and unlocking the gate, they said to him: "Come along in!" If these men-at-arms had been in easy circumstances, they would have been very handsome; but they had suffered such privations, going without food and sleep, that they were in an amazingly poor state. For while he had found the land outside bare and laid waste, he discovered little enough inside; because, wherever he went, he found the streets devastated and saw the houses in ruins and not a man or woman there. In the town were two churches which had formerly been abbeys: one for nuns, who had been terrorised, and the other for monks, who had been made distraught. He did not find these churches at all well decorated or provided with hangings: instead he saw their walls cracked and fissured and their towers unroofed, while the living quarters lay open by night as by day. Nowhere in the entire fortress was there any mill grinding or oven baking, no wine or loaf, and nothing that could be sold to make a single penny. Thus he found the fortress waste, empty of bread and dough, wine, cider and ale.

1774 The four men-at-arms led him to a great hall roofed in slate, and there helped him to dismount and disarm. A serving-lad then came down one of the staircases from the hall, bringing a grey cloak, which he placed on the knight's shoulders. Another stabled his horse in a place where there was only a small amount of wheat, hay or oats, for there was no more in the house. The others had him climb a stair ahead of them leading into the very handsome hall. Two gentlemen and a maiden came to meet him. The hair of the gentlemen was greying but not altogether white, and they would have looked in their prime, full-blooded and vigorous, had they not been dejected and grief-stricken.

1795 The maiden approached, more elegantly adorned and more graceful than any sparrowhawk or parrot. Her mantle and tunic were of dark purple cloth spangled with gold, and the ermine trimmings were far from shabby. The mantle had at the neck a black sable border flecked with white, which was neither too long nor too broad. And if I have ever described the beauty with which God has endowed a woman's body or face, I should now like to do so once more and without a word of a lie. She was bare-headed, and her hair was such that anyone seeing it would have thought it entirely of pure gold, were that possible, for it was so blond and shining. Her brow was high, white and smooth as if it had been made by hand, carved from stone, ivory or wood. The eyebrows were shapely and well-spaced, and the eyes in her head were bright, sparkling with laughter and not close-set. Her nose was long and straight; and in her face the white flushed with crimson was more attractive than heraldic red on silver. To see people's hearts stolen

away, God had in her created a great wonder, never having made
her equal before or since.

1830 On seeing her, the knight greets her and she him, as do both the
knights with her. Then the damsel takes him courteously by the
hand, saying: "Dear sir, your lodging tonight will certainly not be
such as would befit a gentleman. If I went on to tell you all about
our circumstances and situation, you would perhaps believe I did
so with ill intent, in order to persuade you to leave. But come now,
if you please, and accept the lodging such as it is; and may God give
you better tomorrow!" So she leads him by the hand to a very fine,
long, wide room with a decorated ceiling. They sat down together
on a couch covered with a heavy silk spread. Four, five, six knights
at a time came in and sat in large groups without speaking, but
looking at the one sitting beside their lady and not uttering a word.
He refrained from saying anything because he remembered the
warning given him by the worthy gentleman.

1860 Then all the knights discussed this in whispers amongst themselves. "God!" says each of them. "I'm quite amazed if this knight
is dumb. That would be a great pity, for never was so handsome a
knight born of woman. *He looks extremely well beside my lady,
and my lady beside him too, if only they were not both mute. He is
so handsome and she so beautiful that never were knight and
maiden so suited to each other, and they both seem to have been
made by God for one another, so that He might bring them
together." All those present talked of this at length.

1877 The damsel waited for him to open a conversation with her on
some subject or other until she saw clearly and was convinced that
he would never say a word to her unless she addressed him first.
Then, very politely, she said: "Where have you come from today,
sir?"—"Young lady," says he, "I spent the night with a worthy
gentleman in a castle where I had good, pleasant lodging. It has five
magnificent, strong towers, one big and four small ones: I can
describe everything about it, but I can't tell you the castle's name. I
do know, though, that the gentleman's name is Gornemant of
Gohort."—"Ah, my good friend," says the maiden, "you've said a
splendid thing and spoken in most courtly fashion. May God the
King look kindly on you for having called him a worthy gentleman,
because you never spoke a truer word; for he is a worthy man, by
Saint Richier – I can vouch for that. And let me tell you that I'm his

niece, but I've not seen him for a very long time. Certainly I'm sure that since you left home you've never met a worthier man. He gave you a very happy, cheerful lodging as he well knew how to, worthy and courteous man that he is as well as being powerful and a wealthy man of means. In here, though, there's nothing more than five loaves sent me by an uncle of mine, a prior and a very saintly, religious man, for tonight's supper, and also a cask of reheated wine.* There are no other provisions here but a deer one of my servants shot this morning with an arrow."

1918 She then ordered the tables to be set, which was done; and the company sat down to supper. They did not sit at all long over their food, but it was eaten very heartily. After the meal they split up: those who had kept watch the previous night stayed behind and slept, and those who had to guard the castle that night made themselves ready. There were fifty men-at-arms on watch during the night, whilst the rest went to great trouble to make their guest very comfortable. The person preparing his bed provides white sheets, a very costly coverlet and a pillow for his head. That night every comfort and pleasure one can wish for in a bed were enjoyed by the knight save only for the enjoyment of a maiden, had he wished, or of a lady, had that possibility been open to him. But he knew nothing at all of love or anything else; so, having nothing on his mind, he quite promptly fell asleep.

1945 However, his hostess, shut in her room, finds no rest: he sleeps at ease, but she, involved in a struggle in which she is defenceless, is deep in thought. In her great agitation, she tosses and turns restlessly. Over her shift she donned a scarlet-dyed silk mantle; then, taking her courage in both hands she committed herself to trying her fortune. She did not act irresponsibly, though, but rather determined to go to her guest and tell him part of what she had on her mind. She proceeded to leave her bed, and went out of her room in such fear that she trembled in every limb and was bathed in perspiration. She left the room in tears. Coming to the bed where he lies asleep, she laments and sighs deeply, then she bends down and kneels, weeping so much that she wets his whole face with her tears: she lacks the courage to do any more.

1971 She continues to weep until he wakes and is very startled and amazed to find his face wet. Then he sees her kneeling by his bed, holding her arms tightly clasped round his neck. He was courtly enough to take her at once in his two arms and draw her towards him, saying: "What do you want, my fair one? Why have you come here?"—"Ah, noble knight, have pity on me! I beg you in the name of God and His Son not to think the worse of me for having come here. Despite my being almost naked, I had no foolish, wicked or base intention; for there's no living soul in all the world who is so grief-stricken or wretched that I am not more so. Nothing I have brings me pleasure, and never have I spent a day free of trouble. How great is my misfortune! And I shall never see a night other than this one or any day except tomorrow: instead I shall kill myself with my own hand!

1999   "Of three hundred and ten knights who had manned this castle only fifty are left here;* and of the rest forty-eight have been carried off and killed or imprisoned by a very wicked knight, Engygeron, the seneschal of Clamadeu of the Isles. I grieve as much over those in captivity as over the slain, for I'm quite sure they will die and never manage to escape. So many good men have died on my behalf that I have every cause to mourn. Engygeron has laid continual siege to this place for an entire winter and summer, with his strength growing all the time. Our own has diminished, and our provisions have been exhausted; for there's not enough left in here to make a good meal for one man. So now we're in such a desperate plight that tomorrow, unless God intervenes, this castle will be handed over to him, since it can't be defended, along with myself as a captive. But indeed, before he takes me away alive, I'll kill myself and he'll have me dead! Then I shan't care if he carries me off! Clamadeu, who thinks he will have me, never will in any way, unless he gets me bereft of life and soul; for in a casket of mine I keep a knife of the finest steel, which I intend to plunge into my heart. That's what I had to tell you: now I'll go away and leave you to rest."

2038   Before long the knight will be able to win honour for himself, if he dares, because she came to shed her tears on his face for no other reason, whatever she leads him to believe, than to inspire him to undertake the fight on her behalf in defence of her land, if he has the courage. Then he said to her: "My dear friend, cheer up now tonight! Take comfort and don't weep any more. Come up here beside me and wipe the tears from your eyes. If it please God, He will treat you better tomorrow than you've said. Come into this bed beside me, for it's wide enough for both of us. You shall not leave me before tomorrow!" She replied: "If you were happy with that, I would." Then he kissed her and, holding her tightly in his arms, drew her gently to lie at ease under the coverlet. She let him kiss her and was not, I think, unhappy to do so! Thus they lay all night long, side by side and mouth to mouth until the morning and the approach of daylight. That night brought her such solace that they slept mouth to mouth in each other's arms until daybreak.

2070 With the dawn the maiden returned to her room. Without the help of any maid or attendant she dressed and got ready, waking no one. As soon as they could see daylight, those who had kept watch through the night woke those who were asleep and had them get up from their beds, which they did without delay. At the same time the maiden goes back to her knight with the gracious words: "Sir, may God give you a good day today! I very much doubt if you will stay here long: it would be useless to remain. You'll leave without any regret on my part, for it wouldn't be courtly of me to be at all displeased at that, since we've done you no honour or service here at all. And I pray God that He may have ready for you some better lodging, with more bread and wine and other things, and with better provision than here." He said: "My fair one, it won't be today that I shall go looking for another lodging. First I'll have brought peace to all your land, if I possibly can. If I find your enemy out there, and provided you have no objection, I'll be very loath to have him continue the siege. But should I defeat and kill him, I ask as my reward that you grant me your love as mine alone. I'd take no other payment."

2107 She replies most tactfully: "Sir, you've now requested from me a very poor, small thing; but if it were refused you, you'd suppose it was out of pride, and so I'll not deny it to you. Yet don't say I'm becoming your sweetheart on the understanding and condition that you go and die for my sake, for that would be quite lamentable; because you may be sure that neither your physique nor your age are such that you could withstand or oppose in a fight or battle so hard, strong or big a knight as the one waiting outside."—"You'll see about that today," says he, "for I'm going to fight with him: I'll not be put off by any warning!" The argument she put to him was such that she blamed him, yet with approval; but it often happens that one tends to deny one's real wishes in order, when one sees someone eager to do just what one wants, to increase that eagerness. In this she acts wisely, having put him in mind to do what she strongly blames him for.

2138 Having called for his arms, he asked that they be brought. They were fetched for him. Then he is armed and mounted on a horse which they had made ready for him in the middle of the square. There is no one there who does not look dejected and says: "May God lend you His aid this day, sir, and bring down great misfortune on Engygeron the seneschal, who has totally destroyed this land!" That is the prayer of one and all. They escort him as far as the gate; and once they see him outside the fortress, they all shout with one voice: "Good sir, may that true cross on which God allowed His Son to suffer protect you today from mortal peril, from mishap and imprisonment and bring you safely back to some place that offers you comfort, pleasure and delight!" Thus everyone prayed for him.

2162 Then those in the army, seeing him coming, pointed him out to Engygeron, who was sitting in front of his tent, thinking the castle should be surrendered to him by nightfall or else that somebody would come out to fight him in single combat. Already he had his greaves laced; and his men were very happy, thinking they had conquered the castle and the whole country. *When Engygeron sees him, he promptly has himself armed and trots towards him on a strong, well-nourished charger, saying: "Who sends you here, lad? Tell me what errand you're on. Have you come looking for peace, or a fight?"—"What are you doing in this land, though?" he replies. "You'll tell me first why you've killed those knights and wrought havoc on the whole country." Then the other answered him in an arrogant, insolent tone: "I want that castle evacuated and its keep surrendered to me this very day, for it's held out against me too long. And then my lord will have the maiden."—"Damn this claim," says the young man, "and the one who uttered it! On the contrary, you'll have to renounce every demand you make of her."—"Now, by Saint Peter," says Engygeron, "this is a lot of nonsense you're telling me! It often happens that the one who's not guilty of something pays the penalty for it."

2198 That stung the young man, so he laid his lance in its rest, and they charge at each other as fast as their horses can carry them. With the anger and rage they felt and with all the strength in their arms they make their lances fly apart in splinters and fragments.

Engygeron was the only one to fall, having received a wound through his shield, so that he was in great pain in his arm and side. Then the youth dismounts, not knowing how to attack him from his horse. Once off his horse, he grasped his sword and made for him. I do not know what more I should tell about how each of them fared, or if I should give a blow-by-blow account; but the combat lasted a long time and many stout blows were exchanged until Engygeron fell. Then the young man launched a fierce assault on him until he begged him for mercy.

2236 The youth said there was no question at all of mercy. However, he remembered the worthy man who had taught him not knowingly to kill a knight having once defeated him and got the upper hand. Then the other said to him: "My dear kind friend, don't be so brutal as to refuse me mercy. I fully concede and grant that you have the better of me. You're certainly a very fine knight, but not to the extent that anyone who had not been watching and who knew us both would have believed that you could have killed me in armed combat on your own. But if I testify for you in the presence of my men in front of my tent that you've overcome me in an armed encounter, my word on that will be taken and your honour will be increased above that of all knights before you. And if you have a lord who has done you some kindness or service for which he hasn't been repaid, be sure to send me to him, and I'll go and tell him on your behalf how you've defeated me in battle; and I shall surrender to him as his captive to do whatever he wishes."

2268 —"A curse on anyone", said he, "who asks for better than that! Do you know where to go, then? Into that castle. And you'll tell the fair maiden, my beloved, that you'll never, as long as you live, do her any harm; and you'll put yourself entirely at her mercy, in every respect." The knight replies: "Then kill me, because she for her part would have me put to death, as she longs for nothing so much as my shame and ruin; for I had a hand in her father's death, and I've been a great plague to her by seizing her knights from her and killing and holding them prisoner all this year. Anyone sending me to her would have condemned me to a grim captivity and could do nothing worse for me. But if you have some other friend, man or woman, who has no desire to maltreat me, send me there; for this one would undoubtedly take my life if she got her hands on me."

2292 Then the youth told him to go to a castle belonging to a worthy man, whose name he gave him. In all the world there is no mason who would have described better than he the appearance of the castle. He spoke very glowingly to him of the river and the bridge, the turrets, the keep and the strong surrounding walls until Engygeron recognises without question that he wants to send him as a prisoner to the place where he is most hated. "Dear brother," he says, "I know I'll find no safety there where you're sending me. So help me God, you're wanting to send me to a terrible fate and into terrible hands, because in this war I killed one of his own brothers. You kill me yourself, my dear kind friend, rather than make me go to him! If you force me to go there, it will be to my death." He replied: "You shall go, then, as prisoner to King Arthur. And you will greet the king for me and tell him on my behalf to have you shown the girl Kay the seneschal struck because she had laughed to see me. Then you will give yourself up to her as her prisoner and tell her, if you please, that I hope God won't let me die before I've secured vengeance for her." He answers that he will do him this service efficiently and well.

2326 With that the knight who vanquished him turned back towards the castle, whilst he departs for his captivity and has his standard removed. The army then raises the siege and leaves down to the last man, dark and fair-headed alike. Then the people in the fortress come out to meet the returning youth, though they are extremely upset that he did not take off the head of the knight he had defeated and deliver it up to them. Very joyfully they helped him dismount and disarmed him by a mounting-block; and everyone said: "Since you didn't bring Engygeron back here, why didn't you cut off his head?" He replies to them: "Indeed, sirs, I think that wouldn't have been right of me. He has killed your kinsmen, and I couldn't have guaranteed his safety: you'd have killed him in spite of me. I'd have been extremely ungenerous if, once I had the better of him, I hadn't shown him mercy. And do you know what my conditions were? He'll surrender himself prisoner to King Arthur, if he keeps his promise to me." Thereupon the damsel arrives, overjoyed on his account, and takes him away into her room to rest and take his ease. She shows no reluctance in embracing and kissing him: instead of eating and drinking, they sport and kiss and embrace and talk tenderly together.

2363 Clamadeu, however, is entertaining foolish thoughts, confidently hoping promptly to take the castle undefended. But then he

met on his road a youth in great distress who told him the news of
the seneschal Engygcron. "In God's name, my lord, now things are
going very badly," said the youth, tearing his hair with both hands
in his grief.—"In what way?" Clamadeu replies. "My lord," says
the youth, "I swear your seneschal has been defeated in combat,
and will surrender to King Arthur as his captive; and he's on his
way there."—"Who has done that, lad? Tell me! How could that
happen? Where can the knight come from who is able to make such
a fine, valiant man submit in a fight?" He replies: "My dear good
lord, I don't know who the knight was: I only know I saw him come
out of Beaurepaire wearing a suit of crimson armour."—"And
what do you suggest I do, lad?" says he, at his wits' end.—"Do, my
lord? Why, withdraw; for if you went on, you'd never do anything
about it."

2393 As he said this, a rather greying knight, Clamadeu's major-
domo, came up. "Young man," he says, "no good will come of
that. There's need for wiser and better advice than yours. If he takes
your word, he'll act like a fool: on the contrary, he'll go on, if he
does as I say." He continued: "Sir, you want to know how you
might have both the knight and the castle? I'll tell you precisely;
and it will be very simple to do. Inside the walls of Beaurepaire
there's nothing to drink or eat, and the knights are in a weak state,
whereas we're strong and fit, not thirsty or hungry; and we can
stand a hard fight if those inside dare to come out here to engage us.
We'll send twenty knights to fight outside the gate. The knight, who
is enjoying himself with his fair love Blancheflor, will want to show
his chivalry; and, finding it impossible to restrain himself, he'll be
captured or will die, because the others, weak as they are, will give
him little help. And our twenty will do nothing but keep them
guessing until we come through this valley to take them by surprise
and manage to surround them."—"Upon my word," says Clamadeu, "I really approve of your proposal. We have here some first-
class men: four hundred armed knights and a thousand well-
equipped men-at-arms, and it'll be like capturing dead men!"

2433 Clamadeu sent twenty knights in front of the gate, carrying all
manner of pennons and banners waving in the wind. When those in
the castle saw them, they opened the gates wide as the young man
wished; and in full view of them all he went out to tackle the
knights. Bold and strong, he fiercely meets them all at once, and no

one he strikes has the impression he is a novice at arms! That day he was in good form, disembowelling many with his lance, piercing some through the chest, others through the breast, breaking this one's arm, that one's collar bone, killing one, maiming another, felling this one, capturing that. He gives up the prisoners and horses to those who needed them.* But then they see the main body of the army, which had come up through the valley: there were four hundred armed men on their way, not counting the thousand foot-soldiers.

2460 The defenders took their stand very close to the open gate; and those outside, seeing the loss of their mangled and dead men, drive towards the gate in furious disarray. The defenders, packing their gate in close formation, receive them boldly; but they were few and weak. And the strength of the others was increased by the foot-soldiers who had followed them, to the point where the defenders could not withstand them and withdrew into their castle. Above the gate there were archers shooting into the milling throng, who were fired with eagerness to burst into the castle until a band of them stormed their way in by force. The men above released a gate down on to those below, killing and annihilating all those it caught in its fall. Nothing he might see could have so distressed Clamadeu, for the portcullis had killed and cut off from him many of his men, so he had to stay his hand, since so impetuous an assault would only have been a waste of effort.

2491 Then his major-domo, who advised him, said: "My lord, it's no surprise when misfortune strikes a worthy man. Good or ill happens to every man as the Lord God pleases or decrees. The fact of the matter is that you've lost; but every saint has his feast-day! The storm has broken over you, and your men have become casualties, whilst those inside have won: but you may rest assured that they'll lose in turn. You may pluck out both my eyes if they stay three days in there. The castle and keep will be yours, for they will all submit. If you can stay here just today and tomorrow, the castle will be in your hands. Even the maiden who has refused you for so long will beseech you in God's name to condescend to take her." Then those who have brought them have their tents and pavilions pitched, whilst the others bivouacked and camped out as best they could. The men in the castle disarmed the knights they had captured. They did not shut them up in towers or put them in irons, but only made them give their solemn pledge as loyal knights to accept their imprisonment in good faith and never do them any harm. Those were the conditions of their confinement there.

2524 That very day a gale had driven across the sea a boat carrying a large cargo of wheat and full of other provisions. By God's will it had arrived safe and undamaged before the castle. When the men in the fortress saw it, they sent to ask and enquire who these people were and what they had come for. Then down from the castle went those bound for the boat. They ask who the people are, where they come from and where they are going. They reply: "We're merchants carrying provisions for sale: bread and wine, salted bacon, and we've plenty of bullocks and pigs for slaughter if necessary." The others say: "God be praised for giving the wind the strength to send you drifting here! And welcome to you! Unload your goods, and they will soon be sold at whatever price you dare ask! And come quickly to collect your money, for you'll not get out of receiving and counting the bars of gold and silver that we'll give you for the wheat; and for the wine and meat you'll have a cartload of wealth, and more if need be!" Now the buyers and sellers have done their business well. They set about unloading the boat and have everything sent on ahead to raise the spirits of those in the castle.

2561 When the people inside see the bearers of the provisions approaching, you may be sure they were overjoyed; and as quickly as they could they had the food prepared. Now Clamadeu, idly passing the time outside, will have a long wait, because those inside have beef and pork, salted meat in abundance, and enough wheat to last until the next harvest. The cooks are not idle, and boys light the fires in the kitchens for cooking the meal. Now the young man can take his ease and pleasure beside his love. She embraces him, he kisses her, and they find their joy in each other. As for the hall, that is far from quiet, but full of happy tumult. They all rejoice for the food after having longed for it so much; and the cooks work hard to have them sitting down to the meal, of which they stood in great need. Having eaten, they rise from the tables. But Clamadeu and his men grieve at the news which has reached them of the good fortune of the people inside. They say they must leave, since the fortress can in no way be starved out: their siege of the town has been in vain.

2593 Then the enraged Clamadeu sends a messenger to the castle, without anyone's advice or suggestion, informing the red knight that by noon the next day he will be able to find him alone in the lists to fight with him, if he dares. When the maiden hears the summons to her lover, it makes her sad and angry, since he sends back word that, come what may, he shall have his combat as he requests. The sorrow the maiden shows at this grows ever greater and more bitter; but I think he will never renounce his intention, whatever grief the maiden feels. Every man and woman begs him insistently not to go to fight that man, against whom no knight has ever yet prevailed in a combat. "Sirs," says the youth, "you'll do well to say no more now, because in no way would I give this up for any man in the whole world!"

2618   He thus reduces them to silence, as they dare not speak to him any further on the subject. Instead they retire to bed and rest until sunrise next morning. But they are very sad for their lord as, however much they beg him, they cannot dissuade him. That night his beloved too had pleaded with him a great deal not to go to the combat but to stay there in peace, for they were no longer concerned about Clamadeu or his men. But all that was to no avail, which was highly surprising, because she mixed with her blandishments great tenderness towards him, at each word kissing him so sweetly and softly that she put the key of love into the lock of his heart. Yet there was no possibility at all of her succeeding in deterring him from going to fight the combat: instead he called for his arms. The person he had asked brought them to him as quickly as he could. There was great grief at his arming, for all, men and women alike, were sorrowful. Then, having commended them one and all to the King of Kings, he mounts his northern horse which had been fetched for him. That done, he did not linger long with them. Setting forth without further ado, he leaves then grieving bitterly.

2653   When Clamadeu sees him coming, bent on fighting him, he entertains such foolish ideas that he imagines he will very quickly spill him from the saddle-bows. The heath was fine and level, and on it they were alone together, for Clamadeu had dismissed all his men and sent them away. Each held his lance supported on its rest in front of the saddle-bow, and they charge at one another without a challenge or wasting words. They both had stout, easily handled ashen lances with sharp iron tips, their horses galloped swiftly; and the knights, filled with a mutual and mortal hatred, strike so hard that the boards of their shields are smashed and the lances shatter, and they bring each other to the ground. But they have quickly jumped to their feet again and, coming to grips at once, they fight a long, even contest with their swords. I could tell you a great deal about it, if I wanted to take the trouble; but I do not wish to make the effort, because one word is worth as much as twenty.

2682 In the end Clamadeu had reluctantly to ask for mercy, promising him all he wished as his seneschal had done, except that on no condition would he go as a prisoner to Beaurepaire any more than his seneschal would; nor would he, for all Rome's empire, go to the worthy man in his finely situated castle; but he was quite prepared to go as captive to King Arthur and would also give his message to the maiden who had been so outrageously struck by Kay, saying he intends to avenge her, whoever it may distress or grieve, if God will grant him the strength to do so. After that he makes him guarantee that before the next day's dawn all those shut in his towers shall come out freely and in good health and that, so long as he lives, there will never be an army outside the castle which he does not remove, if he can; nor will the damsel have any trouble from his men or himself.

2709 So Clamadeu went away to his own land. And when he arrived, he ordered all the captives to be released from prison and to be allowed to go in total freedom. As soon as he had given the word his orders were carried out. Here now are all the prisoners given their liberty; and they left at once with all their equipment, nothing being held back. Clamadeu made his way in another direction, travelling on his own. It was the custom in those days, and we find it in writing, that a knight should surrender himself captive with his gear exactly as he left the fight having been vanquished: nothing was to be removed and nothing added. In precisely that fashion Clamadeu takes the road behind Engygeron, who is on his way to Dinasdaron, where the king was to hold court. But elsewhere there was great joy in the castle to which those who had spent a long while in very terrible captivity had returned. The whole hall rings with jubilation, as do the knights' dwellings. In the chapels and churches all the bells peal for joy, and there is no monk or nun who does not give thanks to God. The men and women all go dancing through the streets and squares. Among those in the fortress there is great happiness now that no one is attacking or waging war on them.

2748   Meanwhile Engygeron rides on; and behind him, in the lodgings he had occupied, Clamadeu spent three successive nights. By
way of these lodging-places he followed him all the way to Dinasdaron in Wales, where King Arthur was holding very full court in
his halls. They see Clamadeu approaching fully armed as he was
required to be; and he was recognised by Engygeron, who had
already delivered his message at court and given a full account of
events when he had arrived the previous night, and was being kept
at court as a member of the household and as counsellor. He saw
his lord all covered in crimson blood but did not fail to recognise
him, saying at once: "My lords, my lords, here's an amazing sight!
The youth in red armour, believe me, is sending here that knight
you can see. He's defeated him: I'm quite sure of that because he's
covered in blood. I can pick out the blood from here and him too as
being my lord, whose vassal I am. His name's Clamadeu of the Isles,
and I thought he was such a knight that there was none better in
Rome's empire; but a worthy man may well suffer misfortune." So
spoke Engygeron; and then Clamadeu arrived. They run towards
each other and meet in the middle of the court.

2785   It was at Pentecost; and the queen was seated beside King
Arthur at the head of the table, with many kings, dukes, queens and
countesses present. It was after the masses had been sung, and the
ladies and knights had returned from church. Then Kay passed
through the hall, lightly attired, holding a small cane in his right
hand, and with a cloth cap on his blond head. There was no more
handsome knight in the world, and his hair was plaited in a tress;
but his wicked tongue detracted from his beauty and prowess. His
tunic was of costly material dyed a rich scarlet, with, at the waist, a
finely woven belt whose buckle and trimmings were of gold: I recall
that clearly, for that is how the story describes it. Everyone makes
way for him as he comes through the hall: they all fear his malicious
taunts and evil tongue, and so they clear his path; for it is unwise
not to fear patently obvious vilification, whether sincere or spoken
in jest. Everybody in there was too afraid of his wicked taunts for
anyone to speak to him. Then, as they all looked on, he went up to
where the king was sitting and said: "Sire, if it pleased you, you
might begin to eat now."—"Kay," says the king, "leave me in
peace; for, by the eyes in my head, I shall never dine on such a high
feast-day when I'm holding a full assembly, until some news arrives
at my court."*

2827 While they were talking thus, Clamadeu enters the court to surrender himself as a captive there, coming armed as he was obliged to. He says: "May God save and bless the best king alive, the most bountiful and noble, as is attested by one and all who have been informed of the fine deeds he has accomplished! Now hear me, my good lord," he says, "for there's a message I have to deliver. It saddens me, but I nevertheless admit that I'm sent here by a knight who has vanquished me. On his behalf, I have to give myself up to you as your prisoner, for I have no alternative. And if anyone should wish to ask me if I know his name, I should reply no; but this much I can tell you about him – that his arms are crimson, and he says you gave them to him."—"So help you God, my friend," says the king, "tell me truly if he's in full vigour, free, and hale and hearty."—"Yes, you may be quite sure of that, my dear good lord," says Clamadeu; "and he's the most valiant knight I've ever met. He also told me to speak to the maiden who laughed for him and whom Kay treated so shamefully as to give her a slap on the cheek. But he says he'll avenge her, if God grants him the power."

2864 The fool, hearing what he said, jumps for joy and cries out: "God bless me, sir king! That cuff will be well avenged, and don't think I'm bluffing you; for he'll have his arm broken for it and his collar-bone put out of joint, and there's nothing he'll be able to do about it." Kay, who overhears him, thinks he is talking great nonsense; and you may be sure it is not cowardice that stops him from knocking him senseless, but the thought of the king's presence and the shame of it. Then the king shakes his head and says to Kay: "I'm extremely sorry that he's not in here with me. It was on account of you and your stupid tongue that he went away, to my great grief."

2882 At this, Gifflet stands up on the king's command, together with my lord Yvain, who makes better men of all those who keep his company. Then the king tells them to take that knight and conduct him to the rooms where the queen's damsels are amusing themselves; and the knight bows to them. Those the king ordered to do so take him along to the rooms and point the maiden out to him. Then he tells her the news that is most welcome to her, smarting as she is from the shame she received on her cheek. She had quite recovered from the blow she had taken, but had not forgotten or got over the shame; for only a very base person forgets when he is done some shame or mischief. In a vigorous, steadfast man pain passes and shame remains, but in a base fellow it dies away and cools. Clamadeu has delivered his message. Thereafter the king retained him all his days as a member of his court and household.

2910 Meanwhile, the one who had thwarted his claim to the land and the maiden, the fair Blancheflor his beloved, takes his pleasure and delight at her side. The land too would have been freely his had he wished and had his concern not been elsewhere; but his mind turns back to another occasion, his heart being fixed on his mother, whom he saw fall in a swoon; and he has a greater desire to go and see her than for anything else. He does not dare ask his leave of his beloved, for she forbids and prohibits it, ordering all her people to beg him urgently to stay. But all their pleas are in vain, except that he does promise that, should he find his mother alive, he will bring her back with him; and from then on, he assures them, he will hold the land, and so too he will if she is dead. So he sets off, promising them to return and leaving his charming sweetheart very distressed and sorrowful, as were all the others.

2938 When he made his way out of the town there was such a procession that it might have been Ascension Day or a Sunday; for all the monks, wearing their fine silk copes, and all the nuns in their veils were there. And every man and woman said: "Since you have delivered us from our plight and restored us to our houses, it's no wonder if we grieve at your intention to leave us so soon. Our sorrow is bound to be very deep, and indeed it could not be greater." He said to them: "You mustn't weep any longer now. I shall return, with God's favour; and grieving does no good. Don't you think it's right for me to go and see my mother, whom I left alone in those woodlands known as the Wild Forest? I shall come back, whether she wants me to or not, and nothing will stop me. If she's alive, I'll have her take the veil as a nun in your church; but if she's dead, you'll hold a service every year for her soul, so that God may place it in Abraham's bosom with those of the just. Sir monks and you, fair ladies, that should cause you no trouble because, if God brings me back, I'll reward you handsomely for her soul's sake." At that, the monks and nuns and all the others departed, whilst he set forth, lance in rest and fully armed, just as he came there.

2976 Then all day long he continued on his way without meeting any earthly being, no Christian man or woman able to guide him on his journey. Continually he prayed to the Lord God, the sovereign Father, to permit him to find his mother full of life and health, should it be His will. While he was still offering that prayer, he caught sight of a river as he came down a low hill. He looks at the deep, rushing water and does not dare enter it. Then he said: "Ah, almighty Lord! If I could cross this water, I fancy I'd find my mother on the other side, if she's still alive." So along the bank he rides until he approaches a rock with the water washing against it so that he can go no further. Then he saw, coming from higher up the river, a boat floating downstream; and in it were two men. He stops and waits, assuming that they would drift down until they reached him. Then the two came to a halt and, anchoring themselves very securely, stayed quite still in mid-stream. The man in the front was fishing with a line and a hook baited with a small fish slightly larger than a minnow.

3011 The young man, at a loss as to what to do and where to find a place to cross, greets them with an enquiry. "Tell me, sirs," he says, "if there's a bridge at all over this river." The man fishing replies: "No, brother, I assure you; and as far as I know there's no boat bigger than this one we're in, which wouldn't take five men. You can't cross on horseback for twenty leagues up or down river, for there's no ferry or bridge or ford."—"Then tell me, in God's name," he says, "where I might find a lodging." The man replies: "I imagine you could do with that, and more. I'll give you shelter tonight. Climb up through that fissure made in the rock; then, when you get to the top you'll see in front of you, in a valley, a house where I live close to the river and woods." He immediately climbed up to the top of the crag and, once on its crest, looked all around and saw nothing but sky and earth. Then he said: "What did I come here to find? What nonsense and stupidity! May God now heap utter shame on the man who sent me here! He really gave me splendid directions, telling me I'd find a house when I got up here! You fisherman who told me so really have done me a wicked turn, if you said it out of malice!"

3050 Then, in a valley close by, he saw the top of a tower appear.* You could not have found one so splendid or well situated this side of Beirut. It was square, built of dark grey stone, and flanked by two smaller towers. The hall was in front of the keep, and the galleries in front of the hall. The youth rides down towards it, saying that the man who had sent him there had guided him well; and he is full of praise for the fisherman: finding a lodging-place, he no longer calls him treacherous, dishonest or deceitful. So he makes his way towards the gate, in front of which he finds a lowered drawbridge.

3068 He crossed the bridge and went in to be met by four serving-lads, two of whom disarm him and the third leads away his horse and gives it hay and oats, whilst the fourth puts on him a brand-new mantle of fine woollen cloth. Then they led him up to the galleries; and you may be certain that one could have sought as far as Limoges without finding or seeing any as beautiful as these. The young man remained in these galleries until it was necessary for him to go to the lord, who sent servants to him. He then went with them into the hall, which was square, as long as it was wide. In the centre of the hall he saw, seated on a couch, a handsome gentleman with greying hair. On his head he wore a hat of sable, dark as a black-berry and covered at the crown with purple cloth; and he had a completely matching robe. He was leaning on one elbow; and in front of him was a great fire of dry wood that burned brightly between four pillars. It would have been easy to seat four hundred men, each with ample room, round that fire. The pillars were very strong, for they supported a high, wide chimney of heavy bronze.

3102 The men came before their lord bringing him his guest, one on either side of him. Seeing him coming, the lord greeted him at once with the words: "My friend, don't take it amiss if I do not get up to welcome you, for I'm not able to."—"In God's name, sir, say no more about it," says the young man, "because, as God may give me joy and health, I'm not in the least offended." The worthy man is so concerned on his account that he raises himself as far as he can, saying: "Come over here, my friend. Don't be afraid of me, but sit here beside me without any risk, as I ask you to." The youth sat down at his side, and the gentleman said to him: "My friend, where have you come from today?"—"Sir," says he, "I set out this morn-ing from Beaurepaire: that's its name."—"So help me God," says the worthy man, "you've had a very long journey today. You'll have started out before the watchman had sounded his horn for this morning's dawn."—"On the contrary, prime had already sounded, I assure you," says the youth.

3130 As they were conversing thus, a lad came in through the door of the house bringing a sword* that hung from his neck and handing it to the nobleman. He half drew it, enough to see clearly where it was made, for that was engraved on the sword; and as well as that he saw there that it was of such fine steel that it could never be broken except in one particular perilous circumstance known solely by him who had forged and tempered it. The lad who had brought it said: "My lord, your niece the fair-haired maiden who is so beautiful has sent you this gift: you will never see one more handsome in all its length and breadth. You are to give it to anyone you like; but my lady would be very happy if it were put to good use by the recipient. The man who forged the sword never made more than three, and will die without forging any further sword after this one."

3158   The lord immediately presented this sword to the stranger by its baldric, which was worth a great fortune. The sword's pommel was of the finest Arabian or Greek gold, and its scabbard of gold embroidery from Venice. With all its precious trappings the lord bestowed it on the young man, with the words: "Dear brother, this sword was intended and destined for you, and I'm very anxious that you should have it. But gird it on and draw it!" He thanks him for it and girds it on, but not too tightly, then draws it naked from the scabbard. Then, having looked at it for a while, he returned it to the scabbard. And you may be sure that it fitted splendidly at his side and even better in his hand; and it really seemed that in time of need he ought to put it to valiant use. Behind him he sees some youths standing round the brightly blazing fire. Spotting the one there who was looking after his arms, he entrusted the sword to him; and he took charge of it for him. Then he sat down again beside the lord, who did him very great honour. In there the light was as bright as candles can make it indoors.

3190   *While they were talking of this and that, out of a room came a youth holding a white lance grasped by the middle; and he passed by between the fire and those seated on the couch. And everyone present could see the white lance with its shining head; and from the tip of the lance-head oozed a drop of blood, a crimson drop that ran down right to the lad's hand. The young man who had arrived there that night saw this marvel, but refrained from asking how this thing happened, since he remembered that warning given him by the man who knighted him and taught and instructed him to beware of talking too much. He feared that, had he asked, it would have been thought impolite; and so he did not enquire. Thereupon two other youths came, holding in their hands pure gold candlesticks inlaid with black enamel. The lads carrying the candelabras were extremely handsome. At least ten candles were burning in each candelabra.

3220 A damsel, who came with the youths and was fair and attractive and beautifully adorned, held in both hands a grail. Once she had entered with this grail that she held, so great a radiance appeared that the candles lost their brilliance just as the stars do at the rising of the sun or moon. After her came another maiden, holding a silver carving-dish. The grail, which proceeded ahead, was of pure refined gold. And this grail was set with many kinds of precious stones, the richest and most costly in sea or earth: those stones in the grail certainly surpassed all others. Exactly as the lance had done, they passed by in front of the couch, going from one room into another. The young man saw them pass, but did not dare ask who was served from the grail, for he kept continually in his heart the words of that wise gentleman. I fear he may suffer for this, because I have heard it said that on occasion one may just as easily keep too silent as speak too much. Whether to his profit or for his harm, I know not which, he makes no enquiry and asks nothing.

3254 Then the lord orders the youths to fetch the water and bring out towels. Those whose duty it normally was did so; and the lord and the young man washed their hands in warm water. Then two lads brought a broad ivory table-top, all in one piece according to my source. They held it for a while in front of their lord and the young man until two other lads came with two trestles. The wood of which the trestles were made has two excellent properties that make it, when cut, last for ever. For they were of ebony, a wood which no one expects ever to rot or burn: it is proof against the one and the other. The table was set on these trestles, and the cloth was laid. But what could I say of that cloth? No legate, cardinal or pope ever dined off one so white.

3280 The first course was a haunch of venison in hot pepper sauce. There was no lack of clear, smooth wine to drink from golden cups. A youth carved the peppered haunch of venison in front of them, having drawn it towards him together with the silver carving-dish, then placed the slices before them on a single flat loaf of bread. The grail, meanwhile, passed in front of them once more. And the

young man did not ask who was served from that grail: he refrained
on account of that worthy man who gently warned him not to talk
too much; and this he remembers and has his heart constantly set
on it. But he keeps more silent than he should; for at the serving of
every dish he sees the grail pass before him in full view; and he does
not know who is served from it, yet he would like to know.
However, he thinks to himself that he certainly will ask one of the
lads at the court before he leaves. But he will wait until the morning
when he takes his leave of the lord and all the rest of the household.
So he has put it off and concentrates on drinking and eating. There
is no reluctance to bring the wines and dishes, all deliciously
appetising, to the table. The food was fine and excellent. That
evening the worthy man was served with all the dishes fit for any
king, count or emperor, and the young man with him.

3320 After the meal they both sat up talking together. Then the
serving-lads prepared the beds and the fruit to eat, for there was a
very choice supply: dates, figs and nutmegs, cloves and pomegra-
nates, and, to finish with, electuaries* with ginger from Alex-
andria, pliris archonticum, resumptivum and stomaticum. After
that they tasted many drinks: spiced wine without honey or pepper,
old mulberry wine and clear syrup. At all this, which was foreign to
the young man, he is quite amazed. Then the worthy man said:
"My good friend, it's time to retire for the night. If you don't mind,
I shall go to bed in my apartments in there; and when you please,
you can do so outside them. I have no strength in my limbs and so
shall have to be carried." Four strong, vigorous servants immediately emerge from the room, grasp by its four corners the spread
covering the couch on which the worthy man was sitting, and carry
him where they had to. Other youths had stayed with the young
man to attend him and look after his needs. When he wished, they
relieved him of his hose, undressed him and put him to bed between
fine white linen sheets.

3356 He slept until the break of day next morning, when the household had risen. But when he looked around, he could see no one
there and had to get up by himself, like it or not. So he gets up as
best he can when he sees he has to, and dresses without waiting for
help. Then he goes to retrieve his arms, finding them on the end of a
table, where they had been brought for him. Having fully armed
every limb, he goes round the doors of the rooms he had seen open

the previous night; but he went to them in vain, for he finds them securely shut. So he calls, with much beating and pushing: no one opens for him or utters a word. After a great deal of calling he comes to the hall door. Finding it open, he goes down the stairs to discover his horse saddled and sees his lance and shield by a wall opposite.

3383   Then he mounts and goes searching everywhere, but without finding a living soul there or seeing any squire or serving-lad. So he proceeds straight to the gate and finds the drawbridge lowered as it had been left for him so that, whenever he came there, nothing would stop him from passing straight over. He thinks, seeing the bridge lowered, that all the youths have gone into the forest to check their snares and traps. Not caring to wait any longer, he said he would go after them to see if any of them would tell him, if at all possible, the reason for the lance bleeding and where the grail is carried to. Then he went out through the gate; but before he was right off the bridge, he felt his horse's hooves that were still on it rise high up. His mount then made a great leap; for had it not jumped so well, both horse and rider would have been in a sorry plight. The young man turned his head to see what had happened and saw that the bridge had been raised. So he calls, but without receiving an answer. "Hey!" he says. "You who raised the bridge, say something to me! Where are you for me not to see you? Come forward so I can look at you! Then I'll ask you for information about something else I'd like to know." He was wasting his time talking like that, for no one was prepared to reply.

3422   He then heads for the forest, taking a path where he finds the fresh tracks of horses which had been along it. "I think", he says, "this is the way the people I'm looking for have gone." Then he gallops on through the woods as far as these tracks lead him until he chances upon a maiden under an oak tree weeping, crying out and lamenting like a miserable wretch. "Alas!" she says. "What a plight I'm in! It was an evil hour when I was born! A curse on the time I was conceived, for I've certainly never been so enraged at anything that may have happened! Had God willed it, I wouldn't now be holding my dead lover; for He would have done better to have him alive and me dead. Why did Death, who brings me such distress, take his soul rather than mine? What is life to me when I see the one I loved the most lying dead? With him gone, I really don't care about my life or my body. Oh Death, expel my soul from it, so that it can be maid and companion to his own, should that deign to have it!" In this way she was grieving for a knight she was holding and whose head had been struck off.

3456   Once he saw her, the young man rode straight up to her; and when he came close he greeted her and she him, with lowered head, still not ceasing her mourning. Then the young man enquired of her: "Damsel, who killed that knight lying in your lap?"—"Good sir," the maiden says, "a knight slew him this morning. – But there's one thing that strikes me and I find most astonishing; for, God preserve me, you could ride, so they say, forty leagues in the direction you've come from without finding any good, decent or salubrious place to stay; yet your horse has well-filled flanks and a smooth coat. If it had been washed and curried and bedded down in oats and hay, its belly wouldn't have been fuller or its coat sleeker. And you yourself, it seems to me, have been made very comfortable and well rested last night."—"My fair one," says he, "I swear that last night I was as comfortable as I could possibly be; and if it shows, that's as it should be. But if someone should give a loud shout here and now, where we are, he would be very clearly heard there where I spent the night. You're not very familiar with this district and haven't explored it all, for without any doubt I had the best lodging I've ever had."

3494   —"Ah then, sir, you stayed with the rich Fisher King!"—"Young lady, by our Saviour I don't know whether he's a fisherman or a king, but he's very wise and courtly. There's nothing more I can tell you except that very late yesterday evening I came across two men floating gently along in a boat. One of the two men was rowing and the other fishing with hook and line; and that one directed me to his house yesterday evening and gave me lodging." Then the maiden said: "My good sir, he is a king: I can vouch for that. But he was wounded and indeed maimed in a battle, so that he has not been able to manage for himself since; for he was struck by a javelin right through both thighs, and that still causes him so much pain that he can't mount a horse. But when he wants to enjoy himself or indulge in some pastime, he has himself put in a boat and goes fishing with hook and line. That's why he's called the Fisher King; and he takes his pleasure in this way because it would be quite impossible for him to bear or put up with any other sport. He can't hunt or go wildfowling, though he does have his wildfowlers, archers and huntsmen who go hunting with the bow in his forests. For that reason he's happy staying in this place near here, as no better retreat for his purposes is to be found in the whole world; and he's had a house built that is suitable for a rich king."

3534 —"Upon my word, damsel, what I hear you saying is true; for last evening I was quite amazed by that as soon as I came into his presence. I stood a little way from him, and he told me to come and sit beside him and that I shouldn't think him arrogant if he didn't rise to greet me, because he was incapable of it and lacked the strength. Then I went to sit at his side."—"Indeed, he honoured you greatly by placing you beside him. And tell me whether, when you did sit next to him, you saw the lance whose tip bleeds without there being any flesh or vein there."—"Whether I saw it? Yes, certainly."—"And did you ask why it bled?"—"I didn't speak a word, so help me God."—"Let me tell you, then, that you've acted very badly. And did you see the grail?"—"Yes, very well."—"And who was holding it?"—"A maiden."—"And where did she come from?"—"From a room."—"And where did she go?"—"She went into another room."—"Did anyone go ahead of the grail?"—"Yes."—"Who?"—"Just two youths."—"And what were they holding in their hands?"—"Candelabras full of candles."—"And after the grail, who came then?"—"Another maiden."—"Holding what?"—"A little silver carving-dish."—"Did you ask the people where they were going like this?"—"The question never passed my lips."

3571 —"So much the worse, then, so help me God! What's your name, my friend?" Then he, who did not know his name, intuitively answered that he was called Perceval the Welshman,* not knowing whether he spoke the truth or not. But what he said was true, though he did not know. And when the damsel heard it, she stood up in front of him and said to him: "Your name is changed, my good friend!"—"In what way?"—"Perceval the wretched! Ah, unhappy Perceval, how unfortunate you are now not to have asked all this! For you would have brought such benefit to the good king who is crippled that he would have completely regained the use of his limbs and governed his land; and from that you would have reaped such profit! But now you may be sure that many misfortunes will befall both you and others. You may know that this happened to you because of the wrong you did your mother, for she died of grief on your account. I know you better than you me, for you don't know who I am. I was brought up with you in your mother's home for a very long time. I'm your full cousin and you're mine. And I'm no less distressed at your great misfortune in not learning what was done with the grail or where it's taken than I am for your mother who is dead and for this knight whom I much loved and cherished, since he called me his dear sweetheart and loved me like a noble, loyal knight."

3612 "Ah, cousin," says Perceval, "if what you've told me is true, tell me how you know it."—"I know it", says the damsel, "for a fact, having myself seen her committed to the earth."—"Now may God in his goodness have mercy on her soul!" says Perceval. "You've told me a terrible story. But since she's been buried, why should I go seeking any further? Because I was going that way for no other reason than that I wanted to see her. I must take another road. And if you wished to come with me, I'd be very glad; for this man lying dead here will be of no more use to you, I promise you. The dead to the dead, the living to the living. Let's go off together, you and I. It seems to me great folly on your part to watch over this dead man all alone like this. But let's follow the one who killed him; and I promise and pledge that, if I can catch him, either he'll make me give him best or I him."

3638 Then she, unable to hold back the deep grief she feels in her heart, says to him: "My good friend, on no account will I go away with you or abandon him before I have him buried. If you take my advice, you'll follow that metalled road over there, because that's the way taken by the wicked, ruthless knight who slew my sweet lover. But I didn't say that, so help me God, because I want you to go after him; and yet I wish him as ill as if he'd killed me.

3654 "But where did that sword come from that's hanging at your left side and has never yet spilt a man's blood or needed to be drawn? I know well where it was made and also who forged it. Take care never to rely on it, for it will certainly betray you when you get into a great fight, since it will fly into pieces."—"My fair cousin, one of my good host's nieces sent it to him last evening, and he gave it to me: I think I'm very well off to have it. But you've really alarmed me if what you've said to me is true. Tell me now, if you know: should it happen to get broken, could it be repaired?"—"Yes, but not without great hardship for whoever could find his way to the lake below Cotoatre.* There you could have it beaten out again, retempered and made whole, if chance should lead you there. Go to no one but Trebuchet, a smith of that name, for he made it and will refashion it or it will never be restored, no matter who tries. Make sure that no one else tries his hand at it, for he wouldn't be able to succeed."—"Indeed," says Perceval, "I'd be extremely sorry if it broke." Then he leaves, and she stays behind, unwilling to part from the body of the one whose death fills her heart with grief.

3691 Continuing along the path, he follows a line of tracks until he comes across a thin, weary palfrey going at walking pace ahead of him. The palfrey was so skinny and wretched that it seemed to him to have fallen into bad hands. It appeared to have been overworked and underfed, just as one treats a borrowed horse, which is worked hard during the day and poorly looked after at night. That was how the palfrey looked: it was so thin that it shivered as if chilled to the bone. Its whole neck was bald, and its ears hung down. Every cur and mastiff was anticipating a feast of offal, for it had nothing at all but its hide over its bones. There was a woman's saddle on its back, and on its head the kind of bridle appropriate for such an animal.

3715 On its back was a maiden more wretched than was ever seen. Even so, she would have been very beautiful and attractive had all been well with her; but she was in such a poor condition that of the dress she wore not a palm's breadth was intact: on the contrary, her breasts protruded through the rents in front. It was held together in places with knots and rough stitching. Her flesh seemed hacked to pieces as if by a lancet, cracked and burnt as it was by heat, dry winds and frost. She was bare-headed and without a wimple, so that her face was visible, showing many ugly traces where her continual tears had made numerous tracks, running down to her breast and then flowing over her dress right to her knees. A person in such a plight might well have very bitter grief in her heart.

3740 As soon as Perceval sees her he gallops swiftly towards her. She gathers her clothing tightly round her to cover her flesh; but then she inevitably opened up holes, and by covering herself in one place she closes one hole and opens a hundred. Pale, haggard and wretched as she is, Perceval catches up with her and, as he does so, hears her bitterly lamenting her unhappy and distressing situation.

"Oh God," she says, "may it never be Your pleasure to let me live long in this state! My wretched condition has lasted far too long and I've suffered too much adversity without deserving it. God, as You know well that I have merited nothing of this, send me, if it please You, someone who will relieve me of this distress; or else deliver me Yourself from the man who compels me to live in such shame and in whom I find no mercy. I can't escape from him alive, and he's quite unwilling to kill me. I don't know why he desires my company in this fashion, except that he so hankers after my shame and misery. If he had known for sure that I had deserved it, he should have had mercy on me once I'd paid so dearly for my fault, if I pleased him in any way whatsoever. But I certainly don't please him in the least, when he makes me drag out so hard a life at his heels without caring at all!"

3778 Then, having come up with her, Perceval said: "God save you, my fair one!" When the damsel hears him, she hangs her head and replies in a low voice: "You sir, who have greeted me: may your heart have what it desires – yet it's wrong of me to say that!" Then Perceval, blushing with shame, replied: "Why, damsel, in God's name? Indeed, I don't suppose or believe that I've ever seen you before or wronged you in any way."—"Yes you have!" says she. "For I'm so wretched and in such trouble that no one ought to greet me: I can only sweat with anguish when anybody addresses or looks at me."—"Truly," says Perceval, "I wasn't conscious of this misdeed. I certainly didn't come here to shame or insult you, but this is the way my road brought me. Then, having seen you in such distress, so poor and naked, I'd never have been glad at heart unless I'd learnt the truth: what happened to reduce you to such grief and hardship?"—"Oh sir," she says, "have pity on me! Go away! Be off from here and leave me in peace! It's wrong of you to have stopped here; but it will be sensible of you to flee."

3812 —"I'd like to know", he says, "what fear or threat requires me to flee, when nobody is chasing me."—"Sir," she says, "don't be annoyed, but flee as fast as you can, lest the Haughty Knight of the Heath, who asks nothing better than combats and fighting, should surprise us together. For if he found you just here, he'd certainly kill you on the spot. He's so annoyed when anyone stops me that, provided he arrives in time, nobody who holds me back talking to me can get away with his head. He killed one man only a short time ago. But first he tells them all why he treats me so basely and has inflicted this wretchedness on me."

3831 As they were talking thus, the Haughty Knight emerged from the wood riding like lightning through the sand and dust, shouting at the top of his voice: "It's unlucky for you to be riding along with that maiden! You may be sure your end has come for having kept her back and stopped her for a single pace! But I shan't kill you before I've informed you for what cause, for what misdeed I'm making her live in such great shame. So listen now, and you'll hear the whole story. Quite recently, I'd gone into the woods leaving this damsel in a tent of mine; and I loved no one but her alone. Then, as it happened, a Welsh lad turned up there. I don't know who he was or where he went; but he went so far as to kiss her by force, as she assured me. If she lied to me, then what stood in his way? And if he did kiss her against her will, didn't he have all he desired afterwards? Yes: no man would try to kiss her without doing anything more, for one thing leads to the other.

3860 "If someone kisses a woman and goes no further once they are alone together, then in my opinion it's his own fault. A woman who freely surrenders her lips gives the rest very readily to anybody who seriously makes the effort. And though she may well defend herself, it's well known without any doubt that a woman wants to be the victor in everything except in that single contest when she has the man by the throat, scratching and biting and struggling, yet wishing to be overcome. Thus she defends herself yet grows impatient, being too timid to yield, yet wanting to be taken by force; then afterwards she expresses neither thanks nor gratitude.

3877 "That's why I think he lay with her. And he took from her a ring of mine that she was wearing on her finger and made off with it: I'm annoyed at that. But first he drank and ate his fill of strong wine and good pies that I was having kept on one side for me. For that my love is reaping such a decorous reward as can be seen! Anyone who acts foolishly must pay for it, so that he takes care not to do the same again. I'd really every reason to be annoyed when I came back and discovered this; and I took a firm oath, and quite rightly, that her palfrey would eat no oats or be bled or re-shod, and that she would have no tunic or mantle other than what she was wearing at that time until I should get the better of the person who had raped her, and kill him and cut off his head."

3899 When Perceval had listened to him he gave him word for word
in reply: "My friend, you may know quite certainly that she has
done her penance; for I'm the one who kissed her against her will
and to her great sorrow. And I took her ring from her finger: that's
all that happened – I did nothing more. I also ate, I admit, one of the
pies and half of another and drank as much of the wine as I wanted.
I didn't act foolishly in that!"—"By my head," says the Haughty
Knight, "that's an amazing thing you've said, admitting to this
affair. Now you've really deserved death, having made a true
confession!"—"My death's not yet as near as you think," says
Perceval.

3918 Thereupon, without another word, they have their horses
charge at each other, and clash together so furiously that they
smash their lances to splinters. They both quit their saddles as they
bring each other down; but they quickly jump back to their feet,
draw their swords from the scabbards and exchange great blows.*
The encounter was violent and hard. I do not wish to describe it any
further, since that seems to me wasted effort; but they fight on
together until the Haughty Knight of the Heath gives in and begs
for mercy. Perceval, never forgetting how the worthy man
entreated him never to slay a knight after he had asked him for
mercy, said to him: "By my faith, knight, I shall never have mercy
on you until you have pity on your sweetheart; for she hadn't
deserved the hardship you made her suffer, I can swear to that."
The knight, who loved her more than his own eye, responded:
"Good sir, I'm prepared to make whatever amends to her you
please. There's nothing you can command that I'm not ready to do.
My heart is sad and melancholy because of the hardship I've made
her bear."

3950 —"Then go," he says, "to the nearest house of yours in these
parts and have her bathed and rested until she's cured and well
again. Then make yourself ready and take her, well equipped and
attired, to King Arthur, whom you must greet from me. Then place
yourself at his disposal, just as you are on leaving here. Should he
ask who sends you, tell him it's he whom he made a red knight on
the advice and recommendation of my lord Kay the seneschal.
Then at court you must tell of the penance and suffering you've
made your damsel undergo, in the full hearing of all present, so
that every man and woman hears it, including the queen and her

maidens, of whom she has many beautiful ones with her. But above all the others there is one of them I think highly of, to whom Kay, because she laughed for me, gave such a slap that he quite stunned her. I order you to seek her out and tell her I assure her that I shall never be persuaded to enter any court held by King Arthur until I've so avenged her as to fill her with joy and gladness."

3981   He replies that he will very gladly go there and say everything according to his instructions; and there shall be no delay except for the purpose of first resting his damsel and providing her with whatever she would need. He would be very happy to take Perceval himself to let him rest and to heal and attend to his injuries and wounds. "Go now, and may good fortune go with you," says Perceval. "Concern yourself with other things, for I shall seek lodging elsewhere." With that no more was said.

3996   Neither the one nor the other waits there any longer; but they part without more ado. That evening the knight has his beloved bathed and richly dressed; and he takes such good care of her that she has regained all her beauty. After that they take the direct road together for Caerleon, where King Arthur was holding court, though on a very intimate scale, for only three thousand knights of repute were there! The newcomer, leading his damsel, went to King Arthur to constitute himself a prisoner in the sight of all; and when he had come before him, he said: "Good lord King, I am your prisoner to do whatever you wish. And this is only right and proper, for those were my instructions from the young man who asked and obtained from you crimson arms." The moment the king hears this, he understands very well what he is referring to. "Disarm yourself, good sir," he says; "and may joy and good fortune attend the one who has presented you to me! And be welcome yourself: for his sake you'll be cherished and honoured in my house."

4026   —"Sire, there's one thing I want to tell you before I'm disarmed. Only I'd like the queen and her maidens to come and hear the news I've brought you; for it will never be told until the one has come who was struck on the cheek merely for uttering one laugh – that was her only misdeed!" Thus he finishes what he has to say, and the king hears that he is to summon the queen before him. He does call her; and she comes, and with her all her maidens, holding each other by the hand. When the queen was seated beside her lord

King Arthur, the Haughty Knight of the Heath said to her: "My lady, a knight I esteem highly and who vanquished me in armed combat sends you his greetings. I don't know what more I can say of him; but he sends you my beloved, this maiden here."—"I'm very grateful to him, my friend," says the queen. Then he describes to her all the disgrace and shame he had inflicted on her for a long time, and the suffering she had endured, and his reason for his action. He told her everything, concealing nothing.

4059 They then showed him the girl struck by Kay the seneschal; and he said to her: "Maiden, the one who sent me here asked me to greet you on his behalf. And I was never to remove my leggings and boots from my feet until I had told you that he would forfeit God's aid should he ever on any account enter a court held by King Arthur before avenging you for the slap, the cuff you were given because of him." Then, on hearing him, the fool jumps to his feet and cries out: "Kay, Kay! God bless me, you'll really pay for that, and very soon!" The king for his part follows the fool in saying: "Ah Kay, it was really courtly of you to mock that young man! With your mockery you've taken him from me, so that I don't expect ever to see him again." The king then had his prisoner sit down in front of him. He excuses him from captivity, and after that orders him to be disarmed.

4086 My lord Gawain, who was sitting at the king's right hand, asks: "In God's name, sire, who can that be who, in a single armed combat, defeated such a good knight as this? For I've never heard any knight named in all the Isles of the Sea, or seen or known one who could compete with this one in arms or chivalry."—"Good nephew," says the king, "I don't know him, yet I've seen him. But when I did see him, it didn't occur to me to ask him about anything. He told me to make him a knight on the spot; and, seeing his handsome, attractive appearance, I said to him: 'Gladly, brother; but dismount for a while until you've been brought a set of entirely gilt arms.' Then he answered that he would never take them or dismount until he had red arms. And he added another amazing thing: that he would accept no arms other than those of the knight who was making off with my golden cup.

4114 "Then Kay, offensive as he was, still is and always will be, ever reluctant to say a good word, told him: 'Brother, the king grants you those arms and freely gives them to you, so go and get them at once!' The young man, not understanding the joke, thought he was telling the truth: he went after the knight and killed him with a javelin cast. I don't know how the fight and skirmish began except that the Red Knight from the Forest of Quinqueroi struck him very arrogantly with his lance, I'm not sure why; and then the young man pierced him right through the eye with his javelin, and so killed him and obtained the arms. After that he's pleased me so well with his fine service that, by my lord Saint David whom they worship and pray to in Wales, I shall never lie for two nights together in chamber or hall until I know if he's alive on land or sea, but will set out at once to go in search of him!" As soon as the king had made this vow, everyone was in no doubt that it only remained to start off.

4144 Then you might have seen sheets, bedspreads and pillows packed into chests, coffers filled, packhorses loaded and carts and wagons laden, for they are not sparing in taking with them tents, pavilions and awnings. A learned, well-lettered clerk could not write a list in a whole day of all the harness and other equipment that was immediately made ready; for the king leaves Caerleon as though he is going on campaign, and all the nobles follow him. Not even a maiden is left there without being taken by the queen in a show of opulence and splendour. That night they encamped in a meadow beside a forest.

4162 In the morning there was a good snowfall, and the countryside was bitterly cold.* Early that day Perceval had risen as usual with the intention of seeking adventure and deeds of chivalry; and he headed straight towards the frozen, snow-covered meadow where the king's host was encamped. But before he reached the tents, a flock of wild geese, dazzled by the snow, came flying over. He saw and heard them; for they were honking as they went on account of a falcon that came swooping swiftly at them until it found one of them on its own, separated from the flock. It struck at this one and caught it so hard that it knocked it to the ground. But it was too early in the morning, so it flew off without bothering to pounce and secure it. Perceval begins to spur in the direction he had seen the flight. The goose was wounded in the neck, and from it came three drops of blood, which spread out over the whiteness to look like natural colouring. The goose was not injured or hurt enough to remain on the ground until Perceval arrived shortly after, by which time it had already flown.

4194 When he saw the disturbed snow where the goose had lain and
the blood that was visible round it, he leant on his lance to gaze at
this sight; for the blood and snow together have for him the
appearance of the fresh colouring on his beloved's face. By these
thoughts he becomes carried away; for in her face the flush of
crimson on the white resembled the appearance of these three
drops of blood on the white snow. As he continued to gaze he
thought, to his delight, that he saw the fresh complexion of his fair
love's face.

4211 Perceval spends all the early morning musing on those drops
until squires came out of the tents and, seeing him in his reverie,
supposed he was dozing. Before the king, who was still sleeping in
his tent, awoke, the squires encountered outside the royal pavilion
Sagremor who, because of his rashness, was called the Impetuous.
"Tell me," he says, "without hiding anything: why have you come
here so early?"—"Sir," they say, "outside this camp we've seen a
knight dozing on his charger."—"Is he armed?"—"Yes
indeed."—"I'll go and talk to him," says he, "and bring him along
to the court." Sagremor runs at once to the king's tent and wakes
him. "Sire," he says, "there's a knight outside dozing on the heath
over there." The king then orders him to go, asking urgently that he
should bring him back and not leave him there. At once Sagremor
called for his arms to be produced and asked for his horse too. His
orders were promptly obeyed, and he quickly had himself well
armed. In full armour he left the camp and rode until he reached the
knight.

4244 "Sir," he says, "you must come to the king!" The other does
not move and appears not to hear him. He repeats his words and is
met with silence. He grows angry and says: "By Saint Peter the
Apostle, you'll come there, like it or not! I'm very sorry I ever asked
you to; for that was a waste of my words." Then he unfurls the
pennon wound round his lance, and the horse beneath him springs
forward as he takes his distance opposite the knight, then shouts to
him to be on guard, because he will strike him unless he defends
himself. Perceval glances towards him and sees him coming at the
charge. Then he comes quite out of his reverie and in turn spurs
forward at him. As they clash together, Sagremor shatters his lance.
Perceval's does not break or bend, but he drives it with such force
that he topples him in the middle of the field. And his horse

proceeds to take flight, head in air, making for the encampment. Then those who were getting up in their tents saw it; and whoever did was most upset.

4274 Thereupon Kay, who could never stop himself from making wicked comments, made a joke of it and said to the king: "My good lord, see how Sagremor's coming back! He's holding the knight by the bridle and leading him here against his will!"—"Kay," says the king, "it's unkind of you to mock at worthy men in this way. Now you go there, and we'll see how you'll do better than he." — "Indeed," says Kay, "I'm delighted that you'd like me to go; and I'll bring him back without fail – by force, whether he wants it or not. And I'll make him give his name." He then has himself properly armed. This done, he mounts and goes off to the one who was gazing so intently at the three drops of blood that nothing else concerned him. Kay shouts to him from some distance: "Vassal, vassal, come to the king! You'll come now, by my faith, or else pay very dearly!" Perceval, hearing himself threatened, turns his horse's head and digs in his steel spurs to make for Kay, whose own approach is far from slow. Each of them wants to do well, and there is nothing half-hearted about their encounter. Kay strikes and, as he puts all his strength into the blow, his lance breaks and crumbles like bark. *And Perceval does not lack resolution: he strikes him above the boss of his shield and knocks him down so hard on to a rock that he dislocates his collar-bone and breaks the bone between his right elbow and armpit like a dry twig, just as predicted by the fool, who had often foretold it. The fool's prophecy had come true.

4317 In his agony Kay faints; and his horse takes flight and heads for the tents at a fast trot. The Britons see the horse returning without the seneschal. Then youths mount, and ladies and knights set out and, finding the seneschal in a swoon, are convinced he is dead, whereupon they all, men and ladies alike, began to mourn him bitterly. And Perceval leans once more on his lance, contemplating those three drops. The king, however, was deeply worried about the wounded seneschal. His grieving and sorrow continued until he was told to have no fear, for he will make a complete recovery provided he has a doctor who knows how to go about putting his collar-bone back into place and setting his broken bone. Then the king, who is very fond of him and, in his heart, loves him well, sends him a very expert doctor and two maidens trained by him; and they put back his collar-bone and bandage his arm, having joined the shattered bone. They then carried him to the king's tent and did much to comfort him, telling him he will get quite well again and must not worry about anything.

4349 My lord Gawain then says to the king: "Sire, sire, so help me God, it's not right, as you know well and have yourself always quite properly said and maintained, that one knight should, as these two have done, distract another from his thoughts, whatever they may be. I don't know if they were in the wrong; but what is certain is that they've come to pay for it. The knight was brooding over some loss he's suffered; or his love has been stolen from him, so he's upset and dejected about it. But if that were your pleasure, I would go to see how he's behaving; and should I find him in the situation of having come out of his reverie, I'd ask and beg him to come here to you."

4370 These words enraged Kay, and he said: "Ah, my lord Gawain, you'll lead that knight by the bridle, even if he objects: that will be done if you can manage it and you don't have to fight. You've taken many a captive that way! Once the knight is exhausted and has had enough of the combat, that's when a worthy man should ask permission and have the opportunity to go and gain the victory! Ah Gawain, a hundred curses on my neck if you're at all so foolish that there isn't a great deal to be learnt from you! You're very good at finding a buyer for your words, extremely fair and polished as they are. Will you ever say anything quite outrageous, wicked or arrogant? A curse on anyone who has thought that or thinks it now! I don't! You really could do this job in a silk tunic: there will be no need for you to draw a sword or break a lance. You can pride yourself that he'll do what you want, so long as your tongue doesn't fail you before you've said: 'God save you, sir, and give you joy and health!' Not that I'm trying to teach you anything. You'll know well enough how to smooth him down like stroking a cat; and people will say: 'Now my lord Gawain's fighting fiercely!'" – "Ah, Sir Kay," says Gawain, "you might have put that more politely. Do you want to take out your anger and bad temper on me? I swear I'll bring him back, my dear good friend, if I possibly can. I'll never have my arm damaged or my collar-bone put out of joint, for I don't fancy that kind of payment."

4413 —"Now you go there, nephew," said the king. "That's a very courtly thing you've said. Bring him back if at all possible. But take all your arms, for you shall not go unarmed." That man who has a name and reputation for all the virtues had himself armed straight away and, mounted on a strong, agile horse, came directly to the knight who was leaning on his lance, still not tired of the reverie that gave him great pleasure. However, the sunshine had made two of the drops of blood lying on the snow vanish, and the third was fading away; and so the knight's concentration on them was not as deep as it had been. Then my lord Gawain approaches him at a very gentle amble without any appearance of hostility and said: "Sir, I would have greeted you were I as sure of your feelings as of my own. But I can venture to tell you that I'm a messenger from the king who, through me, desires and requests you to come and speak with him."—"There have already been two," says Perceval, "who were after my life and wanted to lead me off like a captive. I was so engrossed in a very pleasurable thought that anyone forcing me out of it was simply asking for trouble. For just here on that spot were three drops of fresh blood bright against the whiteness; and as I gazed at them it seemed to me that I was seeing the fresh colour of my fair love's face; and I would never have wished to relinquish that thought."

4457 —"Truly," says my lord Gawain, "that was no base thought, but a very courtly, tender one; and whoever turned your heart away from it was wicked and stupid. But now I'm very anxious and eager to know what you would like to do; for I'd be delighted to take you to the king, if that would not displease you."—"Now tell me first, my dear good friend," says Perceval, "if Kay the seneschal is there."—"Yes, indeed he's there. And let me tell you he was the one who jousted with you just now. But the joust cost him so dear that you shattered his right arm, though you don't know it, and dislocated his collar-bone."—"Then I think I've well recompensed the maiden he struck."

4478 When my lord Gawain heard that, he started with astonishment and said: "God save me, sir, you're just the one the king was looking for! What is your name, sir?"—"Perceval, sir; and what's yours?"—"Sir, you may be quite sure that I was baptised with the name of Gawain."—"Gawain?"—"Yes, truly, good sir." Perceval was overjoyed and said: "Sir, I've indeed heard people speak of you in many places, and I would like us two to become friends, if that's pleasing and agreeable to you."—"Indeed," says my lord Gawain, "that pleases me no less than you – more, I think." And Perceval replies: "Then, by my faith, I'll go gladly where you wish, for that's only right; and I have a much higher opinion of myself now I'm your friend." Then they go to embrace each other and set about unlacing helmets, coifs and ventails, and they pull down the mail. So they come rejoicing on their way.

4506 Then some youths, seeing them making much of each other, run at once from a low hill where they were standing and come before the king. "Sire, sire," they exclaim, "my lord Gawain really is bringing the knight, and they're making a great fuss of each other!" There is nobody hearing the news who does not dash out of his tent and go to meet them. Then Kay said to his lord the king: "Now my lord Gawain, your nephew, has the distinction and the honour. The combat was very hard and perilous, unless I'm lying! He's returning just as cheerful as he left, for he never took a blow from anyone else, and no one felt any blow of his, and he hasn't given the lie to anybody. So it's right that he should have the distinction and credit for it, and that people should say he's accomplished what we others couldn't, though we put all our strength and effort into it." So as usual Kay spoke his mind, right or wrong.

4534 My lord Gawain has no wish to take his companion to court in his armour, but wants him completely disarmed. In his tent he has him stripped of his armour; and from one of his own chests a chamberlain of his takes an outfit, which he offers him as a gift. Once he was elegantly dressed in the tunic and mantle, which went admirably on him and suited him well, they proceed together, hand in hand, to the king where he was seated in front of his tent. "Sire," my lord Gawain says to the king, "I'm bringing you the person whose acquaintance, I believe, you would gladly have made a full fortnight ago. I present him to you. See, here he is!"

4554 —"Many thanks to you, dear nephew," says the king, who goes so far as to jump to his feet to greet him with the words: "Welcome, good sir! Now I beg you to tell me what I should call you."—"By my faith, I'll never keep that from you, my good lord king," says Perceval. "My name is Perceval the Welshman."—"Ah, Perceval, my dear good friend, now you've been brought to my court, you'll never leave it if I have my way. Since I first saw you I've grieved over you a great deal; for I didn't know the advancement God had in store for you. Yet it was accurately predicted to the knowledge of my whole court by the maiden and the fool struck by Kay the seneschal; and you've proved their prophecies entirely true. There's now no one in any doubt of the fact that the report I've heard of your chivalry is true."

4579 As he spoke the queen arrived, having heard the news of the young man's arrival. No sooner had Perceval seen her and been told who she was, and had seen coming after her the damsel who had laughed when he had looked at her, than he at once went up to them and said: "May God grant joy and honour to the fairest, the best of all ladies alive, as witness all who see her and all who have seen her!" And the queen replies: "And welcome to you too as to a knight proven in high and splendid prowess!" Then Perceval greets in turn the maiden who had laughed for him; and embracing her, he said: "My fair one, should you need me, I would be the knight whose aid would never fail you." The damsel thanks him for that.

4603 It was with great rejoicing that the king, the queen and the nobles took Perceval the Welshman to Caerleon, where they returned that day.* They spent the whole night in celebration and the following day too before, on the next day, they saw a damsel approaching on a tawny mule, holding a whip in her right hand. The damsel's hair was plaited in two twisted black pigtails; and if what is said and related in the book is true, there was never any creature so completely hideous, even in Hell. You have never seen iron as black as were her neck and hands, and yet that was the least part of her ugliness. For her eyes were two holes as small as those of a rat; her nose was like that of a monkey or cat and her lips like a donkey's or bullock's, whilst her teeth were so yellow that they looked like egg-yolk; and she was bearded like a billy-goat. She had a hump in the middle of her chest, and her spine was crook-shaped. Her loins and shoulders were splendid for leading a dance! She had a lump on her back and hips twisted just like two osiers: splendidly made for leading a jig!

4638 The damsel dashes up on her mule in front of the knights: never before had any such damsel been seen in a royal court! She gives a general greeting to the king and all his nobles, except for Perceval alone; but to him, as she sat on her tawny mule, she said: "Ah, Perceval! Fortune is bald behind, but has hair in front;* and a curse on anyone who greets you or calls down any blessings on you! For when you met Fortune, you did not welcome her: you entered the

Fisher King's house and saw the bleeding lance; yet you found it so hard to open your mouth and speak that you were unable to ask why that drop of blood issues from the tip of its bright head; nor, when you saw the grail, did you ask or enquire what worthy man was served from it. He is a wretch indeed who sees as fine an opportunity as could be wished, yet goes on waiting for a better one to come. You are that wretch who saw that it was the time and place to speak, yet held your tongue, though you had every chance. It is unfortunate for you that you remained silent; for had you asked, the rich king, now in distress, would at once have had his wound quite healed and would peacefully rule his land, of which he will now never hold any part. And do you know the fate of the king who will hold no land or be healed of his wounds? Through him ladies will lose their husbands, lands will be laid waste, maidens left orphaned and helpless, and many knights will perish: all these evils will be of your doing."

4684 Then the damsel said to the king: "Don't be offended, O King, if I leave now, for I must take my lodging far from here tonight. I don't know if you have heard tell of the Proud Castle, but that is where I have to go tonight. In that castle are five hundred and sixty-six eminent knights, and there is none of them, you may be sure, who is not accompanied by his beloved, a noble, courtly, beautiful lady. I give you this information because none who go there fail to find a joust or a combat. Whoever wants chivalric action will not be disappointed if he seeks it there. But if anyone wants to gain the high esteem of the entire world, I think I know the place and locality where it could be best achieved, if there were someone of sufficient daring. On the hill below Montesclaire a damsel is besieged: whoever could raise that siege and rescue the damsel would gain great honour and win universal praise; and the one to whom God granted such good fortune would be able to gird on quite safely the Sword with the Strange Baldric." With that the damsel fell silent, having said all she wished, and departed without another word.

4718 At that my lord Gawain leaps up, saying he will go there and do all in his power to rescue the damsel. And Gifflet the son of Do said that for his part he would go with God's aid before the Proud Castle. "And I shall go and climb the Dolorous Mount," says Kahedin, "and won't stop until I get there." Then Perceval spoke quite differently, saying that as long as he lived he would not spend two nights in a single lodging, or hear news of any adventurous passage without going by way of it, or of any knight worth more than one or two others without going to fight him, until he discovered who was served from the grail and had found the bleeding lance and been told the certain truth as to why it bleeds. He will not give up, whatever the hardship.* Thus up to fifty of them rose, pledging and declaring and swearing to each other that they will not learn of any marvel or adventure without going in search of it, however dreadful the land it was in.

4747 While they were getting ready and arming in the hall, through the door enters Guigambresil bearing a golden shield, on which was an azure band. The band covered precisely a third of the shield, accurately measured. Guigambresil recognised the king and duly greeted him; but instead of greeting Gawain, he accused him of felony, saying: "Gawain, you slew my lord and did so without challenging him. For that you've incurred shame, reproach and blame, and I charge you with treason. And all these lords may be assured that I've not told a word of a lie."

4766 Hearing this, my lord Gawain jumped to his feet covered in shame; and his brother Agravain the Arrogant springs up and restrains him, saying: "In God's name, good sir, don't bring shame on your family! I'll defend you from this blame and disgrace imputed to you by this knight: that I promise you." Gawain replied: "Brother, no man other than myself will defend me from it; and I should act in my own defence, because he's accusing no one but me. But had I done the knight any wrong and was aware of it, I'd be very glad to sue for peace and make him such amends that all his friends and mine ought to be satisfied. Assuming, though, what he's said to be a slander, I contest it and offer my surety either here or wherever he pleases." Then Guigambresil said he would prove foul, base treason against him, before forty days were up, before the King of Escavalon who, in his judgment and opinion, was more handsome than Absalom. "And I," says Gawain, "pledge you that I'll follow you straight away; and there we shall see who'll be in the right."

4797 Guigambresil leaves at once, and my lord Gawain prepares to follow him without delay. Anyone with a good horse and good lance, or a good helmet or good sword offered it to him; but he was unwilling to take with him anything belonging to somebody else. He did take along seven squires, seven horses and two shields. Before he left the court very bitter grief was shown for him, many breasts were beaten, much hair was torn, and many faces were marked with scratches. There was no lady, however prudent, who did not vent her great anguish on his account. Many women and men express their deep sorrow. Then my lord Gawain departs. You will hear me tell at some length of the adventures he encountered.

4816 First he sees a party of knights crossing a heath; and he asks a squire who was following them on his own, leading a Spanish horse and with a shield hung at his neck: "Tell me, squire, who these people are who are going this way." He answers: "That's Meliant of Liz, my lord, a gallant, bold knight."—"Are you his man?"—"No, sir: Droés d'Avés is the name of my lord, who is not at all his inferior."—"Upon my word," says my lord Gawain, "I know Droés d'Avés well. Where's he going? Don't keep anything from me."—"My lord, he's going to a tournament undertaken by Meliant of Liz against Tibaut of Tintagel; and I'd be glad if you went into that castle to join against those outside."—"God!" said my lord Gawain then. "But wasn't Meliant of Liz brought up in Tibaut's house?"

4841 —"Yes, sir, as God's my saviour, for his father loved Tibaut as a dear friend and placed so much confidence in him that, as he lay on his death-bed, he entrusted his small son to him. Then he brought him up and took as good care of him as he could until the day when he courted a daughter of his and asked for her love; but she said she would never grant it to him as long as he was a squire. He, being so eager for it, had himself knighted at once and then resumed his suit. 'Upon my word,' says the maiden, 'it's quite out of the question until you've performed before me so many feats of arms and jousted enough for my love to have been earned dearly; for things one gets for nothing are not as sweet or charming as those one pays for. Challenge my father to a tournament if you want my love, because I want to be quite certain that my love would be well placed if I granted it to you.' As she stipulated, he has undertaken the tournament; for Love wields such great authority over those in his power that they wouldn't dare to refuse anything he cares to command. And you'd be very dilatory if you didn't go in there, because you'd be very useful to them if you were prepared to help them." He answered: "Go now, brother! You'd do well to follow your lord and say no more about it."

4882 He left at once; and my lord Gawain journeyed on, continuing to ride towards Tintagel, since there was no other way for him to go. Tibaut had assembled all his close relatives and cousins and summoned all his neighbours; and everybody had arrived, the high and the low, youths and greybeards alike. Tibaut's close counsellors, however, had advised him against engaging in the tournament with his lord Meliant,* since they were very afraid that he wanted totally to destroy them. So he had all the entrances to the fortress well walled up and cemented over: the gates were tightly blocked with hard stone and mortar and had no other keeper. They had, though, refrained from walling up one small postern, whose door was hardly of glass! It was of copper, made to last for ever, secured with a beam and reinforced with a full wagon-load of iron. My lord Gawain approached that gate, riding behind all his equipment, having either to go that way or turn back, since there was no other road or track for seven full leagues around. Seeing the postern shut, he goes into a meadow enclosed with stakes below the keep, then dismounts under an oak tree, from which he hangs his shields. There he is seen by the people in the castle, most of whom were very unhappy that the tournament had been cancelled.

4922 In the fortress, however, was an old vavasour who was very wise and respected, well endowed in land and lineage; and nothing he said was ever disbelieved there, however it might turn out. He saw the approaching men, as they had been pointed out to him when they were still quite some distance away, before they had entered the enclosure; and he went to Tibaut, saying: "My lord, as God's my saviour I do believe I've seen two knights, companions of King Arthur, coming in here. Two distinguished men command great respect, for even one can win a tournament. And my advice would be for us to go confidently to the tourney, because you have good knights, good men-at-arms and good archers who will kill their horses. I'm sure our opponents will come to joust in front of this gate; and if their pride does bring them here, the gain will be ours and the loss and damage theirs."

4949 Following the advice he gave, Tibaut freely allowed anyone who wished to put on their armour and ride forth fully armed. Now his knights are overjoyed, and squires run for the arms and horses, which they saddle. Then the ladies and maidens go and sit on the highest vantage-points to watch the tournament. Below them in the plain they saw my lord Gawain's equipment and thought at first there were two knights because they saw two shields hanging from the oak. And they say that, having climbed up there so as to see everything, they will be lucky enough to see these two knights who will arm in front of them. That is what some of them said; but there were others who declared: "Good Lord God! That knight has so much equipment and so many chargers that there's quite enough for two; yet he has no companion with him. What will he do with two shields? The knight has never been seen who carried two shields at once." So it seems to them quite amazing if this knight, who is on his own, is going to carry both of the shields.

4981 As they were passing these comments and the knights were riding out, Tibaut's elder daughter, who had instigated the tournament, climbed to the top of the keep. With the older daughter came the younger, who clothed her arms so elegantly that in consequence she was known as the Maiden with the Small Sleeves, since they fitted closely to her arms. Along with Tibaut's two daughters, all the ladies and maidens climb up together. Then the tournament promptly assembled in front of the castle. But no one there was as good looking as Meliant of Liz, according to his beloved, who was saying to the ladies all around her: "Ladies, I've no reason to lie to you: truly I've never looked with as much pleasure at a knight as at Meliant of Liz. Isn't it really a joy and delight to see such a handsome knight? Someone who bears himself so well is just made for sitting on a horse and carrying a lance and shield." Then her sister, who was sitting beside her, told her there was a more handsome one there. That made her furious, and she rose to strike her; but the ladies pulled her back, holding her and keeping her from hitting her, to her great sorrow.

5017 The tournament then begins, with many lances broken and sword-blows struck and many a knight felled. But you may be sure that anyone jousting with Meliant of Liz pays very dearly because, incapable of withstanding his lance, he is knocked to the hard ground. And if his lance is snapped, he delivers great blows with his sword, performing better than any on either side. This fills his beloved with such joy that she cannot keep silent, but says: "Look, ladies, at these marvels such as you've never seen or heard of before! Look at the best young knight you've ever set your eyes on, for he's more handsome and successful than anyone in the tournament!" The little girl said: "I can see one who's more handsome and probably better." At once her sister makes for her, burning and seething with anger, and says: "You wench! Have you had the nerve and misfortune to disparage anybody I've praised? Take this, and be more careful another time!" With that she strikes her so hard that she leaves the print of all her fingers across her face.

5050 The ladies beside her rebuke her severely and pull her away; and then they in turn speak among themselves about my lord Gawain. "God!" said one of the damsels. "That knight under the hornbeam:* why is he waiting to get armed?" Another, more rash, suggested: "He's sworn to keep the peace."* Another followed that with: "He's a merchant. Don't tell me he's interested in tournaments: he's taking all those horses to sell!"—"No," said a fourth: "he's a money-changer and has no desire to share those goods he's bringing with him among the poor young knights today. Don't think I'm lying to you: that's money and tableware in those bags and chests."—"Really, what very wicked tongues you have!" says the young girl. "And you're wrong. Do you think a merchant carries such a massive lance as he's carrying? You've truly hurt me terribly today by saying such devilish things. By the faith I owe the Holy Spirit, he looks far more like a jouster than a merchant or money-changer. He's a knight, and shows it." The ladies say to her with one accord: "No he's not, dear, just because he looks like one. But he passes himself off as one because in that way he thinks he can avoid paying duties and tolls.* He's stupid, though he thinks he's clever; because he'll be caught at it, arrested as a thief, charged with base and foolish larceny and get a noose round his neck for it."

5091 My lord Gawain clearly hears and understands these sneers to which the ladies are subjecting him; and he is very ashamed and annoyed. But he quite properly bears in mind the fact that he has been accused of treason and is obliged to go and defend himself. For should he not turn up for the combat as he has pledged, he will have shamed first himself and then his entire lineage. It was through fear of injury or being captured that he had not engaged in this tourney, though he would very much like to, as he sees the tournament growing continually larger and better. And Meliant of Liz is calling for massive lances to deal even heavier blows. The jousting continued in front of the gate throughout the day until evening. Those who win booty carry it off to where they think it will be safest.

5114 The ladies see a very tall, bald-headed squire holding the stump of a lance and carrying a head-stall over his shoulders. One of the ladies immediately calls him naïve and stupid, saying to him: "Sir squire, so help me God, you're an escaped lunatic to go into that throng plundering stumps and heads of lances, head-stalls and cruppers: you call yourself a squire! Anyone who goes into the thick of things like that has little regard for himself. But down here in the meadow below I can see, very close to you, belongings that are unguarded and unprotected. A man who doesn't look after his own interests when he has the chance is a fool. Just look at that knight, the most good-natured ever born! For if anyone plucked out every hair in his moustache, he wouldn't budge. Now don't despise that booty, but be sensible and take all the horses and other property, for no one will stop you."

5140 So into the meadow he went at once and hit one of the horses with his lance-stump, saying: "Is there something the matter with you, fellow, for you just to watch here all day without having done a thing about piercing shields or breaking lances?"—"Tell me," says Sir Gawain, "what's that to do with you? Perhaps you'll eventually know the reason for my inactivity; but, by my head, that won't be now, for I wouldn't deign to tell you. Be off with you! Get on your way and be about your business!" He does promptly leave him, not being a man who would dare after that to speak of anything that might annoy him. At that point the tourney was suspended; but there had been many knights made captive and many horses killed. Those outside had won the day, those inside gained some booty. When they broke up they agreed to reassemble for tourneying in the lists next day.

5165 So they separated that night, with all those from the castle returning there. My lord Gawain also entered, behind their company, and in front of the gate met that worthy vavasour who had advised his lord to start the tournament; and he very kindly and politely offered him hospitality. "Sir," he says, "your lodging is all ready for you in this castle. Please stay and rest here now, for if you went on, you wouldn't find any good lodging today. So I beg you to stay."—"Thank you, good sir," says my lord Gawain, "and so I shall, for I've heard far worse suggestions." The vavasour leads him to his lodging, speaking of this and that and asking him how it was that he had not taken up arms with them in the tourney that day. He gave him the full reason: how he is accused of treason and is necessarily very afraid of being captured and of being injured and harmed before he can clear himself of the charge; for he supposed he could bring shame on himself and all his friends if, by delaying, he was unable to arrive on time for the combat he had undertaken. The vavasour much respected him for that and told him he approved of it; because if he had avoided the tourney on that account, he had acted sensibly.

5204 So the vavasour takes him to his house, and they dismount. Then the people in the fortress set about rebuking him severely; and they have a long discussion about how their lord might go and seize Gawain. And his elder daughter uses every argument she can possibly produce because of her hatred for her sister. "Sir," she says, "I'm sure you've lost nothing today: on the contrary, I think you've gained far more than you realise, and I'll tell you how. Your only proper course is to order him to be seized; for the man who has brought him into the town won't dare to defend him, living as he does by pernicious deception. By having a load of shields and lances and horses led along with him, he gets out of paying dues because he looks like a knight; and that's how he gets himself exempted when he goes trading. But now give him his deserts! He's at the house of Garin, Berte's son, who has given him lodging. He went past here just a moment ago, and I saw him taking him." In that way she tried hard to have him put to shame.

5236 The lord, determined to go there himself, mounts immediately and heads straight for the house where my lord Gawain is staying. When his small daughter sees him going off like this, she leaves by a back door, not wanting to be seen, and goes very quickly and directly to my lord Gawain's lodging at the home of Sir Garin, Berte's son, who had two very lovely daughters. When these girls see their little mistress coming, they cannot help feeling very happy and showing it without reserve. Each of them takes her by the hand, and they joyfully lead her into the house, kissing her on the eyes and lips.

5255 Sir Garin, however, who was neither poor nor mean, was back in the saddle together with his son Herman. They were both going to the court, as they usually did, in the hope of speaking to their lord, when they came across him in the street. The vavasour greeted him and asked where he was going, to which he replied that he was intending to go to pass the time pleasantly in Garin's own house. "Upon my word," says Sir Garin, "that should cause me no trouble or regrets; and indeed you'll be able to see there the most handsome knight on earth."—"In faith, I'm not going there for that," says his lord, "but to have him seized. He's a dealer with horses to sell who is passing himself off as a knight."—"Never!" says Sir Garin. "That's a foul slander I hear. I'm your vassal and you are my lord, but I hereby renounce my homage to you. Here and now on behalf of myself and my whole family I defy you rather than allow you to commit this base act in my house!"—"It was never my wish to do it, so help me God!" says the lord. "And neither your guest nor your dwelling shall ever receive anything but honour from me, despite the fact that, by my faith, I've been advised and urged very strongly to do the contrary."—"Very many thanks," says the vavasour; "and it will be a great honour indeed for me if you come and see my guest."

5292 At once they draw side by side and proceed to the house where my lord Gawain was staying. When Sir Gawain sees the lord, with his customary great civility he rises to his feet and says: "Welcome!" Both men greet him and then sit down beside him. The worthy lord of the land enquired of him why that day, having come to the tournament, he kept out of the jousting. Sir Gawain freely admitted to him that there was something reprehensible and shameful in his behaviour; nevertheless he went on to tell him that a knight was charging him with treason and he was going to defend himself in a royal court. "You most certainly had a sound reason," says the lord. "But where is this combat to be?—"Sir," he says, "I have to go before the King of Escavalon, and I believe I'm on the direct way there."—"I'll give you an escort who will take you there," says the lord. "And because you'll have to pass through very poor country, I'll give you provisions to take and horses to carry them." My lord Gawain replies that he has no need to accept that; for he will have plenty of provisions, if they can be found for sale, as well as good lodgings wherever he goes and everything he will need. He therefore asks for nothing from him.

5331 With that the lord goes to leave; but as he does so, he sees his small daughter coming from the other direction. She at once throws her arms round my lord Gawain's leg, saying: "Hear me, good sir, for I've come to appeal to you regarding my sister, who has struck me. Please obtain justice for me!" My lord Gawain says nothing, not knowing whom she was addressing; but he put his hand on her head. Then the damsel pulls him to her and says: "I'm telling you, good sir, that I'm complaining to you about my sister, for whom I have no affection or love, because she's treated me quite shamefully on your account."—"How does this concern me, my pretty one?" he asks. "What justice can I obtain for you?"

5350 The worthy man who had taken his leave, on hearing what his daughter was asking, said: "Daughter, who tells you to come appealing to knights?" Then Gawain said: "Dear good sir, is this your daughter, then?"—"Yes," says the lord; "but take no notice of what she says. She's a child, a naïve, silly creature."—"Indeed then," says my lord Gawain, "it would be very churlish of me not to find out what she wants." And he goes on: "Tell me, my good sweet child, what wrong of your sister's can I right, and how?"—"If you please, sir, by bearing arms in the tourney, just for tomorrow, for love of me."—"Tell me then, my dear friend, have you ever before made a request of a knight for any purpose?"—"Oh no, sir"—"Don't pay attention," says the lord, "to anything she says. Don't listen to her foolish talk!" Then my lord Gawain said to him: "Sir, as the Lord God may help me, her childish words are, on the contrary, very apt for so small a girl; and I shall certainly not refuse her but, as it's her wish, be her knight for a while tomorrow."—"Thank you, dear good sir," she says, so overjoyed that she bows down to his feet.

5385 With that they part, and no more is said. The lord carries away his daughter on the neck of his palfrey and asks her why that quarrel had arisen. She told him the whole truth from start to finish, saying: "Sir, I was very upset when my sister asserted that Meliant of Liz was the best and most handsome of them all. And down there in the meadow I'd seen this knight; and so I couldn't help contradicting her and saying I could see someone there who was more handsome. For that my sister called me a stupid wench and gave me a thrashing, much to everyone's disapproval. I'd let them cut off both my tresses right to the back of my neck, though that would really spoil my looks, on condition that my knight should bring down Meliant of Liz in tomorrow's joust. Then my lady sister's bragging about him would be silenced! She's gone on about him so much today that all the ladies are bored by it. But a great gale abates without much rain!"

5415   "Dear daughter," says the worthy man, "because it will be a courtly thing to do, I tell you and give you my full permission to send him some token of affection: a sleeve or wimple, perhaps."* She, being very naïve, said: "Very gladly, as you say so. But my sleeves are so small that I wouldn't dare send them: if I sent him one of them, he might not think anything of it."—"Daughter," says the lord, "I'll give some thought to it. So say no more, for I'm very happy about the whole thing." So saying, he carries her along in his arms, delighted to be holding her tight all the way up to his great hall.

5433   When the other daughter saw him coming holding her in front of him, her heart filled with bitter resentment, and she said: "Sir, where has my sister, the Maiden with the Small Sleeves, come from? She certainly knows plenty of tricks and ruses and hasn't taken long to become an expert at them! But where have you brought her from?"—"And what do you want to do about it?" he says. "You really ought to keep quiet. She's worth more than you, who have pulled her tresses and beaten her, much to my sorrow. You've not behaved in a courtly fashion at all!" She was much taken aback by her father's reprimand and reproach. He proceeded to have a piece of rich, scarlet silk taken from one of his chests, and from it a very long, broad sleeve cut and made. Then he called for his daughter. "Daughter," he says, "get up tomorrow morning and go to the knight before he leaves. You'll give him as a love-token this new sleeve, and he'll carry it in the tournament when he goes there." She answers her father that the instant she sees the light of dawn she will want herself wakened, washed and dressed. With that assurance, her father goes away. Blissfully happy, she begs all her companions not to let her oversleep in the morning, but to wake her promptly just as soon as they see the day break, if they value her love.

5473   They followed her instructions to the letter for, as soon as they saw the first signs of dawn in the early morning, they had her get up and dress. Having got up early, the maiden went off quite alone to my lord Gawain's lodging; but she did not arrive there in such good time that they had not all risen already and gone to church to hear the mass that was sung for them. The damsel waited in the vavasour's house until they had prayed for a long time and heard everything they should. Once they were back from church, the maiden sprang to greet my lord Gawain, saying: "May God save you and grant you honour on this day! But carry for love of me this sleeve I have here."—"Gladly, my dear, and thank you," says my lord Gawain.

5496 After that, the knights did not delay in arming themselves. Having done so, they gather outside the town; and, for their part, the damsels and all the ladies of the castle climbed up on to the walls and saw the companies of strong, bold knights assemble. Ahead of all the rest, Meliant of Liz charges up to the defenders' rank, having outstripped his companions by a full two and a half furlongs. When his sweetheart saw her lover, she was unable to hold her tongue, but said: "See, ladies, here comes the one who is renowned and supreme among knights!" Then my lord Gawain launches forth as fast as his horse can carry him against this man, who does not fear him but completely shatters his lance. And my lord Gawain strikes him so hard that he brings him utterly to grief, knocking him on to his back on the ground. Reaching out for his horse, he takes it by the bridle and hands it to a youth and instructs him to take it to the one for whom he was jousting, with the message that he is sending her his first booty of the day and wants her to have it.

5527 The youth leads the horse, complete with saddle, to the maiden, who, from a window in the tower where she was, had clearly seen the fall of Sir Meliant of Liz. She said: "Now, sister, you can see Sir Meliant of Liz, of whom you were speaking so highly, flat on his back! A knowledgeable person should bestow praise appropriately. Now what I said yesterday is demonstrated and, as God's my saviour, it's plain to see that there's someone of greater worth than he." So she goes deliberately provoking her sister to the point where she leaves her senses and says: "Shut up, wench! If I hear another word from you today, I'll give you such a whack that your feet won't hold you up!"—"Really, sister! Bear God in mind!" says the little damsel. "You shouldn't beat me just because I've told the truth. By my faith, I saw him toppled all right; and so did you, just as clearly as I did. And it's my impression he still hasn't the strength to get up again. Even if you were to burst with rage, I'd still say there's no lady here who didn't see him flailing his legs in the air and falling flat on his back."

5558 Then her sister would have given her a slap if the ladies around her had allowed it; but they did not let her land the blow. They then see the squire coming leading the horse. He finds the maiden sitting at a window and presents it to her. She thanks him more than sixty times and has the horse taken away, while he goes away to convey the thanks to his lord, who seemed to be the supreme master of the tournamant, there being no knight skilled enough to keep his stirrups if he aims a lance-thrust at him. Never was he so keen to win chargers; and that day he made presents of four that he won single-handed: the first he sent to the little damsel; with the second he rewarded the vavasour's wife, who was delighted with it, whilst one of his two daughters received the third and the other daughter the fourth.

5584 Then the tournament breaks up; and my lord Gawain returns through the gate, having achieved the highest honour on either side, though it was not yet midday when he left the fighting. When he returned, Sir Gawain had with him such a great company of knights that the whole town was full of them; for all those who were following him wanted to enquire and find out who he was and what region he came from. He met the damsel right at the door of her house; and without more ado she immediately caught hold of his stirrup and greeted him with the words: "Five hundred thousand thanks, good sir!" Knowing well what she meant, he gave her this open-hearted reply: "Maiden, I'll be white-haired and grizzled before I give up serving you, wherever I may be. I shall never be so far from you that, provided news of your need reaches me, any obstacle will prevent me from coming at your first call."—"Many thanks!" says the damsel.

5612 While they were exchanging these words, her father arrived on the scene and tried his hardest to have my lord Gawain remain there that night and lodge with him. First, though, he asks and begs him to tell him his name, if he is prepared to. Sir Gawain excuses himself from staying, but does tell him: "Sir, my name is Gawain. Never was my name concealed wherever I've been asked for it; but I've never yet given it without first having been asked." When the lord heard that this was my lord Gawain, his heart was filled with joy; and he said to him: "Do stay, my lord! Accept my service tonight, for yesterday I gave you none at all; and never in my life, I swear to you, have I seen a knight I'd so much wish to honour." He begged him insistently to stay, but Sir Gawain rejected all his pleas.

5638 The little damsel, who was neither foolish nor wicked, then takes him by the foot and, kissing it, commends him to God. My lord Gawain asks her what she meant by that. She answered that she had deliberately kissed his foot so that he would remember her again wherever he might go. And he said to her: "Have no fear, my fair friend, that, so help me God, I shall ever forget you when I leave here!" With that he departs, having taken leave of his host and the other folk, who all commend him to God.

5656 That night my lord Gawain spent in the hospice of a monastery, having everything he needed. Very early the next day he resumed his journey and rode until he passed by some hinds grazing at the edge of a forest. He told Yvonet, who was leading one of his horses (the best of them) and carrying a very strong, stout lance, to stop. He then asked him to bring him the lance, tighten the girths on the horse he was leading, take his palfrey and lead that. Wasting no time, Yvonet promptly gives him the horse and lance. Then, heading round after the hinds, he used so many tricks and wiles that he caught a white one by a thorn bush and brought his lance down across its neck. The hind leaps like a stag and gets away, with him following. He chased it until he would just about have caught and stopped it, had not his horse completely lost a shoe from one of its front hooves.

5686 My lord Gawain then sets off after his baggage, since he feels his horse limping under him, which greatly annoys him; but he does not know what makes it lame, unless it has caught a tree-trunk with its hoof. He at once called Yvonet and ordered him to dismount and attend to his horse, which was limping very badly. He does as he is bid, immediately lifts one of its hooves and, finding a shoe missing, says: "My lord, it needs to be shod; so the only thing to do is to go along gently until we can find a smith to put a new shoe on."

5703 They then travelled on until they saw some people coming out of a castle and along a paved road. In front were some with their clothes hitched up, lads on foot with dogs on leashes and, behind them, huntsmen carrying bows and arrows; and they were followed by some knights. At the rear of all the knights there came two mounted on chargers, one of whom was a young man more elegant and handsome than all the rest. He was the only one to greet my lord Gawain, grasping him by the hand with the words: "Sir, I offer you hospitality: go the way I've come and stop off at my residence.

This is just the right time of day to take lodging, if you don't object. I have a very courtly sister, who will be delighted to receive you. This companion of mine you see at my side, sir, will take you there." He then said: "Go along, my good friend: I'm sending you after this gentleman to take him to my sister. Greet her first of all and then tell her that I ask her that, for the sake of the love and great trust we should have in each other, if ever she loved any knight, she should show love and affection for this one and do as much for him as for me, her brother. She should keep him such agreeable company as will not displease him until our return. Then, once she has given him a kind reception, hurry and follow us, because I'd like to return to keep him company just as soon as I can."

5748 With that the knight sets off and conducts my lord Gawain to a place where everyone hates him mortally. But, never before having been there, he goes unrecognised and does not think of being on his guard. He notices the situation of the fortress overlooking an arm of the sea and sees its walls and a keep so strong that it fears nothing. And he gazes at the whole town and its very good-looking inhabitants, and at the money-changers' tables entirely covered with gold, silver and coinage; and he sees the squares and streets thronging with good workmen occupied in various trades. With their different crafts one makes helmets, another hauberks, this one saddles and that one escutcheons, this man bridles and that one spurs, whilst others burnish swords; these people full cloth and those weave it, some card it, others shear it. Some for their part smelt silver and gold, others make beautiful, costly objects: cups, goblets and bowls, enamelled jewellery, rings, belts and buckles. One might well have gained the firm impression that there was a continual fair in the town for it to be so full of goods: wax, pepper, scarlet material, vair and grey furs and all manner of merchandise. As he eyed all these things and gazed around, they continued on to the keep, where lads spring forward to take charge of all the horses and other equipment.

5788 The knight enters the keep alone with my lord Gawain and leads him by the hand into the maiden's chamber, saying to her: "My fair friend, your brother sends you his greetings and bids you see that this lord is honoured and served; and don't do it grudgingly, but just as whole-heartedly as if you were his sister and he your brother. Now don't be mean about doing whatever he wants, but generous, liberal and open-hearted. See to it, then, for I'm off, as I must follow your brother into the woods." She, in her delight, said: "A blessing on the one who sent me such company as this! Anybody lending me so handsome a companion scarcely hates me, and I thank him for it. Good sir," the maiden continues, "come now and sit beside me! Because I find you good-looking and attractive, and to meet my brother's request, I'll provide you with very pleasant company."

5815 The knight stays with them no longer, but leaves at once. My lord Gawain remains behind, certainly not complaining of being alone with the maiden, who was most courtly and beautiful and so well mannered that she did not suppose she would be spied upon because she was alone with him. They both engage in love-talk, for if they had spoken of anything else they would have been really wasting their time. My lord Gawain asks insistently for her love, saying he will be her knight for the rest of his life; and, far from refusing him, she agrees with alacrity. But just at that point, to their great misfortune, there entered a vavasour who recognised my lord Gawain; and he found them kissing and having a very joyful time together.

5837 As soon as he saw how they were enjoying themselves, unable to hold his tongue, he shouted at the top of his voice: "Shame on you, woman! And may God destroy and confound you for allowing yourself to be fondled and kissed and embraced by the man you should hate most in the entire world! You wretched, foolish woman! You're really doing your duty well! For you ought to be drawing his heart from his breast with your hands, not your lips. If your kisses touch his heart, then you've drawn his heart from his breast; but you'd have done far better to tear it out of him with your hands – that's what you should be doing. If a woman does any good, hating what's bad and loving what's good, then there's nothing of the woman about her: after that, anyone calling her a woman is wrong, because in loving only good she loses that name. But you are a woman, as I see plainly; for the man sitting beside you killed your father, and you kiss him! When a woman can enjoy her pleasures, she cares little about anything else." Having said that, he dashes off before my lord Gawain had spoken a word to him.

5869 The damsel falls to the paved floor to lie for a long while in a swoon. Then Sir Gawain, very upset and troubled at the fright she has had, raises her up. When she came round, she said: "Oh, now we're finished! Through you I'll die unjustly today, and so will you, I think, because of me. I suppose the citizenry of this town will soon arrive, and in no time there will be over ten thousand of them gathered in front of this keep. But there are plenty of arms in here, and I'll soon have you fitted out with them: one good man could defend the ground floor of the keep against a whole army." In her apprehension she ran immediately to fetch the arms; and once she had fully dressed my lord Gawain in the armour, they were both less fearful. There was, however, one snag in that there was no shield for him. So he took a chessboard as a shield, saying: "My love, I'll not ask you to go and look for any other shield for me." With that he tipped the chessmen onto the floor. They were of ivory, ten times bigger than other chess pieces, and of harder bone. Whoever may turn up now, he is confident he will manage to hold the door and entrance to the keep; for he is girt with Escalibor,* the best sword ever, that cuts through iron like wood.

5905 The vavasour had gone down from the keep and found a gathering of local people all seated side by side: the mayor and magistrates and a crowd of other townsmen who had certainly not been taking purgatives, so stout and paunchy were they! The vavasour arrived at the double, shouting: "To arms now, gentlemen! Let's go and seize the traitor Gawain, who killed my lord."—"Where is he? Where is he?" they all ask.—"I swear", says he, "that I've found him, that proven traitor Gawain, in the keep, where he's having a fine time embracing and kissing our young lady; and she's not objecting at all, but likes it and is very willing. But come along now, and we'll go and catch him! If you can hand him over to my lord, he'll be very pleased with your service. That traitor has deserved the most shameful treatment. Even so, take him alive, because my lord would rather have him alive than dead, and quite rightly, for a dead creature fears nothing. Rouse the whole town, and do your duty!"

5934 The mayor got up straight away, followed by all the magistrates. Then you might have seen bloodthirsty commoners taking up axes and halberds; this one takes a shield without any straps, that one a winnowing basket. The town crier makes the proclamation, and all the people assemble, with the bells of the community ringing so that no one stays behind: there is no one so craven that he does not take a pitchfork or a flail, pick or club. Never was there such an uproar in Lombardy when they go to kill snails!* There is nobody base enough not to go and take some weapon with him. Now my lord Gawain is a dead man, unless the Lord God gives him guidance!

5952 The damsel boldly prepares to help him and shouts at the townsfolk: "Hey, hey, you rabble, you mad dogs, you stinking menials! What devil has called you up? What are you after? What do you want? May God never give you joy! So help me God, you'll never get away with this knight in here. Rather than that, please God, there will be I don't know how many of you killed and maimed. He hasn't flown in here or come by some secret passage: my brother sent him to me as a guest, and I was strongly urged to do as much for him as I would for my brother in person. Do you consider me base, then, if at his request I give him my company and a pleasant, happy time? Just hear that, those of you who are prepared to listen! For that's the only reason why I welcomed him so warmly, and nothing more foolish entered my mind. So I'm all the more annoyed with you for treating me so shamefully as to come against me to the door of my chamber with drawn swords and without having the least idea why. And if you can say why, you haven't spoken to me about it, which I find quite despicable!"

5984 While she was giving them a piece of her mind, they were forcing the door, hacking it to pieces with hatchets they were carrying, and splitting it in half. Then that gate-keeper inside defended it stoutly against them: with the sword in his hand he made the first of them pay so dearly that the rest were terrified, and none of them dared to come forward. Each man looks after himself, fearing for his head. There is no one bold enough to brave that gate-keeper and come on, and nobody will lay a hand on him or advance a single step. The damsel furiously hurls at them the chessmen lying on the stone floor. She gathers her clothes tightly about her and tucks them up, swearing in her rage that, before she dies, she will have them all destroyed if she can.

6007 The commoners retreat, declaring that they will bring the tower down on them unless they surrender, whilst their defence gets better and better as they fling great chessmen at them. Many take to their heels, unable to withstand their attack. Then they set about undermining the keep with steel picks, as if to demolish it, since they dare not attack or fight at the door, which is well held against them. Please believe me that the doorway was so narrow and low that two men could not pass through it together, except with very great difficulty. That is why one good man was able to hold and defend it well; and for cleaving unarmed men to the teeth and spilling their brains it was unnecessary to call for any better gatekeeper than the one who was there!

6028 The lord who had given him hospitality was unaware of all this; but as soon as he can he returns from the woods where he had been hunting. The townsfolk were continuing to hack round the keep with steel picks. Here now comes Guigambresil, who knows nothing of these happenings, galloping at top speed into the fortress; and he is quite taken aback by the din and noise of hammering made by the commoners. He was ignorant of the fact that my lord Gawain was in the castle. Then, when he did find out, he forbade anyone, whoever and however bold he might be, to dare to remove any stone if he valued his life. They say they would certainly not stop for him, but would bring the tower down there and then on him himself, if he were inside with that man. When he hears that his prohibition is fruitless, he decides to go to meet the king and bring him along to this disturbance provoked by the townsmen, as the king is already on his way back from the woods.

6057 When he meets him, he tells him: "Sire, your mayor and magistrates have brought great shame on you: they've been attacking your keep since this morning and are knocking it down. Unless they pay for it and make amends, I'll be far from grateful to you. As you well know, I'd charged Gawain with treason, and he's the man you've given lodging in your residence; so it would be only right and proper that, as you've made him your guest, he should suffer no shame or harm there." The king answers Guigambresil: "That he'll not do, high steward, once we've arrived! I'm most annoyed and grieved by what's happened to him. I can't be surprised if my people have a mortal hatred of him; but since I've given him hospitality, I shall protect him, if I can, from being himself seized or injured." So they come to the keep and find the people all round it making a great uproar. The king ordered the mayor to leave and take the townspeople away. They go off and not a single one stayed behind, that being the mayor's wish.

6088 In the square was a vavasour, a native of the town, who acted as adviser to the whole country, being a man of great good sense.

"Sire," he says, "now you need good and loyal advice. It's no wonder that the man who committed the treachery of killing your father has been attacked in here because, as you know, he's quite properly an object of mortal hatred here. But the fact of your giving him hospitality should protect and safeguard him from being captured or put to death here. And unless anyone wishes to break his word, Guigambresil, whom I see there, should safeguard and protect him because he went to lay the charge of treason against him in the royal court. It's quite evident that he had come to defend himself in your court. But I propose a postponement of this duel for one year and that he should go away to look for the lance whose tip bleeds constantly* and will never be wiped so clean that a drop of blood does not hang from it. He must either hand that lance over to you or again surrender to the kind of captivity he's in here. Then you'll have a better reason for keeping him prisoner than you'd have at this moment. I think you'd never be able to subject him to so severe a trial that he wouldn't come through it very successfully. One should inflict the maximum harm one can contrive on the object of one's hatred, and I can't give you any better advice on how to plague your enemy."

6129 The king takes this advice. He went to his sister in the keep and found her extremely angry. She rose to meet him, as did my lord Gawain who, whatever fear he may have felt, did not turn pale or tremble. Guigambresil went up to him and, having greeted the maiden, who had gone pale, spoke a few empty words: "Lord Gawain, Lord Gawain, I'd granted you safe conduct, but had gone to the length of telling you never to be so bold as to enter any castle or city in my lord's possession if you could readily avoid it. You should not now complain of what has been done to you here."

6149 The wise vavasour then said: "May the Lord God help me, sir, all this can be put to rights. If the commoners attacked him, to whom should one complain about that? That case would be debated until the great Judgment Day. The matter will be resolved instead according to the decision of my lord the king here: through me he issues the command that, unless either you or Gawain object, you both postpone this combat for one year; and my lord Gawain is to go away, provided that my lord has his oath that, in a year's time and no later, he will surrender to him the lance whose tip sheds tears of bright blood. It is written that a time will come when the whole realm of Logres, which was formerly the land of ogres, will be destroyed by that lance. My lord the king wishes to have his oath and pledge on this."

6174 —"Indeed," says my lord Gawain, "I'd rather submit to death or languish for seven years in here than take an oath or pledge him to do that! And I'm not so afraid of dying that I wouldn't rather suffer and endure an honourable death than live in shame and perjure myself."—"Good sir," says the vavasour, "you'll never incur dishonour, as I'll explain to you; nor do I think you'll ever be the worse for it. You'll swear to do all in your power to seek the lance; but if you don't bring it back, you'll return into this keep and be absolved from the oath."—"In those terms you state," he replies, "I'm prepared to take the oath."

6194 A very precious reliquary is at once brought out for him; and he takes the oath to devote his every effort to seeking the bleeding lance. In this way the duel between him and Guigambresil is put off and postponed for a year. He has escaped from great danger by getting out of that! Before leaving the keep, he took leave of the maiden. He also instructed all his squires to return to his land, taking back all his horses except for Gringalet. So the youths part from their lord and go off. I do not wish to say any more of them or the grief they display. At this point the tale says no more about my lord Gawain, but begins to speak of Perceval.

6217 *Perceval, as the story told us, had been so forgetful as not to remember God. April and May passed five times, that is five whole years, without his entering a church or worshipping God on His cross. He remained like that for five years, yet did not cease to pursue deeds of chivalry; and he went in search of strange, terrible and difficult adventures, finding so many that in them he gave good proof of himself. Within five years he sent sixty distinguished knights as prisoners to King Arthur's court. In this manner he passed five years without ever turning his mind to God.

6238 At the end of those five years he happened to be passing through a wilderness travelling, as was his custom, fully armed, when he encountered three knights and with them as many as ten ladies, with their heads hooded, all walking barefoot and wearing hair-shirts. At the sight of this armed man approaching, grasping a lance and a shield, the ladies, who were doing penance on foot for the sins they had committed, were astounded. One of the three knights stopped him and said: "My dear good friend, don't you believe in Jesus Christ, who laid down the New Law and gave it to Christians? It's really not right and proper and indeed is very wrong to bear arms on the day when Jesus Christ was slain."

6261 Then Perceval, who was quite oblivious to the day or time or season, so dispirited was he, replies: "What day is it today, then?"—"What day, sir? Don't you know, then? This is Good Friday, the day for worshipping the cross and weeping for one's sins; for today the One who was sold for thirty pence was hanged on the cross. He who was free of all sins saw those which ensnared and tarnished the whole world; and so He became a man because of our sins. Truly He was both God and man; for the Virgin bore a son conceived by the Holy Spirit, in whom God assumed flesh and blood, so that the Deity was clothed in human flesh: that is a certain fact. And anyone who does not believe it to be so will never look upon His face. He was born of the Virgin Lady and assumed the form and soul of a man together with His holy deity; and, truly, on such a day as today He was put on the cross and delivered all His friends from Hell. That was an extremely holy death, which saved the living and restored the dead from death to life. In their envy the false Jews, who should be killed like dogs, wrought their own harm and our own great good when they raised Him on the cross: they achieved their own perdition and our salvation. All who believe in Him should be doing penance today. Today no one who believes in God should carry arms in the field or on the road."

6301 —"And where are you coming from now in this manner?" asks Perceval.—"From near here, sir: from a worthy man, a holy hermit who lives in that forest; and so holy a man is he that he lives by the glory of God alone."—"In God's name, sirs, what were you doing there? What were you asking for? What were you seeking?"—"What, sir?" says one of the ladies. "We were asking his guidance on our sins and made confession there. We performed there the greatest duty that any Christian wishing to approach God can undertake." What Perceval had heard made him weep; and he felt an urge to go and speak with the worthy man. "I should very much like to go there," says Perceval, "if I knew the path and the way to take."—"Anyone wanting to go there, sir, should take this path straight ahead, in the direction we've come from, through the thick, dense woodland, looking out for the branches we tied together with our own hands when we went there. We left such signs so that anybody going to the holy hermit wouldn't lose the way." With that they commend each other to God without any further questioning.

6333 Perceval sets out on his way, heaving heartfelt sighs because he felt he had sinned against God, for which he was deeply repentant. Weeping, he makes his way through the woods. When he reached the hermitage, he dismounted and disarmed, tethering his horse to a hornbeam, and then entered the hermit's cell. The hermit he found in a small chapel, in fact, together with a priest and an acolyte, just beginning the highest and most moving service that can be held in holy Church. Perceval falls to his knees as soon as he enters the chapel; and the good man, seeing him weeping meekly with his tears running from his eyes down to his chin, calls him to him. Perceval, greatly afraid he has sinned against God, seizes the hermit by the foot, then joins his hands and bows down before him, begging him for counsel, since he has great need of it. The good man bids him make his confession, for he will never have remission unless he has confessed and repented.

6364 "Sir," he says, "for fully five years I've not known where I was or loved God or believed in Him, and have done nothing but wrong in that time."—"Ah, my good friend," said the worthy man, "tell me why you've done this; and pray God to have mercy on the soul of His sinner."—"Sir, I was on one occasion at the Fisher King's home, and I saw the lance whose head bleeds without any doubt; but I asked no question about that drop of blood I saw hanging at the tip of the shining head; and after that I've truly made no amends. And as for the grail I saw there, I don't know who is served from it; and ever since my grief has been such that, had I had my way, I would gladly have been dead. For I've forgotten God as a result and never called on Him for mercy or ever done anything, as far as I'm aware, to earn it."—"Ah, my good friend," said the worthy man, "now tell me your name." And he told him: "Perceval, sir."

6390 On hearing this, the worthy man, who recognised the name, said: "My brother, a sin of which you know nothing has done you great harm: that was the grief your mother felt when you left her. For she fell in a swoon to the ground at the end of the bridge in front of the gate; and of that grief she died. It was through having incurred that sin that you came to ask nothing about the lance or the grail, as a result of which you have suffered many misfortunes. And you may be sure you wouldn't have survived as long as this had she not commended you to the Lord God. But so potent was her plea that for her sake God has watched over you and kept you from death and captivity. Sin stopped your tongue when you saw before you the lance-head which has never ceased to bleed and didn't ask the reason for it. And when you failed to find out who is served from the grail, that was pure foolishness. The person served from it is my brother: your mother was my sister and his. And the Rich Fisherman, believe me, is the son of that king who has himself served from the grail. But don't imagine he has pike, lamprey or salmon: he's served with a single consecrated wafer brought to him in that grail – that supports his life in full vigour, so holy a thing is the grail. And he, whose life is so spiritual that all it needs is the host that comes in the grail, has been there for twelve years like that, without leaving the room which you saw the grail enter.

6432   "Now I wish to impose and prescribe a penance on you for your sin."—"Good uncle," says Perceval, "I want that with all my heart. As my mother was your sister, you should really call me nephew, and I call you uncle and love you all the more."—"That's true, good nephew. But listen now: if you're concerned for your soul, repent sincerely and, as your penance, go each morning to church before anywhere else. That will be to your benefit, so don't fail to do so on any account. If you're in any place with a minster, chapel or parish church, go there when the bell rings, or earlier if you are up. That will never do you any harm: on the contrary, it will greatly profit your soul. And if mass has begun, it will be all the better for you there; so stay there until the priest's singing and chanting is finished. If you're prepared to do this, you may yet increase in merit and gain honour and paradise. Love God, believe in God, worship God. Honour worthy men and women; and stand in the presence of priests – that's a service that costs little, and which God truly loves, since it stems from humility. Should a maiden or widow or orphan seek your aid, then provide it, for that will stand you in good stead: such good deeds have integrity; and you'll do well to help them, so make sure nothing prevents you. I want you to do all this for your sins, if you wish to recover all the probity you used to have. Now tell me if you're prepared to do it."—"Yes, sir, very willingly."

6476 —"Now I ask you to stay here with me for two whole days and, in penance, take the same food as I have." Perceval agrees to everything. Then the hermit whispered a prayer in his ear over and over again until he had memorised it. In that prayer were many of the names of our Lord,* including the most important of them, which must not be uttered by human tongue unless they be named at times of mortal fear. Having taught him the prayer, he forbade him to pronounce the names under any circumstances other than when he was in dire peril. "Nor shall I, sir," says he. So he remained there and heard the service, to his joy. After the service he worshipped the cross and wept for his sins. That night the food he ate was as the hermit wished: nothing but beet, chervil, lettuces, cress and millet, with bread made of barley and oats, and clear spring-water. His horse had straw and a bowlful of barley. That is how Perceval came to the recognition that on that Friday God was put to death and crucified. Then at Easter, Perceval received communion in very worthy fashion. — At this point the tale speaks no further of Perceval; and you will have heard a great deal about my lord Gawain before you hear me telling of him again.

6519 After his escape from the keep where the townsfolk had attacked him, my lord Gawain travelled on until, one morning between nine o'clock and noon, he came riding towards a hillock and saw a big, tall oak tree, whose thick foliage gave good shade. Hanging from the oak he saw a shield, with a lance standing upright next to it. He hurries towards the oak until beside it he can see a small northern palfrey,* the incongruity of which greatly amazes him, because it seems to him that arms and a palfrey do not go together. Had the palfrey been a horse, he would have supposed that some knight or other, roaming the country in search of a reputation and honour, had climbed that hillock. Then he looks under the oak and sees sitting there a maiden who, he supposes, would have been very beautiful had she been happy and in good spirits; but she had her fingers thrust into her tresses in order to tear out her hair, and was making a great show of sorrow. She was grieving for a knight, whom she kissed again and again on the eyes, forehead and mouth. On approaching, my lord Gawain sees that the knight is wounded, with his face cut to ribbons and a very serious sword-wound in his head; and the blood was running in great streams down both his sides. The knight had fainted many times from the pain he felt before finally lying quietly.

6560 When he came there, my lord Gawain did not know whether
he was dead or alive, but asked: "Fair lady, how does that knight
you're holding seem to you?" She replied: "You can see his wounds
are terribly dangerous: he'd die from the very least of them." He
went on: "If you don't mind, my fair friend, wake him up, for I'd
like to ask him for information about how things stand in this
country."—"I'd not wake him, sir," says the maiden. "I'd rather
have myself flayed alive, because I've never been so fond of any
man, or will be as long as I live. When I see him asleep and resting,
I'd be a very stupid wretch to do anything he might hold against
me."—"Then upon my word," says my lord Gawain, "I'm determined to wake him myself!"

6582 With that he turns his lance round and, with the butt, touches
him lightly on the spur. In waking him, he did not annoy the knight,
for he shook his spur so gently that he did not hurt him: on the
contrary, the knight thanked him and said: "Sir, I give you five
hundred thanks for having shown such consideration in nudging
and waking me without my suffering any harm. But for your own
sake I beg you not to go on any further than this, for that would be
very foolish of you. Take my advice and stay here."—"Stay? Why
should I?"—"I'll tell you why, by my faith, since you want to hear.
No knight who has ever gone that way by road or field has been
able to come back; for that's the boundary of Galloway,* which a
knight can't cross and then return again. None other than myself
has ever come back from there, and I've been reduced to such a
sorry state that I doubt if I'll live until tonight. For I encountered a
gallant, bold knight who was both strong and fierce: I've never
found one so valiant, or pitted myself against one so strong. It
would therefore be better for you to turn back than to go down this
hill, because it would be too difficult for you to return."—"By my
faith," says my lord Gawain, "I've not come here to go back again.
People would properly put it down to disgraceful cowardice on my
part, now that I've undertaken the journey, if I turned back at this
point. I shall go on until I understand and see for myself why no one
can return from there."

6624 —"I can tell you have to do it," says the wounded knight.
"You'll go there because you're set on increasing and enhancing
your honour. But if you didn't object, I'd very much like to make a
request of you: should God grant you that privilege which no

knight has so far managed to obtain and I don't think any will ever come to achieve, neither you nor anyone else under any circumstances, then I'd ask you to come back this way, please, and see if I'm dead or alive, any better or any worse. If I'm dead, then I beg you in the name of charity and of the Holy Trinity to take care of this maiden and keep her from any shame or hurt; and may it please you to do that, because God never made or wished to make a more noble or good-hearted person." My lord Gawain promises him that, provided nothing like imprisonment or some other adversity should prevent him, he will return his way and give the maiden all the help he can.

6657 So he left them and journeyed on without stopping, over plains and through forests, until he saw a very strong castle with, on one side, its own large seaport and navy. This extremely noble stronghold was worth little less than Pavia. On its other side was the vineyard with, below it, the great river girdling all its walls as it flowed past into the sea. In that way the castle and town were entirely enclosed. My lord Gawain crossed the bridge into the fortress; and having climbed to the strongest point in the whole castle, in a courtyard under an elm tree he found a sweet maiden, whiter than snow, examining her face and mouth in a mirror. She had crowned her head with a narrow circlet of gold brocade.

6682 My lord Gawain spurred his horse to an amble in her direction, whereupon she calls to him: "Steady, steady, sir! Gently now! You're really coming at a crazy pace. You shouldn't be in such a hurry to waste your mount's turn of speed. Anyone who makes haste to no purpose is stupid!"—"God's blessing on you, maiden," says my lord Gawain. "Now tell me, my fair friend, what came into your head when you were so prompt to remind me to go easily, without having any reason?"—"Oh yes, knight, I do have one, I swear; because I have a good idea of what you're thinking."—"What's that?" he says.—"You want to seize me and carry me off down there across your horse's neck."—"You're quite right, damsel!"

6702 —"I knew it," she says. "But damn the one who thought that! Don't you dare think of putting me on your horse! I'm not one of those naïve, foolish women who provide fun for knights who carry them along on their horses on their chivalric expeditions. You'll not carry me off! Even so, if you dared, you would be able to take me with you. If you were prepared to go to the trouble of bringing me my palfrey from that garden, I'd go along with you until such time as you suffered misfortune, grief and affliction, shame and disaster in my company."—"Is anything more than courage needed for this, my fair friend?" he asks.—"Not as far as I know, vassal," says the maiden.—"Ah damsel, if I go there, where shall I leave my horse? For it won't be able to cross that footbridge I see."—"No, knight: give it to me, and you go over on foot. I'll look after your horse for you, so long as I'm able to keep it. But hurry back, because I wouldn't be able to do anything about it if it grew restless or was taken from me by force before you returned."—"That's true," he says. "But you'll not be held responsible if it's taken from you, nor if it escapes; and you'll never hear me say otherwise."

6741 So he hands it over to her and sets off, deciding to take all his arms with him; for if in the garden he finds anyone wanting to deny him the palfrey and stop him from taking it, there will be some commotion and fighting before he comes back with it. He then crosses over the bridge and finds a large crowd of people watching him in amazement and saying: "May a hundred devils burn you, maiden, for having acted so wickedly! May you suffer misfortune yourself, for you never had any affection for a worthy man! You've had so many good men beheaded, which is a grievous shame. You, knight, who are intending to lead away that palfrey, you don't know now the troubles in store for you if you lay your hand on it. Ah, knight, why are you going towards it? You'd certainly never go near it if you knew the great shame and misfortunes and hardships that you'll encounter if you take it away." So they all said, men and women alike, wanting to deter my lord Gawain from going to the palfrey and rather to have him turn back. He hears and clearly understands what they say, but has no intention of giving up on that account. Instead he continues on, greeting the groups of people, who all join in returning his greetings in a way that suggests that they share for him feelings of great anxiety and distress.

6778 Then my lord Gawain goes up to the palfrey and puts out his hand with the intention of taking it by the bridle, for it lacked neither bridle nor saddle. But a tall knight sitting under a green-leaved olive tree shouted: "Knight, you've come for the palfrey in vain. Don't lay a finger on it, for that would be very presumptuous of you! I don't, however, wish to oppose you or forbid you to take it if you really want to; but I advise you to go away again, because if you do lay hands on it, you'll find very strong opposition in another place."—"I'll not give up because of that, good sir," says my lord Gawain; "for I've been sent here by the maiden who is looking at herself in her mirror under that elm tree, and if I didn't lead it back with me, what would have been the point of my coming here? I'd be shamed on earth as a craven recreant."—"Then, dear brother, you'll suffer for it," says the tall knight; "for by God the sovereign Father to whom I'd wish to surrender my soul, there never was a knight who has dared to take it, just as you want to, who hasn't suffered the disaster of having his head cut off. And I'm very much afraid that will happen to you. By forbidding you to take it, I didn't mean any harm. If you want to, you can take it away and I'll not stop you, nor will anybody you see in here; but if you're so bold as to take it outside here, you'll be taking a very dangerous step. My advice is not to, because you'd lose your head for it!"

6820 Having heard this, my lord Gawain does not stay there an instant longer. He drives the palfrey, whose head was black on one side and white on the other, across the footbridge ahead of him. It was able to cross it easily, having often been over before and being well trained and taught to do so. Sir Gawain then took it by its silken rein and came straight to the elm where the maiden was gazing at herself in her mirror, having let her mantle and wimple fall to the ground in order to see her face and body more easily. Sir Gawain presents the saddled palfrey to her, saying: "Now come here, maiden, and I'll help you to mount."

6840 "May God forbid", she says "that you should ever speak, in any court you may take me to, of holding me in your arms! If with your bare hand you'd held or handled or felt anything about me, I'd consider myself disgraced. It would be a terrible thing for me if people told or learned that you'd touched my flesh: I'd rather have my skin and flesh sliced to the bone – I can tell you that here and now! Let me have the palfrey at once, for I can well mount it on my own and want none of your help. And may God grant me this very day, as I expect, the sight of you incurring great shame before nightfall! Go wherever you like, you'll never come any closer to touching my body or clothes; but I'll keep following along behind you until I cause some dire and shameful calamity to befall you.

And I'm absolutely certain that I'll bring you to grief: you can't escape that any more than death."

6869 My lord Gawain listens to everything the arrogant damsel says, and does not utter a word, but gives her her palfrey, whilst she leaves him his horse. Sir Gawain then bends down in order to pick her mantle up from the ground and put it on her. The damsel, who was not slow or timid in saying shameful things to a knight, watches him. "Vassal," she says, "what concern of yours are my mantle and wimple? By God, I'm not half as simple as you think. I really have no desire for you to serve me, for your hands aren't clean enough to pass me anything I put on or wear round my head. Are you fit to handle anything that touches my body, my mouth, my forehead or my face? May God never grant me any honour again if I'm ever at all inclined to accept your service!" So the maiden mounted, having put on and fastened her garments; and then she said: "Now then, knight, go wherever you wish, and I'll keep following until I see you disgraced because of me; and, please God, that will be today!" My lord Gawain remains silent and says nothing in reply.

6904 Quite ashamed, he mounts, and they ride away. With bowed head he makes for the oak tree where he left the maiden with the knight who was in desperate need of a doctor to tend his wounds. My lord Gawain knew better than any man how to heal wounds; and in a hedgerow he sees a herb that is excellent for relieving the pain from injuries. He goes and picks it and, having done so, rides on until he finds the maiden lamenting beneath the oak. As soon as she saw him she said: "My dear good sir, now I think this knight is dead, because he doesn't hear or take anything in any more." Sir Gawain dismounts and finds his pulse extremely strong and neither his mouth nor his cheek too cold. "Maiden," he says, "this knight is alive, you may be sure of that, for he has a good pulse and is breathing well and isn't mortally wounded. I've brought a special herb which I expect will do him a lot of good and will partly alleviate the pain from his wounds as soon as he feels it; for it's written that there's no better herb for applying to wounds, and that its power is such that if it were tied against the bark of a diseased tree, so long as it wasn't completely withered, its root would recover and the tree would regain the ability to come into leaf and blossom.

6944 "Your lover will no longer be in danger of dying, my damsel, once we've applied some of this herb to his wounds and bound it on well. But we need a wimple of fine material to make a bandage."—"I'll give you one at once," she says, by no means unhappy to hear this. "It will be the one I'm wearing, because I've brought no other with me." She took from her head the very fine, white wimple; and my lord Gawain cuts it up as necessary and binds on to all of his wounds some of the herb in his possession, with the maiden helping him to the very best of her ability.

6962 Sir Gawain does not move before the knight sighs and speaks, saying: "May God reward whoever has restored my speech, for I was very much afraid of dying without confession. A whole procession of devils had come here to get my soul. Before I'm buried, I'm very anxious to be confessed. There's a chaplain I know close by; and if I had something to ride, I'd go to him to give a full account of my sins in confession and then take communion. I'd never fear death having once taken communion and been to confession. But do me a service now, if you don't mind: give me the nag of that squire who's trotting this way."

6984 When my lord Gawain hears this, he turns round and sees an unpleasant-looking squire approaching. What was he like? I shall tell you. He had tousled red hair that stood stiffly on end like an angry porcupine's; and his eyebrows were similar and covered the whole of his face and nose down to his moustache, which was long and twisted. He had a slit for a mouth and a wide, forked, curly beard. His neck was short and his chest humped. Sir Gawain would like to approach him to see if he could have the nag; but first he says to the knight: "Sir, so help me God, I don't know who this squire is. I'd rather give you seven chargers, if I had them with me, than his nag, whoever he may be."—"Sir," says the knight, "you may be sure that the only thing he's after is to bring you trouble, if he can."

7010 Then my lord Gawain goes over to the approaching squire and asks where he is bound for. Far from politely he replied: "What's it to you, fellow, where I'm going or where I've come from? Whatever way I'm going, I wish you yourself every misfortune!" Sir Gawain at once gives him his just deserts by slapping him with his open palm; and, what with the mail on his arm and the eagerness with which he strikes, he upends him and empties his saddle. When he tries to get up, he staggers and falls down again. He collapsed a good seven times or more, and I am not joking, on a smaller patch of ground than the length of a pinewood lance. Then when he did get up he said: "You struck me, fellow!"—"Yes," says Gawain, "I did strike you, but I haven't done you much harm. All the same, I'm sorry I hit you, as God's my witness; but that was a very stupid thing you said."—"I'm still very ready to tell you how you'll pay for it: you'll lose the hand and arm with which you dealt me that blow, because you'll never be forgiven for it!"

7041 While this was happening, the wounded knight's heart, which had been very faint, revived; and he said to my lord Gawain: "Let that squire be, good sir, for you'll never hear him say anything that reflects honour on you. You'll be sensible to leave him. But bring me his nag, then take this maiden you see beside me, tighten the girths on her palfrey and help her to mount. For I don't want to stay here any longer but, if I can, I'll mount on the nag and then go to look for somewhere I can confess; because I want to keep going until I received the last sacrament, after confession and communion." My lord Gawain immediately takes the nag and hands it over to the knight, whose sight had returned and cleared, so that he saw Sir Gawain and recognised him for the first time. Then Sir Gawain took the damsel and with courtly politeness seated her on the northern palfrey.

7071 While he was doing this, the knight took his horse, mounted it, and started to make it prance to and fro. My lord Gawain watches him galloping all over the hill and laughs in amazement; then, amid his laughter, he said: "Upon my word, sir knight, it's extremely foolish of you to prance around on my horse as I see you doing. Get off it and give it to me, because you could easily do yourself harm and make your wounds open." He replies: "Be quiet, Gawain! Be sensible and take the nag, for you've lost the horse! I've put it through its paces for my own benefit, and I'll take it away as my own property."—"Shame on you! I come here to help you, and you'd do me wrong? Don't make off with my horse, for that would be treachery!"—"Gawain, by a similar wrong and whatever the result for me, I'd like to get my two hands on the heart in your breast!"—"Now I'm reminded", Gawain replies, "of a proverb that runs: 'Good deeds bring broken necks.' But I'd very much like to know why you'd want to have my heart and are taking away my horse, for I've never wished nor done you any harm in my whole life. I didn't think I'd deserved this from you, because as far as I'm aware I've never seen you before."

7109 —"Yes you have, Gawain: you saw me somewhere and brought shame on me. Don't you remember the man on whom you inflicted the ordeal of making him eat for a month with the dogs, against his will and with his hands tied behind his back? You can see that was a stupid thing to do because now it's brought you yourself great shame!"—"Are you then that Greoreas who took that damsel by force and had your will of her, despite the fact that you well knew that in King Arthur's land the safety of maidens is guaranteed, the king having assured them of safe conduct and thus protection in his charge? I don't think it credible that you hate me for this 'misdeed' or seek my harm on account of that, since I did it in the exercise of rightful justice as established and maintained throughout the king's land."—"Gawain, you exacted that justice on me, as I well remember. Now you're in the position of having to suffer my own: I'm going to take Gringalet away, as that's the best vengeance I can take at this moment. You'll have to swap it for that nag you knocked the squire off, for you'll get nothing else in exchange!" With that Greoreas leaves him and dashes off at a fast amble after his sweetheart, who was riding quickly away.

7145 Then the malicious maiden laughed at my lord Gawain and said: "Oh vassal, vassal, what are you going to do? Now it may well be said in your case that the world never lacks silly fools. God preserve me, it's really good fun following you! You'll never go anywhere without my being delighted to follow you! If only the nag you took from the squire were a mare! I wish it were, you know, because your disgrace would be all the worse." At once my lord Gawain, having no alternative, mounts the stupid, trotting nag. It was a hideous beast: it had a thin neck, a big head, long dangling ears and all the defects of old age, with a mouth having one lip a good finger's length from the other. Its eyes were clouded and dim, its hooves covered in sores, and its flanks hardened and cut to ribbons by spurs. The nag was long and thin with a skinny rump and crooked spine. The reins and bridle headpiece were made of light cord, and the saddle, which was far from new, had no cover. Sir Gawain finds the stirrups too short and weak for him to dare to put any strain on them.

7178 "Aha! Things are going really well now!" says the sarcastic damsel. "Now I'll be happy and delighted to go anywhere you wish. Now it's only right and proper that I should gladly follow you for a week or an entire fortnight or three weeks or a month. Now you're well kitted out astride a fine charger and look every inch a knight fit to escort a maiden! And for a start I want to enjoy myself watching your discomfort. Give your horse a little dig with your spurs to try it out; and don't be afraid, because it's very fast and spirited! I'll follow you; for the arrangement is that I'll never leave you until you're brought into disrepute, as you certainly will be." He replies: "Sweet friend, you can say what you like; but it's not proper for a damsel over ten years old to be so abusive. She should rather be polite, courtly and well-mannered if she has the sense to learn."—"What, knight? Are you rash enough to want to teach me a lesson? I'm not interested in your teaching. Just get going and hold your tongue; for you're just as well off now as I wanted to see you!"

7212 So they ride on until evening, with neither of them saying any more. He goes ahead and she behind; but he does not know what he can do with his nag, being unable to get it to run or gallop, however hard he tries. Whether he likes it or not, it carries him at a walk; for if he digs in his spurs it gives him a very hard ride, shaking up his stomach so much that he cannot bear under any circumstances to go at more than a walking pace. In this way he travelled on the nag through wild, desolate forests until he reached flat country with a deep river so broad that no cast from a sling, mangonel or catapult could have reached the other side, and no crossbow could have shot across it.

7233 Above the water on the opposite bank was situated a very skilfully constructed fortress,* exceedingly strong and powerful. I have no wish to permit myself a lie: the castle was so splendidly founded on a cliff that no man alive ever set eyes on so mighty a stronghold; for on a rocky outcrop was set a vast palatial hall built entirely of dark marble. This hall had fully five hundred windows, all filled with ladies and damsels looking at the meadows and gardens in bloom before them. Most of the damsels were dressed in samite and were wearing silk tunics of various colours all trimmed with gold. Thus the maidens were placed at the windows, where their shining heads and elegant figures appeared, seen from outside from the waist up.

7258 Then that most malicious creature in the world, preceding my lord Gawain, came straight to the river. She stops and dismounts from the little piebald palfrey; and by the bank she finds a boat, attached with a lock to a stone block. There was an oar in the boat, and the key to its lock was on the block. The wicked-hearted damsel gets into the boat, followed by her palfrey, which had done so many times before. "Now, vassal," she says, "dismount and get in here with me along with your broken-down horse, which is skinnier than a chicken, and then pull up this barge's anchor; because you're in for a really bad time unless you cross this water quickly or else can swim very fast."—"What's that, damsel? Why?"—"You can't see what I can see, knight; for if you did, you'd very quickly take to your heels." My lord Gawain immediately looks round and sees a fully armed knight approaching across the heath. He asks her: "Tell me, my friend, if you don't mind: who is this man sitting on my horse that was stolen from me by that traitor whose wounds I healed this morning?"

7294 —"I'll tell you, by Saint Martin," says the maiden happily. "But you must know for a fact that I wouldn't tell you for anything if I saw the least advantage in it for you. But as I'm sure he's coming for your misfortune, I'll not keep it from you: that's Greoreas's nephew, whom he's sent after you; and I'll certainly tell you why, since you've asked me. His uncle has ordered him to follow you until he's killed you and presented him with your head. That's why I advise you to dismount unless you want to meet your death here. So get in here and flee!"—"I'll certainly not flee because of him, damsel: no, I'll wait for him."—"Indeed I'll not forbid you to," says the maiden, "but shall say no more. For you'll really charge and prance about in fine fashion in front of those lovely, attractive maidens leaning at those windows over there! On your account they're delighted with their vantage-point, as it's because of you they went there. Spur on, now! They'll be overjoyed, for you're seated on a fine charger! You truly look like a knight bent on jousting with another!"—"Whatever price I have to pay, maiden, I'll never flinch but ride against him; for if I could get my horse back, I'd be very pleased."

7331 He makes for the heath straight away, turning his nag's head towards the man coming spurring across the sandy flats. Then my lord Gawain awaits him, bracing himself so firmly in the stirrups that he breaks the left one clean off. So, removing his foot from the right one, he waits like that for the knight, because the nag does not move and he cannot make it stir however hard he spurs it. "Alas," says he, "a nag's a sorry mount for a knight wanting to perform feats of arms!" Meanwhile the knight spurs towards him on his horse, which by no means limps along; and he gives him such a blow with his lance that it bends in an arc and snaps clean across, with its head sticking in Gawain's shield. My lord Gawain strikes against the rim of his shield with such a thrust that he cleaves right through shield and hauberk and brings him down on to the fine sand. Stretching out a hand, he holds back the horse and leaps into the saddle. He was delighted at this turn of events, and felt such joy in his heart that never in his whole life had he been so elated by a success. He heads back for the maiden who had got into the boat, but without finding a trace of either her or the craft. He was very annoyed to have lost her like that and not to know what had become of her.

7371 While he was thinking about the maiden, he saw a skiff approaching from the direction of the castle steered by a ferryman who, when he reached the landing-place, said: "Sir, I bring you greetings from those damsels, along with their request that you should not withhold from me my due." He replies: "May God bless the entire company of damsels and you too. As far as I'm concerned you'll never lose anything to which you have a rightful claim: I've no desire to wrong you. But what due are you asking me for?"—"Sir, you've felled here before my eyes a knight whose charger I should have. Unless you want to do me a wrong, you should hand over the charger."

7392 Gawain replied: "My friend, it would be too great a hardship for me to pay this due, because then I'd have to go on foot."—"Really, knight! Now those maidens you see consider you very unjust and think it very wicked of you not to give me my due; for never has it happened or been told that a knight was brought down at this landing-place to my knowledge without my getting his horse; or, if I didn't have the horse, I didn't fail to get the knight." Then my lord Gawain said to him: "My friend, you're free to take the knight, because I present him to you."—"By my faith, sir," says the ferryman, "I'm not interested in that gift. I fancy you yourself would find great difficulty in taking him if he had a mind to defend himself against you. Nevertheless, if you're valiant enough, go and take him and bring him to me, and you'll have discharged your debt to me."—"My friend, if I dismount, can I trust you faithfully to take care of my horse?"—"Yes, certainly," he says. "I'll look after it for you in good faith and return it to you willingly; and I'll never wrong you in any way as long as I live: on that I give you my solemn word."—"For my part", says he, "I'll believe that of you on your promise and assurance."

7429 He at once dismounts from his horse and hands it over to the ferryman, who takes it, saying he will look after it faithfully for him. Then, with drawn sword, my lord Gawain makes for the knight, who could do without further trouble, since he was so badly wounded in the side that he had lost a great deal of blood. My lord Gawain rides up to him. "Sir," says the knight in great alarm, "I've no reason to hide it from you: I'm so badly wounded that I don't need anything worse. I've lost a gallon of blood, and put myself at your mercy."—"Then get up!" he says. The knight does struggle to his feet; and Sir Gawain leads him off to the ferryman, who thanks him for him. Then my lord Gawain asks him for information, if he has any, of a maiden he had brought there and where she has gone. The ferryman replied: "Don't you worry about that maiden, sir, wherever she may go; for she's no maiden at all — no, she's worse than a devil and has had many knights' heads lopped off at this crossing-place. But if you'd take my advice, you'd come straight away to stay in such a lodging as I have, because it wouldn't be in your interest to stay on this riverbank, as it's wild country, full of very strange things."—"If that's what you propose, my friend, then I'll accept your advice, whatever may happen to me."

7469 Following the advice of the ferryman, who led his horse on board for him, he got into the boat; and they set out and came to the opposite bank. The ferryman's house was close to the river and was fit to receive a count: Gawain found it most comfortable. The ferryman takes his guest and his captive inside and entertains them as lavishly as he can. Sir Gawain was served with everything a worthy man might need: for supper he had plovers, pheasants, partridges and venison; and the wines were strong and clear, white and red, new and old. The ferryman was delighted with his prisoner and his guest. After they have finished eating, the table is cleared away and they wash their hands again. That night my lord Gawain had just such a host and lodging as he would wish, for he greatly appreciated the ferryman's service, which afforded him much pleasure.

7494 The next morning as soon as he could see daylight, he duly got up as was his custom. The ferryman rose too out of friendship, and they both went to lean at the windows of a small tower. Sir Gawain ran his eye over the very beautiful countryside: he saw the forests and the plains and the castle on its cliff. "My host," he says, "I'd like to ask and enquire of you, if you don't mind, who is the lord of this land and the castle over there." His host gives him a prompt reply: "I don't know, sir."—"You don't know? What you say is astonishing, because you're one of the castle's dependants and have a very large income from it, yet you don't know who its lord is!"—"I can tell you quite truly," he says, "that I don't know and never have done."—"Tell me then, good host, who defends the castle and guards it?"—"It has excellent protection, sir: five hundred bows and crossbows always ready to shoot. Should anyone want to cause any trouble there, they would never stop or tire of shooting, so cunningly are they devised.

7527 "But I'll tell you this much about the situation: there's a queen there who is a very distinguished, rich and wise lady of extremely high lineage. The queen came to live in this land, bringing her immense treasure of silver and gold, and she built this mighty residence you see before you. She brought with her a lady of whom she is very fond, calling her queen and daughter; and that lady also has a daughter, who is no disgrace or shame to her line, because I don't think there is anyone under heaven who surpasses her in beauty and refinement. The hall there is very well protected by magic and enchantment, as you're about to learn, if you'd like me to tell you. There in the main hall a clerk, expert in astronomy, whom the queen brought with her, established such great marvels that you never heard of their equal; for no knight can enter there and remain alive and well for the time it takes to cover a league if he is full of greed or at all tainted with deceitfulness or avarice. No coward or traitor survives there; and the faithless and perjurers cannot last there, but die in no time.

7563 "But there are many squires there, gathered together from numerous lands, who are serving their apprenticeship in arms. There are well over five hundred of them, some with beards and some without: a hundred with neither beards nor moustaches, another hundred just growing beards, and a hundred who shave and trim their beards every week; and there are a hundred there whiter than wool and a hundred who are just turning grey. There are also elderly ladies there without husbands or lords but, after the death of their husbands, very wrongfully disinherited of their lands and fiefs. There too are orphaned damsels with the two queens, who keep them very honourably. These are the people who frequent the hall and apartments of the castle; and they're waiting for something quite absurd which couldn't even happen, namely for the coming of a knight who will support them, returning their fiefs to the ladies, giving husbands to the maidens and making the squires knights. But the whole sea will freeze over before a knight is found able to stay in that great hall; for he would have to be ideally handsome and wise, quite free of greed, valiant and bold, with a noble and loyal heart, without baseness or other wickedness. If such a man could come, he would be able to have the lordship of the castle. He would restore their lands to the ladies and bring to an end the deadly wars, he would marry off the maidens, dub the squires knights and remove forthwith the hall's enchantments."

7605 This information was most pleasing and welcome to my lord Gawain. "My host," says he, "let's go down; and let me have my arms and horse again without delay, because I want to stay here no longer, but am leaving."—"Where for, sir? Do stay, and may God preserve you, for today, tomorrow and longer still!"—"Not at this time, host: but my blessing on your house! No: I'm off, so help me God, to see the maidens up there and the wonders inside."—"Say no more, sir! Please God you'll not act so foolishly, but take my word and stay here."—"Be quiet, host! Do you take me for a craven coward? May my soul never find a place with God if I ask for any advice on the matter!"—"Upon my word, sir, I'll speak no more of it, because that would be a waste of effort. As you're so set on going, go there you shall, to my great regret. I must guide you there, though; and you may be sure you could have no one better than I to conduct you. I should, though, like to ask you one favour."—"What favour, host? I'd like to know."—"Agree to it in advance!"—"My dear host, I'll do as you wish, as long as it involves me in no shame."

7638 He then orders his charger to be brought, all ready to ride, from the stable, and asks again for his arms, which are fetched for him.

He arms and mounts and makes to leave; and the ferryman also gets ready and mounts his palfrey, wishing to guide him faithfully to where he is reluctant for him to go. They ride until, at the foot of the stairs in front of the great hall, *they find, seated on his own on a bundle of rushes, a man with one good leg and an artificial one made of silver, or silver-plated, and banded at intervals with gold and precious stones. This one-legged man's hands were by no means idle, for he was holding a small knife and was busy whittling an ash stick. The man did not speak a word to them as they passed in front of him, nor did they say anything to him. But the ferryman drew my lord Gawain to him and said: "Sir, what do you think of this man with the artificial leg?"—"Upon my word," says Sir Gawain, "that leg is certainly not of aspen wood, for it looks magnificent to me."—"Yes, in God's name," says the ferryman, "for that one-legged man is rich and has a very large, handsome income. You'd really hear news that would greatly disturb you, were I not accompanying and guiding you."

7676 So they both passed on until they reached the great hall. It had a very lofty entrance; and its doors were costly and beautiful for, as the story confirms, all the hinges and hasps were of pure gold. One of the doors was of ivory, and its surface was finely carved, whilst the other was of ebony and carried similar decoration; and each was embellished with gold and precious jewels. The hall was paved with slabs of many different colours, green and scarlet, indigo and dark blue, expertly fashioned and highly polished. In the centre of the hall was a bed with nothing of wood about it, for it was made entirely of gold except for the cords, which were all of silver. What I tell of the bed is no fabrication. At each intersection of the cords a bell was hanging. Over the bed was spread a great coverlet of heavy silk material; and in each of its posts was set a carbuncle that shone more brilliantly than four brightly burning candles. The bed stood on little carved dogs that were pulling grotesque faces, and the dogs on four castors that moved so freely and swiftly that if anyone gave the bed a slight push with just one finger it would run all over the hall from one end to the other. To tell the truth, the bed was such that never was one like it made for king or count, or ever will be; and it was placed in the very centre of the hall.

7717 I want you to believe me when I say that in the hall there was nothing made of chalk: the interior walls were of marble and at the

top were windows with such clear glass that anyone looking carefully could see through it all those entering the hall as soon as they
passed the door. The walls were painted in the richest and choicest
colours that could be imagined or made. But I have no wish to
relate or describe every detail. In the hall there were a full four
hundred windows closed and a hundred open. My lord Gawain
went about the hall, up and down and hither and thither, scrutinis-
ing it carefully.

7735 Having looked everywhere, he called to the ferryman and said:
"My good host, I see nothing in here to make the hall too frighten-
ing to be entered. What do you say about it? What did you mean by
telling me so forcefully not to come and see it? I'd like to sit on this
bed and rest for just a short time: I've never seen such a luxurious
bed."—"Ah, dear sir, may God forbid that you should go near it!
For if you should approach it, you'd die the worst death that any
knight ever experienced."—"What should I do, then, host?"—
"Do, sir? I'll tell you, as I see that you've a mind to preserve your
life. When you were about to come here, I asked you in my house
for a favour, though you didn't know what. Now I want you to do
me that favour, namely to go back to your land and tell your friends
and your countrymen that you've seen a great hall richer than any
known to you or to anyone else."

7766 —"Then I'll say that God hates me and I'm dishonoured as
well. Nevertheless, host, it seems to me that you mean well in saying
that; but I assure you that on no account will I refrain from sitting
on that bed and seeing the maidens I saw last evening leaning at the
windows." The ferryman, drawing back in order to strike the
harder, replies: "You'll see none of the maidens you speak of. Just
you go away again the way you came here, because that sight is not
for you under any circumstances! Yet, may God protect me, the
maidens and the queens and ladies are seeing you clearly at this very
moment through those glass windows from where they are in the
rooms beyond."—"Upon my word," says my lord Gawain, "even
if I don't see the maidens, I'll at least sit on the bed, because I really
don't believe that a bed like that should have been made unless
either a noble gentleman or a fine lady were to lie there. And,
whatever may happen to me, I'm going to sit there, upon my soul!"

7796 Seeing he cannot prevent him, the ferryman stops his pleading.
However, he has no wish to stay in the hall long enough to see him

sit on the bed, but instead makes off, saying: "Sir, I'm exceedingly concerned and upset about your death, as no knight ever sat on that bed and left it alive; for that's the Wondrous Bed, on which no one sleeps or dozes or rests or even sits and ever gets up again alive and well. It's a terrible shame that you'll leave your life there in pledge without it ever being redeemed or bought back. As I can't get you away from here by my love or my arguments, may God have mercy on your soul, for my heart couldn't bear seeing you die!" With that he left the hall, and my lord Gawain sat down on the bed armed as he was and with his shield at his neck.

7821 When he has taken his seat, the bed-cords give out a screech and all the bells ring, making the whole hall resound. Then all the windows open and the marvels are disclosed and the enchantments revealed; for through the windows come flying bolts and arrows, and more than seven hundred of them strike my lord Gawain on the shield without his knowing who was responsible. The nature of the enchantment was that no man could see where the bolts came from nor the crossbowmen who were shooting them. As you may well imagine, there was a mighty din as the crossbows and bows were discharged. At that time Sir Gawain would have given a thousand marks not to be there. But suddenly the windows shut again without anyone pushing them. Then Sir Gawain pulled out the bolts which had stuck in his shield and had inflicted numerous wounds on his body so that it was bleeding profusely.

7849 However, before he had extracted them all, he was confronted with another trial; for a churl kicked at a door, the door opened, and a ravenous lion, a strong, fierce, huge, astonishing creature, leaps through that door out of a vaulted chamber to attack my lord Gawain with great ferocity and fury. It plunges all its claws into his shield as if into wax and knocks him to his knees. But he jumps up, immediately draws his naked sword from its sheath, and deals the lion such a blow that he cuts off its head and both its feet. Then Sir Gawain was delighted, for the feet stayed hanging from his shield by the claws, one dangling right inside, the other on the outside. Having slain the lion, he resumed his seat on the bed; and his host, beaming with pleasure, returned to the hall to find him sitting on the bed. He said: "Sir, I assure you that you've nothing more to fear. Take off all your armour, because by your coming here the marvels of the hall have ceased for ever; and, God be praised! you'll be served and honoured by the people in here, the young and the grey-haired alike."

7885 Then a crowd of young men appeared, very smartly dressed in tunics; and, falling to their knees, they said: "Good, dear, kind lord, we offer you our services as to one whom we have long awaited and for whom we have greatly yearned."—"And it seems to me I've delayed too long to serve your interests!" At once one of them took charge of him for some to set about disarming him while others went to stable his horse, which was waiting outside. Then, as they were removing his armour, a maiden came in. She was very beautiful and attractive and wore a gold circlet on her head, where the hair was as bright as the gold, or even brighter. Her face was white, its colouring enhanced by Nature with a pure crimson hue. The maiden was very comely, beautiful and well proportioned, standing tall and straight. Behind her came other very elegant and lovely maidens. Then one single youth entered, a robe fastened at his neck and wearing a tunic, mantle and surcoat. The mantle was lined with ermine and with sable as dark as a blackberry, the outside being of a fine crimson woollen material.

7918 My lord Gawain looks in wonder as the maidens approach and cannot help jumping to his feet to greet them with the words: "Welcome, maidens!" The first bows to him and says: "Dear good sir, my lady the queen sends you greeting and bids all her people to hold you as their rightful lord and to come and serve you. I shall be the first sincerely to offer you my service, and these maidens here all recognise you as their lord, having greatly longed for your coming. Now they are happy when they see you, the best of all worthy men; and it only remains for us, sir, to be ready in your service." As she says this, they all kneel and bow as if to pledge themselves to serve and honour him. He promptly has them rise again and then sit down, being delighted to see them, partly because of their beauty and even more because they are treating him as their prince and lord. He is joyful as never before at the honour God has done him.

7950 The first maiden then stepped forward and said: "My lady sends you this robe to put on before she sees you because, not lacking in courtliness and good sense, she supposes that you've endured great hardship and suffering and become very hot. Try it on, then, and see if it fits you well, for wise people after being hot guard against the cold, since it brings on chills and stiffness. That's why my lady the queen sends you an ermine robe so that you'll not suffer from the cold; for just as water turns to ice so, when one shivers after being hot, the blood coagulates and clots." Then my lord Gawain replies with all the courtliness in the world: "May that Lord in whom no goodness is lacking save my lady the queen and your own kindly-spoken, courtly and charming self! I suppose the queen to be most considerate when her messengers are so courteous. She knows very well what is necessary and fitting for a knight when she sends me this robe to wear, for which I thank her. Do express to her my deep gratitude."—"So I shall, and gladly, I promise you," says the maiden. "In the meantime you can put it on and look at the features of this countryside from the windows; or, if you wish, you could climb that tower for a view of the forests, plains and rivers until I return."

7991 With that the maiden leaves; and my lord Gawain dons the very costly robe, fastening it at the neck with a clasp that hung from the collar. Then he chooses to go and see the viewing-points in the tower. He and his host go together, and they climb a spiral staircase at the side of the vaulted hall until they reach the top of the tower. They then see the country all around, which is beautiful beyond description. Sir Gawain gazed at the river and the level tracts and the forests full of animal life and, looking at his host, said: "My God, host, I'd be very happy staying here and going hunting and shooting in those forests over there."—"My lord," says the ferryman, "you may as well say no more about that, because I've often heard it said that the man so favoured by God as to be recognised here as master, lord and protector would never, according to the established convention, leave this house, rightly or wrongly. Therefore you needn't talk of hunting or shooting, because this is where you stay, never to leave again."—"That's enough of that, host," says he, "for I'd go out of my mind if I heard you say any more about it! You may be certain that I could no more live here for seven days than for seven score years unless I could go out as often as I wanted."

8033 He immediately went down and back into the hall. Highly indignant and pensive, he sat down on the bed again with a very sad, doleful expression on his face until the return of the maiden who had been there before. When my lord Gawain saw her, angry as he was, he got up to meet her and greeted her straight away. She sees the change that has come over his speech and manner and plainly realises from his appearance that something has irritated him; but, afraid of showing that she has noticed anything, she says: "My lord, when it pleases you my lady will come to see you. But the meal is ready and, if you wish, you may eat either down here or upstairs." Sir Gawain replies: "My fair one, I don't feel like eating. May personal calamity strike me if I eat or enjoy myself before I hear news to cheer me up, for I really need to hear it!" The maiden immediately went away again in great alarm; and the queen summoned her and asked what news she had.

8065 "My dear grand-daughter," says the queen, "in what state and condition have you found the good lord whom God sent here to us?"—"Ah, my lady, honoured queen, I'm full of mortal grief and affliction for that good, noble-hearted lord; for you can get nothing out of him but angry, irritable words, and I can't tell you why because he didn't tell me, and I neither know nor dared ask him. But I can tell you this much about him: the first time I met him today I found him so courteous, eloquent and cheerful that you couldn't tire of hearing him talk or seeing his happy face. Now, suddenly, his manner is so different that I think he'd rather be dead, because he hears nothing that doesn't annoy him."—"Don't worry about it, grand-daughter, because he'll quickly calm down as soon as he sees me. However great his anger is, I'll soon rid him of it and replace it with joy."

8093 The queen then made for the hall accompanied by the other queen, who was very happy to go; and in their wake they brought a full two hundred and fifty damsels and at least as many youths. No sooner had my lord Gawain seen the queen approaching holding the other by the hand than his heart told him (for one's heart often has such intuition) that this was the queen of whom he had heard. But that he could readily guess by her white tresses that hung down to her hips; and she was dressed in heavy white silk delicately worked with golden flowers. When my lord Gawain sees her, he does not delay in going to meet her; and he greets her and she him.

8114 She then said: "Sir, after you I am mistress of this castle. I leave the lordship of it to you, though, for you have well merited it. But are you of King Arthur's household?"—"Yes indeed, my lady."—"And are you, I'd like to know, one of the knights of the guard, who have performed many deeds of prowess?"—"No, my

lady."—"I believe you. Tell me, then, do you belong to the company of the Round Table who have the highest reputation in the
world?"—"My lady," said he, "I should not dare to call myself one
of the most highly reputed: I neither rank myself among the best,
nor do I think I'm one of the worst." She replies: "Good sir, that's a
very courtly thing to say, ascribing to yourself neither the honour of
being the best nor the worst of the blame. Tell me now, though,
about King Lot:* how many sons did he have by his
wife?"—"Four, my lady."—"Name them for me."—"My lady,
Gawain was the eldest, and then came Agravain, the arrogant one
with strong hands. The names of the last two are Gaheriet and
Guerrehet."

8143 The queen responded: "Sir, so help me the Lord God, those are
their names, I believe. And would to God they were all here
together with us! But say, now, do you know King
Urien?"*—"Yes, my lady."—"And has he a son at court?"—"Yes,
my lady, he has two of high renown: one is named my lord Yvain,
of the courtly, polished manners; and when I can see him in the
morning I'm the more cheerful throughout the day, so prudent and
courteous do I find him. The other is also called Yvain, but is not his
full brother, and so is called the Bastard; and he gets the better of all
knights who join in combat with him. They are both at court and
are extremely gallant, wise and courtly."

8164 —"And King Arthur, good sir," she says, "how is he
now?"—"Better than ever: fitter, more agile and stronger."—
"Upon my word, sir, that's just as it should be, because he's a young
man, King Arthur: if he's a hundred, that's all he is – he can't be any
older. But I should also like to hear from you just about the queen, if
you don't mind: how is she faring and getting along?"—"Indeed,
my lady, she's so courtly, so beautiful and so wise that God never
made a race or realm where so lovely a lady could be found. Since
God created the first woman from Adam's rib no lady has enjoyed
such renown. And it is only right that she should: just as the wise
master instructs little children, so my lady the queen teaches and
educates the whole world; for from her all goodness derives, stems
and is passed down. No one can possibly leave my lady without
having received good guidance. She knows well the worth of each
individual and how to treat him in order to please him. No man
performs a good or honourable deed without having learnt it from

my lady; and no man will ever be so dejected that he goes away
from my lady in low spirits."

8199 —"Nor will you leave me so, sir."—"My lady," he says, "I
really believe you; for before seeing you I didn't care what I did,
because I was so dispirited and miserable. Now I'm so completely
happy and joyful that I couldn't be more so."—"Sir, by God to
whom I owe my birth," says the queen with the white tresses, "your
happiness will grow twice as great yet and your joy continue to
increase and be with you always. And since you're now in a happy,
cheerful mood and the meal is prepared, you can eat when you
please and wherever you like: if you wish you can eat upstairs or, if
you prefer, you can come to dine in the rooms below."—"My lady,
I have no desire to exchange this hall for any room, since I've been
told that no knight ever sat to eat in it."—"No one, sir, who came
out again afterwards or remained alive here for as long as it takes to
cover a league or even half of one."—"Then, my lady, this is where
I shall eat, if you give me permission."—"I give it you gladly, sir;
and you'll be the very first knight ever to have eaten here."

8229 With that the queen departs, leaving with him two hundred
and fifty of her loveliest maidens to dine with him in the hall, serve
him and gratify his every wish. Squires attended him cheerfully at
table, some completely white-haired, others turning grey and others not. Still others had no beards or moustaches; and two of these
knelt before him, one doing the carving, the other pouring the wine.
My lord Gawain had his host sit close by his side. The dinner was
not short, for it went on for longer than a day lasts around Trinity;
and it was dark, murky night and many great torches had been lit
before that meal was over. During dinner there was much conversation, and after they had eaten there were many dances and
rounds before they retired to their beds, everyone putting all their
energies into the merrymaking for their beloved lord. Then, when
he wished to retire, he lay down on the Wondrous Bed. One of the
maidens placed a pillow beneath his head, ensuring that he slept in
comfort.

8263 When he woke the next day, a robe of ermine and samite had
been made ready for him; and the ferryman of whom I have spoken
came to help him that morning when he rose, dressed and washed
his hands. Also present at his rising was the prudent, beautiful,
gifted, wise, eloquent Clarissant, who afterwards went into the

apartments of her grandmother the queen, who spoke to her and asked: "By the faith you owe me, grand-daughter, has your lord got up yet?"—"Yes, my lady, a long time ago."—"Where is he, then, dear grand-daughter?"—"He went up the small tower, my lady, but I don't know if he's come down since."—"I wish to go to him, grand-daughter, and if it please God, this day will bring him nothing but good, joy and happiness." The queen rose at once in her desire to go to him.

8286 She went until she saw him up at the windows of a turret, where he was watching a maiden and a fully armed knight coming across a meadow. Here now from the other direction come the two queens, side by side, to where my lord Gawain was on the lookout; and they found him and his host positioned at two windows. "Sir," say the queens together, "may your rising be a happy one, and may this day bring you joy and gladness! May this be granted by that glorious Father who made of His daughter His mother!"—"May you be given great joy, my lady, by Him who sent His son to earth to exalt Christianity! But, if it should be your pleasure, come over to this window and tell me who a maiden can be who is coming this way accompanied by a knight bearing a quartered shield."

8310 —"I'll tell you that straight away," says the lady on seeing them. "That's the person who came here with you last evening, and may hellfire burn her! Don't concern yourself with her, though, because she's a most arrogant, wicked creature. And I beg you too not to take any notice of that knight she's bringing; for you may be quite sure he surpasses all knights in courage. A combat against him is no game, for he's put many a knight to death at this crossing-place before my very eyes."—"My lady," he says, "I should like to go and speak to the damsel and ask your leave to do so."—"May it not please God, sir, that I should grant you leave to come to harm! Let her go on her own business! That damsel is an offensive individual. If it's God's will, you'll never leave this hall on such a foolish errand. You should never go out of here unless you want to do us a wrong."

8334 —"Really now, noble queen, you thoroughly alarm me! I'd consider myself poorly rewarded with this castle if I couldn't leave it. May it not please God that I should stay a prisoner in it like this for long!"—"Ah, my lady," says the ferryman, "let him do as he wishes. Don't keep him back against his will, for he might die of

grief."—"Then I'll allow him to leave," says the queen, "on condition that if God protects him from death, he'll come back again
tonight."—"My lady," says he, "don't be offended; for I shall
return if I possibly can, but I do ask and beg one favour of you, if it's
your pleasure and will, namely that you don't ask me my name for a
week, if you have no objection."—"Then, sir, since that's your
wish," says the queen, "I'll do without knowing, because I'd not
like to incur your hatred. Yet that would have been my first request
of you, to tell me your name, had you not forbidden it." So they
came down from the turret; and squires run to give him his armour
so that he may be armed. Then they brought out his horse; and,
fully armed, he mounted and rode to the crossing-place, the ferryman going with him. They both enter the boat, and oarsmen row
them from that bank across to the other, where my lord Gawain
disembarks.

8372 The other knight then said to the pitiless maiden: "My dear,
this knight coming armed in our direction – tell me, is he someone
you know?" The maiden answered: "No, he's not; but I'm quite
sure he's the one who brought me here yesterday." Then he replies:
"As God's my protector, he's the very man I was looking for! I'd
been very much afraid he'd escaped me; for no mother's son of a
knight goes through the passes into Galloway who, provided I
happen to see him and meet him face to face, is ever able to boast
anywhere else that he's come back from this country. Now God has
let this one come to me, he's certain to be taken captive."

8392 The knight charges at once without issuing any challenge or
threat, spurring on his horse, and with his shield firm on his arm.
Then my lord Gawain heads for him and strikes, wounding him
very seriously in the arm and side. But the wound was not mortal,
for the hauberk was so tough that the whole lance-head could not
penetrate it. He does, however, drive the tip of its point a whole
finger's length into his body and knocks him to the ground. He gets
up again and, to his great distress, sees his blood running from his
arm and side over the bright hauberk. So he ran at him with his
sword, but very quickly tired, and was unable to resist any further
but had to ask for mercy. Then my lord Gawain accepts his
assurances and hands him over to the ferryman, who was waiting
for him.

8414 The malicious maiden had dismounted from her palfrey.
Gawain comes up and greets her with the words: "Mount again,

my fair friend, for I'll not leave you here; but you shall come with me over that river I have to cross."—"Oho, knight!" she says. "What proud behaviour now! You'd have had your fill of fighting if my lover hadn't been tired because of old wounds he's received: your extravagant talk would have been thoroughly silenced, and you wouldn't now be bragging so much but would be as quiet as a king checkmated in the corner! But admit the truth: do you think you're worth more than he just because you've beaten him? You've often seen the weak overcome the strong. However, if you'd leave this crossing-place, come with me under that tree, and then do something that my lover whom you've put in that boat used to do for me whenever I wished, then I'd freely grant that you're as good a man as he, and I wouldn't despise you any more."—"Maiden," he says, "I'll not fail to meet your wish by going as far as there." She replied: "May it not please God that I see you return from there!" With that they set off, she ahead and he following.

8450 Then the maidens and ladies in the great hall tear their hair, rend and rip their clothes, and say: "Alas, how wretched we are! Alas, why are we still alive when we see on his way to death and ruin the man who was to have been our lord? The malicious maiden is leading him along with her, vile creature that she is, to the place from which no knight returns. Alas! Now affliction has replaced our great good fortune in having been sent by God the one who was versed in all good things and in whom nothing, neither courage nor any other virtue, was lacking." Thus they lamented for their lord, whom they watched going with the malicious maiden.

8470 She arrives with him beneath the tree; and when they had come there, my lord Gawain called to her, saying: "My fair one, tell me now if I can be released from my obligation or if you wish me to do more. Rather than lose your favour, I'll do it, if it's in my power." Then the maiden said to him: "Do you see that deep ford over there with the very high banks? *My lover used to cross it; and I don't know any less steep place."—"Ah, my fair one, I'm afraid that would be impossible, because the bank is everywhere too high to get down."—"You wouldn't dare cross it," says the maiden; "I'm sure of that. Indeed it never entered my head that your heart was stout enough for you to dare cross over there, because that's the Perilous Ford, which no one unless he's an absolute prodigy dare cross on any account."

8498 My lord Gawain takes his horse up to the bank and sees the deep water below and the bank rising sheer. The river, though, was narrow; and seeing this, Sir Gawain said his horse had jumped many wider ditches. He thinks too that he has heard it said and reported in various places that anyone able to cross the deep channel at the Perilous Ford would obtain the highest honour in the world. Then he distances himself from the river and comes back at full gallop to leap across; but, not having been properly set for the jump, he is short and lands in the very middle of the ford. His horse swam until it got all its four feet on land; and then, putting a great effort into its leap, it launches itself up to land on that very high bank. Once on the bank, it stood quite still and quiet, unable to stir; so Sir Gawain, finding his horse quite exhausted, was forced to dismount. This he proceeded to do. Then he decided to remove its saddle; so he took it off and turned it over to dry it. Once the saddle-cloth was off, he wiped the water from the horse's back, flanks and legs.

8534 He then replaces his saddle, mounts and rides on at a very slow walk until he sees a knight hunting on his own with a sparrowhawk and two small retrievers in the field planted with trees in front of him. It would be impossible to tell how very handsome the knight was. When my lord Gawain came near him, he greeted him with the words: "Good sir, may God who made you more handsome than any other mortal give you joy and good fortune!" The other was swift to reply: "It is you who are good, valiant and handsome. But tell me, if you don't mind, how you've come to leave the malicious maiden alone over there. Where has her escort gone?"—"Sir," he replies, "a knight bearing a quartered shield was accompanying her when I met her."—"And what did you do?—"I defeated him in combat."—"So what became of the knight afterwards?"—"I took him to the ferryman, since he claimed he should have him."

8560 —"Indeed, dear brother, he told you the truth. That maiden was my sweetheart, though not in the sense that she ever deigned to love me or consent to call me her lover. And I swear to you that I never kissed her except by force and never had my way with her at all, because I loved her against her will. I robbed her of a lover she used to go about with, killing him and taking her away; and I did my utmost to serve her. My services were in vain, because just as soon as she could she found an opportunity to leave me and adopted as her lover the man from whom you've just taken her. He's no mean knight, but extremely valiant, so help me God. Yet from then on he never summoned up the nerve to come anywhere he thought he would find me. But today you've performed a feat that no knight has the courage to attempt; and because you dared to accomplish it, you've won through your valour all the honour and praise in the world. When you leapt the Perilous Ford, that needed great boldness; and it's a fact, you may be sure, that never before has any knight survived it."

8592 —"In that case, sir," says Gawain, "that damsel lied to me in telling me and giving me to believe that her lover crossed it once a day for love of her."—"She said that, the faithless hussy? Oh, she should be drowned in it, for she's possessed by the devil to have told you such a tale! She hates you, there's no denying it, and wanted to have you drowned in the deep, roaring water, did that demon – may God confound her! But now give me your word and the same pledge as I give you: if you choose to ask me anything, whether to my joy or sorrow, I'll on no account conceal the truth from you, if I know it; and you for your part will also assure me that in no circumstances will you lie about anything I want to know, if you can tell me the truth."

8615 They made this mutual pact; and then my lord Gawain was the first to put a question. "Sir," he says, "I want to ask about a city I can see over there: to whom does it belong, and what is its name?"—"My friend," he replies, "I can indeed tell you the truth about that city, for I hold it quite freely and owe nothing for any part of it to any mortal man: I hold it from God alone, and its name is Orqueneseles."—"And your name?"—"Guiromelant."—"Sir, you're a very valiant, gallant man, as I've indeed heard, and lord of a very great land. But what's the name of that maiden about whom no good word is spoken near or far, as you yourself maintain?"—"I can", he says, "assure you that she's much to be feared, for she's very malicious and scornful; and for that she's called the Haughty Maiden of Logres,* her birthplace, from which she was brought when she was small."—"And her lover who has gone, like it or not, to be the ferryman's prisoner – what's his name?"—"I tell you, my friend, that that man is a wonderful knight; and he's called the Haughty Knight of the Rock* on the Narrow Way and is guardian of the passes into Galloway."—"And what's the name of the castle that's so lofty and splendid and beautiful on the other side, which I left today and where I ate and drank last evening?"

8653 When he asked that, Guiromelant turned away from him as if in sorrow and started to go off. Gawain makes to call him back: "Sir, sir, speak to me and remember your word!" Then Guiromelant stops, turns his head towards him and says: "A curse and damnation on the hour I saw you and pledged you my word! Go away! I release you from your promise, and you free me from mine in exchange, because I was thinking of asking you for some information about that place on the other side; but I fancy you know as much about the moon as about that castle."—"Sir," he says, "I was there last night and slept in the Wondrous Bed, which no other bed can match, for no one has seen its equal."—"By God!" says he, "I'm quite astounded at the news you give me. Now it's great entertainment and a pleasure to listen to your fictions: it's as good listening to a story-teller as to you! It's plain to me you're a minstrel – and I thought you were a knight and had done some valiant deed over there! Still, let me know whether you did perform some bold deed, and what you saw there."

8687 Then my lord Gawain told him: "Sir, when I sat on the bed, there was a very great commotion in the hall. Don't think I'm lying to you, but the bed-cords screamed out and a set of bells hanging from them rang; and the windows that were closed opened of their own accord; then I was struck on the shield by bolts and polished arrows. And it still has in it the claws of a great, fierce lion with a bristling mane that had been chained up in a vaulted chamber for a long time. That lion was set on me, released by a churl; and it hurled itself at me so violently, struck my shield and dug in its claws so hard that it couldn't pull them out again. If you think it left no signs, just look at the claws still here! For, thank God, I sliced off its head and feet at the same time. What do you make of this evidence?"

8713 Hearing this, Guiromelant dismounted with all speed and fell to his knees, joining his hands together and begging him to forgive the foolish things he has said. "You have my full pardon," says Gawain, "so mount your horse again." He does so, thoroughly ashamed of his foolishness, and says: "Sir, as God is my protector, I never imagined that anywhere, near or far, there could be any knight who might ever have the honour that's fallen to you. But tell me whether you saw the white-haired queen and enquired of her who she is and where she's come from."—"I never thought to do so," he replies; "but I did see her and speak to her."

8732 —"Then I'll tell you," he says; "for she's King Arthur's mother."—"By the faith I owe God and His power, as far as I'm aware King Arthur has had no mother for a long time, not for a good sixty years, to my knowledge, and even for much longer than that."—"Yet it's true, sir: she is his mother. When his father Utherpendragon was laid to rest, it came about that Queen Ygerne came to this country bringing with her all her treasure and had constructed on that rock the castle with its splendid, rich hall, as I've heard you describe it. And I'm sure you saw the other queen, that tall, handsome lady who was King Lot's wife and the mother of that man on whom I wish continuing disaster – the mother of Gawain."

8753 —"My dear sir, I know Gawain well and venture to say that this Gawain has had no mother for at least a good twenty years."—"That's who she is though, sir, and don't doubt it; for she followed her mother here pregnant with a child, that very beautiful, tall damsel who is my beloved and, I'll not disguise the fact, the sister of that man on whom I'd wish God to bring the greatest shame! Truly he'd not get away with his head if I got the upper hand over him and had him on the spot here as I have you, because I'd slice it straight off! His sister wouldn't help him and stop me from tearing the heart out of his breast with my bare hands, so deeply do I hate him."

8772 —"Upon my soul," says my lord Gawain, "you don't love in the same way as I do. If I loved a maiden or lady, for her sake I'd love and serve all her family."—"You're right, I agree. But when I remember how Gawain's father killed mine, I can't have any sympathy for him. And he himself with his own hands killed one of my first cousins, a gallant, valiant knight. Since then I've never found any opportunity to avenge him. But do me a service now: go back to the castle and take this ring and give it to my sweetheart for me. I want you to pass it to her from me and tell her that I have such faith and trust in her love as to suppose she would rather have her brother Gawain die a bitter death than that I should have hurt even my smallest toe. Just greet my sweetheart from me and give her this ring for me, her lover."

8800 My lord Gawain then placed the ring on his little finger and said: "Sir, by the faith I owe you, you have a courtly, wise sweetheart, a noble woman of high birth, beautiful, attractive and good-hearted, if she accepts the situation as you've expressed and described it." Guiromelant replied: "Sir, you'll do me a great favour, I assure you, if you take my ring as a gift to my dear love, for my love for her is deep and strong. And I'll reward you for this by telling you the name of the castle, as you asked me to: this castle, if you don't know, is called the Rock of Chanpguin.* Many fine, costly green and blood-red cloths are woven there along with many excellent woollen materials, and much buying and selling goes on. Now I've told you everything you wished, without telling you a word of a lie; and you too have given me good information. Is there anything more you have to ask me?"—"No, sir, other than for my leave to go."—Then he said: "If you don't mind, sir, you'll tell me your name before you're free to leave me."

8829 My lord Gawain then said to him: "Sir, I'll not keep my name from you, so help me God: I'm the man you hate so much – I'm Gawain."—"You're Gawain?"—"Yes, indeed, King Arthur's nephew."—"By my faith, you're either too bold or too foolish in telling me your name, knowing I hate you mortally. Now I'm very vexed and sorry that I don't have my helmet laced on or my shield held ready at my neck; because if I were armed as you are, you may be certain I'd cut off your head at once and not hold back for anything. But if you dared wait for me , I'd go and get my arms and come back to fight you, bringing along three or four men to watch our duel. Or, if you wish, we can make another arrangement: we can wait for a week and, on the seventh day, come to this place fully armed. You should have sent for the king and queen and all his people; and I for my part will have assembled my own company from my whole kingdom. In this way our combat won't be fought in secret, but will be watched by all those who have gathered here. For a combat between two men as worthy as we are held to be shouldn't be held surreptitiously: on the contrary, it's only right that there should be many ladies and knights in attendance; for when one of us is overcome and everybody knows about it, the victor will win a thousand times more honour than if he alone knew."

8871 —"Sir," says my lord Gawain, "I'd gladly be content with less than this, if it were possible and you were happy for there to be no combat. For if I've done you any wrong, I'm very willing to make such amends as will be reasonable and fair in the eyes of both your friends and mine." He replied: "I've no idea what can be reasonable about your not daring to fight with me. I've made two proposals, so adopt the one you prefer: if you dare, you'll wait for me while I go to get my arms; or else you'll summon all your supporters from your land for one week hence. For King Arthur's court will be in Orkney at Pentecost according to the news I've had; and that's no more than two days' journey from here. Your messenger will be able to find the king and his people all in readiness there. You'd be wise to send word there; for one day's delay is worth a hundred shillings." He replies: "As God is my saviour, the court will definitely be there: your information is quite correct. Here's my hand as a pledge that I'll send there tomorrow or before I sleep a wink."

8902 —"Then, Gawain," he says, "I'll take you to the finest bridge in the world. That river is too fast-flowing and deep for anything alive to cross or leap to the opposite bank." My lord Gawain replies: "I'll look for no ford or bridge, whatever may happen to me, lest the wicked damsel should put it down to cowardice. No, I'll keep my promise and go straight across to her." Then he digs in his spurs, and the horse jumps freely and without hesitation across the water. When the maiden who had so lashed him with her tongue saw him cross in her direction, she tethered her horse to the tree and came towards him on foot. She has changed her feelings and attitude, greeting him quite submissively and saying she has come to him to ask his mercy as one conscious of her guilt, since he has undergone great hardship on account of her.

8927 "Good sir," she says, "listen now to the reason for my being so arrogant towards all the knights in the world who have taken me with them. I'd like to tell you, if you don't mind. That knight, God curse him! who spoke to you on the other side wasted his love on me, because he loved me and I hated him, since he caused me great distress by killing, and I'll not disguise the fact, the one whose sweetheart I was. He then supposed he was doing me honour by trying to win me over to his love; but he got no benefit from that, because as soon as I had the opportunity I escaped from his company and joined up with the man whom you took me from today, not that that matters at all to me. But for so long after death snatched my first lover from me I've been so crazed, so overbearing in my speech, so base and stupid that I never cared whom I went

about offending; in fact I did it deliberately, hoping to find somebody so quick-tempered that I'd make him sufficiently angry and
furious with me that he'd hack me to pieces, since for some time I've
longed to be killed. Now, good sir, exact such punishment that
never will any maiden, having heard of my fate, dare to speak
shamefully to a knight again."

8964 —"My fair one," says he, "what good would it do me to
punish you? May it never please the Son of the Lord God that you
should suffer harm at my hands! Come along now and mount, and
we'll go to that mighty castle. See: the ferryman's waiting at the
crossing-place to take us over."—"I'll obey your every wish, sir,"
said the maiden. With that she climbed into the saddle of a small,
long-maned palfrey; and they came to the ferryman, for whom it
was no trouble or effort to take them across the river.

8979 Then the ladies and maidens who had been lamenting bitterly
for Gawain see them coming. All the squires in the great hall had
also been out of their minds with grief. But now their rejoicing
exceeds any there has ever been. To wait for him the queen had
taken her seat in front of the hall; and she had had all her maidens
join hands to dance in celebration. As a welcome for him they begin
their revelling with singing, dances and rounds. Then he arrives and
dismounts in their midst. The ladies and maidens and the two
queens embrace him and address him most joyfully, then gaily
remove the armour from his legs and arms, breast and head. They
showed great joy in turn to the maiden he had brought with him,
with everybody, men and ladies alike, serving her for his sake, not
at all for hers. Still rejoicing, they made their way into the hall,
where they all sat down.

9005 My lord Gawain then took his sister and seated her beside him
on the Wondrous Bed, whispering to her in private: "My damsel, I
bring you from beyond that crossing-place a golden ring with a
brilliant green emerald. A knight sends it to you with his love and
greetings; and he told me you're his beloved."—"Sir," she says, "I
well believe you; but if I have any love for him at all, I'm his
sweetheart from a distance, because he's never seen me nor I him
except across this river. A long while ago, though, he did give me his
love, and I'm grateful to him for it; and yet he's never crossed to this
side. However, his messengers brought requests for my love until,
I'll not deny it, I granted it to him. I'm not yet his sweetheart to any

greater extent."—"Ah, my fair one, he actually boasted that you would far rather have my lord Gawain, your natural brother, dead than have him hurt his toe."—"What, sir? I'm quite astonished how he could say such a stupid thing! By God, I had no idea he was so uncouth. He's really been very rash to send this message. My brother, alas, doesn't know I'm born and has never seen me. Guiromelant was wrong to say that, because, by my soul, I'd no more want his misfortune than my own."

9043 While the two of them were having this conversation, the ladies were waiting for them; and the old queen said to her daughter seated beside her: "My dear daughter, what's your opinion of that lord sitting next to your daughter, my grand-daughter? He's been whispering to her for a long time, I don't know what about. But I'm very pleased at that; and we have no grounds for worrying, because it's a sign of fine breeding to be attracted to the most beautiful and prudent lady in this hall, and he's quite right. Would to God she were his wife and pleased him as much as Lavinia pleased Aeneas!"—"Ah, my lady," says the other queen, "may God grant that he so sets his heart on her that they become like brother and sister, with such mutual love between them that they are both as one flesh!" By her prayer the lady means that he should love her and take her as his wife. She does not recognise her son: they will indeed be as brother and sister, for once they are both aware that she is his sister and he her brother, there will be no other kind of love between them; and from that their mother will derive a joy different from the one she anticipates!

9074 My lord Gawain conversed with his beautiful sister until eventually he turned and called a youth he saw to his right, the one appearing to him the most alert, prudent, diligent, sensible and capable of all the squires in the hall. He goes down into a room with just this youth following him. When they were in there together, he said to him: "Young man, I suppose you're very prudent, sensible and resourceful. If I tell you a plan of mine, I warn you to keep it quite secret, which will be to your advantage. I intend to send you to a place where you'll be received with great joy."—"My lord, I'd rather have my tongue torn from my throat than have a single word that you want concealed prised from my lips."

9097 —"Then, brother," he says, "you'll go to my lord King Arthur, for my name's Gawain and I'm his nephew. It's not a long or

difficult journey, for the king has set up his court to celebrate
Pentecost in the city of Orkney. If the journey there is very costly for
you, rely on me. When you come before the king, you'll find him
very depressed; then when you give him greetings from me, he'll be
overjoyed. There won't be a single person there who will not be
happy to hear your news. You'll tell the king that by the faith he
owes me, he being my lord and I his vassal, on no account must I fail
to find him on the fifth day of the festival encamped in the meadows
below this tower. There too should be the entire company attending his court, those of high rank and those of low; for I've undertaken a combat against a knight who considers neither me nor him
of much worth. He's none other than Guiromelant, who has a
mortal hatred of him. You'll also tell the queen that she must come
here because of the firm faith that should exist between us, since
she's my lady and my friend. When she hears the news, she won't
fail to bring, for love of me, the ladies and maidens who will be at
her court that day. But I'm very afraid of one thing: you may not
have a good enough hunter to carry you there quickly." He replies
that there is a big, speedy one that is strong and excellent and which
he can take for his own use. "Then I'm not worried," says Sir
Gawain.

9142   The youth then leads him quickly to some stables, and takes
and leads out some strong, well-rested hunters, one of which was
equipped to be ridden on a journey, because he had had it newly
shod and it lacked neither saddle nor bridle. "By my faith," says my
lord Gawain, "you're well off for equipment, young man! Go now,
and may the King of Kings grant you a good journey there and back
and keep you on the right road!" So he sends the squire off,
accompanying him as far as the river and ordering the ferryman to
take him across. This the ferryman does without needing to tire
himself, as he had plenty of oarsmen. Once across, the youth took
the direct road for the city of Orkney: anyone who knows how to
ask the way can travel the world!

9167   Then my lord Gawain returns to his residence, where he stays
with great joy and pleasure, for everybody there loves and serves
him. The queen had the water heated for baths in five hundred tubs,
into which she had all the squires go to wash and bathe. Robes had
been tailored for them; and they were all ready for them when they
left the baths. Their cloth was woven with gold thread, and they

were lined with ermine. The young men kept vigil in the church, standing and never kneeling, until after matins. In the morning my lord Gawain, with his own hands, fastened on each of them the right spur and girt on the sword, giving them the accolade. After that, he had a company of at least five hundred new knights.

9189 The youth, meanwhile, journeyed until he reached the city of Orkney, where the king was holding such a court as was fitting for that special day. As they watch the youth, the cripples and the scurvy folk say: "He's coming on important business. I fancy he's bringing news and some message to court from far away. Regardless of what he may report, he'll find the king quite deaf and dumb, for he's overcome with grief and anguish. And who will there be now to advise him when he's heard what the messenger wants?"—"Now then!" some say. "What business is it of yours to talk about the king's affairs? You should be full of alarm and dismay and distress when we've lost the man who sustained us all for God's sake and from whom we received all that bounty out of love and charity." In this way throughout the city my lord Gawain's absence was lamented by the poor people, who loved him dearly.

9215 *The youth passed on and continued until he found the king sitting in his great hall with a hundred counts palatine, a hundred kings and a hundred dukes seated round him. The king was dejected and pensive to see his great company of nobles but no sign of his nephew. In his distress he fell in a swoon. The first to manage to reach him to raise him up was scarcely idle, for they all ran to support him. My lady Lore* was sitting in a gallery and saw the grief shown throughout the hall. Leaving the gallery, she came down to the queen in a very distressed state. When she saw her, the queen asked her what was the matter.* 9234

GLOSSARY OF TECHNICAL
AND ARCHAIC TERMS

BAILEY: outer walls of castle or space between outer and inner walls.

BALDRIC: sword-belt hung from shoulder to opposite hip.

BARBICAN: outer defensive tower of castle.

BEZANT: gold coin current in Europe in the Middle Ages, first struck in Byzantium.

BRAZIL-WOOD: a red dye-wood from the East.

BUCKLER: small round shield.

CARBUNCLE: mythical light-emitting gem.

CASTLE: the Old French *chastel* was normally a fortified town (translated in different contexts as 'castle', 'stronghold' or 'fortress').

COIF: a close-fitting skull-cap of mail worn under the helmet.

COMPLINE: the seventh and last canonical hour; the service at that time.

DANISH AXE: long-bladed battle-axe.

ELL: varying measure of length (about a yard).

FATHOM: measure of six feet.

FURLONG: 220 yards.

GALLERY: Old French *loges* were balconies or open galleries forming vantage-points on the upper floors of buildings.

GREAVES: leg-armour.

HALBERD: spiked battle-axe.

HAUBERK: coat of mail reaching to the knees.

LEAGUE: varying measure of distance (about three miles).

LISTS: enclosed area for jousting.

MANGONEL: machine for casting stones, etc.

MARK: (a) measure of weight (8 ounces) for gold and silver; (b) gold or silver coin.

NOCK: a piece of horn at the butt-end of an arrow, having a notch to take the bow-string.

NONE: ninth hour of the day or 3 p.m.

PALFREY: horse for ordinary riding, especially for ladies.

PLIRIS ARCHONTICUM: electuary (see note to *Perceval* l. 3327).

PRIME: first hour of the day or 6 a.m.

PSALTERY: stringed instrument played by plucking.

QUINTAIN: post for tilting at, often with a pivoting cross-piece to strike the unskilled tilter.

REST (in phrase "lance in rest"): support holding butt of lance when lowered for charging.

RESUMPTIVUM: electuary (see note to *Perceval* l. 3327).

ROTE: stringed instrument played with a bow.

SAMITE: heavy silk material.

SCARLET: rich woollen cloth, not necessarily of red colour.

SENESCHAL: steward or major-domo of a noble household.

STERLING: English silver penny (early coins being marked with a star).

STOMATICUM: electuary (see note to *Perceval* l. 3327).

SYMPHONIA: a kind of stringed instrument.

TERCEL: male falcon.

THERIAC: potion made with honey.

TIMBREL: early tambourine.

VAIR: blue-grey and white squirrel fur.

VAVASOUR: lesser vassal, vassal of another vassal.

VENTAIL: mail protecting the lower part of face and neck.

VESPERS: the sixth canonical hour; evening.

VIELLE: early fiddle.

WIMPLE: linen covering for head, cheeks, chin and neck.

NOTES

The line numbers refer to the Foerster and Roach editions. Works mentioned in abbreviated form are listed fully in the Select Bibliography. Only the first line is given for passages discussed.

EREC AND ENIDE

1. Chrétien's prologue, following rhetorical tradition, opens with a proverb. In line 9 he names himself for the only time as Crestiiens *de Troies*. The author of *La Mule sans frein* seems to play on this by adopting the name Paiens de Maisieres in his own prologue, itself closely modelled on Chrétien's. What was the adventure story from which Chrétien fashioned *une mout bele conjointure* (line 14)? Comparison with the mabinogi *Gereint Son of Erbin* suggests that it was probably a French or Anglo-Norman tale not very different from the Welsh.

37. The white stag was no doubt originally an otherworld beast. Though Chrétien may not always have realised it, his sources contained many features from the supernatural world of Celtic myth. These he tended to rationalise as far as possible.

83. Chrétien nowhere gives more details of the Round Table, first mentioned by Wace in his *Roman de Brut*.

109. In the Welsh story Gereint was late for the hunt because he had overslept. If this was the situation in Chrétien's source, here is a typical instance of the French poet's concern to raise the courtly tone of his narrative.

313. King Yder, an ally of Arthur, is not to be confused with Yder son of Nut, Erec's opponent in the sparrow-hawk contest.

402. Several motifs run through this romance. Reference to Enide's dress is one of them.

413. In scholastic tradition Natura (Nature) was represented as the creator of human beauty.

424. Though heroines of romance are conventionally blonde, Iseut was especially renowned for the radiance of her hair. Chrétien knew the Tristan story well and claims in *Cligés* to have composed a story of Mark and Iseut. Had this survived it would probably have been the earliest extant version of the legend. This honour is usually accorded to the *Tristan* of Thomas, an Anglo-Norman contemporary

of Chrétien. A Norman poet, Béroul, composed a further version late in the century.

515. In the Welsh *Gereint* the host explains that he had wrongfully deprived his nephew of his possessions, and that in revenge the nephew had later taken all his property, including an earldom and this town.

684. The maiden's silence is an important motif throughout much of the romance; and Chrétien preserves it here, even at the risk of making her appear too passive while her future is being arranged for her.

710. Foerster saw here the implication that charms and enchantments were sometimes used when a knight was armed.

720. The leap into the saddle without using the stirrups was an indication of the knight's vigour and zeal.

743. Here for the first time Erec and Enide are seen riding together. This will become another leitmotif in the romance. It will later be ironical to recall the crowd's words concerning the honour reflected by the maiden on her escort.

1248. When Morholt, Iseut's uncle, claimed tribute from King Mark, he was slain by Tristan on an island unnamed in the early versions of the story, but identified, as here, as St Samson's Isle in the prose *Tristan* and *Merlin*.

1482. Chrétien is here concerned with depicting a love-match between partners equal in merit and beauty. *Fine amor* is frequently presented in lyric and romance. Often known as "courtly love", it is in broad terms a love situation between persons of noble rank and is portrayed according to certain literary conventions sometimes borrowed from the southern troubadours, sometimes from Ovid. Constant features are the worth and beauty of the lovers which should serve, as here, as a source of mutual inspiration, and the need for utter fidelity. In some cases (as commonly in the troubadour lyric) the lady is of higher station than the lover, may be married, and plays the dominant role in the relationship. Chrétien was to illustrate such a relationship in *Lancelot* and to some extent in *Yvain*. In *Erec*, however, he presents an ideal love leading to, and ultimately continuing within, marriage. The present scene shows each of the lovers totally engrossed in the contemplation of the other, with Chrétien thus able to preserve the motif of the maiden's silence.

1526. Here Perceval of Wales (*li Galois*) makes his first

appearance in Arthurian romance. In Chrétien's *Conte du Graal* he will become the hero of the Grail quest.

1691.   This roll-call of Arthur's leading knights is of great interest to students of Arthurian romance, containing as it does the first mention of Lancelot of the Lake and other names familiar from later texts. *Gereint* contains a comparable list of the hero's companions when he left Arthur's court for his own lands (*The Mabinogion*, trans. Jones and Jones, p. 247); and a much longer enumeration of Arthur's warriors figures in the early *Culhwch and Olwen* (ibid., pp. 100–7). For the knights mentioned in *Erec* see the works by L.-F. Flutre and G. D. West listed in the Bibliography.

1793.   Arthur expounds the duties of a ruler as set out in other works of the period, e.g. the Latin and vernacular "miroirs de princes".

1844.   *Ci fine li premerains vers*. This line has been much discussed, *vers* normally being a term from lyric poetry meaning "couplet" or "strophe". One may suspect that Chrétien's source contained a phrase like those found at intervals in the first part of *Gereint*, e.g. "Their story so far" (*The Mabinogion*, trans. Jones and Jones, p. 244).

1874.   *Outre-Gales* or *Estre-Gales* perhaps = Strathclyde. The towns of Montrevel and Roadan (cf. lines 1335, 1339) have not been firmly identified.

1932.   Like the list of Arthur's knights (lines 1691–1750), this enumeration of his vassals contains names and allusions that are obscure to us. Some may have been gleaned from tales of Celtic provenance circulating in Chrétien's day.

1957.   Morgan the Fay, usually identified as a sister of King Arthur, is one of the more mysterious figures of Arthurian romance. She was credited with special skills in medicine. Nothing more is known of her relationship with Guingomar.

2016.   For the ceremony of dubbing young men as knights see Jean Flori, "Pour une histoire de la chevalerie: l'adoubement dans les romans de Chrétien de Troyes", *Romania* 100 (1979), pp. 21–53. Chrétien's descriptions may actually have contributed to the development and significance of the ritual.

2031.   It is a habit of Chrétien to delay the naming of some of his chief characters: other examples are Lancelot, Laudine (in *Yvain*) and Perceval. In the Middle Ages great importance was attached to names and their symbolic significance, as frequently appears in the romances.

2075. On Iseut's marriage night her maid Brangien took her place in the bed of King Mark, Tristan's uncle.

2081. This might seem an inappropriate moment to recall Psalm XLII. 1 (Vulgate XLI. 2): "Quemadmodum desiderat cervus ad fontes aquarum, ita desiderat anima mea ad te, Deus."

2131. i.e. York and Edinburgh.

2219. Foerster assumed a missing couplet here, supposing unnecessarily that it was Gawain who was said to take the horses and knights. It seems more reasonable to understand that though Erec's main concern was with glory, he took the knights and horses in order to discomfit his opponents.

2434. Chrétien here introduces the crucial theme of Erec's recreance. In Gereint the hero was criticised for abandoning the life of the court for his love, whereas Erec withdraws principally from tournaments and active chivalry. The reverse situation will be explored in Yvain.

2496. Enide's fateful words have an increased impact since they are the first we have heard her utter.

2576. In the Welsh story Gereint suspects his wife of infidelity. Of this there is no hint in Chrétien.

2580. In the mabinogi Gereint ordered Enid to don her worst dress. That Chrétien knew this version of the story seems confirmed by some apparent echoes of it which he introduces into his Conte du Graal (see Owen, The Evolution of the Grail Legend, pp. 133–4). Why then does he make Erec call for Enide to wear her finest dress? It might be thought that, having avoided any suspicion of infidelity, he wants to show his hero determined to put his chivalric virtue to the proof in the presence of Enide, the innocent cause of his recreance, at her most radiant. Whereas Gereint wishes to both prove himself to his wife and test and punish her, Erec, less self-assured, seeks to test himself as much as Enide.

3678. Though dwarfs often play sinister or unflattering roles in the romance (cf. the one encountered by Erec at the beginning of his adventures), Guivret, whom he now meets, is entirely noble. This interesting character, perhaps descended from some Celtic deity, seems to be related to the dwarf-king Auberon (Shakespeare's Oberon), who first appears in the epic Huon de Bordeaux. See

Vernon Harward, *The Dwarfs of Arthurian Romance and Celtic Tradition*, Leiden, 1958).

3955.   Gringalet (usually referred to as *le Gringalet*) is the traditional name of Gawain's horse. It may be derived from the Welsh *ceincaled* 'handsome-hardy' or possibly *guin-calet* 'white-hardy'.

3959.   In this episode Kay the seneschal is seen for the first time in French romance in an unfavourable light, though Chrétien was probably merely elaborating his lost source (cf. *Gereint*). Whereas Kay is respected in Arthur's court and has many true knightly qualities, he is apt to appear surly, sarcastic, prompt to make mischief among the knights, even on occasion showing a streak of cowardice. In three of Chrétien's poems (*Erec, Yvain* and the *Conte du Graal*) the seneschal is unceremoniously up-ended by the hero after treating him in an insulting manner. In some respects he acts as a foil to the bland and ever-courteous Gawain, as we see here. A further feature that appears in this episode, later to be used on several occasions by Chrétien, is the incognito encounter. A number of elements from this scene were re-used in the *Conte du Graal*, where Perceval, like Erec, comes across Arthur and his entourage by chance and has to be cajoled into the king's presence by Gawain.

4264.   It being the eve of Sunday, no meat was eaten.

4469.   The blow cleaving an opponent in two is described more often in the epic *chansons de geste* (e.g. the *Chanson de Roland*) than in the romance.

4616.   Enide's ensuing lament is couched in rhetorical terms much favoured in the literature of the day. There may be here some influence from the early French version of the Pyramus story, with Enide, like Thisbe, calling on death and contemplating suicide. A similar scene is enacted, more humorously, by the lion in *Yvain*. It is interesting to find here Enide proclaiming the virtue of silence, whereas in the *Conte du Graal* it was to be Perceval's silence that had dire consequences for him in the Grail Castle. Chrétien's love of dialectic is often seen not only in his own or his characters' inner debates, but also when he tests such general principles in action. Enide's reply to the Count that she is both wife and lover to the wounded Erec (line 4687) may be thought to reflect Chrétien's own ideal of true love continuing within marriage.

4772.   The legality of this marriage would be suspect, even if Erec were not still alive. In the whole episode Enide's steadfast loyalty to her supposedly dead husband may be contrasted with Laudine's more practical reaction to her bereavement in *Yvain*.

4918. Erec's forgiveness of Enide may be seen as concluding happily the main theme of the romance; the hero's recreance through love and his atonement and testing of Enide (cf. lines 5136–8; and note the re-enactment of the marriage night in lines 5245–59). Why, then, did not Chrétien bring his romance to a speedy close, instead of protracting it for a further two thousand lines? It could be argued that he wished to complete his hero's rehabilitation in the eyes of the world by adding a further, supreme, test of his valour. Even so, one has the impression that from this point his narration becomes more diffuse and leisurely, as if there were a "target-length" he wished to achieve. To judge from his other complete romances, this would be in the region of 7,000 lines.

5316. The palfrey presented to Enide is clearly no ordinary animal. Although nothing similar appears in *Gereint*, it may be compared with the parti-coloured beasts found in Celtic mythology. Enide's earlier mount given her by her cousin may likewise have had supernatural origins (see Loomis, *Arthurian Tradition and Chrétien de Troyes*, pp. 105–8).

5337. The allusions in the following lines and in line 5891 may be to the story of Aeneas as found in the Old French *Roman d'Eneas* (ca. 1160), although it is likely that the well-schooled Chrétien also knew Virgil in the original Latin.

5464. The name and nature of this adventure have given rise to much debate. In the mabinogi a hedge of mist is said to enclose "enchanted games", though Gereint's only test is to fight the defending knight. There, as in Chrétien, the hero sounds a horn to complete his exploit, and it is probable that both elements in the name Joie de la Cort had suffered corruption in Chrétien's source and that the second related to the horn (*cor*). The whole episode seems ultimately derived from some otherworld adventure, the mysterious remnants of which Chrétien used to suit his own purposes.

5495. For the inhabitants of a place of peril attempting to deflect the hero from the danger see also *Yvain*, lines 5107 ff. (the entry into the town of Pesme Avanture). This was to become a commonplace in Arthurian romance.

5571. From this point Chrétien's authorial interjections regarding his telling of the story become more frequent, strengthening the impression of a self-conscious spinning out of his material.

5778.   It is strange that Chrétien should here name as examples of prime bravery three Saracens prominent in the Old French epic.

5891.   Lavinia of Laurentum, daughter of Latinus, was Aeneas's wife.

6056.   The *don contraignant*, or granting of a request before knowing its terms, is a common motif in Arthurian romance (see, for instance, *Lancelot*, lines 156 ff.)

6121.   Having adopted the name Joie de la Cort for the adventure, Chrétien makes much play on the idea of joy (including the reference in line 6188 to a probably fictitious "Lay of Joy"). Erec's victory is shown to bring great joy to all who learn of it. Some would maintain that this is the true climax of the romance, since it shows Erec passing from his earlier self-centred chivalry to a state of social awareness that prepares him for the assumption of the kingship. Certainly he, like other of Chrétien's heroes who performed acts of liberation (Lancelot, Yvain, Perceval, Gawain), is accorded quasi-religious veneration by those who benefit (lines 6369 ff.). Another lesson that Chrétien seems to underline in the episode is that withdrawal from society into a private world of love is to be deplored and can only lead to disaster. This, of course, was the fault of Erec as well as Mabonagrain, though the latter's withdrawal was more complete and deliberate and was unsanctioned by marriage (cf. lines 6294 ff.).

6259.   Chrétien is fond of producing unexpected relationships as a device which, though melodramatic to our eyes, he probably saw as adding cohesion to the narrative.

6549.   The coronation was to be held at Christmas. As the story opened at Easter and the wedding took place at Pentecost, Chrétien has used the three major festivals to mark the main stages of his narrative. His choice of Nantes for the coronation may have been prompted by the investiture there by Henry II Plantagenet of his son Geoffrey as Duke of Brittany. That ceremony took place on Christmas Day 1169.

6738.   Macrobius was a Roman Neoplatonic philosopher and grammarian of the early fifth century known mainly for his *Saturnalia* and a commentary on Cicero's *Somnium Scipionis*. Chrétien probably invented this ascription to him of the account of the robe portraying the four Liberal Arts that constituted the Quadrivium.

6801.   *Barbioletes*: these strange creatures have not been identified.

CLIGÉS

1.   Chrétien's reference to his earlier works is not altogether clear. *Erec et Enide* has of course survived. *Les comandemanz Ovide* has been taken to refer to Ovid's *Remedia amoris*, but it seems possible that along with *L'art d'amors* it denotes the *Ars amatoria*. This translation has been lost, as has the work on Mark and Iseut (presumably some story from the legend of Tristan, though it is curious that he is not named). The metamorphosis mentioned by Chrétien is almost certainly Ovid's tale of Philomela or Philomena (*Met.* VI, 426–674), and it is probably his version that has come down embedded in the late thirteenth-century *Ovide moralisé* (ed. C. de Boer, Paris, 1909). The Shoulder Bite (*Le mors de l'espaule*) was apparently a treatment of the story of Tantalus's son Pelops, also mentioned by Ovid (*Met.* VI, 403–11). Both Chrétien's familiarity with Ovid and his interest in the Tristan story have left their mark on *Cligés*, the former largely in the matter of style and the psychology of love, the latter by prompting a number of disapproving references as well as by suggesting certain important elements of the plot. Chrétien's attempt to justify Fenice vis-à-vis Iseut may reflect a rivalry between him and his contemporary, Thomas of England, whose own *Tristan* appears to antedate *Cligés*.

18.   Chrétien's reference to his source must be treated with some reserve, since this was probably composite. The central story of the woman who feigns death, identified in one version as Solomon's wife, was well known in the Middle Ages and passed eventually into Shakespeare's *Romeo and Juliet* (for this legend see Henri Hauvette, *La "Morte Vivante"*, Paris, 1933). A thirteenth-century text, *Marques de Rome*, conserves a version in which the hero is named as Cligés, and which may well stand close to Chrétien's own main source. Apart from this, however, he used a variety of other material, and the first part of *Cligés* seems largely his own invention. The Church of St Peter of Beauvais was burnt down in 1180, to be replaced by the present thirteenth-century cathedral. We know little of the contents of the library in Chrétien's day.

30.   The *translatio studii* topos (the passage of learning from the ancient to the modern world) is frequently found in the middle of the twelfth century. On the whole of this prologue, see Tony Hunt, "Tradition and Originality in the Prologues of Chrestien de Troyes", *Forum for Modern Language Studies* VIII (1972), pp. 320–44.

154. The knight's duty to maintain his reputation by active chivalry is a recurring theme in Chrétien's romances and especially prominent in *Erec* and *Yvain*.

193. Largess is a knightly virtue constantly stressed in medieval literature. It is fittingly recommended here, since Alexander's great namesake was traditionally held to be its finest practitioner.

431. Count Angrés and his treason seem patterned on Mordred's betrayal of Arthur as recounted in Wace's *Roman de Brut* (1155). For Wace's overall influence on Chrétien see Margaret Pelan, *L'Influence du Brut de Wace sur les romanciers français de son temps*, Paris, 1931.

445. Chrétien may have chosen the name Soredamors with its elements meaning "blonde" and "love" to point the parallel with the golden-haired Iseut. The love of Alexander and Soredamors, like that of Rivalen and Blancheflor in *Tristan*, is recounted as an introduction to the main subject-matter. It is told in the precious "Ovidian" manner in vogue at the time, but perhaps deliberately exaggerated here by Chrétien to the point of humour (see especially Haidu, *Aesthetic Distance in Chrétien de Troyes*). The long monologues in particular offer the poet the chance of deriving gentle amusement from the casuistical heart-searchings of the young lovers.

549. This and the following lines contain an elaborate play on the words *la mer* "sea", *amer* "to love" and *amer* "bitter", and appear to be imitated from Thomas's *Tristan*.

1076. Ganelon, who in the *Chanson de Roland* brought about the defeat of Charlemagne and the peers at Roncevaux, was regarded in medieval eyes as a traitor second only to Judas in villainy. Like Angrés, Ganelon had been given an important charge by the king acting on his barons' advice; and Chrétien seems to have developed this whole episode under the influence of the *Roland* (see D. D. R. Owen, "Chrétien and the *Roland*" in *An Arthurian Tapestry: Essays in Memory of Lewis Thorpe*, ed. Kenneth Varty, Glasgow, 1981, pp. 139–50).

1142. A ritual bath was an essential preliminary to being dubbed knight.

1158. The motif of the golden hair by which the beloved is recognised was found by Chrétien in the Tristan legend. He was to use it again in *Lancelot*, ironically it seems in view of *Cligés*, lines 1643-5.

1352.   To spare the life of a defeated opponent was part of the chivalric ethic. The king, on the other hand, was following the code of feudal justice in requiring the execution of traitors. In this episode the unusually vengeful Arthur seems modelled on the Charlemagne of the *Roland*.

1443.   Ganelon was executed by being torn asunder by four horses.

1700.   In the *Chanson de Roland* we learn how God stopped the sun in the heavens to enable Charlemagne to defeat the Saracens. Chrétien probably had this miracle in mind here.

2088.   The corpses are not recognised as they are totally encased in armour.

2302.   The queen here surely expresses Chrétien's own view of love and marriage, with which we may contrast the adulterous relationship between Tristan and Iseut.

2536.   This reference to the story of Thebes probably reflects Chrétien's knowledge of the *Roman de Thebes* (ca. 1155).

2621.   Tristan's mother, Blancheflor, similarly followed her husband to the grave. The main parallels with the Tristan legend are found in this second part of the romance, where the hero enters into an illicit relationship with his uncle's wife. Scholars have described *Cligés* as an anti-*Tristan* or even a hyper-*Tristan*.

2653.   In making Alis's proposed bride the daughter of the German emperor, Chrétien seems to have been inspired by recent events, which he manipulated for his own artistic purposes. Between 1170 and 1174 the emperor Frederick Barbarossa had sought to effect an alliance with the Byzantine emperor Manuel Comnenus, involving the marriage of his own son with the Greek princess. Henry the Lion, Duke of Saxony and Bavaria, took part in these negotiations; but they came to naught, and Henry incurred the hostility of Barbarossa, though not as the result of any amorous involvement. See Frappier, *Cligès* (Cours de Sorbonne), pp. 39–40.

2725.   The choice of the name Fenice is significant, as will appear, since the phoenix was regarded in the Middle Ages as a symbol of resurrection.

2766.   Chrétien could have known the Narcissus story from an Old French version as well as from Ovid, *Metamorphoses* III, 339–510.

3002.   The word "Thessala" was used with the meaning

"sorceress", "witch" (cf. Pliny, *Natural History* XXX, 2). Thessala's role has some points of similarity with that of Brangien, Iseut's maidservant, in *Tristan*, including her part in administering the magic potion.

3031.   Medea, the wife of Jason, was the great sorceress of Greek legend.

3145.   This outburst of Fenice against the love of Tristan and Iseut might be thought to epitomise Chrétien's own views on love, marriage and adultery as they emerge from his work as a whole. That he could justify on legal grounds the lovers' confidence in the innocence of their relationship as it develops here is shown by David J. Shirt in "*Cligés* – A Twelfth-Century Matrimonial Case-Book?", *Forum for Modern Language Studies* XVIII (1982), pp. 75–89.

3848.   This topos of the upside-down world was inherited by the Middle Ages from Antiquity (see E. R. Curtius, *European Literature and the Latin Middle Ages*, London, 1953, pp. 94–8).

3865.   Whether or not there were actual "courts of love", as has been surmised, Marie de Champagne and her circle seem to have been much preoccupied with the "customs and practices" of courtly love and would have appreciated Chrétien's somewhat detached analysis of its situations and problems.

4410.   The following monologue is a good example of those passages in *Cligés* which, smacking of Chrétien's training in dialectic, elicit from readers widely differing appraisals. For some it is dull, heavy and pretentious, whereas Peter Haidu thinks it "a literary triumph, an extraordinary portrayal of a young girl's dreaming which . . . verges on the stream-of-consciousness technique of modern novelists. The sentimentality which might be a danger is averted by a gentle suffusion of irony" (*Aesthetic Distance in Chrétien de Troyes*, p. 78).

4765.   Cligés defeats in the tourney both Lancelot and Perceval, whom Chrétien was later to make the invincible heroes of two of his romances.

5062.   Cligés is not, of course, King Arthur's nephew, but the son of his niece and so his great-nephew (cf. lines 4220, 5303–4 and 6673, where I translate *oncle* as "great-uncle").

5324.   What St Paul in fact said was: "Quod si non continent, nubant; melius est enim nubere quam uri" (I *Corinthians* vii, 9). Surprisingly, Chrétien also misquotes scripture in the prologue of the

Conte du Graal, ascribing to St Paul a paraphrase of a verse from St John.

5555. John's marvellous tower appears to owe much to the "Salle aux Images" or Hall of Statues in Thomas's *Tristan*, a splendidly furnished cavern containing an image of Iseut, which Tristan had had fashioned by a serf. On another level, in view of the religious allusions that appear a little further on, it might be equated with Paradise.

5714. The curious association of God's name with that of Cligés sets the tone for the ensuing series of parallels, which can only be deliberate on Chrétien's part, between Fenice's shammed death and liberation and the crucifixion, burial and resurrection of Christ (see D. D. R. Owen, "Profanity and its Purpose in Chrétien's *Cligés* and *Lancelot*" in *Forum for Modern Language Studies* VI, (1970), pp. 37–48, and in *Arthurian Romance: Seven Essays*). The main parallels, supported by various details, are: the scourging and piercing of the palms watched from a distance by many women; the entombment in a newly prepared sepulchre, which is sealed and guarded; the guards' sleep and the removal of the "body"; the lapse of time between "death" and "resurrection".

5818. Salerno was famous for its medical school throughout the Middle Ages and has a claim to the distinction of being the first university in Europe.

5876. The legend of Solomon deceived by his wife, which may be the earliest form of the "feigned death" theme, was widely known in the Middle Ages.

6223. Cligés's ignorance of the potion is surprising; but A. G. Van Hamel considered that Chrétien introduced it at this point in order to provide a motive for a long lament by the hero corresponding to that of Iseut over Tristan's body in Thomas's poem (*Romania* 33 (1904), pp. 483–4).

6704. The *Porz d'Espaingne* are the Pyrenean passes familiar from the Roland legend.

6753. For Chrétien's ideal of perfect love continuing within marriage, cf. *Erec*, lines 4684–7.

6762. Whatever the extent of Chrétien's humour and irony in the rest of the romance, it is hard to believe that he intended us to take this somewhat gratuitous epilogue seriously.

LANCELOT

1.   Marie, who in 1164 had married Count Henri of Champagne, was the daughter of Eleanor of Aquitaine and Louis VII of France. It is assumed from this prologue that Chrétien had connections with her court, at least at the time he composed *Lancelot* and *Yvain* (see John Benton, "The Court of Champagne as a Literary Centre", *Speculum* XXXVI (1961), pp. 551–91). On the prologue and its ambiguity see J. Rychner in *Vox Romanica* 26 (1967), pp. 1–23, Tony Hunt in *Forum for Modern Language Studies* VIII (1972), pp. 320–44, and Jean Frappier in *Romania* 93 (1972), pp. 337–77. Is it to be taken seriously (the humble poet's praise of his patroness), or as being deliberately humorous in its exaggerations and sophistry? The question can be extended to the whole romance. Is Chrétien wishing to give a serious and sympathetic illustration (some would say exaltation) of the adulterous form of courtly love? Or are the excesses of such a love soberly criticised with occasional flashes of humour? Or is the whole romance conceived as a burlesque designed to ridicule not only an uncontrolled passion, but the lover himself?

26.   *Matiere et san* is usually taken to mean the source material and the treatment of it or meaning supplied by the poet. Lines 26–7 could, however, be interpreted: "The Countess prompts and inspires him to do it."

34.   This is the first known mention of Camelot. Its location is still a matter of debate (for a recent discussion see Geoffrey Ashe, *Camelot and the Vision of Albion*, New York, 1971).

150.   Guenevere's self-abasement before Kay contrasts strikingly with her attitude at the beginning of *Yvain*.

211.   A variant reading is *Ha rois* ("Alas, king"). Foerster reasonably assumed that the queen is here addressing her absent lover Lancelot, who appears in line 273, but is not named until line 3676.

369.   This momentary triumph of reason over love is unique for Lancelot. Chrétien's own attitude appears from his other works to be that reason and restraint or *mesure* play an important part in true courtly love.

434.   The mounted Gawain and the cart pass into the hall (cf. lines 993 ff.). To ride into a castle hall is treated as a sign of youthful impetuosity when Perceval does it in the *Conte du Graal*. *Lancelot* is unusually rich in similarly incongruous situations.

548.   Here we find Gawain in what was to become his familiar

role of philanderer, if we may so interpret Chrétien's rather coy remark.

557.   The knight on the litter is Kay.

641.   Though we do not possess Chrétien's main source for *Lancelot*, the earlier *Vita Sancti Gildae* by Caradoc of Lancarvan tells a clearly related story of how Melwas, king of the summer land, abducted Queen Guenevere to Glastonbury. It seems we are dealing with the debased version of a Celtic otherworld myth. What appears to be an episode from another form of the story is portrayed on an archivolt of Modena cathedral, probably carved in the early twelfth century.

718.   It was the lover's duty to reflect on his beloved at all times. The love reverie, which here causes Lancelot some embarrassment, is treated more lyrically and seriously in the *Conte du Graal*, where Perceval is rapt in thoughts of Blancheflor.

935.   Her fears, misunderstood by Foerster, are explicable in terms of the custom described in lines 1314 ff.

1068.   The following episode admits of no logical explanation, and one suspects an origin in a tale of the supernatural. *Lancelot* has been much criticised for such incoherences as this; but one must allow the possibility that Chrétien deliberately exploited incongruity in this romance in the service of a burlesque intention.

1313.   Logres: Arthur's kingdom, England or part of England.

1355.   Foerster assumed a lacuna here, with the sense having originally been completed by a relative clause, now missing from all MSS.

1364.   Ysoré, the name of several legendary Saracens, provides Chrétien here with a convenient rhyme.

1472.   See note to *Cligés*, line 1158. How seriously are we to take Lancelot and his behaviour under the influence of love?

1723.   The dispute between the young knight and his father shows some similarities with the later quarrel between King Bademagu and his son Meleagant.

1841.   With the following episode there begins a series of apparent borrowings from the account of Christ's crucifixion and harrowing of Hell as found in the *Gospel of Nicodemus* (see D. D. R. Owen in *Forum for Modern Language Studies* VI (1970), pp. 37–48, and in *Arthurian Romance: Seven Essays*). Why Chrétien should suggest this equation between Lancelot and Christ is puzzling. Is it in order to increase his hero's stature in our eyes, or through its very incongruity to make him appear the more ridiculous? At least we can be sure that here, as in the similar equation in *Cligés*, Chrétien intended no blasphemy.

2063. The vagueness of the situation and topography of Bademagu's kingdom of Gorre may reflect its likely otherworld origins. The name has been plausibly explained as a corruption of Old French *voirre* "glass", since Glastonbury, the scene of Guenevere's legendary abduction, was variously known as the City or Isle of Glass (cf. *Erec*, lines 1946–7). The general lack of geographical precision in much of this romance is not necessarily an indication of carelessness on Chrétien's part, contributing as it does to the air of incongruity and mystery that he appears to be consciously cultivating.

2332. This is one of several places in *Lancelot* where Chrétien uses motifs of which variations appear in *Yvain*. He is believed to have composed the two romances concurrently (see the note to *Yvain*, line 3706).

2706. In *Yvain* the hero and Esclados are commended for avoiding striking each other's horse (lines 855–8).

3021. Though the Sword Bridge has distant analogues in Celtic legend, its description here seems to owe more to the testing bridge of Hell as found in various pious legends (see D. D. R. Owen, *The Vision of Hell*, Scottish Academic Press, 1970). A similar structure appears in *La Mule sans frein*.

3374. This reference to the ointment procured by Mary Magdalene, Mary the mother of James, and Mary Salome to anoint Christ's body reinforces the impression that Chrétien's mind is turning on the events of the Crucifixion and Harrowing at this point.

3501. Along with Salerno (see *Cligés*, line 5818) Montpellier was renowned in the Middle Ages for its medical studies.

3676. Lancelot is here first mentioned by name (cf. note to *Erec*, line 2031).

3821. For Chrétien's knowledge of the Pyramus story see notes to *Erec*, line 4616, and *Yvain*, line 3496.

3937. With the release of the captives (corresponding to Christ's liberation of the souls in Hell) the reminiscences of the Harrowing cease.

4053. The stepfather was often a treacherous figure in medieval legend: this was Ganelon's relationship to Roland.

4670.   The literary expression of courtly love often used the imagery of Christian worship, whilst pious texts such as hymns to the Virgin might use the terminology of courtly love. We have already seen that Chrétien was not averse to a startling mingling of the sacred with the profane. Cf. also lines 1472 ff.

4758.   The episode of the bloodstained sheets and resultant misleading oath was probably borrowed by Chrétien from the Tristan story (see Loomis, *Arthurian Tradition and Chrétien de Troyes*, pp. 250–3).

5125.   This is not the only time Chrétien shows Gawain suffering such indignity, for in the *Conte du Graal* he also lands in a river.

5790.   Once captured, knights could take no further part in a tournament, and those who had taken the cross were debarred from participating. On this debated passage see William Henry Jackson, "*Prison et croisié*. Ein Beitrag zum Begriff *arme ritter*", *Zeitschrift für Deutsches Altertum und Deutsche Literatur* CI (1972), pp. 105–17.

5808.   Ignaures and his amorous prowess is the subject of an anonymous lai.

6094.   This reference to the law of salvage is obscure and may result from a corrupt MS. reading.

6132.   According to Godefroi de Leigni's statement at the end of the poem, it was from about this point that Chrétien, for some unknown reason, left the romance for him to finish.

6607.   This passage and lines 6700–9 come strangely from the mouth of Lancelot. A. H. Diverres suggests that the hero may have exchanged the love of the queen for that of Bademagu's daughter, assuming that Godefroi's conclusion corresponded to Chrétien's intentions (see "Some Thoughts on the *sens* of *Le Chevalier de la Charrette*" in *Forum for Modern Language Studies* VI (1970), pp. 33 ff., and in *Arthurian Romance: Seven Essays*).

6724.   Cf. note to *Erec*, line 720.

6777.   Cf. Erec's arming (*Erec*, lines 2624 ff.).

6802.   Bucephalus was the horse of Alexander the Great.

7124.   Nothing further is known of Godefroi de Leigni.

YVAIN

1. For the structure and originality of the prologue see Tony Hunt, "The Rhetorical Background to the Arthurian Prologue" in *Forum for Modern Language Studies* VI (1970), pp. 1–23, and in *Arthurian Romance: Seven Essays*. The Welsh mabinogi *Owein* (*The Lady of the Fountain*), probably deriving from a common source, has no such prologue.

7. *Carduel en Gales* = Carlisle, Wales being taken to include Strathclyde, the British kingdom of N.W. England and S.W.Scotland.

56. Yvain and his father King Urien may have been historical figures of the sixth century living in the kingdom of Rheged, situated in northern England and southern Scotland (see Rachel Bromwich in *Bibliographical Bulletin of the International Arthurian Society* 15 (1963), pp. 86–7). Both are mentioned by Geoffrey of Monmouth and Wace.

57. R. S. Loomis saw in Calogrenant (who appears as Cynon in *Owein*) a doubling of the figure of Kay (Cai-lo-grenant = "Kay the grumbler": see *Arthurian Tradition and Chrétien de Troyes*, p. 275). Kay's churlishness is emphasised by Chrétien in this opening scene, and his insults are used as a leitmotif in the first part of *Yvain* as later in the Perceval section of the *Conte du Graal*.

189. The Forest of Broceliande with its marvellous spring of Barenton is in Brittany, not in the vicinity of Carlisle as would appear from Chrétien's romance. For the Broceliande localisation Chrétien is probably indebted to Wace, who speaks of the spring in his *Roman de Rou* (ed. A. J. Holden, Paris, 1970-73, lines 6373-98). An earlier version of the story, however, may well have placed the spring in southern Scotland, where it appears in a related legend (see Loomis, *Arthurian Tradition . . .* , pp. 289–93).

288. The rustic, of whose ugliness Chrétien gives a conventional description, can probably trace his ancestry back to a figure of the Celtic otherworld, and similar beings are found in Irish and Welsh legend. With Chrétien, however, he becomes an almost credible character, lacking such supernatural traits as are found in *Owein*.

368. The rustic is unfamiliar with Calogrenant's courtly language, claiming to know nothing of any *avanture*. Some critics would see Chrétien's main message in *Yvain* as being a criticism of the chivalric quest of adventure from motives of personal glory rather than responsible social endeavour.

395. The belief in the storm-making properties of the spring of Barenton, already reflected in Wace, persisted into modern times (see Frappier, *Étude sur Yvain . . .* , pp. 85–7).

459. Trees covered with sweetly singing birds are found in various Celtic legends, but with this one there is a particularly close parallel in the Latin *Navigatio Sancti Brendani* (*The Voyage of St Brendan*) and in its Anglo-Norman redaction by Benedeit.

596. Nureddin was the Sultan Nureddin Mahmud, who fought the Crusaders and died in 1173 or 1174. Forré was a legendary pagan king. Knights are often shown making exaggerated boasts after dinner.

723. Yvain's secret departure breaches courtly etiquette, since he should first have obtained the king's leave. Chrétien seems to have been at pains to provide him with as much justification as possible, including making him Calogrenant's cousin (there is no relationship in *Owein*) and so placing his family honour at stake. There will be later references to Yvain's double purpose: to avenge Kay's insults and his cousin's shame.

907. Despite the added mechanical and other detail, this scene is less easy to visualise than in *Owein*, where the hero is imprisoned between the two gates and later escapes into the town with the maiden. It seems as if Chrétien was trying to obtain a rather theatrical unity of place, but in doing so introduced some architectural anomalies.

1180. This is our first record of the widespread popular belief that a corpse's wounds bleed afresh in the presence of his slayer (cf. Shakespeare's *Richard III*, Act 1, Sc. 2).

1361. Chrétien's fondness of this kind of paradox is one example among many of an essentially intellectual attitude to the predicaments of his characters. In *Yvain* this raises the question of how seriously he treated the love theme and whether we are entitled to see in it the main interest of the romance. Nevertheless, in the following scenes he does his best to make Laudine's sudden remarriage psychologically plausible within the limits allowed by his source-story. His development of the role of Lunete is especially skilful: she has much of the character of the soubrettes of later theatrical tradition. The whole situation, though not its treatment, may be compared with that in the earlier *Roman de Thebes* (ed. L. Constans, Paris, 1890, lines 223 ff.), where Jocaste quickly agrees, at her nobles' request, to marry Edipus, her husband's murderer.

1885. As chalk was used in the preparation of furs, the implication here is that the robe was brand-new.

2139. There is no indication in *Owein* that the lady returns the hero's love. Chrétien shows a reciprocal passion in keeping with the principles of courtly love.

2151. Chrétien here follows his frequent practice of delaying the naming of his chief characters until long after their first appearance (cf. Esclados, named only in line 1970, and Lunete in 2415). This is the only line where Laudine's name occurs; and most of the MSS speak merely of *la dame de Landuc*. It is possible that *Laudine* is derived from a form of "Lothian", and that in a more primitive version of the legend she hailed from that part of Scotland (see Loomis, *Arthurian Tradition . . .* , pp. 302–3). Nothing is known of Landuc, or of Duke Laudunet (perhaps also linked with "Lothian") and his lay.

2228. In *Owein*, Cei (= Kay) was twice overthrown by the hero, who then defeated each of the party in turn except for Arthur and Gwalchmei (= Gawain). With the latter he fought a drawn duel, which Chrétien has reserved for the climax of his romance (lines 5991 ff.)

2420. Gawain here shows, perhaps for the first time in Chrétien (though see *Lancelot*, lines 548 ff.), that flirtatious streak which was to be developed in the second part of the *Conte du Graal* and led in later literature to a deterioration in his reputation.

2484. The warning of the danger of recreance through love (Erec's fault) is fittingly put into Gawain's mouth. The crisis to which it leads is the reverse of that which formed the pivot of Chrétien's first romance. It is natural to construe his intention in these two works as being to show the two opposite dangers against which a married knight must be on his guard. One must remember, however, that the essentials of the two situations were already present in Chrétien's sources.

2564. The relationship between love and hate is used as a recurrent theme in *Yvain*.

2677. Yvain has overstayed his leave by some six weeks. Owein, on the other hand, was granted three months' absence and stayed away three years; and unlike Yvain, he did not remember his pledge until after the messenger's arrival.

2814. Yvain's flight to the woods and his life there show some similarities with Tristan's primitive existence in the Forest of Morrois as related in all the main versions of that legend. The hermit may be compared with Ogrin of the Tristan story.

2953. For Morgan the Wise (= Morgan the Fay) see the note to *Erec*, line 1957.

3228. The hilly Forest of Argonne is on the N.E. border of Champagne.

3235. Durendal was Roland's famous sword wielded by him at the Battle of Roncevaux (Ronceval).

3243. In the second part of his romance, Chrétien several times emphasises, as here, Yvain's potential qualities as a husband. In this way he helps to keep the theme of the hero's love and marriage in our minds during the later adventures.

3341. The rescue of the lion is structurally the central episode in *Yvain*. What significance Chrétien attached to it is by no means clear. The seekers for allegory see in the struggle between fire-breathing serpent and lion an evident figuration of the combat between good and evil, especially as medieval symbolism usually equated the lion with noble qualities and even with the Deity. On the other hand, Chrétien did not invent the episode, which is in *Owein* and seems ultimately to derive from the story of Androcles, perhaps as told by Peter Damian in the eleventh century. Moreover, though the medieval public could hardly escape the symbolic associations, the fact that Chrétien treats the story with a good deal of humour may make one less inclined to pursue weighty allegories than to question his total seriousness, not only here but even in the romance as a whole.

3392. The lion's comic obeisance is not found in *Owein*; but there the wild beasts behave in similar fashion before the giant herdsman.

3496. This scene contains an amusing parody of the lovers' suicides in the story of Pyramus and Thisbe, probably known to Chrétien in an Old French version (cf. note to *Erec*, line 4616). The conversation through the crack in the wall (lines 3566 ff.) is an evident borrowing from the same source.

3706. This and two further references to Guenevere's abduction (lines 3918 ff. and 4740 ff.) are taken by scholars as an indication that *Yvain* was composed at much the same time as *Lancelot*, where the full story is told.

4291.   The incognito motif (already initiated at line 3728) seems to have been Chrétien's invention, probably designed to prepare for Yvain's duel with Gawain. The sobriquet "the Knight with the Lion" is not used in *Owein*, nor does the hero deliberately keep his identity secret.

4347.   The lady is not present at this duel in *Owein*. There the hero, with the rescued Luned, goes to her dominions, whence he takes her to Arthur's court, and their marriage is resumed.

4443.   Yvain here states the principle underlying the trial by combat (the *iudicium Dei*), a motif exploited by Chrétien on several occasions, notably in Lancelot's final encounter with Meleagant, Yvain's duel with Gawain later in this romance, and that to which Gawain is summoned in the *Conte du Graal*, lines 4758 ff.

4703.   This situation seems to have been devised by Chrétien in order to introduce the combat between Yvain and Gawain. It is unknown to the Welsh story.

4730.   Gawain's part in the affair is rather questionable and his desire for anonymity never explained. Whether or not this is due to unusually careless motivation on Chrétien's part, the fact remains that here we see Gawain for the first time over-impetuous in championing ladies. Exploited by Chrétien in his last romance, this is a characteristic that will become very familiar to later writers.

4819.   The fact that Chrétien here presents Yvain as a champion of women might imply that he sees his hero atoning for his desertion of Laudine for worldly prowess by henceforth devoting his chivalry to the service of the fair sex.

5107.   The following episode appears in a short and very different form as the concluding adventure of *Owein*. Chrétien seems to have amplified it from his own reading and observation and incorporated in a modified form some material present in the first part of *Owein*. For the warnings addressed to the hero see the note to *Erec*, line 5495.

5188.   There follows one of the most discussed scenes of the romance. It is commonly supposed that Chrétien is here protesting against the exploitation of female labour in the developing silk industry of Champagne or in the workshops to be found in seignorial courts. Whether or not this was his purpose, it is possible to distinguish the elements from which he built up the scene: the captive maidens figured in his main source; the Isle of Damsels (*Isle as Puceles*) seems a recollection of some tale of the Celtic otherworld, with its associated motif of the annual tribute (cf. the Tristan legend); the working of silken cloths probably figured in his source, as in *Owein*, in the castle where the knights received hospitality before the adventure of the fountain.

5308.   The girls only received *quatre deniers de la livre*, fourpence in every pound earned. There were twelve *deniers* in the *sou* and twenty *sous* in a *livre*. They were thus allowed only a sixtieth of their real earnings.

5394.   Chrétien returns here to the theme of his prologue.

5423.   The sleeves of shirts and other articles of dress were detachable and sewn on each time the garment was put on clean.

5512.   These two demon "champions" (line 5575) do not appear in *Owein*. Their equipment is that of contestants in a judicial combat.

5780.   With the almost divine aura given to the saviour-knight compare the reception of Erec after the Joy of the Court adventure, of Lancelot after his defeat of Meleagant, and of Gawain after his braving of the perils of the Wondrous Bed.

6001.   This rather precious debate takes up in allegorical terms the love-hate theme (see note to line 2564). One has the impression here, as in *Erec*, that Chrétien is spinning out his story in order to achieve a particular quota of lines (cf. note to *Erec*, line 4918). The duel with Gawain nevertheless provides an admirable climax to Yvain's adventures, partly because it shows his prowess to be once more second to none, and partly since we see him standing against the man who had lured him from Laudine's side.

6046.   By deploying Hate against Love, Yvain and Gawain, whose mutual affection makes them Love's friends, are also his enemies.

6761.   The *dénouement*, which seems to be Chrétien's own, is cleverly contrived though psychologically unsatisfying. Laudine is persuaded to take Yvain back by a stratagem, just as Arthur had tricked the elder sister into recognising the injustice of her action. The final reassurance that love was restored and endured is scarcely enough to persuade us that Chrétien has not been more interested all along in the formal conditions and etiquette of courtly love than in the psychology of a deep human relationship.

PERCEVAL

My translation is based on the edition by William Roach, with only major departures from his text noted below. Roach has retained Hilka's line numbering.

1.   Opinions are divided as to whether the prologue, with its praise of Christian charity, has any direct relevance to the interpretation of the romance or whether it is merely a deftly turned appeal by the poet to his patron's generosity. See Frappier, *Chrétien de Troyes et le mythe du Graal*, Ch. V, and Tony Hunt, "The Prologue to Chrestien's *Li Contes del Graal*", *Romania* 92 (1971), pp. 359–79.

13.   Philip of Alsace became Count of Flanders in 1168 and died on the Third Crusade at the siege of Acre in 1191.

49.   Chrétien ascribes erroneously to St Paul the statement in I *John* iv, 16: "Deus caritas est; et qui manet in caritate, in Deo manet, et Deus in eo." Cf. the note to *Cligés*, line 5324.

67.   The "book" Chrétien mentions as his source has prompted much conjecture. I have proposed as its likely contents some form of the Fair Unknown legend, itself exploiting Celtic material that can be traced back to Welsh and Irish myth. It was probably in French or Anglo-Norman and may have been in prose or verse. See Owen, *The Evolution of the Grail Legend*.

197.   There is word-play here between *lance* = "lance" and "throws".

343.   I have translated eighteen lines of doubtful authenticity (343–60: "'But now please tell me . . . or think I ever shall!'"). Found in only two MSS, they are printed by Hilka but not by Roach. The hero's ignorance of his name and true identity is a primitive feature found in Irish and Welsh tradition.

419.   The Isles of the Sea have been plausibly identified with the Hebrides.

436.   The wound through the thigh, like those suffered by the Fisher King (see lines 3509 ff.), is often seen as symbolising infertility.

823.   Bleeding was practised in the care of horses (cf. line 3893).

851.   Geoffrey of Monmouth is the first to mention the giant King Rion, whose cloak was made from the beards of defeated enemies.

915.   This Yvonet is not necessarily the person of the same name who later appears briefly as one of Gawain's attendants (line 5664).

1034.   The prophecies of the laughing maiden and fool confirm Perceval as a predestined hero. The medieval fool or jester was paradoxically regarded as a source of wise pronouncements.

1369.   Perceval had not of course been knighted by Arthur; nor had he been by Yvonet, who was apparently a squire, and as we learn from a derivative episode in Guillaume le Clerc's *Roman de Fergus*, "nobody can make a knight unless he is also a knight" (lines 1178–9).

1538.   Saint Julian was venerated as the patron saint of travellers.

1866.   The knights' opinion that the pair are admirably matched might well have anticipated their eventual marriage had the romance been completed.

1914.   To improve the condition of inferior wine it was removed from the cask and heated.

1999.   The situation seems to be that, of the original 310 defenders, 212 were killed in the fighting, 48 captured and put to death or imprisoned, and 50 remained to defend the castle.

2173–5.   ("When Engygeron . . . trots towards him"): I have used Hilka's text for these lines, of which the first two are not in Roach.

2454.   As well as the horses, the recipients would gain the potential ransom value of the prisoners.

2822.   King Arthur's refusal to eat on a high feast-day before hearing some news of an adventure was to become a common motif in later romance.

3050.   The sudden appearance of the Grail Castle together with the strange circumstances of Perceval's departure from it (lines 3356 ff.) are often taken as evidence of its supernatural nature. Typically, however, Chrétien leaves us free to draw our own conclusions.

3130.   On the subject of this mysterious sword and its probable Celtic antecedents see Frappier, *Chrétien de Troyes et le mythe du Graal*, pp. 109–13. It offers further evidence for the predestined course of Perceval's career. See also the note to line 3675.

3190.   The following much-debated scene contains the first appearance in literature of the Grail. Later to be identified with the vessel in which Joseph of Arimathaea caught the crucified Christ's blood, it is here presented simply as "a grail" (Old French *un graal*, meaning a deep, wide dish). Similarly the lance, though a mysterious object, is as yet not recognisably the weapon with which Longinus pierced Christ's side. Even the radiance does not necessarily come from the vessel but could be associated with the damsel bearing it (cf. *Cligés*, lines 2749 ff.). A Christian interpretation of the scene must therefore rely on such evidence as may be found elsewhere in the romance (see the note to line 6217) and in later texts. For a consideration of the main theories and of possible Celtic sources see Frappier, *Chrétien de Troyes et le mythe du Graal*.

3327. On these electuaries (medicinal concoctions with honey or syrup to stimulate appetite, aid digestion, etc.), see Hilka's note to lines 3327–30.

3573. Perceval's discovery of his name by intuition is clearly a significant moment in his development, since a man's name was believed to be an integral part of his personality (cf. Perceval's mother's insistence that one knows a man by his name, line 562).

3675. We know nothing more of the smith Trebuchet, who forged and can repair the sword. His home, Cotoatre, has been plausibly identified with "Scottewatre", the medieval name of the Firth of Forth.

3926. After this line Roach prints the following passage of twenty lines found in three MSS: "First Perceval struck him with the sword he had been given because he wanted to test it. With it he dealt such a mighty stroke on the top of his steel helmet that he broke in two the Fisher King's good sword. The Haughty Knight felt no fear, but repaid him with a great blow on his striped helmet, knocking off the flower decorations and gems. Perceval is very dejected over his sword which has failed him. Immediately he draws the one that had belonged to the Red Knight, and they attack each other on equal terms. And he took all the pieces of the other and put them back in the scabbard. Then they begin a cruel fight, greater than which you never saw." These lines appear to have been gauchely added to Chrétien's text by an interpolator anxious to show the breaking of Trebuchet's sword.

4162. The following episode of the blood-spots on the snow, perhaps of ultimately Celtic inspiration, shows Perceval in the role of the sensitive courtly lover, an important stage in his chivalric apprenticeship. For Chrétien the poetic symbolism of the scene plainly outweighed the implausibility of a snowbound countryside near Caerleon some time after Pentecost (cf. line 2785).

4307. Here, as earlier in the tent-maiden episode, Chrétien seems to be re-using material from the Erec story (for the toppling of Kay cf. *Erec*, lines 4026 ff., and also *Yvain*, lines 2240 ff.). For his repeated use of motifs see Brand, *Chrétien de Troyes* . . . .

4608. Now that the quality of Perceval's chivalry has been recognised by King Arthur and Queen Guenevere, and with even a new-found eloquence appearing in his speech, his apprenticeship might be considered at an end. The Loathly Damsel charges him not with a present flaw in his character but with a past failing; so we might expect some process of atonement to govern his later adventures. On the likely Celtic prototype of the sinister damsel see Loomis, *Arthurian Tradition . . .*, pp. 375–9 and 415–17.

4646. That Fortune has hair in front but is bald behind is a commonplace of medieval school tradition.

4741. The abrupt switching of the focus of interest from Perceval to Gawain encourages the theory that each character was to be the subject of a single romance and that at the time of his death Chrétien was working concurrently on two such poems, the unfinished portions of which were subsequently run together at about this point to produce the surviving text.

4893. Though he fostered Meliant, Tibaut is his vassal, whereas the vavasour (line 4922) is Tibaut's own vassal.

5055. Though one would expect "oak", *charme* ("hornbeam") is attested by the rhyme.

5058. Knights might renounce fighting at certain specified times (the so-called truce of God) or on other occasions, e.g. before participating in a judicial combat or when they had taken the cross preparatory to going on a crusade.

5085. These dues were levied on merchants, but knights were exempt.

5415. Ladies' sleeves were detachable (cf. note to *Yvain*, line 5423) and were often carried in tournaments by their favoured knights (cf. *Erec*, lines 2140–41).

5902. Escalibor or Excalibur is the sword normally associated with King Arthur, as already in Geoffrey of Monmouth. We are not told why Gawain should be carrying it here.

5946. The Lombards' bold enthusiasm for hunting snails was commonly alleged as a mocking reference to their supposed cowardice.

6113. The bleeding lance which Gawain is to seek appears to be the one associated with the grail in the first part of the romance and which Perceval had vowed to find again. In lines 6168–71 we learn of the prediction that it will one day destroy Logres, probably Arthur's kingdom (see the note to Lancelot, line 1313). The differences in its presentation in the two sections lend weight to the theory of their original independence.

6217. The following episode, describing Perceval's penitential visit to his hermit-uncle, has provoked much controversy. Although it is found in all the surviving MSS, such features as the clumsy manner of its insertion and its disruption of the story's chronology, the fact that Perceval is vouchsafed the answers to the unasked questions, and the awkward relationships that are disclosed have led to the questioning of its authenticity. At issue in the debate is the question of whether the grail was for Chrétien a sacred object and hence the degree to which Perceval's apprenticeship and final quest is a spiritual process, perhaps to be contrasted with Gawain's more worldly chivalry.

6484. The hermit's prayer reflects a medieval belief regarding the many "secret" names of God and Christ, which gave added efficacy to any prayer in which they were used.

6530. I translate Hilka's *norrois*, "northern", in preference to Roach's variant *noiret*, "blackish", since that is the almost unanimous reading referring to the same palfrey in line 7069.

6602. Galloway had a bad reputation in Chrétien's day, as indicated by a couplet added at this point in four MSS, where it is described as "a very evil land with very perverse people".

7233. The nature of this mysterious castle, later named as the Rock of Champguin (line 8817), will be progressively, if only partially, revealed. Initially appearing as a kind of "castle of maidens", it was, we learn, established and is governed by women, though peopled also by squires. We are soon told of its supernatural defences associated with the marvellous bed, which acts as a test for the ideal knight. The facts that it lies beyond water and that the chosen knight, once lord of it, may never leave suggest that, although notionally located in Galloway, it may have otherworld connotations; and this is finally confirmed when certain inhabitants are identified as people long dead (lines 8732 ff.). For the suggestion that it shares with the equally mysterious Grail Castle a prototype in Celtic legend see Owen, *The Evolution of the Grail Legend*, pp. 146 ff.

7650. The origins in Celtic myth of this strange figure have been convincingly argued by Loomis, *Arthurian Tradition . . .* , pp. 445–7.

8135. King Lot, variously described as ruler of Norway, Lothian and the Orkneys, had married Arthur's sister Anna. Another of his reputed sons was Mordred, not mentioned here.

8149. King Urien, according to Geoffrey of Monmouth, was King Lot's brother and hence Gawain's uncle.

8481. Hilka's edition includes here four lines (8482–5) missing from six MSS and not in Roach. The translation of Hilka's lines 8481–9 is: '"My lover used to cross it whenever I wished and would go and pick for me the flowers you see in the trees and meadows there."—"How did he get across, maiden? I don't know where the ford is; and I'm afraid the water's too deep and the bank everywhere too high to get down."'

8639. I adopt the majority reading *Logres* instead of *Nogres* as in Roach.

8647. Roach's MS has *Passage* for *Roche*.

8817. Variants are *Canguin* (Roach) and *Sanguin* (four MSS).

9215. This scene may contain an element of parody of the swooning of Charlemagne at the loss of his nephew in the *Chanson de Roland*.

9227. *Lore*: variant *Lores* in Roach.

9234. In most of the extant MSS this line is followed by the First Continuation with no break or indication of a change of authorship. One MS marks the end of Chrétien's work by inserting the note "Explycyt Percevax le viel", and another with the words "Explicit li romanz de Perceval".

Everyman
A selection of titles

*indicates volumes available in paperback

Complete lists of Everyman's Library and Everyman Paperbacks are available from the Sales Department, J.M. Dent and Sons Ltd, Aldine House, 33 Welbeck Street, London W1M 8LX.

ESSAYS AND CRITICISM

Arnold, Matthew. *On the Study of Celtic Literature*
*Bacon, Francis. *Essays*
Coleridge, Samuel Taylor
  * *Biographia Literaria*
    Shakespearean Criticism (2 vols)
*Emerson, Ralph. *Essays*
*Milton, John. *Prose Writings*
Montaigne, Michael Eyquem de. *Essays* (3 vols)
Paine, Thomas. *The Rights of Man*
Spencer, Herbert. *Essays on Education and Kindred Subjects*
*Swift, Jonothan. *Tale of a Tub and other satires*

HISTORY

*The Anglo-Saxon Chronicle
Burnet, Gilbert. *History of His Own Time*
*Crèvecoeur. *Letters from an American Farmer*
Gibbon, Edward. *The Decline and Fall or the Roman Empire* (6 vols)
Green, John. *A Short History of the English People* (2 vols)
Prescott, W.H. *History of the Conquest of Mexico*

LEGENDS AND SAGAS

*Beowulf and Its Analogues
*Chrétien de Troyes. *Arthurian Romances*
*Egils saga
 Holinshed, Raphael. *Chronicle*
*Layamon and Wace. *Arthurian Chronicles*
*The Mabinogion
*The Saga of Gisli
*The Saga of Grettir the Strong
 Snorri Sturluson. *Heimskringla* (3 vols)
*The Story of Burnt Njal

POETRY AND DRAMA

*Anglo-Saxon Poetry
*American Verse of the Nineteenth Century
*Arnold, Matthew. *Selected Poems and Prose*
*Blake, William. *Selected Poems*
*Brontes, The. *Selected Poems*
*Browning, Robert. *Men and Women and other poems*
 Burns, Robert. *The Kilmarnock Poems*
*Chaucer, Geoffrey. *Canterbury Tales*
*Clare, John. *Selected Poems*
*Coleridge, Samual Taylor. *Poems*
*Donne, John. *The Complete English Poems*
*Elizabethan Sonnets
*English Moral Interludes
*Everyman and Medieval Miracle Plays
*Everyman's Book of Evergreen Verse
*Gay, John. *The Beggar's Opera and other eighteenth-century
      plays*
*The Golden Treasury of Longer Poems
*Hardy, Thomas. *Selected Poems*
*Herbert, George. *The English Poems*
*Hopkins, Gerard Manley. *The Major Poems*
 Ibsen, Henrik
    A Doll's House; The Wild Dick; The Lady from the Sea
    Hedda Gabler; The Master Builder; John Gabriel Borkman

*Keats, John. *Poems*
*Langland, William. *The Vision of Piers Plowman*
*Marlowe, Christopher. *Complete Plays and Poems*
*Milton, John. *Complete Poems*
*Middleton, Thomas. *Three Plays*
*Palgrave's Golden Treasury
*Pearl, Patience, Cleanness, and Sir Gawain and the Green Knight
*Pope, Alexander. *Collected Poems*
*Restoration Plays
*The Rubáiyát of Omar Khayyám and other Persian poems
*Shelley, Percy Bysshe. *Selected Poems*
*Six Middle English Romances
*Spenser, Edmund. *The Faerie Queene: a selection*
*The Stuffed Owl
*Synge, J.M. *Plays, Poems and Prose*
*Tennyson, Alfred. *In Memoriam, Maud and other poems*
 Thomas, Dylan
   Collected Poems, 1934–1952
   The Poems
   Under Milk Wood
*Wilde, Oscar. *Plays, Prose Writings and Poems*
*Wordsworth, William. *Selected Poems*

RELIGION AND PHILOSOPHY

---

*Bacon, Francis. *The Advancement of Learning*
*Berkeley, George. *Philosophical Works including the works on vision*
*The Buddha's Philosophy of Man
*Chinese Philosophy in Classical Times
*Descartes, René. *A Discourse on Method*
*Hindu Scriptures
*Kant, Immanuel. *A Critique of Pure Reason*
*The Koran
*Leibniz, Gottfried Wilhelm. *Philosophical Writings*
*Locke, John. *An Essay Concerning Human Understanding (abridgment)*
*More, Thomas. *Utopia*

Pascal, Blaise. *Pensées*
Plato. *The Trial and Death of Socrates*
*The Ramayana and Mahábhárata

SCIENCES: POLITICAL AND GENERAL

Aristotle. *Ethics*
*Castiglione, Baldassāre. *The Book of the Courtier*
*Coleridge, Samuel Taylor. *On the Constitution of the Church and State*
*Darwin, Charles. *The Origins of Species*
Harvey, William. *The Circulation of the Blood and other writings*
*Hobbes, Thomas. *Leviathan*
*Locke, John. *Two Treatises of Government*
*Machiavelli, Niccolò. *The Prince and other political writings*
*Malthus, Thomas. *An Essay on the Principle of Populations*
*Mill, J.S. *Utilitarianism; On Liberty; Representative Government*
*Plato, *The Republic*
*Ricardo, David. *The Principles of Political Economy and Taxation*
Rousseau, J.-J.
  Emile
  The Social Contract and *Discourses*
*Wollstonecraft, Mary. *A Vindication of the Rights of Woman*

TRAVEL AND TOPOGRAPHY

Boswell, James. *The Journal of a Tour to the Hebrides*
*Darwin, Charles. *The Voyage of the 'Beagle'*
*Hudson, W.H. *Idle Days in Patagonia*
*Stevenson, R.L. *An Inland Voyage; Travels with a Donkey; The Silverado Squatters*
*Thomas, Edward. *The South Country*
*White, Gilbert. *The Natural History of Selborne*